CLASSICS OF SEA POWER

The Classics of Sea Power series makes readily available, in uniform, authoritative editions, the central concepts of the naval profession. These major book-length works in the words of the masters have been chosen for their eloquence and timelessness, and express the important themes of strategy, operations, tactics, and theory.

The editors are pleased to claim for this, the latest addition, not one great work but two. We expect that Colin Gray's introduction, with his rich insights on joint littoral warfare, will become as valuable as Charles Callwell's own peerless treatise, which Gray admires so much and explicates so ably. The two together are unrivaled for their relevance to modern amphibious warfare and the link between land and sea in regional conflicts.

Callwell's *Military Operations and Maritime Preponderance* and Gray's introduction are both "undiscovered" classics. This conundrum is explained as follows. Callwell's book, published in 1905, was soon set aside and forgotten because it came at the end of a century of British imperial experience in regional wars, aptly termed "small wars" by Callwell. From 1905, the year of the Russo-Japanese War, until 1945 professional attention centered on preparation for and conduct of war between great powers. Then from 1945 to 1990, the Cold War captured the imaginations of military writers. But now, as Colin Gray himself observes, *Military Operations* reads as a modern book, attuned and instructive for the twenty-first century. In his words, it has been published as a Classic of Sea Power "not because it is, but because it should be" recognized as influential.

Colin Gray gives Callwell the interpretation he deserves: discerning, wide-ranging, and thoroughly current. In Gray we find a reader's companion of references old and new, footnotes for modern context, collations of Callwell's apt insights for today, and a well-researched assessment of the men and events of his period.

Gray is first on scene among modern military writers to cover joint littoral warfare at once timelessly and contemporaneously. We expect that his introduction will itself be a root source of clear, concise thinking on joint operations for generations to come.

Callwell and Gray together are keel and rudder for understanding joint warfare, sea-land cooperation, and service harmony past and future.

SERIES EDITORS

John B. Hattendorf
Naval War College
Newport, Rhode Island

Wayne P. Hughes
Naval Postgraduate School
Monterey, California

Military Operations
and Maritime Preponderance

C. E. Callwell (Courtesy of the Director, National Army Museum, London)

C. E. CALLWELL

Military Operations and Maritime Preponderance: Their Relations and Interdependence

With an Introduction and Notes by
Colin S. Gray

NAVAL INSTITUTE PRESS   Annapolis, Maryland

This book was originally published in 1905 by William Blackwood
and Sons, Edinburgh and London.

Introduction and notes copyright © 1996
by the United States Naval Institute, Annapolis, Maryland

ISBN 1-55750-341-9

Printed in the United States of America on acid-free paper ∞

03 02 01 00 99 98 97 96   9 8 7 6 5 4 3 2
First printing

The three memoranda in Appendix 1 (PRO WO 106/DF/E2/6, PRO WO 106/46/DF/E2/6/B, and PRO WO 106/44/E1/7) are Crown Copyright and reproduced with the permission of the Controller of Her Majesty's Stationery Office.

CONTENTS

Editor's Note and Acknowledgments	ix
Thinking Joint: A British Way in Warfare	xi
Introduction: Sir Charles E. Callwell, KCB—An "Able Theorist" of Joint Warfare	xv
Notes to Introduction	lxii
Military Operations and Maritime Preponderance	1
Appendix I. Toward Continental Commitment, 1905: Three Callwell Memoranda	445
Appendix II. Charles E. Callwell: Summary of a Military Life	457
Appendix III. Selected Publications of Charles E. Callwell	463
Appendix IV. Textual Notes	467
Index	497

EDITOR'S NOTE AND ACKNOWLEDGMENTS

Although Charles E. Callwell, the author of *Military Operations and Maritime Preponderance,* was careful in his historical research and use of historical illustration of his argument, he was not at all careful to provide references for his sources in a standard form acceptable to scholars of a later generation. The editor has decided not to burden the text with footnotes on every person and event mentioned in the text in passing. It is editorial policy as a general rule to footnote only what is important with reference to the book as a work on amphibious warfare or such other matters as are of particular interest. The notes to the editor's introduction and to Callwell's text include a full citation for an authority on its first appearance in either location.

When a strategic theorist and commentator upon contemporary matters of defense ventures into military history he needs all the help he can get. My debts are heavy indeed.

My first debt is to John B. Hattendorf and the Naval Institute Press for their bold decision to trust me with this enterprise. I must record my gratitude to Paul Wilderson of the Press for his tolerance of the time I took to complete the task.

The number of friends, colleagues, acquaintances, and strangers who have been badgered with my requests for information about Callwell is legion indeed. In particular I would like to thank Tim Moreman, Richard Holmes, Ian

Beckett, Allan Millett, Williamson Murray, Humphrey Crum-Ewing, A. P. Thornton, Jonathan Bailey, R. J. Wyatt, and P. S. Walton. A special note of thanks is owed to John Gooch of the University of Leeds, who did everything that a card-carrying military historian could do to save a modern strategist from himself. Any errors by the editor that remain are strictly the fault of the editor.

John Montgomery, Librarian of the Royal United Services Institution, was most helpful, as was Robin Smith of the Department of Manuscripts, National Library of Scotland (for the Blackwood Papers), and James Taylor of the Imperial War Museum. In addition I am grateful for the assistance of the staff at the Liddell Hart Centre for Military Archives, King's College London (for the Hamilton Papers), at the London Library, and at Brynmor Jones Library, University of Hull.

I thank Sir Ian Hamilton for permission to see the Hamilton Papers, and the Public Record Office at Kew for their advice and assistance in locating materials in War Office files. With reference to the photograph of Captain Charles E. Callwell that graces this book, it appears here courtesy of the Director, National Army Museum, London.

Special thanks are due the director and staff of the Royal United Services Institution in London for their assistance in placing an advertisement for information on Charles E. Callwell in the *RUSI Journal*. Penultimately, I wish to express gratitude to my assistant and student, Ernest Moore Garcia III, for his cheerful journeying on my behalf in quest of elusive Callwelliana.

Last, but anything but least, my wife, Valerie, and daughter, Antonia, have coexisted with my Callwell obsession. No praise can be too high for such devotion.

THINKING JOINT: A BRITISH WAY IN WARFARE

The Fleet and Army, acting in consort, seem to be the natural Bulwark of these Kingdoms.
>Thomas More Molyneux,
>*Conjunct Operations; or Expeditions That Have Been Carried on Jointly by the Fleet and the Army, with a Commentary on Littoral War*
>(London, 1759)

The close relations which must exist between our navy and our army are beginning to attract an attention more commensurate with their importance. The theory is gaining ground that maritime command is the paramount condition upon which the employment of the land force in time of war depends. And the great strategical principle that in virtue of supremacy upon the oceans bodies of troops, insignificant as compared with the legions which Continental Powers can put into the field, may sometimes decide tremendous issues, is becoming a basis of our national policy.
>Charles E. Callwell,
>*The Effect of Maritime Command on Land Campaigns Since Waterloo*
>(Edinburgh, 1897)

Still it is hoped that if the book proves nothing else, it will at least prove afresh how great is the importance in a land like ours of cordial, close, and constant cooperation between its navy and its army, not only when the nation is actually engaged in war, but also when Imperial questions of defence are under discussion and come up for decision in time of peace.
>
> Charles E. Callwell,
> *Military Operations and Maritime Preponderance: Their Relations and Interdependence*
> (Edinburgh, 1905)

An army supported by an invincible navy possesses a strength which is out of all proportion to its size. Even to those who rely on the big battalions and huge fortresses, the amphibious power of a great maritime state, if intelligently directed, may be a most formidable menace: while to the state itself it is an extraordinary security.
>
> G. F. R. Henderson,
> *The Science of War: A Collection of Essays and Lectures, 1891–1903*
> (London, 1906)

From the nature of the strategical problems we [British] have to deal with in war, I think we may deduce that the soldier and the seaman should *"Think amphibiously!"*
>
> George Aston,
> "Combined Strategy for Fleets and Armies; Or 'Amphibious Strategy,'"
> *Journal of the Royal United Service Institution*, July–December, 1907

It may be said without exaggeration that, on a large scale, there can be no British war strategy that is either purely naval, or purely military, it must always be "amphibious" in the sense that it must consider the armies and fleets of both sides.

> George Aston,
> *Sea, Land, and Air Strategy: A Comparison* (London, 1914)

Both we and our forbears have been accustomed to think of our military power as amphibious, but I venture to suggest that the chief criticism which our descendants will have to make of our conduct of the Great War will be that we did not make the best use of our amphibious power, and in fact we first turned ourselves voluntarily into a land power, and began to think of our amphibious power afterwards.

> F. Maurice,
> *British Strategy: A Study of the Application of the Principles of War* (London, 1929)

Amphibious flexibility is the greatest strategic asset that a sea-based power possesses. It creates a distraction to a continental enemy's concentration that is most advantageously disproportionate to the resources employed.

> B. H. Liddell Hart,
> "Marines and Strategy," *Marine Corps Gazette*, July 1960

The British Army is a projectile to be fired by the Navy.
> Sir Edward Grey,
> quoted in Arthur Marder, *From the Dreadnought to Scapa Flow: The Royal Navy in the Fisher Era, 1906–1919. Vol. I, The Road to War, 1906–1914* (London, 1961)

Our geography forces us not to choose between one strategy or the other [continental or maritime], but to achieve the optimum balance between the two, as we [British] have always had to do.

> Lord Carver,
> "Continental or Maritime Strategy:
> Past, Present and Future,"
> *RUSI Journal* (Autumn 1989)

INTRODUCTION

Sir Charles E. Callwell, KCB — An "Able Theorist" of Joint Warfare

Military Operations and Maritime Preponderance: Their Relations and Interdependence—hereafter *Military Operations*—may be the best study of joint warfare that has ever been written, though the list of plausible candidates for that award is not a long one.[1] Although scholarly opinion on the military career of Major-General Sir Charles Edward Callwell, KCB, (see Appendix II for a chronology of Callwell's life and career) is distinctly mixed, appreciation of his virtues as a theorist is more unified in praise. In a recent essay, British historian Hew Strachan notes that the military theorists of the late Victorian British army were inclined to focus on continental evidence, not the actual experience of British imperial campaigns. Strachan proceeds thus:

> The single significant exception to this generalization is Charles Callwell, a gunner officer who fought the Afghans and the Boers, and whose book *Small Wars*, published in 1896, is the only major attempt to synthesize Britain's colonial military experience. Callwell also wrote about the relationship between sea power and the army long before Corbett or Liddell Hart. His oeuvre embraced both arms of British strategy, and he can consequently lay claim to being the father of a much more genuine "British way in warfare."[2]

If Strachan is correct in holding *Military Operations* in such high regard, why is it that Callwell, all too fairly, is mentioned with honor by Hervé Coutau-Bégarie in an essay on "unknown, or insufficiently known, naval thinkers"?[3] *Military Operations* bears the stamp of its epoch, but then which works of strategic theory do not?

Many a good book dies; *Military Operations* rests in a numerous company. But, an era such as the present, which is almost religiously "joint," in ethos at least, cannot afford to neglect the educational service of the few outstanding books that can be made available. The "Classics of Sea Power" series of the Naval Institute Press therefore is effecting a long overdue resuscitation of a work that has not previously been reissued in any form whatsoever since its publication in 1905.

It is interesting to note that another book in this series registers the judgment that "prior to the middle of the twentieth century no one had set forth in writing the second half of the maritime theory of warfare, the exploitation of control at sea toward the establishment of control on the land." The author of that sweeping conclusion, Rear Admiral J. C. Wylie, is wrong.[4] Callwell's *Military Operations* goes a long way toward setting forth what Wylie claims was not accomplished until the 1940s. Indeed, as editor of this neglected classic I am amazed at the fact of neglect. Unlike, say, deterrence theory or arms control, joint warfare in the form of "amphibious strategy" is a field singularly short of instructive historical or theoretical works that plainly are first-class in quality. Notwithstanding the irony of some wholly undeserved guilt by association with the Gallipoli fiasco, the absence of apparent intellectual connection between Callwell—and his Royal Marine Artillery virtual "echo," Major-General Sir George Aston—and the U.S. Marine Corps in the 1920s and 1930s is remarkable.[5] Some historians of the amphibious warfare doctrine of the U.S. Marine Corps as first developed by Lt. Col. Earl H. "Pete" Ellis in 1921, and subsequently formalized in the *Tentative Manual for Landing Operations* of 1934, seem totally unaware of Callwell's writings. For example, when discussing the approach taken in the USMC schools after their establishment in 1921, Col. Robert D. Heinl, Jr., informs us that

> there was recognition that the subject of landing operations needed the same applied study and reduction to technique devoted to other forms of warfare. There were mistakes and false beginnings, but there was also progress. Starting with Gallipoli as the classic object-lesson, and *in the entire absence of a source of positive material, except the Ellis plan,* the problem was dissected into its component parts by segregation and analysis of the major mistakes made in the Dardanelles.[6]

It is strange that "Pete" Ellis, or Lt. Gen. John A. Lejeune, USMC, would appear to have been as ignorant of Callwell's *Military Operations and Maritime Preponderance* as have been many of the later historians of the development of the U.S. Marine Corps' amphibious warfare doctrine.[7] The need for detailed study of, and practice in, landing operations is stated as strongly as could be in Callwell's final chapter (chapter twenty-three). Somewhat parochial historians of the Marine Corps would appear to have missed the immediate, albeit British, intellectual antecedents to "Pete" Ellis. An important reason why the innovators of the offensive amphibious mission in the U.S. Marine Corps in the 1920s should have been respectfully familiar with *Military Operations and Maritime Preponderance* was because Callwell already was well known to them as the leading practical theorist on small wars. The U.S. Marines' 1940 manual on small wars drew upon Callwell explicitly.[8] Successful opposed landings were conducted long before Tarawa on 20 November 1943, and sound thinking on the tactical, operational, and strategic arts of joint, then meaning amphibious, warfare long predated 1921.[9] It is relevant to this essay to quote the following judgment by a leading (American) historian of British theory and practice in amphibious warfare. "In balance, Callwell's book

[*Military Operations*] was a very judicious study. By 1905 he had written about many of the things that would later cause the failure of the Dardanelles campaign. It is no mean feat to produce a critique of a campaign ten years before that campaign is fought."[10]

In their justly celebrated history, The *U.S. Marines and Amphibious War,* Jeter A. Isely and Philip A. Crowl demonstrated a less than secure grip on some of the British dimension to the history of their subject. In summary form the authors present the four-item claim that "the British had failed to take the Dardanelles because of faulty doctrine, ineffective techniques, poor leadership, and an utter lack of coordination between the services."[11] The first claim is erroneous—British amphibious doctrine in 1915 probably was sound enough.[12] The second claim, of ineffective techniques, is possibly correct though probably misleading in that the naval and military assets of the expeditionary force were poorly equipped for their tasks, almost regardless of quality of "techniques."[13] Certainly it would be true to claim that the British army and navy had neglected the technological dimension to amphibious warfare. The claim of poor leadership is plausible at all levels—tactical, operational, strategic, and political. The final claim, of poor interservice, or joint, coordination, is correct but, again, somewhat misleading. While it is obviously accurate to argue that the several naval and then the military assaults on the Dardanelles' defenses were not effectively coordinated, it is less obvious that this uncoordinated condition was the fault of the army or the navy. The navy was challenged, and initially drafted, to attempt to force a passage through the Dardanelles in the context of an unavailability of military support. Later, the army was summoned, first to effect an unopposed landing and mopping-up campaign in support of a presumed successful naval assault, and only second to mount a forcible entry onto the Gallipoli peninsula.[14]

INTRODUCTION

Readers of Callwell's *Military Operations* will find much of the basis for a doctrine of amphibious warfare; registration of the significance of the techniques necessary for success in opposed landings (for example, effective naval gunfire support: Callwell was an artilleryman by branch of service); and the placing of emphasis upon the need for effective coordination between the services. Indeed, on the final page of *Military Operations* Callwell cites coordination of authority and "harmony in the council chamber and the theater of operations" as "perhaps the most important lesson to be learnt from the many interesting and remarkable campaigns in which circumstances have brought into contact fighting forces afloat and fighting forces ashore" (466). In other words, Callwell got it right long ahead of the practical demonstration in 1915 of what would and would not work in contemporary conditions.[15]

The attempt in 1915 first to force the Dardanelles with naval force alone, and then to seize the Gallipoli peninsula with a military expedition, unjustly cast a shadow over Callwell's career. Callwell's professional knowledge of the military problems posed by the Dardanelles almost certainly was deeper and more extensive than was that of any other British soldier before 1915. While a staff captain in the intelligence department of the War Office he had attempted some spying of the Dardanelles forts; he was the principal author of the extremely prescient December 1906 General Staff memorandum "Upon the Possibility of a Joint Naval and Military Attack upon the Dardanelles;"[16] in 1914–1915 he was director of military operations in the War Office during both the "planning" and execution phases of the actual adventure itself; and in December 1915 he drafted the memorandum for the incoming chief of the general staff (Field-Marshal Sir William R. Robertson) that provided the formal basis for that new CIGS's recommendation to the cabinet that the Gallipoli peninsula should be evacuated completely.[17]

INTRODUCTION

With reputations at stake in the aftermath of ignominious defeat, Callwell's testimony was critical in the subsequent official enquiry into the reasons for failure—the search for scapegoats, inevitably.

Military Operations can be approached from two perspectives. First, it can be treated as a classic of sea power; which is to say, in this case, as a timeless superior contribution to the short list of insightful books on sea-land cooperation particularly at the operational and tactical levels of warfare. Second, *Military Operations* can be read as an interesting, richly detailed, period piece. In this second perspective the book is indeed *the* example of advanced British thinking on joint warfare before the Great War.[18] *Military Operations* as period piece was completed in February 1905, during the Russo-Japanese War, immediately prior to the conduct by the British army's nascent general staff of the crucial war game with a continental scenario, just prior to the serious consideration of France as a military ally in war with Germany, and considerably prior even to the issuing in January 1907 of the orders for the organization of what was to become the British Expeditionary Force (BEF) of future fame and no little legend. Nineteen Five was a momentous year for British military thought and, to risk exaggeration, for British defense planning.[19] Col. Charles E. Callwell, an assistant director of military operations on the newly created general staff in the War Office, personally was at the crossroads of the strategic developments of that year. Moreover, he appeared to march down more than one strategic road within a short space of time, as the memoranda reproduced in Appendix I attest.

The life, career, and exciting times of Charles E. Callwell are fascinating topics that merit appraisal in this essay; however, they are not the reason why *Military Operations* is reprinted here as a "classic of sea power." It is important that the book should be read as a source of wisdom on joint warfare that happens to have been written by a particularly broad-minded British artilleryman in 1904–1905. Judgment on Callwell himself as a player in the process of strategy-making, on the wisdom of the European continental shift, or lurch, in British military intentions after 1905,[20] and on any aspect of British military and naval performance in the Great War, should be kept apart from consideration of this book. Of course, *Military Operations* is a period piece, but it is much more than that. This reissue of the work is an endeavor to rescue it from undeserved obscurity, while also protecting it from preemptive capture by historians.

Paradoxically, perhaps, *Military Operations* reads as a rather more modern book in the 1990s than it would have in, say, 1911–1912, with the general staff's endorsement of a continental European destination for the BEF. To a strategic context wherein it was expected that multimillion-man armies would be locked in continental warfare, the operational, let alone tactical, relevance of military force from the sea was not immediately evident to many people. Later, the disaster of Gallipoli understandably encouraged British military professionals to adopt negative views of amphibious operations in *grande guerre*. The conduct of amphibious—and, more broadly, joint—warfare was, of course, imposed upon Britain (and the United States, as geostrategic legatee) by the continental expulsion effected in 1940, and upon the United States by the maritime character of the Pacific theater of operations. The strategic logic of most of the Cold War years, with its latent menace of continental Eurasian events triggering a nuclear Armageddon, again seemed to call into fundamental question the significance of Callwell's subject. Who cares about joint warfare if World War III would comprise an explosive gallop from a massive clash of armor in West-Central Europe to an intercontinental nuclear exchange-holocaust?

This is not the place to revisit arguments over the now blessedly strictly hypothetical relevance of land-sea cooperation in the Cold War. But, plainly, it is appropriate to observe that the joint warfare discussed so extensively in *Military Operations* is apparently rendered strategically much more salient by the extant absence of the menace of a great war. Even though Callwell had much to say in *Military Operations* that was to prove relevant to each of the three great wars of this century, there is little doubt that the strategic assumptions of 1904–1905 behind the book fit better the condition of the 1990s than they did the Cold War decades, or even the years of *great* pre-nuclear war. This is a book full of interest to a United States committed to advance forward from the sea.[21]

Who was Charles Edward Callwell and what can be said about his military career? In particular, why was it that a man born in 1859, who had outstanding intellectual gifts (for example, passed in first place into the Staff College in his year of entry, was an exceptional linguist, demonstrably able analyst and, eventually, even a good prose stylist), who had some varied experience of war, who exemplified proper Victorian imperial attitudes (Callwell was intelligent, not progressive—on India, say), and who enjoyed the respect and even close friendship of men of power and influence, was never trusted with the field command of more than four hundred soldiers?[22] Brian Bond notes in his study of the Staff College that "all the future Army Commanders of the First World War were column commanders in South Africa."[23] In company with such men as Herbert Plumer (b. 1857), Julian Byng (b. 1862), Henry Rawlinson (b. 1864), and Edmond Allenby (b. 1861)—to cite but some—Callwell was a column commander in South Africa. Unlike his apparent peers of 1899–1902, however, Callwell never commanded troops again in war and, as a passed over full colonel, retired in 1909 (he had been militarily generally unemployed and on half pay since late 1907).

The mystery, if such it is, deepens, in that although Callwell was judged dispensable in 1907, he was sufficiently respected by his peers to be brought back as a "dug-out"—from genuine retirement, he was even off the reserve officers' list—in August 1914 to accept the poisoned chalice of appointment as Henry Wilson's replacement as director of military operations (DMO) in Lord Kitchener's War Office.[24] As well as being Wilson's choice for DMO, in late 1915 he was invited by Douglas Haig to serve as his military secretary,[25] while Robertson, the new CIGS (as of 23 December 1915), and later Wilson as CIGS, employed Callwell in a series of odd-job roles for the War Office that were by no means trivial in content or implied trust.

To save these pages much space-consuming narrative, a detailed summary of Callwell's military career is provided in Appendix II. Most probably because he left no tranche of papers—at least none that historians have unearthed to date—there is quite literally no biographical literature on Callwell. The most extensive discussion located in the course of preparing this essay are the six pages largely devoted to the content of *Military Operations* by James L. Stokesbury in his 1968 dissertation, "British Concepts and Practices of Amphibious Warfare, 1867–1916," and David R. Massam's 1995 dissertation, "British Maritime Strategy and Amphibious Capability, 1900–1940."[26] It may be an eloquent comment upon Callwell's control of his ego that he succeeded in writing no fewer than three volumes of memoirs without revealing anything of much interest about his professional ambitions, satisfactions, and disappointments, or about the character and achievements of his professional allies and foes. Unfortunately, his memoirs, while noting his relative success as a journalist after 1907, do not even mention his professional military writings. One has sympathy for Keith Neilson, who, in his study of Anglo-Russian relations in the Great War, wrote as follows:

> Another important omission is General Charles Callwell. As Director of Military Operations (DMO) at the War Office

from 1914 to the end of 1915, Callwell was at the centre of military deliberations concerning Russia. As well, he was intimately connected with providing munitions for Russia, serving on the War Office's Russian Purchasing Committee and later with the Ministry of Munitions and Milner Committee. There is no doubt that Callwell should be a member of the élite, but the absence of any private papers for him and the fact that the official War Office files that dealt with his Russia activities no longer exist has made his inclusion impossible.[27]

Callwell's name appears, en passant, in dozens of contemporary memoirs, but hardly ever is he the subject of interest. There is no doubt that his identifiable contribution to the course of events was, at most, distinctly modest. He was a minor character, albeit a minor character who occupied positions very close indeed to the contemporary movers and shakers of high policy and strategy. It is not controversial to argue both that Callwell was a talented military author—a quality recognized at the time—and that, with a single possible exception, he demonstrated competence, if not flair, throughout his career in the army.

Ian Beckett is plausible when he suggests that "in the context of his overall career, Callwell was not especially outstanding although he was regarded by that *eminence grise* of prewar military politics, Lord Esher [Esher was endorsing the opinion of Charles A'Court Repington], as an 'able theorist' and one of only twelve out of 32 officers serving in the War Office intelligence department worth retaining in 1904."[28] It may seem strange to some readers to judge an overall career "not especially outstanding" when it is capped by seventeen months' service as DMO in the War Office during Britain's greatest ever continental war. The truth was that "Charlie" Callwell had been a lifelong friend of the extant DMO, Henry Wilson, who was scheduled to serve as sub-chief of the general staff with the BEF's general headquarters in France.

Callwell was regarded generally as a steady hand, certainly a very experienced one, but the "Sirdar," Lord Kitchener, as de facto "supremo" of the British military effort, was not one to use his staff, even had he known what a general staff was supposed to do.

It is tempting to seek to analyze Callwell's career as a study in failure. In the second volume of his memoirs he reports that "I was, after eighteen months of unemployment, [early in 1909], appointed to a staff appointment of relatively low standing in view of my position on the colonels' list."[29] As a consequence of this confirmation of his lack of prospects for further promotion, because—we can infer—of the loss of face in such an appointment, and because he had "got into the trick" of journalism, he sent in his papers.[30] The lack of surviving evidence of bitterness in a man well known to have a sharp tongue and a fluent pen suggests that Callwell most likely was long resigned to a career foreshortened below general officer rank.[31] It required intervention by the first British continental commitment since the 1850s to catapult Callwell from the station of one deeply retired to honorary (1914), then substantive (1917), Major General with KCB to boot!

A biographer of Callwell, rather after the fashion of a historian examining the record of the British Army of 1914–1918, is unsure whether to label the cup of professional achievement half-empty or half-full. It is true that he did not achieve field command in the greatest continental war in British history. Compared with others in his age cohort (for example, Smith-Dorrien, Plumer, Haig, Byng, Allenby), as a practical soldier Callwell certainly failed to rise as high as he must have hoped. On the British Army in Callwell's time, Bond offers the thought that although "not for a moment would I deny that the Army had serious deficiencies, but I consider it fairer to dwell on the improvements it made in the light of the Boer War rather than on the limitations which were exposed in and after 1914."[32] A general European war was anticipated in the crisis slide from Morocco in 1905 until Bosnia-Herzegovina in 1914, but the war that came was not the one for which the British Army had prepared, and—alas—"none [of the British CIGSs] marked 4 August 1916 on his calendar as *der Tag,* by which the Expeditionary Force should reach the peak of perfection."[33]

In Chapter Ten of *Military Operations,* writing prior even to an assumption of an anti-German continental alliance with France, Callwell had sensible words to offer about both the limited direct value of naval power vis-à-vis continental warfare, he reminded readers of the protracted character of the Napoleonic wars *after* Trafalgar, and he made noticeably prescient comments on the likely contemporary resilience of great continental powers. Notwithstanding these, and other like (for example, on technical advances in weaponry [see pp. 216, 235, 339–40, 358, 407]), sound appreciations, it is not particularly useful, and it is not the purpose of this introductory essay, to test *Military Operations* for its score on judgments-predictions in the light only of the events of 1914–1918.

Callwell's military career is more easily summarized (see Appendix II) than explained. Born of Anglo-Irish parents he was, insofar as the limited personal evidence available reveals, entirely conventional in his political and social attitudes. He attended Haileybury College (as did the eventual Field-Marshal Allenby), passed without difficulty into the Royal Military Academy Woolwich, and performed there with sufficient distinction to be allowed to choose between a commission in the engineers or the artillery (he chose the latter). Callwell served with credit in the Second Afghan War (1880), he was present in-theater for the final phase of the First Boer War (1881), and subsequently did his duty in regimental soldiering with the Royal Field Artillery (RFA) in England and India until he passed (in first place) in 1884 into the less than militarily stellar Staff College (1885–1886).[34] After Staff College—in which period he first made his mark as a military theorist with his gold-medal essay for the RUSI (Royal United Service Institution)[35]—Callwell served five credit-worthy years (1887–1892) in the intelligence department of the War Office.[36] This tour of duty enabled him to develop and exploit his facility with languages, his taste for foreign travel, and some vocation for gentlemanly spying (from Tangier to Constantinople). Following his London-based staff duties in intelligence, he performed four years of regimental artillery duty elsewhere in England (1892–1896) before being posted to a garrison artillery command in Malta (1896–1899). While based in Malta Callwell arranged to be "attached" to the Greek Army fighting the Turks (May 1897).

In December 1899 Callwell and his battery (16, Southern Royal Garrison Artillery [RGA]) were ordered to South Africa. In South Africa he served first with Buller in the campaign to relieve Ladysmith, subsequently he commanded the field artillery in desultory Boer-chasing in the Western and Northern Transvaal, and then, on 31 July 1901, he was offered his big chance, command of a column under Sir John French in N. W. Cape Colony. *The Times* obituary claims that "he commanded a mobile column not without credit" during the period August 1901–May 1902,[37] but on two or three occasions there is reason to believe he failed to satisfy French.

After South Africa Callwell had a brief spell of garrison command in Ireland and England before being appointed to his second spell of War Office duty, which began in the Autumn of 1903. From Autumn 1904 until October 1907 he served in, and then as head of, what became the strategical section of the directorate of military operations on the newly organized general staff. In these three critical years Callwell was a participant-observer in and of the dramatic switch in orientation of the British Army from a primarily imperial, to a primarily European continental, role. In his capacity as ADMO, MO1 (assistant director of military operations, military operations first [strategical] section: sub-sections—operations; imperial defense; army deployment; British possessions other than the U.K., India, and Africa; Egypt, Sudan, and Africa),[38] he wrote, or at least signed, a number of notable—even, dare one say—historic, memoranda and studies. In particular, Callwell endorsed or wrote the contradictory memoranda on "British Military Action in Case of War with Germany," dated 28 August and 30 October 1905, as well as a somewhat skeptical, more personal memorandum on the same topic, dated 7 December 1906,[39] and the Dardanelles memorandum to which reference has been made already. It was during this period of duty in the War Office that he published *Military Operations*.

For reasons discussed speculatively immediately below, the then fifty-year-old Colonel Callwell sent in his papers early in 1909, following eighteen months of official unemployment on half-pay. In August 1914 he was summoned from his retirement activities as military journalist and author to take Henry Wilson's place as DMO in the War Office on the mobilization of the BEF, the consequent mass decamping of general staff officers to general headquarters in France, and the assumption of direction of the military war effort by Lord Kitchener. There is no reason to doubt that Callwell performed the duties of director of military operations as well as Kitchener would allow, though almost certainly not as well as the country really required at that time. An unflattering appraisal of Callwell as DMO has been offered by John Gooch.

> Potentially the most influential post was that of Director of Military Operations; unfortunately its occupant, Major-General Callwell, was in many ways another Wolfe-Murray. . . . Kitchener never discussed strategic questions with Callwell, who neither sought nor got an opportunity to put forward his views opposing a naval action at the Dardanelles.[40]

Which is, of course, quite damning. Whether or not it is wholly fair is another matter. In July 1916 Callwell stated his problem in a way that both has the ring of truth and does not necessarily invite the charge of moral cowardice. Callwell wrote to Brade that

> Lord Kitchener did not approve of the naval attack upon the Dardanelles. Nobody at the War Office who knows what was going on did. He however accepted the Admiralty view [which is to say, effectively, Winston Churchill's view, as First Lord] more or less under protest. On the other hand, he did not expect the Turks to put up the fight they did when military operations commenced believing that they would give way when they realized that we meant business; and that was where the War Office went wrong. *I felt considerable doubt on the point, but could not of course set my opinion on a question so closely connected with the Oriental character against his.*[41]

Close reading of Callwell's autobiographical books, and of such of his relevant letters as have survived, leads to the conclusion that he was a political realist, skilled in getting along with all manner of eccentric personalities with oversized egos, including those of his intimate personal friend Henry Wilson, and Lord Kitchener. A fair-minded reading of Callwell's *Experiences of a Dug-Out, 1914–1918*, and of his biography of Sir Henry Wilson, leaves this commentator, at least, in no doubt that his subject knew the strengths and limitations of Kitchener probably as well as any contemporary could and was no toady-yesman.[42]

In common with others, after 1915 Callwell had his reputation to protect as best he could. He had not influenced policy or strategy over the Dardanelles as DMO in 1914–1915, *but* he had been present, as it were, in the War Office at the scene of the crime, and he was well known to be the military expert on the Dardanelles' defenses. Perhaps he could not have influenced policy or strategy? But, did he try? Could he have tried? And could he have influenced operations even in aid of a policy and strategy course of which he disapproved? Gooch has drawn attention, fairly enough, to optimistic private correspondence written by Callwell to William Robertson on the subject of the naval attempt to force passage. This was indeed "myopic," as Gooch suggests.[43] But it is well to remember that Callwell's judgment on the inadvisability of an effort to force passage had been consistent from his 19 December 1906 memorandum, certainly through to the "decidedly discouraging" advice that he offered Winston Churchill on the subject on 3 September 1914.[44] Moreover, as suggested earlier in this essay, the final (inter alia) chapter of *Military Operations*, from 1905, comprises powerful commentary on how, and by inference how not, to conduct amphibious operations.

Callwell may not have been the stuff of which bureaucratic heroes are made, but an optimistic "wobble" in early March 1915 on the prospects for the naval forcing of the Dardanelles stands out as the exception, not the rule, to his typically sound views on the subject. It is perhaps too easy to forget that in the early months of the Great War Kitchener was the policy and strategy maker for Britain—if anybody in London could be, given the alliance with France—and he had been much impressed by the effects of naval bombardment against Egyptian forts at Alexandria in 1882.[45] Furthermore, Kitchener (and most others) was much underimpressed with the recently demonstrated combat prowess of Turkish soldiers; he found it expedient to believe Churchill on the tactical power of modern ships against the land. Obviously Callwell could have left the team over the Dardanelles, but he was loyal to his chief, he was deeply professional in most respects, and the country was fighting for its life.

As Kitchener's DMO Callwell had some good reason to fear that, as the War Office expert-in-residence on the Dardanelles, and with the chief lost at sea on 5 June 1916, the finger of blame might point in his direction with regard to specific sins as well as by virtue of some general guilt by bureaucratic association. In particular, Callwell was potentially vulnerable to the charge that the War Office (in which he was, after all, DMO), had dispatched Sir Ian Hamilton to command the army charged to seize Gallipoli with woefully inadequate intelligence.[46] Callwell argued that he was in Kitchener's confidence far more after May 1915 than before, and in a letter to Hamilton referring to his testimony before the Dardanelles Commission, he stated:

> I explained to the Commission that I was not fighting my own corner in the matter, as I was merely making use of the work done by my predecessors in collecting information, but expressed the opinion to them that upon the whole the official reports that were handed to your staff when you left [London] afforded as much information as could reasonably be expected of such a region as you were going to operate in.[47]

In subsequent correspondence Hamilton had resorted to flattery: plainly he was anxious lest Callwell provide argument or evidence in self-defense persuasively supportive of War Office claims to sound conduct. "I believe you [Callwell] to be the most straight-forward and fearless of men whose word I would rely upon with the greatest confidence, just as much if you testified against me as if you were pleading my cause."[48] In his reply to Hamilton, Callwell offered these interesting points.

> A good many years ago, when I was a young officer in the Intelligence department [1887–1892], I did a good deal of spying in the Mediterranean, and the only country I ever found any serious difficulty was in Turkey. I tried Salonika, and Smyrna, and Chanak in the Dardanelles, and found on each occasion the Turks were very much too wide awake for me; quite different from my experience in France and Italy. On that account I really believe it was very difficult to get really good information about the Gallipoli peninsula in peace time, seeing that it was virtually a fortress.[49]

In his excellent book on the Dardanelles, Callwell offered the following excuse for Hamilton not raising last-minute objections to the task that he had been set. "It is easy for critics to say now—after the fact—that this would have been the proper course to adopt. A soldier must be very secure indeed of his ground before he can be justified in taking up an attitude that will completely upset the plans that his Government have commissioned him to carry out in time of war."[50] It is likely that the author had another than Sir Ian Hamilton in mind when he wrote that unheroic, but prudent, observation.

When Sir William Robertson became CIGS on 23 December 1915 he reorganized and revived the general staff. In fragile health—possibly gout and certainly stomach trouble[51]—as well as for reason of association with the old regime at the War Office, Callwell finally retired (again) very early in January 1916. He was in high enough regard, however, to be trusted by Robertson to undertake two politically sensitive missions to Russia (January–February and March–May 1916). Flowing from his Russian experience Callwell became the War Office coordinator for the supply of munitions, initially, to Russia, but later to all of Britain's allies. In 1917 he was asked to stand in for a month as Deputy CIGS (May–June), he was knighted (KCB) and his "honorary" rank of major-general was made substantive. In effect in 1916–1918 Callwell served most ably as an odd-job man for the War Office. After the war he devoted his declining years to military, especially biographical, writing. So highly was Callwell regarded as an author that on 1 March 1921 the Royal United Service Institution awarded him its signal honor of the Chesney Gold Medal

> for his distinguished work in connection with military literature, and more especially for the following works:
> (1) *Effect of Maritime Command on Land Campaigns*
> (2) *Military Operations and Maritime Preponderance*
> (3) *Small Wars: Their Principles and Practice*
> (4) *The Tactics of To-day*
> (5) *The Tactics of Home Defence*[52]

Callwell died in London on 16 May 1928.

To seek to explain why Callwell's military career hit a plateau at the level of colonel produces a dilemma. The problem is a superfluity of plausible explanations, but, for the true embarrassment of the biographer, there is an absence of reliable knowledge. In some regards we do not know what is true and what is not, while in others we do not know which among the black marks against his prospects of promotion was or were decisive. In this essay I can advance understanding, but I cannot settle the question of why Callwell failed to ascend to the pinnacle of command achieved by some of his peers.

Research reveals no fewer than seven reasons why Callwell's military career collapsed some way short of high command. The first explanation is that Callwell "fell into disrepute" because of his errors as commander of a mobile column in the Boer War. Richard Holmes records that "[Sir John] French accused him of letting a commando slip through his fingers and sending in exaggerated reports of Boer strength."[53] In this view, column command in South Africa was the school for the generals of 1914–1918, and Callwell failed to make the grade. (One may reflect on the career connection between service in Mexico, 1846–1848, and high command in the American Civil War).[54] I believe that Sir John French's displeasure was a fact, as necessarily would be widespread knowledge of that fact—and the reason for it—in the very small world of the Victorian and Edwardian army. Study of Callwell's South African performance does not yield judgment critical of the subject, but Sir John was not known for his willingness to view matters in the round or to revise his opinion once formed.[55]

Second, it is possible, even probable, that Callwell's facility with the pen was a significant source of professional limitation. It is paradoxical that although he regarded himself as a military professional, and notwithstanding his detestation of "amateur strategists," politicians, and "Men of Business,"[56] his correspondence of twenty years with his publisher, William Blackwood, is studded with indiscretions. For example, when writing on 6 March 1898 Callwell penned the opinion that "Sir H. Kitchener only understands black troops and there are already mutterings coming down the Nile at the way our regiments are being treated."[57] At this time of writing Callwell was proceeding on the S.S. *Clyde* to Alexandria in the hope of playing some career-promoting role in Kitchener's expedition to Khartoum.[58] The anecdotal, as well as direct, evidence of Callwell's indiscretion of pen and tongue is persuasive but not conclusive.

Third, aside from the probability that Callwell's pen and tongue made him more enemies than friends where it mattered most for potential advancement, there is the stigma of "able theorist" to consider. For a soldier to be summarized as an "able theorist" is a useful sobriquet for staff work, but hardly the general reputation most advantageous for promotion in the company of warriors. Let me hasten to add that although Repington (and Esher) were correct in classifying Callwell as an able theorist, there is nothing in Callwell's record that suggests an absence of warrior virtues. On the evidence, fairly appraised, the *Times* obituarist was correct when he wrote: "neither was he unpractical, nor a mere theorist, for his campaigning record stands above reproach." Sir John French would not have endorsed all of those words, but Callwell's career as a gunner in the field on active service really does speak for itself. Callwell, after all, was the man who took a forty-pounder heavy gun battery up the Khyber Pass to Kabul,[59] and who commanded initially a half-battery of heavy field artillery, later a collection of guns of many calibers, under rigorous campaign conditions in South Africa. Of whatever he may stand accused, "unpractical" theorist is not among the plausible charges.

Fourth, Callwell's evident enthusiasm for amphibious warfare, no matter how balanced its treatment of a truly mutual dependency of army and navy, would not have commended him to all of his peers or superiors. The point is not that mastery by Callwell of the principles of maritime, and even of naval, strategy, was prima facie evidence of disloyalty in an army officer, but rather that his empathy for the significance of "maritime preponderance" was liable to prompt a cultural uneasiness among some, at least, of his military peers. It would be wrong, however, to claim that the continentalist tilt of the General Staff after 1904–1905 was accompanied by disinterest in, let alone a comprehensive distaste for, amphibious ventures.

Fifth, the distinguished imperial historian A. P. Thornton has speculated that Callwell's career was blighted by his success as a theorist in *Small Wars*.[60] He argues that "small wars not only break the rules, which is forgivable, but they violate the conventions, which is not." Thornton says of Callwell that "though he rose to major general, he 'sent in his papers' in 1909 and took to his books. His professional colleagues saw to it that he did not get a field command in World War I."[61] This line of approach is implausible because Britain's late-Victorian army eventually became all but thoroughly persuaded of the need for a doctrine distinctive to small wars as contrasted with doctrine for "civilized warfare."[62]

One could be moved by the first chapter of Tim Travers's *The Killing Ground* to consider the proposition that promotion in the Edwardian army bore little essential relation to merit, but was rather an idiosyncratic product of personal patronage or its absence.[63] Travers undoubtedly is right in pointing to personal connections in explaining promotion in the 1900s. Unfortunately, beyond the column-command incident with French cited above, there is nothing much known today about Callwell's personal friends and foes that can aid a biographer decisively. Furthermore, no matter how well disguised, patronage systems always shape selection to positions of higher command.[64]

Sixth, *faute de mieux,* one is obliged to list the possibility of there being something about Callwell's personal life which limited the reach of his career. There is no evidence surviving of a kind likely to have attracted contemporary censure, but a would-be biographer at least has to consider the possibility that there was some whispered knowledge about the man which was professionally damaging. This is strictly speculation.

Finally, Callwell undoubtedly acquired the reputation of being predominantly a staff officer, even though his record of command was by no means trivial. In the British army in this period it could be difficult for a person known as a staff officer to break out of that mold. Brig. Gen. Sir James Edmonds, the eventual Official Historian of the Great War, acquired a similar reputation.

We do not know, and may never know, why Callwell's career was not capped with a major field command. We do know, however, that he was well regarded by the men whom he commanded in the field in 1900–1901 in South Africa. Callwell happened to be Henry Powell's battery commander—initially 16 Battery, Southern Division, RGA, Fort Ricasoli, Malta, then in South Africa—and therefore the subject of comment in his diary. The observations on Callwell in Powell's memoir are entirely favorable. For example, of Callwell: "he was obviously a man with a sense of humour, and got on well with the men. The war was nearly at an end, but Major Callwell would be missed."[65] Powell had served with Callwell in Malta and then in Natal and the Transvaal. His enlisted-man opinion is worthy of note; he had no obvious reason to be generous in assessment of Callwell in his diary, beyond telling the story as it was.

Charles E. Callwell produced a body of writing distinguished in range of subject, quality and regularity of output, and—increasingly—quality of literary expression. Aside from

INTRODUCTION

Military Operations, which has lurked to date in a wholly undeserved obscurity, Callwell wrote a study whose merit was recognized at the time—*Small Wars: Their Principles and Practice*—and he produced what transpired to be a bold precursor to *Military Operations* with his 1897 book *The Effects of Maritime Command on Land Campaigns Since Waterloo* (hereafter, *Maritime Command*). In addition, among his more notable works, he wrote such terse but instructive studies as *The Tactics of Today* (Edinburgh, 1902), a book written from the field in South Africa about the shocking implications of the arrival of magazine rifles with smokeless powder, and *The Tactics of Home Defence* (Edinburgh, 1908), focused innovatively upon the ways in which Mr. Haldane's newly organized territorial forces—second-line troops—might cope with a foreign invader.

Callwell's least successful literary venture was, alas, after *Small Wars,* by far his best known work. Specifically in *Field-Marshal Sir Henry Wilson: His Life and Diaries* (London, 1927), Callwell revealed both too much and not enough of his lifelong friend, the eccentric, brilliant, intriguing, francophile CIGS from 1918 to 1922. Callwell presented a severely Bowdlerized version of Wilson's private diaries, given shape and some meaning by large chunks of historical narrative and contextual explanation by the author-editor. Subject and author would have been better served had Callwell used his unrivalled personal knowledge of Wilson, and his equally unrivalled access to Wilson's private papers, to pen a proper biography. That Callwell in his later years had outstanding biographical gifts was proven by his balanced study of the conqueror of Baghdad, *The Life of Sir Stanley Maude* (London, 1920). As it is, Wilson's reputation, which always had been of a sharply contested character, suffered more, albeit inadvertently, from Callwell's diary selection, than it deserved. Indeed, Wilson still awaits thoroughly persuasive treatment by a biographer who is empathetic yet clear-eyed.

Callwell's fame as a practically minded military theorist rests principally upon his textbook on imperial soldiering, *Small Wars*. In *Small Wars,* by which Callwell meant war between regular and irregular forces, the author analyzed and prescribed for a class of conflict of permanent interest. Notwithstanding the dated character of some of the tactical-technical discussion, and the density and prolixity of some of the prose, *Small Wars* is a masterpiece. H. R. Bailes is right to observe that Callwell's advice on how to wage war against irregulars descends rapidly into the realm of common sense, but that valid comment could be applied to the writings of many of the world's greatest military theorists, not even excluding Sun Tzu, Clausewitz, and Jomini.[66]

Callwell proffers a rich menu of good advice and sound nostrums. For example, he identifies as the key problem in small wars the difficulty of bringing irregular forces to open battle, let alone open decisive battle.[67] Callwell emphasizes with no little insight the typical strategic weakness, yet tactical strengths of the regular side.[68] It follows, he argues, that where possible, regular forces should choose to fight. Generally speaking, the more substantial the combat the larger the relative advantage of the disciplined regular over the irregular. Callwell lays stress upon the persisting implications of the fact that small wars often are as much, if not more, wars conducted against nature as they are wars against irregular forces.[69] Logistics are no less critical, or less unforgiving if mishandled, in small wars than in civilized wars. Callwell writes convincingly to the effect that

> the conditions of small wars are so diversified, the enemy's mode of fighting is often so peculiar, and the theatres of operations present such singular features, that irregular warfare must generally be carried out on a method totally different from the stereotyped system. The art of war, as generally understood, must be modified to suit the circumstances of each particular case. The conduct of small wars is in fact in certain

respects an art by itself, diverging widely from what is adapted to the conditions of regular warfare, but not so widely that there are not in all its branches points which permit comparison to be established.[70]

Those sentiments should speak volumes to the concerns of those today who wonder whether regular armed forces need to learn a new art form in order to be effective in low-intensity conflict. *Small Wars*, it should be noted, also provides one of the finest aphorisms in all of military literature. "Theory cannot be accepted as conclusive when practice points the other way."[71]

Callwell did not achieve a measure of fame for his pioneering 1897 history of joint warfare—*Maritime Command*—at all comparable to that consequent upon publication of *Small Wars*. In its way *Maritime Command,* particularly when bracketed with *Military Operations* from the next decade, was as bold a work, possibly bolder (because of the interservice complication), than was *Small Wars,* and intellectually as successful. In *Maritime Command* Callwell set out to demonstrate the truth in the commonsensical proposition that maritime superiority, or its lack, could have a profound effect upon the conduct of war on land. Following a scintillating introductory chapter, he performs what, to the best of this author's knowledge, remains the only "joint" strategic history of the major conflicts of the nineteenth century ever attempted.[72] Callwell visits the fall of the Spanish Empire in South America, the long struggle for Greek independence, sundry conflicts between the Ottoman and Russian empires, the Crimean War, the campaigns of Italian and German unification, the American Civil War, and much else of joint interest besides.

Although some of Callwell's analysis appears to a modern reader to be more period-specific than the author believed, still there is much in *Maritime Command,* including its historical analysis, that appears distinctly fresh. For example,

Callwell's praise of the Anglo-French-Turkish campaigns against Russia in 1854–1856 lies more in accord with recent scholarship than does the weight of negative opinion typical of judgment offered earlier in this century.[73]

Many of the themes introduced in *Maritime Command* are developed more fully in *Military Operations* and therefore will not be discussed in detail at this juncture. At the level of general wisdom *Maritime Command* offers the following noteworthy thought: "The effect of sea-power upon land campaigns is in the main strategical. Its influence over the progress of military operations, however decisive this may be, is often only very indirect."[74] That thought is not only interesting and wise; also it is massively useful to those willing to learn.

In *Maritime Command* Callwell lays stress upon what he regards as the quite disproportionate strategic value even of only a modest scale of military threat from the sea.[75] He emphasizes the strategic utility of the initiative that maritime command allows a military force based on the sea, though he warns against the possibility of military incompetence negating some of the potential strategic benefits of superiority at sea.[76] Viewed all in all, *Maritime Command* of 1897 is a scholarly work of great sophistication and intellectual and moral courage. It is difficult enough to write competent narrative history, or competent strategic analysis of why conflict on land or at sea proceeded as they did. An endeavor to explore the strategic consequences of the balance of power at sea for war on land is all but unprecedented. Callwell's strategic analytical efforts in *Maritime Command* and then, in terms more ambitious still, in *Military Operations,* constitute the military theoretical equivalent of an assault on K-2 without oxygen. A good part of the measure of the achievement is provided by the degree of difficulty in the enterprise.

In a letter to his friendly publisher, William Blackwood, dated 18 August 1904, Callwell confided that "I have long had the idea of writing a book on the subject of the connection between sea power and military operations, and have been taking notes to that end." The War Office took a civilized view of the workload appropriate to its assigned officers in those days, notwithstanding the prevalence of reform in fact and spirit as the army began to assume a more professional character. It is not too surprising, therefore, to find Callwell telling Blackwood that "General Lyttleton [CIGS, General Sir Neville Lyttleton] has given me leave to take it [*Military Operations*] definitely in hand while at the War Office." In the same letter Callwell expressed an aspiration common to many authors. "I think there would be a good chance of it being adopted as a text book in the army. Something of the kind is sorely needed in both services."[77] He returned to this theme following publication, when he wrote that "I expect the book will be a good deal studied by officers and will be used as a sort of unofficial text-book."[78] In practice, such interest as the army did show in amphibious operations before the Great War probably is best attributed not to Callwell's *Military Operations,* but rather to the fact that another practical-minded theorist of joint warfare, Col. George Aston, Royal Marine Artillery, served as an instructor at the Staff College in the years 1904–1907. Also one must mention that Henry Wilson was long persuaded of the importance of land-sea cooperation and he was both commandant of the Staff College (1907–1910) and DMO at the War Office (1910–1914).[79]

Prior to the publication of Callwell's *Military Operations* in 1905, Britain's foes in overseas expeditionary warfare had been irregular in military character, second-rate in military efficiency, and eminently evadable at the water's edge for unopposed, "administrative" landings. After 1905, by way of contrast, Britain's most probable—indeed all but formally designated—foe, Imperial Germany, was so powerful on land, and presented so immediate a menace to France, that amphibious operations, opposed or not at the water's edge, appeared distinctly irrelevant.[80] To summarize, the pre–1905 strategic context had recorded a string of British successes in amphibious warfare in exceedingly permissive conditions. The post–1905 strategic context appeared to allow little significant role for such warfare.

Whether or not a book is hailed instantly as a "classic" depends more, or at least as much, upon timing as it does upon inherent choice of thesis and quality of argument. The attentive public, though it did not know it, was waiting in 1890 for Alfred Thayer Mahan's *The Influence of Sea Power upon History, 1660–1783,* just as that public a century later was waiting for Paul M. Kennedy's study of *The Rise and Fall of the Great Powers: Economic Change and Military Conflict from 1500 to 2000* (New York, 1987). The attentive publics most relevant to Callwell in 1905 and immediately thereafter were anything but waiting for a hefty treatise on joint warfare. Navalist opinion, as reflected in a notably hostile review, was not friendly to the theme of interdependence between naval and military power.[81] Callwell's response to his publisher to that hostile review is no more objective than are like reactions by any wounded author, but nonetheless he is not wholly off the mark when he writes that "the 'Times' review of my new book was probably written by Robinson their naval man, and as some of the ideas in it might not commend themselves to the extreme naval school he naturally enough attacked these and ignored the remainder."[82] The *Times* review was a patronizing put-down in no significant way softened by the praise offered with the criticism. Readers were advised that

> his volume will amply repay perusal, though the well-informed student will find not a few accepted principles advanced with the air of new discoveries, and will be apt to think that here and there the author has failed to grasp the true relations of "military operations and maritime preponderance" and has

given a narrow and even misleading connotation to the term "sea power."[83]

Lest we have missed the reviewer's main point, later we are told "that in our judgment Colonel Callwell's grasp of the broad strategic principles which underlie his subject is far from adequate." The reviewer then has resort to the classic device of, on the one hand, approving the author's principal line of argument ("we have no exception to take to his main thesis"), while on the other hand damning it for its all but trite conventionality ("unless it be an exception to say that the truth of the proposition [that preponderance at sea may increase the need for complementary military force] is so obvious to any one who really knows what sea power is that it is hard to see why any one should think it worth while to enunciate it solemnly").[84] In one respect at least the *Times* reviewer is correct, Callwell, for all his care in distinguishing in chapter one between command of the sea and maritime preponderance—today, sea control—can be careless in deployment of his conceptual arsenal. Command of the sea, control of the sea, maritime preponderance, maritime command, maritime control, sea power, maritime power, and naval power seem often to be employed more for the sake of literary variety than strategic exactitude. So much for the bad news. The good news is that Callwell's occasional conceptual indiscipline, if that is what it is, really matters not at all. He is neither confused about "broad strategic principles," nor is he likely to confuse others.

If the navalist-attentive public was unhappy about Callwell's substitution of preponderance for command, and was uneasy about the claims for dependence upon the army that maritime preponderance or command might require, the military-attentive public had few generic grounds for skepticism. The fulsomely congratulatory review in the *Journal of the Royal United Service Institution* must have been gratifying to the author.[85] The problem for Callwell with military

INTRODUCTION

opinion after 1905 was that it rejected authoritatively amphibious endeavors in the prospective struggle with continentalist Germany. Many of Callwell's arguments in *Military Operations* must have appeared not so much wrong as simply beside the point because they addressed, or appeared to address, a different strategic context from that of Britain in 1906–1914. Needless to add, perhaps, the events of 1940 and their geostrategic implications were to demonstrate just how essential, indeed inescapable, an "amphibious strategy" could be even in war against a continental European power of the first class.

Unlike his 1897 study of *The Effect of Maritime Command on Land Campaigns since Waterloo,* in *Military Operations and Maritime Preponderance* Callwell cast his pen loose from the confining security of a historical narrative. Whereas the former is a most innovative venture in "joint" exploration of a century's warfare, the latter, as its subtitle and title proclaim, is an analytical study of the relations and interdependence of military operations and military preponderance.

Military Operations divides unevenly and broadly into two clusters of chapters. Whereas chapters one through eight explain the dependence of navies on military force, chapters ten through twenty-two expound on the theme of the dependence of military force upon navies. Chapter nine is a summary chapter, while the concluding chapter, twenty-three, provides a detailed forward look to the needs of amphibious warfare in terms of equipment, organization, and joint planning and training. Bearing in mind that Callwell was writing about joint warfare primarily for a military, and not for a naval, readership, it is entirely appropriate that most of the text should be devoted to the influence of maritime preponderance upon military operations rather than vice versa.

No writer can be trusted to distinguish the enduring from the more ephemeral elements in his magnum opus. This caveat should apply with particular force when a military author is writing during a war (in this case the Russo-Japanese War), holds a responsible position in the armed forces, and is inclined to take a practical view of his subject. Callwell fares tolerably well in this regard. In his eyes, at least, the cutting edge of *Military Operations* was its argument that maritime preponderance often could be converted into true command of the sea only if military force were applied against an enemy's fortified naval bases. On the basis of recent and current history, Callwell reasoned that a superior fleet would have to call upon military support to wreak definitive ruin upon an inferior navy. His logic was impeccable for the Royal Navy vis-à-vis the German Navy in both world wars, and also for the U.S. and NATO-Allied navies vis-à-vis Soviet naval power in the Cold War. Callwell's diagnosis of the problem was correct; a second-class navy should be expected to seek fortified refuge. Writing in a self-congratulatory vein to his publisher on 18 August 1904, Callwell advised that

> The Japs said they were prepared to lose 70,000 in taking the place [Port Arthur], but they are hardly likely to suffer quite so badly as that. I am rather pleased, as I started the theory last autumn (and was scoffed at by experts) that the great object of our siege ordnance in future would be to attack ships in harbour, however this siege is converting my theory into a fact.[86]

Unfortunately, tactical and operational considerations would not allow for the close and continuous military siege of German naval power in the two world wars. The maturing of air power, including sea-based air power, provided some solution in many instances to the problem of the fortified fleet, but the challenge remained—as Callwell had specified, until the end of the Cold War. Recall the U.S. and NATO-Allied navies' focus upon the Norwegian Sea in the 1980s maritime strategy's vision of threatening Soviet naval assets based on the Kola Peninsula.[87] Unlike the contemporary Royal Navy, Callwell in 1905 identified, and discussed a leading solution to, the problem of how to reach an inferior enemy fleet which declined to sail to certain destruction.

A contemporary review of *Military Operations* ventured the critical thought that "its chief, indeed its only, fault" is the sheer magnitude of a work so "extraordinarily complete."[88] The argument in *Military Operations* proceeds at a distinctly civilized pace and is amply buttressed by a profusion of historical illustration. For those who find the prospect of twenty-three chapters unduly challenging in this hurried age, I can recommend, with some reluctance, a short course of *Military Operations* comprising chapters one, two, three, ten, thirteen, fifteen, eighteen, twenty, and twenty-three. Because the book, by way of contrast to the career of the author, speaks clearly for itself, this essay provides a terse reader's guide in the form of presentation of Callwell's principal arguments, points, and themes in the order in which they appear and, by and large, in the author's own words.

THINKING AND BEHAVING JOINTLY

"Soldiers and sailors in the past in this and other countries, knowing little of each other's duties and objects, often failed properly to appreciate them at times of crisis" (8). "Concord between forces accustomed under normal circumstances to work apart, can only be ensured when emergency obliges them to work together, if there is mutual sympathy and community of thought between them" (20–21). "If there is to be perfect harmony in war between the navy and the army, there must be mutual confidence in peace and mutual understanding of respective functions" (21–22). "In the present day the land-service and the sea-service are alike in this, that both know their own particular business, and know it well. But do they know enough about each other's business?" (22). These observations speak for themselves to any age.

STRATEGY AND TECHNOLOGICAL CHANGE

"While naval tactics and military tactics are constantly going through a process of evolution as the science of producing arms of destruction progresses, the broad principles of strategy ashore and afloat remain unchanged from century to century" (23). Callwell modifies the Jominian-Mahanian[89] ring to those words as follows: "But it is none the less true that the principles of maritime strategy have in the course of years undergone appreciable modifications, in conformity to a certain extent with the advances which have taken place in the craft of the shipwright. Then, again, developments and discoveries in the science of electrical communication are exerting no small influence over the principles governing the application of strategy to modern conditions at sea" (24).

BLOCKADE IN THE TWENTIETH CENTURY

"The exhaustion which pressure from the sea produces on shore may prove to be a less potent instrument in the hands of the stronger navy in the future than it has been heretofore" (31). The two world wars against Germany were to demonstrate the truth in this speculative point.[90]

CONSIDER THE PERSPECTIVE OF THE SECOND-CLASS NAVY

"We, with our vast naval resources and noble traditions of the sea, are inclined to regard the noble art of maritime war solely from the point of view of the stronger side. We are prone to forget that when in any set of operations the conditions dictate the adoption of an aggressive attitude to one belligerent, those conditions may dictate the adoption of a Fabian policy [i.e., a policy of evasion and delay] to the other belligerent. It is often forgotten that the destruction of a hostile Navy cannot easily be accomplished, even when that navy represents only a relatively speaking feeble fighting force, unless it accepts battle in the open sea" (52–53). The ethnocentric error to which Callwell points persists in American (inter alia) strategic debate (over information-age warfare, for one contemporary example, and over the power of a "nuclear taboo" for another).[91]

THE DEPENDENCE OF LAND CAMPAIGNS UPON MARITIME PREPONDERANCE

"But a great land campaign based on the sea—a campaign analogous to the British struggle to maintain its hold upon the revolted American colonies, or to the Crimean War, or to the Japanese invasions of Manchuria—is obviously impossible without naval preponderance. And naval preponderance can only be assured by defeating the hostile seagoing fleets, or else by shutting them up in their fortified harbours and destroying them if they venture to emerge" (63). The North Atlantic was the Western flank both for the Allied siege operations against Germany in both world wars, and from 1945 until 1989 for any NATO defense of peninsular Europe against the U.S.S.R. Loss of Allied maritime preponderance in the North Atlantic would have meant defeat in any of the three greatest conflicts of this century.

MARITIME FORTRESSES FOR THE OVERMATCHED FLEET

"We are too prone to look at naval warfare only from our own point of view. The instincts of self-preservation drive the fleet which finds itself over-matched back under the guns and behind the booms of its coast fortresses. The history of maritime war proves that this is the case on almost every page" (77). Technology and weaponry alter, but the situation defined by Callwell remains. U.S. and U.S.-Allied expeditionary forces in the future will need to destroy or neutralize the naval forces that regional powers will seek to place in bastions (or other forms of sanctuary).

MARITIME FORTRESSES (FLEET BASES) MOST TYPICALLY NEED TO BE ATTACKED FROM THE LAND

"The reduction of a maritime stronghold must generally be effected by attack from the land side" (99). "And the history of maritime war provides abundant instances all pointing to the conclusion that a beaten or inferior navy is best dealt with by operations on land, if these be practicable" (131). Callwell might be amended for today with the addition to, or substitution for, "operations on land" by operations from the air. His point remains valid, however: the securing of maritime preponderance is a joint undertaking.

THE STRATEGIC DESIRABILITY OF DESTROYING, NOT MERELY CONTAINING, THE ENEMY'S FLEET

"Command of the sea may have been secured, with all the enormous advantages which that carries with it; but the naval power of the enemy has not been destroyed, it has only been temporarily eclipsed [it has sought sanctuary under the guns and behind the booms and mine-fields of the fortresses on the coast], and it remains an asset on the balance-sheet when the progress of events leads up to discussion as to the terms of peace" (127). Callwell advises, soundly, that "an aggregate of war-vessels lying secure in fortified harbours 'contains' a far larger aggregate of war-vessels in observation" (127). Although naval forces contained by close or distant blockade duty perform the essential enabling service of allowing friendly elements to use the seas substantially as preferred, still those naval forces are denied by their gaoler duties availability for more positive missions.

HOW CAN MILITARY FORCE HELP THE NAVY?

"But working on a smaller scale [than campaigns against great enemy maritime fortresses], military force may effectively second the efforts of a preponderating navy to gain command of the sea, quite apart from the question of mere maintenance of bases for the fleet. The enemy's isolated naval ports and coaling-stations may be attacked by land. Harbours, advantageous for prosecuting the maritime campaign may be seized [and] held. And if the enemy resorts to commerce-destroying, the surest way of extinguishing the hostile cruisers engaged in the work is to strike at the root of the mischief,—to seize the port where they replenish their fuel and supplies, and to which they take their captured prizes" (166). "So far from preponderance at sea obviating the need for the upkeep of military force, it may increase that need in obedience to what is a strategical law" (167). Readers can effect for themselves minor translation from the terms of 1905 to those more appropriate for today.

THE STRATEGIC UTILITY OF AMPHIBIOUS FORCE
CONTRASTED WITH PURELY NAVAL FORCE

"The ability of amphibious force to inflict grave injury upon the foe is usually immense. The capabilities of purely naval force to cause the adversary damage is often very limited" (170). Because "the seat of purpose is on the land" the success or failure of naval forces at sea can have strategic meaning only for the course and outcome of war ashore.[92] But for amphibious force to be a reality, let alone a reality able to cause "grave damage," naval force first must achieve preponderance at sea. Amphibious force has no inherently immense ability to inflict grave damage, the details of the case at issue must dominate (*whose* amphibious force directed against *which* foe?)

PROTRACTED WAR ENABLED BY MARITIME PREPONDERANCE IS VERY EXPENSIVE

"And there has been a tendency among writers on the subject of sea-power to exaggerate the effect which may be produced by that process of driving an enemy's mercantile flag off the sea and of blockading the hostile coasts, which is a usual corollary to the establishing of maritime preponderance. The process may under favorable conditions be sure. But under any other conditions than those presented by the British Isles it will assuredly be slow" (170). Callwell proceeds to note of the Napoleonic Wars that "that great contest of the sea against the land was protracted to a ruinous extent. It went on for nine exhausting years after the question of preponderance was definitely settled in Trafalgar Bay" (171).[93] In chapter ten, "The Limitations of Sea-Power in Securing the Objects for Which War is Undertaken," the author is admirably realistic about those limitations.

MARITIME COMMAND AND THE SECURITY OF GLOBAL EMPIRES

"If the only route for reinforcements lies across the sea, the whole strategical situation is likely to hinge on the question whether in virtue of maritime command these reinforcements can, or can not, proceed in safety to their destination by ship. And this has been proved over and over again in the history of war" (190). Whether the case was Britain in 1899–1902, 1914–1918, and 1939–1945, or the United States in the world wars, the Cold War, and today, any security venture that requires extensive and reliable overseas transportation must rest strategically upon the great enabling agent of a navy able to secure and sustain maritime command.

SUBMARINES

"Their radius of action is at present limited, and many questions concerning their construction and their capabilities have still to be fully examined by the light of experience. But science advances with rapid strides in these days, and it is reasonable to expect that submarines will, before many years have passed, possess far greater powers of offense than they can at present lay claim to" (235). As a technically trained soldier, Callwell generally was sound on the future threats that lurked in technical progress.

PERILS FOR AMPHIBIOUS FORCE

"The delays which are inseparable from a great transfer of military force from place to place by sea must be taken into account. And the unfortunate position in which a military force is likely to find itself which is dependent upon maritime communications, in case those communications are cut by the development of superior naval resources in the theatre of war on the part of the enemy, must not be forgotten" (244). The British expedition to Gallipoli in 1915 illustrates the force of Callwell's first point above. His second point is illustrated by the condition of disputed—actually shared, albeit between day and night—maritime command that rendered the U.S. First Marine Division so beleaguered in the early months on Guadalcanal in 1942.[94]

MARITIME PREPONDERANCE AND SHIFTING BASES OF OPERATION ON LAND

"That power of shifting the base of military operations from point to point which control of the sea may give, has been already illustrated by the Japanese plan of action in Korea in the early part of 1904" (259). In addition, Callwell cites Russia shifting her bases in the Turkish war of 1828–1829, Wellington shifting his military base in 1813 from the Tagus (Lisbon) to Santander, and the ability of General Sherman in 1864 to rely upon a sea-founded supply base at Wilmington, North Carolina. The operational logic holds for all time. A commanded sea enables land forces to select the coastal base which is militarily most convenient.

AMPHIBIOUS FORCE AND THE INITIATIVE

"The great principle of acting on 'interior lines' is applicable to amphibious warfare to an even more remarkable degree than it is applicable in purely land warfare. Maritime command tends to give, in exceptional measure, to the military commander who can count upon its possession, that invaluable possession in war—the initiative" (263). Callwell emphasizes that "it is important that it should be understood what an advantage an army on board transports enjoys, in the all important respect of time, under normal conditions over that on shore, when a sudden transfer of force from one theatre of war to another is to take place" (269). He argues that "all trace of a hostile army when at sea is likely to be lost for the time being . . . the spot which it is making for can only be conjectured; if there are many such spots it is impossible to be prepared at all; and till the transports appear in the offing and the hostile landing begins, all is doubt and uncertainty" (278). Events from Normandy, through Inchon and the Falklands to Kuwait, attest to the truth in Callwell's argument, even as the development of modern means of land, air, and space transportation, in principle pose novel challenges for amphibious power.

SECRECY AND AMPHIBIOUS OPERATIONS

"All the advantages which an army enjoys when making a maritime descent upon an enemy's shores, are thrown away unless the objective is kept secret. The benefits arising from possessing the initiative disappear. The undertaking loses the character of a surprise" (283). In his study of the Dardanelles campaign published in 1924 Callwell wrote "that although the very essence of an enterprise such as the military conquest of the Dardanelles by a force arriving by sea lay in effecting a surprise, the conditions at the start had been such that the enemy was both forewarned and forearmed."[95]

ARE OPPOSED LANDINGS IMPRACTICABLE?

If "the foe is found prepared and in the right place . . . and if the project be not abandoned . . . one of the most difficult of operations of war has to be ventured upon, an operation which modern tactical conditions has rendered so difficult as to make it virtually impracticable—landing from on board ship in face of the enemy" (283). Further on, Callwell makes clear that his pessimism about opposed landings has limits. "It is not suggested that opposed landings are now impracticable when the force which can be disembarked at one time is greatly superior to that drawn up on shore. If the attacking army is prepared to accept heavy loss, it may succeed" (360). It was the conventional wisdom among the few thinkers about amphibious warfare in this period to believe that "modern tactical conditions rendered seriously opposed landings 'virtually impracticable.'" Callwell explains thus: "Now disembarkation in face of the enemy is a tactical operation, the conditions of which are necessarily governed by questions of armament, and it is one which has grown more and more difficult as firearms improve in precision and as they increase in their range and power" (344). But, when strategic and operational conditions are relatively permissive, the paying of great care and attention to tactical details enables amphibious forced entry to succeed, as the history of World War II in Europe and the Pacific was to demonstrate conclusively.

SEA POWER AND MILITARY FORCE IN A COASTAL ENCLAVE: THE POWER OF DISTRACTION

"One great function of sea-power is to act as a backbone to military force. Thanks to maritime command, a body of troops planted down in some coast district may be able to hold its ground against formidable armies because they are operating far from their proper bases and are subjected to great difficulties as regards maintenance; and by its action an insignificant military force may be draining the resources of a powerful State which is placed at a strategical disadvantage. It is the form in which naval preponderance can perhaps make itself felt in the most decisive way in warfare on land" (308). Callwell's argument here is not without merit, but it does not warrant the star status that he accords it. The logic just quoted is the logic presented in Callwell's 28 August 1905 War Office memorandum for the encouragement of the Admiralty (reproduced in Appendix I). As a powerful idea expressing an important mission for sea-based military forces, this logic of distraction has much to recommend it. But, as the root logic for a generically peripheral way of warfare it approaches an aspiration for a free lunch, or at least for the deriving of vastly disproportionate effect from limited effort and liability.[96]

THE VALUE OF PRECEDENT?

After noting of opposed landings that "nothing of the kind has taken place on a great scale of recent years" (367), Callwell provides examples of success in such operations in the tactical conditions obtaining for warfare in the eighteenth century and just beyond. But, he then proceeds to write: "Numerous examples of successful landings have been given in preceding paragraphs, but all of them date back to a time when battle formations were totally different from those which progress in armament has forced upon the trained soldiery of to-day. They cannot be accepted as precedents for what will happen in future war, and the reason for this is that the evolution in tactical conditions works entirely in favour of the troops repelling an attempted landing, as against the troops making the attempt" (359). Callwell could make mistakes, not that his tactical pessimism was an error at the time of his writing, or for several decades to come, but he was not inclined to be doctrinaire. In particular, and in positive contrast to Mahan and Corbett, Callwell's historical study of warfare in the age of fighting sail did not impede his understanding of the operational and even strategic significance of technical-tactical change.[97]

INTRODUCTION

COMMAND OF INLAND WATERS

"The conditions governing the command of a great river, or of a canal, differ widely from those upon which command of the sea depends. But once that command has been established, its strategical influence over land operations may be very similar to that which so often follows upon maritime supremacy" (416). The dominant British imperial experience in this regard during Callwell's years of service was, of course, the use of command of the Nile to penetrate into the Sudan. Somewhat earlier in the nineteenth century the loss of control of the Mississippi River system had proved strategically devastating to the Confederate States, while much earlier in the century combat on the Great Lakes had helped shape the course of the War of 1812. From the use the Romans made of the Danube, the Rhine, and the Rhone, to the riverine warfare in Vietnam in the 1960s, the truth in Callwell's argument shines forth from historical experience.

ORGANIZATION AND EQUIPMENT FOR AMPHIBIOUS WARFARE

"The land-service and the sea-service can co-operate in many situations which arise in struggles between maritime nations, and . . . they can mutually aid one another in bringing about the triumph of their side. But if the highest results are to be attained, there must not only be confidence and harmony between the naval forces and the military forces,—each must also be organized and equipped for the execution of amphibious operations under the circumstances created by the particular campaigns, and each must be prepared to meet with experiences foreign to normal stereotyped forms of warfare" (431). Callwell argues, unobjectionably, that "the class of vessel by which dominion of the sea is attained in time of war is not necessarily that which is best suited for sustaining military operations ashore" (432). He comments pointedly that "nations where military strength lies in the combination of their fighting resources ashore with predominance afloat, are well advised to organise their armies in a form suitable for over-sea expeditions" (437). Callwell praises the Japanese military organization that events at his time of writing were proving to be effective (against the Russians), and suggests that "they have learned, not only by experience but by intuition, that the essence of amphibious strategy lies in compactness and mobility of the forces employed" (437). The spirit, and even much of the detail, of the final chapter of *Military Operations* is the spirit and detail provided by the leading lights in the U.S. Marine Corps in 1921 and beyond. The Fleet Marine Force established in 1933 was entirely Callwellian in purpose and character, if not in direct provenance.

SHIPPING

"It is pleasant to murmur '*Kriegmobil*' [mobile war] in the ear of an attendant aide-de-camp and to know that, within a week, army corps upon army corps will be converging along the lines of a cunningly contrived system of strategical railways, towards that borderland where a mighty conflict is impending. But what boots all this bustle if the frontier be the sea? These masses of men and vehicles and horses need many transports if their journey is to be continued beyond the coastline of their own country" (440). Callwell points out that a mass army on the then European continental conscripted scale could not be moved immediately by sea. What matters for our purposes is the continuing validity of Callwell's argument that shipping and plans for the sea transportation of military forces need to be kept in balance. "Sealift" caused agonies of anxiety in both world wars and was an ever recurring subject for alarmed commentary and some careful study during the Cold War. The issue has lost little of its vitality in the post–Cold War years. Advances in long-range and intratheater airlift remain systemically constrained by the per-mile costs of combating gravity; overseas bases are dwindling in number and can be subject to entropic terms of use; yet the U.S. sea services plan to operate more and more across and then forward from the sea.

THE NECESSITY FOR JOINTNESS

"It has been the purpose of this volume to show how naval preponderance and warfare on land are mutually dependent, if the one is to assert itself conclusively and if the other is to be carried out with vigour and effect. There is an intimate connection between command of the sea and control of the shore. But if the strategical principles involved in this connection are to be put in force to their full extent, if the whole of the machinery is to be set in motion, there must be coordination of authority and there must be harmony in the council chambers and in the theatre of operations. That is perhaps the most important lesson to be learnt from the many interesting and remarkable campaigns in which circumstances have brought into contact fighting forces afloat and fighting forces ashore" (444). Callwell's "most important lesson" would seem today to have been well learned. In the 1993 words of then Chairman of the Joint Chiefs of Staff, Gen. Colin L. Powell: "We train as a team, fight as a team, and win as a team."[98]

Callwell's *Military Operations and Maritime Preponderance* has been selected for the "Classics of Sea Power" series not because it is, but rather because it should be, a well recognized and influential classic. The acid test for classic status has to be the assessed measure of timelessness of a work.

Military Operations bears the hallmark at the level of detail of its date of birth, but that hallmark does not impair fatally or even very substantially the value of the book as a whole. Indeed, with only minor exceptions, even Callwell's judgments on matters of technical and tactical detail tend to look sound today.[99] For example, the author has entirely sensible comments to offer on such new-fangled devices as wireless telegraphy, submarine mines, and torpedoes. Clausewitz advises that "theory then becomes a guide to anyone who wants to learn about war from books; it will help light his way, ease his progress, train his judgment, and help him to avoid pitfalls."[100] *Military Operations* performs usefully in all those regards.

Military Operations addresses enduring issues of joint warfare in ways, and typically with the provision of answers—he was a practical soldier as well as a writer of books—that should command respect. For the U.S. armed services today the facts that Callwell was British, was writing before the experience of world war in this century, and prior to the demonstration of military air power (not to mention ballistic and cruise missiles and nuclear weapons), really does not matter. In its essential structure, in the answers it provides and in the loneliness of the literature on joint warfare, *Military Operations* is a classic. If *Military Operations* is not a classic of joint warfare then which books are? U.S. Marine Corps' (inter alia) readers can supply for themselves the suitable contemporary detail about weapons and tactics, but in the pages of *Military Operations* they will discover rigorous and persuasive analysis of such topics as the utility of land power and sea power for each other; the limitations of the effectiveness of sea power and land power in isolation; the strategic, operational, tactical, and even administrative flexibility of sea power; the implications of new weapons for amphibious warfare; the need to take the enemy seriously, even when his navy is of the second class (or lower); the challenge of inflicting a truly decisive defeat upon an enemy fleet which is most reluctant to expose itself to trial by battle; the value of joint doctrine, organization, and training; and the necessity for specialized capabilities designed for amphibious warfare.

Charles Edward Callwell intended, more accurately hoped, to write a text book for the British army for the second half of the 1900s. Instead he wrote a classic of military theory on joint warfare that can be read and studied for professional joint benefit today.

NOTES

1. Other works instructive on the amphibious dimension to joint warfare include: Alfred Vagts, *Landing Operations: Strategy, Psychology, Tactics, Politics. From Antiquity to 1945* (Harrisburg, Pa., 1946); Jeter A. Isely and Philip A. Crowl, *The U.S. Marines and Amphibious War: Its Theory and Its Practice in the Pacific* (Princeton, N.J., 1951); John Creswell, *Generals and Admirals: The Story of Amphibious Command* (Westport, Conn., 1952); Merrill L. Bartlett, ed., *Assault from the Sea: Essays on the History of Amphibious Warfare* (Annapolis, Md., 1983), particularly the bibliography, pp. 437–42; M. H. H. Evans, *Amphibious Operations: The Projection of Sea Power Ashore* (London, 1990); and Richard Harding, *Amphibious Warfare in the Eighteenth Century: The British Expedition to the West Indies, 1740–1742* (Woodbridge, Suffolk, Eng., 1991), which is surprisingly useful (especially pp. 1–15, 150–201). A. Lorelli, *To Foreign Shores: U.S. Amphibious Operations in World War II* (Annapolis, Md., 1995), is a welcome addition to the literature. It is unsurprising, though disappointing, to find that a recent popular historical survey of amphibious warfare by a British author does not even mention Charles E. Callwell or his writings. Simon Foster, *Hit the Beach! Amphibious Warfare from the Plains of Abraham to San Carlos Water* (London, 1995).

2. Hew Strachan, "The British Way in Warfare," in David Chandler, ed., *The Oxford Illustrated History of the British Army* (Oxford, Eng., 1994), 423.

3. Hervé Coutau-Bégarie, "De quelques pensées navales inconnues ou insuffisamment connues," in Coutau-Bégarie, ed., *L'évolution de la pensée navale, II* (Paris, 1992), 15.

4. J. C. Wylie, *Military Strategy: A General Theory of Power Control*, introduction by John B. Hattendorf (1889; Annapolis, Md., 1967), 34.

5. George Aston's (1861–1938) many writings are pervasively joint, as one would expect of a marine. See his "Combined Strategy for Fleets and Armies; or 'Amphibious Strategy,'" *Journal of the Royal United Service Institution* (July–December 1907): 984–1004; *Letters on Amphibious Wars* (London, 1911); *Sea, Land, and Air Strategy: A Comparison* (London, 1914); and *Memories of a Marine: An Amphibiography* (London, 1919). There were no noteworthy differences of opinion between Aston and Callwell. Callwell certainly agreed with Aston that "for the most part land strategy and sea strategy (as far as they have been written about at all) have been dealt with in 'water-tight compartments' as separate subjects," and that "in studying war histories we are constantly struck by the influence of distant military operations upon the naval situation, and the converse also holds good." (*Sea, Land, and Air Strategy*, 118, 119.)

6. Robert D. Heinl, Jr., "The U.S. Marine Corps: Author of Modern Amphibious Warfare," in Bartlett, ed., *Assault from the Sea*, 187 (emphasis added).

7. I am grateful to Professor Allan R. Millett of Ohio State University for his expert opinion on this question, which is to the effect that the USMC almost certainly was aware of Callwell's writings on amphibious warfare. Millett is the author of *Semper Fidelis: The History of the United States Marine Corps* (New York, 1982), and *In Many a Strife: General Gerald C. Thomas and the U.S. Marine Corps, 1917–1956* (Annapolis, Md., 1993). Nonetheless, evidence of connection between Callwell's books and the U.S. Marine Corps' innovations of the 1920s and 1930s remains wholly speculative. Certainly the author of the most recent relevant study has not found evidence of any such connection. See David R. Massam, "British Maritime Strategy and Amphibious Capability, 1900–1940," Ph.D. diss., Oxford University, 1995.

8. United States Marine Corps, *Small Wars Manual, 1940* (1940; Manhattan, Kans., n.d.), ch. 3, p. 13. Also see the comment on Callwell in the excellent introductory essay by Ronald Schaffer, "The 1940 Small Wars Manual and the 'Lessons of History,'" especially p. vi.

9. For example, see the positive and negative cases discussed in Creswell, *Generals and Admirals,* chs. 1–7, and Harding, *Amphibious Warfare in the Eighteenth Century.* For a precedent in fiasco, see Gordon C. Bond, *The Grand Expedition: The British Invasion of Holland in 1809* (Athens, Ga., 1979). To reach back still further, on 13 July 960 Byzantine Emperor Nicephorus Phocas effected a successful amphibious operation to seize the island of Crete from the Arabs. See Gustave Schlumberger, *Un emperor byzantin au dixième siècle: Nicéphore Phocas* (Paris, 1890), ch. 2.

10. James L. Stokesbury, "British Concepts and Practices of Amphibious Warfare, 1867–1916," Ph.D. diss., Duke University, 1968, 216.

11. Jeter A. Isely and Philip A. Crowl, *The U.S. Marines and Amphibious War: Its Theory, and Its Practice in the Pacific* (Princeton, N.J., 1951), 5.

12. Stokesbury's claim, in "British Concepts," that there was no British doctrine for amphibious warfare is simply wrong. See *Report of the Naval and Military Conference on Overseas Expeditions*, Public Record Office (PRO), 20 March 1905, WO 33/344. This report and a subsequent manual on combined operations emphasized the need for a "covering force" to capture beaches at night and act to protect the landing of the main expeditionary elements. I am grateful to John Gooch for bringing these documents to my attention.

13. On the strategic implications of the tactical and operational problems with amphibious warfare in World War I, see Paul Kennedy, "Military Effectiveness in the First World War," in Allan R. Millett and Williamson Murray, eds., *Military Effectiveness, Vol. I: The First World War* (Boston, 1988), 332–33, 336.

14. Readers in search of information and opinions on the Dardanelles campaign of 1915 are confronted with an overabundance of choice. Bearing in mind the subject of this essay, I recommend Charles E. Callwell's less than wholly disinterested, but still first-rate, study, *The Dardanelles* (London, 1924). The *Dardanelles Commission, First Report* (London, 1917), and *The Final Report of the Dardanelles Commission* (London, 1919), are indispensable, as is C. F. Aspinall-Oglander, *History of the Great War, Military Operations, Gallipoli*, 2 vols. (London, 1929, 1932). In addition, see Alan Moorehead, *Gallipoli* (1956; Annapolis, Md., 1982); Trumball Higgins, *Winston Churchill and the Dardanelles: A Dialogue in Ends and Means* (New York, 1963); Robert Rhodes James, *Gallipoli* (London, 1965); and Nigel Steel and Peter Hart, *Defeat at Gallipoli* (London, 1994).

15. Isely and Crowl's claim that "*The Tentative Landing Manual* [1934] prepared at Marine Corps Schools was the first attempt to set forth in systematic fashion a detailed treatise on modern amphibious warfare" cannot stand as written in the light of Callwell's 1905 achievement. *U.S. Marines and Amphibious War*, 44.

16. PRO, 19 December 1906, CAB 4/2/92B.

17. Charles E. Callwell, *Experiences of a Dug-Out, 1914–1918* (London, 1921), 106.

18. Given the well documented fact of official recognition of the problem of effecting opposed landings, it may not be true to argue, with

Stokesbury, that "the influence of Aston and Callwell does not appear to have been particularly great before the war." "British Concepts," 338–39.

19. See Appendix I for the relevant chronology in 1905 and for those memoranda drafted and signed by Callwell on army-navy cooperation. In addition to the primary sources consulted, principally the War Office files in the Public Record Office, I found the following works especially useful: Arthur J. Marder, *From the Dreadnought to Scapa Flow: The Royal Navy in the Fisher Era, 1904–1919, Vol. I. The Road to War, 1904–1914* (London, 1961); Samuel R. Williamson, Jr., *The Politics of Grand Strategy: Britain and France Prepare for War, 1904–1914* (Cambridge, Mass., 1969); Neil W. Summerton, "The Development of British Military Planning for a War Against Germany, 1904–1914," Ph.D. diss., London University, 1970; Brian Bond, *The British Army and the Staff College, 1856–1914* (London, 1972); Nicholas d'Ombrain, *War Machinery and High Policy: Defence Administration in Peacetime Britain, 1902–1914* (Oxford, Eng., 1973); John Gooch, *The Plans of War: The General Staff and British Military Strategy c. 1900–1916* (London, 1976); David French, *British Economic and Strategic Planning, 1905–1915* (London, 1982); and John Gooch, "The Weary Titan: Strategy and Policy in Great Britain, 1890–1918," in Williamson Murray, MacGregor Knox, and Alvin Bernstein, eds., *The Making of Strategy: Rulers, States and War* (Cambridge, Eng., 1994), 278–306.

20. A most elegant survey of the continental question in modern British defense planning is Michael Howard, *The Continental Commitment: The Dilemma of British Defence Policy in the Era of the Two World Wars* (London, 1972).

21. As promised in the U.S. Navy publication . . . *From the Sea: Preparing the Naval Service for the 21st Century* (Washington, D.C., September 1992); and in John B. Dalton, Adm. Jeremy M. Boorda, and Gen. Carl E. Mundy, Jr., "Forward . . . From the Sea," *U.S. Naval Institute Proceedings* (December 1994): 46–49.

22. Notwithstanding his intellect, his languages, and his wide knowledge of the world, Callwell was entirely a person of his time and place. He was a deeply conservative late Victorian professional soldier and Anglo-Irish gentleman. His biographical writings are studded liberally with evidence of attitudes and prejudices that would have been thoroughly orthodox in the army of his day. A few examples follow. On British public (that is, private) schools: "But people who have knocked about this Empire of ours and who have seen something of its builders, of its developers, of its administrators great and small, and of its defenders, prefer to judge the great public schools of England and Scotland by

results arising from another form of education practised within their walls, from the form of education which turns the public schoolboy out into the world—a gentleman who plays the game." *Stray Recollections* (London, 1923), 1:24. Or, consider, "Beira is the absolute limit. Steamy, depressing, dago-haunted, and buzzing with mosquitoes. . . ." Ibid., 2:242. If not anti-Semitic, Callwell certainly comes close. "Mohileff was reputed to be about the most Jewish township in Russia, and, judging by the appearance of the inhabitants, that reputation was not undeserved. One had heard a lot about pogroms in the past, but they would not appear to be of the really thoroughgoing sort." *Dug-Out*, 248–49. Or, when commenting on Jews in the cities of North Africa, Callwell writes that "these parasites abounded in all such centres of population, and they throng though regarded with little favour by the Moors and subjected to galling disabilities." *Stray Recollections*, 1:355. Callwell harbored a special distaste for those he insisted upon calling "amateur strategists." He was always ready to remind his readers "that imagination is a deadly peril when unaccompanied by knowledge." *Dug-Out*, 218, 219.

23. Bond, *Victorian Army and the Staff College*, 306.

24. Callwell, *Dug-Out*, 7–8.

25. Robert Blake, ed., *The Private Papers of Douglas Haig, 1914–1919* (London, 1952), 117.

26. Stokesbury, "British Concepts," 210–16; Massam, "British Maritime Strategy," 17–18.

27. Keith Neilson, *Strategy and Supply: The Anglo-Russian Alliance, 1914–17* (London, 1984), 6.

28. Ian F. W. Beckett, "The Study of Counter-Insurgency: A British Perspective," *Small Wars and Insurgencies* (April 1990): 47.

29. Callwell, *Stray Recollections*, 2:245.

30. Ibid.

31. H. de Watteville, the author of the entry on Callwell in J. R. H. Weaver, ed., *The Dictionary of National Biography, 1922–1930* (Oxford, 1937), who knew his subject personally, was in no doubt that Callwell had been his own worst enemy. "[H]e excelled in a form of story (*Service Yarns and Memories* [Edinburgh, 1912]) which was inspired by clever satire of army procedure and War Office routine; this had in truth contributed not a little to his being passed over for promotion" (154). On the anecdotal, but still persuasive, side, I am grateful to Professor A. P. Thornton of the University of Toronto for bringing to my attention a judgment on Callwell by the highly respected Gen. Sir Nevil Macready. Professor Thornton has seen a 1917 letter from Macready to his sister (the Macready's were distant relatives of Professor Thornton's

mother), written on official adjutant-general War Office stationary, claiming that "Charlie Callwell's tongue . . . runs away with him and he makes more enemies than he ought to in the wrong places." Professor Thornton is quoting from memory, but, as he said, "it's the sort of remark that's memorable." Professor A. P. Thornton, letter to the author, 11 November 1995.

32. Brian Bond, "Judgment in Military History," *RUSI Journal* (Spring 1989): 69.

33. Shelford Bidwell and Dominick Graham, *Fire-Power: British Army Weapons and Theories of War, 1904–1945* (London, 1982), 56.

34. See Callwell, *Stray Recollections,* vol. 1, ch. 10. Bond's superb study, *Victorian Army and the Staff College,* may be supplemented with Brian Holden Reid, *War Studies at the Staff College, 1890–1930,* Occasional Papers I (Camberley, Surrey, Eng., 1992).

35. Charles E. Callwell, "Lessons to be Learnt from the Campaigns in which British Forces have been employed since the year 1865," *Journal of the Royal United Service Institution,* 31 (1887): 357–412.

36. Thomas G. Fergusson, *British Military Intelligence, 1870–1914: The Development of a Modern Intelligence Organization* (Frederick, Md., 1986), is indispensable.

37. *The Times* (London), 17 May 1928, p. 18.

38. See organization chart number nine in Fergusson, *British Military Intelligence,* 251.

39. Reproduced in Appendix I.

40. Gooch, *Plans of War,* 306. Gooch draws attention to an entry in the diary of Maurice Hankey (secretary to the Dardanelles Committee/War Council) for 23 September 1915, wherein the diarist records that at a meeting of the Dardanelles Committee Kitchener "sits at the head of the table and talks a lot, and bludgeons everyone into agreeing with him. I was the only one who put up any opposition, the Chief of Staff (Wolfe-Murray—or 'Sheep' Murray as Winston [Churchill] calls him) merely mumbling assent, and Callwell just agreeing." Quoted in Stephen Roskill, *Hankey: Man of Secrets, Vol. I, 1877–1918* (London, 1970), 219.

41. Letter from Charles E. Callwell to Sir R. Brade (no date but certainly July 1916), Papers of Sir Ian Hamilton, Liddell Hart Archives, King's College, London, Private files 17/6/7. Emphasis added. Callwell's claim that Kitchener did not approve of the naval attack could mislead the unwary. On 2 January 1915 Kitchener had mooted the idea of a naval demonstration. Letter from Lord Kitchener to Winston S. Churchill [First Lord of the Admiralty], 2 January 1915, Chartwell MSS 13/46. Also, one should bear in mind that although Churchill could dominate

as First Lord, his certainly was not the only view on the Dardanelles in the Admiralty. Whether or not Callwell would have found it feasible and productive to challenge Kitchener's unflattering views of Turkish military prowess with the opinion of, say, British military attachés who had served very recently in the Balkans, must remain a subject for speculation only.

42. Though anything but blind to Kitchener's faults, Callwell spoke and wrote of him with what seems to this author at least to have been a genuine respect and even affection. See *Dug-Out,* particularly pp. 83–84; and *Stray Recollections,* 2:274–78. Callwell had a way with words. One savors this pen portrait of his chief in 1914–1915. "That a man of action, used to getting things done without discussion and without having to listen to dialectics, as the conqueror of the Sudan had been, should have felt himself embarrassed when cheek by jowl with some of those keen and restless spirits amongst whom his lot was cast in the Cabinet, was hardly to be wondered at. Few men trained to arms can even when they are in the right, even when they know what they are talking about while the masters of words do not, hold their own in argument with lawyers and practised debaters." Ibid., 277.

43. Gooch, *Plans of War,* 313.

44. Callwell, *Dug-Out,* 89; and Aspinall-Oglander, *Gallipoli,* 1:41.

45. In Callwell's opinion, at least. *Dug-Out,* 65.

46. See Aspinall-Oglander, *Gallipoli,* 1:88–90; and Winston S. Churchill, *The World Crisis, 1911–1918* (London, 1938), 1:628–29, n. 1. Potentially damaging to Callwell's reputation was the apparent failure of the War Office to pass on to Hamilton and his very small staff all of the useful information which was available. As James puts the matter: "One of the unexplained mysteries of the whole Gallipoli experience is why the detailed reports on the Dardanelles defences which had been sent to the War Office since 1911 by successive military attachés at Constantinople and vice-consuls at Chanak were not made available to [Major-General Walter] Braithwaite [Hamilton's designated Chief of Staff]." James proceeds to reveal that Lt. Col. C. Cunliffe-Owen, military attaché at Constantinople from late 1913 until the outbreak of war "apparently on his own initiative . . . had carried out a careful survey of the Dardanelles area" and had sent back to the War Office "a stream of information . . . dealing with new armaments" and related matters. Callwell did not make Cunliffe-Owen, personally, or his field reports, available to Hamilton and Braithwaite. James, *Gallipoli,* 53–56.

47. Letter from Callwell to Hamilton, 25 May 1917, Hamilton Papers, 17/4/2/73, p. 2.

48. Letter from Hamilton to Callwell, 29 May 1917, Hamilton Papers, 17/4/2/75, p. 1. A year earlier Hamilton had written to Winston Churchill of his uneasiness over the damage that Callwell might or might not be able to wreak upon his reputation, were he so moved. "Next post brought a friendly letter from Callwell telling me it had been decided to publish nothing at present [of the Dardanelles documents]. So far then all is well, but yesterday's worry [when Hamilton found that the documents he had dispatched to help the Dardanelles enquiry were returned by Callwell without explanation] has been a warning and I don't want to go through it again. Do please then treat Callwell's letter [to Hamilton 12 July 1916, Hamilton Papers, 17/6/14] entirely as a negative guide, and do not on any account say or do anything that will bring him into the affair. . . . Callwell must be a most important witness in whatever sort of enquiry or investigation takes place. He alone of soldiers was habitually with Lord K. not only at the War Council but in his room when all these matters were discussed. If Callwell's sympathy now apparently [altered from 'distinctly'] with us is changed into dislike and mistrust then it will be a very bad business." Letter from Hamilton to Churchill, 13 July 1916, Hamilton Papers, 17/6/17.

49. Letter from Callwell to Hamilton, 30 May 1917, Hamilton Papers, 17/4/2/82.

50. Callwell, *Dardanelles*, 57.

51. Letter from Hamilton to Callwell, 29 June 1916, Hamilton Papers, 17/6/4, p. 1; Letter from Callwell to Hamilton, 5 July 1916, Hamilton Papers, 17/6/6, p. 3.

52. "Appendix: Nineteenth Anniversary Meeting, March 1st 1921," *Journal of the Royal United Service Institution* (February–November 1921): xvii.

53. Richard Holmes, *The Little Field-Marshal: Sir John French* (London, 1981), 114. I have been unable to confirm the alleged facts in the case. Holmes's claimed source, a letter from Col. Douglas Haig to Lt.-Col. Brinsley Fitzgerald (ADC to French) of 3 November 1901, is either a faulty citation or is lurking in some collection other than that specified. My researches in the Fitzgerald Papers at the Imperial War Museum have failed to unearth this story about Callwell. Nonetheless, Holmes is certain that he has seen the now elusive letter and I have no reason to doubt him. Needless to add, perhaps, this could be a matter of huge importance for any endeavor to understand Callwell's career. Callwell's busy life as a column commander in South Africa is recorded in *Stray Recollections,* vol. 2, ch. 19. On pp. 158–62 Callwell recounts several abortive Boer hunts, any one, or ones, of which might have fueled dissat-

isfaction on Haig (who was coordinating the activities of several columns, including Callwell's) or French's part. At least as Callwell tells it, unsurprisingly enough, his achievements and frustrations in a column command in guerrilla warfare merited no particular censure. See Erskine Childers, *The Times History of the War in South Africa, 1899–1902,* vol. 5 (London, 1907), ch. 20; and Maurice Harold Grant, *History of the War in South Africa, 1899–1902,* vol. 4 (London, 1910), chs. 15, 26.

54. See James M. McPherson, "Prologue: From the Halls of Montezuma," *Battle Cry of Freedom: The Civil War Era* (New York, 1988), 3–5. Whereas the American comrades in arms of the 1840s were the enemies in arms of the 1860s, so the reverse was significantly the case for British and Boers when one contrasts 1899–1902 with 1914–1918.

55. I am indebted to Dr. Richard Holmes (author of *Little Field Marshal*) for responding to my questions on this matter.

56. See, for example, Callwell, *Dug-Out,* 101, 156, 186, 218, 230 (amateur strategists); *Stray Recollections,* 2:291, 2:296; *Dug-Out,* 213 (politicians); *Dug-Out,* 129–31 ("Men of Business").

57. Letter from Charles E. Callwell to William Blackwood, 6 March 1898, Blackwood Papers, National Library of Scotland, MS 4671, pp. 135–38.

58. Callwell must have envied the good luck of Major Henry Rawlinson (later General Sir Henry Rawlinson, GOC of Fourth Army, 1916–1917, 1918). "In January 1898 either chance or sound management found him in Cairo, where his wife had been directed for her health. Just then Kitchener was launching his expedition against Khartoum, and proved in need of a staff officer to manage the influx of troops. Rawlinson got the job, so for the first time occupying a responsible position during a major military episode." He performed well and "the favourable impression Rawlinson thus created would soon stand him in good stead." Robin Prior and Trevor Wilson, *Command on the Western Front: The Military Career of Sir Henry Rawlinson, 1914–18* (Oxford, Eng., 1992), 6–7.

59. See Rudyard Kipling's poems about the forty-pounder gun teams: "Many Inventions" (from *My Lord the Elephant*) and "Gun-Bullocks" (from "Her Majesty's Servants," in *The Jungle Book*), collected in *The World of Rudyard Kipling* (Ware, Herts., Eng., 1994), 570, 757, respectively.

60. Charles E. Callwell, *Small Wars: A Tactical Textbook for Imperial Soldiers* (1896, 1899, 1906; London, 1990). Callwell's subtitle was "Their Principles and Practice."

61. A. P. Thornton, "Great Powers and Little Wars: Limits of Power," in A. Hamish Ion and E. J. Errington, eds., *Great Powers and Little Wars: The Limits of Power* (Westport, Conn., 1993), 20.

62. See Howard H. R. Bailes, "The Influence of Continental Examples and Colonial Warfare upon the Reform of the Late Victorian Army," Ph.D. diss., London University, 1980; and "Patterns of Thought in the Late Victorian Army," *Journal of Strategic Studies* (March 1981): 29–45. T. R. Moreman, "The British and Indian Armies and North-West Frontier Warfare, 1849–1914," *Journal of Imperial and Commonwealth History* (January 1992): 35–64, also is relevant.

63. Tim Travers, *The Killing Ground: The British Army, the Western Front and the Emergence of Modern Warfare, 1900–1918* (London, 1987), ch. 1.

64. For a superior example of support for this proposition, see Stephen Badsey, "Faction in the British Army: Its Impact on 21st Army Group Operations in Autumn 1944," *War Studies Journal* (Autumn 1995): 13–28.

65. Henry Powell, *Duelling with Long Toms* (priv. pub. in Ilford, Essex, Eng., 1988), 70.

66. Bailes, "Influence of Continental Examples and Colonial Warfare," 135; and "Technology and Tactics in the British Army, 1866–1900," in Ronald Haycock and Keith Neilson, eds., *Men, Machines, and War* (Waterloo, Ontario, 1988), 36.

67. Callwell, *Small Wars,* particularly ch. 12.

68. Ibid., ch. 7.

69. Ibid., 57.

70. Ibid., 23.

71. Ibid., 270.

72. A possible rival would be Clark G. Reynolds, *Command of the Sea: The History and Strategy of Maritime Empires. Vol. II, Since 1815* (1974; Malabar, Fla., 1983), chs. 10–13.

73. See Basil Greenhill and Ann Giffard, *The British Assault on Finland, 1854–1855: A Forgotten Naval War* (London, 1988); and Andrew D. Lambert, *The Crimean War: British Grand Strategy Against Russia, 1853–56* (Manchester, Eng., 1990), for the best of modern scholarship.

74. Callwell, *Maritime Command,* 29.

75. Ibid., 3.

76. Ibid., 301.

77. Letter from Callwell to Blackwood, 18 August 1904, Blackwood Papers, MS 30102.

78. Letter from Callwell to Blackwood, 30 July 1905, Blackwood Papers, MS 30111.
79. See Callwell, *Field-Marshal Sir Henry Wilson,* 1:70–71; and Bond, *Victorian Army and the Staff College,* 98–99, 254–55.
80. As Bond writes of the years 1906–1910, "it was in these years that British military planning swung powerfully—if not irreversibly—towards intervention in a future continental war on the side of France against Germany. Thus at long last staff officers could be trained with a specific and realistic contingency in mind." *Victorian Army and the Staff College,* 245. See also Appendix I, below.
81. "Military Operations and Maritime Preponderance," *Times Literary Supplement* (London), 14 July 1905, pp. 222–23 (hereafter, *Times* review).
82. Callwell to Blackwood, 30 July 1905.
83. *Times* review, p. 222.
84. Ibid., p. 223.
85. *Journal of the Royal United Service Institution* (March 1906): 381–82.
86. Callwell to Blackwood, 18 August 1904.
87. See Admiral James D. Watkins and others, *The Maritime Strategy* (Annapolis, Md., 1986); Norman Friedman, *The U.S. Maritime Strategy* (London, 1988), ch. 7; and, for a skeptical appraisal, George W. Baer, *One Hundred Years of Sea Power: The U.S. Navy, 1890–1990* (Stanford, Calif., 1994), ch. 17.
88. *Journal of the Royal United Service Institution* (March 1906): 381.
89. Antoine Henri de Jomini, *The Art of War* (1838, 1862; London, 1992), 48; and Mahan, *Influence of Sea Power upon History,* 88.
90. The economic blockade of Germany in World War II, though important, was overshadowed by the course and influence of military events. The effect of the blockade in World War I was more significant and remains, to a degree, controversial as to its strategic effect. The outstanding study is the long-suppressed (from 1937 until 1961) official history, A. C. Bell, *A History of the Blockade of Germany and of the Countries Associated with Her in the Great War, Austria-Hungry, Bulgaria, and Turkey, 1914–1918* (London, 1937).
91. On ethnocentrism see A. J. Bacevich, "Preserving the Well-Bred Horse," *National Interest* (Fall 1994): 48–49. On the "nuclear taboo," see Colin S. Gray, "The Second Nuclear Age: Insecurity, Proliferation, and the Control of Arms," in Williamson Murray, ed., *Brassey's Mershon American Defense Annual, 1995–1996* (Washington, D.C., 1995), 145–48.
92. Wayne P. Hughes, Jr., *Fleet Tactics: Theory and Practice* (Annapolis, Md., 1986), 33–34. Julian S. Corbett, *Some Principles of Mari-*

time Strategy, introduction by Eric J. Grove (1911; Annapolis, Md., 1988), 15–16, also is most relevant.

93. In a book published five years after Callwell's *Military Operations,* Julian S. Corbett expressed much the same thought about the legacy of Trafalgar. *The Campaign of Trafalgar* (London, 1910), 408. Whether or not Corbett was indebted to Callwell on this important matter, there is no doubt but that Callwell got there first.

94. See Frank O. Hough, Verle E. Ludwig, and Henry I. Shaw, Jr., *History of U.S. Marine Corps Operations in World War II. Vol. I: Pearl Harbor to Guadalcanal* (Washington, D.C., n.d.), pt. IV; Richard B. Frank, *Guadalcanal: The Definitive Account of the Landmark Battle* (New York, 1990). Also see Dan van der Vat, *The Pacific Campaign: World War II, The U.S.-Japanese Naval War, 1941–1945* (New York, 1991), 222. "A pattern had developed [by 31 August/1 September] whereby the Americans could do more or less what they wished during the day and the Japanese by night."

95. Callwell, *Dardanelles,* 267.

96. See Corbett, *Some Principles of Maritime Strategy,* pt. I, chs. 3–6; and Basil H. Liddell Hart, *The British Way in Warfare* (London, 1932), ch. 1. The better critical commentaries include Michael Howard, *The Causes of Wars and Other Essays* (London, 1983), 189–207; Hew Strachan, "The British Way in Warfare Revisited," *Historical Journal* 26 (1983): 447–61; Strachan, "British Way in Warfare [1994]"; and David French, *The British Way in Warfare, 1688–2000* (London, 1990).

97. In 1918 Callwell offered the prescient thought that "conflicts to come may be of short duration. They may be signalised by constantly fluctuating strategical situations. In place of lines of entrenchments of vast extent behind which opposing hosts stand on guard, we may see a succession of kaleidoscopic combinations of war executed by mobile, nomadic swarms of men." "Introduction" to Lt.-Gen. Baron von Freytag-Loringhoven, *A Nation Trained in Arms or a Militia: Lessons in War from the Past and the Present* (London, 1918), xix.

98. Gen. Colin L. Powell, "A Word from the Chairman," *Joint Force Quarterly* (Summer 1993): 5.

99. For example, Callwell, *Military Operations,* 24, 117, 216, 340, 358–59, 401, 407.

100. Carl von Clausewitz, *On War,* ed. by Michael Howard and Peter Paret (Princeton, N.J., 1976), 141.

PREFACE.

WRITTEN during the months when the great struggle between Japan and Russia has been in progress, and completed before the issue of the war in the Far East has been finally decided, this volume does not take full cognisance of events which illustrate the relations between naval and military force as few campaigns in modern history have illustrated them. It has, however, been possible to refer to the fall of Port Arthur, which was so essentially the result of action by an army working in concert with, and operating in the interests of, sea-power. And some of the earlier incidents of the remarkable contest have been brought into requisition in support of deductions and in explanation of principles.

C. E. C.

25*th February* 1905.

CONTENTS.

CHAPTER I.

INTRODUCTION.

Command of the sea seldom absolute and undisputed	1
Reason of this	2
The example of the Peninsular War after 1812	3
The subject of which the book treats consists of two separate parts	4
Arrangement to be adopted	4
The subject to be looked at from the soldier's point of view	5
Examples of disagreement and lack of co-operation between foreign armies and navies	5
Mustapha and Piali at Malta	6
Dupleix and La Bourdonais	6
Lally and D'Aché	7
Santiago de Cuba	7
Napoleon's lack of appreciation of naval conditions	8
Contrast offered by Marlborough	9
Unsatisfactory relations between British navy and army before the days of Pitt	10
Drake and Norreys	10
Penn and Venables	11
Cadiz	11
Difficulties of Peterborough	12
Vernon and Wentworth	12
Change in the time of Pitt	13
And later	14
Jealousy between services in eighteenth century	15
Toulon	15
Corsica	17
Walcheren	18

Plattsburg 18
Wellington and the Admiralty 19
Happy relations which have existed in campaigns since
  Waterloo 20
Conclusion 20

CHAPTER II.

THE INFLUENCE UPON MARITIME OPERATIONS OF PROGRESS IN SHIP CONSTRUCTION, OF DEVELOPMENT OF ELECTRICAL COMMUNICATIONS, AND OF THE GENERAL RECOGNITION OF THE RIGHTS OF NEUTRALS.

Fundamental strategical principles remain unaltered while
  tactics change 23
Purpose of the chapter 24
Ancient ships of war 24
The galley, and the introduction of sailing-vessels . . 26
Element of uncertainty in the navies of old . . . 27
Effect of storms and bad weather in the sailing era . . 27
Uncertainty as to time to be taken in a strategical combination in the days of sails 29
Examples 30
Difficulties of blockade in the sailing days . . . 30
Rapidity with which fleets could be created formerly . 32
Fire-ships the forerunners of torpedo craft . . . 33
Introduction of steam does away with many elements of
  uncertainty 34
Question of fog 34
Steam and inshore flotillas for military purposes . . 35
Fundamental principles remain unaltered . . . 36
Effect of introduction of electrical communications . . 37
Example of Nelson's pursuit of Napoleon to Egypt . . 38
Comparison with a parallel situation under modern conditions 41
Influence on strategy of closer observance of the rights and
  duties of neutrals 43
Examples of laxity as to observance of neutrality in the
  seventeenth and eighteenth centuries . . . 45
England and Russia in 1770 47
Position of Portugal 48
Situation in the present day 49
Conclusion 50

CHAPTER III.

THE AIMS AND OBJECTS SOUGHT AFTER IN NAVAL WARFARE.

The general objects aimed at in war	51
Injury inflicted on an enemy by destroying his fleet	51
Further consequences of destroying enemy's sea-power	52
The naval strategy of France and Spain in the War of American Independence	53
First duty of the superior navy to dispose of enemy's fleets	55
The naval policy of the weaker side	55
The case of La Galissonière at Minorca	56
Captain Mahan's view	56
Byng's fleet the "ulterior object" in this case, and not Minorca	59
The weaker side must adopt a defensive attitude	60
The attack and protection of commerce	61
The power to bring military force into play against the enemy's coasts and colonies	63
Conclusion	63

CHAPTER IV.

NAVAL BASES AND FORTRESSES.

The need of bases for a navy	65
Water formerly as indispensable as coal to-day	65
Communications at sea	66
The coal question	
Naval bases always indispensable to sea-power	67
The influence of the acquisition of bases on the progress of British naval power in the Mediterranean	68
Harbours of refuge	74
Importance of possessing naval bases recognised in the eighteenth century	75
Natural harbours and artificial harbours	76
Objects of naval fortresses	77
As refuges for floating force	77
Difficulty of dealing with a hostile naval fortress from the sea	78
Importance to a beaten fleet of having a safe place to retire to	79
Secure bases necessary for carrying out commerce destroying	79

Safe harbours required by merchant ships in time of war	80
Need of secure depots and dockyards .	81
Mauritius in the eighteenth century .	82
Coaling-stations .	84
Importance of naval bases being properly defended .	85
Examples in support of this .	86
Importance of coaling-stations being secure .	87
Fortified naval bases essential to the weaker side .	88
Bases for torpedo craft and submarines	89
Conclusion	90

CHAPTER V.

DEPRIVING THE ENEMY OF HIS NAVAL BASES, CAPTURING HIS MARITIME FORTRESSES, AND ACQUIRING PORTS SUITABLE FOR ANCHORAGES AND DEPOTS, AS OBJECTIVES IN WAR.

The enemy's naval bases as an objective	94
Examples of the capture of naval bases and its influence .	95
Nepheris at time of siege of Carthage	96
Louisbourg	97
Toulon	98
Attack of base sometimes necessary as means of destroying hostile fleet within	99
Attack on hostile bases for commerce destroying	99
Captain Mahan's views on this	100
Martinique and Mauritius	100
Question whether steam has not altered the conditions	101
A captured naval base may form a valuable *point d'appui* for future operations	102
Chance of capturing valuable material	103
Floating naval resources of the enemy which may have to be dealt with in hostile coast fortresses .	104
Conclusion as to attacks on hostile bases	105
Question of securing suitable naval bases during the course of a war	106
Examples .	107
Drake at Lagos .	107
Barrington at St Lucia .	107
Corsica in 1794 .	108
Port Royal in the American Civil War	108
Islands occupied by the Japanese in 1904	109
Conclusion	109

CONTENTS. lxxxi

CHAPTER VI

THE REASON WHY LAND OPERATIONS ARE USUALLY NECESSARY TO DEAL EFFECTIVELY WITH THE NAVAL STATIONS OF THE ENEMY AND TO SECURE BASES FOR SPECIAL MARITIME OPERATIONS.

History proves that land operations are generally necessary to deal with the naval stations of the enemy effectively	110
Floating force generally unsuitable for actual attack upon maritime strongholds	111
Reasons for this	112
Examples of attacks of ships on fortresses	113
Blake at Porto Farina and Santa Cruz	113
Sir C. Shovel at Toulon, and later instances	114
Effect of submarine mines	116
Influence of torpedo craft	117
Improbability of fleet attacking fortresses in future	118
Question of blockade—strategical principle involved	119
Difficulties attending blockade	120
Blocking entrance from within	121
Blocking the entrance to a harbour from without, by blockading fleet	121
Examples of blocking channels	121
Sealing up a harbour by mines from without	123
Conclusions. As naval bases and fortresses may have to be attacked, and as floating force is generally powerless, land operations become a necessity	124
Land operations necessary when a naval base has to be acquired in war	125

CHAPTER VII.

LAND OPERATIONS DIRECTED AGAINST FLEETS AND SHIPPING.

Because naval force when not strong enough to keep the sea naturally retires into defended harbours, a very difficult situation for the stronger fleet is likely to arise	126
The lesson of Wei-hai-wei, Santiago, and Port Arthur	128
Land operations necessary to deal with the fleets in each case	129

lxxxii CONTENTS.

The battle of Mycale 129
Pichegru on the Texel, Sveaborg, Abo, and Sebastopol . 131
Land operations alone can seldom dispose of a hostile fleet 132
Disadvantage under which ships lying in port suffer if
    artillery on shore can be brought to bear against them 132
Examples 132
Messina 132
Ochakof 133
Antwerp, 1814 133
Wei-hai-wei 134
Examples of ships being captured incidentally, as result of
    successful attack on a maritime fortress . . . 134
Tunis, 1535 134
Louisbourg 135
Havana 135
Procida, 1809 135
End of the *Merrimac* 136
Examples of co-operation of land forces with naval forces
    attacking shipping 136
A remarkable Admiralty letter to Wellington . . 137
Camperdown and the Helder Expedition . . . 138
Copenhagen, 1807, an example of land operations being
    undertaken for the purpose of capturing a fleet . 139
Other examples 139
Ferrol, 1800 140
The last echo of Trafalgar 140
Position after Trafalgar 141
The Walcheren Expedition 142
The case of Santiago 143
The story of Newport in 1780, as illustrating the inter-
    dependence between land- and sea-power . . 144
Conclusion 146

CHAPTER VIII.

THE QUESTION OF EMPLOYING NAVAL PERSONNEL ASHORE AND IN LAND OPERATIONS GENERALLY.

Advantages of employing sailors for amphibious operations
    in some respects 148
Question of the *personnel* for defence of naval stations
    being drawn from the sea-service. Arguments in
    favour of the arrangement 150

CONTENTS. lxxxiii

Disadvantages of the plan	151
Landing of sailors in defence of naval bases on emergency	152
Acre, 1799	153
Such incidents exceptional	154
What occurred at Ipsara in 1824	154
Employment of sailors in attack of coast fortresses, and in purely land operations	155
This generally only permissible on a small scale	156
Troubridge at Capua	156
The Admiralty rebuke of Nelson	157
No objection to landing sailors if they can be spared from their proper duties	157
Recognition by Rodney and Nelson of need for military force, for enterprises against maritime strongholds	158
Lord St Vincent's remarkable views	159
Landing guns from fleet for enterprises on shore	160
Conclusion	161

CHAPTER IX.

A SUMMARY OF THE PRINCIPLES EXAMINED IN FOREGOING CHAPTERS.

Summary	163

CHAPTER X.

THE LIMITATIONS OF SEA-POWER IN SECURING THE OBJECTS FOR WHICH WAR IS UNDERTAKEN.

Peculiar position of the United Kingdom in relation to sea-power	168
The higher policy of war	169
Maritime force powerless beyond a certain point	170
The war against the French Empire, 1805-1814	170
The American War of Secession	171
Efficacy of blockade decreased under modern conditions	172
Question of contraband of war	173

lxxxiv   CONTENTS.

Circumstances may limit a belligerent to operations by sea   174
Operations against over-sea possessions of an enemy. The
    question of securing these by means of sea-power
    unaided   175
Such isolation by itself has no military effect . .   176
The question of injuring the enemy by destroying his
    maritime trade   176
The Seven Years' War in reference to this . . .   177
Results of operations against trade depend on amount of
    trade   178
Possession by the British Empire of its great chain of
    naval bases due largely to military expeditions .   178
Command of the sea only a means to an end . . .   179
Influence of popular opinion cannot be left out of account
    in war   180
The lesson of Belleisle and Minorca at the Peace of Paris,
    1763   180
Importance of securing hostile territory during a war .   181
The example of Egypt after the Battle of the Nile . .   182
Conclusion   182

CHAPTER XI.

THE IMPORTANCE OF SEA COMMAND TO SCATTERED EMPIRES IN RESPECT OF CONCENTRATING THE NATIONAL MILITARY FORCES FOR WAR.

Scattered empires almost of necessity have their military
    forces scattered   184
The Ottoman Empire   185
In the Greek War of Liberation   186
In 1828-29   187
In the Crimean War   187
In 1877-78   188
France in the Franco-German War   189
Importance of sea command when outlying portions of a
    scattered empire are involved in war . .   189
Spain and her western empire   191
France and Canada   192
Conclusion   193

CONTENTS. lxxxv

CHAPTER XII.

THE RISKS RUN BY TRANSPORTS AT SEA AND INCONVENIENCES INCURRED BY THE TROOPS IN MOVEMENTS ON BOARD SHIP.

Purpose of chapter	195
Helplessness of transports if attacked in the present day	195
Normal perils of the sea	196
Examples of dispersion of military expeditions on the high seas by bad weather	196
Examples of this in the case of attempted invasions of England in the past	197
Bad weather less mischievous under modern conditions	198
Fogs	198
Carrying troops in fighting-ships	198
Carrying troops in merchant-ships regarded as piracy by the Dutch three hundred years ago	199
Later examples	200
No objection when there is no prospect of a naval action	201
Deterioration of troops on voyages	201
Sir J. Moore's view	202
The doctrine of the "fleet in being"	203
Origin of the expression	203
Torrington's theory a fallacy before the days of steam	205
Examples of military forces being moved across the sea in defiance of "fleets in being"	205
Very few examples to be found of troops in transports being captured	208
Fate of Spanish reinforcements going to South America in 1818	209
Few occasions on which an army has been attacked on the high seas	210
Importance of "fleet in being" over-estimated in the sailing days	211
Explanation of this	212
Nelson's plan in 1798	212
Anson and Hawke	213
D'Estaing and Byron	213
Barrington at St Lucia	214
The effect of the "fleet in being" under modern conditions	215
Influence of torpedo craft and submarines	216
Under modern conditions, movement of troops over-sea, unless maritime preponderance be assured, is more risky than was formerly the case	218

lxxxvi CONTENTS.

Importance of not overrating the danger . . . 218
Fleets of transports attacked by cruisers . . . 219
Japanese action in 1894 and 1904 220

CHAPTER XIII.

THE RISKS AND DIFFICULTIES WHICH ATTEND TROOPS IN EMBARKING AND DISEMBARKING, AND AFTER DISEMBARKATION, OWING TO WEATHER AND OWING TO POSSIBLE ACTION OF THE ENEMY'S NAVY.

Subjects to be dealt with in chapter 222
Bad weather seldom impedes the original embarkation of
   a military force 222
Troops often have to be disembarked where there is little
   protection from the bad weather 223
Examples of landings on a large scale in exposed situations 224
Nature of risks run when landing at exposed localities . 225
Charles V. at Algiers as an example 225
The British descent on Ostend in 1798 . . . 228
Under modern conditions, transports less likely to suffer in
   case of bad weather during a disembarkation than was
   formerly the case. Boats as likely to be damaged as
   formerly 229
Character of coast-line as affecting question of landings . 230
Importance of the question of weather in amphibious operations, and of the nature of available harbours . . 231
Unfavourable landing- and embarking-places cause delay,
   and this may affect military operations . . . 232
Attack by hostile vessels while disembarkation is in progress, or after it is completed 233
Difficulties of attacking transports at anchor in the sailing
   days 234
Improbability of such attacks under existing conditions . 235
Submarines in this connection 235
Intervention of hostile naval forces after the army has
   landed 235
Results of such intervention 236
The story of Yorktown 237
The story of Hubert de Burgh and the French invasion of
   England in 1216 241
Conclusion 243

CHAPTER XIV.

MARITIME LINES OF COMMUNICATION COMPARED TO LAND LINES OF COMMUNICATION.

Importance of communications to an army	246
Drain which communications make on the fighting strength of an army	246
Superiority of sea to land communications	248
Influence of steam on this question ashore and afloat	249
The Turko-Greek War, 1897	249
Sea cannot be used as line of military communications without naval preponderance	250
The Sea of Azov in the Crimean War	250
Japanese action in Korea in 1904 in illustration of use of sea as a line of communications	251
Russo-Turkish wars as illustrating this	252
Campaign of 1828-29 in Asia	253
Campaign of 1877-78 in Asia	256
Campaign of 1828-29 in Europe	257
Campaign of 1877-78 in Europe	258
Power of shifting a maritime base as operations progress	259
Wellington in the Peninsula	259
Sherman in Georgia and the Carolinas	260

CHAPTER XV.

THE LIBERTY OF ACTION CONFERRED BY SEA-POWER UPON MILITARY FORCE.

Introductory remarks	263
Salient and re-entering frontier lines	264
Coast-lines present analogous conditions	264
Salient coast-lines	265
Re-entering coast-lines	266
Calabria in 1806	267
An army in transports is generally in a position to act on "interior lines"	267
To a certain extent, a question depending upon distances and nature of land communications at disposal of opposing side	268

CONTENTS.

The move from Varna to Sebastopol as an example	269
The principle of "interior lines"	270
Illustrations of the application of this in amphibious warfare	271
Suliman Pasha in 1877	272
Examples from the South African War	272
General Sherman's march to the sea as illustration of liberty of action	273
Command of the sea generally assures an army a safe refuge at the worst, when operating in a maritime district	274
Sir J. Moore's campaign in 1808-9	275
An army forced to retreat to the sea need not necessarily take to its ships	276
Command of the sea gives the side which enjoys that advantage the initiative	277
Enemy cannot tell where a blow may fall if plan is kept secret	278
Lord St Vincent and the descent on Minorca in 1798	278
The situation lends itself to the employment of feints and ruses	281
Importance of concealment of design	282
The attack on Brest in 1694	282
The war between Chili and Peru as illustrating liberty of action derived from naval preponderance	283
The campaign of 1859	286
In 1859, and in the South American War of 1879-81, maritime command overcame geographical obstacles	287
The attempted relief of Bilbao	288
Liberty of action, as shown by foregoing paragraphs	288
The campaigns in and round Virginia, 1861-65, as illustration of principles discussed in chapter	289
Opening operations	289
Campaign of 1862	291
Campaign of 1863	292
Campaign of 1864	294
The end	295
Conclusion	296

CHAPTER XVI.

THE HOLD WHICH MARITIME COMMAND MAY GIVE AN ARMY UPON COAST DISTRICTS, EVEN WHEN THE ENEMY IS THE STRONGER IN THE THEATRE OF LAND OPERATIONS.

Power which maritime command gives to maintain a grip on a coast district	297
Tactical and strategical advantages enjoyed by a military force operating with its back to the sea . . .	297
The lines of Torres Vedras	298
British over-sea expeditions before the time of Wellington	299
Sir J. Moore's campaign in the Peninsula . . .	300
Wellington's conception of strategy the true one . .	300
Other examples	301
The Crimean War as an example of this . . .	302
Japan in Manchuria	304
The campaign in Denmark in 1848-49 as illustration of the difficulty of expelling an inferior army from maritime districts, if that army can depend upon control of the sea	305
Conclusion	308

CHAPTER XVII.

THE INFLUENCE OF MARITIME COMMAND WHEN A MILITARY LINE OF OPERATIONS OR COMMUNICATIONS FOLLOWS THE COAST OR RUNS PARALLEL TO IT.

Routes following the line of the coast	309
Liability of such a route to be cut from the side of the sea	309
The defile east of the Pyrenees	310
The Riviera	312
The strategical defile north of the Adriatic . . .	314
Italian campaign of 1848-49	315
The case of an isthmus	316
The Isthmus of Corinth	317
The campaign of 1822 between the Ottoman Empire and the insurgent Greeks	317
The coast route from Egypt to Asia Minor . . .	320
Mehemet Ali's wars against the Sultan . . .	320

CHAPTER XVIII.

THE TENDENCY OF AMPHIBIOUS FORCE TO CONTAIN THE TROOPS OF THE BELLIGERENT WHO IS THE WEAKER AT SEA, AT POINTS WHERE THESE CANNOT ACT.

Reasons for this containing power	323
Examples from early times	324
War of the Spanish Succession	325
Pitt's policy of raids during the Seven Years' War	326
1807 and 1809	327
The Crimean War	328
The war in the Far East	330
Conclusion	331

CHAPTER XIX.

TACTICAL INTERVENTION OF NAVAL FORCE IN LAND BATTLES.

Opportunities for tactical intervention of warships somewhat rare	332
Forms in which such intervention can take place	332
The Battle of Gravelines	333
Bunker's Hill	334
Occasions often arise where lines of operations follow maritime defiles	334
Examples. The Var	335
Loano	336
Muizenberg	336
The case of an isthmus	337
Battle of Nanshan	337
Effect of progress in artillery	338
Effect of steam in place of sails	340
Battle of Miraflores	340
Conclusion	342

CHAPTER XX.

LANDINGS AND EMBARKATIONS IN FACE OF THE ENEMY.

Landings generally take place on an open beach	343
Probable landing-place known to the enemy, and delay likely to arise from bad weather	343

Impression which exists that landings even in face of opposition are generally successful	344
If enemy is prepared, a footing is generally gained at some other point	345
Examples of feints	346
Examples of disembarkation in face of the enemy in early times	347
Julius Cæsar at Walmer	347
Count Guy of Flanders' descent on Walcheren in 1253	348
Louis IX.'s landing at Damietta	349
Later examples	350
Tollemache's attempted landing at Brest	351
Incident near Cadiz in 1702	352
Swedish attack on Kronstadt	352
The landing at Louisbourg in 1758	353
Failure at Lomarie in Belleisle	355
Abercromby's landing in Aboukir Bay	355
The difference between former conditions and those of to-day	358
Reasons for difference	359
Landings at awkward places generally best carried out by sailors	361
Question of landings at night	361
Embarkations in face of opposition. Generally speaking a case of retreat	362
A rearguard operation involved as a rule	363
Turkish embarkation at Malta	364
Difficulties of the operation greatly increased under modern conditions	364
Artillery fire from fleet covering embarkation	365
The affair of St Cas in 1758	365

CHAPTER XXI.

THE SIEGE OF MARITIME FORTRESSES.

Command of the sea of vital importance when a maritime fortress is being besieged	369
Three sets of conditions, from the naval point of view	369
Diverse characteristics of coast fortresses	369
Their influence, as regards importance of naval control in the vicinity	370
Sieges where the attacking side has maritime preponderance	371

The question of blockade	371
Examples of difficulties of blockade. Carthage	372
St Martin's in the Isle of Rhé	373
Siege of St Philip, Minorca, 1781	373
Genoa	374
Port Arthur	374
Warships aiding the besiegers	375
Formerly warships could perhaps aid more effectually than in the present day	377
Landing guns from fleet to assist besiegers	377
Sieges where the naval preponderance has been with the defending side	378
Under such conditions the besiegers must fight their way in	378
The siege of Candia	379
Rosas, 1794-95	379
The siege of Tarragona in 1810	380
The siege of Dunkirk in 1793	381
Acre, 1799	381
Assistance of fleet to garrison	381
Siege of Rosas, 1808, and Tarifa, 1811	382
This depends largely on form of the fortress	382
Gaeta, 1806	383
Relief of a besieged fortress by landing troops in rear of besiegers. Examples	383
Sieges where maritime command has been in dispute	384
Tyre	385
Barcelona, 1706	385
The great siege of Gibraltar	386
Missolunghi, 1822 and 1825-26	387
The siege of Cuddalore	388
Conclusion	388

CHAPTER XXII.

THE COMMAND OF INLAND WATERS AND WATERWAYS, AND ITS INFLUENCE UPON MILITARY OPERATIONS.

Explanation of what is meant by inland waters and waterways	391
Inland waterways are generally commanded from the shore, but inland waters often are not so commanded	391
Inland seas and lakes	393

CONTENTS. xciii

Flotillas on them generally have to be improvised during war	394
Great Lakes of North America	394
Question of shipbuilding in such cases	394
Examples	395
Lake Ontario, 1812-14	395
Lake Erie in 1812-14	395
Command of Lake Erie, and Brock's overthrow of Hull	396
Importance of the bases on Lakes Erie and Ontario	397
Land communications running along a lake	399
Other phases of connection between naval and military operations illustrated by warfare on the Great Lakes	400
Estuaries, straits, rivers, and canals	401
Generally a case of small vessels	401
Only limited number of rivers navigable by fighting craft	402
The campaigns on the Mississippi in the American Civil War	403
Question of current	406
Question whether in future armed river-vessels will be able to run past batteries	407
Submarine mines and torpedoes in river warfare	407
Booms and sunken obstructions	409
Russians on the Danube in 1877	409
Difficulties arising from rivers rising and falling	410
Digging canals	411
Co-operation between flotilla and troops on banks, the essence of such operations	412
Operations below Columbus on the Mississippi in 1862, as example	413
Inland waterways as means of rapidly moving troops for strategical purposes	415
Fortresses on rivers and estuaries	416
Examples of attacks on fortresses so placed, under former conditions	417
Changes introduced by modern conditions	417
The conquest of Canada as illustrating the subject treated of in chapter	418
The general plan of campaign	418
The rival forces and commanders	420
Arrival of Wolfe before Quebec	421
The Montmorency fight	421
Difficulties of both sides	422
Wolfe's great move up stream	422
The surprise of the Heights of Abraham and fall of Quebec	423
An appreciation of Wolfe	424

CONTENTS.

Movements of the other columns	425
Preparations for 1760	426
Lévis' attack on Quebec	426
The relief by sea-power	427
The surrender of Montreal	428
Conclusion	428

CHAPTER XXIII.

SOME POINTS IN CONNECTION WITH EQUIPMENT, ORGANISATION, AND TRAINING OF NAVAL AND MILITARY FORCES FOR AMPHIBIOUS WAR.

Necessity for special organisation and equipment	431
Class of vessel required	432
Question of projectile to be used by ships' guns	434
Observation of gun-fire ashore and afloat	435
Japan the only nation with an army organised for amphibious warfare	436
Question of organisation of field army	437
Importance of portable artillery	438
Advantage of all details being worked out beforehand	439
Principles which must govern the military system of an insular Power	439
Importance of adequate methods of communication and signalling between naval and military forces acting in concert	442
Conclusion	443

MAPS.

		PAGE
I.	MEDITERRANEAN SEA	93
II.	GREECE AND THE ÆGEAN	186
III.	WAR OF AMERICAN INDEPENDENCE AND WAR OF SECESSION	245
IV.	THE RUSSO-TURKISH CAMPAIGNS AND THE CRIMEAN WAR	261
V.	SKETCH ILLUSTRATING THE WAR BETWEEN CHILI AND PERU	284
VI.	VIRGINIA	290
VII.	SKETCH ILLUSTRATING THE WAR OF 1848-49 BETWEEN THE DANES AND GERMANS	306
VIII.	SKETCH OF NORTHERN ITALY	313
IX.	SKETCH ILLUSTRATING THE CAMPAIGNS OF 1833 AND 1839 ON THE SHORES OF THE LEVANT	321
X.	MISSISSIPPI ABOUT ISLAND NO. 10	414
XI.	NORTH AMERICAN CAMPAIGNS, 1756-1814	429
XII.	ENVIRONS OF QUEBEC	429

MILITARY OPERATIONS AND MARITIME PREPONDERANCE.

CHAPTER I.

INTRODUCTION.

IN literature which treats of naval strategy and works dealing with naval and military history it is the practice to speak of "command of the sea" when describing the situation consequent upon the fleets of one belligerent having gained a decided advantage over those of the other, or where the navy of one side is unquestionably superior to that of the other. It is a term in common use, and it will be freely employed in this volume. But "maritime preponderance," the expression used on the title-page, more correctly defines the conditions which ordinarily arise in warfare between States laying claim to a measure of sea-power.

In a struggle such as that recently concluded in South Africa, where the greatest of naval Powers was pitted against two petty republics neither of which had access to the sea, maritime command may be complete and indisputable.[1] Even in conflicts between nations both maintaining fighting forces afloat, it may happen that owing to circumstances the supremacy upon the ocean of one side or the other may be absolute and uncontested for a

Command of the sea seldom absolute and undisputed.

season, or may remain so throughout the whole duration of hostilities. But it is most unusual for a belligerent who enters upon a struggle with warships under his control, to suffer total eclipse at sea or to have his vessels definitively confined to port, no matter how superior the naval forces of the enemy may be at the outset, or how predominant they may become during the course of operations. The expression "command of the sea" has in fact always had a somewhat limited signification. That this is so is proved by history, and it is susceptible of simple explanation.

Reason of this. Victory in a naval combat may arise from the possession of greater naval resources by the winning side during the encounter. It may be the result of superior tactical skill, or of better seamanship, or of more accurate gunnery. But the success is seldom so complete that nothing is left of the beaten fleet. Even after the extraordinarily decisive battles of the Nile and of Trafalgar, a few units of the defeated squadrons were left to fight another day. Certain ships almost inevitably escape and find a refuge in some secure haven, where their injuries can be repaired. They may not seriously endanger the navy or the commerce of the adversary, nor seriously interfere with the combinations of the opposing side. But they are not incapable of mischief, and as long as they exist they are in a position, within restricted limits, to dispute the command of the sea with the enemy—only locally perhaps and for a short space of time, but sufficiently to cause some anxiety to the hostile admirals, and with good fortune to create diversions and possibly to do serious damage.[2]

Moreover, most naval powers are in a position to carry out shipbuilding and to arm merchant vessels during the course of a struggle. The construction and fitting-out of formidable fighting craft may be impracticable—the battleship and cruiser of to-day cannot be improvised at short notice,—but vessels designed to prey upon commerce can be rapidly equipped for service. A formidable armament is not necessary to convert an ordinary merchant steamer into a warship capable of dealing peremptorily with a transport carrying troops if not under convoy. The life of such highwaymen of the sea may be short, they may be tracked down and destroyed before they do any appreciable mischief; but as long as they are afloat they constitute a danger, and while their existence may not rob the opposing belligerent of his maritime preponderance they do tend to deprive him of undisputed command of the sea.

The pronounced supremacy which this country achieved afloat after Trafalgar never attained the ideal perfection of causing the enemy's flag to disappear entirely on the high seas. Even before the outbreak of hostilities with America in 1812 the British fleets by no means enjoyed unquestioned control of the ocean. For although it was possible to ensure the safe conduct of expeditionary forces over sea to the Baltic, to Flanders, and to the Peninsula, and although no hostile squadron dared to put to sea from the great French naval ports, isolated hostile ships were busy striking at our trade.[3] And when trouble arose across the Atlantic, that security enjoyed by transports and by merchant vessels when command of the sea is absolute and complete, was no longer enjoyed under the Union Jack even in the Bay of Biscay and on the coast of Portugal. Soon after the battle of Vittoria five store-ships and a troop transport were captured by the enemy. Reinforcements ready at Gibraltar and Lisbon could not be despatched to Santander for fear of hostile cruisers. "I wish you to be distinctly apprised," wrote Melville from the Admiralty to Wellington in Spain, "that we will not be responsible for ships sailing singly or without convoy between this country and Spain and Portugal, or for any considerable distance along the coasts of these countries." And yet all this time

The example of the Peninsular War after 1812.

the British navy was in possession of the command of the sea, as that expression is understood in its broad strategical sense. Where the prosecution of a military enterprise or the progress of a land campaign is largely dependent upon the free and uninterrupted transport over sea of troops and war material and supplies, it is obvious that the distinction between absolute control of the waters and mere established maritime preponderance is an important distinction, if not a vital one.[4] The expression "command of the sea" is, however, convenient, and it is sanctioned by usage. It will therefore be frequently employed in the following pages.[5]

The subject of which the book treats consists of two separate parts.
The relations which exist between military operations and maritime preponderance have to be considered from two separate points of view. The subject with which the volume professes to treat consists, in fact, of two separate parts. Sea-power in time of war is, under normal circumstances, to a great extent dependent upon the support and assistance of military force. The action of armies is, on the other hand, in certain conditions not unlikely to arise, subservient to and only justified by the existence of a dominant navy.

Arrangement to be adopted.
Therefore in the arrangement of this work the two sides of the question will be kept in some measure distinct. The earlier chapters will endeavour to show the extent to which naval forces must rely upon the co-operation of the military under ordinary conditions of war. The later chapters will treat of the influence of sea-power upon land operations, and will demonstrate the remarkable strategical advantages which an army may derive from the power of traversing the sea at will in virtue of maritime command. A special chapter will be devoted to the question of inland waters. And in the final chapter some technical points in connection with the training and organisation and equipment of the land- and sea-services will be dealt with, suggested by what has gone before.

INTRODUCTION. 5

The subject will throughout be treated from the soldier's point of view. For this reason an attempt will be made to place before military readers the fundamental truths of naval strategy, while it will be assumed that the broad principles which govern the art of war on land are understood. Most of the views set out in the ensuing pages, both as regards naval questions and as regards military questions, are of general acceptance, and are hardly likely to be called in question. It is, however, impossible to altogether avoid controversial topics, and certain opinions which will be expressed and certain deductions which will be made from incidents in the history of war, may perhaps not be approved of by all schools of strategical thought. Still it is hoped that if the book proves nothing else, it will at least prove afresh how great is the importance in a land like our own of cordial, close, and constant co-operation between its navy and its army, not only when the nation is actually engaged in war, but also when Imperial questions of defence are under discussion and come up for decision in time of peace.[6] And before closing this introductory chapter it will not be uninteresting to look back into old records of military and naval operations, and to illustrate by actual examples the evils which arise when military and naval forces, intended to act in co-operation, fail to do so from want of mutual understanding.

The subject to be looked at from the soldier's point of view.

Our own history affords such a multitude of examples of military operations dependent upon sea-power, of conjunct expeditions across the ocean,[7] of attacks upon maritime strongholds, and of the various forms which amphibious war may take under all manner of conditions, that we naturally find in its pages instances in times past of misunderstandings and jealousies between the sister services. And it must be confessed that instances of friction, not unfrequently leading to serious inconvenience if not to

Examples of disagreement and lack of co-operation between foreign armies and navies.

6 INTRODUCTION.

actual disaster, were by no means uncommon in the seventeenth and eighteenth centuries. But we may as well first look farther afield and show that foreign countries can also provide their quota of striking and unedifying examples.

Mustapha and Piali at Malta. The disastrous ending of the great Turkish expedition to Malta in 1565 was in no small degree the direct consequence of the quarrels between Mustapha the general and Piali the admiral. Both appear to have been to blame, and both blundered. "Each was more intent upon depriving his colleague of the honour of success than carrying on the main objects of the expedition," writes the historian of the Knights of Malta, "and each felt that if he were not principal actor at the capture of the island, he would rather the attempt were a failure than that the other should reap the fruits of success." It is only fair to the rivals, who vied with each other in personal gallantry during the furious struggle against the intrepid defenders, to remember that Soliman the Magnificent was apt to adopt drastic measures against centurions who failed.

Dupleix and La Bourdonais. The story of Dupleix and La Bourdonais in India affords a melancholy example of the evils which may arise in war when the military and the naval leader are not in harmony. Dupleix was not, it is true, strictly speaking, a soldier; but in the eighteenth century civilian pioneers of over-sea empire became soldiers by force of circumstances. They administered armies, and framed and executed plans of conquest. La Bourdonais, one of the greatest and most prescient of French sailors, perceived as soon as he reached the Indian Ocean to take command of the naval forces, and acquainted himself with the situation in that far-off region, that upon sea-power must rest the foundations of French sovereignty in Hindustan. Imbued with this idea, he converted Mauritius into a great naval place of arms, he organised and developed his command in those waters with rare skill and forethought, and he prepared everything with such resources as he had at his disposal, for the struggle with England for the control of the East which he knew must come. But when the strife commenced he found himself confronted by an unforeseen difficulty— the suspicion, the jealousy, and the obstruction of the military chief, Dupleix. He was thwarted at every turn. When on his way to attack Madras he asked for 60 guns and for some stores at Pondicherry, Dupleix refused the stores, sent only 30 guns of small calibre, and supplied water so bad that the personnel of the fleet was decimated by dysentery. Eventually the feud came to a head. La Bourdonais returned to his native land, and before the military genius of Clive and the sea-power of England in the Indian Ocean, French dreams of supremacy in Hindustan vanished like the morning mists before the rising sun. And yet Dupleix was a great administrator, a man of vast ambitions, and a diplomatist of a character singularly well suited to deal with oriental races and to dominate them.

A few years later we find Count Lally, the French governor and commander-in-chief, quarrelling with D'Aché the admiral, and D'Aché ultimately leaving the governor in the lurch. Sea-power decided the fate of India.[8] But one cause of the command of the sea in those waters becoming a British asset in the long contest for ascendancy, may undoubtedly be set down to the lack of co-operation and cordiality between the naval and military forces of France on the shores of the Indian Ocean. *Lally and D'Aché.*

It is a matter of common knowledge that during the operations by land and sea around Santiago de Cuba in 1898, the relations between the naval and military commanders were not of a very happy character; and in following the course of the operations it is difficult to avoid the conclusion that co-operation between the services was not so generous and so disinterested as it might *Santiago de Cuba.*

have been. No serious evil resulted, perhaps, from the friction — such as it was. But that there was friction is placed beyond dispute by published despatches and documents.

Napoleon's lack of appreciation of naval conditions. Soldiers and sailors in the past in this and other countries, knowing little of each other's duties and objects, often failed to properly appreciate them at times of crisis. And no more remarkable instance of this can be found than in the person of Napoleon, who, in spite of his marvellous grasp of facts, of his close study of details, and of his genius for adapting his objects and purposes to meet the conditions which presented themselves to him, never mastered the secrets of the element which proved his undoing.[9] Thiers has to admit that even after the lesson of Trafalgar "Admiral Decrès, continuing to place at the disposal of Napoleon professed experience and a superior mind, could not always succeed in persuading him that in the navy, with good will, with courage, with money, with genius itself, it is not possible to make amends for time and long training." On the sea he had indifferent materials to work with,—unsatisfactory and halting admirals, inexperienced captains, inefficient seamen. But he made no allowances for the shortcomings of his navy, which, as far as material was concerned, left little to be desired. A ship was a ship to him, and a fleet a fleet. "Accustomed by forethought and sheer will to trample obstacles under foot, remembering the mid-winter passage of the Splügen made by Macdonald at his command, and the extraordinary impediments overcome by himself in crossing the St Bernard, he could not believe that the difficulties of the sea could not be vanquished by unskilled men handling the ponderous machines entrusted to them, when confronted by a skilful enemy. To quote an able French writer: 'But one thing was wanting to the victor of Austerlitz, — *le sentiment exact des difficultés de la marine.'"* His imperious temper rejected advice, and would brook no contradiction. To a military figure so commanding, counsel even from a Massena seems almost an impertinence; but had Napoleon listened to the representations of his naval experts he might have avoided many grave errors most prejudicial to his fortunes, and he might have been saved much bitter disappointment.

It is interesting to contrast the attitude of Napoleon towards the chiefs of his sea-service with that of a soldier who stands second to him and to no other, the great Duke of Marlborough. After Blenheim and Ramillies, Marlborough was for a time the foremost figure in Europe. Not only was he recognised in that age of strife as a master of the art of war, but by foreign Governments as well as by his own he was acknowledged to be a statesman of the very front rank, as competent to guide the policy of nations in the hour of danger as he was certain to lead armies placed under his orders to victory on the battlefield. The idea that England should hold a commanding position in the Mediterranean did not originate with him. It had been the dream of Charles II. in the early days of his reign, before the duties and responsibilities of kingship began to pall. It had formed one of the main objectives of the policy of William III. to the end. But Marlborough revived it at the proper time, and he made a supreme effort to realise it when, the course of the war all over Europe demanding that a decisive blow should be struck, he conceived the bold project of a great combined operation of war by land and sea for the seizure and destruction of Toulon. To carry this out it was indispensable that British sea-power should be firmly established in the western Mediterranean, and that British admirals should have at their command a naval base farther advanced than the gut of Gibraltar.

Contrast offered by Marlborough.

---

* Mahan, 'Influence of Sea-Power upon the French Revolution and Empire,' vol. ii. p. 141.

But in all his letters on the subject he was studiously careful not to express opinions on technical naval matters, or to assume an attitude which might offend the susceptibilities of the naval chiefs. "There is no one but admits the necessity of having a winter squadron in the Mediterranean, but when all is said and done we must submit to the judgment of the admirals and sea-officers on the safety of the port and other accommodation for the ships-of-the-line." "All the orders that can be given in England must be entirely subservient to the judgment of the fleet." "The sea-service is not so easily managed as that of land. There are many more precautions to take, and you and I are not capable of judging them." He was most anxious that Minorca should be seized, he realised the strategical importance of its noble eastern inlet at a time when Rooke and Shovel and Leake but dimly appreciated its significance; but he was careful to admit that this was a question for the navy to decide, and to express his views on the purely nautical aspect of the question in guarded terms.

<small>Unsatisfactory relations between British navy and army before the days of Pitt.</small>

Marlborough's attitude is especially interesting in view of the fact that in his time the relations between the British land- and sea-services were generally the reverse of cordial, and taking it into consideration that, when the navy and the army were obliged from the circumstances of the case to work together, jealousies and recriminations almost invariably ensued, while disaster, due to lack of mutual co-operation, was by no means unknown. This is made manifest by the following short *résumé* of certain conjunct expeditions undertaken by this country between the Elizabethan era and the time when Pitt laid his firm grasp on the helm of the State in the early days of the Seven Years' War.

<small>Drake and Norreys.</small>

In the days of Drake's and Raleigh's expeditions to the West Indies,[10] those enterprising pioneers of empire were supreme over their fighting men, whether they were soldiers or were sailors. But when an expedition was despatched to Lisbon, with Drake commanding the fleet while Norreys commanded the troops, there was a fiasco.[11]

Cromwell, sturdy, resolute soldier and far-seeing statesman as he was, was not altogether happy in his arrangements for oversea expeditions. When Penn as admiral and Venables as general were despatched in 1655 to wrest the West Indies from the hands of Spain, three commissioners were especially deputed to keep the peace between the two chiefs. The Lord Protector was not unaware that jealousies existed. Before the expedition started he addressed an appeal to Penn which clearly indicated the existence of a doubt in his mind whether the leaders would work in harmony. The appeal had some effect. One of the commissioners was able at an early stage to communicate the gratifying intelligence that the demeanour of admiral and general towards each other at sea was "sweet and hopeful." But when the armament brought up off the coast of St Domingo and the time for action came, the services no longer worked together smoothly. Venables charged Penn with grudging his soldiers food. Penn's comments upon Venables' operations ashore were, not without some reason it must be confessed, of a decidedly caustic character. The expedition proved a disastrous failure. And it is difficult, reading the accounts of what occurred, to avoid the conclusion that, even taking into account the ineptitude of Venables and the inferior class of the troops with which he had to carry out his task, the unsatisfactory result was mainly due to lack of effective co-operation between the army and the navy in operations of which co-operation was the keystone.

In 1702 a great armada was got together by England and her allies destined to attack Cadiz. Generals Bellasis and Sparre were respectively the English and Dutch generals. Sir G. Rooke was at the head of the fleet.

The Duke of Ormonde was in supreme command. Although a landing was effected and some little damage was done to Spanish shipping, the project failed to accomplish its purpose; and its ill-success, while partly due to military mismanagement, was mainly the consequence of quarrels between the admirals and generals. "We are," wrote Colonel Stanhope, "not only divided sea against land, but land against land, and sea against sea. Now if it be true that a house divided cannot stand, I am afraid that it is still more true that an army and fleet each divided against itself, and each against the other, can make no conquests." The force, having ignominiously abandoned the enterprise, was on its way home when intelligence of some shipping in Vigo afforded it an opportunity of wiping out the memory of an episode which, in its detailed history and in its result, affords eloquent testimony of the evil which arises when misunderstandings occur between naval and military forces acting, or supposed to be acting, in concert.[12]

Difficulties of Peterborough. In 1706, the year of Ramillies, when Marlborough was beginning to cast his eyes towards the Mediterranean, that great soldier of fortune, Peterborough, achieved remarkable triumphs in Catalonia and on the Valencian shores. He participated in the relief of Barcelona, and by his daring and originality of conception he gave to the British operations in north-eastern Spain an impetus which augured well for the ultimate triumph of the cause which this country had taken up.[13] Then he proposed an attack upon Minorca. But, as Lord Mahon tells us in his history, "the naval officers, jealous of a landsman's authority over them, were most unwilling to concur with him in any enterprise."[14] The descent on the Balearic Islands was postponed, and the impetuous Peterborough left Spain in disgust.

Vernon and Wentworth. The story of the combined operations of Admiral Vernon and General Wentworth against Cartagena in South America is even more significant than that of Cadiz recorded above.

This expedition, which took place in 1741, was a purely British one. There was no question of co-operation between allies with divergent interests and sympathies, as was the case when the Duke of Ormonde made his essay against the famous Andalusian place of arms. There was no excuse for rivalship and no justification for jealousy. And yet the enterprise was mismanaged from the outset, and the untoward discussions between the admiral and the general were the prime cause of its miscarriage. "Vernon," says Lord Mahon, "would bear no colleague, and Wentworth no master. The latter complained of the slowness in landing tents, stores, and artillery for the troops, by which they were prevented from making an immediate attack and exposed for the night to all the inclemency of the climate. On the other hand, Vernon declared that the general had remained inactive longer than he should, and had committed an unpardonable error in not cutting off the communications between the town and the adjacent country, by which the garrison was daily supplied with provisions." An attempt by the troops to storm one of the works failed miserably, owing largely to bad leadership; and in reference to the reverse Lord Mahon observes: "The conduct of Vernon in this affair has been severely—perhaps too severely—judged. Certain it is, however, that several parts of his behaviour seem not incompatible with a malicious pleasure in the defeat of any enterprise not directed by himself," and hints that it was not till he saw the attempt irretrievably ruined that he sent his boats full of men to the general's assistance. A sorry story indeed![15]

Pitt's advent to leadership was signalised by the unfortunate expedition against Rochefort.[16] In this the admiral, Hawke, did everything in his power to aid the general, Mordaunt. There was no question of lack of co-operation, although the resolute and fiery Hawke had no sympathy with the indecision and lack of enterprise displayed by

Change in the time of Pitt.

the army under conditions which undoubtedly were difficult. But the next venture of the great Minister had very different results, and was marked by the happiest relations between the land- and the sea-service. The capture of Louisbourg, which will be referred to again frequently in later chapters, was a memorable feat of arms, and one in which navy and army worked together with the most cordial goodwill.[17] "The admiral and general," wrote Wolfe, "have carried on the public service with great harmony, industry, and union. Mr Boscawen has given all, and even more than all, we could ask of him. He has furnished arms and ammunition, pioneers, sappers, miners, gunners, carpenters, boats; and is, I must confess, no bad *fantassin* himself." The conjunction of General Amherst with Boscawen was almost like the opening of a new era. Wolfe's wonderful campaign on the St Lawrence the following year would never have been crowned with such brilliant success but for the strenuous support and assistance of Admiral Saunders.

And later. A few years later we find the happy relations between Rodney and General Monckton leading to a notable triumph in Martinique, army and navy in close and cordial co-operation at Havana, and a conjunct expedition to Belleisle capturing that island in spite of rare landing difficulties.[18] In the war which ended with American independence, the services throughout afforded each other loyal support under difficult circumstances, even if in some instances misunderstandings occurred. The successful campaign in the West Indies in 1793 was consequent upon the effective co-operation between Sir J. Jervis (Lord St Vincent) and General Grey. And it is especially interesting to note that St Vincent, when a few years later he organised an expedition against Minorca, ordered Commodore Duckworth, who commanded the escorting squadron, to join in "any other plan of attack or defence" which the general might suggest;

INTRODUCTION. 15

for the great admiral, as will be seen in a later chapter, held somewhat singular views as regards the army and as to army organisation. But certain incidents during that great struggle, which lasted with only one short interruption from the intervention of this country in the French Revolution, up to 1814, go to show that all was not yet as it should be between the sailors and the soldiers, even when called upon to work together in a common cause.

That Wolfe and Boscawen and St Vincent and Monckton should have succeeded in getting the two services to drop their mutual prejudices and to act in unison and harmony is no small credit to those fighters of the eighteenth century, for those prejudices were acute.[19] There was dislike between the services in the upper ranks and in the lower ranks. "At the same time," writes Professor Laughton of this period, "there was between soldiers and sailors a very mutual feeling of jealousy and contempt, which the officers in no small degree shared with their men. It was strong enough, no doubt, on the part of the soldiers, but was even stronger amongst the sailors, who saw favoured and courtly rivals sea-sick and helpless on board ship, but had no opportunity of seeing them in their own field of distinction. The pipeclay, the powdered head, the stiff clothing and etiquette of soldiers were all repulsive to the 'tar' of olden time."* It is well to bear this in mind, when those incidents in the early days of the British struggle against the French Revolution which have given rise to so much controversy are considered—the evacuation of Toulon and the Corsican campaign.[20]

Jealousy between services in eighteenth century.

No act of omission or commission on the part of any British naval or military chief during this great contest perhaps exerted so sinister an influence over the fortunes of the country as Lord Hood's failure to destroy the French arsenal and fleet in Toulon, which had fallen into his hands

Toulon.

* 'Studies in Naval History,' p. 346.[21]

by such a singular chance. And there appears to be no doubt that General Dundas counselled evacuation, some days before this had to be carried out in hot haste under pressure of the Republican army. Hood's position, undoubtedly, was one of rare difficulty. He could not depend upon his allies: "dastardly trash" he bluntly called the Spanish and Neapolitan troops. His Spanish associates had no wish that the fine French line-of-battle ships lying in the port should pass into British hands. He had to bear in mind that this precious material had been surrendered to him by the Royalists in the great naval station, and that these desired neither the destruction nor the seizure by foreigners of so important a national asset. He, moreover, was expecting reinforcements from Austria and from Gibraltar, and these might have enabled the fortress to hold out, had they arrived in time. Finally, he had no confidence in Dundas, who, neither within the doomed stronghold nor later on in Corsica, gave much indication of the gifts of leadership. He was, in fact, confronted by a situation of extraordinary complexity in face of the mighty forces which had mustered to wrest from him what had been placed in his hands by a train of events without precedent.

But the fact remains that he disregarded the advice of his general, and that his general proved to be right. And Dundas, if he was not the man to cope with a great emergency, was a man whose military opinion was entitled to respect. A pioneer among professional soldiers in the British army, he had studied the art of war closely, and he was to be the creator of that system of drill-tactics which enabled Moore and Stuart and Wellington to lead their men to victory against the veterans of France, before many years had passed. The advice of a soldier on what was a purely military question was ignored. And so when the crisis came, when the besiegers broke in, and when all was hurry and confusion, there was no time to fully carry out the work of destruction by fire and by scuttling, even had the Spaniards shown more willingness to perform their share. The nucleus of a formidable fleet, which was to cause Hood himself, and his successors Hotham and St Vincent, no small anxiety, was left intact;[22] and only a few of those naval buildings and storehouses and repairing yards which had been growing up since the time of Colbert in the great Mediterranean place of arms, were rendered useless to the Republican forces.

Whether the somewhat strained relations between the naval and military chiefs during the opening phases of the operations in Corsica were very prejudicial to their successful prosecution is not easy to determine. Bastia, it would seem, fell from hunger rather than in consequence of bluff by the small naval force which was landed when Dundas declined to move against the place. But the jealousy between the services is placed in an ugly light by Nelson's letters, by the diary of Sir J. Moore, and by the actual record of the operations. Nelson distrusted Moore, and before Bastia displayed an almost naïve eagerness that none of the glory—such as it was—should fall to the army. "I wish Moore were a hundred leagues away," he writes from before Calvi, although he appears to have formed a good opinion of Dundas's successor, Stuart. Moore, on the other hand, expresses himself as to Hood in terms which read strangely even in the pages of a private diary; and his inability to understand why the naval service venerated that great sailor is difficult to account for in an intelligent man whose judgment was not warped by prejudice. Hood's claim to command the military forces in Corsica was hardly calculated to allay the friction which existed. But through it all we see that rivalry and jealousy between the sister services which had led to such disastrous results at Cartagena, and which

Corsica.

18 INTRODUCTION.

dated back to the days of the generals-at-sea, to the days of Blake and Monk and Deane and Rupert, those soldiers who transformed the tumultuary marine of the Elizabethan era into the navy of La Hogue and Malaga,[23] and who placed the sea-power of England upon a secure and organised basis. It is due, perhaps, to his early experiences before Bastia and Calvi that Moore during his subsequent fifteen years of strenuous military life was always severely critical of the navy, with which he was to be brought into contact so frequently in his eventful career.

Walcheren.

The recriminations between Lord Chatham the military leader, and Admiral Strachan the naval chief, when the Walcheren expedition made its inglorious return to the shores of England,—recriminations which caused no small scandal, and which provoked a searching examination into the conduct of all concerned,—can hardly be regarded as a case in point.[24] The allegations as to half-hearted co-operation on the part of the navy may not have been wholly without justification. But the campaign on shore was carried on with such dispiriting lack of vigour, and with such total absence of any definite, well-considered plan, that no contributory negligence on the part of the sea-service, even assuming that there was negligence, could have influenced the result of a project which under happier auspices might have accomplished a most important purpose. Nelson himself could not have vitalised an amphibious enterprise undertaken in a spirit so unadventurous, and would have failed to concert vertebrate combinations of war with a military commander so incompetent and a military staff so obtuse.

Plattsburg.

Some years later, when operations in Egypt and Sicily and the Peninsula had obliterated dislikes, and when genuine harmony began to prevail between sailors and soldiers of all ranks, there occurred an episode which deserves recording. For it was the last example in the history of this country of the land-service and the sea-service failing to support each other, and thereby causing a reverse.[25]

The story of Plattsburg is not a pleasant one. The incident occurred in 1814, on Lake Champlain near the border-line between Canada and the United States. The war had been in progress for two years without decisive result to either side, and General Prevost, urged on from home to act with vigour, and reinforced by veteran troops liberated from the Peninsula, was undertaking an advance along the shores of the lake. A flotilla was being improvised by the navy, and this was goaded forward by the general before it was fully ready for an active campaign. Prevost promised to co-operate in a naval attack on Plattsburg, where an American force had entrenched itself and where an American flotilla was lying, favourably placed to beat off hostile war-vessels. The little British squadron attacked that of the enemy, received no support whatever from the army, and was completely and disastrously defeated. In consequence of this *contretemps*, for which the military appear to have been almost entirely to blame, there could no longer be any hope of gaining command upon the lake; and the contemplated advance along its edge was perforce abandoned.

In an earlier paragraph reference has been made to the condition of Wellington's maritime communications after the outbreak of the war with America. The commander-in-chief in the Peninsula always acknowledged in the handsomest manner the valuable services performed by naval officers on the spot: his quarrel was not with the navy but with the Admiralty. But a perusal of his despatches and letters at this time, and of those received by him, suggests to us rather that he lacked appreciation of the difficulties inseparable from naval warfare than that he had good cause for dissatisfaction. Lord Melville, in his first letter, explained clearly in the most temperate language the difficulties in

Wellington and the Admiralty.

which the Admiralty were placed. But Wellington was unconvinced. "For the first time," he wrote, ignoring what had occurred at Yorktown a generation earlier, "I believe it has happened to any British army that its communication by sea is insecure." He complained to the naval officers on the coast of Biscay of the conduct of their superiors, who of course heard of it; and later communications from Melville show signs of considerable irritation. "I will take your opinion," he writes, "in preference to any person's as to the most effectual mode of beating the French army, but I have no confidence in your seamanship and nautical skill." Napier conveys the impression that the interests of the army in the Peninsula were neglected by the Admiralty;[26] but it is by no means clear that he is justified in doing so, and that the degree to which hostile naval activity interfered with Wellington's plans has not been exaggerated. The army was inconvenienced, its security was never endangered.

Happy relations which have existed in campaigns since Waterloo. It is as satisfactory as it is significant that since the days of Waterloo the annals of warlike operations conducted by the British navy and the British army afford no illustrations of lack of co-operation or of serious misunderstandings between the services. During the Crimean War—a campaign conducted by military forces, but founded upon, and buttressed by, sea-power—the harmony between the services was complete. In China the soldier and sailor have more than once been called upon to work together, and they have always supported each other with the utmost disinterestedness and goodwill. During the Mutiny, in Egypt, and more than once in South Africa, naval brigades have been engaged ashore under military leadership with advantage to the army and benefit to the State.

Conclusion. Concord between forces accustomed under normal circumstances to work apart, can only be ensured when emergency obliges them to work together, if there is mutual sympathy and community of thought between them. The soldiers of a great maritime empire, the territories of which are scattered all over the globe, must understand the broad principles of the art of naval war ere they can appreciate the problems of its defence. The *personnel* of a navy which may have to shepherd armies over the seas in time of danger, to set them ashore, and to minister to their wants when ashore, will not perform its duties the less effectively if it realises the difficulties, the limitations, and the purposes of operations on land. Was it a mere coincidence that Lord Keith, whose work in 1780 as a young officer in charge of landing-parties from the fleet before Charleston won warm approbation from so good a judge as General Clinton, and whose tactical handling of a mixed body of British and Spanish troops sent out to stay the approach of the Republicans was the talk of the allied camp in Toulon, should have at the siege of Genoa in 1800 established relations with General Melas such as neither Hotham nor Nelson ever attained to when co-operating with the Austrian forces in the Riviera a few years before? Of what account is the opinion of a British military officer on questions of army organisation who knows nothing of sea-power, and who does not realise that in military operations in theatres of war adjacent to the coast, the question which side possesses maritime preponderance is the dominating factor in the issue?

The need for cordial co-operation between land- and sea-forces in situations where their functions are interdependent has been treated at some length in this introductory chapter. There is little risk now of incidents comparable with the bickerings of Penn and Venables or with the failure of Prevost to support the flotilla before Plattsburg disfiguring our future history. But the story of those discreditable episodes teaches us a lesson which is of value still. If there is to be perfect harmony in war between the navy and the army, there must be mutual confidence in peace and mutual understanding of respective functions. The broad principles of the art of war on land and sea present, after all, no complex problems to an intelligent mind: there is nothing about them that is cryptic, nothing that is obscure. But it is given to few to acquire mastery of them by mere intuition. They must be studied. Among British naval officers the fashion of taking their profession seriously has been in vogue since an era antecedent to the days of Nelson and of Collingwood. And, if it has to be confessed that in the army this becoming fashion is of more recent introduction, it can safely be asserted that in the present day the land-service and the sea-service are alike in this, that both know their own particular business, and know it well. But do they know enough about each other's business?

Ashore there is still a powerful undercurrent of opinion that the fleet cannot be trusted to safeguard the United Kingdom against effective invasion.[27] Afloat are to be found men of light and leading who, steeped in theories of naval strategy bordering on the pedantic, maintain in all good faith that conflict with a maritime opponent can be brought to a satisfactory ending by sea-power without military force. When doctors differ, it is the patient who is apt to come off second best. When naval and military experts quarrel over fundamental questions of defence policy, the country suffers for it. Both cannot be right. Neither may perhaps be wholly wrong. Peradventure the divergence of views between the two schools arises from the fact that each only understands one side of the case, in which they are unwittingly acting as opposing counsel rather than as judicial arbitrators. One point, however, is certain. Concord between fleets and armies when some great emergency arises will avail the Empire little if beforehand in periods of peace there has not existed concord between the representatives of the sister services in the councils of the nation.

CHAPTER II.

THE INFLUENCE UPON MARITIME OPERATIONS OF PROGRESS IN SHIP CONSTRUCTION, OF DEVELOPMENT OF ELECTRICAL COMMUNICATIONS, AND OF THE GENERAL RECOGNITION OF THE RIGHTS OF NEUTRALS.

WAR on land and war on the sea have this in common. While naval tactics and military tactics are constantly going through a process of evolution as the science of producing arms of destruction progresses, the broad principles of strategy ashore and afloat remain unchanged from century to century. The development of tactics is, it is true, reflected to a certain extent in certain phases of strategy. But the differences which can be traced between the art of conducting campaigns in the present era and the art of conducting them under the conditions of two thousand years ago, are in reality apparent rather than real. The orders of battle employed at Marathon and at Salamis by victor and vanquished are only of academic interest to-day, but the story of Hannibal's invasion of Italy may still be profitably studied as an example of the art of war. And that the paramount object in maritime operations is the destruction of the enemy's fleets, was as established a principle of war in the days of Antony and Octavian as it is in the opening decade of the twentieth century.

It is fortunate that this is so when we come to consider operations of naval warfare. Many questions concerning

Fundamental strategical principles remain unaltered while tactics change.

naval tactics remain a subject of controversy, owing to lack of convincing experience with modern fighting-ships and engines of war under all conditions. But naval strategy, and the relations which exist between land operations and command of the sea, are still illustrated most instructively by contests in which the opposing forces, alike on board ship or on *terra firma*, fought with weapons long since out of date. And the laws governing these branches of the art of war have been established in the history of struggles dating back to times so remote that their course is known only to a few students of naval and military records.

Purpose of the chapter. But it is none the less true that the principles of maritime strategy have in the course of years undergone appreciable modifications, in conformity to a certain extent with the advances which have taken place in the craft of the shipwright. Then, again, developments and discoveries in the science of electrical communication are exerting no small influence over the principles governing the applications of strategy to modern conditions at sea. Progress in civilisation, moreover, has tended to more clearly define the relations which should exist between belligerents and neutrals, than in the days of those great naval struggles upon which are founded so many generally accepted theories as to the proper conduct of maritime war. And in this chapter it is proposed to explain very briefly how these three factors—the development of shipbuilding, the introduction and progress of electrical telegraphy, and the more rigid observance of neutrality by non-combatants coupled with increased respect for neutrality shown by belligerents —all combine to mould and to modify the art of conducting operations at sea, and to control the question of combining maritime preponderance with operations on land.

Ancient ships of war. If we take first the question of the gradual development of shipbuilding, we find the art of war assuming definite shape in an age when the fighting-ship was a cumbrous, unseaworthy structure, depending for its motive power upon rowers alone. But in those days fighting forces afloat had more to fear from the elements than from the enemy. In the first Punic War storms on three successive occasions destroyed the fleets which the sea-power of Carthage compelled their rivals to create while the conflict was actually in progress. It was due to the dire effects of a tempest encountered off the Gulf of Volo that the imposing armada of Xerxes was not in a position to succour the Persian army in forcing the Thermopylæ defile between the mountains and the sea. And yet, even looking back to those early days when the fighting-ship was essentially a fair-weather craft, we find that the campaigns of Regulus and Hamilcar Barca most admirably illustrate the interdependence between maritime preponderance and warfare on shore. If records are contrasted, it is discovered that the overthrow of the Persian flotilla in the narrow waters of Salamis exerted an influence over the fortunes of the great Asiatic army which had come to conquer Greece, very analogous to that which the appearance of an allied fleet on the coast of Syria in 1839 exerted over the fortunes of Mehemet Ali's forces when they were threatening to overturn the Sultan's power.

The war-vessels of the ancients were singularly ill-adapted for operations in the open sea. When they ventured far from port they ran grave risk of foundering or of being driven ashore if a gale sprang up. But they possessed certain advantages which to some extent compensated for this. Driven by oars, as they were, they could be manœuvred with remarkable precision in fair weather. A flotilla could force its way into a gulf or harbour to fight the enemy, no matter which way the wind was blowing. In a tactical sense they were more navigable than fighting-ships of a much later date. In consequence of this, naval strategical conditions in that epoch differed somewhat from those of the eighteenth century, when fleets consisted of sailing-vessels, which, if the wind was fair for running in to attack an enemy in harbour, ran great risk of failing to get out again if defeated in the combat. In certain respects the old triremes and quinqueremes of the Greeks and Romans were better adapted for carrying out great combinations of war than the line-of-battle ships of twenty centuries later. The nation with the greater sea-power enjoyed in a measure better prospects of annihilating the maritime resources of the foe then, than in a subsequent era.[1]

The galley, and the introduction of sailing-vessels.

Early sailing-ships depended largely upon oars. The galley which played so conspicuous a *rôle* in the days of the Barbary corsairs, which, after it had gradually been superseded in European navies by the sailing-ships pure and simple, was revived by Louis XIV. to harry the British coasts during the War of the Spanish Succession, which was a feature in the fight for the Baltic between Sweden and Russia in the eighteenth century, and which reappeared in the Mediterranean in 1800 during the siege of Genoa, was a huge rowing-boat supplied with masts and sails. Excellent from the tactical point of view before the days of gunpowder, the galley ceased to fulfil its purpose of representing the primary striking force in fleet actions, as cannon came into common use. The broadside battery took up the space where the oarsmen and galley slaves had toiled, although it did so at the loss of manœuvring power to the ship. The dromon of the Levant, the carracks in which the Spaniards battled with Edward III. and his less imposing craft in the desperate scuffle of "L'Espagnols sur Mer,"[2] the galleons which played so important a part in the naval history of the Tudor days, were all different forms of glorified galley—vessels depending for their motive power partly upon oars and partly upon sails. But as the art of navigation developed, as commerce expanded, and as the progress of discovery opened up new fields for the enterprise of the trader and the ambitions of the freebooter, shipbuilders began to design larger and larger vessels, till these attained a size which forbade the use of oars even as an auxiliary to sail-power. This period coincided with that of artillery coming into prominence. And although galleys flourished in the Mediterranean even in the early part of the eighteenth century, and were sometimes used as auxiliaries to line-of-battle ships and frigates and brigs practically up to the introduction of steam, they latterly only corresponded to the destroyer and torpedo-boat and armed launch of the present day.

The galley, like the trireme, was ill-adapted to ride out a storm or to undertake ocean voyages. William the Conqueror was long delayed by unfavourable weather, and lost part of his flotilla before he succeeded in reaching the shores of Pevensey Bay. In 1385 Jean de Vienne formed a plan of securing a foothold on English shores by erecting a huge wooden fortress at the contemplated landing-place,—the fortress was in sections, and was shipped in seventy-two transports: but a storm arose, the transports were dispersed, many were wrecked, and the fragments of the fortress served for firewood in many a Kentish and Sussex home for months to come. The naval annals of those days abound in examples of fleets of fighting-ships and transports meeting with disaster at the hands of the elements. And this had an important bearing upon the strategy at sea and on land in those times. The element of uncertainty was far greater than in the present day. The balance of maritime power was apt to be upset by some sudden tempest, of which one belligerent navy encountered the full force while the other escaped owing to its floating material happening to be safe in port.

<small>Element of uncertainty in the navies of old.</small>

In the sailing era, which coincided approximately with the seventeenth and eighteenth centuries and with the first

<small>Effect of storms and bad</small>

weather in the sailing era. half of the nineteenth century, fleets and single ships, when handled by expert seamen, ran far less risks from bad weather than was the case in earlier days, although they ventured farther and in less settled weather. The great development of sail-power compelled builders and designers to keep stability constantly in view, and the danger of sinking waterlogged in heavy weather grew less and less. The disasters suffered by the Spanish Armada after the British fleets abandoned the chase in the North Sea arose from the ill-handled vessels running ashore through not being under control: none, undamaged by shot, would appear to have foundered in the open sea. But, on the other hand, the dependence upon the force and direction of the wind for motive power often led to most serious naval disasters. English, Dutch, and Swedish fleets, in which the art of seamanship was familiar alike on the quarter-deck and in the forecastle, suffered heavily on many occasions. In the great storm of 1705 no less than twelve large British ships of war were lost in the Channel.

Moreover, even when the great sailing-ships of the days of De Ruyter and Anson and Lord Exmouth rode out a gale at sea in safety, they often suffered so much aloft that they became for a time mere hulks. In a hurricane off the coast of Nova Scotia in 1757 Admiral Holbourne's fleet lost two ships altogether, and had twelve dismasted: in consequence the contemplated blockade of Louisbourg had to be abandoned. In 1778 Howe's and D'Estaing's fleets, opposed to each other off the coast of Massachusetts, were both dispersed by a sudden storm and both suffered considerably,—an incident which, owing to the strategical situation at the moment alike on shore and at sea, exerted a marked influence over the early course of the war in North America. The risks of damage in bad weather introduced, in fact, a very appreciable element of uncertainty into the conduct of maritime warfare in the sailing era,

UNCERTAINTY AS TO TIME.

and one which does not arise from the same cause in the present day. But a far greater element of uncertainty than this, and one which has almost disappeared under modern conditions, arose out of the fact that the speed which fleets could attain, and the course which they could follow at any juncture, were dependent upon a factor so indeterminate as the strength and direction of the wind.

It is this connection between the strength and direction of the wind and the strategical and tactical manœuvring power of navies in the age of sails which, when we come to apply the history of war to conditions of the present epoch, fixes a great gulf between those days and days of steam. Commanders of armies and of fleets strive to conceal the purpose which they have in view from those opposed to them. In any conflict, whether it be ashore or be afloat, there must always be doubts and questionings as to the position, the objects, and the strength of the adversary. But the general can calculate, at least approximately, the time which it will take his force to reach its immediate destination, provided that there is no interference from the foe. The admiral of to-day knows the speed of his slowest ships, and he can form an accurate estimate of the number of hours' steaming which it will take his fleet to make any point, provided that he meets with no opposition. But in the sailing era nothing could be calculated upon with certainty. Quite apart from what the enemy might do, there was the doubt as to force of the wind, and as to the point of the compass from which it might blow. The art of war is essentially a matter of calculation; and for purposes of calculation determinate premises are the first desideratum. Before the adaptation of steam-power to warships, and to transports detailed for carrying troops and stores, there was an element of chance in everything connected with the mariner's calling which since that time has tended to disappear.

It was formerly impossible to foretell whether certain

Uncertainty as to time to be taken in a strategical combination in the days of sails.

classes of enterprise would be practicable at all, till the fleet arrived within striking distance. Any operation in narrow seas almost inevitably depended on the elements. An illustration of the difficulties and uncertainties of maritime strategy in the sailing days is given in a later paragraph, which contrasts the task of Nelson in 1798 in the Mediterranean when Napoleon made his descent upon Egypt, with the task which a naval commander would have to perform were he confronted with the same problem under the conditions of to-day. But numbers of examples could be quoted to show the extent to which all naval plans were formerly subservient to the weather.

Examples. In 1779 the famous Paul Jones appeared with a privateering fleet within sight of Leith. There was great alarm in Edinburgh, and the citizens were called to arms. But Sir Walter Scott, who was in the city at the time as a young lad, tells us, in the Introduction to 'Waverley,' that "a steady west wind settled the matter by sweeping Paul Jones and his vessels out of the Firth of Forth."

Hoche's famous expedition to the south-west coast of Ireland in 1796 had a very similar experience. The bulk of the armada reached the mouth of Bantry Bay unmolested by the British fleet. But the wind which had favoured the voyage thither from the shores of Brittany, was foul for running up the narrow gulf. Neither commanders nor crews of the French vessels were equal to coping with the problem of beating up the bay, a task of uncommon difficulty even for a fleet in the highest state of efficiency. And, the ship which Hoche himself was in having gone astray, the expedition returned to the French coast baffled, after the strategical difficulty of approaching the shores of Ireland without being set upon by the formidable naval forces gathered under Bridport in the Channel, had been overcome.

Difficulties of In the sailing days the difficulties of blockade, or even of keeping a watch upon a hostile port, were enormous. In bad weather the blockading squadron or the watching cruisers had to run for shelter; then when the weather moderated the enemy could often put to sea before it was practicable to recover station. When the voyage of a fleet for some strategical purpose involved the passage of straits, like those of Dover or of Gibraltar, contrary winds sometimes delayed the completion of the movement for weeks, and the situation in the theatre of operations which the fleet was trying to reach was liable to undergo a complete transformation in consequence. One fleet chasing another might be favoured by the better breeze, or might drop far astern owing to the enemy having the better luck. "For a whole month we have had nothing like a Levanter except for the French fleet," wrote Nelson, when Villeneuve had escaped from Toulon and had passed out through the Straits of Gibraltar ahead of him.

blockade in the sailing days.

Apprehensions as to possible change of weather, the element of chance which the climate in most quarters of the globe introduced into every calculation, the doubts and suspense which necessarily assailed the naval commander in the age of sails, undoubtedly affected strategical principles in a certain measure. In a later chapter, when the question of the "fleet in being" is discussed, it will be shown that theories founded upon the immunity so often enjoyed by over-sea military expeditions in despite of effective hostile sea-power before the introduction of steam, may require modification under the changed conditions of the present day. Lessons to be learnt from the Napoleonic wars as to commerce destroying and the mode of meeting it, may not be quite so applicable to-day.[3] The exhaustion which pressure from the sea produces on shore may prove to be a less potent instrument in the hands of the stronger navy in the future than it has been heretofore.[4] But the broad principles remain unchanged, although the sailing-ship has disappeared as an engine of war, and although steam has obliterated much of the uncertainty which attended naval combinations even within living memory.

Rapidity with which fleets could be created formerly.

There is one very important point in connection with shipbuilding in the old days as compared to the present time of which note should be taken. It is certainly the case that fighting-ships could be built more rapidly and more easily formerly than is possible since the introduction of the modern man-of-war. Moreover, speaking generally, merchant vessels could be more effectively and more readily adapted to the requirements of cruisers, or even of battleships, in the era before the days of steam, than since. The story of the Chilian war of independence and of the struggle of Greece for its freedom, both dating less than a century back, show how fleets could then be improvised capable of contesting command of the sea with navies of long standing.[5] In the era of galleys and of sailing-ships it was undoubtedly the case that, the smaller the type of the fighting-craft of the day happened to be, the more easily could losses be repaired by building anew.

Within a single year of the overwhelming disaster of Lepanto in 1571, the Ottoman Empire had a new fleet ready consisting of no less than 210 sail. Two months after the English fleet was crippled by De Ruyter in the great sea-fight known as the "Battle of the Four Days," it was at sea again and ready for a fresh encounter.[6] The French in 1794 and 1795 built ships with marvellous rapidity at Toulon, although the British occupation of Corsica deprived them of the timber generally used in the great Mediterranean dockyard. The longer time required to create a fleet under modern conditions as compared with those of a former era, has introduced a change into naval conditions during the progress of a war which should not be lost sight of. The destruction of a modern sea-going fleet is a more serious national disaster than it was even in the days of Nelson, because the prospects of creating another fleet to take its place during the term of the war in which the disaster occurs are more remote.[7]

The fire-ships of former days deserve a word of notice. The fire-ship of the past in its duties and objects and capabilities had much in common with the torpedo craft and the submarines of to-day. They were the terror of the fleet at anchor which was unprotected by some sort of boom; but they acted like a drag on a seagoing fleet, just as the destroyer does in the present day in unsettled weather. Their handling demanded the utmost skill and daring, just as does that of the modern torpedo-boat and submarine. That they were awkward craft to handle is evidenced by an attack made with them on some Flemish ships at anchor in 1304 by a French flotilla; for the wind veered after they were set alight, and they drove down upon their own side in a blaze and did great damage. *Fire-ships the forerunners of torpedo craft.*

Fire-ships were always especially effective against inefficient ill-manned fleets. The attacks of the Hellenic fire-ships upon Ottoman squadrons in Chesmé Bay and Tenedos harbour during the Greek War of Liberation were attended with astonishing success.[8] The same was the case when the Spanish Armada was thrown into dire confusion by this means off Calais. But, on the other hand, a French attempt against Admiral Saunders' fleet below Quebec was a complete failure, the skill and coolness of the British sailors proving fully equal to the occasion.[9] In view, however, of the signal success of Admiral Spragge against the Barbary corsairs in the harbour of Bougie in 1671, and of Lord Cochrane's famous attack on the French squadron in Basques Roads in 1808, it would certainly not be safe to assert that these engines of destruction did not constitute a danger even to efficient well-administered squadrons when at anchor. In 1676 Vivonne, intigated thereto it is said by Tourville, attacked the Dutch-

Spanish fleet anchored near Palermo, soon after the death of De Ruyter at Agosto had bereft it of a brilliant leader: the completeness of the French success was largely due to fire-ships, launched when the allied warships were already in difficulties from the more regular attack. Seagoing fleets in the first half of the eighteenth century were almost invariably accompanied by fire-ships, but these gradually ceased to form a necessary complement of such squadrons when they were found to retard the mobility which sailors of the type of Hawke and Howe and Hood looked upon as indispensable.

<small>Introduction of steam does away with many elements of uncertainty.</small>

With the introduction of steam much of the uncertainty as to the time which any given operation will take, which was such an important factor in the naval warfare of the rowing and the sailing days, has disappeared. Just as the movements of an army on shore can be foreseen, as the period required for it to effect a concentration on any particular point can be accurately estimated, and as a scheme of operations for it can be worked out up to the time when it comes in contact with the enemy, so can a naval plan of campaign be elaborated with every probability of calculations of time proving correct up to the juncture when the action of the hostile fleets begins to upset the arrangements. Tempestuous weather will to a certain extent create delays even now in the movements of battleships and cruisers, and it may exert a very important influence on the secondary operations of torpedo craft and submarines; but the greatest element of

<small>Question of fog.</small>

uncertainty in the present day arises from the risk of fog or thick weather, especially in certain latitudes and in certain seas. One of the most tragic disasters in British naval history appears to have been partly caused by fog, when Sir Cloudesley Shovel's flagship and three other vessels were lost on the rocks of the Scilly Isles, and when the admiral himself, on his way home from the Mediterranean full of years and honours, was, it is believed, murdered after swimming ashore. In 1711 an expedition against Quebec under Sir Hovenden Walker came to grief in the treacherous channel north of Anticosti owing to thick weather. Fog would appear to have greatly interfered with the naval operations in the Far East in 1904.

Steam has affected the movements of transports carrying troops and war material to the full as much as it has influenced the operations of actual fighting-ships. Provided that the enemy does not interfere, an army can under present conditions be conveyed across the sea with the practical certainty, apart from the dangers of collision or shipwreck and the chance of delays due to thick weather, that it will reach the coast which forms its goal within a space of time that can be accurately calculated. If the conditions be favourable, this enables what may be called amphibious operations to be carried out with an exactitude and precision unknown half a century ago. But, as will be pointed out in a later chapter, the actual landing of troops and stores from transports is, unless the disembarkation takes place in some well-sheltered harbour, in most respects just as liable to interruption by bad weather as it was in the sailing era. The beaching of boats is as difficult and dangerous nowadays if the sea gets up as it ever was. A lee shore has not, however, the same terrors for a steamer as it had for a sailing-ship, and the modern transport can remain at anchor with steam up in weather which would have compelled such vessels as carried Sir R. Abercromby's force to Aboukir Bay to promptly put to sea.

It should be noted that steam in its adaptation to small craft has greatly altered the conditions affecting the employment of inshore flotillas for military purposes. Small sailing-vessels have always been able to manœuvre close in to shore and to escape from sailing-ships of heavier burthen, not merely because of their shallower draught of water, but also because, from their nature, line-of-battle ships or

<small>Steam and inshore flotillas for military purposes.</small>

frigates could not be risked in minor indentations and coves such as are found on most coasts. Formerly a fleet blockading an enemy's coast could not employ small craft for hunting vessels of the same class in intricate seas, unless there were secure harbours for the little ships to fly to for refuge in bad weather. But the smaller class of gunboat of the present day, which can keep the sea in bad weather, can generally get within gun-range of any hostile vessel under the conditions presented by most stretches of coast.

And that this is a point of considerable importance appears from the following references to the conflicts of a century ago. In 1795, although Admiral Hotham's fleet was supposed to be dominating the Ligurian Sea, the French army operating along the Riviera depended very largely for its supplies on coasters coming from both west and east. In the following year, Napoleon managed to convey his heavy guns for the campaign of Montenotte by small transports from Nice to Savona in spite of the British navy. When in 1799 Napoleon advanced from Egypt into Syria along the littoral of the Levant, a flotilla of small craft coasted along, close in, abreast of the troops: Sir S. Smith, with his squadron of ships-of-the-line and frigates, does not seem to have been able to interfere with these very valuable auxiliaries to the French army, although his capture of the siege-train proceeding direct from Damietta to Acre in light coasters exerted a vast importance over the struggle for that great oriental stronghold. It is difficult to imagine, under the conditions of the present day, a preponderating navy allowing a hostile army to derive such assistance from either sailing-vessels or steamers of small class as the French did on the Riviera and in Egypt a century ago, when men like Nelson and Sidney Smith were present and on guard.

Fundamental principles But although the developments in the art of ship construction which mark the progress of navies from the days

FUNDAMENTAL PRINCIPLES UNALTERED. 37

of Salamis up to the days of Port Arthur have transformed the methods under which maritime war is carried on in many respects, the laws of strategy remain unaltered.[10] The fleet which gained the mastery was in a position to attack and, if hostilities lasted long enough, to destroy the over-sea trade of the enemy in the days of the Romans and Carthaginians just as it is to-day. In former times the inferior navy sought the shelter of fortified harbours just as it does still, the only difference being that such harbours are relatively fewer now than in the age of smaller craft. War-vessels have always been compelled from time to time to seek shelter at some place where they could refit after damage in action or from ordinary wear and tear: repairs in the old days could be carried out in any petty port, now they can only be executed in great dockyards specially designed for the purpose. The broad principle, however, remains the same. Transports conveying soldiers were often, when attacked by fighting-vessels in the age of the Norsemen, little less helpless than they are under existing conditions. Soldiers of olden time when unused to the sea could not handle their weapons to good effect in a scuffle, and this impeded the sailors in the management of the ship: nowadays their transport is sunk under them by a torpedo, or is transformed into a shambles by quick-firing guns. The result is the same in either case. The comparative certainty as to the time which a voyage will take in a modern man-of-war or transport benefits both belligerents, and it does not alter the fundamental truths of naval strategy any more than the introduction of railways alters the laws of strategy on land. Principles remain the same even if their application has undergone some modification.

remain unaltered.

Scarcely less important than the progress in ship construction in its influence over naval warfare is the introduction and development of telegraphy. Electrical communications are a far more dominant factor in maritime

Effect of introduction of electrical communications.

operations than in purely land campaigns, owing to the fact that, as a general rule, the theatre of war at sea is of vast extent, and may indeed cover the greater part of the globe. And the introduction of wireless telegraphy of recent years is a fresh step in advance, of which the full possibilities have perhaps not yet been gauged.[11] Thanks to electricity, each belligerent can watch the movements of the other, can discover the positions of hostile fleets, can be kept informed of the concentration and sailing of military expeditions, and can execute naval combinations to meet each particular case with a celerity and precision unknown before electrical telegraphy was introduced. But the accepted doctrines of naval strategy have not been changed by this: the objects to be sought after remain the same, the methods by which these objects are attained are little different from what they were before.

Example of Nelson's pursuit of Napoleon to Egypt. To illustrate the extent to which modern conditions have modified procedure in naval warfare while the fundamental principles which should govern their conduct remain unaltered, we may take as example that remarkable set of operations which began when Napoleon quitted Toulon for the east, and which ended on that August night when the French fleet was destroyed at its moorings in Aboukir Bay.*

The Directory had cloaked the French designs with the utmost secrecy, and the preparations for the expedition were kept studiously concealed to the last possible moment. But a great army could not be assembled at a place like Toulon, nor could a large fleet of transports be got together, without the news leaking out. Intelligence that something was impending, and that an armada was mustering in the great Mediterranean fortress, had reached England in good time. Its destination remained unknown, nor could its purpose be divined. But, so as to observe what was going forward, St Vincent, who was off Cadiz, was

* The map facing p. 92 illustrates this campaign.

directed to detach a squadron into the Mediterranean, which had been abandoned since Spain cast in her lot with France some months before. And the admiral, ignoring claims of seniority, selected Nelson for the command and despatched him to the Gulf of the Lion, where he arrived on the 17th of May.

Two days later Napoleon's expedition quitted Toulon, profiting by the state of the weather, and proceeded to Genoa. Its departure was not observed by Nelson. From Genoa it sailed south to Malta, and arrived there on the 6th June. In the meantime a reinforcement under Troubridge, sufficient to bring the British Mediterranean squadron up to a strength about equalling Napoleon's escorting fleet, had been despatched from Cadiz. Troubridge joined Nelson off the coast of Italy on the 7th June. But it was not till the 17th that the anxious British admiral learnt that the quarry had a fortnight before proceeded to Malta: he thereupon hastened south, realising that the large armada, of which details began to be gleaned from various sources, had most effectually given him the slip.

Napoleon was unaware that British sea-power was reasserting itself east of the Straits, and his stay at Malta was somewhat prolonged. Having reduced the fortress of Valetta, having installed a garrison in the island, and having arranged for its government as a dependency of France, he sailed for Egypt on the 19th June, shaping his course *viâ* the southern shores of Crete. In those waters he learnt, on the 27th, that Nelson with a formidable fleet had been seen at Naples, and, turning south, the expedition reached Alexandria on the 1st of July. But in the meantime Nelson, hurrying towards Malta, had heard of the departure of the French from that island, had guessed that Egypt was its goal, had made all sail for Alexandria by the shortest line, and had arrived there on the 28th June, four days ahead of Napoleon, whose huge flotilla travelled slowly, and who had steered a much longer course.

Arrived in Egyptian waters and finding nothing there, Nelson was completely in the dark. Full of forebodings, he proceeded along the Syrian coast, thus sailing north-eastwards at no great distance to the east of the line along which Napoleon was at the same time approaching Egypt from the north-west. Finding no trace of the French anywhere, he sailed back westwards, quitting the Levant, steered a course past Crete to Syracuse, and arrived there on the 19th of July. Nothing was known in Sicily of what had become of Napoleon, who all this time was firmly establishing himself in the Nile Delta, and was affording the Egyptians brilliant illustrations of the art of tactics and of strategy on land. Nelson, however, felt convinced that the French must have gone to Egypt after all; and so, having watered his squadron, he sailed from Syracuse on the 24th July straight for Alexandria. On the 1st August he found that great port full of shipping; a few hours later he sighted the enemy's squadron moored in the Aboukir anchorage; and that same night was won the victory of the Nile, which severed the communications of the French army with its native land, and shattered Napoleon's dreams of oriental dominion at a single blow.

It is only right to mention that Nelson, during this remarkable game of hide-and-seek, had practically no vessels suitable for scouting purposes. He had no adequate means of gaining intelligence as to the whereabouts of the slow-moving armada which he was chasing. But for this he could not have failed to ascertain the position of the French at a much earlier date, and he might conceivably have caught the expedition out in the open sea far from port.

Now if we picture to ourselves such a set of operations under modern conditions, we see at once how differently events must have shaped themselves, even assuming Nelson to have been practically without cruisers and to have depended upon stray scraps of news when at sea.

Comparison with a parallel situation under modern conditions.

It is most improbable that Napoleon could have quitted Toulon altogether unobserved, although it is true that Nelson, who then had a very inferior fleet, could not have prevented the departure of the expeditionary force, and probably could not have inflicted any damage upon it until he was joined by Troubridge. But as Troubridge only left Cadiz two days after the French expedition started, the armada should, even allowing for the slow steaming of ordinary transports, have got to Malta two or three days before the two British squadrons could possibly have united anywhere near Sicily. Supposing, however, that Napoleon had attacked Malta, there is no reason to believe that, assuming Valetta to be a modern fortress, he would have brought about its capitulation more quickly in the present day than he actually did in 1798. Therefore, in the very improbable event of the French expedition having, under modern conditions, delayed at Malta at all, there would have been a decisive naval fight off that island; and had Nelson been victorious in this, Napoleon and his army would almost certainly have had to surrender there.

But had Napoleon, on the other hand, gone straight on to Egypt from Sicilian waters, Nelson must, after the junction of Troubridge, have been quite three or four days behind him. The news of the great French armada, passing east from Sicily, would have been telegraphed from Malta and Sicily all over Europe. In the meantime, Napoleon would have heard of Troubridge's entering the Mediterranean, by telegraph through Spain, and he could have been in little doubt that a fleet equal to his own was on his heels. He would almost certainly have steamed straight to Alexandria, and would have landed his army before Nelson could possibly have overtaken him. Leaving Toulon on the 19th of May, the army would probably have been all ashore in the Nile Delta by the 28th, and the great naval battle would probably have taken place in Egyptian waters before the end of that month— *i.e.*, two months earlier than occurred in the actual event.

Everything would, under modern conditions, have hinged on the date of Troubridge's quitting Cadiz. Had he found Nelson before Toulon at a date anterior to Napoleon's putting to sea, the French armada would almost inevitably have been caught in the Ligurian Sea: there could scarcely have been a question of it getting away unobserved. Under the conditions of 1798, on the other hand, Troubridge's presence in the Gulf of the Lion, at the time when the French expedition started, need not necessarily have made the slightest difference. Nelson would, in all probability, have been groping about on the coast of Italy till well on into June, before discovering that Napoleon had rounded Sicily, just the same whether Troubridge was with him from the outset or not.

It would therefore seem to be the case that, under the strategical conditions which presented themselves to Napoleon and to Nelson on the 19th of May 1798, neither the substitution of modern battleships and cruisers for the ships-of-the-line and frigates which they actually had at their disposal, nor the substitution of steamers for the sailing transports in which the army of Egypt actually embarked, nor yet the existence of electrical communications and of wireless telegraphy, would have prevented the French expedition from arriving safely in the Nile Delta. But the descent on Malta would almost inevitably have led to the British fleet gaining contact with the armada which it was seeking, in the vicinity of that island instead of in the Levant, supposing Napoleon to have been so injudicious as to undertake the reduction of its formidable defences on his way to the east. And, had the expeditionary force made no halt at Malta, the decisive naval encounter would, in all likelihood, have taken place within a very few days of the French army arriving in Egypt. Assuming it to have terminated as did the battle of the Nile, Napoleon would have found himself obliged to overcome the resistance of the Mamelukes under the adverse conditions of his isolation being patent to all observers, and of his prestige having suffered a most serious blow before any decisive superiority on land had been established.

The history of war affords few better illustrations of the doubts and uncertainties which beset the naval commanders of a former era, than the chase of Napoleon to the east by the greatest admiral who has ever flown his flag. But when we apply modern conditions to even this extreme case, we find that the broad result of the operations would probably have been much the same to-day as they actually were a century ago. Still, it is important to bear in mind that Nelson, at the outset, was in very inferior force. In the present day, nothing would justify the commander of a military expedition in starting for an over-sea enterprise practically in presence of a hostile fleet equal to its own escort. Many of the examples which will be quoted in later chapters of the safe transport of large bodies of troops across the sea, on occasions where maritime preponderance was not by any means established, cannot be accepted as precedents to-day without reserve. In no respect, perhaps, have the laws which govern warlike operations been more affected by the changes due to the introduction of steam and of electrical telegraphy than in this.

The attitude of neutrals towards belligerents engaged in maritime warfare is not dependent upon any very strict or well-established code even in the present day. There is, *Influence on strategy of closer observance of the rights and duties of neutrals.*

moreover, no tribunal to punish the breach of those unwritten rules on the subject, which are generally acknowledged to form part of international law. But among civilised Powers public opinion is a potent force, the news of any violation of accepted usage travels fast, and the relations between belligerents and neutrals are now controlled to a great extent by well-established precedents. To these precedents nations when at war adhere—at least in principle. It is true that during the Russo-Japanese war incidents have occurred showing that the rights of neutrals are still liable to be trampled upon if those neutrals are unable, or are unwilling, to defend them. Recent events have shown that the governments of States not participating in the conflict may succeed in evading their obligations by stealth, or by acting on the assumption that their conduct will not be actively resented. But, upon the whole, matters in this respect have much changed within the last few decades, and this is a fact of considerable importance as affecting the naval conditions of to-day when they are contrasted with those of former times.

Territorial waters of neutrals are now held to be inviolate. Any act of war within them arouses a storm of protest, not only from the aggrieved neutral State, but also from other nations alarmed lest a dangerous precedent may be established. Neutrals in the present day refuse overtly to supply belligerent war-vessels with coal except within certain limitations. Fighting-ships damaged by storm or in action are only supposed to be repaired in neutral ports sufficiently to render them seaworthy, and their stay is expected not to be of long duration.[12] There is, however, a good deal of elasticity as regards the application of these rules. The whole question is still in an exceedingly unsatisfactory condition; but it is only right to admit that there has been vast improvement since the Napoleonic wars. This is shown by the following examples of laxity as regards the observance of

QUESTION OF NEUTRALITY. 45

neutrality in the seventeenth and eighteenth centuries, which are taken at random from a number of similar instances.

In 1650 Spain and Portugal were at peace, although there was at the time a good deal of latent hostility between the governments and peoples. The English admiral Blake happened to be seeking Prince Rupert, turned sailor, and in the course of his cruise in pursuit he traced that venturesome prince to the Tagus. By various acts of hostility against Rupert he became involved in conflict with the Portuguese. In the operations which resulted against Portugal, Blake freely based himself upon Spanish ports, and he was made welcome there. But all the time Spain remained nominally neutral, and Portugal accepted the situation without making any reprisals. *Examples of laxity as to observance of neutrality in the seventeenth and eighteenth centuries.*

Two years later a very singular incident during the Anglo-Dutch war proved how vague and ill-defined were notions of neutrality in those days. A small squadron under Appleton, guarding a convoy, took shelter in the Tuscan port of Leghorn, and it was there promptly blockaded by the Dutch fleet. Tuscany was at the time a Spanish dependency, and the benevolent attitude of Spain towards the Commonwealth, which had been already displayed in the naval operations against Rupert, was still maintained. The Dutch under Van Galen lay off Leghorn on the watch while Appleton remained inside. But some of the Dutch vessels were allowed to use the port for repairs, so that hostile ships were in the same harbour, but covered by its neutrality and therefore keeping the peace. The distinguished admiral Badiley, coming from the Levant, endeavoured to form a junction with Appleton; but he was foiled in the attempt, and in the desperately-contested action off Monte Cristo his squadron was severely handled by Van Galen. He, however, managed to make Elba with the loss of only the *Phœnix*. The Dutch took the *Phœnix* into Leghorn, and there, within sight of Appleton's sailors, they set to work to repair the damages suffered by the vessel and to fit her out for further action, and they actually captured an English merchantman with her which was brought in triumph into the port. This was a sore trial to the English *personnel* beleaguered in the harbour, and, with the full approval of Badiley, who had managed a visit from Elba, a step was taken by some of Appleton's crews of a drastic and decisive kind. One night two or three English boats' crews rushed the *Phœnix* unexpectedly, got her out of harbour, sailed her past the blockading fleet in safety, and escaped with her to Naples. And the extraordinary contention was put forward that an act of hostility of this kind in no way violated the neutrality of a friendly port, as long as no fire-arms were discharged,—the capture had been effected by surprise, and the work had been done with the cutlass. The Grand Duke of Tuscany, moreover, regarded the whole affair as a joke, chaffed the Dutch for their negligence, and refused to demand reparation from Appleton at the time.

A quarter of a century later, while this country was at peace but while Spain was engaged in war with France, a French commander, the Duc de Vivonne, arrived with a great armament in Tangier, which was then a British possession.[13] He was preparing for an attack upon Cadiz, and he made his arrangements for the operation in the Moorish port without any let or hindrance from the British authorities, remaining in the harbour for a considerable time. As it turned out, the French expedition, instead of attacking Cadiz, proceeded eventually to Sicily, that Mediterranean cockpit of two thousand years' standing, and attacked the Spaniards there. But a belligerent had made use of a neutral port as base for an operation intended against a stronghold almost within sight of the port: the neutral had taken no action, and had not been called to account for inaction.

In 1759 the remnants of Commodore De la Clue's squadron, after its defeat between Gibraltar and Cape St Vincent by Boscawen, was run ashore on the Portuguese coast near Lagos to escape capture. The British admiral, however, ignoring Portuguese neutrality, followed De la Clue up, and he either captured or destroyed every one of the French ships. Portugal was not participating in the war; but the representations made from Lisbon to the Government of St James's met with very scanty recognition, and they drew forth merely formal expressions of regret.

In 1770 Russia was at war with the Ottoman Empire, with which Great Britain was at peace. Captain Mahan thus describes the attitude of this country towards the belligerents in 'The Influence of Sea-Power upon the French Revolution and Empire' (p. 11): "In 1770 British officers commanded Russian fleets and ships, and a British admiral had been permitted to take a place in the Russian Admiralty with the promise of his home rank being restored to him. The Czarina sent a fleet of twenty sail-of-the-line from the Baltic to the Levant. They stopped and refitted in Spithead; Russian soldiers were landed and camped ashore to refresh themselves; English sergeants of marines were employed to drill them; a Russian eighty-gun ship, flying the flag of an Anglo-Russian admiral, was docked in Portsmouth and cut down to improve her sailing qualities. Thus comforted and strengthened they sailed for the Mediterranean; and receiving further damage from the poor seamanship of their crews, they were again fitted at Port Mahon — then an English dockyard — for action in the Levant. When among the hard knocks of the two following years the Russians destroyed a Turkish fleet of fifteen ships-of-the-line in a port of Asia Minor, British lieutenants commanded the fire-ships, and a British commander the covering squadron." It can easily be imagined what a storm would be aroused in the present day were any nation to adopt an attitude of such remarkably benevolent neutrality towards one belligerent during a conflict in which it was not an active participator.[14]

Position of Portugal. Portugal, a weak Power on land and sea, but owing to its geographical position and its extended colonial possessions being in the position to offer tempting harbours of refuge and resort to belligerent war-vessels, frequently suffered under the indignity of having its neutrality ignored and set at nought during the great naval wars of the sailing era.

In 1781, when France was at war with England, the great admiral Suffren, on his way to the Cape of Good Hope, accidentally lighted upon the British Commodore Johnstone anchored in the Portuguese harbour of Porto Praya, in the Cape de Verdes. Suffren stood on no ceremony. He bore down on the hostile squadron, which was quite unprepared for battle, and fell upon it in the neutral port. The fight turned out to be indecisive, and the French squadron, somewhat damaged in the encounter, proceeded on its way southwards. Johnstone remained in Porto Praya for a fortnight refitting after the combat, and he then proceeded towards the Cape in the wake of his doughty opponent. Both parties, in fact, violated Portuguese neutrality according to modern ideas, although Suffren's action in bringing on an engagement within the three miles' limit was more of an aggression against the rights of Portugal than was that of Johnstone in using Porto Praya as a base after he had been attacked in territorial waters.

In 1814, during our war with the United States, an American vessel was captured by a British warship in Portuguese territorial waters. The United States claimed damages from Portugal: their right to compensation was, however, disputed by that country. Many years afterwards, in 1851, the question at issue was settled by the award

QUESTION OF NEUTRALITY. 49

of Prince Louis Napoleon (Napoleon III.), then President of the French Republic. The arbitrator gave his decision in favour of Portugal on the broad grounds that that country was not to blame in the matter, and had not possessed the means of preventing the outrage.

In the present day most harbours of strategical importance situated in what were formerly the great theatres of naval warfare are in possession of civilised Powers. The law of nations as regards neutrals and belligerents is now sufficiently well established to practically close these harbours to the navies of the contending parties. And when a belligerent vessel seeks refuge in territorial waters of a neutral State, it is generally admitted that that vessel must either disarm or must put to sea again after a short stay. This tends to limit one of the many uncertainties which used to beset the naval strategist. But in any determined struggle for mastery of the seas between nations claiming a measure of naval power, the maritime campaign is apt in the present day to extend all over the globe. The trade of seafaring nations is world-wide, and it can be attacked in every ocean. Hostilities are likely to penetrate into waters washing territories remote from civilisation and ruled by potentates who know nothing of the rights of neutrals, and who would have no means of defending their neutrality if they did. A belligerent cannot in the twentieth century base himself upon a neutral port in European, nor yet in North American, waters. The three miles' limit of countries not involved in the dispute only as a rule affords sanctuary for a short time to the vessel which is in danger from hostile enterprise, unless the scene of action is remote; but there are still many parts of the world where the story of the Duc de Vivonne at Tangier and of Boscawen and De la Clue at Lagos may be repeated.[15] The element of uncertainty introduced into naval combinations of war previous to the time of Waterloo

Situation in the present day.

D

by laxity as regards neutrality has diminished in these later days, but it has not wholly disappeared.

Conclusion. It has seemed advisable to draw attention to the influence exerted upon maritime operations in general by progress in ship construction, by the development of electrical communications, and by greater regularity of procedure in questions affecting relations between belligerents and neutrals. In the following chapters many references will be made to episodes of war dating back to days of long ago. If the modifications introduced into naval warfare by changes in these matters are not kept constantly in mind, their bearing upon strategy under modern conditions may not be correctly estimated, and false deductions may be drawn from events in history.

CHAPTER III.

THE AIMS AND OBJECTS SOUGHT AFTER IN NAVAL WARFARE.

INJURY of the adversary may be said to be the primary object in war, and, speaking generally, the purpose of a belligerent is to profit when possible by the damage which may be inflicted. When the process of harming the enemy has been carried far enough, it leads automatically to the achievement of the second and principal object—that of compelling the antagonist to acquiesce in terms of peace favourable to the victor.[1] Naval operations aim at attaining these objects by destroying the hostile fleets, by harassing and, if practicable, annihilating the opponent's over-sea trade, and by striving to establish a maritime preponderance so decisive that military force can be brought into play in the form of descent upon the enemy's coasts and colonies. And if the first of these methods—destruction of the hostile fighting forces afloat—is put in force with sufficient success, the other two methods can afterwards be employed with comparatively speaking trifling risk, and they will afford good prospects of achieving the desired result. *The general objects aimed at in war.*

When the question of injuring the enemy comes to be considered, it must be remembered that a navy of the present day represents a vast sum of actual money. Modern war-vessels are costly, and their loss is in itself, quite apart from its effect on the course of operations, a serious misfortune to a nation. The actual value in cash of the *Injury inflicted on an enemy by destroying his fleet.*

Russian Far Eastern fleet early in 1904 was estimated to be many millions sterling, a sum which the wealthiest communities cannot regard with indifference. So that the financial loss to a State which finds its navy wiped out of existence by superior force will always be a serious one. Still, this is in reality a question of minor importance. It is not on account of the mere financial damage inflicted thereby upon the antagonist that the first great aim and object of naval warfare is to destroy the enemy's fleets.

Further consequences of destroying enemy's sea-power. The definite overthrow of a nation's navy means that thenceforward its maritime commerce is at the mercy of the foe, that its over-sea possessions, should it be a world-wide Power, are cut off from the mother land and are exposed to attack in detail without hope of succour, and that its coasts may at any moment be violated by the armies of an invader who can choose his own time and his own place for the undertaking. And, per contra, the downfall of the fleets of its opponent guarantees to a nation a considerable measure of immunity from molestation for its mercantile marine, it ensures distant colonies from serious depredation, and it relieves the people of all anxiety as to hostile descents in any force upon their coasts. No great principle of the art of war is so clearly established as that which lays down that the destruction of the enemy's navy is, supposing it to be possible, the one paramount object in warfare at sea. British writers on naval subjects always insist upon the importance of this great truth.[2] Captain Mahan proves it upon almost every page of those works of his which have exerted so great an influence over public opinion in this country. It admits, in reality, of no dispute. But there are two sides to every question, and there must be two parties to every conflict. We, with our vast naval resources and noble traditions of the sea, are inclined to regard the art of maritime war solely from the point of view of the stronger side. We are prone to forget that when in any

WAR OF 1778 TO 1783.

set of operations the conditions dictate the adoption of an aggressive attitude to one belligerent, those conditions may dictate the adoption of a Fabian policy to the other belligerent. It is too often forgotten that the destruction of a hostile navy cannot easily be accomplished, even when that navy represents only a relatively speaking feeble fighting force, unless it accepts battle in the open sea.[3]

The failure on the part of the stronger side to follow the correct course in naval strategy is most strikingly illustrated by that great war which lasted from 1778 to 1783 when France, and afterwards Spain, and later still Holland, were all engaged in war with Great Britain at a time when Great Britain was already in the throes of its struggle to maintain its hold upon the North American Colonies. In that struggle the allies were, even allowing for the difficulties which must always attend the combinations of a coalition, decidedly superior at sea. The French navy was in a high state of efficiency. The Dutch navy was formidable, as it always was. The Spanish navy was a force to be seriously reckoned with. This country was hampered by its obligation to struggle doggedly on against a determined, resourceful enemy in a theatre of military operations separated from home by 3000 miles of sea, where success depended in reality almost entirely upon the maintenance of maritime preponderance. "When the initial difficulty of combining their forces was overcome—and it has been shown that at no time did Great Britain seriously embarrass their junction—the allies had the choice open to them when, where, and how, to strike with their superior numbers. How did they avail themselves of this advantage? By nibbling at the outskirts of the British Empire, and knocking their heads against the Rock of Gibraltar."*

In 1783 this country consented to terms of peace which, quite apart from the American Colonies, involved some

The naval strategy of France and Spain in the War of American Independence.

---
* 'Influence of Sea-Power upon History,' p. 535.

sacrifices. But if the allies emerged from the conflict with some advantage to their credit, they could claim no triumph at all commensurate with the superiority of naval and military resources which they threw into the scale, and that this was the case was due to their gross misuse of their seapower. At one time they were actually in the Channel in superior force, but they made no well-considered attempt to profit by the situation or to deal vigorously with the defending fleet. It is true, however, that the failure of the allied armada to turn their preponderating force to account at that particular juncture was partly due to technical mismanagement. But the true reason for the inadequate results gained by the stronger side is to be found in the explanation that neither the policy of the allied governments nor yet the plans of their admirals were framed with a view to the one great object in naval warfare, that of securing maritime preponderance as the first step towards further operations.[4] Washington had good grounds for his complaints that his French allies afforded him but niggardly support with their navy; for they made no sustained effort to secure the command of North American waters, and their presence in the Chesapeake at the critical time of Yorktown was rather due to happy accident than to the workings of a sound plan of campaign. The coalition wasted its naval efforts upon scuffles for West Indian islands, which Great Britain could not possibly have defended had the allied fleets obtained command of the Carribean Sea. Spain's supreme effort to recover Gibraltar was natural, and it was justifiable in a strategical sense; but the success of the siege hinged upon efficient maritime blockade, and such blockade could not be maintained while British fleets roamed the seas unbeaten and unwatched. The naval policy of the allies was directed towards the achievement of "ulterior objects" rather than towards the destruction of the maritime resources of their antagonist.[5]

Where one belligerent is in a position—owing to the superiority of his naval material, or owing to the greater efficiency of the *personnel* of his fleet, or owing to fortuitous circumstances—to act strategically on the offensive with good prospect of securing definite maritime preponderance, the history of war proves it beyond possibility of doubt that the right course for that belligerent to pursue is to devote his energies at sea to wiping out the hostile fighting fleet. Once that object has been achieved, the harrying of the enemy's commerce can be carried on with impunity, his over-sea possessions can be dealt with decisively, and it may even be possible to bring military force into play with vital effect. Before that object has been achieved the pursuit of "ulterior objects" is only justifiable when it does not endanger the prospects of the naval campaign. This was the plan followed by the British Admiralty during the wars of the French Revolution and the Empire, by St Vincent and by Nelson. It was due to their firm adherence to fundamental principles of the art of war that Napoleon's over-sea projects were frustrated, that the colonial possessions of France and her allies were wrested from them before the negotiators met in conclave at Amiens or at Vienna, and that a comparatively small British army operating in the Peninsula cost the great conqueror more in men and money than did any one of his great campaigns upon the Continent up to his fatal expedition to Moscow.

<small>First duty of the superior navy to dispose of enemy's fleets.</small>

But if the true policy for the belligerent with the stronger navy admits of no dispute, that which the weaker side should adopt is not so obvious as regards the question of "ulterior objects." Here there can be no obligation to devote all efforts to the overthrow of the enemy's fleets, for there is no prospect of overthrowing them. On the contrary, the object is rather to avoid engagements unless some happy chance brings about a local naval superiority, and to injure the antagonist by other means if possible.[6] And as an illustra-

<small>The naval policy of the weaker side.</small>

tion of this may be quoted the case of Minorca in 1757, the historic interest of which is so greatly wrapped up in the fate of Admiral Byng, but the strategic interest of which lies rather in the action, or perhaps it should be said the inaction, of his antagonist M. la Galissonière. Captain Mahan, in 'The Influence of Sea-Power upon History,'* deals with this remarkable episode of war in some detail, and we take the liberty to differ with his conclusions.

The case of La Galissonière at Minorca.

The story of what occurred is familiar. A formidable conjunct expedition was secretly got together in France under the Duc de Richelieu at a moment when British naval power was practically unrepresented in the Mediterranean. It descended on Minorca, invested Fort St Philip which dominated the harbour of Port Mahon, and reduced the British garrison to serious straits. A fleet was hastily got together in England, which was apparently somewhat ill-equipped, it was placed under command of Admiral Byng, and it was despatched to the Mediterranean with orders to relieve the imperilled fortress. Byng encountered the French fleet, which had acted as escort to the Duc de Richelieu and which approximately equalled his own, in the vicinity of the island. An indecisive action took place, in the course of which the British squadron was so manœuvred as to be at a tactical disadvantage. Byng retired to Gibraltar, leaving Minorca to its fate, and the French admiral, accepting the situation, let his opponent sail away unmolested. "How if a' will not stand?" "Why, then, take no note of him, but let him go; and presently call the rest of the watch together, and thank God you are rid of a knave." That about represents the attitude adopted by M. la Galissonière.

Captain Mahan's view.

Captain Mahan, in accounting for the course followed by the French commander, writes as follows: "The true reason is probably that given and approved by one of the French authorities on naval warfare.† La Galissonière considered

* Pp. 285 *et seq.* † Ramatuelle.[7]

the support of the land attack on Mahon paramount to any destruction of the English fleet, if he thereby exposed his own. 'The French navy has always preferred the glory of assuring or preserving a conquest to that more brilliant, perhaps, but actually less real, of taking some ships, and therein has approached more nearly the true end that has been proposed in war.' The justice of this conclusion depends upon the view that is taken of the true end of naval war. If it is merely to assure one or more positions ashore, the navy becomes simply a branch of the army for a particular occasion, and subordinates its action accordingly; but if the true end is to preponderate over the enemy's fleets and so control the sea, then the enemy's ships and fleets are the true objects to be assailed on all occasions. A glimmer of this view seems to have been present to Morogues when he wrote that at sea there is no field of battle to be held, nor places to be won.[8] If naval warfare is a war of posts, then the action of the fleets must be subordinate to the attack and defence of the posts; if its object is to break up the enemy's power on the sea, cutting off his communications with the rest of his possessions, drying up the sources of his wealth or his commerce, and making possible a closure of his ports, then the object of attack must be his organised military forces afloat—in short, his navy. It is to the latter course, for whatever reason adopted, that England owed a control of the sea that forced the restitution of Minorca at the end of the war."

The great American writer is not perhaps here quite at his happiest. He preaches a convincing sermon; but is he not preaching it from the wrong text? "Exclusiveness of purpose is the secret of great successes and great operations," says Napoleon, and this was the view taken by La Galissonière. If the French admiral considered the support of the land attack on Mahon paramount to any destruction of the English fleet, supposing that he thereby exposed his own, he was perfectly right. Where he seems to have failed was that he might apparently have defeated the squadron of Byng without risking the French position in Minorca. But he could not be aware of the vacillating character of his adversary, and he probably gave the opposing fleet credit for a state of efficiency to which it could not properly lay claim. In 1756 the French had only sixty-three ships-of-the-line to the British one hundred and thirty. How could a local victory in the Mediterranean have redressed the balance? It is suggested that a naval triumph at this juncture might have aroused enthusiasm for naval development in France. That is after all a matter of conjecture. But the importance to that country of the acquisition of Minorca is not a matter of conjecture, it is a matter of fact which is writ large in the records of the time.

We read in 'The Lost Possessions of England' that "so long as we retained Port Mahon the war insurances of cargoes sailing out of Marseilles had ranged from fifty to seventy-five per cent of their value. Immediately after the success of the French expedition insurance rates dropped to fifteen per cent." Owing to the loss of Minorca, Boscawen, on guard over De la Clue in Toulon, was compelled, after his fleet had incurred some damage in an encounter with the shore batteries, to repair back to Gibraltar to refit, and so he unwittingly allowed the French commodore to quit the Mediterranean in safety in his hazardous attempt to join Admiral Conflans at Brest. Minorca was the bait by which Choiseul lured Spain into an alliance four years later, which, if it benefited the latter Power little, served at least to divert a portion of British military and naval resources from enterprises against France. And although it is true in a sense that England's control of the sea forced the restitution of the island at the end of the war, the acquisition of the Duc de Richelieu aided by La Galissonière was a precious asset in the hands of the French Government when the terms of peace came under discussion.

The fact is that, as the situation presented itself to the French admiral when he met with Byng, the "ulterior object" was not Minorca. The "ulterior object" was Byng's fleet. Suffren, or Tegethoff, or Hawke, would perhaps not in the same circumstances have let the British squadron go so easily, but would have added a naval victory on the high seas to the triumph of capturing Minorca. A quarter of a century later another French admiral, De Grasse, was outside Chesapeake Bay with twenty-four sail-of-the-line completing the investment of Cornwallis in Yorktown, when the British admiral Graves with nineteen sail was trailing his coat to draw the French fleet into a close action. But De Grasse would not be tempted, and Yorktown fell. De Grasse probably would have beaten Graves in a pitched battle, but he wisely forbore, realising that Cornwallis's army was the true objective. This point has been argued at some length because, however unsound may be the doctrine conveyed in the passage which Captain Mahan quotes from Ramatuelle when it is applied to a belligerent possessing naval resources superior or equal to those of the adversary, the procedure approved in that passage may be a wise one to follow when the circumstances are different. The destruction of the enemy's fleet is only the paramount object in naval war, if that destruction be practicable. If it be impracticable,—if to attempt it means that the navy undertaking the task will in all probability be destroyed itself, leaving the enemy supreme upon the waters,—then the doctrine as to the viciousness of "ulterior objects" falls to the ground, because the objections to devoting attention to those objects cease to exist.[9]

OBJECTS OF NAVAL WARFARE.

That the definite adoption as a settled policy on the part of France of the principles extolled by Ramatuelle was a mistake, few will now dispute. To this may be attributed not only the unsound strategy which prevailed during the War of American Independence, and which has been commented on on p. 53, but also the neglect on the part of the French Government to create a navy of sufficient strength to cope single-handed with the rival nation across the Channel,—a neglect which led to the virtual extinction of the French over-sea possessions before the long contest between the two western Powers came to a close. But we are here dealing not with the influence of naval power upon the growth of nations, but with the situations which arise in actual war. To ensure that the problems which present themselves to the naval strategist when hostilities are actually in progress may receive correct solution, it is necessary to bear in mind that one belligerent is generally stronger than the other at sea, and that the weaker side must shape its course accordingly.

The weaker side must adopt a defensive attitude.

The inferior navy must in time of war act, as it were, on the defensive. And it must be remembered that a defensive attitude has certain especial advantages in naval warfare which are not so apparent in operations on land. A fleet which declines to encounter the enemy on the high seas retires into a defended port and awaits its opportunity. There it can refit, it can replenish its stores, and it runs no risks from wind or weather; and all this time the hostile war-vessels are out in the open, cruising and on the watch, so as to be ready to act should it decide to issue from the fortress. If the superiority of the stronger navy is not very marked, the disadvantages which it suffers from being obliged to keep at sea while that opposed to it can be kept fully prepared for action but moored off some well-equipped dockyard, may in course of time reduce its superiority to the vanishing point. Still, the belligerent whose fighting

COMMERCE DESTROYING. 61

fleets abandon the high seas for a time, abandons his commerce during that period and risks the loss of his over-sea possessions. What is once lost cannot be regained except by a naval triumph carrying with it maritime preponderance. And the natural disinclination of any nation laying claim to sea-power, as also of any commander with a powerful fleet under his orders, to adopt the policy of scuttling into harbour without fighting, even when confronted with superior force, generally brings it about that the weaker belligerent has been roughly handled in the early stages of the war, and that the relative disparity between the contending navies has been accentuated thereby.[10]

A word is necessary on the subject of the attack and protection of sea-borne trade in war. The damage or destruction of the enemy's maritime commerce has at the beginning of this chapter been indicated as one object of naval warfare, and what one side endeavours to injure the other side must endeavour to protect. *The attack and protection of commerce.*

It is not proposed here to go into all the pros and cons of the controversy between the school which advocates commerce destroying as a primary objective in naval operations, and the school which holds that the side which beats the hostile fighting fleets and drives them off the sea inevitably and almost automatically protects its own mercantile marine, and is in a position to sweep out of existence that of the enemy. Mere commerce destroying can never inflict vital injury unless it takes the form of sustained effort, and it cannot take that form unless it has naval preponderance at its back.[11] Owing to the enormous volume of its sea-borne trade and the huge development of its mercantile marine, the British Empire has more to fear from this form of attack than any other Power, and it must take steps accordingly. To afford protection to its swarms of merchant vessels in time of war with a maritime nation, especial precautions must be observed and an enormous fleet of cruisers must be maintained. And yet the main safeguard of this mass of floating wealth is not found in the cruisers which the nation has at command, but in the battleships upon which it must depend for the assertion and maintenance of its naval superiority over the floating forces of the enemy.[12]

Captain Mahan, in those fine chapters of his which deal with the warfare against commerce during the epoch of the French Revolution and Empire, makes this plain. Commerce-destroyers must have secure bases from which to issue for their forays. Merchant vessels sailing under cruiser convoy are reasonably immune against attack from such craft. Sailing under convoy means, however, delay and inconvenience, and it may lead to the flooding of the market with goods at one moment and its starvation at the next.[13] The whole subject is almost as intricate in its varying phases and possible developments, as it is illustrative of what is the use and what is the abuse of fighting power afloat. But the one dominating factor in deciding the extent to which this form of war may prove successful is to be found in the relative strength and efficiency of the rival battle-fleets.

History proves that this is the case. The relative tonnage of the mercantile marine owned by the British Empire, by France, by Holland, and by Spain, when compared in 1815 after a century and a half of combat for the dominion of the seas, places it beyond a doubt. Enormous numbers of British trading vessels were captured by hostile cruisers during those struggles; but the enemy's flag was, in most cases, almost driven off the sea ere the conflict ended and the commercial community as a whole profited thereby, apart from the drain on national resources which war naturally brings in its train. The question of commerce destroying and commerce protection is, from the point of view of the interdependence between military operations and naval preponderance, to a certain extent a side issue. But the principles of naval strategy are intimately bound up with it, and in sketching the aims and objects sought after in warfare at sea some reference to it has been thought necessary.

It was stated at the beginning of the chapter that one of the principal purposes of naval warfare is to establish a maritime superiority so decisive that military force can be brought into play in the form of descents upon the enemy's coasts and colonies. The strategical aspect of this question will be examined from the military point of view in later chapters, and the advantages enjoyed by an army based upon the sea and utilising the facilities presented by maritime communications will be set out in detail. But operations of this class are in the main dependent upon the possession of naval preponderance, and such naval preponderance can only be secured by destroying or by definitively neutralising the battle-fleets of the enemy. It is true that military force dependent upon sea-power can sometimes achieve appreciable successes in despite of the enemy possessing a superior navy, as Richelieu did at Minorca in 1756. And, as in that case, a blow may be struck which may in some measure compensate for the almost inevitable sacrifices which a maritime nation will suffer in war against a power stronger afloat. But a great land campaign based on the sea— a campaign analogous to the British struggle to maintain its hold upon the revolted American Colonies, or to the Crimean War, or to the Japanese invasions of Manchuria— is obviously impossible without naval preponderance.[14] And naval preponderance can only be assured by defeating the hostile seagoing fleets, or else by shutting them up in their fortified harbours and destroying them if they venture to emerge.

The power to bring military force into play against the enemy's coasts and colonies.

The subject briefly touched upon in this chapter is one of paramount importance in any general treatise on the

Conclusion.

art of war,—a term which, alike in this country and on the Continent, has been too much reserved for questions of a purely military character. But as this volume is concerned only with certain phases of strategy and tactics, a mere outline of the fundamental principle which should govern naval warfare suffices. In the two next chapters various points in connection with bases for fleets, and with strongholds for the security of fighting-ships and mercantile marine in time of war, are dealt with. That these subjects are treated in so much more detail is not because they overshadow in importance the principles set out in the above paragraphs, but because it is in the "war of posts" that the dependence of sea-power upon land-power asserts itself, and that military force comes to the aid of naval force.[15]

CHAPTER IV.

NAVAL BASES AND FORTRESSES.

FIGHTING power afloat demands a system of maintenance and supply which is in some respects even more elaborate than the system required by an army on shore; and it must be remembered that a navy uses up food and fuel, and that it suffers depreciation, even during times of peace. The fouling of its surface under water decreases the fighting value of a warship from day to day as it lies at its moorings in harbour. Efficiency of *personnel* can only be ensured by evolutions at sea which involve expenditure of coal and wear and tear of engines. The winds and the waves beat on the battleship and on the gunboat when they are on cruise in time of peace, just as relentlessly as they do in time of war. Ships must be docked and cleaned from time to time, whether they have been engaged or not in warlike enterprise. Apart from damage which may arise in actual action, war merely increases an existing strain,—it does not create the strain. The need of bases for a navy.

Before the introduction of steam the chief requirements of ships of war, apart from food for the crews and ammunition for the guns, which of course are also necessaries in the present day, were sails, spars, cordage, and water. These were the articles which had to be replenished after every cruise and on the termination of every extended operation. The boilers nowadays supply water by condensation, and coal takes the place of the sails and Water formerly as indispensable as coal to-day.

spars and cordage which had formerly to be replaced. But it is worthy of note that if stores of coal are absolutely indispensable under modern conditions to enable a fleet to keep the sea, replenishment of water was equally indispensable in the sailing era. The question of filling up the tanks was often a source of gravest anxiety to the naval commander, and it not unfrequently to a serious degree interfered with the execution of projects of war. In naval records there are constant references to watering. An efficient *personnel* could improvise fresh gear aloft after a hurricane or at the end of a hotly-contested combat, without proceeding to port. But water could only be obtained by communication with the shore.

<small>Communications at sea.</small> Strategical combinations on land hinge, as it has often been expressed, on the communications of armies. These communications follow roads, or railways, or in some cases navigable rivers. Their course is as a rule clearly defined, and on the route or routes which they traverse there is constant traffic backwards and forwards between the army at the front and the base or bases from which the army draws its supplies and ammunition and reinforcements, and to which it returns its sick and wounded. But on the sea lines of communication are only determinate when they happen to traverse defiles like the Straits of Malacca or the Dardanelles, or when, owing to their length, it is incumbent on vessels moving along them to put into port on the way.[1] In the sailing days the fact that in certain seas and certain localities the wind blows normally from a particular direction, compelled ships navigating some quarters of the globe to adhere to well-established routes. In the age of steam, however, the line of communication from one point to another is generally the shortest line which avoids the adjacent coasts, although there may be, and there usually indeed is, no compulsion to follow that line. The communications of an army can be cut by the

enemy anywhere, but those of a fleet can only be cut at certain points. A fleet, moreover, is self-contained for a far longer time than an army, although the period during which it can operate without replenishing supplies depends upon the rate at which it has to steam and upon the nature of the vessels of which it is composed.

The dependence upon the power to replenish its coal-bunkers chains a modern ship of war to the point where its fuel supplies are situated, and it has in consequence only a certain radius of action—a radius of action which in the case of the battleship or cruiser is calculated in thousands of miles, but which in the case of torpedo craft is calculated in hundreds, and in the case of the submarine is calculated in tens of miles.[2] The coal-stores need not necessarily be retained in port. A supply can be despatched in colliers to some appointed rendezvous at sea. But unless fighting-ships are actually accompanied by colliers carrying sufficient fuel to maintain them for whatever length of time the operation they are engaged on may be likely to take,—and the fleet depending upon colliers under its own wing is in a position analogous to that of the army, so well known to the British soldier, which is merely an escort to its own transport,—these fighting-ships must have a base. And, as a matter of convenience, the base for coal generally becomes a base for food and minor stores as well, it sometimes becomes a base for ammunition, and if it combines with its functions of a depot the functions of a repairing yard including a dry dock, the efficiency of the fleet affiliated to it can be maintained for an almost unlimited time, provided that the fleet meets with no serious mishap at the hands of the enemy. *The coal question.*

Bases have in all times and in all ages been a necessity to navies. In days of old fleets had to be revictualled and watered, although cleaning and repairing demanded no very elaborate arrangements. Since war-vessels reached a size *Naval bases always indispensable to sea-power.*

which forbade their being hauled up on to any ordinary beach after the manner of the fishing-smack of to-day, safe places became necessary where they could be deliberately careened from time to time. The introduction of cannon and gunpowder made ammunition depots a necessity. The coal question is a newer development, which has been referred to above. And the fighting-ship has now developed into a machine so elaborate, so complicated, and so delicate, that it can only be maintained in a state of proper efficiency by dint of constant renovation and frequent overhaul. So that well-equipped bases have become more indispensable than ever under modern conditions, and their strategical importance is at the present time of great significance in war.

The influence of the acquisition of bases on the progress of British naval power in the Mediterranean. Nothing could better show the value of naval bases to fleets in war than the records of our, at one time somewhat checkered, career as a Mediterranean Power; and a short account of this will serve to illustrate the subject and will throw light upon many subjects to be touched upon further on in this volume. There is a map at the end of the chapter.

The British navy first became a force to be seriously reckoned with in that great tideless sea in the days of Cromwell, and at a period when we possessed not one single spot upon its shores. Badiley and others were allowed to use neutral ports like Leghorn as bases while operating against the Dutch, and this, it will be remembered, gave rise to the singular affair mentioned on page 46. When Blake was acting against the Barbary corsairs he was a welcome guest on the coasts of Italy and Sardinia, for he was fighting the common enemy of Christendom. The peculiar conditions, and the laxity which prevailed on the question of neutrality, thus made the maintenance of a British fleet within the Straits possible for a time. But it had no fixity of tenure as long as it possessed no definite *point d'appui* anywhere nearer than the British Isles, and the course of events soon made this obvious alike to friends and foes. In 1665 Spain offered Sir W. Temple a base in Sardinia, and in 1675 Sir J. Narborough was allowed to make use of Malta for a time. But ere this an event had occurred which for a time planted the flag of England firmly on the fringe of the coveted sea. In 1665 Tangier came to Charles II. as a marriage portion. And it is to the credit of that sovereign that when he came to his own again, and in the early days of promise ere the problems of government had ceased to interest and ere his conduct had alienated his subjects, he realised with prompt intuition that the Mediterranean was a proper field for British enterprise, and that this Moorish city which looks across towards Gibraltar must turn out to be an acquisition of extraordinary value politically and strategically, if full use was made of it as a naval base.

But the opportunity was lost. Nothing prospered under Charles II. Its maintenance was costly, the mole did not progress, the Moors were always a menace, and they often became a serious danger. Finally, after twenty-three years, this strategically almost priceless harbour, this gateway into a land which remains to the present day a land of promise, was incontinently abandoned by a nation which had not yet risen to its opportunities nor yet realised its destiny.

The mainspring of the foreign policy of William III. was opposition to the schemes of aggrandisement entertained by Louis XIV., and from an early period in his reign he looked towards the Mediterranean as affording a favourable opening for operations against the French king. As long as he was in alliance with Spain the English fleet could base itself upon Valencian and Catalonian ports. But William found his admirals most averse from wintering in these waters and depending on the hospitality of a foreign Power in the season of bad weather. "I would much rather have chosen to live on bread and water," wrote Russell, the hero of La Hogue, when apprised at Malaga that he was not to return to England when the winter season approached, and shortly before the Peace of Ryswick the squadron was perforce recalled at a time of threatened invasion of England.[3] It had, however, exerted no small influence upon the course of the war then in progress between France and Spain. It had saved Barcelona for the time, and had held a formidable invading army in check. But no sooner did it quit those waters than the French advanced afresh over the border, and the great port and fortress speedily fell.

A few years later all Europe was convulsed by the quarrel over the Spanish Succession, in which Great Britain was leagued against Louis XIV. This time the fleet found no Spanish ports at its disposal when it was despatched to the Mediterranean under Rooke. It was to have captured Cadiz and to have retained the city when taken, William III. and Marlborough both attaching great importance to the possession of the splendid harbour; but the attempt failed, as has been already related on p. 12. Two years elapsed and then Rooke, again in these waters and seriously hampered by the want of a base, found himself in a position to undertake an enterprise of momentous consequence. Whether the initiative was due to him, or to some of his subordinate admirals, or to the Duke of Hesse, is immaterial. On the 4th August 1704 he attacked and took the Rock of Gibraltar, and thereby secured to his country what it above all things required for the development of its naval power, a footing in the waters of southern Europe.

This great stroke was speedily followed by another. Marlborough, whose strategical genius and foresight are perhaps more clearly displayed by his action in this matter than by even those brilliant combinations of war which led to the triumphs of Blenheim, of Ramillies, and of Oudenarde, was thoroughly imbued with the Mediterranean idea. He perceived that, to secure to the navy the power of action in these waters, some suitable harbour within the Straits must be obtained. Even at a time when Barcelona and other Spanish ports were, thanks to alliance with one of the contending parties in that country, at the disposal of the British fleet, Marlborough was insisting upon the importance of obtaining a base. And so, largely as a consequence of the persistence of the illustrious soldier who was fighting far away in Flanders, Minorca with its splendid harbour of Port Mahon was captured in 1707 as the result of a well-planned and admirably executed *coup*. "It will be to France in the Mediterranean," prophesied General Stanhope, who commanded the troops, "what Dunkirk has been in the Channel."[4] And for half a century British sea-power was the determining factor in most military events which occurred in the south of Europe.

Then suddenly, like a bolt from the blue, came the Duc de Richelieu's descent upon Minorca, and the fall of the fortress after Byng had failed to relieve its garrison. During those years so disastrous to France,—when her colonies in America and the West Indies were being wrested from her, when her power in the East Indies came to an end, when her fleets were dispersed in the Atlantic and their remnants were destroyed among the shoals of her storm-driven Biscay coast,—the Mediterranean remained open to her trade and replenished her ebbing resources, because there was no British naval base within the Straits. At the period of greatest triumph, when the nation was bewildered with its own victories and when conquest was being added to conquest, Great Britain's power in one important quarter suffered a decided check. That misfortune in the Mediterranean which heralded British participation in the Seven Years' War left its mark up to the Peace of Paris. In virtue of that treaty, however, Minorca was restored by the French.

During the war in which France and Spain and Holland ranged themselves alongside the revolted American Colonies, the naval position of this country was too critical to admit of operations in the Mediterranean. Desperate efforts were made by the allies to capture Gibraltar without success; but Minorca was taken by the Duc de Crillon, and when the conditions of peace were agreed to in 1783 that island was after eighty years' tenure in foreign hands restored to Spain. The consequences of its loss were at once felt when Hood in 1793 found himself so unexpectedly in possession of Toulon. For when driven from that place, and when its observation by a British fleet became an imperative obligation, the British admiral found himself without a base, and it became necessary to wrest Corsican ports from the hands of the French, because the occupation of Minorca was precluded by its being in the hands of our nominal ally, Spain. But Corsica required a considerable garrison, and Elba, which was occupied about the same time, was never really made secure: their retention was entirely dependent on the presence of a supporting squadron. So that when Spain in 1796 threw in her lot with revolutionary France, and when the naval position in the Mediterranean in consequence became decidedly critical, both islands had to be abandoned, the fleet under Sir J. Jervis withdrew to Gibraltar,[5] and the British navy was again in the position which Marlborough had deplored nearly a century before.

The withdrawal was, however, of short duration. Early in 1797 Jervis gained his famous victory over the Spanish fleet off Cape St Vincent. Then a year later, Nelson was, under the circumstances already detailed on p. 39, sent back to Toulon to watch Napoleon, the friendly attitude of what is now Italy securing Leghorn, Naples, and Sardinian and Sicilian ports to the British fleet in case of need. After the destruction of the French Mediterranean fleet at the Battle of the Nile, and before the reduction of Malta, St Vincent and Keith and Nelson could always rely on the ports of Southern Italy, and used them as if they were their own. In 1798 Minorca was recaptured from Spain, and its possession proved of great value to the British military and naval forces at the time of the siege of Genoa by the allies in 1800, and of their subsequent operations on the coast of Tuscany and Piedmont. With Minorca and Malta in our hands, the command of the Mediterranean was undisputed at the time of the Peace of Amiens. This enactment, however, included the remarkable provision that not only was Malta to be restored to the Knights of St John, but that Minorca was to be restored to Spain—the act of a weak-kneed ministry and of a nation weary of war.[6]

Happily for the Empire, an excuse was found to continue in occupation of Malta, so that when war broke out afresh a year later its splendid harbour and formidable fortifications afforded the British fleet an ideal base in the heart of the Mediterranean,—a base which commanded the narrow seas between Sicily and the north-eastern corner of the Barbary States, and which acted as a *point d'appui* for operations in the Adriatic and in the Levant. In the two critical years after the commencement of hostilities Nelson was, moreover, enormously benefited by having at his disposal in addition that fine anchorage within the Maddalena Islands north of Sardinia, which Italy has of recent years converted into a great maritime place of arms. During the long years of war after Trafalgar the fact that the British fleet had generally not only Malta but also Sicily at its command, assured consistency to its naval preponderance in the Mediterranean without throwing an unduly serious strain upon the maritime resources of the country, which were already so severely taxed in the more open seas.

Since the acquisition of Malta the position of the British

Empire as a leading Mediterranean power has never been questioned either in peace or war, and the possession of the two fortresses of Gibraltar and Valetta fixes that hold upon the waters of southern Europe which Charles II. dreamt of, and which Rooke and Leake and Stanhope, instigated by Marlborough, first definitely secured.[7] Naval warfare is not a war of posts. But its true object, the breaking of the enemy's power at sea, cannot be achieved without posts. And the history of the Mediterranean since the days of Blake shows how greatly maritime preponderance depends upon the possession of bases whither fleets can repair to make good damages, to replenish stores and ammunition, and to rest during periods when the conditions of the campaign permit them to lie in port.*

Harbours of refuge. In the earlier periods of the sailing era, harbours of refuge were considered absolutely essential to fighting fleets to hibernate in; and anchorages whither squadrons could repair in tempestuous weather were always an essential for the conduct of any set of operations, down to the time when steam superseded sails. It was not, indeed, till the latter part of the eighteenth century that all-year-round naval campaigns became the order of the day.[8] The harbour of refuge did not necessarily constitute a naval base, where stores were collected and where damage received by the weather or at the hands of the enemy could be made good. A squadron could take shelter under the lea of a shore in the enemy's hands with impunity, provided the enemy had no artillery on the spot. But the obvious convenience of combining the port of refuge with the base of supplies and the repairing depot naturally brought it about that maritime powers selected roomy harbours, sheltered in all weathers—

* Mr Julian Corbett's 'England in the Mediterranean' gives us a most admirable account of the development of British naval power in these waters in the early days: it is perhaps not too much to hope that these two volumes are merely a first instalment of a history carrying the story down to later times.[9]

BASES IN THE EIGHTEENTH CENTURY. 75

like Cadiz and Toulon and the Cove of Cork,—fitted them out with building-yards and victualling establishments, fortified them against attack by sea and if necessary against attack by land, and made of them a home for their warships in time of peace and a naval base for their fleets in time of war. And as colonial expansion progressed, naval requirements in far-off lands led to the creation of naval bases in distant seas, equipped more or less elaborately according to the circumstances of the case. Thus Spain designed great maritime places of arms at Cartagena in South America and at Havana in Cuba; France established the naval bases of Louisbourg in North America and Fort Royal in Martinique; while England, up to the time of the War of the Spanish Succession, rested content with New York on the far side of the Atlantic, the port of Tangier having been abandoned ere it had developed into a sure and trustworthy prop of fighting sea-power in foreign waters.

During the wars of the eighteenth century the value of naval bases became manifest, and their acquisition by conquest was often the chief feature of a campaign. The transfer or restoration of these important strategical positions was the subject of the most noteworthy clauses in the treaties of peace which put an end to hostilities.[10] And at the time of the French Revolution each of the great maritime powers—Great Britain, France, Spain, and Holland—possessed a number of fortified ports in different parts of the world, where not only their fighting-ships but also their merchant vessels could take refuge in time of danger, and where the former found the stores and ammunition which they needed, and could get their spars and rigging renewed after the stress of an active campaign. First-class dockyards were generally then, as now, confined to home ports. The gradual increase in the size of line-of-battle ships and frigates from the Elizabethan era up to the time of Napoleon made it more and more necessary that navies should have repair-

Importance of possessing naval bases recognised in the eighteenth century.

ing yards under government control constantly at their disposal, the facilities afforded by commercial ports sufficing less and less to meet the growing requirements. But it must be remembered that it is only of late years that the types of the fighting-ship and the merchant-ship have drawn so far apart, that great commercial ports like Hamburg, or Liverpool, or Alexandria, can now only serve as fleet bases if they have railway communication with a naval dockyard.

Natural harbours and artificial harbours. Modern science and engineering skill make it possible to create harbours where no natural harbours exist. But formerly the existence or otherwise of natural harbours on a coast exerted an extraordinary influence on the course of naval campaigns. During the great wars of the eighteenth century France was without a good natural harbour in the Channel. Napoleon strove to remedy this deficiency by acquiring Antwerp, but the acquisition was made too late to avert the downfall of the sea-power without which his plans could never reach fruition. The nature of the Dutch harbours was such that the great line-of-battle ships of Nelson's time could not use them without considerable difficulty: in consequence of this lack of deep-water ports the type of fighting-ship used by Holland was latterly smaller than that found in the British navy, and the significance of this contrast in material was made manifest when the last great sea-fight between the old rival maritime nations took place off the sands of Camperdown.[11] But science and engineering skill avail a country little without money. The construction of first-class naval harbours of the type of Portland and Cherbourg is a very costly undertaking. The lack of great inlets of the sea like Sydney or Rio de Janeiro may, it is true, oblige a maritime nation to resort to the expedient of creating artificial ports for the service of its maritime fighting-forces; but a navy which is starved as regards its *personnel* and its floating

OBJECTS OF NAVAL FORTRESSES. 77

material, to allow of the requisite funds being provided to create for it bases of an elaborate character, is likely to spend much of its time in those bases when the war-clouds burst.

The question of naval bases is closely interwoven with that of maritime fortresses. In considering the subject of fortresses, those special problems which arise from coal requirements, and from the warfare of torpedo craft and submarines, will for convenience be dealt with separately. Fortresses will in the first instance be discussed as refuges for floating force when threatened by a superior fleet, as havens of shelter for merchant shipping endangered by hostile cruisers, and as protection to dockyards, repairing stations, and depots required for the maintenance of warships in an efficient condition: speaking generally, it is only in the last form that they are necessary to the stronger side at sea. And in this chapter questions of land defence are left out of account, as being of military rather than of naval consequence. *Objects of naval fortresses.*

In the last chapter it was pointed out that the British people are inclined to forget that the destruction of an inferior hostile fleet is not easily accomplished unless it accepts battle in the open sea. We are too prone to look at naval warfare only from our own point of view. The instincts of self-preservation drive the fleet which finds itself over-matched back under the guns and behind the booms of its coast fortresses. The history of maritime war proves that this is the case on almost every page. However much it may conflict with theories as to the art of war afloat, and however much it may outrage the senses of the enemy of all forms of fixed defence, naval operations will hinge in the future, as they have hinged in the past, upon maritime strongholds.[12] Victory in a great fleet action is the ideal. Blockade—using the term in the sense of *As refuges for floating force.*

observation, not of actual shutting in — is the normal experience.

Difficulty of dealing with a hostile naval fortress from the sea.

The question of attacking and defending coast fortresses and of blockade is dealt with in the next chapter. Suffice it to say here that any adequately defended port of suitable conformation affords to ships of war which may be driven into it, or which may retire into it of their own accord, a satisfactory refuge against attack from the sea. If within the harbour there are dry docks, repairing yards, and depots of warlike stores and of supply, the fugitive vessels can be placed in a state of thorough efficiency ere they proceed to sea again, while the enemy, on the watch to pounce down upon them, is suffering wear and tear and losing fighting value out at sea. Kinsale and the Tagus sheltered Prince Rupert against Blake in the Commonwealth days.[13] Over and over again the two great maritime fortresses of Brest and Toulon have shielded the navy of France. The flotillas and armadas of the Ottoman Empire have been disappearing into the Dardanelles before the enemy for five hundred years.[14] Revel and Sebastopol and Port Arthur have in different times served as refuges to Russian fleets in time of war,—the fox who goes to ground is safe as long as the hounds get no outside assistance from terrier or spade.

The open battery with gigantic ordnance supersedes the casemate and the bastion, as these superseded the crenelated battlement and Genoese castle. The modern ironclad replaces the ship-of-the-line, as this replaced the galleon and galley. And yet one function of the maritime stronghold remains much the same as in medieval times—it can still act as a place of security for naval force when overmatched; and we find the story of Van Galen off Leghorn and of Boscawen watching Toulon reproduced in Manchuria in the opening years of the twentieth century.[15]

And under modern conditions, and in accordance with

theories and practice of modern war, it perhaps assumes greater importance in this capacity than formerly. The vital significance of strenuous pursuit after successful action at sea was not realised fully before the days of St Vincent and of Nelson. The defeated Armada was allowed to make its perilous voyage round the north of Scotland unmolested,—and it must be admitted that in this case the attitude of the British sailor chiefs was justified by the event. Tourville, after his success at Beachy Head, let the inferior Anglo-Dutch fleet sail up Channel almost undisturbed.[16] Rodney, after his great victory over De Grasse, made scarcely an attempt to pursue the beaten enemy.[17] Now that it is an accepted principle of tactics that mere defeat of the opposing squadron is not enough, but that the vanquished foe must be followed relentlessly and if possible utterly destroyed, the existence of friendly fortresses offering a refuge to the beaten side assumes great importance. The British fleet was so damaged aloft in the desperate fight at Trafalgar that it is perhaps doubtful if the proximity of Cadiz made any great difference in the number of the allied ships which escaped destruction or capture; but eleven sail of the twenty-three which quitted the fortress the day before the great sea-fight, were back there, seriously damaged but in safety, the day after the battle. *Importance to a beaten fleet of having a safe place to retire to.*

Secure havens of refuge are especially necessary to a belligerent who proposes to adopt the naval policy of commerce destroying, without having maritime preponderance as a basis for the operation.[18] The commerce-destroyer's function is to attack defenceless shipping, not to fight with the war-vessels of the enemy. The career of mischief which craft of this class are likely to enjoy cannot in any case be very prolonged. But if they have no stronghold to fly to when the hostile cruisers heave in sight, their existence above water will almost certainly be very speedily cut short. *Secure bases necessary for carrying out commerce destroying.*

The nation which falls back upon the *guerre de course* confesses itself beaten at sea before a shot is fired: if it possesses no fortified ports scattered over the face of the globe, the amount of injury which it succeeds in inflicting upon its antagonist by such irregular and invertebrate operations of war will probably be infinitesimal.

<small>Safe harbours required by merchant ships in time of war.</small>

Coast fortresses have at all times served as temporary asylums for merchant vessels when threatened by the frigates and galleys of the enemy. In the old days, before the electric telegraph came into prominence, when the naval situation in the vicinity of one port was often quite unknown to commanders at another a few hundred miles away, ships laden with specie and produce of great value were often intercepted close to such havens of refuge by cruisers lying in wait, which were themselves safe from molestation owing to the acquisition of local maritime command. It was, however, the practice to move great trading fleets under strong escort from one defended harbour to another, and a convoy would sometimes wait for weeks and even months for a favourable opportunity ere it moved on another stage. The consequence was that a great assemblage of shipping, representing with the cargoes on board a vast sum of money, was often gathered in a fortified haven of refuge, offering a tempting bait to a daring squadron commander. Some of the most stirring episodes in British naval history have arisen out of attacks upon merchant vessels when in security, or in supposed security, in strongholds on an enemy's coast.

The capture of the Spanish silver ships in the strongly fortified harbour of Santa Cruz in the Canaries by Blake in 1657 is a remarkable example of such an enterprise, and the attack upon the French galleons in Vigo Bay by Rooke and Ormonde in 1702 was one of the most notable successes of the War of the Spanish Succession. When Havana was taken in 1762, the treasure and merchandise on board the fleet of Spanish trading-vessels in the harbour was valued at over two millions sterling,—the naval and military commanders each got over £120,000 in prize money! One object of Nelson's attempt upon Santa Cruz in 1797 was the capture of a galleon laden with specie which was believed to be in the port.

In the present days of world-wide traffic the possession of fortified ports conveniently situated with reference to the great routes which trading vessels follow, is obviously of advantage to a Power which possesses a mercantile marine liable to be seriously attacked by a hostile navy capable of disputing the command of the sea. The true defence of maritime commerce is naval preponderance; but such preponderance takes time to achieve, and it is not achieved by shepherding merchantmen across the ocean, but by destroying the enemy's fleets or driving them off the sea. While this process is in course of execution the merchant ships of the belligerent possessing the preponderating naval force may be harried by hostile cruisers, and the maintenance of safe havens of refuge whither they can repair till great naval operations have cleared the air is an obvious, and may prove an economical, means of tempering the dislocation of commerce, and of reducing the financial loss which is certain to occur on the outbreak of hostilities.

But the naval base—for reasons to be stated farther on, the naval base and the maritime fortress are practically synonymous terms—has other purposes to serve than that of refuge for fighting-ships or trading vessels. In the present day more than ever, fleets must have conveniently situated depots and dockyards. The modern man-of-war is a complicated engine. Strategical and tactical conditions are, moreover, so greatly governed nowadays by questions of speed, that a navy which has not docks at its disposal in the theatres of operations when it is to act in war, fights after a time with one arm tied behind its back. A few

Need of secure depots and dockyards.

F

months' immersion reduces the number of knots which a ship can steam to such an extent that she may for the time being become virtually useless for purposes of battle. The damage which a fleet will sustain in a well-contested action can only be effectively repaired in a properly equipped dockyard. And the enormous expenditure of ammunition likely to take place in a modern sea-fight can only be made good if depots of warlike stores exist in convenient situations. The gun of the present day, moreover, has only an ephemeral existence when once it gets to work, and it must be replaced after firing a limited number of rounds if its accuracy is to be depended upon.

<small>Mauritius in the eighteenth century.</small> The value of naval bases, and also the extent to which in the sailing era fleets could dispense with them even after heavy fighting, is well illustrated by certain phases of the French attempts in the last century to contest maritime supremacy in Indian waters with the sea-power of England.

La Bourdonais, whose relations with Dupleix have already been referred to as an example of the evils which arise when soldiers and sailors quarrel, was in 1735 the naval governor of the French islands of Mauritius and Bourbon. Realising the importance to his country of a good naval base in these seas, he set to work, and by his fertility of resource and his indomitable determination he created elaborate repairing and fitting yards in the former island. There he collected abundant stores of timber and formed ample depots of supplies, and he gradually developed its chief port until it grew to be a great naval station. But for his administration, ability, and foresight it is doubtful if he himself, or at a later date D'Aché, could have made any attempt to contest maritime supremacy with the British fleets on the coast of the Carnatic. Bases alone will, however, never create sea-power. The home Government failed to send out sufficient ships. It neglected to despatch stores which could not be improvised in those remote waters. And it disappointed its naval representatives in that it failed to provide that material and moral support which was indispensable if they were to cope on equal terms with their doughty opponents in Indian waters, even had they enjoyed cordial assistance from Dupleix and Lally. Mauritius, moreover, was situated at a considerable distance from the main theatre of operations.

The work of La Bourdonais was allowed to fall into decay by his successors. Still, when Suffren in 1781 proceeded to the East Indies to attempt to revive French sea-power in that quarter, he was able to effect some repairs at Mauritius before proceeding to Madras on his difficult task. The French admiral, without a naval base, fought three well-contested actions with Admiral Hughes, in each of which his ships suffered damage. His ingenuity and untiring energy enabled him to effect the necessary repairs without returning to the Isle of France. "After the action of the 6th," we read in Mahan, "Hughes found at Madras spars, cordage, stores, provisions, and material. Suffren at Cuddalore found nothing. To put his squadron in fighting condition, nineteen new top-masts were needed, besides lower masts, yards, rigging, sails, and so on. To take the sea at all, the masts were removed from the frigates and smaller vessels and were given to the ships of the line, while English prizes were stripped to equip the frigates. Ships were sent off to the Straits of Malacca to procure other spars and timber. Houses on shore were torn down to find lumber for repairing the hulls."* Under modern conditions a fleet after three actions would hardly be in a position to keep the sea, in face of another of equal strength which was in a position to repair its damages in port, unless it had some base to lean upon. Suffren's great performance illustrates the difference between the sailing era and the days of steam in this respect,

* 'Influence of Sea-Power upon History,' p. 451.

although this does not detract from the brilliancy of his achievements.

Coaling-stations.

The question of coal is of paramount importance in modern combinations of war at sea. Without an ample coal supply the most powerful fleets become non-effective and the speediest cruisers are soon reduced to immobility. It has been pointed out in an earlier paragraph how seriously the presence of colliers must hamper a sea-going fleet. If the fleet is to act decisively and is to carry on operations over an extended theatre for any considerable length of time, great stores of coal conveniently situated for the service are indispensable. And in consequence of this, coaling-stations have become one of the essentials of sea-power.

It is obvious that well-sheltered harbours are desirable as coaling-stations. That the coaling-station should also contain stores of other kinds and means of executing repairs, is clearly a convenience to war-vessels resorting thither to replenish fuel. And so it comes about that, as a rule, the coaling-station is also a naval base, and conversely that great stores of coal are generally collected in dockyards and maritime arsenals. But while all naval bases contain great stores of coal almost as a matter of course, coaling-stations, especially those formed actually during the course of a war, need not necessarily be naval bases in other respects, and in many cases no naval establishments other than those connected with the stores of fuel are formed in them.

Coaling-stations at points conveniently situated with regard to the great arteries of maritime commerce are in the present day the only sound foundation upon which a *guerre de course* can be built up. Formerly a frigate or privateer, well supplied with sails and ropes and stores, could remain almost indefinitely in distant seas, completely cut off from its base. The cruiser or armed steamer of to-day must keep in touch with her coal supplies, being practically prohibited by international law from replenishing fuel at a neutral port. Access to a coaling-station is therefore essential if commerce destroying without maritime preponderance is to have any effect at all.

The function of the maritime fortress as a place of refuge for fleets and cruisers and merchantmen has already been discussed; but fortifications are also a necessary adjunct to mobile naval force, quite apart from the question of their affording asylums for ships endangered by the enemy. Dockyards, arsenals, and coaling-stations must be secured by fixed defence, unless the navy which they serve is so absolutely certain of maritime preponderance that they have nothing to fear from hostile attack by sea. Otherwise measures for their safety will hamper that freedom of action which fleets must enjoy if they are to be employed to the best advantage, and there will always be risk lest, in consequence of a deft and daring stroke on the part of some insignificant hostile force, a naval station which is indispensable if war is to be carried on effectively, may suffer irreparable damage.

Importance of naval bases being properly defended.

In the present day of torpedo-craft warfare it is customary to attach torpedo-boats to certain fortified harbours as part of their permanent defence. To this there is no objection. The torpedo-boat forms no part of a sea-going fleet.[19] But to chain battleships and cruisers to naval bases so as to strengthen their power of resistance is false strategy on the part of any navy which hopes to command the sea in time of war. "Our great reliance is in the vigilance of our cruisers at sea," wrote St Vincent, "any reduction in the number of which, by applying them to guard our ports, inlets, and beaches, would in my opinion tend to our destruction." Naval bases must be able to stand alone for a time against any attack which is likely to be made upon them. The extent to which insufficient defences of an important naval station may tie the hands of a fleet commander is well illustrated by Hughes and Trincomalee in 1782, and by Keith and Minorca in 1798.

<small>Examples in support of this.</small> Trincomalee was captured by the British just a month before Suffren appeared off Madras. It afforded an excellent harbour, and, except for the locality being at the time somewhat unhealthy, it made an almost ideal base. But there was no time to place it in a state of defence. In the campaign which followed, "Trincomalee unfortified was simply a centre round which Hughes had to revolve like a tethered animal; and the same will always happen under like conditions."* This concise summary of Captain Mahan's of what occurred, admirably describes the inconvenience suffered by the British admiral. When the Cingalese port was captured by Suffren during the course of the operations, that able and energetic seaman took good care at once to place its environs in a state of defence, and to leave a garrison sufficient to secure it from anything in the shape of a *coup de main*.

When Minorca was captured by Commodore Duckworth and General Stuart in 1798, no proper steps were taken to place the defences in a state of readiness, or to detail an adequate garrison to hold the fortress. It came about that a few months later Admiral Bruix escaped with a formidable fleet from Brest and made his way into the Mediterranean. British domination of the sea was at once placed in jeopardy. The preponderance which had been gained for the British by Nelson at the Nile appeared to have passed over to the French and Spaniards, inasmuch as a Spanish fleet had about the same time got out of Cadiz and reached Cartagena. Lord Keith, upon whom the command of the British navy devolved at this critical juncture owing to Lord St Vincent's ill-health, was placed in a position of great anxiety, and his embarrassment was augmented by the responsibility of

* 'Influence of Sea-Power upon History,' p. 430.

guarding Minorca. "It is very hard," he wrote to Nelson, "that I cannot find these vagabonds in some spot or other, and that I am so shackled with this defenceless island." The truth was that Keith subordinated the primary objective of seeking out the hostile fleet and dealing with it, to the ulterior objective of watching over an important seaport, the securing of which at a proper time had been neglected. His strategy was at fault. But all commanders are human and are liable to errors which horrify the arm-chair strategist, who is hampered by no responsibility and is fortified with that knowledge which in war so often comes after the event. Had Minorca been safe against a *coup de main* it is probable that a great sea-fight would have taken place in the western Mediterranean with the combined fleet of the allies. As it turned out, they withdrew unharmed from the Mediterranean, as soon as Bruix realised how little dependence could be placed upon the Spanish squadron.

In the present day, when an adequate and secure coal supply is so essential to a fleet, a naval commander might be compelled to remain on guard over his coaling base even when opposed to inferior naval force, rather than leave that base wholly unprotected. Were his stores of fuel destroyed by a hostile raid his fleet would at once become immobile and useless, and the weaker antagonist would be left in control of local waters. Minorca in 1799 was not essential to Keith. But had his fleet been a modern fleet, and had his only coal reserves been lying unprotected on the wharves of Port Mahon, there would have been some justification for his allowing his strategical dispositions to be dominated by solicitude as to the island. It is for this reason that coaling-stations should be fortified. But the same principle holds good in less degree as to any naval base, and when this base is a first-class dockyard, possessing all the requisites for equipping and maintaining a powerful fleet, the fortifications ought to be designed to withstand a determined attack, because an enemy has sufficient inducement to make a determined attack. The multiplication of fixed defences is an unsound and vicious military policy; but every port which is necessary for the maintenance and replenishment of a fleet should be able to hold out for a time independent of that fleet, otherwise it becomes a source of anxiety, and it shackles the naval commander in his combinations.

Fortified naval bases essential to the weaker side.
And to the weaker belligerent at sea strongly fortified bases are an essential, whether the naval policy proposed aims at great operations of war or at mere commerce destroying. Without such bases the inferior navy cannot exercise over that opposed to it the containing influence which is its one trump card; it cannot with its four battleships, safe under the guns and behind the mine-fields of a great fortress, keep five or six battleships of the enemy occupied, wearing out their machinery, exhausting their crews, and losing mobility from day to day owing to prolonged immersion without facilities for docking.[20] The doctrine of the "fleet in being" will be referred to in a later chapter dealing especially with troops at sea; but it is an accepted principle of naval strategy that such a fleet must be treated with respect, that it must be watched and neutralised, and that it must be pounced upon and dealt with instantly should an opportunity offer.

The commerce-destroyer, possessing practically no fighting value but demanding frequent replenishment of fuel, must have fortified bases to act as shelters whither it can flee from time to time when the hostile cruisers are on its track and its coal-bunkers have been exhausted. If the naval stations on which it depends are destitute of defences, they will inevitably be captured at once by the enemy who possesses command of the sea. Then the commerce-destroyer is left without loophole of escape and robbed of the only means by which its mobility—its only asset for the purpose of war—can be maintained unimpaired. And it must be borne in mind that the *guerre de course,* although it usually contemplates destruction rather than capture, may be more profitable and effective if the vessels attacked are seized and retained than if they are sunk and their cargo is lost. But unless there be some safe haven to take the prizes to, retention becomes impracticable, and the commerce-destroyer is forced to adopt the course of inflicting injury without corresponding gain.[21]

The question of bases for torpedo craft and submarines stands somewhat apart from that of bases for sea-going fleets, and of harbours of refuge for a mercantile marine imperilled by hostile ships of war. The functions of the destroyer, of the torpedo-boat, or of those submersible vessels the potentialities of which are still obscured by lack of full knowledge, differ materially from those of the battleship, the cruiser, or the gun-vessel. Tactically these essentially modern craft act in principle upon the offensive. But strategically they act either on the offensive or on the defensive, according to the general naval situation. In defence of a fortress or of a coast-line, these mosquitos of the sea are designed to sally out and harass a hostile fleet which may be blockading or observing the fortress, or to swoop down upon a flotilla of transports with troops on board destined for a landing on the coast-line. On the other hand, they may be called upon to act strategically on the offensive by forcing their way into some defended harbour of the enemy, or by falling upon an opposing squadron moored in some anchorage. But whether they are acting on the offensive or on the defensive, their powers are limited by their peculiarities as ships.

Their coal consumption is so abnormally heavy, relative to their capacity, that their radius of action without replenishing bunkers is very small. The space of time during which they can act is, in the case of torpedo craft, confined to the hours of darkness and, in the case of submarines, circumscribed by their nature. They are ill-suited for work in the open sea in heavy weather. And the result of this is that the base from which they emerge must be, comparatively speaking, close to their objective. For this reason torpedo-boat stations designed for defensive purposes must be dotted at short intervals along the coast-line which they are intended to protect. And if the craft which they nourish and shelter are intended to act offensively, the stations must be established within striking distance of the maritime fortresses, or defended anchorages, or harbours of refuge of possible antagonists. Vessels of this class require little space, and they draw but little water. The type of port especially adapted to their service and security differs widely from that demanded by sea-going fleets or ocean steamers,—a large harbour is not necessary, although if well sheltered it is not objectionable. Suitable localities for torpedo-boat stations are not difficult to find, provided that their geographical position meets with strategical requirements. But these requirements are not easily fulfilled, except where the stations are intended merely for defence. The difficulty as to bases places one of the greatest limitations upon the effectiveness for war purposes of the torpedo-vessel and the submarine when designed to act strategically on the offensive.[22]

Conclusion. Dominion of the sea in time of war is a lofty ideal for a maritime nation to keep in view. To the sailor nurtured in traditions of naval victory far and wide, control of the great waters appears to be essentially a question of floating force — as indeed it is. The harbour for occasional rest and relaxation in time of peace, the broad ocean when hostile squadrons dare to dispute the mastery,—that represents the spirit which impels a navy on towards triumph in the hour of action. But however distasteful dependence on the shore may be, however much expenditure upon dockyards and stationary establishments may seem to outrage the fundamental principle of war that victory is achieved by fleets and not by masonry and cement, naval bases are none the less an indispensable corollary to combatant resources. And these bases carry fixed defences in their train by the irresistible force of circumstances.

There has been in this country a kind of crusade against fixed defences, a crusade for which there is some justification. But because the fortification of defended harbours has been carried to excess, and has in some cases been developed in utter defiance of strategical conditions governing the particular locality, that is no reason for going into the other extreme and hampering mobile force by burdening it unduly with the guardianship of the shore establishments which are vital to its efficiency, and with the protection of ports of call to which the mercantile marine instinctively flies in the early days of a maritime contest. The primary object of overthrowing the hostile sea-going fleets, or in driving them to their lairs, is best accomplished by concentration of fighting strength. And concentration of fighting strength means the abandonment for the moment of certain seas. If there are no defended posts in those seas a single hostile cruiser may inflict serious injury on commerce, and may even throw serious difficulties in the way of ultimately recovering domination within their area. That is looking at the question from the point of view of a paramount navy. But there are nations whose aggregate of war-vessels does not mount up to a total which can justify confidence in their beating fleets opposed to them under all possible contingencies: in discussing the problems which arise in the art of naval warfare, the position of the weaker side cannot expediently be ignored. To such nations the possession of maritime fortresses affords a guarantee that their navy will not be wiped out of existence within a few weeks of embarking on hostilities, and that their over-sea commerce may not be destroyed, possibly for good and all, by the seizure or the sinking of the whole of the trading fleet simply because there is no safe spot outside of neutral waters where it can take shelter.

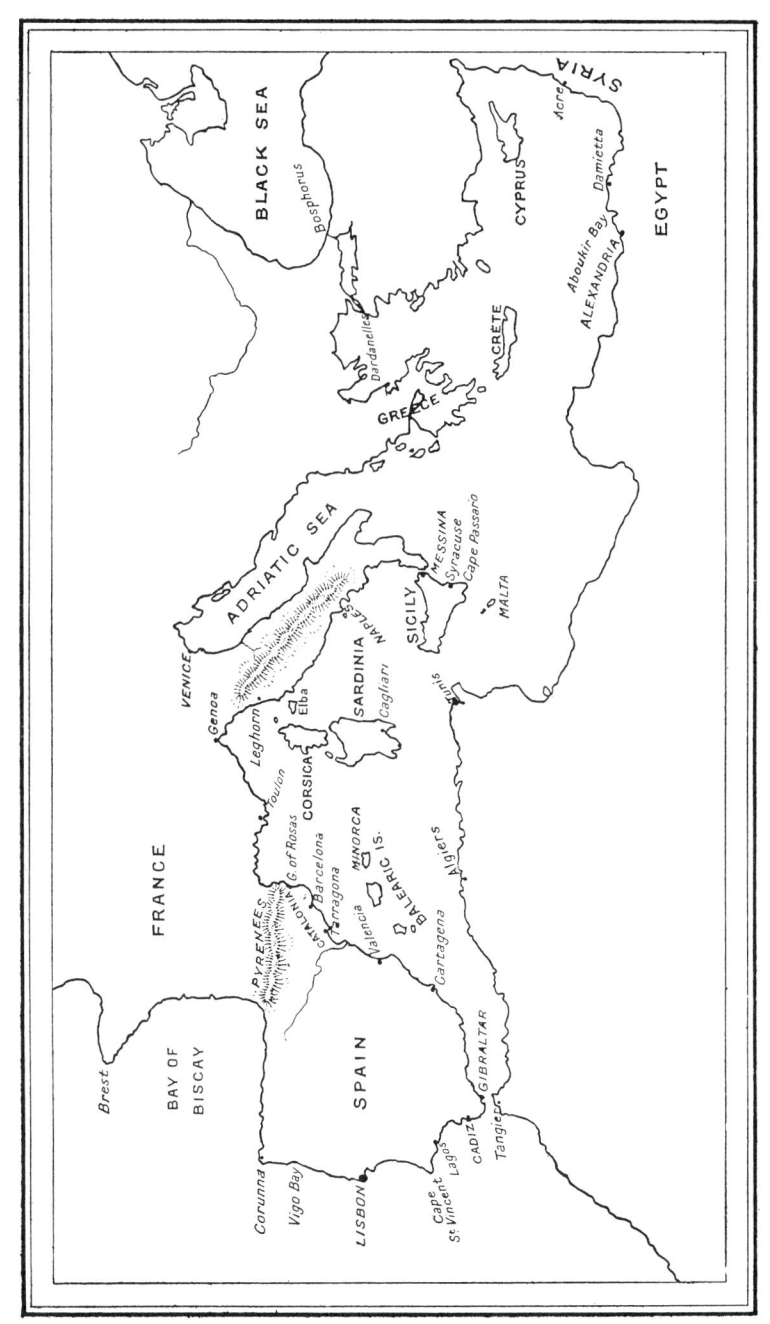

MEDITERRANEAN SEA.

CHAPTER V.

DEPRIVING THE ENEMY OF HIS NAVAL BASES, CAPTURING HIS MARITIME FORTRESSES, AND ACQUIRING PORTS SUITABLE FOR ANCHORAGES AND DEPOTS, AS OBJECTIVES IN WAR.

The enemy's naval bases as an objective.

THE extent to which a navy depends upon bases has been explained in the last chapter, and the reasons for fortifying the stations and dockyards upon which mobile fighting-forces at sea rely in time of war have been discussed. The mobile fighting-forces must always be the decisive factor in naval warfare, and in a certain sense they form the best defence for their own bases. But the belligerent with the inferior maritime resources may be unable to safeguard his naval stations by the indirect method of operations in the open sea, and may have no course open to him except to withdraw his war-vessels into port. The stronger navy may uncover the harbours where its stores are collected and its repairing establishments are located, in the course of the campaign. It is in cases such as this that the bases of the enemy offer a natural objective, if the conditions admit of offensive operations being undertaken against them.

One means of achieving victory in war must always take the form of enterprises set on foot to deprive the antagonist of that which is essential.[1] And as dockyards, coaling-stations, and fortified harbours under certain circumstances become absolutely essential, and as they are always likely to be useful, their capture is from the strategical point of view a legitimate undertaking. Preponderance approaching to sea command will not, it is needless to say, be attained in a conflict between maritime nations by attacks on posts alone. Supremacy must first be won out in the open; attacks on posts come afterwards.[2] Under certain conditions of distribution of the fighting-forces, operations against some hostile naval base may, it is true, be justified at the outset of hostilities—when, for instance, the capture of an ill-defended coaling-station by a *coup de main* automatically expels the enemy from some particular sea. But such a situation may be regarded as abnormal. It is generally at a later stage that the question of attacking and defending bases comes into prominence, and that operations of this class may assume a paramount importance in the conduct of the campaign.

It must be remembered, moreover, that naval stations captured from the enemy may serve as valuable *points d'appui* for the prosecution of further operations by the victorious side. It will be proved by examples that successful attack on such ports may often offer ulterior advantages, quite apart from the damage which their loss inflicts upon the foe. It will further be pointed out that, for the effective accomplishment of combinations at sea, it may be indispensable to seize and to hold points of strategical importance within hostile territory which may not have been regarded as naval stations by the adversary, and which may not have been equipped for such a purpose. In the next chapter it will be shown that there are grave difficulties in the way of neutralising the maritime strongholds of the enemy by blockade, and that attack in some form or other is the surest method of depriving the opponent of whatever benefits he may derive from them.

The Duc de Richelieu's successful descent on Minorca has been referred to in chap. iii. This was a remarkable example of the capture of a naval base at the outset of a war, and of its loss causing very serious inconvenience

Examples of the capture of naval bases and its influence.

to the belligerent, whose navy largely depended upon it for maintenance in the Mediterranean. When the island was again taken by the French in 1780 the consequences at the time were less momentous, because the British fleet was then too weak, relatively to the navies opposed to it, to act vigorously in the waters of Southern Europe. It has been shown on p. 72 how the loss of this excellent naval base was to influence the naval operations of Lord Hood and his successors in the early years of the war against the French Revolutionary Government.

Nepheris at time of siege of Carthage. The siege of Carthage provides us with a striking illustration from ancient history of the need of depriving hostile war-vessels of their base, even when preponderance has been secured at sea. At an early stage of the great siege the Romans, who had crossed the Mediterranean in great force,— thanks to their naval superiority,—closely invested the city on the land side. The blockade by their war-vessels was, however, very ineffective at first. The garrison was constantly being revictualled by a Carthaginian flotilla based on the port of Nepheris: this appears to have been somewhere to the south, but the coast-line has considerably altered since those days, and the exact locality is doubtful. So that in spite of the naval superiority of the invaders the beleaguered city was not suffering from serious want, and the siege was making but moderate progress, when Scipio arrived upon the scene. The great Roman general soon made his presence felt, and he began by taking prompt measures to cut off the stream of supplies at its source. He determined that special operations must be forthwith undertaken against Nepheris. He himself took command of the military expedition detailed to attack the place, he speedily captured it, and he laid it in ruins. From that time forward Carthage began to be in dire straits for want of food.

Here we see decisive results ensuing from the destruction of a hostile naval base in the days of the quinqueremes, and

LOUISBOURG. 97

at an epoch when naval warfare was still confined to narrow seas. It is probable that one reason for the inability of the Roman flotilla to deal effectively with the weaker one opposed to it in the Bay of Tunis, was the want of a suitable harbour well situated as a *point d'appui* for the object in view; the crews from Italy, moreover, did not know the coast. The story of Louisbourg, however, illustrates the same principle in its application to ocean warfare, and in the sailing days.

Louisbourg, a commodious harbour in the island of Cape Breton, had been converted by Louis XV. into a great naval fortress and base for French sea-power in North America. It afforded a refuge to French war-vessels in those waters, it contained within its precincts the means of equipping and revictualling a fleet, and it also from its position threatened any hostile attempt to penetrate into the great estuary of the St Lawrence which led into the heart of what was then New France. In times of war with England it, moreover, provided a lair for the privateers and commerce-destroyers which were engaged in preying upon the floating trade of the British North American Colonies.

In 1745 Louisbourg was captured by a military expedition from those colonies, in co-operation with a fleet under Admiral Warren. The French Government realised at once how seriously the loss of their great naval station in North America must affect a position across the Atlantic which obviously depended upon the maintenance of sea-power. Desperate efforts were therefore made to recover the place. An expedition from Europe actually landed in Cape Breton. But the French navy, even when actually in superior force, could not, owing to the lack of a *pied à terre*, make its power sufficiently felt in those stormy seas to recover preponderance in Nova Scotian waters. An attempt to retrieve what had been lost proved unsuccessful, and Louisbourg remained in British possession up to the conclusion of hos-

G

tilities. But then the famous stronghold was, to the not unnatural chagrin of the people of Boston and New York, restored to France by the peace of Aix-la-Chapelle, in exchange for Madras which had been captured by La Bourdonais. The influence which its capture had exerted on the course of the war had been very marked, both in its effect upon the great naval operations of the campaign and upon the security of British commerce in the Western Atlantic. And although Louis XV. greatly strengthened the place, elaborated its defences and multiplied its armament, it became at once an obvious objective to the elder Pitt when that statesman was entrusted with the reins of government soon after the outbreak of the Seven Years' War.

A first attempt, undertaken with insufficient forces, proved abortive,—it indeed can hardly be said to have got beyond the initial stage. But in 1758 the renowned stronghold fell to Boscawen and General Amherst, and its acquisition proved the first step towards the conquest of Canada. Deprived of their naval base, the French were unable the following year to dispute the command of the north-west Atlantic with the British fleets, or to interfere in any way by naval force with the operations of the expedition up the St Lawrence which captured Quebec.

Toulon. It is easy to imagine the great effect which the successful execution of the combined enterprise against Toulon, which was planned by Marlborough in 1707, would have had upon the War of the Spanish Succession. The destruction of the naval arsenal and dockyard, which served at once as a haven of refuge and as a secure base to French floating force in the Mediterranean, would inevitably have crippled their sea-power in those waters for many years. Had Lord Hood been able to demolish all the building-slips and to burn all the naval depots and stores in 1794, it is probable that no expedition to Egypt would ever have been attempted by Napoleon.

It has often occurred in war that operations have been undertaken against some great maritime stronghold, not merely with the object of destroying its naval establishments and of depriving the hostile fleets of its use as an asylum when in peril and as a base of replenishment and repair, but also for the purpose of actually dealing with warships which may be lying within the defences. The cases of Sebastopol half a century ago, and of Port Arthur in 1904, are examples of this which naturally come to mind. The presence of a fleet within a place of arms adds considerably to the difficulty of capturing it, whatever means may be employed to bring about its downfall. But on the other hand, inasmuch as the mobile naval forces of the enemy form the primary objective in warfare afloat, the fact that hostile fighting-vessels have taken refuge in the fortress offers a strong inducement for undertaking operations against it. As explained later, the reduction of a maritime stronghold must generally be effected by attack from the land side. And in chap. vii. it will be shown how often it occurs that when an inferior or a beaten navy betakes itself to the shelter of defended ports, its final destruction has to be effected by intervention of military force. *Attack of base sometimes necessary as means of destroying hostile fleet within.*

In the last chapter it was shown how dependent upon naval bases must be any organised system of commerce destroying. This being the case, it follows that the loss of these bases must prove most prejudicial to the prosecution of this form of naval warfare. The most effectual antidote to the *guerre de course* was formerly indeed found to be operations directed against the shelters, whither the cruisers or privateers which preyed upon trade fled when in danger, where they took in the supplies which had been expended, and where they could be fitted out afresh for further mischief. It is because their bases were certain to be closed to them sooner or later, that commerce-destroyers as a rule enjoyed so short a life in the sailing days. *Attack on hostile bases for commerce destroying.*

100   CAPTURING BASES AND FORTRESSES.

<small>Captain Mahan's views on this.</small>

Captain Mahan is emphatic on this point. Speaking of the attacks which were made upon our maritime trade in West Indian waters at the end of the eighteenth century, he says: "In a contest between equal navies for the control of the sea, to waste military effort upon the capture of small islands, as the French did in 1778, is a preposterous misdirection of effort; but when one navy is overwhelmingly preponderant, as the British was after 1794, when the enemy confined himself to commerce destroying by crowds of small privateers, then the true military policy is to stamp out the nests where they swarm."* This was also well illustrated at an earlier date in the same quarter.

"In the previous January"—this was in 1762, at the time of the British capture of Havana—"the West Indian fleet, under the well-known Rodney, had acted with the land forces in the reduction of Martinique, the gem and tower of the French islands and the harbour of an extensive privateering system: it is said that fourteen hundred English merchantmen were taken during this war in the West Indian seas by cruisers whose principal port was Fort Royal in Martinique. With this necessary base fell also the privateering system resting upon it."†

<small>Martinique and Mauritius.</small>

In the war against the French Empire Martinique again served as a base for commerce-destroyers till it was captured in 1809,—it had been captured in 1794, but had been restored to France by the Peace of Amiens. After its fall Guadaloupe became the refuge for the French cruisers, till that island was also captured in the following year. In the meantime British trade was suffering very appreciably from the depredations of hostile vessels in the Indian Ocean. This was attributed to the failure of the convoy system and to the extraordinary difficulty of hunting down the enemy's

---

* 'Influence of Sea-Power on the French Revolution and Empire,' vol. ii. p. 252.

† 'Influence of Sea-Power upon History,' p. 314.

commerce-destroyers in these extensive and distant seas. But in the years 1810-11 the captures of merchantmen greatly decreased, and this was owing to the adoption of a fresh strategical policy. Blockade had failed. Convoys had failed. Our trade with the East was imperilled, and serious losses were falling upon the trading community. So "the British Government reverted most properly to the policy of Pitt by directing expeditions against the enemy's colonies, the foreign bases of their sea-power, and in the absence of great fleets the only possible support upon which commerce destroying can depend; with whose fall it must also fall. The island of Bourbon and of France (Mauritius) capitulated in 1810, the same year that saw the surrender of Guadaloupe, the last survivor of the French West Indian Islands. This was followed in 1811 by the reduction of the Dutch colony of Java. Thus an end was put to the predatory warfare which had been successfully carried on against the British trade in India for a number of years."*

The same fundamental principle of naval warfare, that the *guerre de course* can be best checkmated by capturing the bases on which the cruisers of the enemy depend, is illustrated to a certain extent by the American Civil War. In that protracted contest the commerce-destroyers of the Confederates inflicted serious injury upon the sea-borne trade of the Federals, who throughout the struggle enjoyed a decisive maritime preponderance. The capture of Confederate ports on the Atlantic coast-line and in the Gulf of Mexico turned out to be the most effective method of counteracting the efforts of the Southern States to damage the commerce of the Union by guerila warfare. But this proved to be a slow process, and it remains to be seen whether in campaigns of the future the principle of attacking the commerce-destroyer by seizing the commerce-

marginal note: Question whether steam has not altered the conditions.

* 'Influence of Sea-Power on the French Revolution and Empire,' vol. ii. p. 217.

destroyer's base or bases will necessarily be the most satisfactory mode of protecting threatened trade.

The fast-steaming cruiser, which will henceforward be the instrument for the *guerre de course*, will have a difficult game to play if it operates in the vicinity of the great ocean routes. Its radius of action is limited by its coal supply. Every ship that has sighted it will report its whereabouts at the next port of call, and the news will be communicated in all directions by the telegraph cable. Wireless telegraphy will make its concealment from the hostile warships which will be on the watch for it, still more difficult. Some attention was attracted by the Vladivostok cruisers in 1904 which caused annoyance in Japanese waters, and which for a long time encountered no opposition; but these vessels were operating in a theatre which Japan was compelled to abandon to them owing to the general strategical situation, they had a secure base to retire to, and, considering the advantages which they enjoyed, the most striking feature about their campaign against commerce was the insignificant results which it achieved.

Much of the success credited to the French commerce-destroyers in the West Indies and the Indian Ocean in the Revolutionary and Napoleonic wars was due to the privateering system, which has been abolished by the Declaration of Paris. It seems extremely doubtful if the experiences in those seas a century ago are altogether applicable to the conditions of the present day. But occasions may yet arise in future when the seizure of the base or bases will prove to be the best means of checking an undoubted evil. Such seizure will certainly be effective. The question is whether, as a general rule, the object cannot be more easily attained by the operations of cruisers in the open sea.[3]

A captured naval base may form a valuable point   A naval base generally coincides with a satisfactory and well-sheltered harbour. In consequence of this, its acquisition during the progress of hostilities may in later stages of the campaign prove of great service to the navy which has *d'appui for future operations.* captured it, or has assisted in its capture. This was the case when the Bailli de Suffren captured Trincomalee from us in 1782. That excellent Cingalese port had previously served as a base to Admiral Hughes; but having secured it, the French commander promptly adapted it as a base for himself. When Admiral Elphinstone (Lord Keith), acting in concert with General Craig, captured the Cape Peninsula in 1795, he secured a most valuable naval base for the further naval operations of a struggle which was to last for seven years longer. On the other hand, Louisbourg was dismantled after its capture in 1758: owing to its proximity to the better harbour of Halifax, it was of no use to the British navy. Maritime strongholds captured in time of war would not, in fact, generally be maintained as bases by the successful belligerent for the rest of the campaign unless they happened to be situated at a considerable distance from the nearest *point d'appui*. It is obvious, however, that if a hostile dockyard, or coaling-station, or maritime fortress, is so situated that its acquisition will provide a needed base, there is a strong incentive for undertaking operations against it, quite apart from the damage which its loss inflicts upon the enemy.

And there is another argument for attacking hostile naval *Chance of capturing valuable material.* bases. Apart from the probable presence within the precincts of their defensive zone of hostile fighting-ships,—a point to be dealt with in the next and subsequent paragraphs,—it may be the case that naval stores of great value will be found in them. Thus 12,000 tons of coal were seized in the fortress of Khertch when it was taken by the allies in 1855. As the defenders will always endeavour to destroy war material and supplies before the place falls, a sudden attack will be more likely to promise useful captures than more deliberate methods, although the tactical situation must of course govern the procedure in each particular case. And yet the history of war abounds in examples showing the difficulty of rapidly destroying great quantities of stores in an emergency, and of the hesitation on the part of commanders to order it in time. Just as the French in 1870 delayed to blow up the Vosges tunnels till too late, so the commander of a maritime place-of-arms shrinks from destroying the docks, and structures, and machinery erected by his country at great cost, if there be the remotest hope of saving them. The situation at Toulon in 1794 was no doubt extraordinary and unprecedented; but the story of the evacuation will always serve as a signal illustration of how much may be abandoned to the enemy who compasses the downfall of a great naval base. And at the time of writing, the question whether the naval material captured by the Japanese in Port Arthur will be of use to them during the remainder of the war is still a matter of conjecture.

Floating naval resources of the enemy which may have to be dealt with in hostile coast fortresses.

And this brings us to the question of the floating naval resources of the enemy which may be captured in a naval station. As a result of the attack on Copenhagen in 1807, which led to the capitulation of that ancient capital, the whole Danish navy was carried off to England. Operations directed against a maritime fortress because a hostile squadron has taken refuge within its zone of defence have been a feature of amphibious warfare since ancient times. Messina, Cadiz, Brest, Sebastopol, Port Arthur, and innumerable other naval strongholds harbouring "fleets in being," have been the scene of blockades and attacks by land and attacks by sea. Changes in war material, progress in ship construction, and modifications in naval tactics, make no difference in this. Mobile naval force which has taken refuge in a coast fortress acts as a magnet to the mobile naval force, and also sometimes to the mobile military force, of the opposing side. It cannot be ignored. It must be watched, or bottled up, or captured. Hostile naval bases, merely as naval bases, need not necessarily be taken seriously; but if, in addition

CONCLUSIONS AS TO CAPTURING BASES. 105

to their stores and repairing-yards and depots of supply, they contain ships of war, whether these be formidable ironclads, or be unprotected commerce-destroyers, or be merely torpedo craft, they must be dealt with in some form or other. This is a fundamental principle of the art of naval warfare which in no way clashes with the law that the destruction of the enemy's fighting-power afloat is the primary objective. The doctrine of the "fleet in being" will be dealt with in a later chapter, as the phrase had its origin in a reference to the over-sea transport of a military force. But any fighting-ship, left to itself, constitutes to a certain extent a danger, and is "in being." It may be impracticable to capture it or to destroy it in its fortified haven of refuge, or even to forbid its exit, but it can and must be kept under observation.

This question of attacks on fleets in harbour will be dealt with at greater length in the next two chapters. The extent to which such operations have governed naval warfare in the past, and are likely to govern it in the future, has not always been fully appreciated by writers dealing with the principles of sea-power. For the purposes of this chapter it is sufficient to point out that, where some defended harbour of the enemy is serving as a *point d'appui* to a hostile fleet or to hostile commerce-destroyers, its capture is often a legitimate and desirable objective, but that when that defended harbour is sheltering a formidable hostile squadron its capture becomes sometimes an imperative necessity. In their results, and in the scale of the operations framed to achieve their downfall, the attacks on Guadaloupe in 1794 and on Mauritius in 1810 were insignificant undertakings compared to the invasion of the Crimea for the purpose of destroying Sebastopol with all that it contained, or to the Japanese campaign against Port Arthur when in Russian hands. But in all four cases the sea-power of an enemy was attacked and was seriously damaged, not out on the

Conclusion as to attacks on hostile bases.

great waters but at a point where it was linked to the shore.

Enterprises against the naval bases of the adversary, the destruction of his maritime arsenals and his dockyards, the reduction of his strongholds on the coast, are, then, often justifiable, and are sometimes unavoidable, in war. Operations of this character will not secure to a belligerent command of the sea, if they are allowed to prejudice those great strategical combinations which lead to the defeat of the mobile naval forces of the enemy. But when, as in the case of Minorca in 1756, the side with the weaker navy seizes a favourable moment for dealing effectively with some important coast fortress of the antagonist, the result may exert appreciable influence over the subsequent course of the campaign, and may check the establishment by the enemy of that undisputed maritime supremacy which is the highest purpose of naval warfare. Undisputed maritime supremacy, amounting to definite command of the sea, may possibly not be achieved without capturing at least some of the naval bases of the beaten foe.

Question of securing suitable naval bases during the course of a war. The strategical conditions of naval warfare are often such that one of the belligerents has no suitable base for his fleets to depend on in the theatre of actual warlike operations, even when having at command the fighting resources necessary for acquiring a harbour adapted to the purpose. The natural course under such circumstances is to select a suitable port and to seize it. In some cases, as shown above, the desired naval station may be gained by wresting a coast fortress from the adversary: an undertaking of that kind will, however, generally involve a considerable expenditure of power, and it may take some time to bring to a satisfactory conclusion. The object will usually be more readily gained by simply occupying some suitable unfortified harbour in hostile territory, and by taking the necessary steps to secure this by improvised works of defence.

In 1586 Drake had been playing the corsair with brilliant effect and with consummate skill in Spanish waters. He had swooped down upon the merchant flotilla sheltering in fancied security in Cadiz harbour, and had dealt Spain a deadly blow within the precincts of her greatest and most historic fortress. Then he had turned homewards, hoping for further plunder and intent on gaining some information as to the great hostile flotilla known to be gathering at Lisbon. But he wanted water and he required an anchorage. So he proceeded to Lagos; and when he there found an old castle perched on a precipice overhanging the sea, he went to work with characteristic energy and daring, stormed the stronghold, toppled its guns into the sea to be retrieved by the ships, and established a comfortable base in an ideal position for harrying trade. Lying there for some little time, he used to sally out and surprise the passing merchant ships of Spain, securing valuable booty in the process. Then he proceeded up the Portuguese coast and looked into the Tagus, where he spied a scene of great activity and ascertained that the Armada was in a forward state. Overtaken by a storm which caused him serious damage, he returned to Lagos, and he spent nine busy days in his captured base, refitting for the voyage home. Then he started for the Channel by a circuitous course, picking up on the way a great Portuguese galleon crammed with treasures from the East, and was enabled to lay an attractive store of plunder at the feet of good Queen Bess, who in these matters was apt to judge by tangible results, and who sometimes even deigned to accept a share of the spoils.

Examples. Drake at Lagos.

In 1778, at a time when the British and French navies were disputing the command of West Indian waters, Admiral Barrington seized the French island of St Lucia,

Barrington at St Lucia.

108 CAPTURING BASES AND FORTRESSES.

which lies next to Martinique. The harbour of Gros Ilot, at the northern end of St Lucia, offered an ideal anchorage for watching the French naval base at Fort Royal, and its retention during the following three years of war was of the utmost service to the British fleet.

Corsica in 1794.

The occupation of Corsica in 1794, after the evacuation of Toulon, has been already referred to in chap. iv. In this case it was necessary, so as to secure a naval base, to undertake serious land operations against bodies of troops posted in fortresses, and to accept the inconvenient responsibilities of suzerainty over a most turbulent people. The British land- and sea-forces proceeded thither in compliance with an invitation from the Corsicans themselves, but till the French garrisons had been dealt with the island was, to a certain extent, hostile territory. The operations against San Fiorenzo, Bastia, and Calvi involved some sacrifices. Paoli and his Government did not prove as tractable as was desirable, considering that the British naval and military forces in the Mediterranean might at any moment be called upon to make some great effort. And the incident as a whole affords a remarkable illustration of the singular situation which may arise when the prosecution of naval warfare calls for the seizure of positions ashore.

Port Royal in the American Civil War.

In 1861, in the early days of the American Civil War, the Federals found it imperative to secure some Atlantic port in the Southern States. A depot for coal and other supplies was required for the use of the numbers of vessels of all kinds which had been detailed to blockade the islands and harbours and sounds along the Confederate coast. The spacious inlet of Port Royal, between Savannah and Charleston, was selected. A fleet was told off to convoy transports thither, with 12,000 men on board under General Sherman. Possession of certain posts and islets within the extensive harbour was gained by the expeditionary force after some fighting, and its use was thus secured to the

Federal navy. Port Royal was held by troops of the North till the end of the war as a naval base. It proved of immense value during the prolonged and arduous blockade of a lengthy and deeply indented coast-line. It served, moreover, as a starting-point for a military expedition against Charleston in 1865.

At a very early stage of the war against Russia the Japanese seized some islands in the vicinity of Port Arthur, and made use of them as an advanced naval base during the operations which followed. The limited radius of action of destroyers and torpedo-boats makes the possession of such a base very necessary if it is proposed to use these vessels offensively against ships of the enemy lying in port. And where a fighting fleet is engaged in blockade, or is in observation of some hostile maritime stronghold, it is obviously advantageous that there should be at hand some port or anchorage where fuel and ammunition and supplies can be replenished with convenience and despatch. *Islands occupied by the Japanese in 1904.*

Naval warfare is not a war of posts, in the sense that the action of a fleet is under ordinary circumstances to be subordinated to questions as to their attack or defence of posts. But the attack and defence and occupation of posts has been a feature in naval warfare since the days of the Phœnicians, and it will continue a feature in naval warfare till the reign of universal peace. De Ruyter in the Medway, arrested in his career of destruction by Upnor Castle; Suffren intent upon the capture of Trincomalee; Hood, "the greatest of the sowers," devoting a main portion of his fleet to gain a secure footing in Corsica; Rodney sailing out to fight his great fight with the Comte de Grasse from St Lucia, captured two years before; an army equal to that of Napoleon at Waterloo, and practically the whole fighting sea-power of Japan, ranged around a maritime stronghold harbouring a shattered fleet,—can it be said that posts exert no influence on naval warfare? *Conclusion.*

CHAPTER VI.

THE REASON WHY LAND OPERATIONS ARE USUALLY NECESSARY TO DEAL EFFECTIVELY WITH THE NAVAL STATIONS OF THE ENEMY AND TO SECURE BASES FOR SPECIAL MARITIME OPERATIONS.

History proves that land operations are generally necessary to deal with the naval stations of the enemy effectively.

IN chap. iv. the relations of naval bases to mobile floating force have been discussed. In chap. v. it has been explained how during the course of hostilities at sea it may become necessary or desirable to deprive the enemy of the use of his bases, the reasons why it may be expedient to undertake enterprises against his strongholds on the coast have been pointed out, and it has been shown that circumstances may arise which compel a belligerent to seize harbours and anchorages situated in the adversary's territory, so that they may become available for the prosecution of the plan of campaign. In this chapter the design is to establish the principle that in the war of posts land operations can seldom be dispensed with, and that amphibious force must generally be brought into play in some form.

The purposes for which maritime nations have erected strongholds on their shores have in reality varied little since the early days of history. As havens of refuge for ships of war and ships of commerce when placed in jeopardy by the enemy or by the elements, and as secure depots of supply and places of repair, their function has not altered much in principle in the gradual evolution of the art of war. And it will be found on examination that the methods adopted for wresting them from hostile hands, or for counteracting their influence, have not in reality changed much either in their principles. The Romans tried to shut up the Carthaginian fleet in Carthage by erecting a dam across the mouth of the harbour; Admiral Togo sinks ships in the channel of Port Arthur with a like end in view. Blockades of fortresses—successful in some cases, unfortunate in others—were a feature in maritime warfare in the age of the galley and in the era of sails, just as they are in the modern days of armour-plating, of high explosives, and of triple-expansion engines. Ever since the cannon came into prominence afloat and ashore, naval places of arms have been subject to bombardment from the sea, and have replied with their shot and shell to the challenge of the enemy's ships. And land attacks upon fortified seaports have taken the place of attack by fighting-vessels, or have been executed in conjunction with attack by fighting-vessels, in all times and all ages.

Against attack from the sea the coast fortress opposes the fire of its batteries, and the obstruction to the advance of hostile ships which is comprised in boom and mine defence. Under modern conditions night operations by torpedo craft to force a passage into the harbour have come into prominence. But in whatever form the assailants deliver their blows from the side of the sea, the history of war tends to discredit the principle of pitting floating force against the fixed defences on shore.[1] A formidable fleet can of course crush a relatively feeble fortress, and it will probably suffer little damage in the process. Rooke in 1704 beat down the fire of the Gibraltar batteries with his ships, and captured the Rock with a few boats' crews. Lord Exmouth destroyed the coast defences of Algiers by bombardment in 1817. The allied fleets in 1855 overwhelmed the granite gun emplacements and casemates of Sveaborg, and laid the place in ruins. As a general rule, however,

Floating force generally unsuitable for actual attack upon maritime strongholds.

the action of ships against defended harbours takes the form rather of blockade and observation than of actual assault.

<small>Reasons for this.</small>
And the reasons for this are twofold. In the first place, naval operations against a maritime stronghold are generally undertaken mainly to deny its use to the warships of the enemy, or to prevent any of the warships of the enemy which are within from issuing forth; and it is in many cases feasible to achieve these objects by some kind of blockade. And in the second place, shore defences enjoy in actual combat marked advantages over ships, so much so that it is seldom justifiable to risk battleships or cruisers in an attempt to overcome the resistance of a naval place of arms by attack from the sea. To the artillery of the defence a vessel at sea affords an admirable target. Ships are vulnerable quite apart from their armament and *personnel*, while batteries ashore are only vulnerable in their armament and *personnel*. "When, therefore, circumstances permit ships to be pitted squarely against fortifications,—not merely to pass swiftly by them,—it is only because the builders of the shore works have not for some reason, possibly quite adequate, given them the power to repel attacks which they might have had."* Contact with a submarine mine may, moreover, send the finest fighting-vessel to the bottom in a moment, carrying with it potential force in engines of destruction, and *personnel*, and mobility, which cannot be replaced within the space of time usually required to decide the fate of a campaign. Nelson did not hesitate to challenge the forts of Copenhagen with his fleet when a great object was to be gained thereby—the destruction or capture of the Danish navy; but he objected to laying ships against the walls of Calvi, because the end did not justify the means. In the fighting for the possession of Port Arthur the participation of the Japanese sea-going fleet was confined

---

* Mahan, 'Lessons of the War with Spain,' p. 50.[2]

in the main to long-range bombardments of the harbour and docks and forts; the ships were never risked except against the Russian squadron when it issued from the besieged fortress, and thereby afforded opportunity for a fight at sea.

Still, the circumstances of the case will sometimes demand, as in the case of Copenhagen, that an actual attack shall be delivered upon a fortified port by ships of war. Such a situation is especially likely to arise where some of the enemy's fighting-vessels have taken refuge in the place, and where therefore the fleet making the attempt must be prepared for resistance, additional to that which the batteries and other forms of fixed defence can offer. And a few examples of attacks of this character may be of interest. *Examples of attacks of ships on fortresses.*

In 1654 Blake, who was engaged in coercing the Dey of Tunis, found the piratical fleet of that potentate lying in the harbour of Porto Farina, between Goletta and Biserta. The entrance into the harbour was protected by batteries mounting a number of guns, and the corsair chiefs were confident that their galleys were in perfect safety in the landlocked bay. But Blake stood in cleared for action, overpowered the batteries by superior gunnery aided by the smoke which impeded the fire of the Moslem gunners owing to the direction of the wind, and destroyed the flotilla of the enemy under the guns of the fortress. The daring displayed by the British admiral, and the remarkable success which attended his enterprise, caused a great sensation in Europe. *Blake at Porto Farina and Santa Cruz.*

Two years later he attacked the fortified harbour of Santa Cruz in Teneriffe. The Spanish treasure-ships were lying under the protection of its frowning battlements. The convoying fleet was anchored in front of the galleons, so that its guns bore on the entrance to the harbour. The fortifications were of a formidable character, bristled with cannon, and were in good repair. Moreover, the wind blows right into the Bay of Santa Cruz as a rule, and an attacking fleet of sailing-ships which got into the harbour and failed to overcome the defences was very unlikely to get out again, even in a disabled state. But Blake was not deterred by the formidable difficulties of the enterprise from making the attempt. He sailed right in, and after a desperate struggle destroyed the galleons and burnt or sank every ship in the Spanish fleet. Then he was favoured by rare good fortune, for the wind shifted, and the whole British squadron, although considerably knocked about, succeeded in getting out of the harbour in spite of the fire of the batteries, having performed one of the most remarkable exploits in the history of war. The victorious fleet then sailed for England. But Blake, broken in health and suffering constantly from an old wound, sank from day to day on the voyage home; and the greatest of the soldier-admirals died within sight of the coast of Devon, and only a few hours before his flagship entered Plymouth Sound.

Sir C. Shovel at Toulon, and later instances. Sir Cloudesley Shovel in 1707 participated with his fleet in a general attack on Toulon made by an army under the Duke of Savoy. But although the fire of the ships caused considerable damage to the sea-batteries, the issue was decided on the land side; for a successful sortie compelled the assailants to fall back, and necessitated the abandonment of the enterprise. But during the wars of the latter half of the eighteenth century and the opening year of the nineteenth century, there are not many instances of ships attacking formidable land defences, apart from the memorable battle of Copenhagen. Some of Pocock's ships suffered very severely in an attack on Morro Castle during the combined operations against Havana in 1762, which ended in the capture of the fortress and city. In 1790 a Swedish fleet sailed into the fortified harbour of Revel and attacked the batteries and a hostile squadron lying near them; but when the contest was at its height and victory hung in the balance, the wind shifted, and the assailants only escaped by desperate efforts and after the loss of three of their ships. The great bombardment of Gibraltar by the French and Spanish fleets was almost wholly without result, the floating batteries of the allies indeed being almost all destroyed. At the capture of Monte Video in 1806 the fleet nearly used up the whole of its powder. The heavy expenditure of ammunition in such operations is, from the naval point of view, one of the strongest objections to their being undertaken. One reason for the indecisive character of Rooke's fight with Toulouse off Malaga appears to have been that the British fleet was short of ammunition after its successful attack on Gibraltar.

In later days Admiral Stopford's attack upon Acre in 1840 affords a remarkable example of ships overcoming formidable batteries manned by determined troops. But the fleet was on this occasion aided by the fact that the sills of the embrasures did not admit of the guns on shore being depressed sufficiently to bear upon it when it lay to, close in: a lucky shell, moreover, blew up the main magazine, causing great loss of life and terrible confusion. The blowing up of the main magazine was a very usual incident in the defence of strongholds included in the ancient Ottoman Empire. The attack of the allied fleets upon the harbour defences of Sebastopol failed to make much impression on the fortress. Admiral Farragut's great attack upon the forts guarding the extensive harbour of Mobile in 1864, and his destruction of the Confederate flotilla higher up, was rather a case of running past formidable defences than actually attacking them from the sea. The operations of Admiral Persano's powerful fleet against the feeble Austrian defences on the island of Lissa in 1866 were marked by losses and damage to ships which were quite out of proportion to the advantage gained: the inopportune arrival of Tegethoff on the scene, and the sea-fight which ensued, prevented a definite conclusion being arrived at in an undertaking which showed a singular lack of strategical insight. Admiral Dewey's victory in Manilla Bay, striking as it was, was over shore batteries that were out of date, over mines that did not go off, and over war-vessels in every way inferior to those of the attacking squadron: the enterprise turned out to be a far less difficult one than it appeared to be, and its merit lies rather in the fact of its having been attempted than in its actual execution.

There are exceptions to every rule. But the verdict of history accords with the view which is generally held by naval and military experts in the present day, that the opposition of valuable fighting-ships to batteries on dry land is not in accordance with sound principles of strategy or of tactics.

<small>Effect of submarine mines.</small> And the development of submarine mining makes attack upon coast fortresses from the sea far more difficult than it was before this form of fixed defence came into prominence. In considering the efficacy of the submarine mine in the war of posts the history of maritime campaigns of the past affords little guidance. The subject is, comparatively speaking, a new one, and it is only of recent years that these engines of destruction have become a formidable bar to the passage of ships. Captain Mahan tells us that when the Union gunboat *Cairo* was sunk by a mine in the Mississippi, "torpedoes had hardly yet come to be looked on as a respectable mode of warfare, especially by seamen, and the officer who laid these and was looking on when the *Cairo* went down, describes himself as feeling much as a schoolboy might whose practical joke had taken a more serious shape than he expected." Two years later the monitor *Tecumseh* was sunk by a mine during the attack on Mobile harbour; but others of the ships of Farragut's fleet fared better, the mines were heard "knocking against the bottom of the ships and the primers

snapping," but none of these exploded. This is a different story from that of the *Petropavlosk* at Port Arthur forty years later.[3]

Admiral Sampson's refusal to attempt to force the mouth of Santiago harbour when called upon by General Shafter to aid him, was due to the perfectly justifiable fear of the Spanish mines. And the operations of the Japanese fleet before Port Arthur suggest that when this form of defence exists, fighting-ships do not attempt to force a passage through the field. It is unnecessary to go into the technical subject of removing mines and of countermining, methods by which it may be possible to clear a passage. But there is perhaps no phase of warlike operations ashore or afloat in which the question of moral effect is so predominant as in the employment of engines of destruction below the surface of the sea. The fear of mines exerts an influence as great as do the mines themselves. Their position is unknown. Their existence may be a mere matter of conjecture, but the warship of to-day is much too valuable for it to be placed in the deadly peril which it incurs when it traverses a mine-field controlled by a vigilant foe.[4]

It does not, however, follow that mine-fields necessarily form part of the defences of a maritime fortress which is to be attacked. Fixed submarine mines are adapted rather for passive than for active defence. They are wholly inapplicable to some situations owing to technical conditions which it would be out of place to go into here. But upon the whole it is safe to assert that this class of protection to a naval stronghold enhances very considerably the difficulty of attacking it from the side of the sea.

Nor do torpedo craft redress the balance in favour of the sea against the land. These hornets may sting the battleship or the troop-transport out at sea, or lying at anchor, if they are insufficiently protected. But the Far

Influence of torpedo craft.

Eastern war shows that a squadron which has taken refuge within a modern fortress, manned by a determined and efficient garrison, is not easily assailed by destroyer or torpedo-boat. The boom, the mine-field, the quick-firing gun, and the searchlight between them bar the way. The Japanese onslaughts on the Chinese fleet in the harbour of Wei-hai-wei in 1895 afford ample proof that operations of this class may easily succeed if the fortifications and their adjuncts be defective, or if the *personnel* be unequal to its responsibilities: it is not, however, suggested that mobile naval force cannot assail land defences, if the relative power of these be far inferior to that of the attacking fleet.

<small>Improbability of fleet attacking fortresses in future.</small>

We are, however, entitled to conclude that under the normal conditions of amphibious war the attitude of the navy of one belligerent towards the maritime strongholds of the other will be one of reserve. Fleets will not actually attack hostile fortresses; they will rather aim at blockading them in some form. With modern guns of great range it may sometimes be possible to bombard the ships, or dockyards, or depots which the defence-works of the fortresses are guarding, without exposing the vessels conducting the bombardment to serious danger from the batteries on shore. Such procedure does not, however, amount to actual attack. Nor is it likely to achieve very decisive results. And that it involves risk is shown by the *Huascar*, in the Chilian bombardment of Callao in 1880, having been pierced by a projectile below her armour when rolling in the swell, and being only saved from foundering by her bulkheads. Bombardment may be very effective when a naval station coincides with a great town, because the inhabitants may bring inconvenient pressure to bear on the commandant: the tendency of the day is, however, to avoid the close vicinity of important seaports, if possible, when selecting the site for a dockyard or naval base.

In a struggle for the upper hand afloat, the destruction

of the fighting sea-power of the adversary is the dominant objective. The close blockading of an inferior fleet which has sought refuge in a maritime fortress—close blockading, that is to say, in the sense of shutting the inferior fleet in and forbidding its egress—is not in accordance with the fundamental principles of naval strategy. On the contrary, the commander of the naval forces cruising off the stronghold, or lying in wait at some convenient point in its vicinity, is animated by the hope that the enemy will come out and afford an opportunity for a combat at sea. "I beg to inform your Lordship," wrote Nelson to the Admiralty, "that the port of Toulon has been never blockaded by me; quite the reverse. Every opportunity has been offered the enemy to put to sea, for it is there we hope to realise the hopes and expectations of our country." The belligerent with the greater naval resources only seals up hostile squadrons in the havens of refuge where they have sought safety, under special circumstances,—when, for instance, there is a question of transports passing within striking distance of hostile warships lying in port. This is a point which is often misunderstood by military men and others not conversant with the naval art of war. Where a maritime fortress is being besieged by land and sea a strict blockade by war-vessels is essential, so as to keep supplies or relief from getting in by ship to aid the garrison; but blockade of that kind is directed against the approach of vessels from without, not from within: it would not, moreover, often involve the employment of formidable fighting-ships,—this point will be referred to again later, in the chapter on sieges. Even under such circumstances it would only be desirable to deny exit to a hostile fleet within the fortress, if the siege was progressing so satisfactorily that the downfall of the place and of the fleet with it had become a certainty, or else in case it was for some special reason essential that the neighbouring waters

Question of blockade—strategical principle involved.

should be absolutely free from any enemy's ship for the time being.

Difficulties attending blockade. Not only is the blockade of a stronghold on the adversary's coasts, with the idea of shutting hostile vessels in, rarely a sound procedure from the strategical point of view, but it is in reality almost impracticable as an operation of war. In the sailing era and also in earlier days, blockades, when they were enforced, had constantly to be raised owing to bad weather. This was the case when Prince Rupert escaped from Kinsale in 1649; and numberless instances have occurred since. In the case of Brest, so often blockaded by British fleets in the eighteenth century, the fact that the squadron lying outside could not maintain its station in heavy weather from the west, was to a certain extent compensated for by the difficulty which attended the ships of war inside in beating out against the wind. The introduction of steam has in great measure obviated the obstacle to the maintenance of an effective blockade created by the elements. But, on the other hand, with the battleship and cruiser of to-day has come the torpedo-vessel, a dangerous enemy to a squadron lying off a fortress which includes such craft in its defensive resources. And the fact that modern warships driven by steam-power can escape from a port in any weather and moving at a high-rate speed, makes the theoretical blockade an undertaking so difficult as to be almost impracticable, except as a measure of merely a few hours' duration. "Few," writes Captain Mahan, "realise the doubts, uncertainties, and difficulties which attend such operations as the 'bottling' of the Spanish fleet by Admiral Sampson; for bottling a hostile fleet does not resemble the chance and careless shoving of a cork into a half-used bottle,—it is rather like the wiring-down of champagne by bonds which cannot be broken, and through which nothing can ooze."

Closing the entrance of a harbour from within, although

sometimes adopted by the defending side, as at Sebastopol where line-of-battleships were sunk by the Russians to keep the allies out, was unusual during the great naval wars which followed the golden age of maritime discovery. Supposing that there are fighting-ships within the fortress, the forming of an obstruction by scuttling ships in the entrance to the place necessarily prevents these ships from getting out. It is essentially a measure of passive defence, and in view of the disinclination of attacking fleets to brave the dangers of running the gauntlet of shore batteries, it is a measure which is seldom necessary. *[Blocking entrance from within.]*

Admiral Togo has shown us that when the entrance to a defended harbour is comparatively speaking narrow, it may be possible to absolutely seal that entrance up for a time from outside by sinking suitable vessels in the fairway. The heroism displayed by the Japanese naval *personnel*, which after many abortive attempts succeeded in blocking the passage at a critical juncture, has excited general admiration; but it has also made manifest the rare difficulty of such an operation. The attempt to close the entrance into Santiago harbour in 1898 failed. The bottling process is in any case out of the question if the channel be of more than a given depth. The obstructions are certain to be removed by the defenders of the fortress before long, and the gateway by which the imprisoned war-vessels can get out to sea will not be permanently denied to them. As a temporary expedient for scotching a "fleet in being" the plan of sinking vessels may serve. But it does not dispose of the fleet. *[Blocking the entrance to a harbour from without, by blockading fleet.]*

The tactics of Admirals Sampson and Togo in the matter of blocking the entrances to Santiago and Port Arthur attracted a good deal of attention because of their apparent novelty. But those commanders were in reality only reviving forgotten methods in a new guise, as is shown by the following episodes in ancient and medieval history. *[Examples of blocking channels.]*

After the Romans had established a close blockade of Carthage by land and sea and had disposed of the port of Nepheris as mentioned on p. 96, Scipio still found some difficulty in preventing the Punic flotilla within the harbour from sallying out and bringing in provisions. So he constructed a dam across the mouth of the port at the cost of much labour and of many lives. But while he was making his dam the obstinate garrison were, unknown to him, digging a canal which formed a new outlet. And in the end the naval situation was decided, not by the fleet of the defenders being sealed up, but by its being overthrown and finally disposed of in a fight outside.

In 1379 there was strife between the rival maritime republics of Venice and Genoa. Venice on its archipelago of islands lies within a great lagoon shut off from the Adriatic by a gigantic spit 30 miles long, known as the Lido. Through the Lido there are only a very few gaps affording navigable channels. The Genoese had gained the upper hand at sea, had occupied Chiogia at the southern end of the lagoon with a considerable army, and in view of the approach of winter had assembled their flotilla within the lagoon and were preparing for an attack upon Venice itself. The prospect of a struggle for life and death with formidable fighting-forces excited the utmost consternation in the sea-girt city, but all classes rose to the occasion. A patriot named Pisani was, by popular acclamation, placed in command of the Venetian galleys and of the levies. All sorts and conditions of the citizens seconded his efforts to strike a decisive blow at the menacing foe. And he justified the confidence reposed in him by adopting a plan, at once bold and original, for dealing with a great emergency. The Genoese fleet being inside the lagoon, Pisani sallied out into the Adriatic and corked up the outlets by means of sunken vessels from the outside. That done, he was easily able to cut off the supplies and communications of the enemy by sea. A Venetian land force in the meantime threatened communications between Chiogia and the west. The tables were thus completely turned upon the armada which had come full of confidence to conquer the capital of the Doges; for it was blockaded itself, and it was soon reduced to serious straits by hunger and by loss of the initiative. There was plenty of stirring work in galleys and some interesting fighting on land; but the tide set steadily against the forces of the western republic, and six months after Pisani scuttled a few ships in the channels through the Lido, the entire Genoese armament surrendered.

In 1436, during the reign of Henry VI., Calais, which was then an English dependency, was assailed by the Duke of Burgundy, who closely besieged the fortress. A relieving expedition was despatched across the Channel, and the military portion of this landed in the vicinity and moved towards the place. The Duke did not despair of beating off these troops; what he mostly feared was that the English fleet would get into the harbour, pour in supplies, and prove a powerful auxiliary to the garrison; so he prepared vessels filled with stones to sink in the entrance and to thus complete his line of contravallation against the efforts of the armament destined to succour the besieged city. But the defenders divined his plan, and they managed to set fire to the craft intended to close the channel before these could be got into position. Thereupon the Duke, realising that there was no prospect of success unless the English fleet could be kept out, struck his tents and departed.

Sealing up the entrance to a harbour by sinking ships in the channel, although effective enough for a time, seems a crude method of attaining the desired end in these days of scientific warfare. And at Port Arthur the plan—more conformable with modern usage in technical tactics—of laying mines in front of the harbour, was tried with considerable success. But the future will probably show that

Sealing up a harbour by mines from without.

neither sunken vessels nor submarine mines can be depended upon to shut up mobile naval fighting-forces in a fortress, if their commander is determined to emerge. It is a generally accepted principle in land warfare that obstacles are only genuine obstacles when they are under fire, and this holds good also afloat. Sunken ships or mines deposited at the mouth of a fortified harbour by the attacking side can be removed by the defenders, as long as they are not protected by the guns of the blockading fleet; and they cannot usually be so protected without exposing that fleet in some measure to the fire of the batteries on shore. The cork can be forced into the bottle; but it will be blown out again by the pressure inside if the contents are sound.

Conclusions. As naval bases and fortresses may have to be attacked, and as floating force is generally powerless, land operations become a necessity. And so, reviewing what has been stated in previous paragraphs of this chapter and putting them in their concisest form, the position of the fleet operating against a naval base or maritime stronghold is this. It cannot attack its defences without considerable risk, and long-range bombardment is unlikely to cause the defenders serious damage. It cannot absolutely seal it up by blockade, or by closing up the entrances. Therefore it cannot by itself destroy what the place contains, whether it be docks, or stores, or repairing yards, or shipping; nor can it make certain of preventing the issuing of that shipping from the harbour, should the strategical object be to shut the shipping in. It follows, then, if the place is to be dealt with decisively, if its functions as a naval station are definitely to cease, and if the vessels which its batteries and booms and mine-fields make secure are to be destroyed or are to become prizes of the victor, that land operations must be resorted to. If the history of maritime warfare be studied it will be found that, for one purely naval success against a coast fortress such as that of Blake at Santa Cruz or of Exmouth at Algiers, there are a dozen where land operations have brought about its fall. And this last point, the question of land operations to deal with floating forces of the enemy which cannot be disposed of by naval power alone, is of such importance and is illustrated so vividly by records of past conflicts, that it will be treated of especially in the next chapter.

There is one other point to refer to. In the last chapter it was shown that in the prosecution of naval warfare not only have the bases and fortresses of the enemy to be taken into consideration, but that bases have sometimes to be acquired during the course of this conflict. In the examples quoted—Drake at Lagos, Suffren at Trincomalee, the Japanese in the islands near Port Arthur, and others—land operations in some form have almost always been necessary. Rooke captured Gibraltar by landing-parties from his fleet. When Minorca was taken a few years later, the operation was, on the other hand, carried out by a considerable military force under General Stanhope in conjunction with Sir J. Leake's fleet. Malta, which Napoleon was so anxious to secure as affording a foothold for his navy in the middle Mediterranean, did not offer a strenuous resistance when he seized it on his way to Egypt, but its downfall was due to land operations, not to attack from the sea. Whether a great military expedition is needed to effect the object, or whether the point can be secure by a few boat-loads of bluejackets, the principle is the same. Land operations are indispensable, as a rule, if resistance is to be expected.

Land operations necessary when a naval base has to be acquired in war.

CHAPTER VII.

LAND OPERATIONS DIRECTED AGAINST FLEETS AND SHIPPING.

Because naval force when not strong enough to keep the sea naturally retires into defended harbours, a very difficult situation for the stronger fleet is likely to arise.

FLEETS which find themselves overmatched or which have been vanquished in combat retire, if they can, to the refuge of some fortified port. There they can repair damages which have been sustained, there they can replenish ammunition and stores which have been expended, there they may be able to dock vessels requiring cleaning, and there the *personnel* can be rested and gaps in its establishment can be filled up. While thus at rest, sheltered within a defended harbour, a fleet, or even a single warship, unless so much injured as to be unseaworthy or to have no fighting value, constitutes a certain potential force, and may be able to issue forth on a favourable opportunity to prosecute operations of war in the open sea. Therefore the victorious navy which has swept the warships of the adversary back into the zone where they are protected by fixed defences, cannot ignore them thenceforward. Far from it. It is imperative that they should still be kept under observation, unless they can be destroyed or captured.

It is the foundation of policy in war that decisive victory can only be achieved by the practical annihilation of the fighting-forces of the enemy.[1] That is the object to be aimed at strategically and tactically. The purpose for which hostilities were originally undertaken may be attained without a triumph so complete in a military sense. A belligerent will generally acknowledge defeat, and will sue for peace

ATTACK ON FLEETS FROM THE LAND. 127

before being reduced to a state so desperate. But as long as hostilities last, the side which gains the upper hand must not rest content with merely overcoming the navy and the army opposed to it; it must endeavour to destroy them, to demolish or seize the material, and to place the personnel *hors de combat* as killed, or as wounded, or as prisoners.

Therefore when naval warfare takes its normal course, when one side has gained maritime preponderance and more or less controls the sea, while the floating fighting-forces of the other side have sought sanctuary under the guns and behind the booms and mine-fields of the fortresses on the coast which are almost certain to be available, an awkward problem is likely to present itself to the successful fleet. It may be obliged to surrender the initiative and assume an attitude of mere observation, or otherwise it may have no option except to risk the dangers of attacking the enemy's strongholds, unless operations can be undertaken against these from the land side. Command of the sea may have been secured, with all the enormous advantages which that carries with it; but the naval power of the enemy has not been destroyed, it has only been temporarily eclipsed, and it remains an asset on the balance-sheet when the progress of events leads up to discussion as to the terms of peace.[2] The difficulties attending action from the side of the sea against maritime strongholds have been explained in the last chapter. The virtual impossibility of shutting up fighting-ships in port by blockade has been pointed out. If operations on land in some form are impracticable, command of the sea may be again in dispute at any moment, the enemy enjoying the advantage of being able to choose his own time.

And an aggregate of war-vessels lying secure in fortified harbours "contains" a far larger aggregate of war-vessels in observation. This is not due solely to the fact that there must be a preponderance of force outside at each point, ready to be brought into play should the fleets inside emerge from their shelter. It follows also from the inevitable wear and tear on the material of the squadrons watching the fortresses. This tends to reduce the fighting efficiency of the fleets on guard, and to oblige a proportion of the units of which they are composed to be constantly absent undergoing repair. In the sailing era, and in the days of the great blockades of Brest and Cadiz and Toulon, when wars lasted for years, the disadvantages under which the blockading fleets laboured as regards material were, as a rule, more than compensated for by the greater efficiency secured for their *personnel* by keeping the sea in all weathers. But under modern conditions of recruitment and careful training in peace time, of campaigns brought rapidly to a conclusion, and of the mechanic supplanting the typical seaman, it seems doubtful if the *personnel* of the fleet in port will suffer in efficiency to at all the same extent as was the case in an age which has passed away.[3]

The lesson of Wei-hai-wei, Santiago, and Port Arthur.

There have been three notable wars in recent years in which both belligerents have enjoyed a measure of sea-power, and in which naval operations have played a prominent part in the struggle. And in each of these wars the question of final maritime control has been decided by land operations. In the struggle between China and Japan the Chinese fleet, worsted in the Bay of Korea, sought refuge in Wei-hai-wei, and a Japanese army had eventually to be disembarked on the shores of Shantung for the special purpose of helping the Japanese navy to destroy that fleet. The order to Admiral Cervera to put to sea from Santiago may have been a strategical blunder; but it was brought about by the fear of General Shafter's approaching army, of an army which was sent against Santiago for the express purpose of dealing with the Spanish squadron lying secure within its defences. The story of Port Arthur and the sunken Russian fleet is the most striking episode of war which has occurred since organisation, superior training, and an intelligent anticipation of coming events, brought the German armies to the gates of Paris a generation ago; and it proves incontestably the dependence of sea-power upon military force.

The dominant note at Wei-hai-wei and Santiago and Port Arthur from the strategical point of view was that military force employed on shore in each case brought about the destruction of a fleet. And this was no mere accident arising from the especial conditions which may always influence some particular campaign. It was not the result of breech-loading guns, or of armour-protected vessels, or of mines moored under the sea, or of modifications in tactics consequent on progress in the science of armament. Its cause is to be found in a principle of naval warfare which dates back to the most ancient times,—the principle that fighting-fleets must gain their victories at sea, and cannot under the normal conditions of a maritime struggle destroy the naval forces of the enemy when these take shelter under the wing of fixed defences. The action of Blake at Santa Cruz, of Nelson at Copenhagen, and of Farragut in Mobile Bay, afford interesting and valuable examples which show that to this as to every other rule in war there are exceptions. But they do not disprove the rule. *Land operations necessary to deal with the fleets in each case.*

More than two thousand years have passed since the great Persian conqueror Xerxes brought his hordes from Asia Minor across the Dardanelles, and advanced through Thessaly on ancient Greece. Abreast of the great army moved a huge flotilla, carrying supplies and destined to wipe out of existence any fighting-ships which the Greeks might possess. But the Asiatic monarch had not reckoned upon the powers of his antagonists on land, still less had he reckoned upon their resource and skill and bravery at sea. His flotilla, already damaged by storm and injured in action, suffered overwhelming defeat at Salamis. And the entire plan of campaign, entered upon with such con- *The battle of Mycale.*

I

fidence and prepared for on such a Homeric scale, was wrecked, before the vast military forces gathered for the invasion had suffered a single defeat or had even met with serious check,—for the fight of Thermopylæ was not of real strategical significance. Xerxes made his way back to Asia Minor, leaving Pausanias to continue the struggle in Greece as best he could. But what became of the remains of the Persian fleet? It retired to the island of Samos, still a formidable armament. There the Phœnician contingent departed for the Syrian coast. Weakened by its departure and fearing destruction by the Greek navy, which was roaming the Ægean, should they give the enemy an opportunity of fighting afloat, the Persian sailor chiefs crossed over to the Asiatic coast where a large army was assembled, hauled their ships up high and dry on shore, and built up a fortress round them.

But the Greeks had learnt the virtues of sea-power on the day of Salamis, they were resolved that no other Persian king should follow in the footsteps of Xerxes and Darius, and they determined that the hostile flotilla which had shunned encounter on the waters should be attacked on dry land. Disembarking in the vicinity of Mycale, where the hostile host was drawn up on guard over its beached flotilla, they marched boldly against the enemy, and after a desperate combat utterly defeated him. They burnt the ships, and they thus put a final end to that formidable navy which had enabled the barbaric princes of the East to violate the soil of Attica, and which had nearly converted the free republics of Hellas into dependencies of an Asiatic empire. The crude plan of dragging the inferior fleet on to the shore proved no more effective security when there was a possibility of land attack, than the retirement into a fortified harbour proved in the case of Wei-hai-wei and Port Arthur. And the history of maritime war provides abundant instances all pointing to the conclusion that a beaten or inferior navy is best dealt with by operations on land, if these be practicable.

The seizure of the Dutch fleet in the Texel by Pichegru in 1793 with cavalry and horse artillery dashing across the frozen Zuyder Zee, must be regarded as a *tour de force* rather than as a legitimate exposition of the art of war. The capture by the Russians in 1808 of part of the Swedish galley fleet at Sveaborg, and the burning of the remainder by the Swedes themselves at Abo, were due to the invaders of Finland selecting the season when the Gulf was frozen over for their advance: such conditions are no doubt abnormal, but the upshot was that Swedish naval power was very gravely damaged by military action long before Admiral Saumarez arrived to support the Scandinavian kingdom with a powerful British squadron. The sinking of the Russian fleet in Sebastopol was not wholly due to fear of military force,—Prince Mentschikof's orders that the ships were to be scuttled was no doubt prompted in the first place by the dread lest the allied fleet might actually try to force its way into the harbour past the formidable batteries; but the Tsar's generalissimo in the Crimea also realised that the approach of the French and British armies menaced his ships with total destruction, for the place was at the time practically without land defences. In all these cases the circumstances have been unusual. But the annals of past warfare furnish the searcher with abundant instances of fighting-forces afloat going down before the display of fighting force on shore when there has been nothing abnormal in the strategical situation. And these are at once so interesting and so instructive that a selection from them will be given,—the cases where the capture or destruction of war-vessels was a mere minor incident in an operation being distinguished from those where their capture or destruction was the main object for which the operation was undertaken.

Pichegru on the Texel, Sveaborg, Abo, and Sebastopol.

132 ATTACK ON FLEETS FROM THE LAND.

Land operations alone can seldom dispose of a hostile fleet.

It is obvious that land operations alone can seldom inflict serious injury upon fighting-ships, for they will put to sea if there is no fleet outside to stop them. Cases have, it is true, occurred where vessels seriously injured in an action or by bad weather have fallen as prizes to troops on shore without naval assistance. And supposing a naval station to be successfully attacked from the land side, ships in course of construction would naturally fall into the hands of the victors. But as a general rule a triumph of this nature is the result of co-operation between forces ashore and forces afloat, each service bearing its share in the fighting to be accomplished and in the credit to be won.

Disadvantage under which ships lying in port suffer if artillery on shore can be brought to bear against them.

Ships have always been placed at a great disadvantage when lying in port if guns are brought up to bombard them from the shore. Even in the present day battleships at anchor must suffer severely from high-angle fire by artillery far less powerful than their own ordnance. This fact has been brought into great prominence by the successful shelling of the Russian battleships and cruisers in Port Arthur; but there is nothing new in it. Guns have always played a part in land operations for several centuries, and in most cases where such operations have led to the capture or destruction of hostile fighting-ships, artillery has exercised a special influence over the fate of the doomed vessels. The following examples bring this point out especially, and are deserving of attention.

Examples. Messina.

In 1719 Messina was held by a Spanish army. In its harbour were lying some Spanish ships, the remnants of a fleet which had been defeated the previous year off Cape Passaro by Admiral Byng.* The place was being besieged by an Austrian and Sardinian army, and it was blockaded

---

* Father of the unfortunate admiral who in 1756 "fell a martyr to political persecution at a time when bravery and loyalty were insufficient securities for the life and honour of a naval officer."[4]

by Byng's fleet. When the crisis came, and when the portents all pointed to the speedy fall of the stronghold, Byng insisted upon a battery being erected for the special purpose of bearing upon and destroying the ships. This demand was complied with, and the result fully justified expectations. The British admiral feared that his allies might consent to a capitulation of the fortress which would admit of the ships receiving safe-conduct to Spain; and with a proper regard to sea-power he took steps to prevent such a contingency. The objective of the Austrians was the expulsion of the Spaniards from Sicily; the objective of the British was the curbing of Spanish naval power.

In 1788 the Russian general Potemkin was preparing to besiege the Turkish fortress of Ochakof at the mouth of the Dnieper,—the Ottoman Empire included the northern shores of the Black Sea in those days. But the Russian battering-train had not arrived, so Potemkin employed his time in bombarding a Turkish fleet which was lying under the guns of the coast batteries of the stronghold. The result was that the flotilla of the enemy was completely destroyed. Ochakof itself, however, held out for many months, and the stronghold only succumbed at last to a desperate assault, delivered at the moment when a terrific explosion of the main magazine had thrown the garrison into panic and confusion.

In 1814 General Graham (Lord Lynedoch) was sent with an expeditionary force to the Scheldt to co-operate with the Dutch and with a Prussian army. In the course of the operations, which were not crowned with much success, an attempt was made to destroy by bombardment a French fleet lying in the basin of Antwerp. No great injury was inflicted on the ships, only two being disabled, but all of them suffered a good deal in their spars: the failure was, however, largely due to the wise precaution taken by the French to cover their decks with timber and turf. Most

134 ATTACK ON FLEETS FROM THE LAND.

of the Dutch mortars, moreover, gave out after firing a few rounds.

Wei-hai-wei. When the Japanese in 1895 captured part of the fortress of Wei-hai-wei from the land side, they succeeded in turning some of the guns of the captured batteries upon the Chinese fleet. This was in consequence obliged to move to a more exposed anchorage, where the Japanese torpedo-boats were able to act against it with far-reaching effect.

Examples of ships being captured incidentally, as result of successful attack on a maritime fortress. It often happens that a land attack directed especially against a maritime fortress or naval base with the object of wresting the place from the enemy, leads incidentally to the capture of ships of war which have taken refuge in the harbour. Thus Mauritius was assailed by General Abercromby* and Admiral Bertie in 1810, with the especial object of depriving the French of a base for their privateers which were harrying our trade; but some ships of war were taken when Port Louis capitulated. A stroke of this kind may be merely subsidiary to another enterprise. The land operations may not have been undertaken for the purpose of injuring hostile floating force. But it is none the less the case that a more or less serious blow has been dealt at shipping of the enemy, and dealt by fighting-forces ashore. And therefore the following examples of the capture or destruction of ships of war in fleets, in consequence of land operations undertaken mainly with other objects in view, are deserving of note.

Tunis, 1535. In 1535 that restless, public-spirited, and powerful potentate, the Emperor Charles V., undertook an expedition on a great scale to the shores of Tunis to drive out Barbarossa and his dreaded corsairs. A landing was effected near Goletta, the fortress which guarded the entrance of the

---

* Sir John, son of Sir Ralph Abercromby. He enjoyed the singular experience of being captured with his staff by a French privateer on his way from Ceylon to the Cape to take command of the expedition. He was recaptured, however, by H.M.S. *Boadicea*.[5]

great lagoon of Tunis, and after severe fighting the place was carried by storm. As a result of its fall the whole of the pirate flotilla in harbour, amounting to over one hundred galleys, was captured. The Emperor afterwards prosecuted a vigorous and successful campaign in the interior, and for the time overthrew the power of Barbarossa in that region.

When the great French stronghold and naval base of Louisbourg was taken in 1758 by General Amherst's army in co-operation with Boscawen's fleet, six ships-of-the-line and six frigates were either captured or destroyed in the harbour. It is interesting in this connection to find Wolfe writing: "In another circumstance, too, we may be reckoned unlucky. The squadron of men-of-war under De Chafferault failed to put into the harbour of Louisbourg, where inevitably they would have shared the fate of those that did, which must have given an irretrievable blow to the marine of France, and delivered Quebec into our hands, if we chose to go up and demand it." *Louisbourg.*

When Havana was taken in 1762 by Albemarle, nine sail-of-the-line were captured, and five others were destroyed. In addition to the enormous prize in treasure and merchandise taken in the city, and to the deadly blow delivered against Spain in wresting out of her grasp the focus and trading centre of the Pearl of the Antilles, the fall of Havana was equivalent to a great British naval victory at sea. *Havana.*

In 1809 a British military force from Sicily was transported to the vicinity of Naples with the view of creating a diversion to draw down French forces from the north. The operations were not of a very brilliant or effective kind on shore. But incidentally the islands of Ischia and Procida were taken, with their batteries. In consequence of this forty Neapolitan gunboats, which had contemplated passing through the narrow channel between the islands and the mainland, were stopped, and, their line of retreat being *Procida, 1809.*

closed to them inshore, they were captured by the British squadron which escorted the expeditionary force.

<small>End of the Merrimac.</small>
For two months after its famous duel with the *Monitor*, the *Merrimac* lay off Norfolk navy yard, which was in Confederate hands, and occasionally steamed out and menaced the Federal fleet in Hampton Roads. But then a force of Union troops marching across country arrived in the vicinity. The fall of Norfolk being certain, the question arose what was to be done with the *Merrimac*. Owing to her draught of water it was impracticable to take the ironclad up the James River, where she would have been safe; egress to the open sea was barred by Federal ships of war; so she was burnt by her commander to prevent her falling into the enemy's hands.

<small>Examples of co-operation of land forces with naval forces attacking shipping.</small>
Many examples could be cited of the co-operation of forces on land affording great assistance to a fleet in operations against hostile shipping. Thus when Admiral Rooke in 1702 attacked the West India galleons in Vigo harbour under protection of a French squadron, his success was in no small measure due to 2500 soldiers under Ormonde, who landed and who carried a fort covering the boom by assault. But history provides us with so many instances of land operations on a great scale having been undertaken for the express and avowed purpose of capturing or destroying hostile ships of war, and these illustrate so forcibly the dependence of a navy upon military assistance to secure for it definite and assured command of the sea under certain conditions, that such cases as Vigo need not be considered at length. General Shafter's army was despatched against Santiago, not because the place was of itself of prime importance, but because Cervera's squadron was there and could not be attacked by the American fleet except at considerable risk, or after successful countermining operations. The Japanese would probably have attacked Port Arthur in 1904 even had there been no Russian fleet there: the

fortress offered an obvious objective quite apart from the sentiment connected with it. But the force detailed to operate in the promontory of Kwang Tung would have been smaller; in all probability the stronghold would have been merely invested, and it would have been reduced slowly and deliberately by starvation; and the interest of the whole world would not have been centred upon siege operations for which there is scarcely a parallel, and on the devotion of an army making its first essay in war against a great Power, for which there is no precedent.

But before recording some especially remarkable instances of land forces being put in motion for the express purpose of dealing with fleets and ships of war when secure, or virtually secure, from naval attack, it will not be out of place to quote a pregnant and illuminating passage from an Admiralty letter written in 1813. This was written after twenty years of almost uninterrupted maritime conflict,—of a conflict in the course of which Nelson had risen out of comparative obscurity to a position which no sailor has attained before or since. It was written at a time when Hood was yet living, and when St Vincent was still looked up to as the greatest naval personality in the country. It was written at a time when Collingwood had but recently succumbed to overwork on active service; at a time when Pellew and Hardy were flying their flags and carrying on the work of controlling the sea in face of opposition which was insidious rather than direct; at a time when, if ever, the art of naval warfare was adequately appreciated and applied by the British navy. The letter has been referred to already in an earlier chapter in connection with another subject. Lord Melville, in explaining to Wellington in his despatch of the 28th July the difficulties with which the Admiralty was beset, wrote: "The employment of a body of troops to destroy the shipping in some of the enemy's ports in France or America would at once liberate a large

A remarkable Admiralty letter to Wellington.

portion of our naval force and diminish greatly the public expenditure, but would *you* think we were acting wisely in making these diversions, unless we could secure at the same time, without the possibility of failure (which I apprehend cannot be done), the means of maintaining to the fullest extent our military superiority in the Peninsula." The First Lord here honestly and straightforwardly admitted to the great soldier the limitations placed on naval mobile force. There were hostile "fleets in being" which could not be dealt with by pressure afloat. Pressure was required on shore, and the means of applying that pressure were lacking because there were not sufficient troops to carry out the task.

<small>Camperdown and the Helder Expedition.</small> How such pressure can be applied on shore had been demonstrated in strange and dramatic fashion fifteen years before. We are not accustomed to look back upon the operations of the Duke of York's army in Holland in 1799 with marked complacency; on the contrary, they have been held up to a certain amount of ridicule for a hundred years. They were adorned by no Minden or Dettingen or Malplaquet. Their conduct, except at the outset when Abercromby was at the helm, was not signalised by refreshing vigour or by conspicuous enterprise, and they terminated in a somewhat ignominious withdrawal by agreement with the enemy. But they were far from being without effect.

Two years before, in 1797, a great British victory had been gained over a Dutch fleet off these coasts. Tactically it was more decisive than St Vincent or the memorable sea-fight of the 1st of June. In its completeness it was only to be eclipsed by Trafalgar and the Nile. After Camperdown, Admiral Duncan returned to England with eleven ships of war as prizes, carrying 668 guns.

But when the expeditionary force in 1799 secured the Helder, several Dutch line-of-battle ships and frigates lying

THE HELDER AND COPENHAGEN. 139

there surrendered at once. And, in consequence of the passage into the Zuyder Zee being secured, Admiral Mitchell was enabled to pass in and to summon the rest of the Dutch fleet to surrender, which it promptly did. This was indeed one of the objects for which the expedition had been undertaken, an object which naval force unaided could not possibly have attained. Although the seamen of Holland had borne themselves as gallantly as ever at Camperdown, their sympathies were not with France,—it was hardly to be expected that Pichegru's dramatic seizure of the fleet a few years before would be forgiven. Officers and crews were disaffected when Mitchell bore down upon them, and they refused to fight. The British navy gained no glory from the affair, but their prizes amounted to twenty-five vessels with 1190 guns—about double what was taken by Duncan at Camperdown. "The greatest stroke that has perhaps been struck in this war has been accomplished in a few hours, and with trifling loss," wrote Moore exultingly from Holland.

A very few years after the affair of the Helder another striking example of the employment of land forces to capture a fleet occurred in northern Europe. Into the peculiar political conditions which gave rise to the expedition to Copenhagen in 1807 it is needless to enter. The object of the enterprise was to capture the Danish fleet. In 1800 Nelson had by brilliant daring and skill achieved practically the same object with ships alone.[6] But the risk of that memorable undertaking had been great, and the British Government on the second occasion wisely resolved to bring military force into play, so as to help the fleet in the task: 27,000 men were landed, the city was invested and bombarded, and Denmark was compelled to surrender her navy by capitulation.

Copenhagen, 1807, an example of land operations being undertaken for the purpose of capturing a fleet.

The following further illustrations of the employment of land forces on enterprises undertaken for the special

Other examples.

140 ATTACK ON FLEETS FROM THE LAND.

purpose of operating against hostile ships of war which cannot be satisfactorily dealt with from the side of the sea, are worthy of note.

<small>Ferrol, 1800.</small> It had been ascertained in England in 1800 that there were six Spanish ships-of-the-line lying in Ferrol, waiting to put to sea. A conjunct military and naval expedition under General Pulteney and Admiral Warren was therefore fitted out, which was despatched to Galicia to deal with the squadron before it should emerge. After an isolated fort had been silenced by the ships, the army was landed and gained some trifling successes. But Pulteney came to the conclusion that the fortress was too strong to be attacked, and he thereupon re-embarked the troops. Many of the naval officers present considered a land attack practicable; Moore, on the other hand, who saw the place in 1804, did not; but there can be no question that the fall of the fortress would have meant the capture or destruction of the Spanish squadron. It is interesting to note that two of the six vessels which it was the object of the expedition to put out of action, fought five years afterwards at Trafalgar.

<small>The last echo of Trafalgar.</small> The "last echo" of that great fight, as Captain Mahan expresses it, was heard in 1808. Seven ships of Villeneuve's ill-fated fleet were still lying in Cadiz, where they had sought and found refuge after the terrible October day three years before. A change had come over the political situation. The somewhat half-hearted support afforded by Spain to Napoleon in his struggle against British sea-power had been replaced by open enmity on the part of a people whose patriotism would not brook the humiliation which the Emperor wished to impose upon their country, in reducing it to the level of a dependency of France with a Buonaparte for sovereign. Admiral Rosily, who commanded this remnant of the once formidable French fleet, hearing of the uprising of Spain against the usurper, removed his vessels out of range of

the batteries of Cadiz,—to put to sea was out of the question, as Collingwood and Cotton were on the watch outside. General Dalrymple now proposed to send a military force from Gibraltar to capture Rosily's doomed vessels. But the Spanish chiefs preferred to perform the task unaided; they erected special batteries to bear upon the French fleet at its new anchorage, and after some show of resistance it surrendered unconditionally.

The numerous examples cited in this chapter show clearly how dependent upon land operations a navy often is to set a seal upon the successes which it has gained at sea. The victorious fleet hunting the vanquished foe across the waters is brought up short by the shore batteries of some hostile stronghold into which the quarry flies for safety. Napoleon after the downfall of the sea-power of France in Trafalgar Bay abandoned all hope of contesting maritime supremacy in the open sea with the island kingdom which he had hoped to invade and to crush, as he had crushed Austria on the Danube and the Po, and as he was to crush Austria and Prussia in the immediate future. But the dockyards of Toulon and Brest were not idle all this time. Antwerp was absorbed, and was created a first-class naval station. There were during the later years of the war a goodly number of formidable fighting-ships lying in French ports, the watching of which strained even the mighty maritime resources of the British Empire.[7] It was these ships, secure in their well-defended harbours, which aroused the anxiety of the naval authorities in Whitehall,—an anxiety which was voiced in Lord Melville's despatch quoted on pp. 137, 138. They could not be got at except by land operations, and there were no troops available to put land operations in force once the Peninsular War was in full swing. But the Walcheren Expedition, undertaken before the bulk of the country's military strength was absorbed in Spain and Portugal,

Position after Trafalgar.

was directed against this latent floating force, and its story has therefore an interest all its own.

The Walcheren Expedition. The Walcheren Expedition has often been quoted as an example of military ineptitude, and it was, up to 1899, distinguished as being the occasion of the despatch of the largest army that had ever at one time quitted British shores for a campaign abroad. The force which proceeded to the Scheldt consisted of nearly 40,000 men. Its preparation and equipment cost a vast sum of money. The hopes of the country were centred upon it.

The objective of this great armament was the destruction of the formidable fleet which Napoleon was creating at Antwerp and Flushing, to burn the elaborate naval establishments constructed there, and to put an end to a serious maritime danger threatening the sea-power of this country. There were in the Scheldt nineteen French vessels in commission or building, and the precise purpose of the enterprise committed to Lord Chatham and Admiral Strachan was to capture these or to burn or to sink them, and to demolish the dockyards, building-slips, and arsenals which had grown up under the Emperor's directions. The ignominious failure of the undertaking can be attributed partly to lack of proper intelligence service, partly to the unfortunate season selected, and partly to the fact that the whole plan had been the talk of England and the Continent for some weeks before the expedition sailed. But the French were unprepared, and the master-mind controlling the military destinies of the Empire was engaged on the Danube in a critical campaign. The real cause of the disaster to the British army—for it practically amounted to a disaster—was the deplorable lack of energy and initiative displayed by its inexperienced and incapable leader. There seems to be no doubt whatever that had this great army been handled with skill, had it acted with promptitude, and had its plan of action been conceived on sound strategical lines, it would have captured the greater part of the enemy's fleet. French military writers freely admit this. Napoleon himself at St Helena expressed the same view in unmistakable terms. The fact that the enterprise was wholly unsuccessful—for the capture of Flushing and the damage done to the naval establishments there was an insignificant achievement in view of the scale of the expedition—does not make it the less interesting as an example of land operations directed against sea-power, and in the main against actual floating force.

There has not perhaps been a conflict in the history of war in which the question of sea-power has played a more predominant part than in the duel between Spain and the United States in 1898. The fate of the ill-protected American coast from Florida to Maine, of Cuba and of the remainder of the Spanish Antilles, of the Philippines, and of Spanish possessions which, as events turned out, only felt the strain of the struggle very indirectly, was wrapped up in the rival navies. And yet we find Admiral Sampson telegraphing from before Santiago on the 7th June: "If 10,000 men were here, city and fleet would be ours within forty-eight hours. Every consideration demands immediate army movement." On the 31st May General Shafter had been ordered to proceed to Santiago with his force to act so as "to capture or destroy the garrison there, and cover the navy as it sends its men in small boats to remove torpedoes, or, with the aid of the navy, capture or destroy the Spanish fleet now reported to be in Santiago harbour"; but the force had not then been ready to start. The struggle was essentially a question of sea-power. But land operations were none the less found necessary to establish maritime command for the United States, and they affected that object in singularly dramatic fashion when Admiral Cervera was forced out of his asylum into the arms of the American fleet.

The case Santiago.

The story of Newport in 1780, as illustrating the interdependence between land- and sea-power.

The subject of the interdependence of fleets and forces on land is illustrated vividly by one especially interesting phase of the war in North America which lasted from 1777 to 1783, and which hinged throughout to so remarkable an extent upon the question of command of the sea. No fleet was captured by an army as at the Helder or in Port Arthur. But the record of what occurred proves how close a connection often arises in war between military and naval operations, and a short account of the events will form a fitting epilogue of this chapter.

During 1778 and 1779 the French navy, upon which Washington so justly founded his hopes of ultimate success in the great struggle against the land- and sea-forces of Great Britain, proved a sore disappointment to the American colonists. D'Estaing came and went, and came again, and again left; and while this was going on, the British forces gradually regained the position of predominance which they had lost for the time when Burgoyne was compelled to surrender at Saratoga.

But on the 12th July 1780 there arrived in the splendid harbour of Newport a French armament of seven sail of the line under the Chevalier de Ternay, escorting five thousand troops under Rochambeau, and new hope was infused into the despondent ranks of the patriot forces. At the moment De Ternay was superior to Admiral Arbuthnot, the British naval commander in these waters. But only three days later Admiral Graves arrived at New York with reinforcements sufficient to give Arbuthnot a decided numerical advantage, and to enable him to assume a blockade of observation over Newport.

General Clinton, commanding the British army at New York, was anxious to attack Rochambeau at once, if transports could be prepared to convey a force to the vicinity of Newport. But there was a serious want of harmony between Arbuthnot and himself. Sufficient transports were not made available. Precious hours were allowed to slip by. And the French commander soon rendered his position so secure that an attack on him by land promised little prospect of success, and that the British general abandoned all idea of falling upon the newly arrived armament before it was in a position to resist. Washington was anxious that Rochambeau should co-operate with the colonial forces in land operations against Clinton about New York; but solicitude for the safety of De Ternay's fleet, cooped up as it was in Newport harbour, held the French general fast. And so some weeks passed by, neither side feeling in a position to act offensively.

Then in September Rodney arrived with some ships from the West Indies, and the British naval superiority over De Ternay became more marked than ever, the combined forces of Rodney and Arbuthnot being sufficient to annihilate his seven ships had he ventured to sea. A Blake or a Cochrane would have attacked the French fleet in the harbour in spite of the batteries, which, if they were not perhaps very formidable, at least called for respect. But Rodney, an admirable tactician and a great admiral, was by disposition cautious. His health had suffered in the West Indies, and, although he was yet to see the day when the commander-in-chief of a mighty hostile fleet was to occupy one of the cabins of his flagship as a prisoner of war, he was already an old man. He consulted with Clinton, who was not now in a position to spare so large a force for purposes of co-operation as he had been when the French first arrived two months before. Clinton wrote: "As to land operations against the French force at Rhode Island, I must give it as my opinion to you, sir, as I did to Admiral Arbuthnot, that as long as there was an appearance of a *coup de main*, before the enemy was entrenched or reinforced, I thought an attempt practicable, and with 6000 men I should have made it; but when I found the enemy had at least fourteen days to prepare against it, I naturally gave up all hopes of a *coup de main.*" So De Ternay was allowed to remain with his "fleet in being" in Newport. Rodney departed. A large portion of Rochambeau's force was gradually withdrawn to co-operate with Washington. And when some months later the Comte de Grasse, summoned by Washington and Rochambeau from the West Indies, arrived on the coast of North America, the squadron which had lain so long in Newport harbour slipped out, joined the main French fleet, and participated in the triumph of the allies at Yorktown.

Thus Rochambeau, with the land force which had arrived under convoy of De Ternay's squadron, improvised what was virtually a stronghold and haven of refuge for that squadron when it was in danger. But Newport only served as a secure shelter for the French fleet because, for a variety of causes, the British did not undertake land operations against the place. On the voyage across the Atlantic De Ternay's ships-of-the-line had safeguarded Rochambeau's troops; but when the armada reached Rhode Island their *rôles* were reversed, and the army became guard and escort to the fleet. This caused inconvenience and disappointment to the hard-pressed colonists, because they had counted on active assistance of French soldiery against Clinton's veteran forces. The security of De Ternay's squadron was, however, rightly held to outweigh all other considerations, for the ultimate fate of the revolted colonies depended upon the question of maritime command; but for the moment the question of maritime command depended upon military dispositions.

Conclusion. Writers on naval subjects sometimes hardly seem to realise the extent to which fleets are obliged to lean upon land forces, and how subservient during the actual progress of a campaign the conditions of sea-power must under certain conditions be to operations on shore. If this feature of war be not taken into account, false strategical theories may be arrived at, and a dangerous naval policy may be adopted at a critical time. That the conception of the Walcheren Expedition was in accordance with sound principles, however much its execution may have failed, is illustrated by the action of the Russians in sinking their fleet in Port Arthur harbour when land attack made the place untenable. The last echo of Trafalgar, heard when the guns of the Spanish patriot army opened on Rosily's fleet at their anchorage in the port of Cadiz, has its counterpart in the catastrophe to the Chinese naval forces after Japanese military resources were brought into play at Wei-hai-wei. The influence of land operations over the question of acquisition and maintenance of maritime command may easily be exaggerated, but it cannot safely be ignored.

CHAPTER VIII.

THE QUESTION OF EMPLOYING NAVAL PERSONNEL ASHORE AND IN LAND OPERATIONS GENERALLY.

Advantages of employing sailors for amphibious operations in some respects.

IN previous chapters it has been shown that defended naval stations are a necessary adjunct to sea-power, that land operations for the purpose of depriving the maritime forces of the enemy of the bases on which they depend are often indispensable, and that it at times becomes necessary and desirable to act from the land side against the fleets and shipping of the enemy which have taken refuge in port. The question therefore arises whether the *personnel* charged with the manning of fixed defences, and the *personnel* detailed to operate ashore against the bases or floating force of the antagonist, should be naval or should be military.

There are certain obvious advantages in employing sailors on amphibious enterprises. For landing from boats in broken water, seamen are incomparably superior to soldiers. In any disembarkation or embarkation of a fighting-force, it is essential that the management should be in the hands of men accustomed to the sea. And it stands to reason that, supposing the entire force be made up of naval *personnel*, the arrival and departure of the expedition will work more smoothly than when two separate and distinct services are acting in co-operation, no matter how thorough may be the concord between them. Naval brigades, British and foreign, have frequently performed most admirable service ashore, and our own history provides almost innumerable examples of this. Adaptability to circumstances is a characteristic of those who go down to the sea in ships and whose dwelling is in the great waters, all the world over; and the soldier who has enjoyed the privilege of serving alongside a contingent of the Royal Navy in military operations, cannot fail to appreciate the fertility of resource and ingenuity in surmounting obstacles which is invariably displayed alike by the bluejacket and by his highly trained superiors.

It is worthy of note, however, that in the old days this was not so much the case, although in the Penn-Venables operations in the West Indies, under the Cromwell *régime*, the sailors on shore undoubtedly behaved far better than the undisciplined military rabble with which they were associated. Jack did not always shine in land fighting two centuries ago, as appears from a quaint report by Admiral Montague, a soldier who was partnered by Cromwell with Blake in 1656, to see what could be done against the coasts of Spain. "We had then some debate of Gibraltar," he writes, "and there appeared no great mind to it in regard of hardness and want of land men formed, and officers and numbers of men too, all of which are real obstacles as you may judge upon the description of the place and the number and quality of our men; and, to say the truth, the seamen are not for land service unless it be for a sudden plunder. They are valiant, but not to be ruled and kept in any government ashore. Nor have your sea officers much stomach to fight ashore." This was just before Blake with this same *personnel* vanquished the Barbary corsairs at Porto Farina, and made the power of England felt in the Mediterranean as it had not been felt since the time of the Crusades. Whatever doubts there may have been as to the capabilities of the naval *personnel* of that time when on land—and Montague as a soldier may have been prejudiced, —the crews who fought under the flag of Blake claim our warmest admiration as daring and efficient seamen when on board ship.

A few years later we find Rooke capturing Gibraltar with his ships' crews, while the accompanying military force was yet some miles away; and during the eighteenth century the sailors and marines of the British fleet over and over again performed most admirable service on shore. Although no doubt in some measure due to the development of discipline and to the growth of *esprit de corps*, this change from the conditions of an earlier era may perhaps also be attributed to another cause. It is not impossible that association with the military at Cadiz, Toulon, Minorca, and elsewhere, served as a useful training during that transition period between the era of the Dutch wars and the days of "the great Lord Hawke," during those years when the question still remained nnanswered whether this country was, or was not, to be mistress of the seas.

The general question of the employment of naval *personnel* on shore, from the point of view of expediency, can best be considered under two separate headings. In the first place, there is that subject of so much controversy,—the question whether naval stations should or should not be controlled and garrisoned by sailors, and this deserves to be discussed on its merits. Then, in the second place, there is the important point of offensive operations; and it is desirable to deal shortly with the arguments for and against the trusting to maritime forces alone such operations as the British attack on Cartagena in the Spanish Main in 1740, or as Napoleon's attack on Malta in 1798, or as the allied enterprise against the great Russian naval station of Sebastopol known as the Crimean War.

Question of the personnel for defence of naval sta- There is a great deal to be said for the theory that naval stations and naval bases should be entirely in the hands of the navy. The arguments in favour of the arrangement

SAILORS IN FIXED DEFENCES.   151

at first sight seem to be very strong. When coast defences in the shape of batteries mounting powerful ordnance, of submarine mines, of search-lights, and of quick-firing guns to repel torpedo-boat attacks, are under control of soldiers, there is always risk of misunderstandings with the navy. Difficulties arise as to signalling, and as to the line of demarcation between military and naval responsibility; and in time of war the friendly vessel may conceivably be mistaken for a foe. This question should not, moreover, be regarded from the naval point of view alone. Any duties of a sedentary character are prejudicial to the general efficiency of an army. Responsibility for manning the fixed defences required for the maintenance of sea-power is a veritable millstone round the neck of military authorities charged with the duty of organising and maintaining an active and efficient army. From the soldier's point of view everything pertaining to a navy, or subservient to a navy, should be in naval charge.   *tions being drawn from the sea-service. Arguments in favour of the arrangement.*

But there is another side to the picture. The sailor's true place is on the sea. Was the superiority established by the British navy over the navy of France and the navy of Spain in that long succession of struggles which lasted from the days of Drake to the peace of 1814, due to better ships, to better armament, to better dockyards? Was it not rather attributable to the crews who manned the fleets and to the maritime aspirations and inclinations of the British nation? It was the personal factor which decided the issue, it was the seamanship of the commanders and the nautical experience of the complements which gave them victory.[1] French ships were better designed and better found; Spanish ships were, as mere fighting-machines, to the full as powerful. But the place for a navy is out on the great waters, its drill-ground is the sea. Those capacious harbours of Toulon and Cadiz and Brest served not merely as havens of refuge to the maritime forces of France and   *Disadvantages of the plan.*

Spain when the enemy was on the prowl or when the tempests blew. They served also as the permanent abiding place of the French and Spanish fleets. And so when the day of battle came one side was in its element, the other side was not.

Garrison duty in a maritime stronghold is bad training for military troops for war, but it is still worse training for the *personnel* of a navy. To man the defences of naval stations, either the land-service or the sea-service must be sacrificed. But the sea-service suffers most; and if this fact be thrown into the scale it outweighs any advantages which may arise from that somewhat more efficient co-operation of the shore defences with the fleet, which may be expected when the batteries and other forms of fixed defence are in naval hands. And it must be remembered that naval stations have generally to be defended by land as well as by sea. It has been made clear in earlier chapters that when a maritime stronghold is assailed, the attack generally falls upon the rear of the fortress and not upon its sea front. An effective land defence involves almost of necessity the use of mounted troops. The garrison of a great place of arms like Portsmouth, or Spezia, or Port Arthur, in time of war exceeds in strength the *personnel* of a formidable fleet. Nations so situated that naval efficiency is a consideration altogether secondary to that of military efficiency, may be justified in binding their marines and seamen to the shore, and in turning their commodores into brigadiers. It is an arrangement inapplicable to the conditions of the British Empire.

Landing of sailors in defence of naval bases on emergency. It is true that on many occasions naval *personnel* has been landed to aid in holding maritime fortresses. In 1680, just before Tangier was taken over, that city was suddenly attacked in great force by the tumultuary forces of the Moorish Sultan; but the British admiral, Herbert,* who

---
* Afterwards the Lord Torrington of Beachy Head.

happened to be in the roads with his fleet, landed a force of sailors who beat off the assailants and saved the place. French seamen contributed greatly to bring about the protracted defence offered by Louisbourg in 1758: their ships had been sunk in the harbour mouth, and they were thus available to man the entrenchments on the land side of the fortress. One of Cochrane's most brilliant exploits was his maintenance with a handful of his sailors of the castle at Rosas in 1807, when the greater part of the defences of the Spanish stronghold had been long since captured by the French besiegers. And the magnificent defence of Sebastopol was in no small measure due to the exertions of Admiral Kornilof and of the crews landed from his fleet, at a time when what was to grow up into a mighty stronghold under the eyes of the allied armies was, apart from its coast batteries, little better than an open town. In each of these cases naval *personnel* performed invaluable service on shore at a time of great emergency, and under circumstances when absence from the ships to which the *personnel* belonged was not injurious. And the same conditions prevailed at Acre in 1799.

A specially striking illustration of the services which sailors may render ashore in defence of a fortress is afforded by the action of Sir S. Smith when that historic stronghold was assailed by Napoleon. Before regular siege operations had been commenced, Smith's little squadron had performed a signal service in capturing the French siege train, somewhat injudiciously despatched by sea from Damietta. The sight of the friendly flag had kept the defenders in heart as the battlements crumbled and as the enemy crept nearer day by day. At the crisis, when Turkish reinforcements were actually within sight but becalmed in their transports, and when Napoleon was making his final desperate attempt to force his way through the breaches, the British commodore brought his sailors ashore to assist in holding the place, and their timely succour just turned the scale in favour of the hard-pressed garrison.

Such incidents exceptional.

But in all these cases the services of the naval *personnel* ashore have been lent merely temporarily, or else they have been called for to preserve their ships against the terrors of attack from military operations. When a fleet is endangered by the approach of the enemy on land, as the Spanish fleet was at Messina in 1817, or as the French fleet was at Louisbourg in 1758, or as the Russian fleet was at Port Arthur in 1904, there are obvious, and indeed imperative, reasons for bringing guns and crews from the vessels to help to keep the foe at a distance. That is quite a different question from permanently charging marines and sailors, whose proper place is afloat, with the manning of batteries on shore, whether these bear out to sea or bear inland. And although the following example presents a somewhat abnormal state of affairs, it is none the less interesting as showing what evils may sometimes arise when the hands are withdrawn from fighting-ships to serve in land defences, even when those land defences are in undoubted danger.

What occurred at Ipsara in 1824.

Ipsara is a small and sterile island lying out in the Ægean, the inhabitants of which have for generations been noted for their nautical skill and their piratical exploits. In the Greek War of Independence the Psariots from the very outset took the lead in the maritime struggle against the Ottoman navy. For this reason their island home became a very natural and proper objective for the fleets of the Sultan to operate against when an opportunity offered; and in 1824 a powerful squadron, convoying transports carrying some 14,000 troops, bore down upon it from the Hellespont, meaning mischief.

Canaris, the renowned Hellenic seaman leader, was off the island at the time, and there happened to be lying in the port a number of fighting-ships at anchor. He urged upon the Psariots the advisability of meeting the Turkish armada on the sea, and vied with his sailors in eagerness for the fray. But the magistrates and notables not only ignored this salutary counsel, but they also took a singularly unfortunate step. Fearing that the crews might put off from shore, and might possibly escape to sea and leave the island to its fate, they withdrew a large part of the *personnel* of their fighting flotilla from the ships to man the land defences, and they actually went to the extreme length of removing the rudders from the vessels to ensure that they would not quit the port. In spite of this senseless proceeding on the part of the authorities, the Greek ships, undermanned as they were and almost unmanageable for want of proper steering-gear, got out into the open water and made so desperate a fight of it with the far superior Ottoman fleet that there seems little doubt that, but for the ill-advised course adopted by the local executive on shore, the Turks would never have effected a landing at all, and would have been obliged to return, baffled of their prey. But the fatal diversion of the naval *personnel* from its true functions, coupled with the disastrous action taken as regards the rudders, brought it about that the flotilla was dispersed and that the Ottoman troops succeeded in getting ashore. The island was speedily captured, the whole of it was laid waste, and those of the inhabitants who were not put to the sword were carried off into slavery.

We have not, however, to consider this question of the employment of naval *personnel* on land only as one concerning the defence of bases and the garrisoning of strongholds on the sea. It has frequently occurred in wars of the past that marines and sailors have been utilised on shore in attacking fortresses. They have often been detailed for purely land operations. And to meet the case of descents on a small scale on an enemy's coasts when the force is early to re-embark again, there are undoubted advantages in employing landing-parties from a fleet in preference to a military

Employment of sailors in attack of coast fortresses, and in purely land operations.

force. It will generally prove a more convenient arrangement. The actual disembarkation will certainly be more rapidly and satisfactorily accomplished. And it may be assumed that in such cases fighting men on foot, supported possibly by light guns dragged by hand, will be able to effect all that is necessary.

<small>This generally only permissible on a small scale.</small>

But no sooner does the operation become a serious military undertaking than the employment of soldiers becomes in every way preferable. A large body of men cannot be disembarked from a fleet without prejudicing its fighting efficiency. For campaigns ashore on any extensive scale mounted troops and mobile artillery will almost always be required, and a properly organised transport and supply service are indispensable. And when the enterprise is of such a class as the attack on Toulon in 1707, or the operations directed against the French ships and naval establishments in the Scheldt in 1809, it becomes entirely beyond the available strength of any navy constituted on the generally accepted lines, to carry out the work. The army which took Port Arthur far exceeded in numbers the total establishments of the naval *personnel* of Japan. And there is also the question of tactical organisation and of training and leadership to be taken into account. The sailor, all the world over, is quick and adaptive. Naval officers with a natural talent for leading troops on shore, such as Lord Keith displayed at Charleston and Toulon, may be able to dispense with the prolonged experience in peace and war on land which makes the general. But the place for the seaman is on board ship, and his withdrawal from his proper sphere, except under special circumstances or for a short period of time, is to be deprecated inasmuch as it is a waste of power.

<small>Troubridge at Capua.</small>

Captain Troubridge's famous expedition to Capua, his unconventional methods of approaching a fortress, and his conspicuous success in what was a military undertaking pure and simple, adorn a page in the brightest annals of our navy.² But Bosquet's oft-quoted remark as to the Light Brigade charge might be applied to it—" C'est magnifique, mais ce n'est pas la guerre." While Troubridge and his gallant force were wrapt up in a land campaign, the fleet was denuded of *personnel* at a time when the strategical situation in the Mediterranean did not justify any weakening of floating force. Nelson would never have countenanced such an enterprise had not his judgment been warped by his infatuation for that political anachronism, the Kingdom of the Two Sicilies, which led him to disobey Lord Keith's orders that he was to send all ships he could spare to Minorca.

To the weighty rebuke sent to the great admiral for flouting his superior the Lords of the Admiralty added: "Although in operations on the sea-coast it may frequently be highly expedient to land a part of the seamen of the squadron to co-operate with and to assist the army, when the situation will admit of their being immediately re-embarked if the squadron should be called away to act elsewhere, or if information should be received of the approach of an enemy's fleet, yet their Lordships by no means approve of the seamen being landed to form a part of an army to be employed in operations at a distance from the coast where, if they should have the misfortune to be defeated, they might be prevented from returning to the ships, and the squadron be thereby rendered so defective as to be no longer capable of performing the services required of it; and I have their Lordships' commands to signify their directions to your Lordship not to employ the seamen in like manner in future." This puts the case against the employment of naval *personnel* on purely military enterprises concisely and with unanswerable force.

The Admiralty rebuke of Nelson.

A few years later, after Abercromby's landing at Aboukir, Keith sent so many of his sailors ashore to aid the military

No objection to landing

158   NAVAL PERSONNEL ASHORE.

sailors if they can be spared from their proper duties.

in their difficult advance on Alexandria that his fleet was almost crippled for want of men. Fortunately, however, a Turkish squadron arrived on the Egyptian coast just at the time when the insufficiency of *personnel* on board the British warships was making itself seriously felt. When there is no question of serious operations at sea there is, of course, no objection to withdrawing part of the *personnel* of a fleet even for operations far inland: examples of this are afforded by the famous achievements of Peel in the Mutiny and by the naval brigades which served in the late South African war. And the French were fully justified in 1870 in depleting their fleet, which was practically without occupation owing to the circumstances of the conflict, so as to reinforce their overmatched army striving vainly to stem the tide of invasion in their eastern provinces. But the correct policy, as long as maritime preponderance is in any way in dispute, appears to be to leave offensive operations on land to the military, and only to employ seamen ashore in special emergencies.

Recognition by Rodney and Nelson of need for military force, for enterprises against maritime strongholds.

And most great sailors have fully realised this, and have acted on this principle. When Rodney in 1780 was returning to the West Indies from the North American coast he wrote: " In vain have I solicited for a body of troops to sail with me and act in the West Indies; fully convinced as I am that if that could be obtained, that a port might be taken in Martinique and rendered tenable, which would deprive the French fleet of the power of sheltering themselves in the Bay of Fort Royal, and enable H.M. fleet to anchor with safety in the said bay." Nelson, when concocting his plan to attack Santa Cruz, was keenly desirous of securing the assistance of 3000 men under General De Burgh, who were on their way from Elba to Lisbon. It was on this occasion that, disappointed in his hopes of military assistance, he gave vent to that oft-quoted complaint, " Soldiers have not the same boldness in undertaking a political measure that we have: we look to the benefit of our country, and risk our own fame (not life merely) every day to serve her; a soldier obeys his orders and no more." Mahan provides us with a striking picture of Nelson's anxiety to get troops to Malta in 1799, when the siege of Valetta was proceeding but slowly and the fate of the island seemed to be hanging in the balance.

Against the view that a military force is the necessary complement to sea-power, and that the employment of naval *personnel* on shore is, except under abnormal circumstances or in cases of emergency, a misapplication of force, is, however, to be set the opinion of one of the greatest of admirals, Lord St Vincent. And his attitude in this matter is the more remarkable when we remember the story of his career, when we recall that as commander of the sloop *Porcupine* he spent hours in close communion with Wolfe on the afternoon before that great soldier went out to fight his last fight, when we bear in mind his cordial relations with the military in the West Indies in the early part of the Revolutionary War, which brought no small credit to the British flag in that quarter, and when we take into consideration that in the case of Duckworth's despatch to Minorca in 1798, already quoted on page 14, he showed such generous confidence in the commander of the military expedition. In 1797 St Vincent submitted a memorandum to the Admiralty suggesting steps to be taken in view of a prolongation of the war. He admitted in this paper that artillery stood apart, but he added, "I hope to see the day when there is not another foot soldier" (other than marines) "in the Kingdom, in Ireland, in the Colonies." His theory was that any work which infantry might be called upon to perform on shore would be as well carried out by marines, and that marines formed a reserve of *personnel* for the sea-service which infantry did not. But St Vincent came

Lord St Vincent's remarkable views.

prominently to the front at a time when British enterprises on land were generally entirely subsidiary to naval operations, and when any bodies of troops set on shore to fight rarely mustered more than a few hundred men. The memorandum was written from off Cadiz before the Egyptian campaign; it was composed some weeks before an army was despatched to the Helder to capture the Dutch fleet, and at a time when the latest illustration of British military operations on an important scale was furnished by that campaign in Flanders memorable rather for the vigour of language heard in the bivouacs than for the results which the troops achieved.*

Landing guns from fleet for enterprises on shore. To a certain extent the objection to employing naval *personnel* on shore, if there be any danger that war-vessels may be left short-handed in the event of the enemy approaching, holds good even more strongly as to landing guns from a fleet. And in the present day, when the ordnance mounted in fighting-ships takes time to remove and replace, this objection has greater force than it used to have. But many examples could be quoted of artillery from on board ship being used with great effect on land, especially in the sieges of maritime fortresses. Thus at the attack on Toulon in 1707 Sir Cloudesley Shovel landed one hundred guns from his fleet, there being no siege train available: some of these guns were captured by the French in a vigorous sortie. When General Clinton attacked Charleston in 1780, he depended for guns entirely upon ordnance landed from Admiral Arbuthnot's squadron.

* In later life the admiral was much concerned about the growth of "militarism" in the country. He regarded the formation of the United Service Club after the battle of Waterloo with the gravest suspicion, held such an association of fighting men to be unconstitutional, and peremptorily refused to allow his name to be added to the list of candidates at its inception. As a member of that institution, the author feels justified in expressing satisfaction that the great seaman's forebodings have not been vindicated by its subsequent record.

CONCLUSION.

Rooke, after taking Gibraltar, disembarked a large amount of naval guns, so as to secure the Rock against hostile enterprises for the time being.

This question of the employment of naval *personnel* ashore has been treated in some detail, because one purpose of this volume is to establish the principle that sea-power is generally dependent up to a certain point upon military force, and that it may in certain conditions be reduced to impotence without its aid. It has been shown in certain of the foregoing chapters that the attack and defence of fortified ports must often play a part in the prosecution of naval warfare. It has been proved, by examples of what has actually occurred in conflicts of the past, that even the stronger navy cannot wholly dispense with the support of posts on shore, while the weaker navy is obliged, by the irresistible force of circumstances, to retire under the wing of strongholds within friendly territory, should there be any such available. Therefore the attack and defence of fortresses must be a feature in contests for maritime control, and their maintenance in peace time must be a source of national expenditure, and must involve the retention of combatant *personnel* of some kind within their precincts.

It has been shown that the final destruction of fleets which may have been worsted in the first instance in fight at sea, or which may be too lacking in power to attempt to dispute for mastery with those opposed to them at all, is frequently accomplished by the intervention of land forces, and that it sometimes can be accomplished by no other means. And the examples of Copenhagen, of the Walcheren expedition, of Sebastopol, and of Port Arthur, —besides others less striking and not so well known,— have been quoted as proving that the land forces necessary to achieve the desired result may have to be organised on a great scale, may have to consist of mounted as well as of

Conclusion.

dismounted troops, and may have to be equipped as armies are equipped for military campaigns, and not as landing-parties are equipped for the execution of some petty enterprise. Naval *personnel* is incapable of carrying out operations of this class unless it is organised especially for the purpose, to the detriment of efficiency on its proper element. Whether the plan of burdening floating force with the guardianship of fortresses is expedient or not is, perhaps, susceptible of argument. But there can be no question that in many of the situations which arise in maritime war, navies must trust to the co-operation of armies on shore if they are to perform the task for which they exist.

CHAPTER IX.

A SUMMARY OF THE PRINCIPLES EXAMINED IN FOREGOING CHAPTERS.

THE purpose of the last six chapters has been to explain **Summary.** the dependence of navies upon military force in time of war. There is a connection between land-power and sea-power which sailors and soldiers alike are apt to overlook, and which extreme schools of naval thought and of military thought sometimes try to ignore,— a connection which is, from the point of view of strategy, of the utmost consequence to maritime nations when engaged in war. In some situations the influence over the course of naval warfare exerted by land operations, and by the expenditure of purely military force, may be almost imperceptible; in others it may be paramount. But it will rarely be the case that this influence does not make itself felt to some slight extent. Its possibilities can never be wholly left out of account in framing a plan of maritime campaign, nor can they be entirely neglected in putting in execution those great combinations of war which decide the issue in struggles for sea-power. In this chapter it is proposed to summarise very shortly the lessons which previous chapters have attempted to teach in reference to the underlying principles which govern naval warfare.

The great aim in naval warfare is to secure what is called command of the sea. That object is either attained by destroying the fleets of the enemy if it be possible, or else by driving them into port and then mounting guard over them so as to be in a position to fall upon them in superior force should they dare to emerge. That is the groundwork of the general scheme of operations which the stronger navy endeavours to carry out, if it be controlled by capable leaders. But to carry such a scheme out, the stronger navy is to a certain extent tied to the land. It must have its depots and repairing-stations; and if the ports where these have been established be wholly undefended, a raid by a very insignificant naval force may destroy the stores, may wreck the docks, and may place the fleets depending upon them in a position of serious difficulty, if it does not indeed reduce them to absolute impotence. Its naval bases may also in some cases be open to land attack coming from such a direction that sea-power is unable to provide against it. Thus the belligerent enjoying maritime preponderance is to a certain extent dependent upon fixed defences on shore, although these need not necessarily be elaborate or costly, and although they may not perhaps absorb a large *personnel*.[1]

But the weaker side at sea stands on a very different footing with regard to fixed defences. If its floating forces accept battle, they will be defeated and may even be destroyed. Without naval strongholds which are sufficiently formidable to compel the respect of the hostile fleets, its maritime power must speedily cease to exist. The only sound plan of action for its ships of war to follow is for them to retire into coast fortresses, to remain there on the alert, and to lie under shelter of their guns prepared and on the watch for an opportunity. Once they have accepted the situation, they are in a position to take full advantage of the inconveniences which the enemy must inevitably suffer during the prolonged and damaging process of maintaining a close or a watching blockade. Expressing it in very general terms, it may be said that a fleet hidden within a fortress is virtually safe against attacks from a fleet outside; and it may be said that the fleet outside cannot prevent the fleet inside from putting to sea if it so wills it. Exceptions will of course often occur, and have often occurred; but that may be taken to be the broad rule. The inferior navy, or the navy which has suffered overthrow during the course of hostilities, is entirely dependent upon fixed defences and upon forces on shore to protect it from total destruction.

Had France, the weaker side at sea during the wars of the Revolution and Empire, been powerless on land, Bridport and St Vincent and Cornwallis would not have been obliged to lie off and on, in fair weather and in foul, for months and months, watching the French armament in Brest; nor would Nelson have spent the two most anxious years of his strenuous life maintaining a position of observation with a "crazy fleet" ready to destroy or to pursue Latouche Tréville should he put to sea from Toulon. The operations would have assumed a totally different aspect. Armies would have been sent from the Channel ports destined to attack the great maritime fortresses of the French from the rear, and either to drive the warships sheltering within them to sea and into the arms of the squadrons waiting for them outside, or else to destroy those "fleets in being" at their moorings. The great military strength of France guaranteed it to the Directory, to the Consulate, and to the Empire, that the national navy would not cease to exist, and that it would remain a menace to the sea-power of the victors of St Vincent and the Nile.

And so it comes about that even the navy which is paramount upon the ocean may have to trust to land operations, if maritime control is to be abiding and assured. The enemy's floating forces lurk in harbour. To get at them, armies must be brought into play. It is when one side possesses preponderating resources both afloat and ashore in a struggle between seafaring nations, that the issue at sea is decided rapidly and beyond possibility of dispute. Such was the case in the wars between Japan and China, and between the United States and Spain.

The actual attack of armies upon fleets, of which the Helder campaign of 1799, the Crimean War, and the Japanese operations against Port Arthur in 1904, are such remarkable examples, demands as a rule a great display of military force; and the available resources of the belligerents may forbid such combinations of war. But, working on a smaller scale, military force may effectively second the efforts of a preponderating navy to gain the command of the sea, quite apart from the question of mere maintenance of bases for the fleet. The enemy's isolated naval ports and coaling-stations may be attacked by land. Harbours, advantageous for prosecuting the maritime campaign, may be seized and held. And if the enemy resorts to commerce-destroying, the surest way of extinguishing the hostile cruisers engaged on the work is to strike at the root of the mischief,—to seize the port where they replenish their fuel and supplies, and to which they take their captured prizes: it may be a waste of power, it may be taking a sledge-hammer to knock in a tin tack, but it is bound to prove an effectual method of scotching the evil. And it is the natural consequence of the strategical conditions governing sea-power when it is acting on the offensive and when it is acting on the defensive in war, that the belligerent with the preponderating navy pays small attention to fixed defences, while the belligerent with the inferior navy is compelled to expend force upon them and to devote large sums to their equipment and maintenance. Therefore when the stronger side afloat is driven by the course of the campaign to deal with the fixed defences of the enemy, those fixed defences may be by no means easy to neutralise and to overcome.

The very fact of possessing overwhelming naval forces compels a nation to maintain military forces, if its naval forces are to have full scope for effective action when hostilities take place. The dominating position attained by the British fleets as a consequence of Trafalgar led up to Napoleon's transformation of Antwerp into a great naval station, and to the Walcheren Expedition which was to destroy that naval station and all that it contained. So far from preponderance at sea obviating the need for the upkeep of military force, it may increase that need in obedience to what is a strategical law.

If we consider the art of war only from our own point of view, we are apt perhaps to set undue store on ideals, and to reject altogether points of secondary, but none the less of practical, importance. At sea there may be no field of battle to be held, nor places to be won.[2] But even the purely naval issue may not be decided at sea. The final object of attack in maritime warfare should always be the organised forces afloat of the enemy, but those organised forces may be afloat in harbour. The enunciation of sound strategical doctrine does not necessarily establish a dogma which is infallible, nor set up an image which can under no circumstances be broken. For a generation the British army has been learning in the great school of experience that theory and practice are not one and the same thing in war on land. May not the sister service perhaps find some day that this same distinction arises when the contest is on the sea?

CHAPTER X.

THE LIMITATIONS OF SEA-POWER IN SECURING THE OBJECTS FOR WHICH WAR IS UNDERTAKEN.

Peculiar position of the United Kingdom in relation to sea-power.

THE United Kingdom stands in relation to the question of sea-power in a position which is unique. Within a relatively restricted area, of which some portions are comparatively speaking unproductive, is collected a huge population dependent for its unexampled prosperity and its widely distributed riches upon commerce and manufacture. But the British Isles are not self-supporting; the food of the people and the raw material for the factories come in large part from over the sea. Thus it comes about that the security of its maritime trade is a question of such paramount importance to the country that it outweighs all other military and naval considerations. The national existence depends upon the fleet. It is a fact which admits of no dispute, and which is accepted universally.

One consequence of this is, however, that there is in certain quarters an inclination to assume that naval preponderance in war is of more momentous consequence to other nations, differently situated, than is actually the case. No prominent people, not even the Japanese, are situated as the inhabitants of the United Kingdom are. No other great portion of mankind relies so absolutely upon the safety of its mercantile marine and on the uninterrupted flow of supplies from over the sea into its many harbours. But this is often overlooked even by the experts, and so an idea has spread abroad that, because maritime disaster in war means to this country almost irretrievable ruin, the potentialities of naval force for deciding the issue of a conflict between belligerents, otherwise situated, are greater than they really are.[1] It is too readily assumed because some formidable foe, or collection of foes, on the ocean might conceivably compel the British nation to admit defeat and to accept the consequences however disastrous, that mere naval collapse, with what it brings in its train, will drive Powers, whose dependence on freedom of the sea is far less absolute, to submit and to crave for peace. To that fine preamble to the Naval Discipline Act which declares that it is "the navy whereon, under the good Providence of God, the wealth, safety, and strength of the Kingdom chiefly depends," we all subscribe. Why? Because the navy serves us as a shield. It is because the people of this land have good cause for their trust that the shield will prove impenetrable in the hour of danger, that the shield will secure the shores of the United Kingdom against violation by an invader, and will assure food to the millions who are powerless to intervene in defence of their country, that the Royal Navy is held in such veneration.

But the gladiator who enters the arena equipped with nothing but a shield may fail to win the plaudits of the amphitheatre. There is in war a higher military policy than that which is comprised within the general meaning of the term strategy. Strategy is a problem for the ministries of war and marine to con over, a question for the admiral and the general to answer. Military policy, on the other hand, is a question for the government to decide and for the nation to approve.[2] When a nation appeals to the final tribunal of actual combat with any confidence of securing a favourable verdict, it must set up for itself some loftier ideal than that of merely averting a catastrophe or of warding off the blows of its antagonist. It

The higher policy of war.

may assume a posture of defence; but it must be prepared to strike, and if the struggle is to be brought rapidly to a satisfactory conclusion, it must be prepared to strike hard. The ability of amphibious force to inflict grave injury upon the foe is usually immense. The capabilities of purely naval force to cause the adversary damage is often very limited.[3]

<small>Maritime force powerless beyond a certain point.</small>

Fleets and cruisers may destroy those opposed to them if they are fortunate. Given a reasonable superiority of force added to capable management, and they are sure after a time to enjoy the practical control of the sea. They can ruin an enemy's maritime commerce. They can blockade the sea-board of the opposing belligerent. But their capacity for damaging the foe stops with the shore,—it is limited to the effect which may be caused upon the hostile community by cutting off the sources of supply from oversea. These sources of supply may be vital to the existence of the people; they may be of, comparatively speaking, no importance. A country like the United Kingdom, to which its over-sea trade is its life's blood, can be brought to its knees at once by the action of a stronger navy. A country like Austria-Hungary, which is virtually self-supporting, which is begirt by productive territory, and which possesses only a modest mercantile marine, may be inconvenienced by hostile sea-power, but will never be crushed by it alone.

<small>The war against the French Empire, 1805-1814.</small>

And there has been a tendency among writers on the subject of sea-power to exaggerate the effect which may be produced by that process of driving an enemy's mercantile flag off the sea and of blockading the hostile coasts, which is a usual corollary to the establishing of maritime preponderance. The process may under favourable conditions be sure. But under any other conditions than those presented by the British Isles it will assuredly be slow.[4] Captain Mahan has, in his second volume of the 'Influence of Sea-Power upon the French Revolution and Empire,' provided us with a masterly account of the triumph of the maritime forces of the United Kingdom over a nation numerically far stronger, possessing vast resources within its borders, and dominated by a master-mind. But that great contest of the sea against the land was protracted to a ruinous extent. It went on for nine exhausting years after the question of naval preponderance was definitely settled in Trafalgar Bay. And can the events which overshadowed Europe from 1805 to 1814 justly be summed up as a contest of the sea against the land? During those nine years of bloodshed Napoleon twice traversed central Europe to tread underfoot the formidable military empire of Austria. His armies overran North Germany, and overcame the fighting-forces of Prussia nursed in the traditions of Frederick the Great. They besieged and took maritime strongholds on the shores of the Baltic. They defeated the hosts of the Tsar in the basin of the Vistula. Finally they melted away in the great frost-bound plains of Russia, and France, her vitality sapped by military sacrifices almost unprecedented in history, was driven to create new armies which were to go down before a continent in arms. France was not pitted against the British people alone, but was pitted against all Europe. And can even the prolonged duel between the two nations facing each other throughout this period in the west be described as merely a contest of the sea against the land? From the time when Sir J. Moore's advance towards Burgos overthrew Napoleon's strategical plans in Spain, British military power by means of land operations—of land operations which were, it is true, founded upon naval supremacy—came to the assistance of the fleets and cruisers which were so slowly dragging the great conqueror down.[5]

And the American War of Secession furnishes another example of the limitations of sea-power in deciding within a reasonable time a campaign, where the conditions were eminently favourable to its effective employment. The States of the Confederation were poor in natural resources.

The American War of Secession.

172   LIMITATIONS OF SEA-POWER.

They depended for their military stores to a great extent upon imported war material, and their wealth lay in the export of their agricultural produce.[6] The naval forces of the Union enjoyed control of the sea, and they soon established a moderately effective blockade, which tightened its grip from month to month and from year to year as the struggle drifted on. And yet the desperate contest lasted from 1861 to 1865, and was eventually decided by the great numerical superiority of the Federal fighting-forces on land. The influence of maritime command over the military operations was enormous, because as the war went on the Northern army commanders made it to a certain extent the basis of their combinations. But had the Union States not possessed a huge preponderance as regards population, had the Federal navy not accepted the *rôle* of an auxiliary to the army in the Mississippi and performed that *rôle* with consummate self-denial, had the troops of the North not worked hand in hand with their warships in the Virginian campaigns, sea-power alone would not have eventually decided the issue, and the United States would not be the wonder of the world to-day.

Efficacy of blockade decreased under modern conditions. And it must be remembered that the economic conditions of the present day, the development of railway and canal communication, and the improvements which have taken place in methods of commercial intercourse between adjacent countries, tend to restrict the effect of naval pressure on a continental as opposed to an insular State.[7] Formerly, before the introduction of the locomotive, and when good roads were few and far between, the difficulties of moving goods from place to place by land were of course far greater than they are now. At the present time the result of blockading the coasts of a maritime State which is in land contact with neutral territory will merely be that its imports are derived from a fresh source, and that its exports are diverted into a new channel. Maritime closure cannot even prevent goods which must necessarily make a voyage to reach their destination, from entering the closured territory if its borderland touch on neutral soil.[8] A German blockade of the shores of Spain would not prevent American produce from reaching that country, unless it were brought in Spanish ships; nor could it hinder cargoes in neutral vessels from being discharged in the Tagus and from crossing the Spanish frontier by rail. Dislocation of trade necessarily means financial loss and increased cost of living, because certain necessaries rise in price owing to their arriving in the country by less convenient routes than they did before the blockade: the force of the pressure depends upon the circumstances of the case, the geographical conditions, and so forth. But the situation created by the sea-power of the British Isles, when thrown into the scale against Napoleon in the early part of the nineteenth century, would be far less damaging to France under existing conditions than it was a hundred years ago. Now the centres of industry and population of our neighbours across the Channel are in close railway communication with central and eastern Europe. Continental Europe is self-contained. The blockade of the coasts of any State included therein may be an inconvenience to the State,— it may constitute a menace to its prosperity and a check to its advancement,—but such blockade will hardly suffice by itself to coerce that State into sacrificing what it believes to be its rights, or to drive a self-respecting people into purchasing peace by appreciable concessions.[9]

Then there arises also, in this connection, the awkward problem of contraband of war and of rights of neutral shipping. Situated as the British Government was in its contest with Napoleon, the position was too grave, the consequences involved too serious, for it to stand on much ceremony with regard to neutral trade. The Berlin and Milan Decrees, and the British Orders in Council to counteract their effect, created a state of affairs that is not likely

Question of contraband of war.

to occur again. One result of the drastic measures adopted by the Power which commanded the sea was, however, to involve it in hostilities with the United States at a most inconvenient time. The indeterminate condition in which the question of contraband of war now stands in international law is a constant source of doubt and anxiety to belligerents, and of inconvenience and danger to neutral nations. But the signs of the times point towards the admission that neutral cargoes will be immune from seizure in future wars, provided they do not consist of genuine war material or of coal. They will be immune, that is to say, if the belligerent making seizures contrary to that principle is not prepared to face grave complications.[10] And this tends to decrease the efficacy of that form of coercion, produced by checking the flow of imports by sea into a hostile country and of exports from it, by means of naval force, which has in wars of the past proved at times so useful a weapon of offence.

Circumstances may limit a belligerent to operations by sea.

It may of course happen that a nation engaged in war is, by the circumstances of the case, obliged to confine its action to the sea. It may have no military forces at its disposal capable of acting effectively on land against the enemy. There may be no objective ashore worthy of attention. It may be impossible owing to geographical conditions to bring an army into play. If so, there is no help for it. The operations of war must then be confined to enterprises against the hostile navy, to the harrying and, if possible, the total destruction of the adversary's over-sea trade, and to the blockade, if it be practicable, of the enemy's coasts; and by these means it may eventually be found possible to bring hostilities to an end on advantageous terms. But the struggle is almost certain to be exhausting and protracted,—it has been shown in earlier chapters how limited are the powers of a preponderating navy in dealing with a hostile fleet which shuns encounter. And while the war drifts on from month to month the political conditions may undergo a change. New antagonists may come into the field. And prospects of ultimate success may fade away in face of coalitions which would never have taken practical shape, had the contest between the original combatants been decided by more vertebrate combinations of war.

In these days when great nations seek expansion in territories separated from the motherland by vast expanses of ocean, their foreign possessions may fall to an enemy preponderant at sea. But it does not by any means follow that they will so fall if the enemy has no other striking force at his disposal than ships of war. The isolation of an island by hostile fleets does not necessarily mean its surrender, any more than does the mere blockade of an inland fortress ensure its capitulation. It is in either case a question of the resources available in the place, and of the effectiveness of the blockade. Take, for example, those two highly-prized dependencies of the Crown—Malta and Ceylon. Malta, an island, or rather group of islands, of very small area, has a large population, forms practically one great fortress, has a sufficient and highly efficient garrison, but is not self-supporting as regards food-supplies. Ceylon is an island of great extent with a long coast-line, has only a very small garrison relative to its size, but produces sufficient food for the support of its population. Owing to its limited dimensions, an effective blockade of Malta might be easily established by a hostile Power commanding the Mediterranean, and the colony might in consequence be starved into surrender: an attack upon the island, whether by land or by sea, or both, would on the other hand be a formidable enterprise in view of its elaborate defences. But an effective blockade of Ceylon would be a most difficult undertaking, and it would lead to no result beyond causing inconvenience to the wealthier classes and loss to the commercial community. The conquest of the island by an enemy controlling

Operations against over-sea possessions of an enemy. The question of securing these by means of sea-power unaided.

the sea, on the other hand, would not probably demand any great expenditure of force, or involve any very difficult military operations.

Such isolation by itself has no military effect.

The isolation of the over-sea possessions of a great maritime nation does not damage those possessions in a military sense, unless they are attacked. Unless fighting takes place there is no expenditure of ammunition, and there is no wastage in *personnel* owing to wounds or to the diseases inevitable in campaigning in the open field. Sea-power unaccompanied by land operations can, as a rule, only bring about the fall of an enemy's colonies if these are not self-supporting, and if in that case an effective blockade can be established. Mere naval preponderance will not bring it about without blockade, unless neutrals admit the principle that food-stuffs are contraband of war, and this cannot be depended upon. If neutrals admit that principle—a not very probable contingency—a few cruisers may perhaps suffice to stop supplies. Otherwise there must be a properly established blockade, demanding a great expenditure of naval force for a somewhat doubtful object. And the whole history of war upon the seas goes to show how difficult it is to maintain a really effective blockade. In the chapter on sieges it will be shown that it is almost impossible for ships to entirely close the avenues of maritime approach, even to a stretch of coast-line so restricted as what is included in the sea front of an ordinary fortress. And the principle of starving the civil population of some remote colony included in the dominions of a belligerent into submission, seems a little out of date. The theory that a belligerent who controls the sea can strike a vital blow at the opponent through his distant colonies does not in fact bear examination, unless it be understood that military force is to be brought into play as an adjunct to naval power.

The question of injuring the

The amount of damage which can be inflicted upon an antagonist by operations against his maritime trade obviously depends upon the volume of that trade. The value of the mercantile marine and the development of over-sea commerce varies greatly in the case of different nations, and they are not necessarily proportionate to the importance or to the resources of a country as a whole. The prosperity of the British Empire, almost its existence indeed, depends upon the security of its merchant shipping. But there are other great and powerful nations whose wealth is not to be found afloat, but is to be found on shore. These cannot be appreciably injured by the action of commerce-destroyers on the high seas, nor by that steady pressure of a dominating navy which gradually sweeps the merchant flag of the weaker maritime State off the ocean. Effective offensive action against nations such as these must be undertaken by armies on land, or not at all.[11] *enemy by destroying his maritime trade.*

And the great results achieved in the past by belligerents who have gained control of the seas in their onslaughts upon the trade of maritime opponents have not always been achieved by naval power alone. In the inspiring and oft-quoted inscription on the monument to Chatham in the Guildhall, we read how that illustrious statesman advanced the nation to a high pitch of prosperity and glory by "commerce for the first time united with and made to flourish by war." But this country did not amass wealth and multiply its resources at the expense of France and Spain in the days of Quiberon and Quebec and Havana, merely by seizure of their trading vessels. It was because the sources from which they drew their wealth from over the seas under their own flags were wrested out of their hands by British military force, that the riches of the East and West Indies, and of lands far off across the ocean, were diverted into the coffers of merchants in London and Bristol, and other English cities. Apart from the conquest of Canada and from the overthrow of French authority in the East Indies, we mainly benefited in that great war at the cost of our adversaries by "filching *The Seven Years' War in reference to this.*

M

sugar islands "—to borrow Sheridan's gibe of a generation later. Naval power did, it is true, at first intercept the produce of the Antilles, in its transit across the seas to enrich the parent States which at the outset of the struggle owned the most fruitful portions of the archipelago. But as the communications became insecure, and as cargoes were seized at sea, commerce gradually ceased. It was then that war in the West Indies became a war of posts, that island after island was captured, and that their wealth was drawn into the treasury of Great Britain, and afforded to the victorious maritime nation the sinews of war not only for its own operations but also for those of its ally the kingdom of Prussia.

Results of operations against trade depend on amount of trade. A navy which becomes paramount at sea during the course of a campaign may be able to inflict crushing damage upon the enemy by operations against maritime commerce. But the severity of the injury must depend upon the volume of that commerce. And even in the case of the Seven Years' War, which is generally regarded as affording the most remarkable example of the successful adoption of this policy, it was not sea-power alone, but the judicious conjunction of sea-power with military force, which achieved such surprising results.

Possession by the British Empire of its great chain of naval bases due largely to military expeditions. The unique position of the British Empire as a naval power is not entirely due to its unrivalled fleet of ships of war. It is also due, although in very inferior measure, to that wonderful chain of naval bases and stations which gives it a *pied-à-terre* in every ocean and in every sea. Did these precious possessions fall into our hands by accident or by right of conquest? And, if they are ours in virtue of operations of war, were those operations purely naval? Halifax and Bermuda and Esquimalt were gained by peaceful settlement. Hong Kong was ceded by China after the first Chinese War. Singapore was relinquished by arrangement with a local rajah. But what of the others? Jamaica was captured by a military force under Venables whose relations with Penn at St Domingo have been subject of reference on p. 11. St Lucia fell to a military expedition. Malta was taken after a prolonged siege. Colombo is ours by right of conquest from the Dutch. Simon's Bay was secured by a conjunct military and naval undertaking. Mauritius was captured by an army despatched expressly for the purpose. In every case the operation was founded upon sea-power; but it was a military operation for all that. Gibraltar stands alone. It was taken by a naval force practically unaided, for the Duke of Hesse's soldiery who landed at the head of the bay hardly contributed to the fall of the stronghold. Gibraltar is the one exception which proves the rule.

"To the sailor," writes Mr Corbett, "the aim of naval strategy must always seem to be the command of the sea. To the soldier and the statesman it is only a means to an end. For them the end must always be the furtherance or the hindrance of military operations ashore, or the protection or destruction of sea-borne commerce; for by these means alone can governments and populations be crushed into submission. Of the two methods, that of military pressure must always come first, where resources allow, just as an assault, where practicable, is always preferable to the lengthy blockade. If, therefore, it is possible to give sudden emphasis to vital military operations by momentarily and without due risk abandoning the sailor's preoccupation—by ceasing for a moment to aim solely at the command of the sea—a bigoted adherence to it may become pedantry and ruin the higher strategy of the campaign."* Wholesome words, these, from one of the "blue-water school" who has not allowed an intimate acquaintance with the story of the sea to develop bias, and who realises that if a maritime nation is to do great things in war its navy and its army must go hand in hand.

Command of the sea only a means to an end.

* 'England in the Mediterranean,' vol. ii. p. 242.

Influence of popular opinion cannot be left out of account in war.

The higher strategy of a campaign will always be, to a certain extent, prejudiced, if indeed it be not absolutely governed, by the impulse of national sentiment and by the force of the national will. The master of the art of war may scheme and calculate, may plan the profoundest combinations for prospective operations afloat and for prospective operations ashore, but it is the people who sanction or who disapprove. The influence of popular opinion sways the Government of a country whether its institutions be autocratic or be liberal, and it is the Government which issues the fiat what the soldier and the sailor are to do. There were no board schools in England a century and a half ago when the country was ablaze because Minorca fell. Not one man in fifty can have had a clear perception where Minorca was, not one man in a thousand realised its worth. And yet people who had never heard of it before swelled with indignation that a British possession, a dependency of the Crown, should have passed into an enemy's hands by act of war, and the whole nation clamoured for a victim. There is an important lesson to be learnt from this. It is that a nation which is inspired by patriotic instincts prizes all portions of its territory without regard to their actual intrinsic value, that a blow aimed at some remote province or island belonging to it inflicts a grave, even if it be in a sense an imaginary, injury upon that nation, and that the effect of capturing places from an enemy which are strategically insignificant may exert a remarkable influence over the fortunes of the belligerents and over the result of the contest.

The lesson of Belleisle and Minorca at the Peace of Paris, 1763.

The Seven Years' War opened with this grave disaster to the British arms. Towards its close a joint naval and military expedition on a small scale succeeded in capturing the island of Belleisle, off the coast of Brittany. As a possession the island was of little use to this country either in peace or in war. Lacking a good harbour, and exposed to the full force of the Bay of Biscay storms, its rocky shores afforded scanty shelter to ships of war, or to trading vessels even of the smallest tonnage. From the strategical point of view the attack on it partook of the nature of a pinprick, but as a move in higher military policy it was forceful and effective. For when the peace plenipotentiaries met in conclave, Belleisle was a pawn for the British Minister to bargain with. It was integrally as much a part of France as Islay is of Scotland. Its possession by a foreign nation, and especially by a nation then so much hated as were the British people, was to the French insufferable. So the Government of George III. claimed Minorca in exchange for this almost worthless island; the British representative, indeed, actually asserted that their country was getting the worst of this bargain; and the country, by playing upon the patriotic sentiments of a spirited people, thus recovered the splendid harbour of Port Mahon in the Mediterranean, which had been lost seven years before.

Holding in occupation hostile territory is, in fact, an important step towards a satisfactory settlement of the question which has given rise to the quarrel. The destruction of the enemy's fleets may be impracticable. The overthrow of the opposing armies may be out of the question. But it may nevertheless be possible by good fortune or by good management to seize some portion of the adversary's dominions, and the success may just turn the scale and lead to ultimate triumph. This principle is well illustrated by the position of Egypt before the Peace of Amiens. The delta of the Nile is certainly not worthless, and it properly belonged not to England but to the Ottoman Empire. But it was a cardinal point of the British policy that Napoleon should have no foothold in the Levant. And, although the French army under Menou was strategically in an impossible position, although it was cut off from France by the British fleets without hope of succour, and was weary of sojourn in a

Importance of securing hostile territory during a war.

foreign land, it was in possession. Therefore Abercromby was sent to attack it and to turn it out of the country. No difficulties were made over the terms of capitulation after the British army had gained the upper hand. The object was to deprive Napoleon of a valuable asset when negotiations for peace were instituted, and that object was achieved when the French army was shipped back to France from the Egyptian shores.

The example of Egypt after the Battle of the Nile.

Reference to that disastrous expedition of Napoleon's to the land of the Pharaohs forms a fitting ending to this chapter. There are other lessons to be learnt from it with reference to the subject under discussion besides what it teaches as to the importance, as a question of general military policy in war, of holding in occupation territory which happens to be in dispute, even if the tenure be precarious. The perilous situation of the French in the delta after the battle of the Nile is often quoted as an illustration of the risks which are run by armies undertaking an over-sea enterprise without being assured of maritime command. It is an example of a military force isolated and with its communications cut, for lack of sea-power. Nelson's victory in Aboukir Bay was decisive almost beyond all precedent. It placed the expeditionary force under Napoleon in a position of the gravest perplexity. But that force managed nevertheless to retain its hold on Egypt for three long years, and a British army had to be shipped out, and had to be landed in the country to wrest it from the hands of France. The story of that attempt of Napoleon's to create an oriental empire under his sway, makes manifest at once the strength and the weakness of preponderating naval power; it illustrates at once the influence of maritime command, and the bounds within which the potentialities of maritime command are restricted.

Conclusion.

There is a dangerous idea prevalent in this country, that because a dominating navy is the best safeguard for its security, the complement of sea-power, military force, is of altogether secondary importance to a State so situated. The attitude taken up by soldiers of prominence on the subject of home defence, an attitude which has helped to throw the true functions of the army for so long into the background, has contributed to this. An insular Power with great fleets at its command may be justified in trusting to its battleships and cruisers to guard not only its sea-borne trade, but also to ensure its shores against invasion. But that is defence, mere passive defence. In this chapter an attempt has been made to show that naval resources unaided cannot, under the ordinary conditions which arise in warfare between maritime nations, inflict upon an enemy the amount of injury requisite to bring about collapse. Command of the sea is, as Corbett so well expresses it, merely a means to an end, and that end is attainment of the object for which the war was undertaken.[12]

Sometimes war is undertaken for the express purpose of conquering territory. If so, military force must perform its share in the struggle. Sometimes it is undertaken to destroy naval forces which have grown into a menace to future prosperity. If so, sea-power unaided may be unable to accomplish the task. Sometimes, and more often, the war arises out of some quarrel, or is the result of rivalry between nations. And then the purpose which either side has in view, is to achieve such measure of success as will lead up to an advantageous peace. Success means injury to the enemy in the form of exhaustion financially, of securing some material guarantee at the enemy's cost, or of acquisition of hostile territory. And this kind of success is generally beyond the scope of naval force to accomplish, unless indeed the contest be protracted to a dangerous length, and unless the victorious belligerent is prepared to emerge from the struggle ruined if triumphant.

CHAPTER XI.

THE IMPORTANCE OF SEA COMMAND TO SCATTERED EMPIRES IN RESPECT OF CONCENTRATING THE NATIONAL MILITARY FORCES FOR WAR.

Scattered empires almost of necessity have their military forces scattered.

EMPIRES covering great areas are generally, in a geographical sense, split up into distinct territories, and these themselves are often separated from each other by wide areas of sea. And when this is the case, it follows almost as a matter of course that one central government or one powerful nationality is dominating subject alien races, and that military forces have to be maintained in outlying provinces to preserve order and to uphold the flag. History shows, moreover, that it is the accepted practice for world Powers to develop the local fighting resources of countries which have been annexed or have been occupied, so as to provide a ready means of swelling the total military forces available for some great war, and of furnishing local troops to deal with provincial disturbances should they break out. And so it comes about that the armies belonging to empires like Rome of old, like Spain of two centuries ago, and like France and Russia to-day, are always to a certain extent widely dispersed; and that to effect imposing concentrations of troops for war in any one portion of the empire, it is often necessary to transport large detachments with their impedimenta over the sea.

The risks run by transports conveying military *personnel* and military stores, if command of the sea be not reasonably well assured, will be explained in the next two chapters in some detail. Here it is sufficient to say that if troops and war material are to be freely moved by ships during the progress of a campaign, maritime preponderance is essential, and that the belligerent shackled by the inferior navy is almost entirely precluded from using communications across the sea for military purposes. A scattered empire which cannot place dependence upon its fighting fleets may, in a purely military campaign, find masses of its men locked up in distant provinces where they are useless for the purpose of the operations in progress, simply because the risk is too great to transfer them to the theatre of war in transports. It may, moreover, have precious dependencies wrested from it, because the maritime situation forbids the despatch of reinforcements even when ample reinforcements may be available.

The history of the wars in which the Ottoman Empire was engaged during the nineteenth century illustrates this with peculiar force. Early in the century the Sultan's dominions included the whole of the Levant, included Greece, extended round three sides of the Black Sea, and stretched along the southern side of the Mediterranean to the borders of Morocco. This vast territory was almost destitute of good communications. The fertile and populous areas were separated from each other by vast stretches of desert, and by barren, mountainous, unproductive tracts. And a glance at the map on p. 93 shows to what extent the tortuous trace of the Adriatic, the Ægean, the Black Sea, and of the Mediterranean itself, served to break the empire up. To move armies by land from Tripoli or from Egypt to Macedonia, or from the Dalmatian border to Palestine, or from the mouths of the Danube to Armenia, involved marching for hundreds of miles through roadless and inhospitable regions. To make such transfers of force across the sea merely involved the collection of sufficient shipping, and a voyage of a very few days.

The Ottoman Empire.

186   SEA-POWER AND SCATTERED EMPIRES.

In the Greek War of Liberation. In the Greek War of Liberation the question of maritime supremacy was in dispute, and in the early phases of that prolonged struggle the Porte encountered great difficulties in moving the fine fighting material of Asia Minor round the north of the Ægean through Thessaly into the revolted provinces. So much was this indeed the case that, but for the valuable support by sea and land of Mehemet Ali, viceroy of Egypt, the Hellenes unaided would almost certainly

have thrown off the Ottoman yoke. But Egypt, developed by the masterful Pasha into a prosperous principality, represented formidable naval as well as military resources. And when, after the Turkish troops and Turkish fleet had suffered many humiliations, Mehemet Ali was induced by his suzerain lord to throw his fighting-ships and his well-armed and disciplined soldiers into the scale, the Greeks were speedily reduced to almost desperate straits. Thanks to sea-power, the regiments and batteries from the Nile Delta and from Palestine were shipped across the Western Mediterranean and planted down in the Morea. And, had it not been for the intervention of the British, French, and Russian fleets at Navarino, at a moment when the revolted nationality was at its last gasp, the Ottoman forces would certainly have restored the Sultan's authority in Greece.

The battle of Navarino destroyed Turkish naval power for the time, and immediately after that "untoward incident" the Russo-Turkish war of 1828-29 broke out. In that campaign Russia enjoyed the command not only of the Black Sea but also of the Ægean; and thus the Ottoman Empire, already exhausted by its efforts to subdue the Greeks, entered upon a struggle against its historic northern foe under most adverse conditions. The Sultan Murad was fighting with one arm tied behind his back. He could not draw troops freely from Africa to reinforce the army on the Danube, because transports ran the utmost risk of capture in crossing the Mediterranean. Corps destined to operate in the Asiatic theatre of war at the eastern end of the Black Sea could not be conveyed by ship from the Bosporus to Batoum or to Trebizond, but had to march through the mountains of Anatolia and Kurdistan to reach Armenia.* It was entirely due to sea-power that Russia was able to push her army almost to the Golden Horn, and that Paskievich achieved such brilliant results round Kars and Erzerum. But this sea-power perhaps exerted its influence with the greatest effect in that it denied to the Ottoman Empire the power of putting forth its full military strength.

In 1828-29.

In the Crimean War the Sultan, propped up on his tottering throne by the allies, made no attempt to utilise to the full the military resources of many outlying provinces over which he claimed a sovereignty. Before the interven-

In the Crimean War.

* See map on p. 261.

tion of Great Britain and France some troops had, however, been brought to Bulgaria from across the Mediterranean, in which Russia had no ships of war. That struggle does not throw light on this question of the importance of maritime command to a scattered empire for the purpose of concentrating its military forces, to at all the same extent as the war of 1828-29; and the conflict which began a quarter of a century after the destruction of Russian maritime power in the Black Sea at Sebastopol illustrates the principle much more forcibly.

In 1877-78. During the war of 1877-78, the Turks enjoyed the advanage of controlling the Black Sea and also the Mediterranean; and it is due to this alone that the effete oriental empire was able for so long to keep at bay the vastly superior military forces of the Tsar. For the Sultan was able to concentrate almost the whole of his military resources on the Armenian frontier and in Bulgaria at an early stage of the war, with the exception of the Egyptian contingent and of one important detachment which was to play a highly dramatic part at a later stage. An army was left to deal with revolted Montenegro, and this arrived on the scene at a most opportune moment: this move of Suliman Pasha's troops from the Adriatic to the Ægean, and their despatch from Enos to the Shipka Pass at a critical stage of the campaign in Bulgaria, affords one of the most remarkable illustrations of the benefits which a belligerent may derive from maritime command during the progress of a war on land, which is to be found in the history of modern war. But for the facilities for moving his soldiers from outlying provinces of his vast empire to the European and Asiatic theatres of war, which the steamers at the disposal of the Sultan placed in his hands, his pashas could not have met the Russian generals on anything approaching to level terms; nor would either the tactical skill of Mukhtar Pasha in Armenia, or the strategical insight and dogged resolution of Osman

Pasha north of the Balkans, have stayed the forces of invasion from the north for months had these distinguished soldiers not controlled great bodies of troops drawn from far and near.

The wars of 1828-29 and 1877-78 are admirable examples of the importance to a scattered empire, threatened at vital points, of being able to assemble its land forces from distant provinces by means of ship transport.[1] And this same principle is also well illustrated by the Franco-German War, during which France was supreme at sea, and during which her naval superiority indirectly aided her to an extent that is not sufficiently appreciated.[2] When that stupendous conflict broke out, Napoleon III. was maintaining a large force of excellent troops in Algeria, where so many of the generals of the Second Empire had won their laurels, and there was also a French contingent located in the Papal States. At a very early period of the war the garrisons both of North Africa and of Rome were almost entirely withdrawn, so as to swell the armies vainly endeavouring to stem the tide of German invasion. This transfer of force was rendered possible by the French control of the Mediterranean, and was effected without the slightest difficulty. The conflict in the northeast was too one-sided, it is true, for a few brigades to change the issue, but they nevertheless exerted an appreciable influence over the first part of the campaign. Algerian soldiery acquitted themselves gallantly at Wörth, and a brigade from the Eternal City, which just missed the catastrophe of Sedan, was one of the few remnants of the French regular army to aid in the defence of Paris.

France in the Franco-German War.

France in 1870, and the Ottoman Empire in certain phases of its wars against the revolted Hellenes and against Russia, alike gathered in their isolated detachments for central defence by sea. But the importance of naval control is even more strikingly displayed when a scattered empire is

Importance of sea command when outlying portions of a scattered empire are involved in war.

threatened, or is assailed, in provinces lying far removed from the centres of its fighting power. For when that is the case the menaced territory will generally be weakly defended. The garrisons of outlying colonies and dependencies are seldom large, and they often consist of troops of no great combatant capacity. If, then, reinforcements cannot be despatched to the point of danger, a disaster, the extent of which is only bounded by the importance of the territory in jeopardy, may occur. If the only route for reinforcements lies across the sea, the whole strategical situation is likely to hinge on the question whether in virtue of maritime command these reinforcements can, or can not, proceed in safety to their destination by ship. And this has been proved over and over again in the history of war.

Few conflicts have been more remarkable or more instructive than the South African War which lasted from 1899 to 1902. Many of its incidents were of an exceptionally striking character. It affords one of the most illuminating examples of guerilla warfare on record. Strategical and tactical lessons of the utmost value can be deduced from its story. But not the least distinguishing feature of that memorable struggle was the illustration which it afforded of the concentration at one threatened point in the dominions of a world-wide empire, of its military forces drawn from all quarters of the globe, thanks to that empire possessing absolute and undisputed command of the sea during the progress of hostilities. And this principle has received fresh demonstration in the great struggle in eastern Asia. For want of sufficient naval power the Russians have in their war with Japan been compelled to depend solely upon a single line of rail, many thousands of miles in length, and have been unable to put in the field more than a fraction of that gigantic army which the Tsar can mobilise, but which he cannot move in the required direction for lack of means. The histories of Spain and of France prove the impossibility, without adequate naval resources, of preserving over-sea dominions in war against a maritime nation if the enemy can bring military force into play.

Spain originally acquired her empire in the western hemisphere by the overthrow of local principalities, and by the conquest of some of the inferior races which peopled the American continent at the time of its discovery. She lost her vast western empire, partly by the revolt of her far-off provinces when these developed and began to feel their own strength, and partly by their absorption into the dominions of hostile great Powers stronger than herself. But in every case the lack of sea command was the all-important factor in robbing her of her dependencies. This becomes manifest when the history of the decline of Spanish authority in Central and Southern America is studied. And the question is especially well illustrated by what occurred when those States of the Southern Pacific, Chili and Peru, emerged from the wreck of the Empire of Charles V. and took their place as independent republics. Chili gained her liberty by creating a fleet. As long as Spain was able to land armies on the lengthy coast-line of this essentially maritime province, the gallant endeavours of the people to shake off the yoke of despotism led only to useless bloodshed and to fruitless sacrifice. But when an inspiration seized the Chilian patriots and they suddenly improvised a navy which was able to hold its own at sea, freedom was their immediate reward. Then, not content with having achieved their own emancipation, they hurried to the assistance of Peru and liberated their northern neighbours as easily as they had freed themselves. Bereft of maritime control, Spain could not despatch transports to the Pacific ports, and she lost her fairest possessions because when the crisis came she was unable to reinforce her garrisons. It is a remarkable story, and one of transcendent interest to nations dreaming of world power.

Spain and her western empire.

The dramatic creation of the Chilian navy may excite the imagination, the exploits of Cochrane may arose our enthusiasm. But it was not by raids, and bombardments, and cuttings out, that Chili and Peru became independent nationalities. It was because the parent State with its infinitely greater military resources could not bring those resources into play against its defiant children, owing to the control of the local waters having slipped from its grasp.

Spain lost her South American dependencies by the action of those dependencies themselves, and as a consequence of being unable to send military forces to the centres of disturbance owing to the perils of the sea. Great Britain lost her American colonies under somewhat analogous conditions, although in that case it was the navies of France and Spain and Holland which closed the seas to the despatch of reinforcements, while on land the colonists in the main worked out their own salvation. But the transfer of Canada from France to Great Britain stands on a different footing. For on this occasion the distant and isolated province was conquered from outside, although its transfer to a hostile nation was mainly caused by the inability of the parent State to send succour to its colony across the sea.

France and Canada. The story of Louisbourg has already been told on p. 97. We have seen how Louis XV., after its first capture by the New England colonists, made desperate efforts to recover the island of Cape Breton: two distinct expeditionary forces were despatched across the Atlantic to effect this purpose. But British superiority at sea prevented the arrival of one, and it seriously hampered the movements of the other; and France only recovered her position in North America in virtue of the Peace of Aix-la-Chapelle.

During the opening years of the Seven Years' War the decisive naval superiority of Great Britain made it impossible for the government of Louis XV. to send reinforcements to New France. Therefore it came about that the armies of Amherst and Wolfe and Murray, armies of no great numerical strength, operating in a very extended theatre of war, and opposed to brave troops under capable leadership strenuously supported by a patriotic people, were able to overcome the gallant resistance of the garrison, and to add the basin of the St Lawrence to the British Empire. In a later chapter it will be indicated how in that remarkable succession of campaigns the victors relied upon the mobility conferred by sea-power and upon the support accorded by the fighting fleet. But the issue of the conflict was in reality primarily due to the inability of France, in spite of her great military resources, to land the comparatively small number of troops which would have sufficed to give her generals, Montcalm and Lévis, a fighting superiority on land. And the cause of that inability was the loss of command of the sea.

And so it has ever been. A scattered empire, if its distant colonies and dependencies be not knit to the mother country and to each other by communications enabling its military strength to be concentrated at any point where the realm is threatened, whether by internal disorders or by external attack, must fall to pieces. If these communications lead across the ocean they must be protected by an adequate navy. For lack of sea-power Spain has dropped down from the proud position of dominating a whole continent, and owning what was at one time the most wealth-giving archipelago in the world, to the position of a second-class power. It was due to maritime weakness that France was deprived of her Indian empire when it was little more than a conception of dominion to come.

Conclusion.

The maintenance of the British Empire on its present basis depends primarily upon sea-power. And this is not merely because a paramount navy is essential for the security of its maritime trade and its huge mercantile marine, but because military forces must be maintained to defend its colonies and dependencies and may have to be strengthened in the hour of danger. The army must be distributed over its vast area and must be kept up to adequate strength, so as to preserve its possessions against disorder from within and against aggression from without. Facilities must exist for moving these military detachments from colony to colony and from province to province when emergencies arise. And owing to geographical conditions these transfers of troops must take place over-sea, which becomes impossible without naval preponderance in time of war.

CHAPTER XII.

THE RISKS RUN BY TRANSPORTS AT SEA AND INCONVENIENCES INCURRED BY THE TROOPS IN MOVEMENTS ON BOARD SHIP.

IN this chapter it is proposed to discuss the difficulties and dangers which beset troops on board ship while in transit across the sea and in port, and to point out the risks run by transports and freight-ships engaged in conveying warlike stores and supplies for armies operating in the field. In the next chapter the risks run in disembarkation, and after disembarkation, owing to change of maritime conditions, will be dealt with. These dangers are partly attributable to the chances of bad weather, fog, errors in navigation and so on, which beset the mariner in time of peace, and they are partly due to the possible action of the enemy afloat and ashore.

Purpose of chapter.

Transports filled with troops are in the present day to all intents and purposes helpless against attack. In the Greek and Roman era, and at a later date when fighting-ships took the form of galleys and analogous craft depending partly upon oars and partly upon sails for motive power, soldiers on board ship could use their arms, could engage in the hand-to-hand combats which took place when rival vessels grappled, and were not always clearly distinguishable from the naval *personnel*. But with the gradual development of artillery, troops when afloat have more and more degenerated into becoming purely passengers, unable to offer resistance if the vessel they are in is engaged by the enemy.

Helplessness of transports if attacked in the present day.

And under existing conditions the troop-transport, unless it can escape from the foe by superior speed, is absolutely at the mercy of insignificant torpedo craft or gunboats, should they assail it. The modern steamer possesses no power of offence, it affords no protection against even the smaller natures of ordnance carried by fighting-ships, it has no searchlights to observe the approach of torpedo-boats at night: its only hope of security, therefore, lies in its engines, if these be of sufficient power to drive the ship faster than the assailant can go—and such conditions are seldom found in vessels chartered for the conveyance of troops. The sinking of the *Kowshing* at the opening of the Chino-Japanese war, and similar incidents of a later date in the same seas, serve as striking illustrations of the helplessness of the troop-transport when attacked.

<small>Normal perils of the sea.</small>

But before further considering the dangers to which troops are exposed when at sea owing to the action of the enemy, the question of the normal perils of the sea should be dealt with. It has been already explained in chapter ii. how progress in shipbuilding and in the art of navigation tends to lessen the dangers which war-vessels run from the action of the elements, and this applies equally to transports conveying troops. The introduction of steam has altered the whole aspect of the question in so far as foul weather is concerned; but the risk of fogs, and the delays and inconveniences incurred therefrom, are as serious as ever. Any great movement of troops across the sea is still therefore liable to be interrupted and to be retarded by unfavourable climatic conditions, to an extent which may seriously interfere with their employment to good advantage on shore.

<small>Examples of dispersion of military expeditions on the high seas by bad weather.</small>

A few examples of delay or danger to, and of dispersion of, military expeditions on their passage across the sea owing to bad weather may be of interest, although they date back to a bygone age. In the latter part of the thirteenth century—Marco Polo and others who record the facts differ as to the exact date — the Tartar emperor Kublai, grandson of Genghis Khan, despatched a colossal force to conquer Japan. Authorities differ as to its strength and as to the exact story of what actually occurred; but all are agreed that the expedition met with an unprecedented catastrophe, owing to a hurricane in which the greater part of the flotilla disappeared. The first attempt to relieve Malta from Sicily during the great siege by the Turks failed because the succouring flotilla was overtaken by a storm soon after leaving Syracuse: this scattered the shipping, drove several transports ashore, and compelled the whole armada to put back into port to refit. Richard Cœur de Lion's armament destined for Palestine suffered very severely in the same waters.[1]

So much has been written at various times on the subject of a possible invasion of the United Kingdom, that it is of interest to note how often expeditions destined against its shores have miscarried owing to the transports being delayed or dispersed by storms, which need not necessarily have brought about the failure of the enterprise had the troops been conveyed in steamers: it is not, however, suggested that such invasion is feasible as long as the country's first line of defence, the navy, is maintained at its proper standard of strength and efficiency. William the Conqueror was at his first attempt driven back by strong winds to the coast of Normandy, and his bold venture was much delayed by this *contretemps*. The Duke of Richmond (Henry VII.) made an attempt to reach England from Brittany with 5000 men two years before his success at Market Bosworth, but his flotilla was dispersed by a gale in the Channel. William of Orange's first effort failed owing to the same cause. Ormonde's great expedition from Coruña in 1718, destined to replace the Old Pretender on the throne, was driven back by a hurricane in the Bay

Examples of this in the case of attempted invasions of England in the past.

of Biscay, and the project was abandoned in consequence. Charles Edward started from Calais in 1744 with 7000 men; but his armada met with tempestuous weather—many vessels were lost, the expedition put back, and the enterprise was postponed till the following year, when the Prince, accompanied by only a meagre retinue, made his appearance on the shores of Scotland. We have seen how Hoche's elaborate project failed, largely owing to adverse winds in Bantry Bay.

<small>Bad weather less mischievous under modern conditions.</small>

In the present day rough weather may render embarkations or disembarkations impracticable, but it would rarely seriously interfere with the passage of troops across the sea. The modern transport can be expected to ride out a storm, and is not likely to be seriously delayed by high winds and a heavy sea. Men and horses suffer from the effects of the buffetings to a certain extent, and they deteriorate in some measure in military efficiency; but owing to the speed at which steamers travel, and to the conveniences enjoyed under modern conditions by troops at sea, there is no comparison between the depreciation suffered by an army performing a voyage to-day, and the depreciation which an army would have suffered in making the same voyage a century ago.

<small>Fogs.</small>

The danger caused by fogs has already been referred to. Thick weather is especially prevalent in certain seas and in certain seasons, and when encountered it must cause delay and it may cause disaster. The frequent occurrence of fogs in the Yellow Sea and Sea of Japan added considerably to the difficulties of the Japanese during their operations in Korea and Manchuria in 1904, and it influenced the military situation to a certain extent in the opening days of the war.

<small>Carrying troops in fighting-ships.</small>

It used formerly to be a very common practice to carry troops in fighting-ships. In the epoch anterior to the gradual evolution of regular navies there was often, indeed, no very clear distinction between the fighting seaman and the fighting landsman when at sea. The Spanish Armada was to land 6000 men to aid the Duke of Parma in his invasion of England; but from the somewhat vague instructions given to the Duke of Medina Sidonia, these 6000 men would appear to have been part of the fighting complement of the ships.

A few years later a singular incident occurred, which was to show that a theory existed in those days that in time of war troops must be conveyed across the sea in fighting-ships, and not in ordinary trading vessels, or, as we call them now, transports. Some Spanish reinforcements were being brought by sea to the Netherlands conveyed in neutral English and German merchant ships from Atlantic ports. The little flotilla, which was not sailing under convoy, fell in with a Dutch squadron under Admiral Haultain in the Channel. This promptly gave chase, captured some of the vessels, and drove the rest under the guns of Dover into territorial waters, where pursuit was checked by the English gunners,—England was not concerned in the struggle between Spain and the States-General, but it is not impossible that the violation of neutrality would have been less promptly resented had the culprits not been Dutch; James I. was favouring a Spanish policy, and the country regarded the commonwealth which had sprung so suddenly into existence as a commercial community, with mixed feelings. Haultain took drastic measures against the unfortunate soldiers who had fallen into his hands. He had them bound together, two and two, and then, by signal from his flagship, they were all simultaneously tossed into the sea to feed the fishes. This act strikes one in the present day as one of wanton barbarity, which the embittered nature of the contest in Flanders in no way palliates; but the contention appears to have been that the troops were pirates, because they were travelling in trading vessels and not in ships of war. It was the first time that Spanish troops had tried to

Carrying troops in merchant-ships regarded as piracy by the Dutch three hundred years ago.

reach the scene of action by this method, and it seems to have been the last.

Later examples.
In the middle of the seventeenth century there came to be a much clearer distinction between the troops carried on board fighting-ships and the crews of those ships. And the practice of transporting large bodies of soldiers on board men-of-war who are destined for military purposes, has since that time grown more and more unusual. At the same time, many examples could be quoted of troops being conveyed in war-vessels, and of being present in naval actions in consequence, at a much later date.

At the battle of Texel in 1673 between Prince Rupert and De Ruyter, there were 6000 troops on board the Prince's fleet, destined for land operations in the Netherlands. When Elphinstone in 1796 captured the Dutch warships in Saldanha Bay, there were 2000 infantry and artillery on board the prizes.

The troops which were to land in Ireland under Hoche on the occasion of that brilliant soldier's famous but unfortunate venture, were all carried on fighting-ships. The whole scheme hinged on evading the British fleet, and shipping was somewhat scarce in French ports. Six hundred men were carried on each of the ships of the line, and 250 on each of the frigates. Had the armada been brought to battle in the open sea, its naval *personnel*, which was far from efficient, would have found these crowds of sea-sick soldiers a terrible burden.

The most remarkable example of the conveyance of troops on men-of-war in modern times is afforded by the expedition to the Crimea in 1854. When the allied forces left Varna, practically the whole of the French and Turkish war-vessels were employed as transports owing to lack of shipping. The British squadron acted as escort. There was at the time a powerful Russian fleet in Sevastopol, and the risk run was in consequence very great.

When there is no prospect of a naval action the chief objection to transporting troops in fighting-ships is, that there is very limited accommodation for men and none for horses. It has often occurred in times of emergency that a few hundred men have been transported from one place to another in a battleship or cruiser at a moment when there has been no question of encountering the enemy at sea: a battalion was brought from Mauritius to the Cape in this manner at a period when troops were urgently needed early in the late South African war. But the ordinary practice is to convey troops in transports, except in military movements on an insignificant scale and under unusual circumstances. It is the most convenient and satisfactory procedure, and when there is any risk of a naval engagement the objections against taking up the limited space which is available on a man-of-war with passengers are so serious, as to render the plan almost unjustifiable.   *No objection when there is no prospect of a naval action.*

Troops kept for any length of time on board ship lose their fighting efficiency to a certain extent. They deteriorate. Men lose their marching power, and horses and transport animals not only lose condition, but may become entirely unserviceable for a considerable time if the circumstances happen to be unfavourable. The extent to which this is the case depends not only upon the length of the voyage, but also upon the efficiency or otherwise of the arrangements, upon the space allotted to man and beast, upon the climate, and upon the weather. In the present day troops enjoy far greater comfort at sea than they did in the sailing era, and they therefore suffer less depreciation within a given time on board ship than they used to formerly: moreover, as voyages are more rapid, the troops are a considerably shorter period on board in traversing a given distance than they were in the Peninsular or even in the Crimean days. But even now an army conveyed by ships from one point to another is not so capable of sus-   *Deterioration of troops on voyages.*

tained effort when it arrives as it was when it started, and it may not fully recover the effects of the voyage for some little time after it disembarks.

Sir J. Moore's view.

It is interesting in this connection to note that Sir J. Moore, than whom few soldiers of this or any other country have enjoyed so extensive and varied an experience of military expeditions over-sea, held strong opinions as to the deterioration which an army suffers on a voyage. At the commencement of his famous campaign in the Peninsula, which ended at Coruña, the question came up for consideration whether the force under his orders should proceed from Lisbon by sea or by land to unite itself with the reinforcements which were to be landed in Galicia. He decided on the latter course. "The passage by sea is precarious," he wrote in his diary, "an embarkation unhinges." Communications in Portugal at the time were most indifferent, the Tagus afforded exceptional facilities for getting his force on board ship, and in Galicia there was no lack of well-sheltered ports to land at: the relative advantage of the sea route as against the land route were, in fact, in this case, unusually marked. Yet the general, who had taken part in campaigns with British troops in Corsica and the West Indies, and Egypt and Sicily, who had been present at the attempted landing at Cadiz, and who had taken an army to Sweden, chose the rough routes over the hills and valleys of Portugal, in preference to a voyage which would probably not have lasted more than two and three days, from one of the finest natural harbours in the world to a coast on which only a few miles apart were to be found Ferrol and Vigo and Coruña, with Oporto also available on the way. And if the same case presented itself in the present day, it must be remembered that the superiority of the modern transport over the sailing-vessels of Sir J. Moore's time is no greater than is the superiority of the communications by road and railway in Portugal by which an army would move now over the tracks which led north-eastwards from Lisbon in the year 1808. The inconveniences suffered on board ship, and the depreciation which takes place in fighting efficiency, must not of course be exaggerated. On short voyages it may almost be ignored. But when the effect of maritime command upon land campaigns is examined, it is important not to forget that there are some drawbacks to the movement of troops by sea. These drawbacks are perhaps not so serious as to very appreciably lessen the value of such maritime command, but they must not be left wholly out of consideration.

We now come to the somewhat controversial subject of the risks which military forces run while on the high seas owing to acts on the part of the enemy. Extreme views are entertained with regard to this question in certain quarters. And this will be a convenient place to examine into the doctrine of the "fleet in being" which has been the subject of so much discussion among naval strategists of late years. *The doctrine of the "fleet in being."*

The term "fleet in being" is applicable to any aggregate of fighting-ships which, as Sir W. Laird Clowes defines it, is "potential";[2] and this definition is in accordance with Mahan's more elaborate explanation: "A 'fleet in being' therefore is one the existence of which, although inferior, on or near the scene of operations, is a perpetual menace to the more or less exposed interests of the enemy, who cannot tell when a blow may fall, and who is therefore compelled to retard his operations until that fleet can be destroyed or neutralised."[3] Although this is a question of purely naval strategy, the expression itself was first used in connection with the possibility of a great military expedition across the seas, and it is from that point of view that it will be discussed and illustrated here.

The origin of the expression dates back to a memorable event in the days of William III. After the battle of Beachy Head, when Lord Torrington, consequent upon an indecisive *Origin of the expression.*

action with the very superior French fleet under Tourville in the Channel, retired to the Thames, the admiral was called to account and was tried by court-martial. In his defence he said, "Had I fought otherwise our fleet had been totally lost, and the kingdom laid open to invasion. . . . As it was, most men were in fear that the French would invade, but I was always of another opinion, for I always said that whilst we had a fleet in being they would not dare to make an attempt." Torrington assumed that the French, masters of the Channel, did not despatch a military force to the shores of England because of the existence of his inferior fleet beyond the Straits of Dover. But the truth seems to have been that Louis XIV. was not ready to undertake an invasion at the time. It is difficult to see how in the sailing era an inferior fleet, so inconveniently situated as Torrington's was, could have prevented the landing of an army from the ports of Normandy or Brittany on the south coast of England, or how it could even have made certain of approaching the scene of action during the time that the army was afloat. Once the army was disembarked the French with their stronger naval power could have fairly calculated on keeping its maritime communications secure.

The disaster to the Spanish Armada was due to the ignoring of the English fleet; and it is interesting to observe that when a large but inefficient Franco-Spanish fleet was for a time, in 1779, practically in command of the Channel, the Spanish commander Cordova advocated troops being put across without defeating the opposing naval forces under Admiral Hardy, while the capable French chief D'Orvilliers would not acquiesce in so hazardous a proceeding. Upon the whole, however, the history of war since the days of Beachy Head tends to show that the "fleet in being" affords but an illusory guarantee to a nation against over-sea invasion of its shores, if that fleet be as inferior to that which the enemy can bring into play as Torrington's was. The examples which can be adduced are, however, almost without exception, cases of the transport of armies in sailing vessels, in despite of hostile warships depending upon sails and not upon steam. Up to the time of the Russo-Japanese war there has been no case of the transport of an army across the seas under modern conditions in face of a "fleet in being" such as is defined by Mahan and Sir W. Clowes. The Chinese navy in 1894, even before its defeat in Korea Bay, was so wanting in any form of enterprise as hardly to be "potential." The *Merrimac* was effectually neutralised by the *Monitor* and the rest of the older-fashioned war-vessels of the Federals, at the time when M'Clellan invaded Virginia from the Yorktown peninsula in 1862. It will be shown further on that the tactical naval conditions due to steam and to torpedo craft and submarines, considerably modify the situation as regards the question of conveying a military force in ships, when there is a potential hostile flotilla in the theatre of operations. But, up to within half a century ago, actual experience in war proves that Torrington's "fleet in being" theory was a fallacy. Belligerents have over and over again not only "dared to make an attempt" of despatching expeditionary forces over the sea when maritime command was not absolutely secured, but they have achieved far-reaching military successes by taking the risk. Without going back further than the Seven Years' War, the following examples may be quoted in proof of this. *[Torrington's theory a fallacy before the days of steam.]*

In 1756 Minorca was attacked by the Duc de Richelieu's expedition, as already narrated on p. 56. There was at the time no immediate prospect of molestation by a British fleet. But the probability of interference ere the fortress on the harbour of Mahon was captured was fully foreseen, and the danger to the army was appreciated. Had Byng defeated La Gallissonière the whole French expeditionary force would probably have had to lay down its arms; but, as it turned out, "the fleet in being" had not the slightest effect. *[Examples of military forces being moved across the sea in defiance of "fleets in being."]*

The following year Lord Loudon undertook an expedition against Louisbourg from New York, the fleet escorting his transports being decidedly inferior to that within the harbour of the fortress. The attack was abandoned owing to the formidable nature of the enterprise, a decision for which the general was much blamed at the time. The troops were, however, safely withdrawn, and they got back to New York unmolested by the French "fleet in being." The incident was a very singular one. For a French vessel, having despatches on board designed to convey the impression that the garrison of the place and its state of preparation rendered it more formidable than it really was, had been purposely thrown in the way of the British fleet. The attempt was abandoned, not because of the risk at sea, which would appear to have been very real, but because of the risk on land, which was probably not nearly so great as faulty intelligence painted it to be.

The arrival of De Ternay's squadron and of Rochambeau's 5000 troops at Newport has been already referred to on p. 144. This force was conveyed across the Atlantic in defiance of the British navy in American waters. The armada was actually engaged in mid-ocean by Commodore Cornwallis with a squadron inferior to that of De Ternay, but the convoy was unharmed.

In 1781, at the time that Lord Cornwallis was cooped up in Yorktown by Washington on land and De Grasse on the Chesapeake, General Clinton actually embarked 7000 men at New York to attempt the relief of his threatened subordinate. The escorting fleet was decidedly inferior to that of the French admiral. As it turned out, however, Yorktown had capitulated before the succouring force reached the vicinity of the Chesapeake, and this retired in safety to New York.

Hoche's expedition actually reached the mouth of Bantry Bay in spite of Lord Bridport's formidable forces in the

Channel.[4] The project failed, in so far as effecting a landing was concerned, owing partly to bad luck as regards wind and partly to the inefficiency of the nautical *personnel* engaged in the enterprise. But the "fleet in being" had no effect upon the venture.

Napoleon's safe arrival in Egypt with a large expeditionary force in 1798, after a prolonged voyage, has been already dealt with on pp. 39, 40, and Nelson's failure to intercept the unwieldy lethargic armada has been discussed.

In 1825, after the Greek War of Liberation had been in progress for four years, and when the revolted nation had upon the whole fully held its own against the naval and military forces of the Sultan, Ibrahim Pasha, son of the Egyptian viceroy, succeeded in landing with a small but formidable army in the south of the Peloponnesus. Up to that time the Greek flotilla had maintained itself with brilliant success against the powerful Turkish navy. But it happened that, at the time of Ibrahim's descent, the disinclination of the revolutionary crews to remain for long periods at sea had brought it about that the "fleet in being" was not ready to act. For two years subsequently the Egyptian army prosecuted a more or less active campaign in southern Greece, although maritime command was throughout in dispute. And there can be no question that, but for the intervention of the British, French, and Russian fleets and their destruction of the Ottoman navy in the Bay of Navarino, the military force which had crossed the Mediterranean in defiance of a potential fleet, and which had managed to maintain itself while its communications were constantly jeopardised by that fleet, would have eventually stamped out the revolutionary movement by overthrowing the ill-equipped and inefficient Greek armies, and would have re-established the authority of the Caliph over the whole country from Thessaly to Cape Matapan.

The case of the transfer of the allied army from Bulgaria

to the shores of the Crimea in 1857 has already been mentioned.[5] It is probable that in this case Admiral Kornilof in Sebastopol overrated the strength of the escorting fleet, and that he was unaware that the French and Turkish fighting-ships were virtually mere transports. But this remarkable operation of war affords a striking refutation of the doctrine of the "fleet in being." The British and French naval commanders-in-chief were both opposed to the invasion of the Crimea: their objections were not, however, based upon the potentialities of the Russian squadron in the great fortress against which the army was to act. Kornilof proved himself to be an able and determined fighting man before many weeks had passed away. The allies undoubtedly accepted very serious risks. But the fact remains that they were not hindered from undertaking the hazardous enterprise by the existence of a "fleet in being"; that, as it turned out, the landing was effected without interference; and that the campaign as a whole achieved its object.

Very few examples to be found of troops in transports being captured.

Other illustrations could be given. But the above suffice to show that in the sailing era military commanders were not deterred from undertaking expeditions across the sea even when there was a potential hostile fleet threatening the operation, and that naval commanders were prepared to accept the responsibility which such enterprises imposed on them. "We may fight their fleet," wrote Nelson in 1796 when a French descent on Tuscany was anticipated, "but unless we can destroy them, their transports will push on and effect their landing. What will the French care for the loss of a few men-of-war? It is nothing if they can get into Italy." And in the annals of the century which passed between the capture of Minorca by the Duc de Richelieu and the fall of Sebastopol, it is remarkable how very few instances are to be found of the interception of military forces at sea by the warships of the enemy.

Napoleon's great expedition to Egypt was, as narrated on p. 40, very nearly cut off at Alexandria before it even reached its destination,—an admiral of less impetuous temperament than Nelson might have remained on that coast from the 28th June to the 1st July. There were other examples of narrow escapes, and on one or two occasions small expeditionary forces were actually caught at sea. In 1798 a force of 3000 French troops, carried on board of a weak squadron under Commodore Bompart, attempted a descent on Lough Swilly; but the armada was intercepted by a fleet under Commodore Warren, was promptly attacked and was signally defeated, the greater part of the force being captured: the celebrated Wolfe Tone was among the prisoners. But this is one of the very few instances of an expedition of this character failing either to reach its destination or else, as in the case of Hoche's attempt upon the south-west coast of Ireland, returning to its starting-point without serious interference from the hostile navy. The following incident is, however, worthy of notice as an example of a "fleet in being" dealing most decisively with a military force on the high seas, although the circumstances were entirely out of the ordinary.

In 1810, what is now Chili revolted against the authority of Spain, and for eight years the struggle continued more or less without interruption. At first the Chilians gained a certain measure of success, and they, indeed, for a time established their independence; but, thanks to their sea-power, the Spaniards overthrew the patriot government and re-established their ascendancy. Then in 1817 a small revolutionary force came over the Andes from what is now Argentina, and drove the army of occupation back into its coast fortresses. There followed a desperate campaign against Spanish reinforcements which were brought round by sea from Lima, in which the Chilians gained the upper hand, and thereupon the patriot leaders suddenly conceived

Fate of Spanish reinforcements going to South America in 1818.

the idea of creating a navy. An East Indiaman lying in Valparaiso was converted into a fighting-ship, stood boldly out of the harbour, and successfully attacked two Spanish war-vessels lying outside. Three more merchantmen were armed with all speed, and then the little squadron sailed away south with a great purpose in view. Large reinforcements of troops from Europe were, it was known, coming round Cape Horn, and these were escorted only by a single frigate. The frigate was attacked and taken; then, one by one, the transports as they sailed northwards wholly unsuspecting danger were rounded up and captured; and eventually only three out of the eleven which had formed the original flotilla quitting Spain managed to get into Callao in Peru. Still this brilliant and, as it turned out, decisive success was in reality due mainly to surprise. When the Spanish troops were despatched from Cadiz there was no idea of a "fleet in being" threatening their voyage through the southern Pacific.

Few occasions on which an army has been attacked on the high seas.

This case in South America is one of the very few where in modern times an important military force has been dealt with by a hostile fleet while on the high seas. Considering the number of occasions on which expeditions have been despatched across the seas, it is remarkable how few examples can be found of their being seriously interfered with by the warships of the enemy. It is interesting to note, however, that on the occasion of what was perhaps the greatest naval encounter in the history of war, a large army, carried in the vessels of one of the contending sides, appears to have suffered very little harm. This was at the battle of Ecnomus in the first Punic war, fought soon after the Romans first asserted their sea-power in open fight with the rival nation. Determined to carry the war into the enemy's country, Rome despatched an enormous armada from Sicily to make its way to Libya for an attack on Carthage. The flotilla consisted of 330 sail, with 100,000 sailors; the soldiers carried on board amounted to 40,000. A Carthaginian fleet of about equal strength attacked this imposing armament, and a desperate fight ensued in which the Romans proved victorious. They continued on their way, watched by the hostile fleet, and a landing was safely effected on the opposite side of the gulf of Tunis to where Carthage stood, the Punic flotilla having been drawn up near the city to oppose a disembarkation there, and being apparently unable to get across the gulf in time to interfere with the actual landing.

If we accept the teachings of history we cannot escape from the conclusion that in ancient days and in the sailing era the "fleet in being" had not the terrors for a flotilla of transports at sea that have sometimes been imputed to it. It was indeed the practice to move considerable bodies of troops by ship, even when maritime preponderance rested with the enemy. But before pointing out how modern conditions modify the strategical aspects of this question, it will be worth while examining why it was that in the sailing days it often happened that, even when an assemblage of helpless merchantmen crammed with soldiers met with hostile ships of war, they so often escaped unscathed.

Importance of "fleet in being" over-estimated in the sailing days.

The landsman who endeavours, even on paper, to manœuvre a thirty-two-gun ship—to say nothing of a "seventy-four"—is not unlikely to "miss stays," if he does not commit some yet more outrageous nautical impropriety. The evolutions of men-of-war used to be somewhat complicated before the introduction of steam, and the phraseology employed adds to the difficulties of the layman in attempting to follow their intricacies. But there must be some explanation for the fact—for a fact it undoubtedly is—that formerly, even when the "fleet in being" ceased to be a bogey, and when it actually appeared in the offing to the consternation of troops sailing under convoy, the convoy generally got off scot-free. With the utmost diffidence we put forward the following interpretation of what in the present day seems almost a phenomenon.

Explanation of this. Owing to the comparatively speaking slow movements of fighting-ships in the sailing era, and to their dependence upon the direction of the wind, it was generally impossible for them to get at a convoy without being intercepted in good time by its escort. The escort could always, whether the assailants were to windward or to leeward of the flotilla as a whole, interpose itself between the enemy and the transports, and could at least delay attack on them. Speaking generally, transports could outsail line-of-battle ships, although they could not outsail frigates. Therefore supposing, for example, a military expeditionary force escorted by six ships-of-the-line and four frigates was attacked by a fleet of twelve ships-of-the-line, and could not avoid action altogether, the prospect was that there would be a partial fleet action in which the escort would be worsted, but that the convoy would be untouched. If, on the other hand, the composition of the fighting fleets were reversed, then the escorting squadron with its great superiority in ships-of-the-line would probably accept battle, trusting to keeping the frigates at a distance by superior gun power and certain of defeating the enemy's ships-of-the-line if these ventured to attack. In either case the transports stood a good chance of escaping untouched. It was when the escorting fleet was inferior, not only in ships-of-the-line but also in frigates, that the convoy ran the greatest risk. Nelson, writing to Sir W. Hamilton on the 17th June 1798 while hunting for Napoleon, said that if he met the enemy at sea, the convoy would get off, because he had no frigates.

Nelson's plan in 1798. We know from Sir E. Berry that Nelson during that famous chase had arranged, if he met the great French armada—there were in it no less than 248 transports of very varying size and sailing qualities—that his fleet should be divided into three detachments. One was to consist of six, and two were to consist of four, line-of-battle ships. Two detachments were to fight the escorting fleet, while the other was to fall upon the convoy. As regards material, Bruey's fleet was practically equal to the British fleet; Nelson was therefore contemplating fighting the French escort with inferior forces for the sake of striking a blow at Napoleon's transports. This is an interesting point, because such dispositions were unusual, although it is true that there was scarcely a precedent for so great a prize in the shape of troops at sea being offered to an attacking squadron.

Naval history in the sailing days tends to show that if the escorting fleet was prepared to sacrifice itself, the convoy generally escaped. Anson, it is true, not only defeated La Jonquière in 1747, practically destroying his squadron, but also took nine of the thirty merchantmen which he was escorting. Hawke, on the other hand, in the same year, while with his fourteen ships-of-the-line he completely defeated Commodore L'Etendeur's nine ships-of-the-line, let the convoy escape. In both these cases the convoy, consisting as it did only of merchantmen, was an "ulterior object" as compared to the fighting-ships. This of course hardly applies to the case of Napoleon's great flotilla of transports in the Mediterranean. *Anson and Hawke.*

In 1779, the French admiral D'Estaing captured the British island of Grenada in the West Indies with a fleet and a military force. Admiral Byron with a similar armada hastened from Barbadoes to relieve the island, but, arriving too late, he found the French fighting fleet at anchor and the hostile troops already disembarked. D'Estaing at once got under way, and Byron, leaving his convoy of transports hove to in rear and to windward, bore down upon the hostile *D'Estaing and Byron.*

squadron, which was somewhat stronger than his own. In the partial action that ensued Byron was upon the whole worsted. But D'Estaing made no attempt to get between the British admiral and his helpless convoy, and not a single transport was taken. D'Estaing was a soldier converted into an admiral; he was no seaman, was a poor tactician, and to an almost singular extent lacked what may be called strategical grip. The incident therefore loses some of its interest. But the fact remains that a flotilla of transports escorted by a fighting fleet came upon a superior fighting fleet, that an action was fought in which the enemy upon the whole gained the upper hand, and that nevertheless the convoy was untouched. Taking into consideration that the British armament had the weather-gauge, it is by no means certain, however, that even a more skilful commander than D'Estaing would have succeeded in inflicting injury on the British transports.

Barrington at St Lucia. Six months before the action off Grenada there had occurred an incident which illustrates the position of a convoy of transports under escort in the sailing days, when caught at anchor by a superior fleet. In December 1778 a fleet under Admiral Barrington, accompanied by transports carrying 5000 men under General Meadows, proceeded from Barbadoes to the French island of St Lucia. The troops landed and secured the northern end of the island, and by rapid well-concerted movements they obliged the garrisons to surrender within a few hours. But on the afternoon of the next day D'Estaing arrived with a fleet double the strength of Barrington's. The transports were lying in an open bay. The situation seemed in the highest degree menacing. But during the night the British admiral anchored his battleships in a long line outside of the transports, secured the ends of the line by batteries on shore, and awaited the attack of D'Estaing's fleet. The French admiral next day twice stood down the line cannonading at long range, but he made no close attack: he then sheered off and landed a military force. This force was, however, repulsed in an assault on the position of the British troops, and the British were left in possession of St Lucia. It is worthy of mention that at this time the practice of attaching fire-ships to sea-going fleets had fallen into disuse: D'Estaing had not thus at his command the most potent weapon which then existed for assailing a flotilla of vessels at anchor.

Twenty years later Nelson was to show that a fleet stationary in an open bay could be dealt with effectively by a sea-going fleet even in the sailing era. Barrington's position at St Lucia was a far more dangerous one than that of Brueys in Aboukir Bay, for his strength was greatly inferior to that of D'Estaing, and his transports were moored under his wing while those of Brueys were safe at Alexandria. In those days naval ordnance had a very limited range, and a cannonade such as D'Estaing satisfied himself with could do but little damage to the transports lying behind the barrier formed by his ships-of-the-line, even supposing that it had caused injury to these latter. Under the conditions of the present day, unless the escort were moored at a considerable distance outside the transports, these might suffer very severely from a bombardment. It is one of those situations which tactical developments have completely transformed, and where experiences of a century ago afford little guidance in the present day.

This question of transports and escorts in the sailing days has been dealt with at very considerable length. Viewed as a whole, the examples which have been quoted tend to the conclusion that under the conditions which then obtained the doctrine of the "fleet in being" does not bear examination. Transports at sea, no doubt, ran a certain amount of danger if hostile warships were at large; but they seldom actually encountered fighting craft, and if they did they very often managed to escape scot-free. But it *The effect of the "fleet in being" under modern conditions.*

is important to clearly understand how greatly the introduction of steam and the development of fighting-ships of all kinds in the last half century, coupled with the establishment of cable communication and the installation of wireless telegraphy, have modified the strategical aspect of the conveyance of troops over the sea when maritime command is not assured. The good fortune which played so conspicuous a *rôle* while Napoleon was making his hazardous voyage from Toulon to Alexandria, which aided Hoche's armada to make the coast of Kerry, and which was not altogether absent when the allies reached the shores of the Crimea without seeing Kornilof's fleet, cannot be expected to smile on an expeditionary force in the future. Movements and concentrations cannot in these scientific days be so easily concealed from the enemy either on sea or on land as they used to be. And a multitude of transports escorted by a fleet of fighting-ships will not enjoy the same prospects of escape if an enemy's squadron heaves in sight, as convoys did in the days of L'Etendeur and Byron. Steam has introduced an elasticity as regards movements which did not exist in the sailing era. The effect of a modern cruiser with its formidable ordnance and its fish-torpedoes getting among a flotilla of steamers with troops on board while the battleships are in hot fight on the horizon, might be very serious. Its discharges would be infinitely more damaging than anything that a frigate with its round-shot was able to do against vessels of the class usually told off to convey military detachments in the eighteenth century. There would in the present day be a justification for Torrington's theory of the "fleet in being" in the Thames while a superior navy roamed the Channel, such as did not exist when that theory was first enunciated.

Influence of torpedo craft and submarines. And this leaves out of account those terrors to the unarmed transport—the destroyer, the torpedo-boat, and the submarine. The radius of action possessed by such craft is, it is true, somewhat limited. In a case analogous to that above quoted of Barrington at St Lucia, where a fleet of ships-of-the-line and of transports at anchor in an unprotected bay was threatened by a superior squadron of fighting-ships, and where both sides were operating in a theatre of naval war far removed from home, it might easily be the case that neither of the fleets was accompanied by torpedo craft. But anywhere within their radius of action a flotilla of torpedo-boats or destroyers is a most effective "fleet in being" as against a military expedition over-sea. Torpedo-boat stations afford an invaluable protection to a coast-line against hostile descents. What occurred at Port Arthur at the outset of the Russo-Japanese war shows the risks run, even by fighting-ships provided with search-lights and quick-firing guns and anti-torpedo nets, if they are assailed by a swarm of these hornets of the sea when anchored in the open. The situation of a flotilla of helpless transports attacked under like conditions would be desperate. And although a fighting fleet when under weigh at night has not perhaps very much to fear from the enterprise of torpedo-boats, that does not apply to at all the same extent to an assemblage of merchant steamers engaged in conveying any considerable military expeditionary force across the sea. The failure of the Russian torpedo craft within Port Arthur to interfere in the least with the disembarkation of a great Japanese army on the coast, less than one hundred miles distant from where they were lying, is one of the most singular circumstances in the story of the war in the Far East. The fact that the channel into the harbour of the fortress was temporarily blocked against the exit of battle-ships and cruisers does not account for what remains, at the time of writing, a mystery.*

* It is not proposed to discuss at any length the, till recently somewhat controversial, topic of a possible invasion of England. The views of the moderate "blue-water school" on this subject find general acceptance at last, and no

Under modern conditions, movement of troops over-sea, unless maritime preponderance be assured, is more risky than was formerly the case.

Under modern conditions it is undoubtedly the case that the movement of troops and military stores by sea in time of war is a more delicate operation, if maritime preponderance be not fully assured, than it was in the days of the great naval wars which created the British Empire. Although, apart from the possible action of the enemy, steam and the vast improvements which have taken place in shipbuilding greatly facilitate the maritime transport of men and animals and material, although voyages are rapid and almost independent of weather, although arrangements for embarkation and disembarkation are generally adequate, although the great size of modern steamers favours the keeping of units together and reduces deterioration *en route* to a minimum, there is more danger from the enterprises of hostile ships of war than was formerly the case. But while fully admitting that this is so, it is important that the danger should not be exaggerated.

Importance of not overrating the danger.

"Do not make pictures for yourselves," wrote Napoleon, exasperated at the caution of his sailor chiefs. "All naval operations since I became head of the Government," he wrote another time, "have always failed because my admirals see double, and have learnt—where, I do not know—that

advantage would be gained by rekindling the smouldering ashes of a discussion which has closed. But it may be pointed out that, when the advocates for the maintenance of a great army for home defence founded their arguments upon the possibility of a temporary loss of command of the Channel, they overlooked what is in reality a second line of defence. Assuming the seagoing fleet which guards the shores of the United Kingdom to have been "lured away," or to be absent cruising, the transports conveying the invading army would still be a prey to those detachments of torpedo-boats which are stationed at various points round the coast. The neutralisation of these by a hostile fleet controlling the Channel would be a mere matter of time, it is true. But, in the controversy which raged so long, those who hesitated to put their trust in the Royal Navy always admitted that the invaders could only hope for a fleeting opportunity. Should the British navy suffer a serious disaster in battle in home waters and lose command of the sea, its torpedo craft would assuredly not protect the country from invasion. But were such an untoward event to occur, the enemy would not need to undertake the operation,—the British isles would be starved into submission without it.[6]

war can be made without running risks." Military operations, using the term in its widest sense, are essentially a game of hazard. The skilled commander, whether he be a seaman or a soldier, endeavours to reduce the element of chance within safe proportions. Such an enterprise as the transfer of the Allied army from Varna to the shores of the Crimea in 1854, while a formidable "fleet in being" lay in Sebastopol, would, under the conditions of the present day, be a most hazardous undertaking. But the chief who shrinks from moving troops by sea past an insignificant naval force which is effectively contained by an alert and powerful squadron, is not likely to achieve great ends in war. The departure of General Shafter's army from Tampa for Santiago was delayed six days by a false report that three Spanish war-vessels had been sighted off the north coast of Cuba, although an effective escort squadron was assembled waiting to accompany the transports. "It is as a threat," says Mahan, "that the fleet in being is chiefly formidable." And it is important to distinguish in such cases between the substance and the shadow.

The terrors of the situation, should a fleet of transports carrying troops and military material encounter a hostile cruiser, are generally depicted in glowing colours. The impotence of the soldiers to avert a catastrophe, the grave loss of life which is likely to arise, the probable destruction of stores which may be urgently needed in the theatre of war, all tend to make a lurid picture. But a fleet of transports ought not to be without some kind of escort capable of occupying the attention of the intruder. And, even assuming that there is no escort, it is by no means certain that more than one or two units in the fleet will suffer. A steamer cannot be extinguished in a moment unless by a torpedo, and for it to be struck by a torpedo the enemy must have got to close range. An unarmoured vessel will seldom be crippled by mere cannonade till some little time has elapsed.

Fleets of transports attacked by cruisers.

This of course depends greatly on the gun-power of the cruiser, and upon the respective speeds of the vessels; but the exploits in commerce destroying and the attacks on transports in the Sea of Japan by Russian warships in 1904, do not point to the conclusion that the steamer attacked is necessarily disposed of at once.

If a solitary cruiser assails even an unprotected flotilla of transports, it must take its victims one at a time; and while it is dealing with one the others disperse. What happens when a terrier gets loose among a swarm of rats in an open field? One rat is pounced upon in an instant, worried, and flung aside expiring; another is snapped up after a brisk scamper, and is demolished like the first; a third is run down fifty yards away, and is left a corpse upon the battlefield; the rest—the rest have scattered off in all directions. And it must be remembered that the activity of the terrier as compared to the rat is far greater than the speed of the cruiser as compared to the transport. The sinking or the capture of one or two transports must always be a serious disaster,—the risk of it cannot be faced with a light heart; but the theory that the movement across the sea of military force becomes impossible, because there may happen to be one or two hostile fighting-ships at large, is inadmissible unless war is to be degraded to the position of mere peace manœuvres.

Japanese action in 1894 and 1904.

The Japanese in 1894, and again in 1904, have afforded to the world an object-lesson on this subject. In each case they commenced the transport of troops to Korea from the very outset. In 1894 their fleet did not bring the Chinese navy to battle till many weeks had elapsed, during which thousands of men had poured across the sea into Korea. In 1904 they dealt the Russian fleet a severe but not a decisive blow within a few hours of deciding upon war, and then proceeded to transport a huge army from home ports to the mainland of Asia. In neither case were they frightened by the "fleet in being," although careful not to ignore its existence. But in neither case did they venture to plant down an army actually in the Liaotung peninsula till the hostile navy was practically reduced to impotence —in the one case by defeat at sea, in the other by the blocking of the narrow entrance to Port Arthur. Masters of amphibious strategy, they have known when to venture and they have known when to hold their hand. As an illustration of the art of war this feature of the great struggle in Eastern Asia stands apart, commanding attention and establishing precedent.

CHAPTER XIII.

THE RISKS AND DIFFICULTIES WHICH ATTEND TROOPS IN EMBARKING AND DISEMBARKING, AND AFTER DISEMBARKATION, OWING TO WEATHER AND OWING TO POSSIBLE ACTION OF THE ENEMY'S NAVY.

Subjects to be dealt with in chapter. THE dangers and difficulties to which transports conveying troops and warlike stores and supplies are exposed do not necessarily end when they reach the point of disembarkation. Nor are the troops free from risks due to maritime conditions, while landing and after they have landed. Considerable difficulties will often attend disembarkation. After the force is ashore, its sea communications may be cut. And tempestuous weather may supervene when part of the army is on land and part is still on board ship, bringing about separation, and laying open that fraction which has disembarked to be attacked by hostile military forces while the rest of the troops are afloat and unable to participate in the conflict. It is not proposed in this chapter to consider the question of disembarkation in face of the enemy, or to deal with landings generally: these questions will be considered at a later stage. Here we have to do with the question of interruption from the weather, and with the difficulties which arise in landing troops under ordinary conditions of war; and we have, further, to examine into the effect of loss of naval preponderance while an army is landing, or after it has landed.

Bad weather Unfavourable weather does not often seriously impede

EMBARKING AND DISEMBARKING. 223

the original embarkation of a military force for service over-sea. As a rule, such an operation takes place in a selected harbour where storms have little effect, and where all facilities exist for putting troops and stores rapidly on board. This is not, of course, always the case; but, as a rule, a country despatching an expedition across the sea is at least able to give it a good start from a reasonably commodious port. When the embarkation takes place in an open roadstead like Port Elizabeth, there is, of course, risk of delay in tempestuous weather. At the worst, however, the transports can put to sea, and the troops which have been unable to get on board remain safely on shore. *seldom impedes the original embarkation of a military force.*

But the disembarkation at the other end of the voyage is not always so simple an operation. If it is merely a case of transfer of military force from one point to another, the embarkation and the landing both being in friendly territory, there may be no difficulty. It is when this force has to be put on shore in an enemy's country, that there is considerable likelihood of the point of disembarkation being inconvenient and even being dangerous. The harbours will probably be in occupation of the enemy — unless, owing to the circumstances of the case, the adversary can offer no military opposition, it would generally be the case that any favourable ports would be found occupied by hostile forces ready to contest the actual landing. Harbours of the best class are indeed very often fortified. Supposing the antagonist to be on guard and capable of resistance, it will probably be found necessary to put the troops on shore at some point on the coast where there may be very inadequate shelter, and where there are no conveniences for carrying out a disembarkation. If we examine history, we find that expeditionary forces undertaking descents upon an enemy's coast-line have rarely at the *Troops often have to be disembarked where there is little protection from the bad weather.*

outset made good their footing at a natural or at an artificial harbour.

There have been exceptions to this, of course. Venables' force destined against Santiago in Cuba, in 1741, landed in the fine inlet of Guantanamo—so far from the objective, as it turned out, that it never got there. Wolfe in 1759 landed far up the estuary of the St Lawrence, only a mile or two below Quebec. Napoleon landed at Alexandria. And the numerous descents of Federal armies upon the shores of Virginia during the War of Secession were made within the creeks and bays and estuaries opening out upon that huge land-locked arm of the sea, the Chesapeake. As a rule, however, where it is a question of disembarking on an enemy's coast, the landing, at least in the first instance, takes place at less convenient spots.

Examples of landings on a large scale in exposed situations. Leaving out of account operations on a minor scale, like the British and the French descent upon Minorca in the eighteenth century and the attacks upon the French coast during the Seven Years' War, it is still found that undertakings of this character, even on a great scale, very frequently open with a landing on some more or less exposed beach, or within some by no means well-sheltered inlet or bay. Abercromby's army disembarked on the shores of the bay of Aboukir. Sir A. Wellesley's first landing in the Peninsula was in the ill-protected estuary of the Mondego. The French army invading Algeria gained its footing upon the open coast at Sidi Feruch. The locality where the allies landed in the Crimea was a roadstead fringed by a long stretch of beach. The points where the Chilian army disembarked in Peru preparatory to its final advance on Lima in 1880 were in no sense harbours. And the Bay of Quinteros, near Valparaiso, where the Constitutionalist expeditionary force landed in 1881 before its final triumph over Balmaceda, offered little protection against bad weather. The Japanese army for attacking Port Arthur in 1894, and again in 1904, made its descents at exposed portions of the coast of Liaotung.

The risks run from bad weather when an ill-sheltered spot is selected for disembarkation are considerable. Delays are likely to occur. The boats are liable to be damaged. And if it comes on to blow from a dangerous quarter the operation may be interrupted, and the transports may even have to put to sea leaving such detachments as may have landed more or less in the lurch. It is rarely, if ever, the case that a large expeditionary force can depend upon a locality of this class as a permanent base: the army may effect its original landing, but it must subsequently secure some reasonably good harbour if it is to draw its subsistence and its ammunition from over the sea. Thus Wellesley, although landing at the mouth of the Mondego, always aimed at securing the fine harbour of Lisbon in due course. The allies in the Crimea marched from north of Sebastopol inland, round the head of the inlet which forms its harbour, to the south side of the fortress, so as to secure the inlets of Kamish and Balaclava as bases. And the Japanese after a time secured the well-sheltered bay of Talienwan in both their campaigns against Port Arthur.

Nature of risks run when landing at exposed localities.

The story of Charles V. at Algiers has not lost its value as a lesson in the art of war with the passing of the centuries. It seems a long way to go back, to select, as an illustration of the dangers which may beset an army disembarked upon an enemy's coast, an incident which startled Europe a generation before the ill-starred attempt of the Spanish Armada against Elizabethan England. But there is not perhaps in the history of the world a more striking example of an operation of war of this class meeting with disaster, owing to bad weather after the initial difficulty of gaining a footing on shore had been got over. And, as in this chapter the question of the risks which the expeditionary force runs after landing owing to hostile naval power

Charles V. at Algiers as an example.

P

has also to be considered, it is interesting to note that the two most prominent figures of their respective eras, Charles V. and Napoleon, each met with a serious military reverse after having successfully planted down an army on the shores of an enemy's country. The one, Charles V., failed because he had disregarded the chance of storm. The other, Napoleon, failed because he had not secured the command of the sea.

It was in 1541 that the great Emperor Charles V. embarked upon his famous expedition against Algiers. His armada consisted of 500 sail manned by 12,000 sailors, and carrying 24,000 soldiers. The force was admirably equipped, it consisted of excellent troops, and his prospects of dealing a decisive blow at the focus and centre of the power of the Barbary corsairs would have been excellent, had he not made one great mistake. He started on this enterprise too late in the year to be able to count upon that fine weather which generally prevails in the Mediterranean during the summer months.

Nor were there wanting influential counsellors who bade him beware. The Pope, who earnestly desired the chastisement of the Algerian pirates, and whose keen insight into military affairs entitled his opinion to respect even from a leader so experienced as the Emperor, was full of forebodings. Andrea Doria, the old Genoese sea-dog who was to command the fleet, and who had been battling with corsairs and infidels in all quarters of the Mediterranean for half a century, was an expert on matters nautical whose views it was dangerous to flout, and Doria was dead against the campaign at so late a season as September. Nobody wanted to brave the winds and the waves on the exposed North African coast, in the fall of the year. But Charles V. thought of his triumph gained in Tunis some years before— it has already been referred to on p. 135—and, being one who tolerated no opposition, and who possessed unbounded confidence in his own judgment and his own skill, he silenced the expostulations of his advisers, and imperiously insisted that the great expedition should start.

The bulk of the troops landed safely one fine day in September a few miles from Algiers, and the Emperor forthwith led them on against the hostile stronghold, only to find that its capture would prove a less easy task than had been anticipated. That night there was one of those terrific rain-storms which occur at infrequent intervals in that region. The soldiers had landed without impedimenta, and they therefore suffered severely from the want of shelter. They were dispirited by their experience, they were alarmed by the sight of the surf on the beach, and they showed no great stomach for assaulting the formidable battlements of the city when the day broke. Moreover, owing to the heavy swell, the Emperor was unable to land any of his heavy artillery, or of his stores, or of his food. So the army lay before the corsair capital two days, suffering great privations, harassed by the enemy, and losing confidence from hour to hour. Then on the third night there arose a tempest such as even Andrea Doria had never encountered before in his voyagings. One hundred and fifty transports and fifteen fighting galleys were wrecked, thousands of sailors were drowned, and the admiral only saved the rest of the huge flotilla by withdrawing it to a fairly sheltered anchorage which was three days' march distant from the Emperor's rain-sodden bivouacs.

The bad weather, rain and wind, continued. The army was starving. It was in no condition to hurl itself upon the fortifications which guarded the great Moslem centre of piracy in the Mediterranean, and the only course open to Charles V., whose bearing under the crushing misfortune was not unworthy of a mighty sovereign, was to march his men to his fleet and transports, where they lay tossing in the swell ten leagues away. The usually dry watercourses had been converted into foaming torrents. His men were famished, and exhausted with exposure. Swarms of cutthroats hung on his rear, massacring those who could not keep up with the column, and constantly threatening to fall upon the dwindling legion and to roll it up. But the undaunted Emperor fought a desperate rearguard action for miles, kept the foe at bay, and eventually with a remnant of his force reached the point where his flotilla lay at anchor awaiting him.

There it was found that so many transports had foundered or had gone ashore that the horses could not be taken on board, so these had to be destroyed. The re-embarkation was effected without especial difficulty, for the enemy was cowed by the stubborn resistance met with, and had learnt to respect the prowess of the Christian legions. The expedition sailed away again to Europe unmolested, but having lost a large proportion of its ships, a large proportion of its men, and the whole of its horses. And the Emperor may, perhaps, be accounted fortunate that the disaster, serious as it was, did not attain the magnitude of a total annihilation of the land force which the elements had so grievously beset, and that he himself did not leave his bones in the land of the Barbary corsairs.

The British descent on Ostend in 1798.

A somewhat similar incident, although on a much smaller scale—one which, however, cannot upon the whole, owing to the peculiar circumstances of the case, be described as a disaster to the expeditionary force—is worth narrating. It occurred at a much later date.

In 1798 it was ascertained in England that a large army was gathered in threatening array on the northern coast of France, and that a number of great boats were being built in the Scheldt: intelligence, moreover, came to hand that the canals leading from that river to Ostend and to Dunkirk were being enlarged to admit of their passage. It was therefore determined to attempt the destruction of the sluice gates at Ostend, and a small military expedition was despatched under naval escort to put this design in execution. The force landed without difficulty, and it effectually destroyed the locks and gates. But just as the work was completed the enemy approached in force, and when it was decided to re-embark it was found that the wind had risen ominously, that an awkward surf was beating on the beach, and that communication was cut off with the attendant fleet. News of the British descent brought up more French troops, who hurried to the scene. On the morrow the sea had not moderated, the enemy had gathered in great strength, and after offering a creditable resistance the little force was eventually obliged to surrender. It had effected its object; but the story of its being unexpectedly cut off from its transports by a change of weather serves as a valuable illustration of the perils to which troops who have landed in hostile territory may sometimes be exposed by the action of the elements.

Under modern conditions a disaster so serious as that which befell Charles V.'s fleet and transports would not be likely to occur. If a gale arises steamers lying off an exposed coast put out to sea. They are indeed in little danger as long as they have steam up. But an army landed as the Emperor's was on an open beach would, under the same circumstances, be just as much cut off from its ships in the present day as it was three and a half centuries ago. The lesson to be learnt from that fatal expedition to the Barbary coast is, in fact, of value still. Boats are no more able to land or to embark men and stores and horses on a surf-beaten strand in the days of steam, than they were in the sailing era or in the age of galleys. An army which lands on an exposed coast is always liable to be separated from its ships by bad weather. Therefore when a disembarkation takes place under conditions of this character, it behoves the commander to see to it that reserves of supplies

Under modern conditions, transports less likely to suffer in case of bad weather during a disembarkation than was formerly the case. Boats as likely to be damaged as formerly.

are put on shore with the troops, assuming that the country cannot provide for their wants should they be cut off by a change of weather. And the troops first landed should be organised and equipped so as to be independent for a time, and they should be of such strength as to be able to resist any hostile attack which is likely to be made while the state of the sea may prevent reinforcements arriving from the transports. The terrible straits in which Charles V. found himself in front of Algiers were due in some measure to his own lack of foresight, to the army being disembarked without artillery or supplies or equipment: had half the force been landed with a reasonable amount of impedimenta of this kind, it could certainly have maintained itself for several days, and it might have awaited the calming of the sea necessary for the remainder to join it in comparative security.

It is interesting to note that at the Court of Inquiry on the Convention of Cintra it transpired that, after the whole of the troops and stores had disembarked in the estuary of the Mondego and at adjacent points on the coast of Portugal, only thirty or forty boats remained serviceable. All the rest were damaged beyond repair, and those which could still be used had only been maintained in sea-worthy condition by desperate exertions on the part of the carpenters of the fleet.

Character of coast-line as affecting question of landings. The character of the coast-line of a country governs the question of disembarking troops and stores even more than the weather does. On this point an ordinary map is often most delusive. The existence of bays and indentations by no means ensures good landing-places: they may assume a very different aspect when closely examined on a chart. It often happens, moreover, that when there is deep water close in, cliffs rise abruptly out of the sea. Localities where stretches of beach conveniently accessible for boats are to be found, may have shoal water forming a barrier in front of them extending miles out to sea. Estuaries are often inaccessible owing to the existence of bars across their mouth. And protected anchorages fringed by a suitable shore may be situated at a spot where, owing to lack of communications inland, an expeditionary force could achieve nothing, even supposing it to be safely landed. On a map the invasion of Manchuria from the Gulf of Liaotung or from Korea Bay seems to present few difficulties; but the actual number of points where a landing on a great scale is feasible happens to be extremely small. Along the 240 miles of Portuguese coast from the Minho to the Tagus there were only three localities at all suitable for the disembarkation of Sir A. Wellesley's forces in 1808,— the estuary of the Douro held by the French, the mouth of the Mondego where the army actually landed, and Peniche, where there was a small fort which was garrisoned by the enemy. In many parts of the world, especially in the tropics, the approach of boats, even to points on the shore where there is a shelving and convenient beach, is absolutely forbidden for many months in the year by persistent surf,—surf which is not so much the result of local atmospheric disturbance as of a swell which sets in from the ocean, and which waxes and wanes for no very apparent reason.

It is necessary to draw attention to the influence which weather may exert upon disembarkations, and to point out how greatly the nature of the littoral may affect the operations, because these questions tend to limit the liberty of action enjoyed by the belligerent who commands the sea in a theatre of military warfare adjacent to the coast. In later chapters the enormous advantages will be explained which maritime control often confers when an army conducts a campaign in sea-girt territory, and the subject will be illustrated by many examples from the history of war.[1] But it must not be supposed that the strategical conditions can in *Importance of the question of weather in amphibious operations, and of the nature of available harbours.*

such a case be correctly estimated by a mere cursory examination of the map. Fogs and currents and shoals may sway the movements of military commanders absolutely, even though it may be indirectly. The sufferings of the British troops in the Crimea in the winter of 1854-55 were not attributable to the rigours of climate prevailing in the Tauric Chersonese alone: they were very largely the direct result of the great hurricane of the 14th of November which caused such havoc alike to transports and to the fighting-ships of the allies, in the ill-sheltered harbours of Balaclava and Kamish. Mercantile ports and anchorages are selected by the seafaring community in virtue of their convenience and of their security from the nautical point of view. They are the outcome of essentially maritime conditions. But military forces may have to depend upon landing-places for troops and stores which, owing to lack of protection, or to difficulty of approach, or to shallowness of the water near the shore, would be scouted by the masters of trading vessels. The troop-transport and the freight-ship are in fact liable to be exposed to greater risks than those arising from the normal perils of the sea, which every mariner necessarily encounters in the prosecution of his calling: this, moreover, altogether leaves out of account the possible action of hostile men-of-war or of insidious torpedo vessels.

Unfavourable landing- and embarking-places cause delay, and this may affect military operations.

The question of time is of great importance in all operations of war. Except under unusually favourable conditions —when the work of embarkation and disembarkation is being carried out in some first-class port, for instance—there must be delay in getting any large force of all arms on board ship, or in getting such a force off board ship; and a delay of this kind may be very prejudicial to the general plan of campaign. From the strategical point of view there is a vast difference between moving an army corps by sea from Torquay to Clacton-on-Sea, and moving that same army corps from Southampton to Hull: in the one case the operation is

ATTACK WHILE TROOPS ARE LANDING. 233

dependent upon the weather at two different points, in the other case the state of the weather is almost immaterial. And even assuming the elements to be propitious, the time taken in the one case will be far longer than in the other, although the distance traversed is approximately the same. In later chapters it will be shown what liberty of action the commander of a military force conducting a campaign in a theatre of war adjacent to the sea enjoys, as long as he can depend upon maritime command and can move his troops or portion of his troops from point to point in ships. But it is important to bear in mind that the facilities for carrying out such operations are greatly dependent upon the nature of the landing-places; and if these landing-places happen to be at exposed localities, the state of the weather on the day when an embarkation or disembarkation is to take place may damage the best-laid schemes, and it may ruin the most promising plan of campaign.

When the effect of intervention by the naval forces of the enemy during a disembarkation comes to be considered, it is necessary to distinguish clearly between mere raids on the part of hostile ships of war which may for the moment have eluded the vigilance of the friendly fleet controlling the theatre of maritime operations, and the appearance on the scene of opposing war-vessels in such strength as to be able to dispute command of the sea.[2] It has been shown in chap. ii. that in the later stages of the Peninsular War Wellington was appreciably inconvenienced by French and American cruisers and privateers, and that these to some degree menaced his communications with home ports. Annoyance of that sort is, however, obviously a very different matter from the actual severance of the communications of an army based on the sea by a preponderating hostile navy. The British army advancing on the Pyrenees was merely placed in a position on all-fours with that which so often *Attack by hostile vessels while disembarkation is in progress, or after it is completed.*

arises when military forces are engaged in operations against guerillas—when its convoys bringing up supplies are harassed and its stragglers are cut off. It was worried, but it was not endangered.[3] Had, however, the British navy lost general control of the Channel and of the Bay of Biscay at that time owing to some misadventure, the army could have drawn no reinforcements, nor munitions of war, nor equipment, nor forage, nor food, from over the sea, and it would have been compelled to depend wholly upon the sterile districts in which it was operating for the replenishment of supplies of all kinds. Maritime command is, as has been pointed out earlier, a question of degree. It is rarely absolute in favour of either belligerent when the contest is between nations both of which claim some measure of sea-power.

The intrusion of hostile ships of war upon the scene while a military force is actually disembarking obviously comes at a most inopportune time, if they cannot be kept at bay by the escorting squadron. The transports will probably be at anchor. Part of the troops may have landed. Portions of regiments may have reached the shore while the rest of the corps is still on board ship. Even steamers take some time to weigh and get to sea, and a solitary hostile cruiser appearing at such a moment with nothing to stop it might do incalculable mischief. Still, an incident of this nature would be unusual, and, as a matter of fact, scarcely a single case of the kind has occurred in modern times.

Difficulties of attacking transports at anchor in the sailing days.

In the sailing days there was often considerable risk involved in bringing an attacking fleet into action effectively against shipping lying in the vicinity of the shore, even when the transports were not adequately guarded by friendly war-vessels. It was necessary to get to comparatively speaking close quarters for the guns to tell, and unless the wind was coming from a favourable quarter, and unless extremely skilful seamanship was displayed, the assailants ran considerable risk of getting into serious difficulties.

Under the conditions of the present day there should likewise be appreciable difficulty in dealing a blow at transports engaged in landing troops. For, assuming the scouting to be adequate and wireless telegraphy to be in use, an army in the act of disembarking ought to get sufficient warning of the approach of the enemy to take measures for its security. There should be plenty of time for the transports to get under weigh, even if a portion of the troops were for the time being abandoned to shift for themselves on shore. If reasonable precautions are taken, attack from the sea while boats full of helpless soldiers are actually plying to and fro between the steamers and the shore ought to be impossible by day. And disembarkation by night within the radius of action of an enemy's torpedo craft is not likely to take place, except in the form of a mere desultory raid on a comparatively speaking small scale. *Improbability of such attacks under existing conditions.*

The coming of the submarine has, however, introduced a new factor. These novel engines of war are effective by day, and they are especially dangerous to vessels at anchor. Their radius of action is at present limited, and many questions concerning their construction and their capabilities have still to be fully examined by the light of experience. But science advances with rapid strides in these days, and it is reasonable to expect that submarines will, before many years have passed, possess far greater powers of offence than they can at present lay claim to. The disembarkation of a military force anywhere within the area over which submarines from an adjacent hostile naval station can roam, must inevitably be a hazardous undertaking; and there are good grounds for believing that this obstacle to landings will become more and more serious as the years go by. This is, however, a matter of conjecture: there is at present no precedent to act as a guide in forming conclusions. *Submarines in this connection.*

It has been remarked above that the interruption of an actual landing by the enemy's war-vessels is unusual. Very *Intervention of hostile naval forces after the army has landed.*

few examples of such an occurrence can be found in modern history. But the intervention of hostile naval forces after disembarkation has been completed, or else at a time when an army which is operating in hostile territory happens to be largely, if not wholly, dependent upon the sea for its line of communications, is by no means an unknown episode of war. A situation of this kind may be brought about by political changes which unexpectedly bring some great access of strength to the enemy's naval resources, as was the case when Ibrahim Pasha, fighting in the Peloponnesus, found the sea-power on which he relied wiped out of existence by the allied fleets at Navarino. Or it may result from a hostile victory at sea, as was the case when Napoleon found himself in Egypt cut off from home by Nelson's victory in Aboukir Bay. But, whatever be the cause, an army thus isolated must be placed in a position of some difficulty, and it may find itself in a position of the utmost danger.

Results of such intervention.

It was pointed out in chap. x. that, in spite of the fact that the British navy controlled the Mediterranean, and that it was making all communication between France and the Nile delta most precarious, the army which Napoleon had succeeded in planting down at Alexandria and with which he had conquered Egypt, managed to maintain itself on Egyptian soil for three years, and that the military forces under Menou had ultimately to be deal with by Abercromby's military expedition. But although the French army was in a sense marooned all this time in the land of the Pharaohs, it was marooned in a land of plenty. It did not require to draw its supplies from over the sea. The arsenal at Cairo even afforded it some aid in replenishing warlike stores. The strategical injury suffered by an army if its communications are cut, varies according to the extent to which the army is dependent for its existence upon those communications. If the theatre of war be productive, and if there be little or no fighting, an army may be completely isolated and may yet suffer little harm. Ibrahim Pasha in Greece was operating in a land devastated by years of war, and he was pitted against guerillas fighting among rugged mountains eminently suited to their tactics. When his communications by sea were severed, his forces were not only exposed to the terrors of starvation, but they were also exposed to the risk of losing all military efficiency owing to lack of warlike stores. It is doubtful if he could have prosecuted a successful campaign after Navarino, even had the Sultan not abandoned all attempts to coerce the Greeks in view of the attitude of the Great Powers. There is a great difference between the strategical position of Ibrahim after the allies destroyed his supporting fleet, and that of Napoleon and Kleber and Menou in Egypt after the battle of the Nile, although in either case an army which had planted itself down in hostile territory had its maritime communications severed by the intervention of hostile fleets.

Our own history provides us with a most instructive example of the dangers to which an army is exposed, which has based its campaign upon the sea but which sees maritime command pass into the hands of the enemy. The story of the operations is full of interest, and it illustrates many aspects of the art of war. Only an outline sketch of what occurred will, however, be given here. *The story of Yorktown.*

For the first three years of the great struggle between the revolted American colonies, aided somewhat capriciously as they were by the French, and the naval and military forces of Great Britain, the mother country held her own. Saratoga, humiliating disaster as it was, had shown the British military authorities on the spot the stuff which the rebellious colonists were made of, and it had convinced them that this was to be a serious campaign. The home government was of the same opinion. Reinforcements arrived. A definite plan of operations was concerted with the navy. And while the main British military forces maintained themselves in the north about the Hudson, detached bodies of troops, handled with vigour and manœuvred with skill, operated with considerable success in Georgia and in the Carolinas. But as the French naval forces gradually gathered strength, and as their co-operation with the levies under control of Washington became better defined, the difficulty experienced by the British in prosecuting a campaign in the southern States grew apace. And in the end the indeterminate condition of the question of command of the sea led to catastrophe to the army of occupation in the surrender at Yorktown.*

In the summer of 1780, after numerous successes in actual battle, Lord Cornwallis, who commanded the detached force in the south, found himself at Wilmington, and was there obliged to make his choice between two alternatives. The strategical situation was such that it was open to him to move back southward towards Charleston, whence he had come. Or else he was in a position to direct his march against Virginia, and to endeavour to reassert British authority in that prosperous State; and in taking this direction he would be approaching New York, where the main army under Clinton was located. Unwilling to give to his operations a direction which might be interpreted as a retreat, he resolved to advance north-eastwards towards the Chesapeake.

Up to this time the British navy had, upon the whole, controlled the Atlantic along the North American sea-board. Twice over D'Estaing had appeared on the coast, to be foiled on one occasion by the skill and vigilance of Howe, and on the other to waste his opportunities in inept, blundering operations against Savannah. Clinton in the north could therefore still count upon sending reinforce-

* The map facing p. 244, and the sketch of Virginia on p. 290, illustrate the operations.

ments from time to time to the southern States, and Cornwallis in consequence based his plans upon command of the sea, and trusted to shipping to supply him with ammunition and equipment, and to supplement the food and forage available in the districts which he was to traverse. And so it came about that when the British general made his way into Virginia early in 1781, he found the renegade Arnold there waiting for him with a small force which had been detached from New York. La Fayette, whom Washington in his anxiety for his native State had despatched to the scene, was opposing Arnold, and desultory operations, not unaccompanied by rigorous reprisals, were in full swing. But even when united with some of Arnold's troops, and after receiving further reinforcements from the Hudson by sea, Cornwallis was not strong enough to carry out an effective campaign in a difficult country which was inhabited by an intensely hostile population. So that finding himself unable to make any headway, he eventually assembled his army in the Yorktown peninsula, with his back to the Chesapeake, and there awaited developments.

These developments proved to be entirely beyond his control. For Washington had induced De Grasse, with a formidable fleet which had been for some months in the West Indies, to come to his assistance; he had arranged with the French naval and military chiefs a brilliant combination of war; and scarcely were the defensive works which the British commander was constructing on the Virginian peninsula fit for occupation, when Cornwallis found himself surrounded by land and by sea. The American general, concealing his plans and movements to the last most skilfully from Clinton at New York, had transferred his land forces round to the Chesapeake. De Grasse took up position in that great estuary, and obstinately refused to be lured out of it by Admiral Graves. Cornwallis was first blockaded and then besieged by a greatly superior army, which pushed its approaches with such determination that the British troops could only hold their ground by dint of hard fighting and heavy expenditure of ammunition. And then, when the situation was becoming critical, his gun ammunition gave out.

The British commander had conducted his defence with great spirit. He had made frequent sallies, some of which, however, had not been altogether fortunate. He had lost heavily, and it is very doubtful if he could have successfully withstood the assault which was impending when he determined to capitulate. But had Wellington been in Washington's place he would probably have described his triumph as a "damned close thing." De Grasse was very fidgety about his position in these narrow waters. Clinton, with 7000 men, was actually embarking to come round by sea to the aid of his hard-pressed subordinate, and it is difficult to say what might have happened had he actually got to the Chesapeake. Maritime command was in dispute in the North Atlantic, and a highly complex strategical situation had arisen. But the fate of Cornwallis was decided by the fact that his opponents had managed to secure naval control actually on the spot, and it was the dominating personality and the military genius of Washington which governed the issue. He it was who framed the plan and carried out its most essential details. He it was who was responsible for overcoming the greatest difficulties which stood in the way of its effective execution. He, by sheer force of character and strength of will, overcame the reluctance of his coadjutor De Grasse to maintain his station in the Chesapeake, and induced the admiral to play the game out to the end.

The story of Yorktown is especially interesting because the disaster to the army based on the sea which found its communications cut, appears in this case to have been largely attributable to the fact that ammunition could not be replenished, although the disproportion between the British force and that of the allied colonists and French was so great, that in an assault Cornwallis's resistance might have been overborne even had this not been the case. An army thus isolated does not necessarily succumb provided that it has food enough and that it has sufficient munitions of war in the magazines; and if it is not called upon to fight, a lack of munitions of war, supposing such lack to exist, need not make itself felt.

Before leaving this subject it is worth recalling an incident in the early English history, which affords a striking illustration of the position in which military forces are placed when operating in a hostile country and based upon the sea, if their maritime communications come to be in jeopardy. Between the tactical conditions of those days, whether ashore or afloat, and those of the twentieth century there is, it is true, little in common. Social life has undergone a complete transformation since that stirring age. The theatre of war has changed almost out of recognition. Out of the England of medieval times has grown up a mighty empire. But the story has its strategical value still, and its chief episode possesses an interest which grows and grows as the years pass by, for it signalises the birth of the greatest force placed at the disposal of any nation since the decline and fall of Rome—the sea-power of this land.

The story of Hubert de Burgh and the French invasion of England in 1216.

In the year 1216 the barons of England, weary of King John,—of his instability of character and of his uncertain temper,—offered the crown to Prince Louis of France. The prince arrived on the shores of Kent accompanied by an imposing array of knights and men-at-arms, and escorted by a fleet under a chieftain who appears to have combined the function of pirate with that of dignitary of the church, Eustace the Monk. The enterprise was for a time crowned with remarkable success. Except at Dover, where the even then ancient castle was stoutly defended by Hubert de Burgh, Louis carried all before him in the south-east, and having borne down resistance in that quarter, pressed north to overcome the disheartened and unwilling forces which were gathered there under the banner of King John.

Then suddenly King John died. The barons rallied to the cause of his child-successor. The French pretender suffered a crushing defeat at Lincoln; and, in the hopes of retrieving the situation and of recovering the ground which he had lost, he summoned vast reinforcements from across the Channel to come to his aid. These assembled at Calais, the requisite flotilla for their transport was got together, special fighting-ships were collected, and the whole armament put to sea under Eustace the Monk. But the passage of the imposing armada to the shores of England was not to be unopposed. Hubert de Burgh had called upon the seamen of the Cinque Ports to gather their ships together, and to equip them for the fray. They answered readily to the summons of the trusty leader whose defence of Dover Castle had marked him out as a man for a great crisis. And when the French fleet, running towards the North Foreland before a fair wind, was well up the Straits, Hubert boldly sallied out, tacked across towards Calais to get the weather-gauge, and then, bearing down straight upon the enemy, he utterly defeated the French—Eustace the Monk himself being among the slain. Thus, not only were the reinforcements, which Louis' position imperatively demanded, for all practical purposes wiped out of existence—the "fleet in being" in this case actually attacked a military force at sea—but his communications with France were gravely imperilled. The prince therefore gave up the contest, and was permitted to withdraw across the Channel by the barons, who were more intent upon getting rid of him and upon re-establishing order in the distracted kingdom, than upon following up

CONCLUSION. 243

Hubert de Burgh's great naval victory to its strategical conclusion.

The limitations of sea-power as regards bringing war to an end were pointed out in chap. ix., and the case of the French army in Egypt after the destruction of Bruey's fleet was cited as an example. It is interesting to note that in the cases quoted above to illustrate the danger which an army, dependent upon maritime communications, runs in the event of the enemy securing naval control, hostile land operations have always contributed to bring about the result. Prince Louis' endeavour to secure the English crown was, it is true, frustrated by the victory of Hubert de Burgh and the Cinque Ports' flotilla in the Dover Channel; but this was only after the pretender had met with a disaster on shore and at a time when the military forces of the barons were gathering against him. Had Washington not appeared with a superior army in Virginia, De Grasse with his warships in the Chesapeake would not have obliged Cornwallis to surrender at Yorktown. Ibrahim Pasha need not have abandoned his campaign in the Peloponnesus after Navarino, had no guerilla bands harassed his forces and thwarted his movement at every turn. In estimating the influence of maritime preponderance over land campaigns, care must be taken not to exaggerate its power while realising its possibilities.

The importance of naval control in campaigns which have territory bordering on the sea for their scene of action can hardly be exaggerated. It may govern the whole course of the conflict and may decide the issue. One of the chief purposes of this volume is to show why this is the case, and to examine into the causes of that potent influence which maritime command so often exerts over land operations. But when considering this aspect of the subject, it is well to remember that there are two sides to the question. Looking at it from the soldier's point of view, it is necessary to bear in mind the dangers which sometimes beset troops on

Conclusion.

board ship from natural causes, and to recollect the extent to which embarkations and disembarkations are frequently dependent on the weather. The difficulties which are apt to arise in selecting suitable landing-places must not be overlooked. The delays which are inseparable from a great transfer of military force from place to place by sea must be taken into account. And the unfortunate position in which a military force is likely to find itself which is dependent upon maritime communications, in case those communications are cut by the development of superior naval resources in the theatre of war on the part of the enemy, must not be forgotten. These points have been dealt with in this chapter and the preceding one in some detail. The strategist who overlooks them when sifting problems of land warfare in relation to sea-power, may go astray in his calculations.

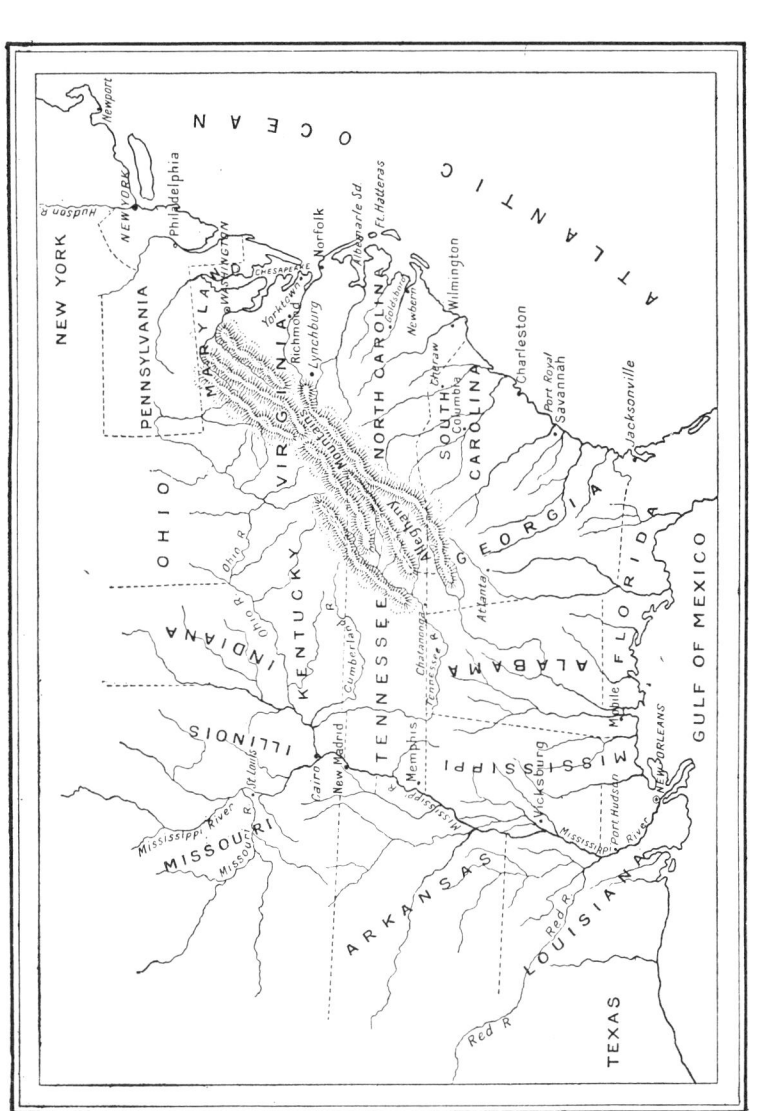

WAR OF AMERICAN INDEPENDENCE AND WAR OF SECESSION.

CHAPTER XIV.

MARITIME LINES OF COMMUNICATION COMPARED TO LAND LINES OF COMMUNICATION.

Importance of communications to an army.

THE art of war on land hinges upon questions of communications. In popular imagination the military commander is ever looking to the front, and contriving plans to beat the enemy in battle; in reality his attention is far more often concentrated upon the roads and the convoys and the depots behind him. Tactical skill and superior numbers avail him little if food runs short or if ammunition comes to an end. His army drags behind it a chain which hampers its every movement, which saps its numerical strength, and the snapping of which may mean irretrievable disaster.

Drain which communications make on the fighting strength of an army.

An examination of the distribution of troops at any period of a campaign almost invariably discloses the fact that a large percentage of the total forces in the field on either side is scattered along the lines of communication of the contending armies. It is often found to be the case that a mere fraction of the total numbers in the theatre of war is actually at the front. Even in such a case as the Franco-German war, where one belligerent achieved triumphs so constant and so complete as to place the campaign in a special niche of its own, the victorious side was compelled to maintain enormous numbers of men in inactivity, far away in rear of the scene of active fighting, and for purposes of actual battle entirely out of the reckoning. When the operations cover a vast area of country, the population of which is particularly hostile, a general may in the end find that the whole of his men are scattered about in posts in rear of that ill-defined line which divides him from his opponent, and may find that he has no force left to strike with, or with which to parry the blows of his antagonist.

Soldiers know this well, and they appreciate the causes which bring such a state of things about. A commander whose communications are absolutely secure, not only from the enterprises of an active enemy having forces at command capable of making a serious incursion, but also from the acts of the people of the country in which the operations are carried on, enjoys an enormous advantage. And if those communications traverse the sea, and if the sea be controlled absolutely by a friendly navy, the result is that his army is entirely emancipated from that disintegrating process which maintenance of a line of land communications almost invariably brings about. The allies before Sebastopol were operating thousands of miles from their bases at home. But not a soldier was required to guard that long line from Kamish and Balaclava through the Black Sea to the Bosporus, and thence through the Hellespont and the Mediterranean to the ports of western Europe. The army of invasion was massed within a very small area, under the eye of the two chiefs, and face to face with the enemy. Wellington was able to meet Napoleon's marshals in Portugal practically on level terms, and this was because his communications only extended a few miles overland, while the rest of the long line crossed the sea. His adversaries, Massena and Marmont and Soult, on the other hand, depended upon indifferent roads, extending back to the Pyrenees, right across Spain. The total French forces in the theatre of war were far superior to those of Wellington; but so large a proportion of them was absorbed in protective duty in rear, that their superiority disappeared when the opposing armies met in action.

A maritime line of communications not only saves the

general in command much anxiety,—it also gives the general more men to put in his line of battle. This is one of the greatest of the many advantages conferred on the belligerent commanding the sea, when conducting a land campaign in a theatre of war near the coast: its importance is sometimes almost inestimable.

Superiority of sea to land communications.

Moreover, quite apart from the question of the saving in troops in rear of the army, communications by sea are often on other grounds preferable to communications by land. In theatres of war where railways are abundant and secure, little difficulty is likely to present itself in maintaining that constant flow of reinforcements and supplies and ammunition from rear to front, which is essential if troops in advanced positions are to be kept efficient and up to strength. An army based on London and operating in Yorkshire would gain nothing by using a maritime line of communications from the Thames to the Humber, in preference to using those great arteries of traffic—the Great Northern and the Midland and the Great Central railways. But if, on the contrary, there are no railways, if roads are bad, if there are unbridged rivers to be crossed and mountain ranges to be traversed, a line of land communications will bear no comparison, from the point of view of convenience, with one of even considerably greater length by sea. In the old days when military forces from England invaded Scotland, their supplies and spare equipment were generally carried by sea, the army used to be accompanied by a flotilla, and the line of operations almost always followed the coast: even so late as the time of Culloden the Duke of Cumberland's line of communications, from his base at Aberdeen forward to Inverness, was by sea. It was the same when Edward I. was operating against Llewellyn in the fastnesses of the Snowdon range: his troops were fed by supplies brought up by sea from the Dee to the mouth of the Conway. When Cromwell in 1649 moved south from Dublin intent upon attacking Wexford, which had been a nest for privateers preying upon English commerce during the great Civil War, his supplies and siege-train were despatched by sea to meet him at the place he meant to deal with in his thorough-going fashion.

Those were days of galleys and sailing-vessels. Steamers are far more certain and rapid in their movements. Railways are, on the other hand, an even greater step in advance over the roads which had to serve for Prince Eugene and for Washington and for Suvarof, than is the modern steam transport over the class of vessel which conveyed Stanhope's force to Spain or Rochambeau to Newport Bay. Where in the present day the theatre of war is a country covered with a network of railways, like France or like the older districts of the United States, the relative advantage of sea over land communications, supposing there to be any advantage at all, cannot be so marked as where the operations are taking place in a land like Turkey or like the hermit kingdom of Korea. It is a question of degree. Even in the opening years of the twentieth century there are still many huge expanses of territory bordering on the ocean where communications are in a most backward state. Land campaigns of the future must in consequence be often very appreciably influenced by the fact that one belligerent or the other is in a position to link his army to its base by sea transport, in place of having to trust to an elaborate system of land transport in a country presenting obstacles to its movement. *Influence of steam on this question ashore and afloat.*

The value of sea communications was well exemplified in the war of 1897 between Turkey and Greece.* In that campaign the Turks had a great superiority of force on land, but they made no genuine attempt to dispute the control of the western Ægean with the Greeks. The Greeks were therefore able to convey reinforcements, munitions of war, and reserves of equipment by ship transport from Athens and other centres, to Thessaly: this was of enor- *The Turko-Greek war, 1897.*

* See the sketch on p. 186.

mous advantage to them. The land routes through the northern parts of Greece are few, and are for the most part indifferent. It is a district cut up by rugged mountain ranges and by deep ravines. There was at the time of the war no railway leading from the Morea to the Turkish frontier. Had it not been for control of the sea, it is doubtful if the Greek army at the front could have been maintained, even in that moderate state of efficiency which was preserved up to the time of its disastrous overthrow at Domokos.[1]

Sea cannot be used as line of military communications without naval preponderance.

The sea cannot, of course, be used as a line of communications if the enemy possesses a preponderating navy on the spot. If a military commander proposes to base himself upon a point on the coast, it is essential that the ships upon which he relies so absolutely shall enjoy at least a reasonable measure of immunity from hostile attack. The maritime route must be secured by combatant sea-power, unless neither belligerent happens to possess a navy; otherwise the troops may be left without ammunition or destitute of stores, gaps which occur in the ranks from death or wounds or sickness cannot be filled up, and in case the theatre of war is unproductive, men and horses are likely to starve. The anxiety caused to Wellington by a few French and American cruisers and privateers has been referred to in earlier chapters. And the case of Yorktown, where the sea communications of Cornwallis were completely severed, serves to show the straits to which an army dependent on such communications may be reduced for want of naval preponderance. The military advantages of the line of communications being a maritime line are often very great; but it is essentially a question of sea-power.

The Sea of Azov in the Crimean War.

During the first few months which elapsed after the allied army landed in the Crimea and commenced siege operations against Sebastopol, the Russian control of the

Sea of Azov was not disturbed. The action of the allies in undertaking a campaign in this great peninsula had come as a surprise to the military advisers of the Tsar. No magazines of supplies had therefore been organised in anticipation of such an eventuality, to feed a great army in the country. Land communications leading from the grain-growing portions of the huge empire to the scene of action were of enormous length. And the question of food might have paralysed the action of the defending forces coping with the sudden invasion, but for the failure of the British and French fleets to at once force their way through the Straits of Khertch. Control of the waters beyond made it possible for Prince Mentschikof to draw supplies by water from the corn-lands of the Don. And the result of this was that, when the belated naval expedition into the Sea of Azov easily penetrated its inmost recesses, vast stores of food had already been collected in rear of the Russian army within the Crimea. "It was like bursting into a vast treasure-house crammed with wealth of inestimable value," writes a historian of the naval operations. "For miles along its shores stretched the countless storehouses packed with the accumulated harvest of the great corn provinces of Russia. From these the Russians in the field were fed; from these the beleaguered population of Sebastopol looked for preservation from the famine which already pressed hard upon them." It was estimated that enough corn was destroyed by the allied flotilla to supply 100,000 men for four months. But during the previous half-year the magazines in the interior had been stocked from these storehouses on the shore. The Russian maritime communications were in fact cut too late for their severance to exercise a decisive effect.[2]

The great struggle between Russia and Japan in the Far East affords an admirable example of the value of sea communications. The facility with which the very heavy

Japanese action in Korea in 1904 in illustra-

tion of use of sea as a line of communications.

wastage suffered by the Japanese armies in numerous desperate encounters has been made good, and with which sick and wounded have been despatched from the front to the ease and comforts awaiting them in their island home, has been a feature of the campaign. And the plan of operations adopted by the Japanese in the opening phases of the war shows how correctly had been estimated the advantage of shipping over land transport as a means of supply. The base in Korea was shifted forward from estuary to estuary as the ice melted and the troops advanced, till the mouth of the Yalu was at last secured. The fundamental principle governing their action was to push the maritime line of communications as far forward as possible, and to correspondingly reduce the length of the land line of communications. It is one of the many points which at once arrest attention, when the story of the desperate contest in far-off Asia is examined as a study in amphibious warfare.[3]

Russo-Turkish wars as illustrating this.

As an illustration of the advantages of maritime over land communications in an inhospitable, unproductive theatre of war, the Russo-Turkish wars of 1828-29 and of 1877-78 are of especial value. A brief sketch of certain phases of those memorable campaigns will therefore be useful, before closing this branch of the subject. The general course of the operations can be followed on the map facing p. 260. In the first of these wars Russia was paramount in the Black Sea, as a result of the battle of Navarino, where the destruction of the Ottoman fleet had been chiefly the work of the British and French squadrons. In the second of the wars, on the other hand, Turkey enjoyed practically undisputed supremacy in these waters, in consequence of the limits which had been imposed upon Russian naval power by the Treaty of Paris. The territories bordering the Black Sea on the west, south, and east were, during both of these severely-contested struggles, very deficient in communications; there were practically no railways, and there were very few good roads in those districts. And this was, and is indeed still, especially the case in the northern parts of Anatolia and of Armenia, which are rugged, mountainous provinces, entirely destitute of navigable waterways, and which therefore place serious difficulties in the way of the movement of troops. In both wars, moreover, there were fought out two practically independent campaigns, one in Europe and the other in Asia. And it is especially the operations in Asia which serve to illumine the question under consideration, although the course of events in Bulgaria and Roumelia is also instructive.

In 1828 Roumania and Bulgaria still formed integral portions of the Ottoman Empire; its frontier in Europe was the Pruth. And although Circassia was virtually independent, its coast-line was in Turkish hands. Russia had gained a footing in Georgia, but the northern empire was still shut off from the Asiatic shores of the Black Sea by a fringe of Ottoman territory. It is the Asiatic campaign which especially well illustrates the question of communications.

General Paskievich, who commanded the Muscovite armies in the eastern theatre of war from the outset, contemplated offensive operations of the most uncompromising character. A conjunct expedition from the Crimea captured the Turkish fortress of Anapa on the coast at a very early stage; and about the same time Paskievich's right wing, pushing forward rapidly through the hills from Georgia, compelled Poti, after a feeble resistance, to surrender. Thus at the very outset of the campaign the Russian army which was to invade Armenia established itself on the shores of the Black Sea, south of the Caucasus, while the seizure of Anapa gave the Muscovite forces a footing at the extreme end of the Circassian coast. Paskievich's forces were, as regards numerical strength, by no means commensurate with the latent military power of the Russian Empire. His army was small, and in

Campaign of 1828-29 in Asia.

the first instance it was completely isolated. But before winter closed in, this dashing, skilful leader had made himself master of three important frontier strongholds—Akhalkali, Akhalsik, and Byazid; and he had crowned his career of victory by securing possession of the historic fortress of Kars.

During this first year of fighting the Russian forces in Asia had only benefited indirectly from the command of the Black Sea. No regular line of communications was established from Odessa and Sebastopol and the Sea of Azov to the newly-acquired port of Poti. Immediate use was not made of ports which had been captured. But the Sultan, on the other hand, was unable to send reinforcements from the Bosporus to Trebizond by sea, owing to Russia's naval preponderance. The very ill-prepared Turkish army in Armenia depended for its line of communications on bridle-tracks leading for hundreds of miles through a wilderness of hills, and crossing numerous rivers and watercourses by fords which were often impassable. Its communications traversed territory infested with robbers and marauders, whose respect for the soldiery of the Caliph varied with the strength of the convoy escorts, and with the size of the detachments proceeding to the front through the little-known tracts where these freebooters held almost despotic sway.

But in the west, on the other hand, the Russian campaign had been by no means a success. So unfortunate had been his experiences on the Danube, that the Tsar was intent on retrieving the position in the theatre of war where the question of triumph or failure must exert more influence on public opinion than anything likely to occur in a remote corner almost unknown to civilised Europe, and he therefore devoted little attention to the doings of his doughty general in the Asiatic hills. The Sultan, on the contrary, was justified in viewing the course of military events in Bulgaria with some complacency; but the fall of his line of strongholds on the borders of Armenia, and the acquisition by the enemy of a firm footing on the eastern shores of the Black Sea, gave him good grounds for alarm. As a consequence the Porte made great efforts during the autumn and winter to push up reinforcements towards Erzerum by land.

In consequence of the attitude of the Tsar, Paskievich had to content himself with modest additions to his strength. But the Russian accessions came by sea from the northern Black Sea ports to Poti, they suffered little wastage in transit, and they underwent no special hardships by the way. In the meantime the Turkish troops, on their long march through the defiles and mountains of Anatolia and Armenia, dwindled unaccountably away: some were massacred by tribesmen, others deserted, others again fell sick. So that when operations were renewed in the spring of 1829 the numerical odds were not so uneven as might have been expected; and, thanks to maritime command, Paskievich was well supplied with munitions of war, and was at the head of an efficient, well-equipped army. Of this he made the most. For, manœuvring his forces with consummate skill, he utterly defeated the Ottoman forces opposed to him, he thrust his army forward to the gates of Erzerum, he planted the standard of Russia on the citadel of the Armenian capital, and he had pushed a portion of his troops on to within sight of Trebizond when hostilities were brought to a conclusion by the peace of Adrianople.

It is no discredit to Paskievich that his brilliantly successful campaign was in reality the result of command of the Euxine. His prompt seizure of Poti at the very outset of the war was the cause of his being able to bring sea-power into play. But for the reinforcements and supplies and warlike stores which he was able to draw direct across the Black Sea from the magazines and arsenals of Odessa and Sebastopol, his genius for war alone would not have enabled him to fight so successful a campaign against very superior forces. His land line of communications through Georgia, and over the Caucasus, and across the steppes towards the Don, was of such length, and its security was so precarious, that, even had the Tsar been far more intent upon achieving success in Asia than he actually was, little could have reached the theatre of war in Armenia by that route.[4]

Campaign of 1877-78 in Asia.
In the later war of 1877, the situation in Asia at the outbreak of hostilities was very different from what it had been fifty years earlier. Russia had during that half century firmly established herself in Circassia and Georgia. There was a good road over the Caucasus. And within the limits of Transcaucasia was to be found at least a fraction of the stores of warlike material, and at least a proportion of the depots of food and forage, which were requisite if that province was to be a base for a great army. Turkey on the other hand enjoyed on this occasion the advantage of control of the Black Sea, and was in a position to make Trebizond a base. From Trebizond a comparatively speaking short line of land communications led up to Erzerum and Kars. But the great development of communications within the Russian Empire made the broad strategical conditions of the struggle very different from that of 1828-29. It had become possible to move troops from the heart of the huge State to its far-off extremities within a reasonable time. And as there was no comparison between the total military resources which the Tsar could place in the field and those at the disposal of the Sultan, victory in Asia was a mere question of sustained effort.

The Armenian campaign, however, opened most inauspiciously for the Muscovite forces. Under the skilful leadership of Mukhtar Pasha the Turks drove the invaders back in confusion, and arrested the tide of Russian conquest almost before it had begun to flow. But no attempt was made to follow up this triumph. A long pause ensued, which the invaders employed to good purpose in pouring reinforcements over the mountains into Transcaucasia; while their opponents, supine as is the wont of the Oriental, rested on their laurels. When fully prepared, the army of the Tsar pressed forward again in overwhelming strength, captured Kars by a fine feat of arms, and had advanced up to Erzerum before the peace of San Stefano put an end to the war. The Turks had been so hard-pressed in Europe that no troops could be sent to help Mukhtar Pasha; the maritime line of communications did not therefore benefit them in the same way as it had benefited their hereditary foe fifty years before in the same theatre of war. The struggle of 1877-78 in Asia does not, in fact, illustrate the value of a line of communications across the sea as strikingly as that of 1828-29, because the side which enjoyed the benefit of maritime command was beaten. But had the Russian navy been supreme in the Black Sea in the later war, as it had been in the former one, Mukhtar Pasha would certainly not have been at the head of an army in the vicinity of Kars capable of resisting the original Russian army of invasion in the early days of the campaign. His forces would have been numerically inadequate, and they must have lacked almost everything required to make an army an efficient fighting machine. He could not have hoped to inflict upon the forces opposed to him the somewhat humiliating reverse which he actually did inflict.

In Europe the war of 1828-29 naturally followed the coast-line in consequence of the position of Russia on the Black Sea. Possessing the initiative, Russia selected the theatre of operations. The invading army was during the first year under the veteran Wittgenstein: it proved to be ill-organised, and it was badly handled by a commander whose hand had lost its cunning. After crossing the Danube it worked down parallel to the coast as far as Varna, making Kustenji and other points on the shore farther south successive bases. *Campaign of 1828-29 in Europe.*

In the interior it met with little encouragement; and its campaign would have been disastrous but that, before winter set in, it managed to capture the important stronghold of Varna, and thus to secure a valuable maritime base for the future. But its efforts were upon the whole crowned with little success, and at the close of the year Wittgenstein withdrew baffled behind the Danube.

The possession of Varna proved, however, invaluable the following year, when a stronger and better equipped army under a most capable and resolute chief, General Diebich, pushed into Bulgaria. Diebich's campaign was a masterpiece of bold and skilful strategy. The Turks were completely out-manœuvred by the Russian leader, who first defeated them in Bulgaria, and then, securely based on the sea, turned the line of the Balkans and captured Bourgas. Then, based on that useful harbour, the invaders pressed on to Adrianople, and thence proceeded on their progress towards Stamboul, having interposed themselves between the Ottoman army in Bulgaria and the heart of the Sultan's dominions on the Sea of Marmora. It looked for a brief space as if the cross of St Andrew was to be planted in the capital of Othman and Soliman the Magnificent. But under the circumstances the Porte hastened to make peace. The Sultan readily acquiesced in the Russian demands, which, although onerous, were not unreasonable considering the measure of the successes which had been gained alike in Europe and in Asia.

Campaign of 1877-78 in Europe. In 1877-78 the Russians, aided by the efficient military forces of Roumania, advanced in Europe by quite a different line. They crossed the Danube with their main army at Sistova and operated towards the Shipka Pass. From the outset its command of the Black Sea was of great assistance to the Turkish army assembled about Shumla and Rustchuk, inasmuch as its main line of communications ran from Varna to the Bosporus; and for a long time the hosts of the Sultan held their antagonists fast in Bulgaria. But the invaders enjoyed a great superiority of strength, and after encountering some serious reverses and being checked for many months, they disposed of Osman Pasha at Plevna and forced their way over the Balkans, compelling the Turkish forces in eastern Bulgaria to abandon that country and to hasten by sea to the vicinity of Constantinople. The Russian armies, greatly diminished in strength by losses in action and disease, and by the drain of a long line of land communications, advanced to the gates of the capital, and there they compelled the Sultan to make peace. They had achieved a striking success; but in spite of preparations on a great scale for a struggle long foreseen, of starting upon the great venture with a powerful army deliberately collected on the Ottoman borders, and of railway communication which led back from the frontier to the great centres of population, of wealth, and of food-supply in the interior of Russia, the generals of the Tsar had found the approach from Bessarabia to the Golden Horn a task of uncommon difficulty. And the campaign, as a whole, contrasted very unfavourably with that of Diebich, who had taken the field with far less numerical superiority over the foe, but who had been able throughout to base his plans on a maritime line of communication.

That power of shifting the base of military operations from point to point which control of the sea may give, has been already illustrated by the Japanese plan of action in Korea in the early part of 1904. This was also well shown by the Russian campaign in Europe in 1828-29, Kustenji, Varna, and Bourgas successively becoming bases for portions of the army of invasion. But the most striking example of this is the well-known case of Wellington's transfer of base from the coast of Portugal to Santander, when he made his great advance to the Pyrenees in 1813. The long line of communications back to Lisbon had become a serious encumbrance, *Power of shifting a maritime base as operations progress.*

Wellington in the Peninsula.

and the distance which had to be traversed over indifferent roads by somewhat inefficient transport had begun to make the replenishment of stores a matter of considerable difficulty. Quite apart from the benefits to be expected from establishing a base so much nearer to the immediate theatre of operations, this new line of communication brought part of Wellington's forces into a secure position on the flank of Joseph Buonaparte's army, and to this in great measure was due the extraordinarily decisive character of Wellington's triumph at Vittoria. The days of retiring before superior strength to the security afforded by the shores of Portugal were over. "That country," says Napier, "was cast off by the army as a heavy tender is cast from its towing-rope, and all the British establishments were broken up and transferred by sea to the coast of Biscay."

Sherman in Georgia and the Carolinas.   Another notable example of maritime communications permitting a military commander to transfer his base by sea from one point to another in a theatre of war, in furtherance of his general plan of campaign, is supplied by the march of Sherman's army from Georgia towards Virginia in the closing days of the great War of Secession. The general direction of operations can be followed on the map facing p. 244.

Sherman, having advanced from the Mississippi basin through Confederate territory, had reached Savannah, and was resting his forces after their dashing campaign in the environs of that southern city, when he was summoned to come to the aid of his commander-in-chief Grant, before Richmond. There was some talk of his proceeding by sea—which it will be remembered was under Federal control,—but Sherman preferred to move by land, being anxious to make the presence of an enemy felt in the Carolinas, which had up to that time escaped serious invasion. It was, however, impossible to march along the coast, victualling from ships at the numerous petty ports which existed. Charleston had

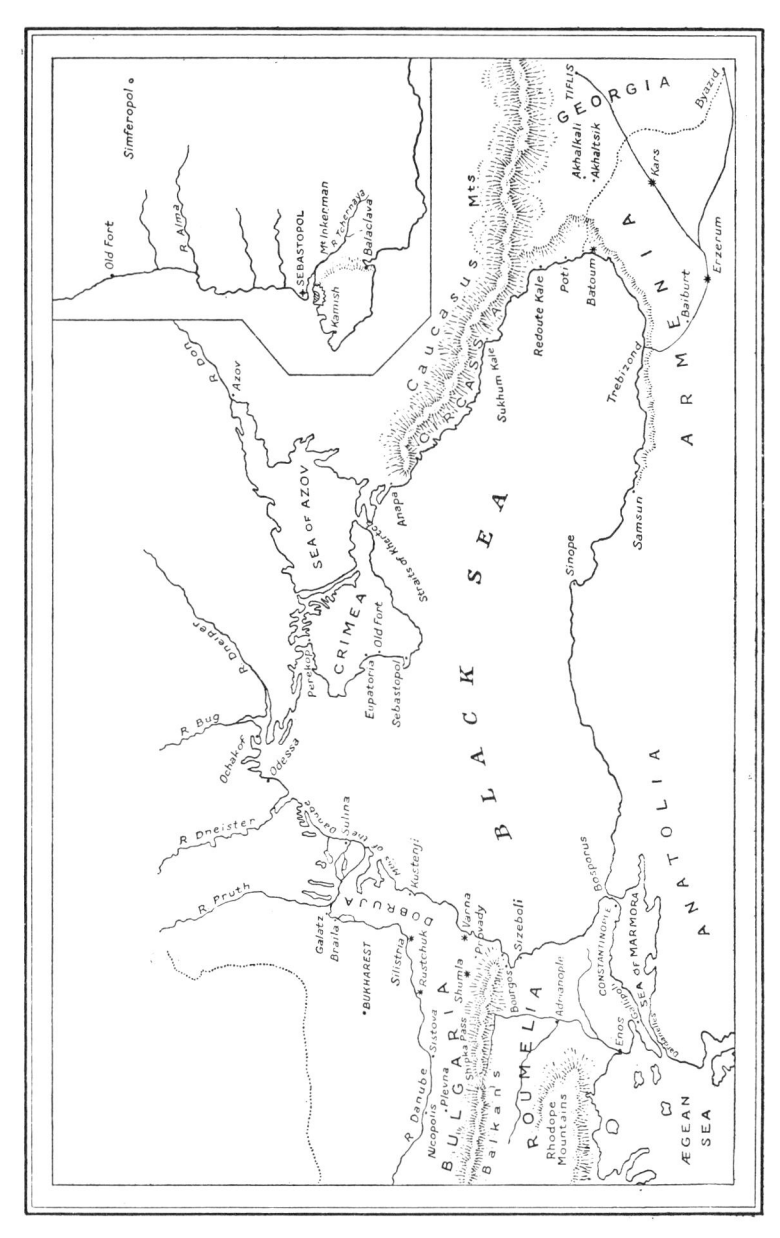

THE RUSSO-TURKISH CAMPAIGNS AND THE CRIMEAN WAR.

to be avoided. The shore districts of South and North Carolina are low-lying and swampy, presenting great difficulties to the movement of an army. It, moreover, was part of the plan to devastate the country traversed, and the tracts near the sea were not sufficiently populous or well-cultivated to make this process a very damaging one to the enemy. Sherman therefore moved by Columbia and Cheraw. But an auxiliary force was despatched by sea to Wilmington to establish a base at that port, and to open up communications with Goldsboro, where the main army was to pass. The commander of this force, Schofield, found the Wilmington-Goldsboro line unsuitable, and so he moved on by sea to Newbern in Pamlico Sound. From there a conveniently short line of communications was opened to Goldsboro, so that when Sherman reached that place he found himself with a new and convenient base for further operations. It was, however, very soon after this that Grant at last overcame the stubborn resistance of Lee in his lines of Richmond and Petersburg, and that the remnants of the famous army of Virginia, retiring on Lynchburg, were surrounded and compelled to surrender. This practically brought the war to an end, so that Sherman's fresh maritime base was only for a short time brought into play.

CHAPTER XV.

THE LIBERTY OF ACTION CONFERRED BY SEA-POWER UPON MILITARY FORCE.

THE principles of strategy, when illustrated by geometrical diagrams, do not present a very fascinating study.[1] That method of examining into the groundwork of the art of war on land is indeed nowadays somewhat out of date. But the form of frontiers, the direction taken by the line of communications of one army operating in the field as compared to the direction taken by the line of communications of the army opposed to it, the relative distance of one body of troops measured in a straight line from the objective as contrasted with the distance of the enemy from that objective,—all these have an important bearing on the question of the liberty of action conferred by sea-power upon military force. The great principle of acting on "interior lines" is applicable to amphibious warfare to an even more remarkable degree than it is applicable to purely land warfare. Maritime command tends to give, in exceptional measure, to the military commander who can count upon its possession, that invaluable possession in war —the initiative. And all these points will be passed in review in this chapter, in their application to the interdependence between land operations and naval preponderance, which forms the subject-matter of this volume.

The works of Jomini, and of Hamley, and of other writers on the art of war, who have examined into the principles

Introductory remarks.

Salient and re-entering frontier lines.

and the application of strategy, have demonstrated the extent to which the course of war may be influenced by the direction followed by the frontier between the belligerent states.[2] They have explained the effect of angular frontiers, of salients and re-enterants, and of rivers and mountain ranges which so often represent the border line between belligerent states. It is only in modern times and in little-known regions that the mathematical line has come to be accepted as a demarcation between territories under separate government. The frontiers of France, of Holland, of India, and to a certain extent of Canada, are angular and tortuous. Frontiers following an even moderately straight line are the exception rather than the rule. They not unusually run along natural geographical features, which twist and turn in all directions. And the result is that well-marked salients and re-enterants are to be found everywhere, the strategical bearing of which is well known to the military expert.

Coast-lines present analogous conditions.

It is the same in the case of the coast-line of most states. Vast promontories occur, and pronounced gulfs and bays. And while the irregular line followed by the frontiers between adjacent states seldom approaches the degree of one state encircling the other, there are many countries, putting islands out of the question, which are nearly surrounded by the sea—Spain, Denmark, and Korea are examples of this. When a belligerent State which has lost command of the sea has a coast-line possible of approach by hostile force, that coast-line becomes the frontier or portion of the frontier between it and the State with which it is at war. Thus in the old days of war between England and Scotland, when the southern kingdom almost always possessed maritime control and was able to land troops in the Firth of Forth or elsewhere at will, the geographical border-line ran from the Tweed to the Solway; but the strategical frontier might almost be said to have coincided with the outline of all Scotland. In the War of Secession the military frontier of the Union ran from within the State of Missouri to the Chesapeake; but the military frontier of the Confederation ran from within the State of Missouri, by the Chesapeake, right round the Atlantic coast and the shores of the Gulf of Mexico, to Texas. For this reason the actual shape of the coast-line, the question whether there are promontories, extensive gulfs, and so on, may become of transcendent strategical importance.

It often happens in the case of land frontiers between countries which are at war, that these follow a natural feature which offers a serious obstacle to the passage of armies. Such obstacles find their counterpart in the cliffs and shallows often found round the shores of a maritime state. Considerable stretches of the coast-line of a country are often virtually unapproachable. Therefore the points where a hostile military force may manage to effect an entrance from the sea are sometimes few and far between.

But it is rarely the case that a State is encircled or nearly encircled by the territories of another. Many States are, on the other hand, encircled or nearly encircled by the sea. Therefore it may be said, speaking in very general terms, that a maritime country is, as a rule, worse situated to repel invasion from over the sea than a country is which has only to repel invasion by land. The coast-line of France is longer than its Belgian, German, Swiss, Italian, and Spanish frontiers added together. Between the length of the coast-lines of Italy and Greece and Scandinavia, and the length of their land frontiers, there is really no comparison. Insular powers like the United Kingdom and Japan have no land frontiers at all.

Acute salients, where the territory of one belligerent juts right into the territory of the other, are unusual in war, although they are not unknown. The northern end of Natal in 1899-1900 presented such a salient. A British

Salient coast-lines.

force posted at Newcastle was liable to be cut off from the south by Boer commandos crossing the frontier, either from the Orange Free State or from the Transvaal, or from both. This created an abnormal situation; but conditions analogous to this often present themselves in the case of a country with an extensive coast-line. A German army invading Jutland might have its communications cut by military forces landed on either side of Schleswig, and a British army operating in Devonshire might be cut off from the rest of the kingdom by forces landed either in the Bristol Channel or in Dorset. The salient land frontier does not necessarily place the troops within the salient at a strategical disadvantage; because they may be in a position to strike, and there are two different directions in which they can strike. But the army in a salient girt by the sea cannot from the nature of the case strike if the enemy has command of the sea, and it is therefore of necessity strategically in a bad position. From the point of view of the belligerent possessing maritime control, the fact that the coast-line of the opposing side presents a salient is necessarily a point to the good.

Re-entering coast-lines. But it is the same when the coast-line of the enemy is re-entering instead of salient. A military force on board ship off the mouth of the Thames, and meditating a descent on English soil, can take its choice of landing on either side of the great re-enterant. It can attack Essex, or it can land in Kent. But the defending forces in Kent and Essex are in a very different position strategically from that enjoyed by the Boers when grouped along the borders of the great re-enterant which their frontiers formed around Natal, for they do not in any way threaten the communications of the enemy. The army operating from the sea, in fact, necessarily enjoys the strategical advantages which the re-enterant frontier of the enemy presents, and it suffers from none of the disadvantages. As, in time of war, the frontier of that nation which enjoys the maritime control is the coast-line of the enemy, it follows that when that coast-line takes the shape of a great gulf or bay, the army of the Power dominating the sea can strike either to the left hand or to the right, while the adversary is compelled to divide his forces.

The operations at the extreme end of the toe of Italy in 1806 illustrate the strategical advantage enjoyed by the side commanding the sea when the military forces of the enemy are operating in a great promontory or salient. The French armies had overrun nearly the whole continental part of the kingdom of Naples, but the British fleet and a British army still secured the island of Sicily. Sir S. Smith, the naval commander, made some raids on the coasts of Naples, which, however, had little effect; and it was therefore decided by him, in concert with the commander of the army, Sir J. Stuart, that a descent in force should be made upon the coast of Calabria. The landing was successfully carried out, and its strategical effect was immediately made manifest; for the French general, Reynier, who was on the shores of the Straits of Messina, found his communications threatened, and he promptly marched northwards. The result was the battle of Maida, in which British soldiers met and completely defeated a superior force composed of the veterans of Napoleon; and the French forces, out-manœuvred strategically and overthrown in action, were compelled to abandon the whole of the toe of the Italian peninsula in consequence. *Calabria in 1806.*

It has been pointed out above what an advantage an army proposing a descent on the shores of some gulf or bay enjoys. Assuming a hostile expeditionary force to be on board ship in the Bristol Channel, it can strike either at South Wales, or else it can aim its blow at Devonshire and Somerset. It can, in fact, act on "interior lines." But the army meditating a descent may in reality be said to *An army in transports is generally in a position to act on "interior lines."*

have the power of acting to a certain extent on "interior lines," whatever shape the coast-line may take. Unless the country which is acting on the defensive against over-sea attack happens to be especially well provided with communications, a hostile military force threatening a descent upon one point of the coast can almost certainly be more rapidly transferred to another point of the coast, than the troops destined to ward off the attack can be moved to meet it. This does not take into account the element of surprise, nor the fact that the attacking army possesses the initiative: even assuming that the defenders have ascertained the new point which the adversary is going to make his objective, the adversary will probably win the race to the spot.

<small>To a certain extent, a question depending upon distances and nature of land communications at disposal of opposing side.</small>

Still, this does not by any means follow as a matter of course, even supposing the land communications to be indifferent. There must be loss of time in a landing even under the most favourable conditions. The distance by land may be very much shorter than that by sea, as for instance, supposing that a hostile army meditating the invasion of Scotland were to appear in the Firth of Forth, and that that army were then to be moved round by sea to the Clyde. But when the coast-line is approximately straight, and when the inland communications are reasonably efficient, and when the actual distance from point to point measures some scores of miles, everything is in favour of the army on board ship as against that waiting for it on shore.

Thus a division of all arms off Barcelona faced by a defending force of the same strength on the coast should be able to get to Gibraltar Bay, and should be on shore, before the bulk of the defending troops from Catalonia could arrive on the scene. The division would in all probability only have to deal with the leading detachments of the enemy on its arrival: this of course leaves the question of surprise entirely out of the question. In actual practice the aspect of affairs would be completely transformed by the fact that the commander of the army at sea would have the initiative, and that he would be able to keep his plans and movements absolutely concealed from the defenders. Were such a case to arise in war, the Spanish troops in the north would not begin to move to the new point of danger till the expeditionary force had made its appearance there. It is important that it should be understood what an advantage an army on board transports enjoys, in the all important respect of time, under normal conditions over that on shore, when a sudden transfer of force from one theatre of war to another is to take place.

The early days of the Crimean War afford a particularly good example of this. When the allies, assembled at Varna, decided to make their descent upon the shores of the Crimea and to attack Sebastopol, the Russian army, which at an earlier date had advanced to the Danube and had undertaken the siege of Silistria, had already fallen back into Bessarabia. The arrival of the French and British armies in Bulgaria, the loss of the command of the Black Sea, and the threatening attitude of Austria, had combined to force the Tsar to abandon all idea of an offensive campaign in the Balkan peninsula. Apart from Mentschikof's army already in the Crimea, there were only available in the European theatre of war the troops which had been withdrawn from Roumania, and which at this time were in Bessarabia and about Odessa. *The move from Varna to Sebastopol as an example.*

The allies began landing at Old Fort on the 14th September, defeated Mentschikof's army at the Alma on the 19th, and on the 26th reached Kamish and Balaclava, having the previous day passed just in the rear of the Russian forces withdrawing eastwards from Sebastopol. The siege of the fortress commenced, and it was prosecuted during October without serious interruption, except on the 25th when the

Russian field army advanced from the east and was repulsed in the action of Balaclava. But all this time a large part of the army in Bessarabia was moving round by land to the vicinity of the threatened stronghold, and six weeks after the battle of the Alma these troops began to arrive at the decisive point. In the early days of November vast reinforcements were arriving near Sebastopol from the north, without the allies being aware of it, or at least without their appreciating the great access of numerical strength to the enemy which had come upon the scene. On the 5th November the Russians attacked in very superior force; but they were defeated in the hard-fought battle of Inkerman, thanks to the stubborn resistance of the British soldiery and to the cordial co-operation of the French after the battle developed. And thus a remarkable combination of war was frustrated. Allowing for the descent upon the Crimea being in some sense a surprise to the Russians, and for the delay in getting the forces gathered about the Dniester into movement, the allies gained more than a month in time over them. The battle of Inkerman was not indeed fought for nearly two months after the expeditionary force left Varna. The rapidity of the Russian march from Bessarabia to the vicinity of Sebastopol has, moreover, always been regarded as a fine feat of endurance, although the movement was to some extent accelerated by the use of country carts to carry a proportion of the men.

The principle of "interior lines." The strategical principle of "interior lines" has been referred to above. In war on land this principle is especially applicable to the case of one army in a central position, operating against two or more armies separated from each other by such a distance that they cannot afford each other tactical support. The army in the centre can deal with those opposed to it in detail, by bringing superior force to bear first against one of the hostile forces and then against another. The usual procedure is to "contain" the divided bodies of the enemy with detachments, and to reinforce these detachments from a central reserve from time to time for a decisive stroke. Napoleon's famous campaign of 1814, and the operations of Lee in Virginia in 1862-63, are among the most striking examples of the application of the principle of "interior lines" recorded in history, and their main incidents are well known to all students of the art of war on land. But a moment's consideration will show that this same principle can be put in force, in what is in reality the same way, by the commander of an army operating in a theatre of operations adjacent to the coast against divided hostile forces, provided that he has transports at his disposal and that he is backed up by a navy which controls the sea.

Numbers of instances of military forces in possession of maritime command putting the principle in force could be quoted from history. In the wars between Russia and the Ottoman Empire, which have so often presented the feature of two separate and wholly distinct campaigns owing to the theatres of operations being divided from each other by the Black Sea, transfers of force from side to side of the great sheet of water have frequently taken place. In 1828 a considerable body of Russian troops, after capturing Anapa on the Circassian coast, was shipped across to Bulgaria, and arrived at a most opportune moment to assist in the siege of Varna. In 1855 Omar Pasha's Turkish army was moved by sea from the Crimea to the Asiatic theatre of war, and was landed at Redoute Kale on the east coast of the Black Sea, with the idea of trying to save Kars by threatening the Russian rear. The campaigns on the Danube and in the Balkans have, however, been generally so wholly distinct from those in Armenia, the distance apart has been so great, and interior communications have been so defective, that the principle of acting on "interior lines" has scarcely been put in force by the belligerent commanding the Black Sea in

Illustrations of the application of this in amphibious warfare.

these recurring conflicts, to the same extent as it has in many other great theatres of war.

Suliman Pasha in 1877. For such is the liberty of action conferred upon an army by control of the sea, that to turn the principle of "interior lines" to account it is not essential that the ocean shall actually, in a geographical sense, intervene between the two separate theatres of land operations. During the Russo-Turkish war of 1877 the Sultan had not only the armies of the great northern Power to deal with, but he was also harassed by the levies and guerilla bands which his revolted provinces, Servia and Montenegro, could bring against him. The Montenegrins, a hardy race of warrior hillmen, were especially troublesome. So bold and aggressive was their attitude that it required a considerable army to hold them in check. But when the Russians, after crossing the Danube, pushed forward suddenly to the Balkans, the Porte realised that its mountainous Adriatic dependency was of secondary importance, and that it must be left to its own devices. This liberated a force of many thousand men under Suliman Pasha: they were promptly shipped round from the Gulf of Cattaro to the Ægean, were landed at Enos, and were thrust northwards to confront the enemy in the Shipka Pass. A great transfer of force from the theatre of war in Montenegro to that in Bulgaria was in fact effected, and it was effected with little difficulty and in a very few days.

Examples from the South African War. During the South African War the power of transferring military force from one point to another by sea, on the principle of "interior lines," was used on two occasions which are worth recalling.

After the relief of Ladysmith, General Hunter's division was moved down by train to Durban. There it embarked, and was transported to East London and Port Elizabeth, whence it was moved up by train to reinforce the main army under Lord Roberts in the Orange Free State. Thanks to command of the sea, it was possible to transfer this considerable body of troops from the Natal theatre of war, which had assumed a secondary importance, to that which was to be the principal one in the British plan of campaign for the future.

In the closing days of the war the somewhat desultory operations in Cape Colony were enlivened by the Boer and rebel commandos concentrating unexpectedly in Namaqualand, in the north-west corner of the country. They captured some of the mining centres in that remote region, and besieged the principal one—Ookiep. The country between Namaqualand and the more developed districts, where the British troops were mainly operating, is so destitute of resources and of water that the relief of Ookiep by a force traversing this arid tract would have been almost impracticable with the resources available. But a column was sent down by train to Cape Town from the interior of the colony, was shipped with some other troops to the coast of Namaqualand, and this force had little difficulty in succouring the beleaguered settlement.

A very remarkable example of the value of maritime command to an army under certain conditions, and of the extraordinary liberty of action which the army may derive from it, is supplied by General Sherman's famous march from Atlanta to the Georgian coast. As an episode of war, it stands almost alone. There is no modern parallel for a great army abandoning its communications completely, and striking off across country as a huge flying column to seek a new base 250 miles off. The Americans are justly proud of the achievement. The Federals at the time regarded it as an extraordinary exploit of war, and held it to be the incident reflecting the greatest credit on their arms and leadership of any operation throughout the war. But when it is dispassionately considered, the memorable march through Georgia does not appear to be so brilliant an exploit after all. *General Sherman's march to the sea as illustration of liberty of action.*

Sherman, coming from the basin of the Tennessee (the

map facing page 244 illustrates the strategical situation), had fought his way to Atlanta from the west in spite of strenuous opposition on the part of a Confederate army under Hood. Hood then suddenly moved round the Federal flank and threatened their communications leading back into the Mississippi basin. The Union commander had no choice open to him except to conform his movements to those of the enemy, unless he could find a new base and then let Hood do his worst in rear. He remembered that friendly ships were blockading the coast, and that if he reached the Atlantic shores he would regain touch with the magazines and arsenals of the north. He knew that he could feed his troops on the fertile country which he would traverse, provided that he made no halt. So he started off for Savannah, left his opponent to his own devices groping about in the southern Alleghanys, and arrived on the sea-coast, having encountered no appreciable opposition, and having left the mark of ruined homesteads and devastated fields upon the State of Georgia, which up to that time had enjoyed almost complete immunity from invasion. Sherman's march to the sea was a remarkable operation of war, rather on account of its novelty than of the intrinsic difficulties involved in its execution. His action in the matter was perfectly natural to a man so fully alive to the broad principles which govern the art of war; and it appears to have been the case that the distinguished general formed a sounder estimate of the character of his exploit after it was over than the bulk of his countrymen, who overrated its difficulties and who exaggerated its importance.

Command of the sea generally assures an army a safe refuge at the worst, when operating in a maritime district.

Another respect in which maritime command confers an extraordinary advantage upon the chief of an army carrying on military operations near the sea is, that he will generally have a secure line of retreat if overwhelmed on land. This permits him to dispose the forces under his orders in positions which might under other circumstances expose them to disaster. It justifies his acting with a vigour and boldness which, under the ordinary conditions of war on land, might gravely imperil the safety of his army. And it affords him a fair prospect, even if his plan of campaign in the interior should miscarry and if he be compelled to fall back upon the sea, of being able at least to maintain a grip upon one small portion of the theatre of military operations, with a view to future events.

The best example of this is afforded by Sir J. Moore's famous campaign in the Peninsula, the story of which, told in so interesting a form by Napier, is known to most British students of military history. Moore's dispositions, his strategy, and his conduct of the memorable retreat to Coruña, have been sharply criticised. There are certain incidents in connection with the operations which even warm admirers of the gallant general find it difficult to wholly excuse. But his bitterest detractor cannot deny that his combinations exerted a tremendous influence over the course of Napoleon's one campaign in Spain, that he compelled the greatest master of the art of war of modern times to abandon well-considered projects and to conform to his movements, and that he has left a mark upon one of the most striking pages in military history which time will not obliterate, and which neither the advance of technical science nor the changes constantly taking place in tactics can ever wipe out.

Moore had advanced in a north-westerly direction into Spain from Lisbon, in conjunction with a detached force from Coruña. Napoleon had fought his way to Madrid; he had established himself there, was organising the country as a dependency of his throne, and in pursuance of his plans his detached armies were pushing their successes all through southern Spain. The French superiority of force over the allies was very great, the situation somewhat critical. Moore, after a pause, suddenly thrust his force forward to a point seriously threatening the enemy's communications with the Pyrenees, and thereupon Napoleon turned on him. A retirement to Lisbon was out of the question, but the British army was nearer to several points on the coast than the French army, and it had got the start. There followed the retreat to Coruña, and the pursuit by the main French army under Soult through the mountains of Leon and Galicia. This drew a large fraction of the forces engaged in overcoming Spanish resistance, away from Madrid, away from the basin of the Tagus, and into a rugged sterile territory, the occupation of which was of little practical advantage to a military force employed in subduing a nation in arms. Moreover, Moore, at bay, with his back to the sea, defeated Soult; and although its commander lost his life, the British army sailed away from the Peninsula having completely out-manœuvred one of far greater strength, and having suffered relatively much less serious losses than the enemy.

The northern coast of Spain is, it must be remembered, very wanting in sheltered harbours. All this took place in the depth of winter. The Bay of Biscay is noted for its stormy seas. Moore's liberty of action was therefore far more restricted than would usually be the case when a general, who is threatened by superior force so placed that it cannot intercept but can only pursue, finds himself obliged to retreat to the coast with the assurance that once on board ship his army will be safe.

An army forced to retreat to the sea need not necessarily take to its ships.
It does not necessarily follow that an army which is thus compelled to fall back to the sea-coast, has no option except to retire to its ships and to abandon the point of embarkation to the enemy. On the contrary, once it has reached the coast, the army will generally be strategically and tactically in a particularly strong position. It cannot be surrounded. Its flanks are secure.[3] Its communications afford the commander no anxiety. It will be shown in the next chapter how a military force which is based on the sea, and which is assured

of maritime command, may sometimes wear a powerful opponent down, and may gain the political ends for which the campaign has been undertaken, without committing itself to any serious operations in the interior. In the short narrative of the campaigns of the great American Civil War given further on, it will be seen how M'Clellan, cut off from one maritime base as Moore was cut off from the lower Tagus, marched like Moore to a new point on the coast. But M'Clellan, when he found himself on the coast, held his ground: he did not promptly embark his army, abandon the point of embarkation, and quit the theatre of war.

But it is the possession of the initiative which in reality gives to the military commander who is based on the sea, and who is confident in possession of sea-power, his greatest advantage.[4] It is the initiative, and what that involves, which affords him to the greatest degree that liberty of action admitted to be of such incalculable value in all combinations of war. The sea has been well likened by Mahan to a great common. Once a fleet of transports has quitted harbour it can move in any direction, and it can appear at any point on the coast of a region where military operations are in progress, or are in contemplation.

Command of the sea gives the side which enjoys that advantage the initiative.

The general awaiting a hostile descent upon the shores of territory which he is charged to defend, can only guess where the blow will fall. He must judge from what he knows of the various localities on the coast, which point the commander of the hostile army is likely to choose for disembarkation. He must, from the few signs which may be vouchsafed to him, interpret the objects and aims which the adversary has in view. Even if he drives the enemy back into his ships after a victorious campaign, the enemy may appear again at some other point, and his task begins all over again. In purely land operations the opposing sides are compelled to follow certain routes, the time that each army will take to get to some particular place can be estimated by the staff of the other, each learns the direction which the other is following by means of reconnaissances, by means of intelligence communicated by spies, from prisoners captured, and by circumstantial evidence which comes to hand from various sources. But all trace of a hostile army when at sea is likely to be lost for the time being. It may be known perfectly well that it has started on its voyage. The time which it may be expected to take to reach any point can of course be calculated. But the spot which it is making for can only be conjectured; if there are many such spots it is impossible to be prepared at all; and till the transports appear in the offing and the hostile landing begins, all is doubt and tension and uncertainty.

Enemy cannot tell where a blow may fall if plan is kept secret.

In the early days of the Russo-Japanese war the army holding Manchuria and parts of northern Korea was for long kept in complete suspense as to what was to be the line of operations which the Japanese would follow, although these were all the time completing their arrangement and were concentrating their forces. The Duc de Richelieu's expedition to Minorca in 1756 came as a complete surprise to the garrison of that island. Nelson was entirely in the dark as to Napoleon's destination when the great expedition embarked at Toulon. When the objective of an expeditionary force proceeding over-sea has been studiously kept secret, it has almost invariably achieved at least an initial success, provided always that it has escaped the perils of the ocean and that it has met with no mishap at the hands of a hostile navy.[5] And the following story is worth recording as showing the importance of not merely keeping the destination of the army hidden from the adversary, but also of actually deceiving him with regard to the objective which is aimed at.

Lord St Vincent and the descent on Minorca in 1798.

In 1798 Lord St Vincent was contriving a descent upon Minorca from Gibraltar, the preparations for which could not be wholly concealed. It was known that there were plenty of troops at Barcelona, but that the garrison of

Minorca itself was weak, and that the defences in Port Mahon were in disrepair. If the Spanish Government were to guess that the enterprise was destined against the peace of the Balearic Islands, it was practically certain that sufficient reinforcements would be sent from Catalonia to enable the commandant to offer a stout resistance, and that steps would moreover be taken to mount guns on the crumbling battlements of Fort St Philip, and to lay in food in anticipation of a possible siege. It was therefore given out at Gibraltar that the armament in process of organisation was destined for some place in the east. Abundant supplies for the troops were shipped on the transports. The force—by no means a large one—was ordered to embark as soon as the supplies were all on board. And at last, after a long day of bustle and hard work, it had been actually arranged that the expedition was to start upon the morrow, when, late at night, there burst upon St Vincent and the governor O'Hara, engaged in final conclave, a bearer of ill-tidings in the shape of an excited, breathless, and perplexed town major. A Spanish spy, he said, had been detected in the fortress, but was still at large. What was to be done in this distressing emergency?

The "Old Cock of the Rock," as O'Hara was called in barracks and by the British community generally, was for seizing the inconvenient intruder at once. But the admiral took another view. "Let him be," said he, "he may be useful"; and a sergeant was sent speeding to the residence of the agent-victualler to summon that functionary and to bring him to the convent forthwith. The agent-victualler, exhausted after a rare day's work, had retired to his well-earned rest, his labours finished, the armada ready. But in spite of his lamentations to the sergeant, he was roused from his slumbers, was brought round to the governor's house half awake, was there told that the authorities had changed their minds and had resolved to send eighteen months' provisions for the force instead of provisions for only a year, and was peremptorily informed that they must somehow be got on board next day. He urged that there were no more supplies available in store, but was directed to seize whatever could be found in the place. He declared that there would be no working-parties, but St Vincent rejoined that he must then impress the Jews. He protested that he had no boats, but this, like every other argument, was overborne by the masterful admiral. Then the agent-victualler rose to the occasion —the thing was urgent, he resolved that he at least would do his share,—and at dawn of day there was such a hubbub on the wharves that all Gibraltar rang with it from the Moorish Castle to Buenavista. Stores were ransacked, boats were impressed, Jews were coerced.[6] Everybody who was not pulling at an oar, or handling a barrow, or staggering under a well-filled sack, was looking on, and advising, and wondering; and in the thick of it all were Lord St Vincent, and the governor, and the spy. All day long the turmoil continued, till late in the afternoon the flotilla weighed and stood across towards Ceuta and the African coast, following the natural course for a voyage to the east. And while the agent-victualler, prostrated with mental and bodily fatigue, was that night sleeping the sleep of the just, the spy, unmolested by provost-marshal and unchallenged by sentinel, had slipped out of the fortress, and was posting through the defiles of Andalusia towards the capital.

The news which he imparted to his employers was of the most satisfactory and reassuring character. It was true that those grim red war-dogs of the Rock were meditating mischief as had been reported, but this time it was someone else's turn. They had strained every nerve to get a year and a half's supplies on board the transports carrying the force which had been mustering for some enterprise. This army was evidently going to seek the bubble reputation in a far-off eastern scene of action—in Egypt maybe, possibly in

FEINTS AND RUSES. 281

Syria, in the Ionian Islands as like as not. Its intentions and its destination were now merely of academic interest to the *caballéros*. There was no necessity for a display of that energy which is so distasteful to the Spanish temperament, and which is so inconvenient to a country of failing financial resources when it involves the laying out of money.

A few days afterwards the British expedition appeared suddenly on the coast of Minorca. The arrangements for disembarkation were admirably carried out. Such resistance as there was, was speedily overcome. And within a week the whole island and the fine harbour of Port Mahon were in the hands of the force which had started from Gibraltar apparently on some oriental mission bent, that force not having lost one single man in gaining the rich prize.

On the occasion of the first start of the allied expedition destined for the Straits of Khertch, from near Sebastopol, the armada at first sailed off in the direction of Odessa. And when a landing is intended at any point it is indeed a very common practice for a feint or feints to be made at other points. The whole expedition is sometimes in the first place brought to anchor at a locality where there is no intention of making the real descent; a show of disembarking troops is made so as to deceive the enemy; and then, while the defenders are hastening to the scene, the flotilla proceeds to sea again. When the Japanese in 1895 made their descent on the coast of Shantung to attack Wei-hai-wei, they first made a feint at a town on the coast seventy miles west of the fortress; and they then steamed off to the real landing-place twenty miles to the east of their objective, having by their ruse drawn off a great part of the Chinese troops in the province to the wrong point.

The situation lends itself to employment of feints and ruses.

When Louis IX. was at Cyprus, preparing to descend upon the delta of the Nile, he spread the report in his army that he meant to land at Alexandria: in consequence of this he found when he arrived at Damietta, the place which he had selected for disembarkation, only a comparatively speaking small force of Saracens to oppose him. The advantage of deceiving the enemy is so obvious, and the conditions so often render such deception particularly easy, that it is strange that precautions of this kind should ever be neglected. And it is still more strange that cases should have occurred where the whole design has been allowed to leak out beforehand, and where the enemy has been forewarned, not only of a descent being intended, but also of the place where the descent is to take place. An English spy in 1757 prepared the French for the contemplated enterprise against Rochefort, for which such costly and elaborate preparations were made, and which ended so ignominiously. And the case of Tollemache's attack on Brest in 1694 is even more remarkable.

There was no real attempt at concealment on that occasion. The objective was known to numbers of people in London. The preparations were of the slowest and most deliberate kind. Louis XIV. was early apprised of what was in contemplation, and was given ample time to send reinforcements to the stronghold, and to have the defences placed in good repair under the eye of the great Vauban himself. There was treachery no doubt, and in this Marlborough was apparently to some extent implicated. But the catastrophe which overtook the rash and impetuous Tollemache was probably not attributable to deliberate treachery on the part of those in high places in England; and there is no evidence which will bear examination, to justify Macaulay's famous denunciation of the greatest soldier of the time: "While the Royal Exchange was in consternation at the disaster of which he was the cause, while many families were clothing themselves in mourning for the brave men of whom he was the murderer, he repaired to Whitehall; and there, doubtless with that grace, that nobleness, that suavity, under which lay hidden from all observers a seared conscience and remorseless heart, he professed himself the most devoted, the most loyal of all subjects of William and Mary."[7] The truth is that Marlborough's letter to the exiled James was only despatched on the very eve of the departure of the expedition from the south coast, and it cannot possibly have influenced the issue of the fight in Camaret Bay. Whatever chance Tollemache may ever have had of achieving success, was thrown away when his destination became common talk many weeks before he ever started. The lesson to be learnt from this memorable incident is that all the advantages which an army enjoys when making a maritime descent upon an enemy's shores, are thrown away unless the objective is kept a secret. The benefits arising from possessing the initiative disappear. The undertaking loses the character of a surprise. The foe is found prepared and in the right place. And if the project be not abandoned, as Tollemache's counsellors urged him to abandon his attack on Brest when the reception which the French had prepared for him became manifest, one of the most difficult of operations of war has to be ventured upon, an operation which modern tactical conditions have rendered so difficult as to make it virtually impracticable—landing from on board ship in face of the enemy.

The war on the Pacific coast of South America, which lasted from 1879 to 1881, affords a very remarkable illustration of the liberty of action enjoyed by the Power commanding the sea, when, owing to the nature of the country, military movements are restricted by topographical and geographical conditions, and when, on the other hand, the territories of the belligerents offer a great extent of coast-line for attack. Chili and Peru present somewhat peculiar geographical features. Both are States with a long seaboard, *The war between Chili and Peru as illustrating liberty of action derived from naval preponderance.*

offering many possible landing-places to the enterprise of an expeditionary force contemplating invasion. And so a brief account of what occurred will help to disclose the relations which establish themselves between military operations and maritime command in a certain class of theatre of war.

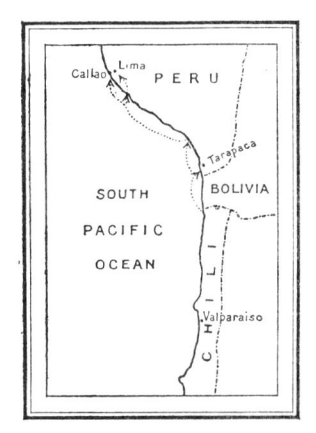

Chili in this war had Bolivia as antagonist as well as Peru. The narrow strip of territory belonging to that inland republic, which came down to the sea at that time, at the outset separated the two main combatants. Chili, and the greater and most prosperous portion of Peru, may be described as a comparatively speaking narrow strip of country lying between the great range of the Cordilleras and the waters of the Pacific Ocean. From the main mountain chain huge spurs jut out towards the coast, forming rugged barriers, which separate from each other the basins of the rivers flowing down from the watershed of the Andes, and which render movement from one basin into another a matter of serious difficulty. The result is that the routes of communication from valley to valley do not run by land,—they run by sea. Transverse roads and tracks are few. And the movements of armies for any considerable distance parallel to the coast-line must inevitably be slow and tedious, where it is practicable at all. The northern end of Chili in 1879—its frontier was extended after the war—was extremely mountainous, and certain portions of the maritime tracts of Peru are almost a desert. The geographical and topographical conditions made it obvious, when the rival republics embarked on the conflict, that the question of naval supremacy would be a factor of paramount importance in deciding the issue; and the course of the struggle proved unmistakably that this was the case.

It took some months for the Chilian warships to overcome the resistance of the well-handled, but much inferior, Peruvian navy; but during this time the military forces of the southern republic were being collected at convenient ports, ready for action. The difficult nature of the country near the frontier made any invasion of Bolivia from Chili almost impracticable; but as soon as maritime command was assured the Chilian army embarked, put to sea, and made a descent upon the fertile district of Tarapaca, situated about 200 miles to the north of the frontier and immediately north of that small strip of Bolivia which then came down to the coast. The resistance of the Peruvian forces on the spot was speedily overcome, and a firm grip was laid upon the smiling province. Then the army re-embarked and descended afresh upon another populous and productive district about 100 miles farther on, and dealt with it in the same fashion. The Peruvians could not tell where the blows would fall, and they could not have concentrated troops to ward the blows off even if they had guessed the enemy's objectives. Local forces actually on the spot did their best to contest the occupation of their soil; but they were necessarily outnumbered, and they never had any prospect of effectually beating the invaders off.

Finally, after some delay, the Chilian army embarked a third time, and it landed on this occasion at two different points not far from the Peruvian capital Lima. The defending forces were necessarily somewhat scattered, having many points to watch. Bolivia was far to the south, and could give no help. Considerable bodies of Peruvian troops had, as might have been expected, been retained in what was obviously the most important portion of the country, and had been concentrated at the point most likely to prove the final objective of the triumphant foe. But even these were unable to resist the Chilian advance for long; Lima was taken after severe fighting; and Peru had no option except to sue for peace, beaten down and trodden underfoot by the combination of sea-power and land-power which the southern republic had thrown into the scale. It is no exaggeration to say that the Chilian naval and military leaders had had the game absolutely in their own hands from the moment that their maritime supremacy was assured. Their opponents had never had a chance ashore, although in actual military strength the antagonists were by no means ill-matched.

The campaign of 1859.

In 1859 Napoleon III. resolved upon aiding Sardinia in the conflict impending with Austria, the confines of which empire then extended north of the Po as far as the Ticino, and thus included the provinces of Lombardy and Venetia. There is a sketch of northern Italy on p. 313. France was separated from the theatre of war in the basin of the Po by the great Alpine chain, which in those days had not yet been pierced by the Mont Cenis railway. Only two good carriage-roads led over the lofty range, and it therefore formed a very serious obstacle to the concentration of the French army in Piedmont. But the allies held undisputed command of the Mediterranean. Large bodies of French troops were therefore embarked at Marseilles and other ports of Languedoc and Provence, and were conveyed to the Italian Riviera by sea. There was railway communication northwards from Genoa, and by this route masses of troops were rapidly poured into the plains of the Po—troops which would have been seriously delayed in reaching the scene of action had the movement been confined to the Alpine passes.

The direction naturally taken by these French forces in their advance was moreover very advantageous to the allies. The Austrian army on the Ticino automatically fronted to the west, and its line of communication ran from west to east. But the army advancing from Genoa threatened the

CAMPAIGN OF 1859. 287

left flank of troops moving forward from Milan towards Turin, and it to a certain extent menaced their communications through Lombardy. The result was that the Austrian invasion of Piedmont came to an abrupt halt at its very outset, that the allies became at once the assailants, and that the battle of Magenta was won by France and Sardinia with an army equal to that opposed to them. But for control of the sea the advantage in numbers must have been on the side of the Austrians till a later date.

The peculiarity of the campaign on the shores of the South Pacific, of which the outline was given above, is that the nature of the country almost forbade purely land operations. The alternating hill-ranges and valleys, the tracts of desert, and the enormous distances to be traversed, would have made it almost impossible for the Chilian army to penetrate far into Bolivia or Peru by simply marching northwards across the frontier, or conversely for the military forces of the allied republics to carry out a decisive campaign by moving across the mountains southwards into Chili. Similarly in 1859 it was the Alps which made the sea-route from French ports to Genoa of such importance. But cases have often occurred in war where advance by land through maritime tracts of country has been difficult or impossible, not so much because of topographical features as because of the presence of formidable bodies of hostile troops which bar the way. At Thermopylæ it was not the defile itself, but the presence of the Lacedemonians in the defile, which checked the Persian host, and had the attendant flotilla been present on the spot the invaders could easily have turned the defile by embarking some detachments and landing them in rear of the defenders. This is another form in which command of the sea may confer liberty of action on a military commander, and an instance of such a transfer of force in later times is worth recording.

In 1859, and in the South American war of 1879-81, maritime command overcame geographical obstacles.

In the course of the Carlist War of 1836 the forces of the

The attempted relief of Bilbao. Pretender invested the town of Bilbao, which lies in the province of Biscay a few miles from the sea. Its relief became a matter of urgent importance, and to effect it the daring and skilful government general Espartero collected a small army at Santander, which lies on the coast some distance to the west, and advanced by the shore route, intending to turn off inland by the road which led direct from the sea up to the beleaguered town. There were British warships on the coast co-operating with the movement, and maritime command was secure. But the Carlists despatched a force to meet the relieving army, and this force was found strongly entrenched in a formidable position blocking the way along the coast. An attack on it, placed as it was, could only have proved successful at great loss of life, and the attempt might easily have proved a disastrous failure. Espartero therefore embarked the greater part of his troops, moved them by sea to the mouth of the valley leading up to Bilbao, thus effectually turning the position which the enemy had taken up, and landed them successfully before any Carlist forces could assemble to oppose him. The relief failed on this occasion, but the operations none the less show what advantages the side commanding the sea possesses in a case of the kind.

Liberty of action, as shown by foregoing paragraphs. The purpose of this chapter has been to demonstrate how great a liberty of action the commander of an army may enjoy who is supported by a preponderating navy, and who is operating in a theatre of war adjoining the sea. It has been explained why it is that, when a body of troops destined for an attack upon the coast-line of an adversary is on board ship and approaching the scene of action, the initiative lies necessarily with its commander and not with those who control the distribution of the defending forces. The troops on board ship can be landed at any point favourable for disembarkation; the enemy must shape his plans to conform with their designs. It has been explained that an over-sea expeditionary force can conceal its projects to the very last moment, and can deceive the adversary by feints and ruses to an extent rarely practicable in operations taking place entirely on land. It has been pointed out that a military force operating in a maritime country will generally, if strategically worsted during the course of the campaign, or if threatened by very superior bodies of hostile troops, have a safe line of retreat to the coast in some direction or other. The extent to which the great strategical principle of "interior lines" is applicable to amphibious warfare has been discussed. And Sherman's march through Georgia, and the overthrow of Peru by the Chilian land and sea forces, have been cited to illustrate what enormous advantages armies may derive from maritime command.

In no great war since the downfall of Napoleon has the influence of sea-power over the course of the conflict on shore been depicted so vividly and from so many different points of view, as in that desperate struggle for the preservation of the Union, which devastated great portions of the United States from 1861 to 1865. An outline account of the operations in and around Virginia during those momentous years, which are of unique interest, will serve as an instructive epilogue to the chapter.

In the War of Secession the Federal side may be said, for all practical purposes, to have enjoyed undisputed command of the sea. As can be seen from the sketch, Virginia is a maritime state bordering on the great inlet of the Chesapeake with its many minor estuaries and creeks. At the time of the war it was a territory with comparatively speaking few roads, it was by no means thickly populated, and it therefore formed a theatre of war not very well adapted for the manœuvring of great armies in the field. Just as Washington was the capital of the Northern side, Richmond became to all intents and purposes the focus and nerve-centre of the South.

The campaigns in and round Virginia, 1861-65, as illustration of principles discussed in chapter.

Opening operations.

And the great campaigns which have immortalised the names of Lee and Stonewall Jackson, and of the ultimate victor Grant, were fought for the possession of what was merely a large country town, which, prior to the outbreak of hostilities, possessed little more than local importance. The Potomac formed the frontier between the contending forces.

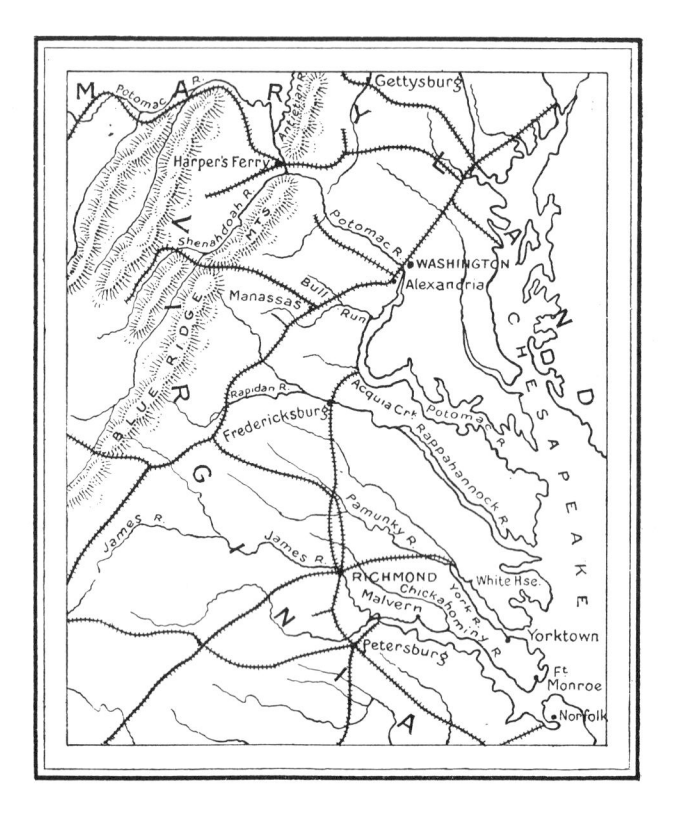

The struggle in Virginia was initiated in 1861 by the advance of a large Federal army from Washington on Manassas, by its disastrous overthrow at Bull Run, by its precipitate retreat back to the vicinity of the capital, and by the abandonment of active operations in that quarter for the rest of the year.

For the campaign of 1862 General M'Clellan was placed at the head of the Union army destined to subdue Virginia. He decided to base his plan of operations upon sea-power, and to attack from the Chesapeake. He was, however, much thwarted in his designs by the apprehensions of the Federal Government as to the safety of Washington. And so it came about that when he landed at Fort Monroe, it was only with a portion of the total forces detailed for the Virginian campaign. His arrangements were, moreover, for a time dislocated by the presence of the famous Confederate ironclad *Merrimac* in the estuary of the James, which he had hoped to dominate with vessels of light draught. His advance was extremely slow, the general line running past Yorktown and along the York river or estuary of the Pamunky, a stretch of water which the Federal navy was able to control. At last, however, his base was established near White House, and from there he commenced his final advance on Richmond.

But stirring events had occurred in the north-west. Stonewall Jackson from the Shenandoah valley had completely out-manœuvred the Federal forces operating in that quarter and in front of Washington. He had suddenly moved southeast, and appearing unexpectedly on the Chickahominy, had joined with Lee in front of Richmond. The united Confederate forces turned M'Clellan's right flank, cut him off from his base at White House, hustled him southwards, and the Federals might have suffered a disaster which would have thrown the ignominious affair of Bull Run entirely into the shade, had not in the meantime the *Merrimac* been destroyed (as has been already mentioned on p. 136), and had not the estuary of the James thus come under control of the gunboats of the North. M'Clellan fell back to Malvern, and there, with his back to the water, stood his ground. Thanks to maritime command, he was able to effect his retreat in a direction widely divergent from his original line of communications, to form a new base, and to establish himself in security on the sea-shore.

The Washington Government were bitterly disappointed by this untoward ending to their strenuous effort. It was therefore resolved to leave M'Clellan on the James, and to push forward a strong force under General Pope from the Potomac by the Manassas line. Lee thus found himself between Pope and M'Clellan in a position to act on interior lines, and he made brilliant use of this great opportunity. He left a force to watch M'Clellan and fell upon Pope, driving him back in utter confusion towards the Potomac. Then, following up his victories with the resolution and promptitude characteristic of the highest type of soldier, he crossed the frontier line at Harper's Ferry and invaded Maryland. But their control of the Chesapeake saved the situation for the Federals. For when Pope was defeated, M'Clellan, with a large part of his force, was hastily brought round by sea from the James to near Washington, and so Lee found himself confronted on the Antietam by an army which was too strong for him. The engagement proved tactically indecisive, it is true. But the Confederate chief gauged the strategical situation too clearly to indulge in any illusions, he withdrew into Virginia, and the campaign of 1862 closed for the time being.

After a pause, during which Lee withdrew practically unmolested to the vicinity of the Rapidan, the Federal forces, now under General Burnside, advanced to the upper Rapahannock. From there they attempted a flank march round Lee's right. The result was the battle of Fredericksburg, in which the army of the Union was again disastrously defeated. But the strategical result of the victory of the South was small, for Acquia Creek offered Burnside a fresh *point d'appui* on the water. And during the winter months the two armies faced each other on the Rapahannock, the Federals based on the estuary of the Potomac.

Campaign of 1863.

Early in the spring of 1863 the Northern army, under

the command of a new general, Hooker, crossed the Rapahannock. But the venture merely led to another mortifying reverse, for Hooker was completely defeated at Chancellorsville, an action ever memorable because during its progress Stonewall Jackson received the wound which cost him his life. Hooker fell back again across the river. Lee now, however, resolved to carry the war into Pennsylvania; he put the Confederate forces in motion, and, making a flank march to the north-west, he crossed the Potomac a second time at Harper's Ferry. The utmost alarm prevailed at Washington and in the Union States generally, when it was found that the army of Virginia, under its illustrious chief, was in Maryland. Every nerve was strained to assemble an overpowering army to stay the advance of the formidable Confederate leader. Troops were gathered from all sides. The forces from the Rapahannock were hastened by sea to Washington, and were hurried north, and a great battle was fought at Gettysburg, in which Lee, decidedly outnumbered, was beaten and was forced to retreat. He succeeded, however, in withdrawing his troops to the upper Rapahannock with little loss other than that suffered in the most severely-contested combat of the war.

No further operations of great interest occurred in Virginia in 1863; but the Federal cause was now strongly in the ascendant in the west. The capture of Port Hudson and Vicksburg during the summer gave to the Northern side complete command of the Mississippi. Their superior resources, coupled with the incalculable advantage they enjoyed in possessing the command of the sea and in being thus in a position to blockade the hostile coasts, and added to the power of harassing the enemy's extensive seaboard by maritime descents, was slowly but surely placing the forces of the Union in a dominating position, and assuring them of ultimate success. During the winter the army destined to invade Virginia from the Potomac was carefully organised, was adequately equipped, was swelled to a total which it had never attained in the days of M'Clellan or Pope or Hooker, and was placed under the command of the famous soldier to whom the Federals mainly owed their triumphs in the west, General Grant.

Campaign of 1864. Grant advanced in 1864 by the time-honoured Manassas line, with the avowed intention of fighting Lee whenever he could, of crushing the Confederates by superior force, and of wearing their resistance down by the process of attrition. Manœuvring constantly by his left, he worked round from the estuary of the Potomac to that of the Rapahannock, thence to that of the Pamunky, and finally, keeping his back constantly to the sea, he reached the James, after many encounters in which Lee invariably displayed consummate art and kept the enemy at bay, but which seriously diminished the numerical strength of the Confederate forces. Grant's huge army astride of the James, with a secure base and in a position to receive a constant flow of reinforcements by sea from the north, had commenced a kind of siege of the entrenched camp of the Secessionist forces gathered about Petersburg and Richmond, when an unexpected incident occurred which was to demonstrate the extraordinary liberty of action sometimes conferred on military forces by maritime command. A Confederate force suddenly came down the Shenandoah valley, crossed the Potomac, and made a dash for Washington. The capital was in a panic, the Government in a state of consternation. But a force which had just arrived from New Orleans by ship to reinforce Grant, was promptly sent on up the Chesapeake and Potomac to the scene of danger. Grant put some of his own troops on the James on board transports and hurried them round to Maryland. Control of the sea, as at the time of the Antietam and of Gettysburg, saved the situation for the Union, and the raiding force, confronted by a far superior army, hastened back to the Shenandoah valley whence it had so suddenly come, foiled in its design.

The vastly superior army of Grant was face to face with Lee's ever-dwindling force all the winter, and for months was unable to make any headway. But early in 1865 the end came. Sherman's victorious operations in Georgia and the Carolinas, the Federal successes in the basin of the Mississippi, and the exhaustion of the Confederate resources in men and money and material, had told their tale, and had made the cause of the South a hopeless one. So that when Grant penetrated the lines of Petersburg, forced his antagonist back towards the west, and enveloped the remnants of the famous army of Virginia at Appotamox, Lee had no course open to him except to surrender, and this brought the struggle to an end.

The end.

Over and over again the genius of Lee and Stonewall Jackson and the devotion of their troops had combined to overthrow the Federal armies on the battlefield, but these had always been saved from irretrievable ruin by their command of the sea. When the vastly superior resources of the North had rendered a repetition of the Confederate triumphs of Manassas and Chancellorsville impossible in Virginia, and when the struggle became merely one of wearing down the weaker side, the great army of Grant was supplied and refreshed with ease by ships coming from the Potomac, from Baltimore, from New York and from Boston, bearing men and munitions of war and food and forage. When in the earlier days Lee had, once and again, crossed the border-line and invaded the territory of the Union, maritime control had on each occasion enabled the scattered Federal forces to act on interior lines and to concentrate to meet him in superior strength at the threatened point. And when the Confederates made their last despairing attempt to dash at Washington from the Shenandoah valley, a transfer of force by sea, causing little inconvenience elsewhere and carried out without the least difficulty, again brought the raiders up short, and compelled them to hasten back to their own territory.

Conclusion. "He that commands the sea," says Bacon, "is at great liberty, and may take as much and as little of the war as he will." The truth of this is written down in the military history of maritime nations. Given naval preponderance and an enemy possessing territory which can be approached by sea, and military force can be brought into play with an immunity from undue risks and a freedom as to choice of objectives and direction of attack, which is very rarely to be found in purely land warfare. The story of Moore in the Peninsula, of M'Clellan on the James River, of the Crimean War and the numerous struggles between the Russian and Ottoman empires around the Black Sea, of Sherman's famous march to the coast, and of the war between Chili and Peru, are, after all, merely fresh illustrations of a strategical principle which dates back to the days of Darius and to the great campaigns of antiquity fought out round the Mediterranean Sea. These modern incidents of war merely serve to endorse the teachings of wars dating back to an epoch long before gunpowder was thought of, and long before even sails were used in ships except as an occasional auxiliary to the bondsmen straining at their oars.

CHAPTER XVI.

THE HOLD WHICH MARITIME COMMAND MAY GIVE AN ARMY UPON COAST DISTRICTS, EVEN WHEN THE ENEMY IS THE STRONGER IN THE THEATRE OF LAND OPERATIONS.

IN no strategical situation are the relations between maritime preponderance and military operations more likely to be emphasised, than when a nation possessing a predominant navy is maintaining a grip upon some locality or district on the enemy's coast. Amphibious force may under such conditions exert an extraordinary influence over the course of the struggle as a whole. And this same principle also holds good where the belligerent controlling the sea is holding on with a land army to some maritime tract within his own territory, the rest of which, or considerable portions of the rest of which, are in hostile occupation. *Power which maritime command gives to maintain a grip on a coast district.*

The tactical and strategical advantages enjoyed by a military force operating with its back to the sea, in possession of a suitable port, and fortified by naval power, are immense. The flanks are secure. Retreat in case of reverse is assured. There can be little or no anxiety as to supplies. Friendly warships may be able to afford assistance in actual battle. Some of the most protracted sieges in history—that of Ostend by the Spaniards which lasted from 1502 to 1505, and the great siege of Gibraltar of much later date, for instance—have been fought out under these conditions. And if the side which is maintaining its footing in virtue of maritime command is in so favourable a position, the *Tactical and strategical advantages enjoyed by a military force operating with its back to the sea.*

adversary will obviously be compelled to put forth great efforts to gain the upper hand; for when one army is from the tactical and strategical point of view decidedly the better placed, that opposed to it cannot hope for victory unless it represents a force stronger in numbers, in armament, or in quality.

<small>The lines of Torres Vedras.</small> No better example of this can be quoted than the case of Torres Vedras. When Wellington fell back to his famous lines in 1810, his army was practically safe once it was within them. The position was naturally one of great defensive strength. The flanks were secured by the estuary of the Tagus on one side and by the Atlantic on the other. The harbour of Lisbon afforded an ideal anchorage for transports and for freight-ships. The French armies under Massena and his brother marshals were, on the other hand, operating far from their base, and were campaigning in a country which was infested with guerilla bands and which had been stripped bare of supplies. Their communications were of great length, and were very far from secure. Merely to have driven the British army out of its fine position, a great superiority of force actually on the spot would have been indispensable; but, in addition to the troops at the front, an immense expenditure of detachments along the routes leading back to the Pyrenees was the inevitable consequence of the strategical situation. While Wellington was resting his relatively insignificant army on the shores of Portugal in anticipation of another campaign, he was all the time wearing out the vitality of a host numerically far superior to his own, and was producing in it that process of wastage which saps the power of a military force in war when casualties from exhaustion and disease cannot be made good. He, in fact, was treading his opponents down by doing nothing. And there is perhaps no portion of the military career of the great Duke which more clearly proves his claim to be accounted one of the foremost of the masters

of the art of war, than the period of the Peninsular struggle when his operations were wearing their least active appearance. The traditions of British strategy were totally opposed to the course which he adopted. His plan of campaign was in defiance of all precedent. It sounded an absolutely new note in the military history of his country.

At the time when Wellington constructed the lines of Torres Vedras no nation could lay claim in modern times to so illuminating a record of military operations based on the sea as England. For a century or more British forces had been making descents on hostile shores in the Mediterranean, in South America, in the Low Countries, almost everywhere in fact where there was an enemy to be found. But with a very few noteworthy exceptions the story of these expeditions had been always the same. The army came, and saw, and went away again.[1] These undertakings had almost invariably been signalised rather by fickleness of purpose than by duration of effort. Peterborough's brilliant exploits during the War of the Spanish Succession, the snaps at the French coast instituted by Pitt during the Seven Years' War, the expedition to the Helder in 1799, the operations in the Kingdom of the Two Sicilies about the time of Maida,—these and many other British campaigns had all presented very similar features. When the enterprise had been deliberately set on foot with the actual conquest of territory and with its subsequent retention in view, as for instance in the cases of Wolfe's campaign on the St Lawrence and of the attacks on the islands of Minorca and Martinique, the operations had sometimes been conducted on sound strategical lines. But where the object had merely been to injure the enemy in a military sense, the combination of land- and sea-power had seldom been turned to account with happy perseverance or with any fixity of design.

British over-sea expeditions before the time of Wellington.

In the last chapter a brief account of Sir J. Moore's

Sir J. Moore's campaign in the Peninsula.

campaign in Spain and Portugal was given in illustration of the liberty of action which command of the sea confers upon a general when in difficulties. Moore undoubtedly at a critical time achieved a remarkable strategical triumph. But it is difficult to avoid the conclusion that his governing idea throughout was to upset Napoleon's plans by a bold demonstration, and then to make for the coast and get away to sea. "If the French succeed in Spain," he had written to Castlereagh from Salamanca, "it will be vain to attempt to resist them in Portugal. The British must in that case immediately take steps to evacuate the country." The idea of holding on to some point on the coast seems never to have been entertained by him. From an early stage in his memorable campaign he would appear to have regarded his presence in the Peninsula in the light of a mere interlude, not in the light of a protracted, far-reaching operation of war. "It is impossible to conceive," says Jomini, "why the English did not defend Coruña. It is not indeed a Gibraltar, but against an enemy who had nothing but field-pieces it surely could have been maintained for some time, the more so as they could at any time throw in succour by sea." No arrangements had been made for remaining in Galicia, nor does such an idea ever appear to have been seriously entertained. The project of transferring the army by sea from Coruña to Lisbon, where there was still a British force in possession, seems never to have been carefully considered. Had Sir A. Wellesley been governed by like theories of strategy, he would never have been Duke of Wellington, and the history of Europe in the early part of the nineteenth century might have been a very different one.

Wellington's conception of strategy the true one.

Napoleon's scheme of operations in the Peninsula was as simple in conception as it proved to be difficult in execution from the time that Wellesley for the second time set foot in Portugal. It was to drive the British into the sea. That their ships would be there to take them back to their own country if necessary, he knew from earlier experiences. He had driven them into the sea at Toulon, but they had sailed away to Corsica. His generals had worsted them amid the dykes and dunes of the north of Holland, but they had been obliged to let the enemy embark and return to England. To a commander accustomed to decisive victories like Marengo and Austerlitz and Jena, these islanders, with their appearances and disappearances, their flittings to and fro, their intangible and irritating strategy, presented a perplexing and vexatious problem. But their methods must at least have appeared to the Emperor such, that they did not require to be taken very seriously. It is possible that he abandoned the pursuit of Moore to Soult at Astorga, foreseeing that there was small prospect of inflicting a serious defeat on the fugitive general,—he did not quit Valladolid on his return to France till nearly three weeks later, after the battle of Coruña had been fought. Wellesley's ideas of war were, however, altogether different from those of his many predecessors in command of British over-sea expeditions, and Napoleon found to his cost that his marshals in Spain and Portugal were now face to face with a commander who, when he was driven back to the coast, held his ground there and defied them to come on.

The strategy of which Torres Vedras represents the type and symbol was not a new departure in the art of war. The difficulty of expelling the military forces of a powerful maritime nation from territory washed by the sea, had been proved long before by the resistance offered by the Venetian colonies to the vast fighting resources brought against them by the Ottoman Empire. It had been proved again at a later date by the enormous difficulties encountered by the Russians in their endeavours to wrest the northern shores of the Black Sea and the country round

Other examples.

the Sea of Azov from the Turks, before the time when they began to dispute the command of those waters with the fleets of the Sultan. The great military strength of successive Tsars had gradually absorbed the eastern shores of the Baltic into the Muscovite realm, and had secured possession of the territory round the Gulf of Finland; but the tide of conquest had risen very slowly until Russia, having succeeded in creating a fighting fleet in the Neva and in sending it to sea, challenged the supremacy of the Swedish fleets in north-eastern Europe. That an army based on the sea, in possession of a favourable harbour and occupying ground suitable for defence, can hold out for ever against superior numbers is not of course the case. The fortress of Candia resisted the Turks for more than twenty years, but it was taken at last. Toulon must have eventually fallen, even had Hood received the Austrian and British reinforcements which had been promised him. But to actually drive the defenders of a maritime district or locality into the sea, supposing the defenders to be backed up by a preponderating fleet, there must be a great expenditure of military force, and there will consequently, almost inevitably, be loss of power in other directions. To contain superior bodies of hostile troops with a numerically feeble army for any length of time is in itself a great object gained, and the longer the process is continued the more important and far-reaching may be the strategical consequences.

The Crimean War as an example of this. The Crimean War is in some respects an even more remarkable example of the application of this principle than the operations of Wellington in the Peninsula. And what is especially singular about the campaign of Sebastopol is, that the mistakes and miscalculations of the allies turned out to be a blessing in disguise. Napoleon III., the British Government, Lord Raglan, and Marshal St Arnaud had no other idea in their minds, when the invasion of Krim Tartary was decided upon and when the Anglo-French army moved against the great Russian stronghold, than to destroy the chief naval station belonging to the enemy in the Black Sea, and to destroy with it the fleet which was known to be sheltering behind its batteries. Under the political circumstances of the time the demolition of the fortifications and docks and arsenals, and the sinking of the warships of the Tsar, offered a very appropriate object for the employment of amphibious power. But, at the best, it meant merely a blow: it did not involve the wearing out of the resources of a formidable adversary by prolonged operations during which he was labouring under a crushing strategical disadvantage. And the signal success achieved in the end by the allies in this Homeric struggle, was in reality due to the fact that the course of events in the Crimea imposed upon them an attitude totally different from that which they had intended to assume.

Had the victorious army advanced straight upon Sebastopol after the battle of the Alma it would probably have captured the fortress with little difficulty. The land defences were then of small account, Mentschikof's chief preoccupation being to get out of the place. Everything was left in confusion, and Kornilof, with his able coadjutor Todleben, had not had time to even initiate that wonderful scheme of defence which was to keep the French and British armies occupied for months. But the invaders skirted in processional array round the head of the Sebastopol inlet, settled themselves on the plateau south of the town, organised their bases at Balaclava and Kamish after a fashion, and then found that what had been on the land side virtually an undefended town, had developed into a great place of arms. The upshot was that an extraordinary military situation was brought about. An army based on the sea and aided by a navy of overwhelming strength, started the siege of a maritime stronghold without even being able to invest it; and to all intents and purposes the position of the invaders came to be almost a counterpart of that which Wellesley had taken up at Torres Vedras in 1810. They had a tract of sea-girt country in their grip, while a mighty military empire was striving to make them relax that grip and was striving in vain.

The siege of Sebastopol lasted nearly a year, and during all those weary months Russia was trying to mass sufficient troops in the Crimea to turn the intruders out. The Tsar's troops had to be moved enormous distances athwart a country almost devoid of communications. Difficulties of supply became very grave in spite of the facilities which had been enjoyed at first for bringing corn across the Sea of Azov, and which had enabled magazines of food to be set up within the peninsula. The allied soldiery suffered terribly, it is true, during the winter,—the losses of the British contingent represented a war wastage almost unprecedented; but the Russian armies suffered infinitely more, and their losses were proportionately far greater. The blow, as a blow, had failed; but the amphibious power of the two western nations maintained an open sore in the Tsar's great empire, which gradually exhausted its strength, and which in the end compelled it to agree to terms.[2]

Japan in Manchuria. The conflict between Japan and Russia in the Far East affords another most remarkable illustration of this important strategical principle. The Japanese, based on the sea and in occupation of the southern portions of Manchuria, enjoy an extraordinary advantage over their formidable antagonists. They suffer little inconvenience as regards supplies, for these come by sea. The gaps in their ranks caused by battle and by sickness are speedily filled up. Their flanks are secure. In the meantime the Russians have to bring their reinforcements and munitions of war and a great part of their food, a fifteen days' journey along a single line of railway. If they lose 10,000 men in action, these can only be replaced by seriously interfering with the regular flow of reinforcements and of stores from Russia Proper. How it all will end cannot be foretold at the close of the first year of war. But the operations which have taken place have proved that as long as Japan controls the sea, she enjoys a tremendous advantage in the theatre of land operations from the point of view of strategy.

An interesting example of the difficulties which attend the operations of a preponderating army engaged in trying to expel hostile troops from maritime districts when the enemy is dominant at sea, is provided by the campaigns of 1848-49 in Denmark. The story of that remarkable struggle of the Danes against the land forces of North Germany is not very well known in this country. Its incidents are not related by German military writers with the same enthusiasm and wealth of detail as are those of Teutonic combats of somewhat later date. But the names of Düppel and Fredericia should be familiar to the British army,[3] for they are connected with events where military force and naval force acting in harmony achieved astonishing results, and which admirably illustrate the potentialities of amphibious strength in war.

The campaign in Denmark in 1848-49 as illustration of the difficulty of expelling an inferior army from maritime districts, if that army can depend upon control of the sea.

In 1848 Schleswig and Holstein still formed a portion of the kingdom of Denmark. The German Confederation was at the time practically without a navy; Denmark, on the other hand, possessed a small but admirably manned fleet, and throughout the war the little kingdom enjoyed the enormous advantage of supremacy at sea. The campaign commenced with the advance of a formidable German army through Holstein into Schleswig, which defeated the Danish force at the town of Schleswig. The Danes thereupon retired into the islands of Funen and Alsen, while the invaders pushed on as far as Kolding in Jutland. But Europe intervened at this juncture, and, by dint of strong diplomatic pressure and of demonstrations on the part of the Baltic States, obliged the Germans to fall back again into Schleswig. As they were retiring, the Danes from the islands suddenly fell upon their flank near Gravenstein, inflicted upon them a humiliating and disastrous defeat, and before the vanquished invaders could recover from this reverse, the victors had retired again to Düppel and had taken up a fortified position there with their back to the sea. Bent on retrieving their laurels,

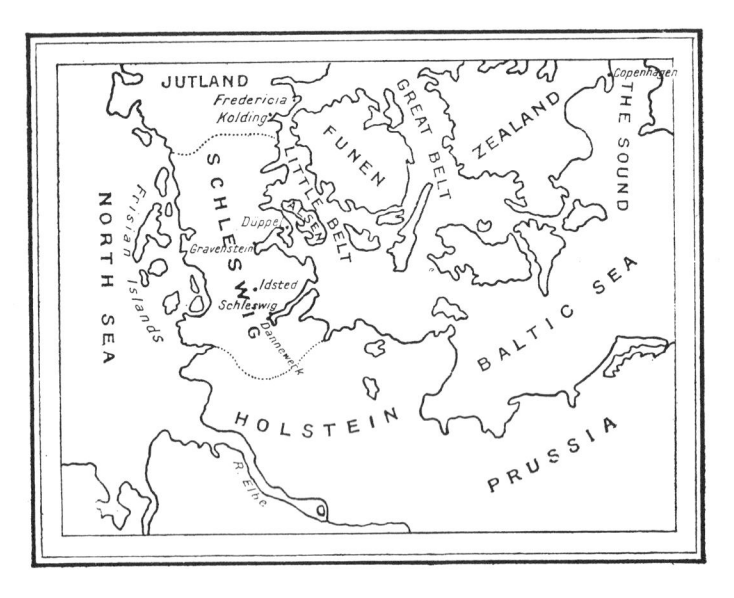

the invaders advanced on Düppel. But the defenders, fighting with their flanks and rear secured by their maritime preponderance, and effectively supported by some ships of war during the actual combat, repulsed the assault with heavy loss. An armistice was thereupon concluded, and peace reigned for a season.

But the truce lasted only for a few months. In the spring of 1849 the Germans advanced in still stronger force than in the previous year. They overran Schleswig and swarmed into Jutland, while the bulk of the Danish army retired into Alsen and Funen as they had done in the first campaign, but maintained a footing on the mainland at Fredericia and at Düppel. The invading army pressed forward against Fredericia, and commenced a regular siege of that not very formidable stronghold on the coast. But before much progress had taken place in the siege, Danish detachments from Funen suddenly disembarked both north and south of the place, and, acting in conjunction with the garrison, fell unexpectedly upon the besiegers. The battle which ensued was singularly decisive tactically: most of the artillery of the Germans was captured, their line was rolled up, part of their baggage-train was taken, and they were driven away in great confusion from the vicinity of the little fortress. It is doubtful, indeed, whether the invaders could have maintained themselves in Jutland at all after the disaster. But a convention soon afterwards brought about the withdrawal of the German armies, and the war between Denmark and the Confederation came to a conclusion.

It is interesting to note that in this war the Danes seem at the outset hardly to have fully realised the advantage of keeping a footing on the mainland at Düppel, and of inducing the enemy to waste his strength on assaults of a position which could not be turned. In the later war of 1864 the defence of this important point was a part of the Danish plan from the beginning. But they had neglected to make the intrenchments really formidable, and had failed to extend the perimeter sufficiently to meet the changed tactical conditions of the day: in consequence of this oversight the lines were captured by Prince Frederick Charles without very serious difficulty. In the later war, moreover, maritime command was to a certain extent in dispute, and this militated seriously against the successful employment of the plan of active defence which had served the hardy Danes so well fifteen years before.

Conclusion.

The liberty of action which the military commander of forces based upon the sea enjoys in a maritime theatre of war was discussed at some length in the last chapter. Liberty of action to a certain extent implies the adoption of capricious methods of war. It suggests sudden landings and unexpected changes of base. It may involve daring advances, and may call for hasty retirements to points on the coast not previously occupied. It confers extraordinary advantages upon an army under a leader who knows how to make the most of his opportunities. And the brilliant strategy of the Danes in their fight against an enemy infinitely stronger than themselves on land, serves to illustrate these principles most admirably. But an even more striking feature in the campaign of 1848-49 is the manner in which the weaker army managed to cling to the mainland of the Cimbric Chersonese. It never relaxed its grip on some part of its coast-line. The bulk of military forces might be withdrawn to the islands, Holstein might be abandoned, Schleswig might be overrun, and Jutland might be in jeopardy, but the defenders always managed to maintain a footing on the continent.

The lesson to be learnt from this is the same as the lesson to be learnt from Torres Vedras and the history of the Peninsular War, from the Crimean War, and from Manchuria. One great function of sea-power is to act as a backbone to military force. Thanks to maritime command, a body of troops planted down in some coast district may be able to hold its ground against formidable armies because they are operating far from their proper bases and are subjected to great difficulties as regards maintenance; and by its action an insignificant military force may be draining the resources of a powerful State which is placed at a strategical disadvantage. It is the form in which naval preponderance can perhaps make itself felt in the most decisive way in warfare on land.[4]

CHAPTER XVII.

THE INFLUENCE OF MARITIME COMMAND WHEN A MILITARY LINE OF OPERATIONS OR COMMUNICATIONS FOLLOWS THE COAST OR RUNS PARALLEL TO IT.

IT is not uncommon to find great lines of communication which are the highways of commerce running along the sea-shore, or else following the general line of the coast and only a few miles inland. Sometimes this follows from the fact that mountain-ranges rise more or less abruptly from the sea, leaving only a narrow strip of comparatively speaking level country. Sometimes the interior is a desert, only the actual littoral is inhabited, and the main artery of traffic therefore naturally skirts the shore. Sometimes it is due to the number of settlements on the coast, and to the routes and roads which are the necessary consequence of ordinary intercommunication between different ports, and which naturally take the shortest line. But where such conditions prevail in a theatre of war, the command of the sea assumes a special strategical importance. Military lines of communication naturally follow main routes, and if main routes run parallel to a coast-line or along a coast-line, the army dependent on them offers its flank to the sea. *Routes following the line of the coast.*

Troops cannot march along a coast road if hostile warships are in a position to sweep it with their guns. A railway running along the shore is at the mercy of landing-parties which can destroy bridges and culverts, can tear up the rails, and can block up cuttings. Even where an important *Liability of such a route to be cut from the side of the sea.*

line of communications does not actually follow the shore, but runs a few miles inland parallel to the general direction of the coast, it is always liable to be cut by small hostile forces disembarked suddenly, and it is obviously exposed to the depredations of an enemy with a preponderating navy. Such a line of communications partakes, in fact, of the character of a military defile exposed on one flank, and an army depending upon it is strategically in a very dangerous position.

The defile east of the Pyrenees.
At either end of the great barrier of the Pyrenees, stretching between France and Spain, there is a defile of this character. And that at the eastern end, where the mountain-range rises abruptly from the shores of the Mediterranean, has played an important part in history, notably during the War of the Spanish Succession and again in 1808. This eastern defile is of considerable length, and, owing to the height and rugged character of the Pyrenees between Languedoc and Catalonia, it has always formed a main line of advance and of communications for armies passing into or out of north-eastern Spain. The road, and now the railway, run generally along the shore, and their uninterrupted use by a military force is almost necessarily contingent on the command of that part of the Mediterranean being in possession of a friendly navy. It is true that the main road for some distance avoids the shore and climbs over the mountains; but its general line from Barcelona to Perpignan runs close to the sea. During the War of the Spanish Succession the British navy did not constantly make its presence felt in these waters,—it will be remembered that in those days admirals were averse to wintering so far from home,—and therefore French armies operating in north-eastern Spain made free use of this important line of communications. But from the earliest days of the Peninsular War the Spanish patriots seriously menaced the security of the route, and when Lord

Collingwood came to their assistance, and when the daring and restless Cochrane appeared upon the scene, a large force of troops had to be detailed by Napoleon to keep open the line upon which all operations in the eastern theatre of war depended.

In the reign of William III., when the policy of maintaining a British fleet in the Mediterranean, which had been allowed to lapse with the abandonment of Tangier, was suddenly revived, the influence of maritime command over the course of operations at the eastern end of the Pyrenees manifested itself in startling fashion. Louis XIV. was at the moment devoting his attention almost entirely to the occupation of Catalonia by forces under command of the Duc de Noailles, whose main objective was to be Barcelona. All was progressing smoothly when Admiral Russell, the victor of La Hogue, suddenly appeared in the Mediterranean with a formidable fleet. His old opponent Tourville, who had been blockading the great Spanish port in anticipation of Noailles' arrival, retired precipitately to Toulon, not venturing to dispute control of these waters with his doughty antagonist. The result was that Noailles, thus left in the lurch, came to a complete standstill, and that the French king's projects in north-eastern Spain were perforce abandoned for the time. A year later, however, the British fleet was definitely withdrawn from the Mediterranean, and thereupon Barcelona soon fell.

Although it is only for a few miles that there is an actual defile between the Pyrenees and the Mediterranean, any military advance from France into Catalonia exposes the flank of the army to the sea for a long distance. Even when the route is not actually exposed to the artillery fire of a hostile fleet lying off the shore, the fact that a general line of advance and of communications runs parallel to the coast makes it a matter of great importance which side enjoys the control of the adjoining waters. For if the enemy be in a position to land detachments at points in rear of the army, this is kept in a constant state of perturbation and anxiety, even when its position does not become one of actual peril. Strong bodies of troops have to be told off to guard the communications and to ward off attacks from the sea. This means dispersion, and it creates a serious drain on the strength of the force as a whole. The indirect effect may be great, even without any aggressive move on the part of the enemy. If, on the other hand, friendly war-vessels are cruising off the coast and the adversary be powerless at sea, one flank of the advancing army is absolutely secured, and therefore the protection of its communications only absorbs half the number of men which are ordinarily required when the line of operations leads straight into the heart of hostile territory across a land frontier. In the one case the communications of the army are especially exposed. In the other they are peculiarly secure.

The Riviera. The Riviera is a district analogous to the maritime strip east of the Pyrenees, and it equally exemplifies the importance of naval control where a line of military operations follows the coast. The peculiar geographical features of this favoured tract of country are well known. It is a winter resort for the wealthy leisured classes from all lands, who are attracted by the charm of its climate and by the beauty of its scenery. From the military point of view it constitutes a very remarkable strategical defile, a defile of great length and a defile of signal importance. And the reason for this can be seen on any good map depicting the topographical features of the frontier provinces of Italy and France. The sketch gives a general idea of the physical geography and direction of coast-line.

The great mountain-range of the Alps creates a most formidable barrier, running from north to south, between the basins of the Po and the Rhone. Close to the Mediterranean, however, it curls round to the east, overhanging the sea, and it forms the Riviera. Armies advancing from France into Italy, or *vice versa*, must either scale the mountains or else must follow the shore. The hill chain of the Alps is so lofty and so rugged that routes traversing it of necessity follow the course of narrow mountain valleys, and they traverse difficult passes. Such routes can be blocked by a mere handful of men in a fortified post; and a military commander always hesitates to attempt the passage of a mountain-range in face of opposition. But

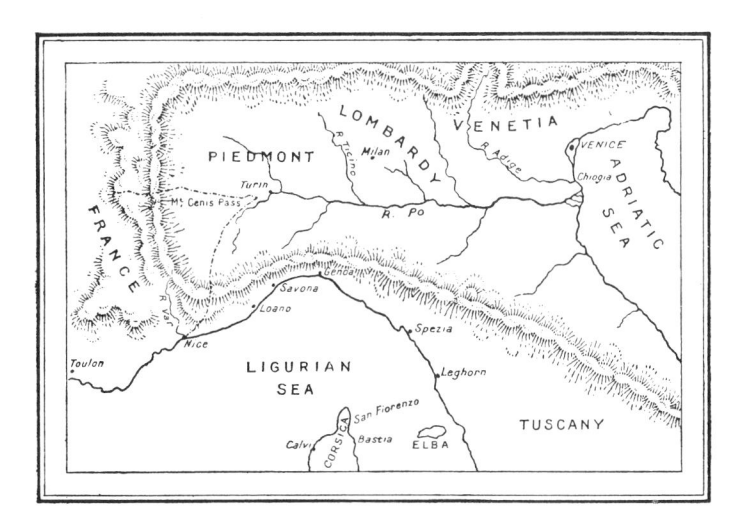

the Riviera also, though to a somewhat less extent, is singularly well adapted to defensive tactics, for the spurs from the main mountain system come down abruptly to the shore, and the streams rushing down to the Mediterranean have cut out deep and narrow valleys between them: there is not a league of ground between the Var and Genoa, nor between Genoa and the neighbourhood of Leghorn, where the defile opens out into the plains of Tuscany, without some natural position for an army to take up. Troops advancing through this district supported by a fleet can, however, turn any position which the enemy has occupied by landing troops in rear of it; and to the belligerent possessing naval preponderance, a line of operations through this remarkable strip of country presents many attractions. The support of Sir Cloudesley Shovel in 1707 greatly assisted Prince Eugene and the Duke of Savoy when they advanced on Toulon through the western Riviera. Mahan has shown how, in 1795 and 1796, the failure of the British fleet to adequately support the Austrian and Sardinian forces in this theatre of operations led first to the overthrow of the Austrian general Devins at Loano, and afterwards enabled Napoleon to work along the coast-line for a considerable distance previous to his sudden dash over the mountains and his victory of Montenotte. For an army to follow the famous Cornice road from Nice to Genoa, or to use that road as a line of communications in defiance of an enemy commanding the sea, may be said to be virtually impracticable in a strategical sense.

The strategical defile north of the Adriatic. Conditions somewhat analogous to those of the Riviera, although the geographical features are not so marked and although the defile is not so narrow, are presented by the stretch of country north of the Adriatic and lying between its shores and the great mountain-ranges to the north. The main line of communications of Austrian armies engaged in the basin of the Po has always traversed this strip of country, the left flank being necessarily exposed to the sea; and on account of this the question of naval control in the Adriatic has often influenced military combinations far up the valley of the Po. Thus we find in 1702 Admiral Rooke ordered to detach eighteen or twenty sail to the Adriatic, because a small French squadron was harassing Prince Eugene's land communications between Lombardy and Austria proper,—the British ships were not, it is true, sent, owing to the general naval situation. The importance of the command of the Adriatic as influencing land operations in the basins of the Adige and Po is also well illustrated by Radetzky's operations in 1848 and 1849 against the Italian principalities headed by the kingdom of Sardinia. A short account of this campaign may be given, as it presents several points of interest.

A great movement was started in 1848 by Sardinia to drive the Austrians out of Lombardy and northern Italy. Most of the states in the Italian peninsula espoused the cause of their compatriots, and threw their naval and military resources into the scale. And the result of this was that Austria, for the time being, lost the command of the Adriatic, and that the veteran Marshal Radetzky, who commanded on the Adige and Mincio, found himself confronted by formidable military forces drawn from most of the dukedoms and principalities and kingdoms into which the land south of the Po was divided up. He could probably have dealt effectively with these, but for insurrectionary disturbances in Venetia which were backed up by support from the sea—for these imperilled his communications. As it turned out, however, internal convulsions compelled the Neapolitan government to recall its land forces and naval forces into southern Italy, and the result of this was that control of the northern Adriatic was recovered by Austria.

Italian campaign of 1848-49.

The influence of this change in the maritime situation soon made itself felt. The rebellion in Venetia was at once got under restraint. Radetzky's communications ceased to cause him anxiety. And the Sardinian army which had swept forward boldly into Lombardy was speedily driven back across the Mincio, beaten and forced to assume the defensive. A truce followed, which lasted through the winter. But hostilities recommenced in 1849, this time under conditions very favourable to the Austrian army. There was no longer any fear from the Adriatic. Reinforcements had arrived from the Danube. And Radetzky, with his communications secure and at the head of a formidable army, advanced into Piedmont and defeated the forces of the House of Savoy at the decisive battle of Novara, which put an end to the conflict. As long as the command of the Adriatic had been in doubt the marshal had been compelled to act on the defensive, and to see portions of Austrian territory overrun by an invader whom he was inclined to despise: no sooner, however, did a friendly navy control those waters than he assumed the offensive, and asserted the superiority of the imperial forces decisively over those of Sardinia and the lesser Italian States.

The case of an isthmus. The importance of maritime command where the line of operations or of communications of an army runs along the coast, or parallel to the coast and at no great distance from it, has been established in preceding paragraphs. But if the line traverses a strip of country with the sea on either side,—traverses an isthmus, in fact,—a preponderating navy is even more essential for its reasonable security. Only an altogether disproportionate expenditure of military force on the flank and communications of the army, indeed, would permit of its progress through a defile of this kind, if the waters on both flanks were controlled by hostile ships of war. On the other hand, supposing the army to be fortified on either hand by friendly flotillas, its position strategically is exceptionally favourable: its rear is secured, and its flanks need cause the commander no anxiety. A narrow strip of land of this kind is, however, seldom of great extent. As a rule, an isthmus merely represents a short defile like that of Suez, or like that near Dalny and Talienwan leading to Port Arthur.

And an isthmus is, it must be remembered, a military defile, quite apart from the question of sea-power. Supposing that neither side possesses naval forces or has any shipping at its command, then the army acting on the offensive has to overcome the resistance of the defenders more or less by frontal attack. Tactically and strategically the situation is all in favour of the defending side. If the assailants enjoy maritime command the position of the defenders becomes almost untenable, but if the defenders control the sea their position must necessarily be singularly secure.

Few defiles have played a more important part in history than the Isthmus of Corinth. The struggles between continental Greece and the Peloponnesus in ancient days often centred round that classic pass. It has been the scene of many an interesting and well-contested combat. And it has always been the case that hosts coming down from the north with the idea of penetrating into the Morea, have run great risks unless they were absolutely assured of the command of the Ægean and of the Gulf of Corinth. When the Russian fleet in 1770 moved into the eastern Mediterranean and roused the Greeks of the Morea to revolt against the power of the Sultan, the Turks, as long as the command of the sea was in dispute, had the utmost difficulty in re-establishing their authority because of the terrors of this famous gorge. In 1821, the first year of the Greek War of Liberation, when the daring enterprise of the Hellenic sailors practically drove the Ottoman navy off the high seas, the Turkish military forces could do little to retrieve the position south of the isthmus. And the campaign of 1822, in which the Caliph put forth all his power to suppress the alarming revolt, is so remarkable that it is worth more than a passing mention.

The Isthmus of Corinth.

The army and navy of the Sultan had suffered many humiliating reverses at the hands of the insurgents during the campaign of 1821, and it was decreed in consequence that a supreme effort was to be made the following year to retrieve the position. A mighty host was to advance from Macedonia. A formidable fleet was equipped for the purpose in the Golden Horn. Turkey in Europe and Turkey in Asia were called upon to do their utmost in providing

The campaign of 1822 between the Ottoman Empire and the insurgent Greeks.

men and ships to accomplish the discomfiture of the giaour. The army was to advance through Thessaly, Bœotia, and Attica, and was to sweep on in irresistible strength into the Morea. The Ottoman navy was in the meantime to brush the Greek fighting-ships from off the face of the Ægean, and when this was done it was in due course to join hands with the military forces on the shores of the Peloponnesus, was to convey supplies to them from the Dardanelles, was to minister to their wants, and was to secure their flanks and their communications with the north. And for a time all went well.

Issuing from the Dardanelles in imposing array, the Turkish fleet threw supplies into Nauplia, which was holding out gallantly against the insurgents, landed troops on several of the revolted islands, and finally appeared off the fertile and populous island of Chios. This was deliberately devastated, most of the inhabitants being put to the sword. While the navy was thus performing its share in the programme, the army was advancing through the defiles of northern Greece, harassed by the guerilla tactics of the hardy mountaineers, losing heavily in indecisive combats, and finally arriving at Corinth considerably the worse for the wear. From that ancient city it turned towards Nauplia.

But a terrible disaster had befallen the Ottoman fleet. After completing its work of ruin at Chios the squadron had anchored opposite the island off the coast of Asia Minor, and had remained there inactive for a considerable space of time, while the Greek mariners were straining every nerve to get together a flotilla fit to offer it battle. For some weeks the insurgent war-vessels cruised off Chios trying in vain to tempt their opponents to put to sea. Then at last one night they attacked the hostile fleet at its anchorage with fire-ships, and inflicted upon it an overwhelming defeat. The Turks were wholly unprepared for such an onslaught. There was a discreditable panic. A few ships were destroyed.

The rest fled precipitately to the Dardanelles, and in consequence of their nocturnal victory the Greeks at a blow regained the mastery in the Ægean. Thus when the Sultan's troops passed on into the Peloponnesus in hopes of meeting a friendly navy with supplies and munitions of war, to make good what had disappeared during their desperately contested advance, they were counting on a broken reed. They found themselves surrounded on all sides, by land and by sea. The Turkish commander entered into negotiations and offered to retire; but the patriot leaders demanded unconditional surrender, a humiliation which the pasha would not endure. He retreated, and in the end only a few half-starved and worn-out soldiers got back to Macedonia to tell the tale of how the great Moslem host, which had marched south a few months before so full of confidence, had fared among the cut-throat hillmen of insurgent Greece.

Defiles such as the Isthmus of Corinth are few. Military operations in the Isthmus of Perekop, which links the Crimea to the mainland of Russia, have never been appreciably affected by the question of maritime command, because the adjoining waters happen to be very shallow. The Isthmus of Suez separates seas which are in other respects so far apart that, up to the present, it has not afforded useful illustrations of this branch of the subject. No great army has ever marched from Central America towards the southern continent through the Isthmus of Panama. The west coast of Schleswig is fringed by reefs and shoals to such an extent that during the war of 1848-49 the Danes were content to attack the German communications from the other side alone. But the position of an army operating in any peninsula must always be, to a certain extent, strategically in a dangerous position if the enemy have control of the sea, and the narrower the isthmus through which its communications run the greater will be its insecurity.

The coast route from Egypt to Asia Minor.

It was pointed out above that cases occur where a great line of communications necessarily skirts the coast because of the interior consisting of desert country. This is found to be the case in parts of Arabia and of North Africa. But the most remarkable case of a main route of commerce skirting the shore for a long distance so as to avoid traversing desolate tracts is found on the coast of Palestine and Syria. By far the most important strategical feature of the south-eastern corner of the Levant is provided by the fact that an army advancing from Egypt into Syria is practically compelled to march almost by the water's edge. Along the shore is a narrow strip of level and fairly productive country, which has been a highway for the passage of trade and of conquering armies for ages. Napoleon, when he advanced into Asia from the delta of the Nile, followed this line. He moved along the coast till he was brought up short by the fortress of Acre, backed by the sea-power of Great Britain. And a generation later the attempt of Mehemet Ali to extend his dominions at the expense of his suzerain lord the Sultan was to produce a very remarkable sequence of operations,—operations which brought home to the Egyptian viceroy with singular force the advantages that an army enjoys when following a line of advance along a coast as long as it has the support of a friendly fleet, and the perils which that army encounters if maritime command passes over into the hands of the enemy.

Mehemet Ali's wars against the Sultan.

When in 1833 Ibrahim Pasha, whose exploits in Greece have been already referred to in earlier chapters, was ordered by his father Mehemet Ali to advance into Syria, the control of the Levant was, owing to events which need not be recorded here, in Egyptian hands. Ibrahim found himself, like Napoleon, obliged to besiege Acre, and that celebrated stronghold very seriously delayed his advance. But the fortress fell in due course, and then the Egyptian commander, pressing on vigorously northwards, overthrew the

Osmanli army at the battle of Homs, captured Aleppo, and pushed boldly over the Taurus mountains into Anatolia. His communications were secure, thanks to sea-power. Supplies were brought to him by ship to Acre, to Beyrout, to Latakia, and to other points. And when the Sultan thrust a formidable army across his path at Konia, Ibrahim inflicted upon this a crushing and disastrous defeat.

The Porte was so much terrified by the victorious progress of the Egyptian forces that, after vainly attempting to get aid from the British Government, negotiations were opened with the hereditary enemy of Ottoman power, Russia. The Tsar readily acquiesced in the proposal that his fleet and troops should prop up the tottering throne of his former foe. Some of his line-of-battle ships appeared in the Bosporus. They were followed by several transports full of troops. Preparations were made to pass the Dardanelles into the Mediterranean. And the consequence was that Mehemet Ali, recognising that this intervention entirely altered the strategical situation and that it would probably lead to the landing of hostile forces on the shores of Syria and in rear of Ibrahim, agreed to evacuate Asia Minor while retaining Syria; and on these terms a peace was patched up.

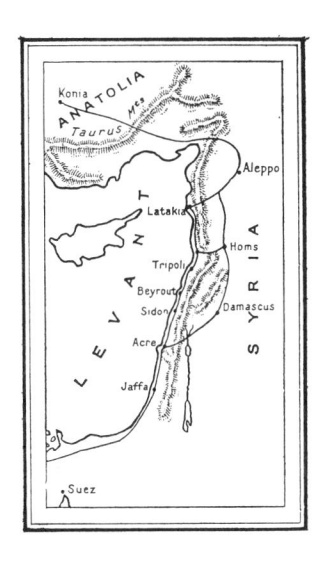

War, however, broke out afresh six years later. The campaign began with the signal overthrow of a Turkish army which was advancing into Syria, at Nezib near the Euphrates. The Turkish fleet from the Dardanelles, moreover, which was to dominate the Levant, treacherously delivered itself up to the Egyptians in the harbour of Alexandria. Thus the prospects of Mehemet Ali and his soldier-son were in the highest degree promising, and Ibrahim was dreaming of triumphs to come which would eclipse even the glories of Konia, when suddenly intervention came from a totally unexpected quarter. Russian readiness to enter the lists after Konia had not been purely disinterested and quixotic: there had been a deal over the business, in virtue of which the Tsar had acquired rights affecting the Dardanelles which the western Powers of Europe viewed with no small concern. So when it looked as if the Osmanlis were again about to collapse before the forces of Egypt, and as if the Eastern question might become acute, the British and Austrian Governments, apprehensive lest Russia should be called in a second time by the authorities at Stamboul, despatched fleets to the Levant to put an end to the strife. The coast was blockaded. Beyrout, Tripoli, and Acre were taken in quick succession. And Ibrahim Pasha found himself in the north of Syria, with the Turks in front of him, and with an aggressive allied fleet practically athwart of his communications. After some negotiations, therefore, the Egyptians consented to fall back to the Isthmus of Suez, the Turkish fleet was restored to the Sublime Porte, and one of the most singular campaigns of the nineteenth century was by mutual consent brought to a close. It was a campaign in which there had been no sea-fight of importance, and in which, till just before its termination, naval operations had been entirely of a passive kind; but it was a campaign which had nevertheless hinged upon the question of maritime command from the very outset, and in which, twice over, the transfer of naval preponderance from one side to the other exerted a paralysing influence over the prospects of an army.

CHAPTER XVIII.

THE TENDENCY OF AMPHIBIOUS FORCE TO CONTAIN THE TROOPS OF THE BELLIGERENT WHO IS THE WEAKER AT SEA, AT POINTS WHERE THESE CANNOT ACT.

THE liberty of action enjoyed by the armies of the belligerent who commands the sea in warfare between maritime nations has been dealt with at length in chapter xv. It has been shown how the side which is assured of naval preponderance can plant its forces down on hostile shores and can withdraw them again at will. It has been explained that such descents naturally partake of the character of a surprise, and it has been pointed out how absolutely the initiative rests in the hands of military forces when they contemplate over-sea operations against hostile territory. The enemy is kept in a state of constant uncertainty. The hostile military forces have to be prepared for attack at many points. And the result of this is that the army of a nation which finds itself open to attack from the sea during the course of hostilities must of necessity be dispersed, and must to a certain extent be scattered over the face of the territory which has to be defended. Portions of it may have to remain on guard far from the real theatre of operations, and great bodies of troops may be contained and may be held in inactivity by mere threats of aggression, and may be held in durance by the anxiety of the central government as to the safety of localities against which action has never been even contemplated by the foe. King-

Reasons for this containing power.

lake well describes this containing effect of naval force when he speaks of the "power an armada can wield when not only carrying on board a force designed for land service, but enabled to move—to move swiftly—whether this way or that at the will of the chief, who thus, so to speak, can 'manœuvre' against an army on shore with troops not yet quitting their ships."

Examples from early times. It is interesting to find this principle recognised and taken into consideration so far back as the days of Xerxes' great invasion of Greece. The Persian monarch was not a little perturbed to learn from the lips of the exiled Spartan king Demaratus that there were thousands of warriors still available to bear arms for the defence of the Peloponnesus, who were of the same descent and were endowed with the same military virtues as those whom the invaders had with such difficulty overcome in the gut of Thermopylæ. He took the renegade into counsel and asked him for his advice. Demaratus saw in his mind's eye his countrymen on guard athwart the Isthmus of Corinth, and he strove hard to persuade Xerxes that the wisest course would be to send a portion of the Persian fleet to the shores of Laconia, which would harry the coast of the Morea and thus entice the Spartans back from the north to defend their own homes. His advice was not taken, it is true. But the scheme of Demaratus was—to use technical phraseology—that the formidable Spartans should be contained in the south of Greece by a demonstration of amphibious force. In making the proposal that worthy showed a creditable insight into the strategical conditions which arise when troops are acting in combination with sea-power.

Many examples of this containing power possessed by troops when they are at sea could be given. History often does not take full account of it, and it is only by close examination of military records, and by ascertaining the dislocation of the army which anticipates attack from the sea, that its importance can be adequately appreciated. Details of garrisons at various stages of a war are by no means easy to obtain, even with regard to campaigns only a few decades old. The data are often wanting, because troops thus kept in idleness attract no attention from the ordinary observer, and excite little interest even in the mind of the contemporary expert. It is therefore by no means easy to produce satisfactory illustrations of an aspect of war which is likely enough to escape attention.

The following example from medieval times is worth recording. In 1385, in the days of Richard II., the French were contemplating an invasion of England. But to attempt such a hazardous enterprise while the sovereign and all his knights and retainers were assembled in the south, was by no means attractive to the *entourage* of the king of France. The remarkable seaman Jean de Vienne was therefore despatched to the coast of Scotland with an armada, so as to denude England of fighting men by drawing these away into that rugged territory; and the plan proved eminently successful. For King Richard, with no less than 80,000 men it is said, was lured right away north to Aberdeen, and England was left at the mercy of a resolute invader. As it turned out, however, the invasion was not attempted, the French apparently having been unable to collect the 600 vessels required to transport across the Channel the military forces which had been assembled to carry out the ambitious design.

The liberty of action which maritime command confers upon military force was proved on numerous occasions during the War of the Spanish Succession. In 1709, at a time when the Portuguese who were in alliance with Great Britain were in dire straits, it was proposed to create a diversion in their favour in Andalusia, with the idea of drawing away part of the hostile forces who were engaged in harrying the country almost to the gates of Lisbon

War of the Spanish Succession.

itself. General Stanhope was therefore shipped round from Catalonia to Gibraltar with the avowed design of attacking Cadiz. But it was found that that historic maritime stronghold was far too formidable a fortress, for the comparatively small force available to assail it with any reasonable hope of success. Stanhope returned therefore to the north-east without undertaking any aggressive operation, and in appearance the transfer of force was little better than a waste of power. "But," he wrote, "though the end for which I left Catalonia cannot be accomplished, yet I am glad to learn by all hands from Portugal that our expedition has not been useless; since by keeping in suspense all the enemy's troops on this coast, it has amused and diverted them from taking advantage of the miserable condition of Portugal."

Pitt's policy of raids during the Seven Years' War.

The numerous British descents and attempted descents on the French coasts organised by the elder Pitt during the Seven Years' War have often been ridiculed by historians, and they would probably have been hotly criticised in Parliament had their author held a less commanding position in that assemblage. "An elaborate expedition, naval and military," writes Carlyle in his rugged trenchant style of the attempt on Rochefort, "which could not 'descend' at all when it got to the point, but merely went groping about on the muddy shores of the Charente, holding councils of war; cannonaded the Island of Aix for two hours and returned home without result of any kind, courts-martial following on it, as too usual."[1] But even this first and especially unfortunate venture was not perhaps so lacking in effect as the biographer of Frederick the Great would have us suppose. Later expeditions for the most part achieved a very limited amount of success, judged by apparent results. Some stores were destroyed at St Malo. A few buildings were demolished at Cherbourg by a force of which the rearguard when re-embarking met with something very akin to disaster. Only at Belleisle was any real solid advantage gained, and, as has been pointed out in an earlier chapter, that storm-driven isle was of practical value to England only in virtue of the sentimental attachment entertained by the French for a portion of their soil fallen into the enemy's hands. None of these enterprises were marked either in their design or in their execution by that fixity of purpose, by that principle of the long arm of maritime command laying a military grip upon some portion of an enemy's coast and compelling the adversary to strain his resources to recover what has been lost, which was discussed in chapter xvi. But in reality Pitt's policy of military raids effected a most important and beneficent purpose.

"There is no doubt," writes Lord Mahon of the first expedition to St Malo, which cannot truthfully be described as a very brilliant affair, "that the damage done to the French shipping had been considerable, and that the apprehension of the approach of this expedition had effectually withheld the French from sending any succours to Germany. This effect was frequently and warmly applauded in Prince Ferdinand's despatches." It is not unnatural that a historian like Macaulay, looking merely to superficial results, should write of Pitt that "several of his expeditions, particularly those which were sent to the coast of France, were at once costly and absurd." But the British Government was pledged to Frederick, and there seems to be very little doubt that these, often ill-conceived and ill-executed, enterprises contained strong forces of the enemy in outlying districts of France,—forces which might, in the great theatre of war around and within the borders of Prussia, have exerted a very evil influence over the fortunes of the illustrious warrior-king.

The containing power of amphibious force was, it should be noted, fully realised by the allies in 1807, and they set no little store by it. Napoleon, having trampled Prussia

1807 and 1809.

underfoot, was operating under considerable difficulties and with a marked absence of those startling triumphs which had adorned his earlier military career, against the formidable military resources of the Tsar in the basin of the Vistula. The failure of the British Government to despatch a respectable land force to the Baltic, a failure which arose out of the fact that transports previously taken up had been fatuously dismissed, caused bitter disappointment on the Continent. It, moreover, evoked criticisms at home which were at once caustic and cogent. "This ill-judged economy was the more criminal," said Canning, "that by having a fleet of transports certainly at command and threatening various points, 20,000 men could easily paralyse three times that force of the enemy." And this principle was just at that very time being put in force by Cochrane in the *Imperieuse* off the coast of Catalonia. By his intrepid energy, by his raids, by his landings, by his wonderful exploit in throwing a small reinforcement into the citadel of Rosas when that important fortress was about to capitulate and offering a further desperate resistance to the overwhelming forces of the enemy, this frigate commander is said to have kept 10,000 French troops marching backwards and forwards aimlessly for weeks. In 1809 an Anglo-Sicilian expedition under Sir J. Stuart appeared off Naples, which was then in French hands. The military successes gained by it were of small account, but the move had the effect of drawing off strong bodies of French and Neapolitan troops from the valley of the Po, where they were operating against an Austrian army under the Archduke John. Having effected his object of indirectly assisting the Austrians, Stuart sailed back to Sicily.

The Crimean War.

No campaign in history has probably been more influenced by this containing power possessed by amphibious fighting resources, than was the war of 1854-55. In that contest Russia was being attacked by formidable land and sea forces on her Black Sea shores. A great hostile army was planted down, slowly but surely compassing the downfall of a maritime stronghold on which great sums had been spent, in which lay the remains of a noble fleet, and in defence of which the troops of the Tsar had undergone many sacrifices and had shown no common devotion. Even if the relief of Sebastopol was rendered extraordinarily difficult by its position and by the exhaustion of supplies in the Crimea, troops were sorely needed at other points of the Black Sea coast in case the allies, taking advantage of their sea-power, should swoop down upon Odessa or some other analogous and important maritime locality. But far away up in the north, upon the Baltic shores, echeloned along the coast-line of the Gulf of Finland, on guard over St Petersburg and Revel and many another centre of commercial enterprise, were thousands and thousands of efficient, well-equipped soldiers, whose presence in the remote southern theatre of war was grievously wanted, but who in their garrisons and cantonments in Lithuania and Esthonia never saw an enemy nor heard the boom of cannon.

The allies at no time contemplated serious military operations against northern Russia. Imposing fleets moved into the Baltic and dominated its waters. Some fortified towns suffered from bombardment. The fortress of Sveaborg was very roughly handled, and Bomarsund was taken. Even the White Sea became the scene of warlike enterprises of a desultory kind. But no real damage was done to the dominions or, except indirectly, to the subjects of the Tsar in these provinces, and the naval operations of the British and French in Baltic waters were upon the whole crowned with but limited success. It was not, however, the mischief which these hostile fleets actually did,—it was the mischief which they might be preparing to do and the possibility of enterprises on land being undertaken under their wing, which kept great Muscovite armies idle in one part of the

Empire, while in another the foe was slowly but surely wearing military resistance down.[2]

The war in the Far East. The extent to which this dread of attack by hostile land forces upon maritime districts open to such enterprises tends to disintegrate the armies of the nation which has lost naval preponderance, was well shown in 1904 in Eastern Asia. Having gained the upper hand at sea, the Japanese invaded Manchuria with forces which were at first decidedly superior numerically to those of General Kuropatkin. The strategical advantages enjoyed by their hardy antagonists made it a question of the very first importance to the Russians to arrest the hostile advance northwards at the earliest possible opportunity, in view of the obvious difficulty which must attend the recovery of ground which had once been lost. The reinforcing of the army south of Mukden thus became a question of the utmost moment. But an army had to be kept inactive around Vladivostok, within easy railway communication of Kuropatkin's overmatched troops in Manchuria, for fear of a Japanese descent in the neighbourhood of that important place of arms. The military authorities at Tokio kept their plans so profoundly secret that, until the winter had created its impenetrable barrier of ice in the waters fronting Vladivostok, the Russians could not be certain that some enterprise would not be undertaken in that quarter. And by that time the want of the troops thus contained by Japanese sea-power, and lost to the army in the field, had come to be far less felt about Liaoyang and the valley of the Sha-ho river than at an earlier phase of the struggle. A stream of reinforcements had been pouring across Siberia during nine months of war, and a huge mass of men was assembled under Kuropatkin's orders in front of Mukden. The amphibious strength of the island empire, in fact, held an appreciable percentage of the inadequate Russian forces fast at the critical time, in a quarter where they did not influence the actual struggle in the slightest degree.

A nation which in time of war gains the mastery at sea, and which possesses an efficient army, has in its hands a singularly potent weapon of offence, if the adversary is penalised in the struggle by an extensive and vulnerable coast-line. The bringing of superior fighting resources to bear at the decisive point is the foundation of strategy and of tactics. To strike at one portion of an enemy's scattered forces with every available man, and so to bring concentration to bear against dispersion, is the highest art of soldiership.[3] If, then, by the very conditions of the case one side is compelled to scatter its troops for the protection of districts which the belligerent possessing the initiative has no intention of molesting, and is thereby driven to weaken his defences at the point selected for attack, the army destined to carry out that attack enters upon its task with excellent prospects of performing it.

Conclusion.

CHAPTER XIX.

TACTICAL INTERVENTION OF NAVAL FORCE IN LAND BATTLES.

Opportunities for tactical intervention of warships somewhat rare. CASES have occurred in all ages of ships of war actually participating in engagements between land forces, and on some occasions naval intervention in a battle ashore has gone far to decide the issue. But there is an obvious reason why such incidents should be somewhat uncommon. One or other of the belligerents is generally superior at sea and in command of the local waters, and the military commander of that side which has no fighting-ships on the spot will naturally avoid an action on ground where those of the enemy may take part in the combat. The obvious course for the side which is fighting without naval assistance is to keep away from the coast, if this be of such a nature that hostile war-vessels can act against the land. Therefore examples of fleets interposing tactically in combats on shore are generally provided only by those campaigns which have taken place in theatres of operations like the Riviera, where the contending armies are constrained by the topographical features of the country to remain near the sea.

Forms in which such intervention can take place. Landings, and sieges of maritime strongholds, are dealt with in later chapters. In this chapter the question to be discussed is the intervention of naval force in land battles in the open field. Such intervention may take the form of disembarkation on an enemy's flank or rear during a fight, or it may take the form of fire from the ship's guns,

TACTICAL INTERVENTION OF SHIPS. 333

or both. Instances could also be quoted of tactical intervention of ships of war when no actual fighting on land is going on, as, for instance, when General Godinot, marching from St Roque to besiege Tarifa in 1810, was constrained by the difficulties of the country to take his siege ordnance along the coast road, and was bombarded in flank by British cruisers from Gibraltar Bay.

As an example of a battle by the sea-shore where a naval force, rather by the moral effect of its intervention than by the actual damage which it inflicted, exerted a remarkable influence over its result, may be quoted the case of the fight at Gravelines in 1558. In this engagement a French army, which had recently achieved a most important success by the recovery of Calais from the English, was confronted on the coast of the Channel by Count Egmont with a mixed force of Flemish, Dutch, and Spanish troops. Egmont had got between the French and their natural base, and each army was during the fight facing to its proper rear: the French forces had their right flank resting on the sea, those of Egmont had their left flank close to the shore. England was at the time at war with France, but no definite arrangements had been come to with Egmont to afford him aid. Motley describes the action as follows: "For a long time it was doubtful on which side victory was to incline, but at last the English vessels unexpectedly appeared in the offing, and ranging up soon afterwards as close to the shore as was possible, opened their fire upon the still unbroken lines of the French. The ships were too distant, the danger of injuring friend as well as foe too imminent, to allow of their exerting any important influence upon the result. The spirit of the enemy was broken, however, by this attack on their seaward side, which they had thought impregnable." In this case naval intervention came as a surprise: had such a contingency been foreseen the French

The Battle of Gravelines.

commander would hardly have taken up a position close to the shore.

Bunker's Hill.

At the memorable battle of Bunker's Hill British ships of war contributed greatly to bring about the dearly bought victory of the regular troops. The provincial forces had during the night occupied and fortified high ground on the far side of the harbour from Boston, and thereby threatened the anchorage and town. The British force crossed the water and delivered an attack, aided by the guns of the warships in harbour. The fighting was of a desperate character, the Colonial levies in this, their first fight, showing a spirit and determination beyond all praise, and the regular troops displaying the disciplined valour which had won admiration from the most experienced soldiers of the age on many continental battlefields. The assailants lost heavily, but they at last found their way into the incompleted entrenchments. During their retirement the Colonials were effectively enfiladed by a man-of-war and by two floating batteries as they retreated over a neck, and this added greatly to that confusion which is inevitable when a tumultuary assemblage of armed men is beaten in action by a regular army.

Occasions often arise where lines of operations follow maritime defiles.

When the line of operations of an army necessarily runs close to the shore, its advance is always likely to be checked by the enemy at some point close to the sea. An engagement follows, and it is always a possible contingency that the navy of the side which commands the sea may be able to intervene in the fray with its gun-fire. If the route be within range of an enemy's fighting-ships it becomes practically impossible for troops to move along it, or to use it as a line of communications, as long as the ships are there. The enormous strategical importance of naval preponderance under such conditions has already been referred to in chapter xvii. And the same principle holds good in a tactical sense, provided always that such

THE FIRTH OF FORTH. 335

combats as may occur have for their battle-ground a site close to the water's edge, and at a point where shoal water does not happen to extend far out to sea.

It has been pointed out in an earlier chapter how in the old days of warfare between English and Scottish armies, command of the sea was generally in the hands of the Southron, and that in consequence of this the invading armies from the south of the Tweed were in the habit of following the coast-line. An important route skirted the southern shores of the Firth of Forth, which played a conspicuous part in that remarkable set of operations in which Cromwell and Leslie were the chief actors, and which led up to the famous fight of Dunbar. We find that at the battle of Pinkie Cleugh, fought near Musselburgh in the reign of Henry VIII., the English fleet greatly aided the invading army in what appears to have been for some time a rather doubtful conflict; for it took the Scottish forces in flank and reverse with its fire as these stood barring the way to Edinburgh, and this threw the clansmen drawn up next the water into confusion.

Ships of war have in like manner often intervened in combats on land in the Riviera, where, from the nature of the case, opposing armies are naturally found on the coast, and where engagements almost necessarily take place in proximity to the sea. Two historic battles fought in this region were greatly influenced by the participation of naval forces while they were in progress, and their main features deserve to be recorded.

A portion of the allied army under the leadership of the Duke of Savoy and Prince Eugene was in 1707 advancing along the Riviera on Toulon, in co-operation with the British and Dutch fleet under Sir Cloudesley Shovel. When this reached the River Var it found a French force drawn up on the far side of the valley to bar the way, and holding the passage across the stream in some strength. In

Examples.
The Var.

the battle which ensued the allied troops attacked the hostile position in front, while some of the ships simultaneously entered the mouth of the river and cannonaded the enemy. Then 600 seamen and marines from the fleet were landed on the right bank of the Var, and vigorously assailed the French right flank. This spirited action on the part of the navy greatly contributed to bring about the victory of the allies, and to brush out of their path the forces which were endeavouring to stay their advance upon Toulon.

Loano.

At the battle of Loano in 1795, French gunboats brought most useful fire to bear on the left flank of the Austrians. At this time the Austrians were relying on the support of the British fleet, which was superior to that of the French on the open sea; and the fact that some of the enemy's vessels were able to contribute towards bringing about the disastrous defeat of General Devins reflects little credit upon Admiral Hotham. "The Austrian generals say, and true," wrote Nelson, who was doing his utmost with an insufficient detachment to aid our allies in the Riviera, "they were brought on the coast at the express desire of the English to co-operate with the fleet, which fleet nor admiral they never saw."

Muizenberg.

Recent events have made the bright little watering-place of Muizenberg, situated on the shores of False Bay south of the Cape Peninsula, familiar to many British officers. The sand dunes and bluffs on which it has sprung up were the scene a century ago of a very spirited fight on shore, in which naval forces participated with most marked effect. Muizenberg lies at the point where the steep declivities which overhang Simon's Bay and the shore for a few miles to the north-east of it suddenly recede from the strand, and where the defile leading along the beach at their foot opens out upon a sandy, undulating, bush-grown country. Admiral Elphinstone and General Craig arrived at Simon's Bay in

1795 with the object of securing the Cape Peninsula from the Dutch. Simonstown was promptly occupied, and then the troops, assisted by a force landed from the fleet, marched along the foot of the hills towards Muizenberg. It was found, however, that the enemy was holding that place in some force, and the nature of the approaches to the hostile position seriously hampered deployment. The Admiral thereupon armed some launches and he improvised a gunboat; these together brought such an effective fire to bear upon the Dutch, that when General Craig advanced to the attack they quickly gave way and the position was secured with no great loss.

In chapter xvii. it has been pointed out how, when the line of operations or of communications of an army runs along an isthmus, the question of maritime command assumes an even more paramount importance than in the case of a defile between the mountains and the sea. It is obvious that where a line of battle extends across a narrow isthmus the presence of warships is likely to be a controlling factor in deciding the result of the engagement. Such military situations seldom occur, it is true, and in cases where a landfight has actually taken place in a defile of this class, shoal water has often prevented naval force from taking any effective part in the combat. Thus the Turkish fleet could not prevent the lines of Perekop from being forced in 1738, the water on either side of the isthmus being very shallow. And when, at the close of the disastrous descent on Quiberon Bay in 1795, by the *emigrés*, backed up by the British fleet, the unfortunate Royalists were hustled back by Hoche across the narrow sandy isthmus which unites it to the mainland into the Quiberon Peninsula, the war-vessels found great difficulty in getting within gun-shot of the land to afford some succour to the fugitives, for want of water.

The case of an isthmus.

But the battle of Nanshan, on the 28th of May 1904, provides a singularly striking example of naval participa-

Battle of Nanshan.

338   TACTICAL INTERVENTION OF SHIPS.

tion in a land-fight on an isthmus. While the Japanese fleet co-operated with their army in its desperate attack on the Russian left on the western side of the narrow defile, a Russian gunboat brought a cannonade to bear on the Japanese left on the eastern side; and an attempt was even made to land Russian marines from five steam-launches, but this was frustrated. The successful assault of the Japanese upon the formidable works on the Russian left must be classed among the most remarkable exploits in the history of modern war. The fighting was of a desperate character, the losses suffered by the assailants were terrible. At the decisive moment the 1st division was brought to a standstill by the hail of bullets. "The situation seemed critical," wrote General Oku in his laconic report, "as a further advance was impossible. Just at this juncture our fleet in Kin-chau Bay vigorously renewed its heavy fire on the left wing of the enemy's lines, and our 4th Artillery Regiment also poured in a cannonade against the enemy's fire." Taking advantage of the opportunity a general advance was made by three divisions, the Japanese infantry performed prodigies of valour, and the works were eventually captured at the point of the bayonet. The Russians in their accounts of this great fight attribute their overthrow mainly to the enfilade fire of the Japanese ships.*

Effect of progress in artillery.   The enhanced range of modern guns necessarily to no small extent favours their employment from on board ship against hostile forces ashore, as compared with the conditions which prevailed even a few decades ago. There is often considerable difficulty in bringing a vessel of even small size within several hundred yards of the beach. A mile or so of shoals was, a century ago, sufficient to prevent the

* That the Russian navy was able, after a fashion, to co-operate with its army on the eastern side of the isthmus, while the Japanese fleet was so effectively pounding the Russian works on the other side, is an illustration of how in naval warfare maritime preponderance may have been established without necessarily carrying with it the command of all local waters.

guns of a fleet from effectively participating in an engagement even close to the water's edge. During the Napoleonic wars, and earlier, sailors might have to look on at their comrades engaged on shore, and might be totally unable to afford them the slightest assistance, except by landing-parties, which the circumstances of the case often forbade. Until very recently naval ordnance could not effectively participate in a battle on land if this were taking place a league or so from the shore, even supposing that there was deep water close in. But the development of gun construction has considerably altered this, and artillery fire from a fleet might now be used with no small effect against troops even some miles off. Apart from the increased range of the ordnance of to-day, modern weapons are in other respects infinitely more formidable than those used at Loano and at Muizenberg. Their fire is more accurate and their projectiles are far more destructive. The result of this is that, even allowing for the sweeping modifications which have taken place in battle formations on land, even allowing for the modern dispersion of troops in action and for the difficulty of detecting their exact position when they are once fairly committed to the fight, the artillery of a war-vessel is likely to exert a great influence over the progress of a fight ashore, so long as the progress of the engagement can be noted from the deck of the ships.[1] Recent events on the South American coast, in Cuba, and in the Far East prove that this is the case.

At the battle of the Alma the Russian army was drawn up in a strong position at right angles to the coast. Its left flank was about two miles from the cliffs which at that point rise abruptly from the sea, the idea in leaving this gap being to avoid the fire of the allied fleets. The space intervening between the line of battle and the sea was only very thinly occupied. It is of interest to read in Kinglake how a great Russian column of eight battalions, which was moving forward to check the advance of the French right at a point less than a league from the shore, came suddenly under heavy flanking fire from some French field-guns which had got into position between the advancing column and the sea, and how General Kiriakof, under the impression that this fire was coming from the warships, withdrew the column just at a moment when it was beginning to cause the French considerable anxiety. The Russian position was within range of guns of the present day from end to end, and a modern fleet would have rendered great part of it quite untenable.

Effect of steam in place of sails.

The introduction of steam, moreover, has greatly improved the chances for warships to co-operate effectively when a battle is going on near the coast. In the sailing days there was often considerable difficulty in manœuvring vessels when near the shore. In such positions they were likely to meet with some serious mishap if the navigation was at all intricate or if the winds were capricious; the breeze was often baffling, and the element of luck necessarily entered largely into the problem. Lord Keith's gunboats were generally of great assistance to the Austrians in 1800 during their operations in the Riviera west of Genoa; but on one occasion, when an affair was shaping itself near Voltri, the ships could not get to their appointed stations owing to a calm, so that their fire was lost to the allied army on shore at a time when it was much needed. Such a contretemps could not occur under the conditions of the present day.

Battle of Miraflores.

One other fight may be mentioned before closing the chapter, because it presents the aspect of affairs under modern conditions, and because it was perhaps the first occasion when long-range artillery fire was used to good effect from the sea in a fight on land. In the closing days of the war between Chili and Peru, of which an outline has already been given in chapter xv., the Chilians, having landed south-east of Lima at two points and having joined their forces, marched along the coast straight for the capital. The Peruvian army was drawn up some miles in front of Lima to bar the way. Its left flank rested on the sea, detachments held an advanced position at a place called Chorillos, and a second and strongly fortified line in rear at Miraflores was occupied in strength. After a sharp fight, in which their fleet gave the attacking troops some assistance, the Chilians drove their antagonists out of their Chorillos position. Thereupon an armistice was concluded, the Peruvian forces holding their formidable intrenchments of Miraflores, while the invaders paused, facing them, in anticipation of negotiations for peace being set on foot.

Next day, however, through some misunderstanding, the Peruvians suddenly opened fire at a time when the invaders were not on the alert. The Chilians were thrown into momentary confusion. Some of the infantry gave way; part of the artillery had hastily to retire for fear of capture. The situation was becoming somewhat alarming, when the fleet most opportunely came to the rescue of the troops on shore. Opening a heavy fire on the works on the left of the Miraflores position and taking them in enfilade, it drove the defenders away from the coast, thereby throwing their forces into confusion on that flank; and this gave just that encouragement to the Chilian army which was required at the moment, and which soon enabled it to recover from its surprise. The ships were nearly 5000 yards from the shore —long range for those days. The shooting was interfered with by a heavy swell, and was not apparently very hurtful to the Peruvians. But the moral effect of the naval intervention at a critical moment was undoubted,—it helped the invaders to turn the tables upon the enemy, to recover from panic, to advance to the attack, to storm the formidable lines, and so to open the road to Lima in spite of the undoubted strength of the Peruvian position and of the unfortunate opening to the battle.

Conclusion.

Maritime preponderance may not always exert a very decisive influence over the course of a struggle on land, even when this is taking place in territory adjoining the sea. Many great campaigns have been contested in such a theatre without any actual fighting taking place near the shore. But if the course of such operations brings the opposing armies into contact actually on the coast, floating force may be able to participate with marked effect in the combat. Exceptional cases may occur, as at Nanshan, where warships are able to aid both sides on land. But the normal situation must be that if a battle takes place on or near the shore, it will be the troops of the belligerent in command of the sea in a strategical sense who will derive tactical benefit from any ships of war present during the conflict, not their opponents. It is one of the many forms in which naval superiority may affect land operations in the course of a war.

CHAPTER XX.

LANDINGS AND EMBARKATIONS IN FACE OF THE ENEMY.

It has already been pointed out in chapter xiii. that the first landing of a military force in a country which is in occupation of the enemy seldom takes place within a harbour. It is safe to assume that the seaports situated on an adversary's coast will be occupied by detachments of hostile troops, and that they will be found to be prepared for defence. The initial disembarkation is therefore generally perforce carried out in some more or less open bay, where there is a stretch of foreshore convenient for boats to be beached, and where the transports which bring the troops across the ocean can ride at anchor within a reasonable distance of the landing-place. The feasibility of the operation of course depends in the first place upon the weather and upon the direction of the wind,—even with a smooth sea there is often sufficient surf to render the beaching of boats impracticable. But we have, in this chapter, to do with action which the enemy may take to prevent the landing, and with the tactical aspect presented by the operation, rather than with the technical difficulties which may arise from broken water or an inconvenient breeze. *Landings generally take place on an open beach.*

The commander of an over-sea expedition meditating a descent upon the enemy's shores enjoys the advantage of initiative, of liberty of action, and of power to employ feints and ruses so as to deceive the adversary as to the contemplated landing-place. But so much depends upon the *Probable landing-place known to the enemy, and delay likely to arise from bad weather.*

weather, that it has often occurred that the army has been unable to commence disembarkation when it has reached its proper destination, that delay has ensued, and that hostile troops, rushed to the spot, have been drawn up in position by the time that landing of soldiers with their impedimenta has become practicable. Amherst's army was kept for six days tossing in the Atlantic off Louisbourg before a single man could get ashore. At the time of the successful British attack upon Belleisle in 1761, landings had to be put off from day to day for more than a week, owing to the heavy sea which is always so likely to get up on small provocation in the Bay of Biscay. The troops were detained off the Helder in their transports for four days before they could be got to land. Nor do modern conditions alter this in the slightest degree. The operation of beaching boats, or of taking them alongside rocky ledges or artificial jetties, is to all intents and purposes the same now as it was in the days of Blake and Barbarossa.

Impression which exists that landings even in face of opposition are generally successful.

It has been declared by writers on the art of war that, if the weather proves propitious, landings are almost always successful, even if opposed. Now disembarkation in face of the enemy is a tactical operation, the conditions of which are necessarily governed by questions of armament, and it is one which has grown more and more difficult as firearms improve in precision and as they increase in their range and power. But even in the past it has by no means always been the case that undertakings of this class have been crowned with success. It is not difficult to find examples of the repulse of military forces disembarking in defiance of the enemy, even in days before cannon existed or small arms were thought of. The first sea-fight recorded in history occurred off Pelusium, situated not far from where Port Said now stands. The story is that an armada from Greece and Asia Minor overthrew the flotilla of Rameses III., and that the fighting-men on board of the victorious squadron thereupon attempted to land. But the lord of Egypt has inscribed on the walls of a temple hard by Thebes what was the sequel to an enterprise begun under such happy auspices. "Those that gained the shore I caused to fall at the water's edge; they lay slain in heaps. I overturned their vessels. All their goods sank beneath the waves." And other examples of failures on the part of landing-parties to make good their footing on shore, in consequence of the action of an enemy barring the way, will be given later, all of which go to show that disembarkations in face of opposition have at every period of history been undertakings of some hazard, and that they have sometimes resulted in grave disaster.

The impression which prevails that this class of operation is generally successful has probably arisen owing to the fact that, by dint of feints at other points, the enemy can so easily be enticed away from the selected spot. The extent to which the liberty of action, which is conferred on military force by sea-power, lends itself to such procedure has already been pointed out in chapter xv. By such means the requisite time may be gained to get at least an advanced guard ashore unmolested, and this can cover the disembarkation of the rest of the army. The anchoring of a few transports for a short time off some possible landing-place may suffice to draw the entire available forces of the enemy thither. Or detachments may even be actually put on shore, so as to make a demonstration and to give greater force to the deception. Then, in case the ruse has succeeded and in case the weather remains favourable, a very few men hurried to the beach at the chosen place may be able to seize ground which is in every way suitable for defence, and may be able to hold this till sufficient troops have reached the land to deal effectively with any opposition likely to be offered after the enemy has recovered from the first shock of surprise.

If enemy is prepared, a footing is generally gained at some other point.

Examples of feints.

When Charles XII., in 1700, was preparing a descent upon the island of Zealand, the military commander, General Stuart, made a secret reconnaissance of the coast and decided upon the point at which the landing was to take place. He then ostentatiously examined several other localities which were obviously well adapted for purposes of a military disembarkation. This induced the Danes to so scatter their forces along the shore, that, when the Swedish landing-parties began to arrive in their boats, there were no Danish troops actually present on the spot to meet them. And by the time a force had arrived strong enough to offer an opposition adequate to cope with the emergency, the invaders had already gained a firm footing on the shore, reinforcements were coming from their ships, and the thing was done.

When Albemarle's force in 1762 was about to make its descent at the spot which had been selected some miles east of Havana, a feint was made of landing marines at a point four miles to the west of the harbour. This feint served to bewilder the enemy, and it largely contributed to bring about the unopposed disembarkation of the main army. Similarly, on the occasion of the descent on Minorca in 1798, which has already been referred to on p. 281, a pretence was made in the first instance of disembarking some miles from the fine land-locked Gulf of Fornelles, although that was the point where the expeditionary force for the most part set foot on shore subsequently. In 1898 General Shafter's army, destined to act against Santiago, carried out its actual disembarkation at Daiquiri, fifteen miles east of the harbour mouth; but a demonstration was at the same time made at Cabanas, a league to the west of the entrance, boats were loaded as if intended to put off to shore, and every means was taken to induce the belief among the Spanish forces that this was the chosen landing-place.

Many other examples of the same kind could be given. Feints of this nature may indeed almost be called a normal feature of descents upon an enemy's coast. The advantage which may be derived from such devices is, however, obvious, and their execution is not generally difficult. The few instances quoted above will suffice to provide one explanation for that immunity from opposition which has so often been enjoyed by armies when gaining a footing on hostile shores, even on occasions when the foe has been well prepared and has been on the watch.

Before discussing the influence which modern artillery and small arms is likely to exert over the question of opposed landings,—nothing of the kind has taken place on a great scale of recent years,[1]—a few examples of such operations even in the remote past will not be without interest. Disembarkations in face of an enemy have by no means always proved successful, either before or since the introduction of gunpowder. Many cases have occurred where undertakings of this character have given rise to most gallant exploits, and where they have been attended by incidents of a highly dramatic kind. They have on occasion provided the historian with material for tales of stirring adventure and sublime devotion. Taken as a whole, however, the evidence of the annals of war down to the time of introduction of rifled firearms, undoubtedly goes far to prove that opposed landings were formerly by no means impracticable, and that troops making such attempts not unfrequently achieved their purpose even under conditions of the most unpromising nature. *Examples of disembarkation in face of the enemy in early times.*

The first arrival of Julius Cæsar on the coast of Kent is a case in point. The Britons were drawn up on the beach somewhere near Walmer in great force, determined to oppose the landing and ready for the fray. Their chariots and their footmen presented an imposing and formidable spectacle, such as might well have made the invaders quail. The Romans were not expert mariners, they were puzzled by the change of tide, and their hearts may *Julius Cæsar at Walmer.*

perhaps have sunk when the character of the enterprise which they were engaged on was made apparent by the summary repulse of their first attempt at landing. The fine soldiership of the ever-victorious consul, however, saved the day for the Roman army. Getting part of his forces successfully on shore on one flank, he rolled the defenders' line of battle up, swept them in panic flight from off the battlefield, and firmly established his standards upon English soil.

<small>Count Guy of Flanders' descent on Walcheren in 1253.</small>

In sharp contrast to that bloody fight upon the Deal and Walmer strand, may be quoted the story of Count Guy of Flanders' attempted landing near the westernmost point of Walcheren in 1253. The Count is said to have had with him no less than 150,000 Flemings. The Dutch, who were his antagonists, had, unknown to him, concealed themselves among the sandhills fringing the beach, where the presence of a hostile host could not be suspected from the sea. Count Guy, an old chronicler tells us, was quite unsuspicious, and he commenced his disembarkation anticipating no immediate opposition. He had already set foot on shore with his advanced guard when the defenders of a sudden rose up, as it appeared, out of the ground, and dashed forward at the charge to meet the Flemings. "The combat was great and lasted for long, for as fast as they disembarked and put their foot upon the ground they were dispatched, and the more they hastened to disembark that they might succour the first landed, the more were slain of them, and there was so much blood spilt in that quarter, of those Flemings that were killed by the Dutch, that it rose above the shoes of them that walked in it. There died of the men 50,000 on the spot, besides those who were drowned, and a great number of persons who were chased like a flock of sheep; these, perceiving the King, cried to him for mercy. The King, remembering the favour of God which had been shown him in this victory, gave them their lives, and permitted them to return to their own country after that the Zeeland peasants and soldiery had despoiled them, and left them naked; and being on the territory of Flanders they gathered the green leaves of trees and other herbage and foliage, with which they covered their nakedness, until they came into a sure place where they might find better."

We may hesitate to accept the statistics. But the vivid realism in the matter of details carries with it the conviction that this medieval combat on the sands was an affair of a sanguinary nature, and that the landing cannot, as an operation of war, be classed as an unqualified success.

A generation later the far Levant was to afford an illustration of a disembarkation in face of the enemy which had a very different termination. The foresight of Louis IX. in announcing before he quitted Cyprus that he contemplated making his descent on Alexandria, has been already referred to. By this means he drew off the majority of his opponents from his real objective, Damietta, which was in those days held to be the key of Egypt. Nevertheless when his armada hove to off that famous stronghold it was perceived that his enemies were not wholly unprepared, and that the standard of the Crusaders was not to be planted on the soil of the Ptolemies without an initiatory combat. *Louis IX.'s landing at Damietta.*

The attitude of the Moslem foemen little resembled that of the stolid Dutch in Walcheren. There was no concealment and no ambuscade. On the contrary, when the line of boats, headed by a barge bearing aloft the banner of the cross, drew nigh to the shore, the Saracen chivalry, goodly to see and decked in gorgeous raiment, caracoled upon the sands, disdaining subterfuges; cymbals and tom-toms discoursed barbaric music; trumpeters arrayed in full panoply of war blared noisy defiance; while the battlements of the ancient fortress were aglow with the rainbow-hued draperies of Zuleikas gazing in rapt admiration upon the unwonted spectacle, and eagerly awaiting the triumph of their sovereign lords. Nor were the approaching knights and their retainers one whit less eager for the shock of battle. The galleys strove in friendly rivalry which earliest should touch the strand; and Saint Louis himself, slinging shield and broadsword round his neck, wrenched himself loose from those who would have held him back, and, plunging waist-deep in the broken waters, floundered ashore dripping and enthusiastic among the very first.

But the Crusaders had no mind for a mere rough-and-tumble scuffle, where superior numbers might avail them little in a situation which essentially demanded order and deliberation. The thing had been thought out. A palisade of shields was set up in hot haste, and was rendered invulnerable by a line of sloping lances firmly stuck into the sand. Behind this improvised defence the horse-boats discharged their living freight, and the head of the invading army formed itself in fighting array. Then, when all was ready, the knights sprang into the saddle, seized shields and lances from their attendant squires, and charged home with irresistible fervour upon the hated foe. The Saracens bore themselves right gallantly in the affray. But they were out-matched, were ridden down, and were driven pell-mell from the field of battle. And so great was the moral effect of Louis' victory on the Damietta beach, that the formidable stronghold hard by opened its gates on the very first summons, and the Crusaders found themselves firmly established on Egyptian territory within a few hours of their flotilla coming to anchor.

Later examples. And when we come down to a later date, to the era of gunpowder and of great sailing-vessels capable of withstanding winter tempests on the broad Atlantic, we still find that landings in face of opposition were by no means always unsuccessful. On the contrary, records of failures in propitious weather which can be ascribed to hostile action are by no means easy to discover. It seems strange that this should be so. A flotilla of open boats drawing near to a beach must have presented an admirable target to small arms and artillery even two centuries ago. Sailing-ships shunned close vicinity to shore even if no shoals obstructed the approach, and they could therefore rarely effectually cover disembarkations with the fire of their guns. But the landings at Louisbourg and Aboukir Bay show that, even when the defenders were fully prepared, this class of operation was, under the tactical conditions of the time, a perfectly feasible one.

Tollemache's disaster at Brest in 1694 has been already referred to in illustration of another branch of the subject. In this case the enemy was collected in strong force and in a fortified position. Formidable batteries had been set up. The initiated eye speedily detected that the enemy was alert and ready, and the naval officers, after careful reconnaissance, were strongly opposed to making the attempt in view of the manifest preparedness of the troops on shore and of their apparent strength. But Tollemache would not hear of abandoning the enterprise; and although he courted reverse when he refused to listen to the advice of those who counselled prudence, he was not wholly responsible for the gravity of the catastrophe. By some inexplicable blunder the hour chosen for the landing was when the tide was on the ebb. The sailors got in the way of the soldiers when the boats reached the beach, and impeded the troops while undergoing the, then somewhat elaborate, process of forming up. Amid the confusion, and while the men were dropping fast under an accurate and well-sustained artillery and musketry fire, the French cavalry delivered a most effective charge. Tollemache himself fell, badly wounded. When retreat was ordered, many of the

Tollemache's attempted landing at Brest.

boats, left high and dry by the fast receding tide, could not be launched, and in the end only a portion of the forces committed to the dangerous venture got back again to the transports lying in the bay. The failure to keep the plan a secret, the refusal to relinquish a project which was obviously hopeless, and the mismanagement which attended the actual disembarkation, combine to make the attempt on Brest one of the most fatuous and ignominious of British expeditions across the sea.[2]

Incident near Cadiz in 1702. Of a landing which took place near Cadiz during the unsuccessful expedition of Rooke and Ormonde in 1702, Lord Mahon tells us that "the descent of the troops was made with more hazard and difficulty than had been foreseen by the seamen, for though the weather appeared calm, there was so high a surf upon the strand that about twenty boats were sunk, as many men were drowned, and not one landed who was not wet up to the neck." They were then charged by a squadron of picked cavalry, the onslaught of which was only beaten off with considerable difficulty. The landing was, however, eventually made good.

Swedish attack on Kronstadt. The fact of the troops being wet through had an unfortunate result on the occasion of a Swedish attack upon the island of Kronstadt a few years later. The fortifications of that reclaimed mud-flat were still in embryo at the time, and the recapture of the island, which had but recently been acquired by the Russians, promised to be a comparatively easy task. Owing to the shallows, the boats carrying the landing-parties could not approach within some distance of the shore. But the Swedish troops, nowise dismayed, sprang out and were wading in towards the beach, when they came upon an unsuspected channel where deeper water took them up to their elbows. Their powder thus got wet. The Russians lay in wait till the assailants reached the strand. They then opened on them with musketry at close range from under cover, to which the Swedes could not of course reply. Finally the defenders drove their antagonists back with much slaughter to their ships, the attempt to recover Kronstadt having ignominiously failed.

Coming down to a somewhat later date, to the era of British over-sea expeditions, the landing of Amherst's army near Louisbourg in 1758 at once rivets the attention. Taking place as it did after the expedition had been lying off the fortress in its transports for some days waiting for a change of weather, and when the French were well aware of what was impending and had taken steps to repel all attempts to reach the shore, it takes a high place among the many brilliant feats of arms which signalised the warfare of the eighteenth century. Feints were made at two points to confuse the defenders. The main landing was designed to take place at a small bay farthest from the town, and of this Mr Bradley gives a vivid account in 'The Fight with France for North America,' from which the following is a quotation.

The landing at Louisbourg in 1758.

"When morning broke upon the short summer night, all was ready for a start, and at sunrise the entire fleet opened such a furious cannonade as had never been heard even in those dreary regions of strife and tempest. Under its cover the boats pushed for the shore, Wolfe and his division, as the chief actors in the scene, making for the left, where, in Kennington Cove, some twelve hundred French soldiers, with a strong battery of guns, lay securely intrenched just above the shore line and behind an abattis of fallen trees. As Wolfe's boats, rising and falling on the great Atlantic rollers, drew near the rocks, the thunder of Boscawen's guns ceased, and, the French upon shore still reserving their fire for closer quarters, there was for some time an ominous silence, broken only by the booming of the surf as it leapt up the cliffs or spouted in white columns above the sunken rocks. Heading for the narrow beach, the leading boats were within a hundred yards of it when the French batteries opened on them with a fierce hail of ball and round-shot. Nothing but the heaving of the sea, say those who were there, could have saved them. Wolfe's flagstaff was shot away, and even that ardent soul shrank from leading his men further into such a murderous fire. He was just signalling to his flotilla to sheer off, when three boats on the flank, either unaware of or refusing to see the signal, were observed dashing for a rocky ledge at the corner of the cove. They were commanded by two lieutenants, Hopkins and Brown, and an ensign, Grant. These young gentlemen had caught sight of a possible landing-place at a spot protected by an angle of the cliff from the French batteries. Without waiting for orders, they sent their boats through the surf, and with little damage succeeded in landing on the slippery rocks and scrambling to temporary shelter from the French fire.

"Wolfe, at once a disciplinarian and a creature of impulse, did not stand on ceremony. Feeling, no doubt, that he would himself have acted in precisely the same fashion as his gallant subalterns under like conditions, he signalled to the rest to follow their lead, setting the example himself with his own boat. The movement was successful, though not without much loss both in boats and men. The surf was strong and the rocks were sharp; many boats were smashed to pieces, many men were drowned, but the loss was not comparable to the advantage gained. Wolfe himself, cane in hand, was one of the first to leap into the surf. . . . As the troops came straggling out upon the beach, full of ardour, soaked to the skin, and many of them badly bruised, Wolfe formed them rapidly in column, routed a detachment of grenadiers, and fell immediately with the bayonet upon the French redoubts. The enemy, though picked and courageous troops, were taken aback, and fled without much resistance."

The side repelling, or attempting to repel, a landing must

always enjoy great opportunities for forming ambuscades. It will be remembered that the Dutch in the case of the bloody fight on the beach of Walcheren, mentioned on p. 348, remained concealed behind the rolling sand-dunes till the proper moment, and that the Russians adopted the same expedient when the Swedes made their disastrous attempt upon the isle of Kronstadt. Similarly the British expedition to capture Belleisle in 1761 commenced its campaign under inauspicious circumstances, owing to the judicious reserve of the defenders in concealing themselves till the last moment, and then adding strength to their blow by delivering it unexpectedly.

Failure at Lomarie in Belleisle.

A landing was at the outset attempted at the southern extremity of the island, with the idea of seizing some works at Lomarie. The works were first bombarded by a squadron of war-vessels; then after a while the boats, full of soldiers, pulled ashore to a beach lying at the foot of some broken ground. The ascent of this declivity proved to be more difficult than had been anticipated. Those of the men who reached the summit were in disarray and out of breath. And the French detachment who held the defences, reserving their fire till it was bound to tell, of a sudden poured in a murderous musketry alike upon the assaulting columns on the beach and on the panting soldiery scrambling up the rocky steep. A party of sixty grenadiers managed to reach the top of the cliffs, but they were there overpowered and forced to lay down their arms. The rest of the British troops were beaten off, hurried to their boats, and made good their retreat with a loss of 400 men. The point selected for disembarkation would appear to have been singularly ill-chosen; but the defenders, who were by no means in strong force, deserve all credit for the judgment displayed in remaining concealed till the proper moment for action.

The most remarkable example of a disembarkation carried out in face of the enemy in modern times is furnished by

Abercromby's landing in

Aboukir Bay.

Sir R. Abercromby's achievement in Aboukir Bay. His force consisted of some 16,000 men, with, however, scarcely any horses—there was practically no cavalry, and the artillery during the subsequent move on Alexandria was hauled along by hand. The transports were lying for six days off the coast before the weather permitted boats to reach the shore. In consequence of this there had been time for a force of 2000 men under Friant to be despatched to the bay by General Menou: that commander has, indeed, been severely and probably not unjustly blamed for not sending more. The French troops were drawn up in a concave semicircle on the sand-hills commanding the beach, while their guns had been placed in battery on a lofty bluff which dominated its whole extent. And the result was that the British chief was confronted with the problem not only of getting his men ashore, but also, at the same time, of assailing a strong position manned by veteran troops.

At nine in the morning of the day of battle signal was made for the boats of the fleet, each of them containing fifty soldiers, to advance towards the shore. The scene in the bay at once became one of intensest animation. Under the command of Captain Cochrane, uncle of the Cochrane of the *Speedy*, of the *Imperieuse*, and of Basque Roads, the whole of the troop-boats, formed up in two lines, made for the shore. Armed craft sustained the flanks. Launches containing field-artillery, with seamen to work the guns, accompanied the boats. Bomb-vessels and sloops of war stood in close to the shore with their broadsides ready. In charge of the whole was that daring and resourceful, if somewhat unconventional, knight-errant of the sea, Sir Sidney Smith. The flotilla contained some 5000 troops, a force representing only about one-third of Abercromby's army, and this illustrates one of the disadvantages under which a military force labours when landing in face of opposition, in that only a fraction of its strength can generally be thrown into the fray at the outset.

No sooner did the first line of boats come within range of Friant's expectant soldiery than a heavy fire of grape and musketry opened from the shore. The surface of the water was ploughed up by the storm of projectiles and bullets. Several boats were sunk. The sailors pulling eagerly at the oars, the infantry huddled between the seats and thwarts, the officers in the stern alert and ready,—all suffered appreciable losses during those terrible moments when the boats were traversing the zone of fire. But nothing could damp the ardour of the two services at this critical juncture. Scarcely had the stems struck the sand than the soldiers poured out on the beach. The 23rd and 40th regiments were the first to get on the move, and without firing a shot they rushed up the heights and carried them at the point of the bayonet, in spite of a stout resistance offered by the French grenadiers. Sir Sidney Smith and his sailors got some guns ashore and hauled them up on the high ground in an extraordinarily short space of time. And, with a firm grip established on ground in the heart of the enemy's position, the battle was in reality won within a few minutes of the first boat touching the strand.

The naval arrangements worked with mechanical precision. Immediately the boats had discharged their freight they were pulled back to the transports in eager haste to bring up reinforcements. A furious charge of French cavalry at one moment threatened to roll up a large detachment of infantry on one flank, but this managed to form square and to maintain itself till supports arrived. Then, before the whole of the attacking army had reached the land, Friant wisely gave orders for retreat, which was carried out in good order although with the loss of eight guns.

The rest of the disembarkation, which took two days to complete, was carried out without molestation.

French historians have been rather inclined to belittle this great feat of arms. But Bertrand pays a generous tribute to the brilliance of the exploit and to the excellence of the naval and military dispositions. "Their debarkation," he declares, "was admirable. In less than five or six minutes they presented 5500 men in battle array. It was like a movement on the opera stage." As an example of a particular class of military operation it stands on a pinnacle of its own in the warfare of modern times. Landings in defiance of a formidable enemy in position have rarely been attempted on so great a scale. There is scarcely a precedent for an enterprise so hazardous and so difficult, leading to startling tactical results within the space, it may almost be said, of a few minutes, and of a disembarkation in face of the enemy virtually deciding the issue of an important campaign almost before it had begun. Once the British army was securely ashore the fate of Egypt was decided. Menou did not, it is true, capitulate without offering a determined resistance between Aboukir and Alexandria; but the result was never really in doubt.

The difference between former conditions and those of to-day.

In the days of Abercromby muskets only carried one hundred yards or so; grape began to lose its effect at a range of over a quarter of a mile; round-shot and shell, the only projectiles of any use beyond that distance, had no great terrors for troops in boats. Under the conditions then obtaining, landing-parties only suffered serious loss when close to the shore, and when actually disembarking and advancing to the attack. A moment's consideration serves to show how completely the great advance which has taken place in the science of armament has transformed the tactical situation when an army endeavours to force its way ashore in face of opposition under modern conditions of war.

Artillery fire could, in the present day, hardly fail to be highly effective against boats some thousands of yards away. Small arms are destructive at over a mile distance. The accuracy and power of modern weapons makes them far more formidable, even at comparatively speaking short ranges, than were Friant's guns and muskets which for a few moments caused the British advanced forces such grievous loss when the boats rushed for the beach fringing Aboukir Bay. Numerous examples of successful landings have been given in preceding paragraphs, but all of them date back to a time when battle formations were totally different from those which progress in armament has forced upon the trained soldiery of to-day. They cannot be accepted as precedents for what will happen in future war, and the reason for this is that the evolution in tactical conditions works entirely in favour of the troops repelling an attempted landing, as against the troops making the attempt.

Open boats move through the water no faster now than they did a century ago, nor do they offer those in them any better cover. If there be field-artillery on shore so placed that ships' guns cannot silence it, transports must lie off at a great distance from the beach, and the time taken by the boats to reach the landing-place will be actually greater than used to be the case. In unopposed disembarkations, like those of the Japanese in Korea in 1904, it is the practice to tow several boats by a single steam-launch; but a group of this sort would afford so large and conspicuous a target for shrapnel-firing guns, that the plan could not safely be adopted if there were serious opposition to be encountered. Unless the transports conveying an army which is to disembark in hostile territory carry a great number of steam-launches,—a number sufficient to take a large force of men at a single trip,—steam does not facilitate a landing in face of an enemy. The speed

Reasons for difference.

with which such launches move through the water is of course advantageous if soldiers are actually carried in them; but unless especial arrangements had been made, there would not be enough available to appreciably shorten the time spent by the troops in traversing the zone of fire, and craft of that class are not generally designed to take many men.

Under the conditions of the present time a military force disembarking in defiance of troops drawn up on shore is almost certain to be under fire for a considerable space of time. And if the adversary be present in strength and be provided with artillery, there must inevitably be heavy loss in the boats before they reach the shore. In the days of muskets and round-shot, on the other hand, landing-parties were only exposed to small-arm fire for a minute or two at most, while actually afloat. In the future the boats will in all probability offer a target for musketry for quite ten minutes, and to shrapnel for fully double that length of time. Under such circumstances an enterprise comparable to that of Abercromby, where about 5000 men attacked 2000 assisted by eight guns, could only succeed if a covering fleet was able to pour in an overwhelming artillery fire upon the position held by the defenders, and if it was able to maintain that fire up to the very last moment.[3] In chapter xxiii. this question of warships covering disembarkations will be touched upon again,— suffice it to say here that it is a matter of opinion whether that class of naval support would prove very efficacious against a determined foe. It is not suggested that opposed landings are now impracticable when the force which can be disembarked at one time is greatly superior to that drawn up on shore. If the attacking army is prepared to accept heavy loss, it may succeed. But the operation is not one to be ventured on with a light heart, or one to be undertaken without counting the cost and without accepting risk of disaster.

SAILORS BEST AT AWKWARD PLACES. 361

In all disembarkations, whether they are opposed or not, naval assistance is indispensable. That is a principle which is universally accepted in the British service. But where landings have to take place on slippery rocks, where in fact the process of getting out of the boats on to the shore presents special difficulties, it is always preferable to detail naval personnel to at least gain a footing on land to start with, and prior to the troops approaching. The soldier is not at his best at this sort of work. The bluejacket and the marine are accustomed to it, and they are not prone to add to the perils and confusion of landing at an awkward place under fire, by falling into the water out of sheer clumsiness. Naval history provides numbers of instances of small landing-parties despatched from ships of war performing brilliant exploits on shore. Such parties have often disembarked in broken water on jetties and ledges of rock, sometimes even by night. Undertakings of this class are scarcely the soldier's business, although the story of Wolfe at Louisbourg, recorded on an earlier page, proves that they are not impossible even to a purely military force. The principle of using marines in the first instances has recently been illustrated by the Japanese in their descent on the Liaotung peninsula; the earliest troops to be sent ashore in Yen Toa bay were two battalions of this kind of infantry. *Landings at awkward places generally best carried out by sailors.*

The tactical difficulties of a landing in face of the enemy are now so serious that, when such enterprises have to be attempted in future, there would seem to be some temptation to make the venture under cover of darkness. But night operations are generally hazardous even on shore. Few military commanders would incur so grave a risk, unless the chosen point of disembarkation had been carefully reconnoitred beforehand, and unless the conditions as regards the nature of the beach and the state of the sea were peculiarly favourable. One cause of Nelson's failure *Question of landings at night.*

362   LANDINGS AND EMBARKATIONS.

at Santa Cruz was that many of his boats missed the mole which was their destination. The first essential, if success is to be achieved in a military undertaking at night, is that there shall be no mishaps and no confusion, and to expect this with a body of troops in the dark, under surroundings to which they are wholly unaccustomed, is unreasonable. Doubtful and dangerous as an opposed landing must always be by day under existing tactical conditions, it would seem wiser to brave the perils which it involves than to jeopardise a military force by launching it upon an amphibious undertaking of this kind by night.

Embarkations in face of opposition. Generally speaking a case of retreat. The moral factor can never be overlooked in war, and it is not unlikely to play a particularly important part when an embarkation takes place in face of the enemy. It is unusual for a military force which has been successful in its operations to take to its transports harassed by the adversary. An army rarely withdraws by sea from territory in occupation of hostile detachments, unless it be yielding to superior force. It does not, of course, of necessity follow that the embarking troops have been beaten, or that they are even in any serious danger. They may be retiring after a mere feint, or they may be performing a part in some profound strategical combination of an offensive character involving transfer of force from one point to another on the coast. But, generally speaking, when an operation of this nature takes place, the soldiers who are returning to their ships are doing so because they have met with reverse, or to avoid reverse, and they are therefore necessarily fighting under depressing conditions. This is unfortunate, because an embarkation in face of the enemy must in itself be a dangerous undertaking. A landing may be effected to a certain extent as a surprise even when hostile forces are drawn up to contest it; but the presence of the transports and boats necessarily discloses the intentions of an army which is contemplating withdrawal by sea, and it marks the spot where the withdrawal is to be carried out. An operation of this class must in its final stages be tantamount to a retreat, and to a retreat executed under circumstances where confusion and misunderstandings are peculiarly likely to arise, and where losses must almost inevitably be encountered.[4]

It is essentially a case for a rearguard—for a rearguard, moreover, which has to hold its ground to the very end and to then make its escape at the last moment under circumstances of the utmost peril. When the embarkation takes place by boats from off a beach, the great military object to attain is that the bulk of the retiring force shall get to its transports without being subjected to heavy fire on the way across the water. If the army is to be put on board ship at quays and jetties in some harbour, it is essential that the ships shall get out of artillery range before the enemy can bring guns to bear on them. In either case the covering troops have a laborious and dangerous task to perform, and their own withdrawal to the transports can hardly fail to develop into an almost desperate enterprise if the foe be formidable and if the hostile commander realises his opportunities. Sir J. Moore's army inflicted so arresting a defeat upon that of Soult at Coruña, that the troops eventually embarked without being exposed to fire, although some of the transports suffered somewhat before quitting the anchorage: on that occasion the British army fought a general action before its departure even commenced. But a mere rearguard could not hope to delay a pursuing force so effectually as this under modern conditions. Nowadays, when boats will be so much longer under musketry and artillery fire than was formerly the case, the effect of the tactical changes which have taken place is to militate very seriously against the prospects of the fugitive army.[5]

A rearguard operation involved as a rule.

Turkish embarkation at Malta.

When, in 1565, news arrived that an army from Sicily had landed in Malta, Mustapha, the Turkish general, embarked with all speed near Valetta, resolved upon a precipitate flight eastwards. Finding, however, that the relieving force was considerably less formidable than had been at first supposed, the Ottoman commander disembarked afresh in St Paul's Bay at the west end of the island, and advanced a second time against the fortress. This was what his enemies wanted. The Christian forces had united, the succoured garrison panted for revenge while the army which had effected the relief was eager to show its prowess, and deliverers and delivered suddenly fell upon the Moslems and drove them back in utter confusion to the shore. Mustapha, however, never lost his presence of mind even when all was at its worst. He managed to detach a rearguard, which was posted so skilfully and which maintained its ground with such fortitude that the main body of the Turks got away in safety from the beach, and the actual re-embarkation was eventually carried out with little loss, in spite of the disastrous overthrow which had rendered a precipitate flight necessary.

Difficulties of the operation greatly increased under modern conditions.

In those days the soldiery when embarking were only exposed to serious loss while on shore, or immediately after getting into their boats. Firearms were still in a primitive condition; and, going back to the time before gunpowder was invented, we find that the risks were still less. The battle of Marathon, and what followed it, affords a remarkable illustration of an army which had been disastrously defeated near the shore escaping to its boats, putting to sea, and still enjoying a measure of fighting efficiency. The Persian commander Doris, with a grasp of strategical conditions and a resolution in spite of untoward circumstances which did him no little credit, sailed from Marathon round Cape Sunium to Phalerum Bay, hoping to find that the Athenians, who had so decisively beaten him, would be devoting their energies to plundering the deserted camp of the invaders. But Miltiades, scenting danger, had made a night march back to Athens. And so when in the morning the Persians prepared to land at the new point, hoping to retrieve their laurels by a dash at the hostile capital, they found the victors of the previous day ready to give them a warm welcome and eager for another tussle. The project was thereupon abandoned, and the Persians disappeared from Greek waters.

When an army is embarking in face of hostile forces the warships which will, it may be assumed, be present to protect the transports may be able to afford the troops great assistance. This depends upon their getting in close enough to use their guns effectively, and if that be practicable they ought generally to be able to prevent the flanks of the rearguard from being turned. When the critical moment arrives for the covering detachments to make their way to the shore, the support of the fleet may save the imperilled remnant from being overwhelmed, and it may compel the pursuers to keep at such a distance that boats can be got away without exposure to severe fire. But unless, owing to there being deep water close in or to vessels of small draught of water being available, the ships can approach within close range of the spot where the troops are embarking, they may be obliged to discontinue fire for fear of injuring their own side, in a combat which is likely to be of a hand-to-hand and somewhat unconventional character. And this is admirably illustrated by an incident which occurred a century and a half ago, but which even in this present day serves as an instructive tactical example. Its remarkable story provides one of the most illuminating illustrations of an embarkation in face of the enemy in the annals of modern war. *Artillery fire from fleet covering embarkation.*

In 1758 an expedition under General Bligh, escorted by a squadron under Commodore Howe, was despatched from *The affair of St Cas in 1758.*

England to destroy the defences of Cherbourg. Should the project contemplated against that place not succeed, the armament was—so ran the King's instructions—to "carry a warm alarm along the coast of France, from the easternmost point of Normandy, as far westwards as Morlaix inclusive." Morlaix is not far from Brest.

Much damage was done at Cherbourg. The expedition then proceeded to continue the work near St Malo. The troops landed and burnt some shipping in a neighbouring port; but the weather was becoming unsettled, Howe declared himself unable to aid in an attack on St Malo itself, and he proposed that the army should march to the sheltered bay of St Cas some miles to the west, and that it should re-embark there. This arrangement was agreed to by General Bligh, and after a three days' march, during which some slight opposition was encountered and which gave the French time to collect forces in the vicinity of St Cas, that point was reached in safety and the embarkation began.

Three brigades and the wounded had been safely got on board the transports, when the French began to press down in force upon the troops not yet embarked. A rearguard of 1500 men under General Drury was formed up to arrest their progress, and the fleet opened such a heavy fire on the advancing hostile colunms that they were for a while checked in their approach. A well-contested engagement thereupon ensued, the British soldiery holding their ground stubbornly and resisting all efforts of their antagonists to get to close quarters. But ammunition began to give out, an attempted counter-attack failed, and in the end a rush was made for the boats, many of which had been destroyed by the French light guns which were playing on them. A desperate struggle ensued on the beach. General Drury, who had been wounded earlier, was drowned, with many others. When the confusion was at its height, Howe, who had already acquired renown as a fighter in the abortive expedition to Rochefort the year before, who was destined to achieve a brilliant reputation in American waters twenty years later, and who was to compass the overthrow of Villaret Joyeuse's imposing armada out on the broad Atlantic on the memorable First of June, came ashore in his own boat to personally superintend the operation of getting the stricken soldiery off the beach, and by his example and his genius for command he to a certain extent retrieved the situation.

When it was impossible to aid the military further, and when all available boats were crammed with fugitives and almost gunwale-under, Howe signalled to his ships to cease their fire, for this fire was injuring friend and foe alike as they fought upon the beach. The remnants of the British troops were thereupon taken prisoner, the total loss to the expeditionary force amounting to 700—about half of the force detailed to cover the embarkation under Drury. The French also lost heavily in the combat, in which both sides bore themselves most valiantly.

Bligh was severely, and perhaps not undeservedly, criticised for not fighting a general action with his whole force before beginning to embark. He appears to have had an army under his command which was fully equal in numerical strength to any bodies of troops which the French had been able to collect to molest him, and he enjoyed a decided advantage as regards organisation and security of flanks. Had he made up his mind to fight a battle he might perhaps have gained a victory tactically as decisive, and strategically as far-reaching, as was Sir J. Moore's triumph over Soult before Coruña half a century later. It is reasonable to assume that a happy issue to such a combat would have permitted him to carry out the subsequent embarkation almost undisturbed, and it is possible that his troops might have got on board without a shot being fired. But one of the disadvantages of retreat must always be the difficulty of obtaining accurate intelligence, and the strength and determination of the enemy very likely were not fully realised. St Cas was far from an ideal anchorage for shipping, and the prospect of heavy weather setting in had to be taken into consideration. That sanguinary encounter on the Breton shore, and the circumstances which surrounded it, serve as a vivid picture of the difficulties and dangers which attend the departure of an army by sea when fighting forces are at hand to speed the parting guest.

CHAPTER XXI.

THE SIEGE OF MARITIME FORTRESSES.

COMMAND of the sea is of vital importance where a maritime fortress is being besieged or blockaded. A stronghold on the coast cannot be said to be fully invested unless the besiegers are seconded in their efforts by naval force shutting the place in on the water side.[1] Without preponderance afloat the troops attacking a place of arms so situated cannot reduce it by famine, and they are compelled to force an entrance through the lines of defence either by the hazardous process of assault or else by the protracted and dubious operations of sapping and approaches. *Command of the sea of vital importance when a maritime fortress is being besieged.*

From the naval point of view three different sets of conditions may present themselves in such a siege: the besiegers may have command of the sea, the garrison may have command of the sea, or control of the local waters may be in dispute. And as the strategical and tactical situation necessarily varies widely according as one or other of these sets of conditions prevails, it will be convenient to discuss each separately. Before doing so, however, it will be convenient to put forward some general observations with regard to strongholds on the coast. *Three sets of conditions, from the naval point of view.*

Maritime fortresses present a great diversity of characteristics, not only as regards their extent and importance, but also as regards their situation. In some cases—Toulon in the present day and Messina under the conditions of two centuries ago are examples—the defended area is *Diverse characteristics of coast fortresses.*

roughly the segment of a circle, of which the land fortifications form the arc and the sea front the chord. Or a fortress may be situated on a promontory or peninsula where the coast defences will naturally cover a greater perimeter than the works which face in-shore: San Sebastian and Gaeta present typical illustrations of this form of stronghold in the time of the Napoleonic wars, and Vladivostok may be cited as an example of more modern date. Then there is the form where the whole of an island, or of a group of islands, is included within the ring of fortifications: the anchorage within the Maddalena group of islands off the Straits of Bonifaccio, which has been created into an Italian fortress, comes under this heading, and Kronstadt, both under the tactical conditions of the past and of the present, affords an instance of a fortress and an island all in one. Finally, there are many fortresses which have played a prominent part in history which are situated on estuaries and navigable rivers: Antwerp, Komorn, and Quebec are examples. The features which arise in the siege of a stronghold of this character will, however, be dealt with in chapter xxii., which is concerned with inland waterways.

Their influence, as regards importance of naval control in the vicinity.

It is obvious that the greater the length of the sea front of a fortress is in proportion to the length of its line of defences on the land side, the more important does the question of maritime command become. Where the whole of an island is fortified, the siege of it is a purely naval operation, although, if it be proposed to actually assault some portion of its defences, the landing-parties might well consist of military detachments. Conversely, if the enceinte or line of works encloses the head of an inlet, there will proportionately be a great extent of land front: this will of course offer considerable freedom of choice as to the exact point for attack, but it will also call for a comparatively speaking large army to invest the place and to push siege works home. And, as the effective blockade of a besieged fortress is always an operation of a difficult and harassing nature, it is clearly advantageous from the naval point of view that the sea front should be as short as possible, supposing the besiegers to have the maritime control. If, on the contrary, the sea be open to the garrison for bringing in supplies and reinforcements, it is manifestly favourable to its prospects of holding out, that it should have a short extent of country to defend on the land side and an extensive sea front.

It is hardly necessary here to go into the question of the size and scale of importance of maritime fortresses. But it may be pointed out that in the present day there is a very general tendency to elaborate the purely coast defences of such places, to pile up the armament of its shore batteries and to multiply the number of these, while trusting to works of a more provisional nature for protection on the land side. Many defended dockyards and naval bases, the retention of which may be of vital moment for the effective prosecution of a maritime campaign or for the denial to the enemy of absolute mastery of the sea, have no permanent fortifications at all facing towards the interior. The tendency of modern tactics in land fighting has been to depreciate the value of elaborately constructed works of defence, and on the other hand to greatly extend the area included within their perimeter.

When we come to consider the principles governing the siege of a coast fortress where the attacking side enjoys the maritime command, the question at once arises how far naval blockade can be said to be effective in the light of definite investment. One means of wearing down the resisting power of a garrison is starvation, and starvation only results when the avenues by which food can reach the place are choked up. An army besieging a stronghold *Sieges where the attacking side has maritime preponderance. The question of blockade.*

in the interior has generally good grounds for confidence that it will be able to cut off all supplies which the garrison may hope to draw from outside: that is an accepted method of compelling the place to surrender. History provides numbers of examples of maritime fortresses blockaded by land and sea opening their gates to the conqueror as a result of famine: the case of Valetta, which was defended for two years by General Vaubois against a land force of Maltese aided by British and Neapolitan troops, and against an Anglo-Portuguese fleet, may be quoted as an example. But the effectual sealing up of all approaches to a fortress from the sea is, generally speaking, a much more difficult operation than closely investing it on the land side. And the experience of war upon the whole goes to show that no amount of vigilance on the part of a blockading fleet can make it absolutely certain that no vessels will manage to evade its scouts and penetrate the defensive cordon. "All the small craft in the British navy could not prevent an occasional entrance of small boats at night into San Sebastian," wrote Melville to Wellington in reply to remonstrances as to the ineffectiveness of the blockade; and although in this case the blockading squadron was admittedly insufficient to perform its task, it is surprising what a large amount of supplies and stores managed to reach the place by sea.

Examples of difficulty of blockade. Carthage. The siege of Carthage was marked throughout by singular and dramatic episodes, and it is clear that, although the Romans were paramount at sea, the garrison managed for a long time, thanks to the daring and skill of its sailors, to replenish its food from boats which slipped into the harbour at night. It will be remembered that, as quoted on p. 96, Scipio was so much impressed with this that he undertook a special campaign against Nepheris as one base of supply for the besieged. The capture of that place improved the prospects of the attacking side, but small craft

DIFFICULTIES OF BLOCKADE. 373

appear still to have got into the harbour from time to time. It was for this reason that the Roman commander undertook the construction of the famous dam across the mouth of the port mentioned on p. 122.

This difficulty of maintaining an effective blockade of a beleaguered fortress, experienced by the Romans in their final effort to destroy the formidable rival power in the western Mediterranean, has since that time manifested itself in many sieges of maritime strongholds. In the case of San Sebastian, referred to above, the British naval force on the spot was so inadequate that its inability to effectively invest the place is perhaps not surprising. But this hardly applies to an incident which occurred nearly two centuries earlier, where a powerful fleet proved unable to exclude blockade-runners from the tiny harbour of a petty fortified port.

The notorious Duke of Buckingham, at the head of a large military force and backed up by a respectable fleet,—fruits of that ship-money which was to tear society in twain a few years later,—was besieging the citadel of St Martin's in the island of Rhé off Rochelle. The little port dominated by the fortress was merely an insignificant indentation in the coast. The defences were not exceptionally formidable. To seal the place up by sea and land would have seemed to be a simple matter, but the flotilla totally failed to stop blockade-running by boats from the French coast. In spite of this, however, food gradually ran short, and the garrison was just about to surrender under pressure of famine, when a number of small craft somehow managed to get through with two months' provisions. In consequence of this, Buckingham hazarded an assault; but his columns were beaten off with heavy loss, and thereupon the English forces withdrew confounded, and abandoned the enterprise. *St Martin's in the Isle of Rhé.*

Another instance is provided by the siege of Fort St Philip in Port Mahon by the Duc de Crillon in 1781. The *Siege of St Philip, Minorca, 1781.*

French were at the time paramount in the Mediterranean, and they were able to detail a number of war-vessels to blockade the harbour. The British garrison was under command of General Murray, a man of rare grit and resolution, who had played an important part at Quebec under similar circumstances twenty years before. Under his sturdy governance the fortress, although closely beset, maintained an active and spirited defence. His confidence was infectious, his resourceful leadership a constant source of worry to the besiegers by land and sea. The blockade was frequently run by vessels bringing provisions, and as a result of their enterprise famine was long staved off. The fortress eventually surrendered after a siege of 170 days, the defenders being accorded every honour by their chivalrous foes. This gallant resistance of a garrison undaunted by the absence of all hope of relief gives to St Philip a high place in that honourable roll of great defences to which Port Arthur has just added another name.

Genoa. Genoa is another stronghold on the sea which has had to yield under pressure of starvation. Massena's fine defence in 1800, in face of the Austrian army under Melas and the British squadron under Lord Keith, was one of the most remarkable episodes of the Napoleonic wars. The British admiral has been often eulogised for the loyalty of his co-operation with his Austrian allies and for the strenuous watchfulness of his blockade. But nevertheless we read in General Thiebault's diary of the defence, "At this period a small barque escaped the vigilance of the enemy's fleet and brought us corn for five days." A few more such barques, and Napoleon descended from the snows of the St Bernard upon the plains of the Po, would have brought the siege to an abrupt conclusion.

Port Arthur. In all the above examples the control of the sea has rested with the besiegers, and their naval supremacy on the spot has been practically undisputed. Like conditions prevailed during the later stages of the siege of Port Arthur; and yet a certain number of junks, and even larger craft, succeeded in reaching the inner harbour in defiance of Admiral Togo's fleet. The Japanese navy has conducted its campaign with such resolution and such foresight, its *personnel* has proved itself so devoted and so efficient, and the importance of closing all avenues of supplies to the beleaguered garrison was so manifest, that it is justifiable to accept the comparative failure of the blockading squadron in this one respect as conclusive proof that it is impossible to wholly prevent succour from reaching a besieged coast fortress by sea. This is in accordance with what was said in chapter vi. as to the difficulty of preventing ships from issuing from a defended harbour. Floating force does not lend itself to the establishment of a barrier, comparable to that which a land army can create with its outposts and defensive positions.[2]

The point has been dealt with at some length. It is one of considerable strategical importance, and the criticisms which have been expressed with regard to the inability of the Japanese fleet to wholly close Port Arthur make it clear that a very general impression exists that naval force can invest a fortress as effectively as military force can. This is not the case. A blockading flotilla cannot absolutely forbid ingress to a harbour. It can make such ingress difficult and dangerous, but it cannot as a general rule render it impossible; and the gradual evolution which has taken place in naval material from the age of triremes down to the conditions which prevail to-day, does not seem to change the relations between besiegers and besieged in this respect.

The presence of warships, supporting an army engaged on siege operations against a defensive position on the coast, may of course exert a great influence over the progress of the undertaking, quite apart from the question of blockade. They may be able to take an active part in the *Warships aiding the besiegers.*

attack. In an earlier chapter the efficacy of bombardment of coast batteries, dockyards, and so forth, from the sea has been discussed, and it has been pointed out that this form of attack seldom achieves important results. But against a fortress which has undergone a prolonged investment, and the garrison of which has been subjected to the anxiety, the exhaustion, and the suffering which the enterprises of an active enemy on land are calculated to cause, bombardment by a fleet may be decisive. It may be the last straw required to break the resolution of the defenders. And this is especially likely to prove the case where the stronghold includes within its area a maritime city with a large civil population. For a city provides a huge target which can be hit by guns firing from a great distance at sea; so that battleships and cruisers may be able to bring their powerful ordnance to bear on it from points where shore batteries cannot reply to them or endanger their safety.

Inasmuch as the extremities of the line of defence works protecting a maritime fortress on the land side necessarily rest on the coast, these works can sometimes be taken in enfilade and even in reverse from the sea. A supporting fleet may be able to greatly assist the besieging army in its operations against those sections of the fortress which abut on the shore, or it may be able to harass the defenders with its gun-fire and may help to secure the assailants against effective sorties. Long-range fire from the United States war-vessels against the land defences of Santiago appears to have given General Shafter's troops some little assistance. The Japanese squadron cruising off Port Arthur was able to give the besieging army occasional support in its difficult task. At the siege of Genoa, already mentioned on p. 374, a frigate and some gun- and mortar-vessels detached from Lord Keith's fleet caused the garrison so much annoyance by their fire, that Massena organised a flotilla of galleys to oppose them: this gave rise to a most stirring combat, the chief galley being cut out one night under the muzzles of the guns of the fortress.

Formerly a co-operating fleet could perhaps aid besiegers more effectually than is now the case, owing to war-vessels being less likely to suffer vital injury from the defenders on shore. Belisarius, the conqueror of Sicily and Justinian's favourite general, when his land forces could not storm the battlements of Palermo, brought his fleet close up to the fortifications on the sea front and assailed the defenders with such a hail of arrows and other missiles fired by marksmen perched on the masts that the place promptly yielded. In the days of round-shot, ships used sometimes to stand close in and to bring their broadsides to bear at very telling range. But even in the eighteenth century it began to be realised that the proper duty of naval force engaged in the siege of a stronghold in conjunction with troops on shore, was primarily blockade. The relations between attacking ships and the batteries of the fortress have already been discussed on p. 112, and it does not seem likely that fleets will in future play a very active part in attacks on coast fortresses.

Formerly warships could perhaps aid more effectually than in the present day.

Where maritime control is assured, a friendly fleet can often come to the assistance of the besieging troops by landing guns to arm batteries on shore. Naval ordnance of the present day is not perhaps so easily adapted to such a purpose as the less powerful guns on simpler mountings of an age that has passed away. But the technical skill, the energy, and the resource, which are available in a efficient squadron, should generally be able to cope with any difficulties which may arise owing to the complications existing in modern artillery material. At the siege of Fort St Philip on the occasion of the first capture of Minorca by British forces in 1708, Sir J. Leake landed a number of guns from his fleet to aid General Stanhope. Admiral Byng similarly provided the Austrian troops attacking Messina in 1719 with ordnance from his squadron. Ship's

Landing guns from fleet to assist besiegers.

guns were used at the siege of Sebastopol, and on many other occasions. During the only great siege of a maritime fortress which has taken place under modern conditions, that of Port Arthur, the attacking side was not sufficiently assured of absolute control of the sea to justify the landing of naval guns on a large scale to aid the army on shore, even had they been required.

Sieges where the naval preponderance has been with the defending side.

So far sieges have only been considered under the conditions of the place assailed being exposed to attack from the sea. But it has often happened in war that a maritime fortress has been invested on the land side while the garrison has all the time enjoyed the support of a friendly fleet, and this obviously creates a totally different strategical situation. The defenders cannot fail to derive enormous advantage from maritime command. They are in a position to replenish their supplies and ammunition and to make good their losses in officers and men, owing to transports and freight-ships being able to enter its harbour unmolested. The ships of war may be able to aid in actual combats with the besiegers. A situation of this kind has often arisen in the past, where a belligerent, dominant at sea, has been striving to maintain a grip on territory which has been menaced by an adversary capable of putting the stronger army in the field. And the circumstances obviously differ widely from those where the besieging side possesses naval control.

Under such conditions the besiegers must fight their way in.

A mere blockade of the stronghold on the land side on the part of the besieging army can never lead to the fall of the place so long as the sea is open. It cannot be reduced by famine, nor are its defensive capabilities likely to be prejudiced by failure of ammunition supply nor by lack of *personnel* to man the works. The result of this is that the besiegers are forced to fight their way through the works into the interior if they mean to capture the fortress, and that they are compelled to adopt active measures. They cannot triumph by merely sitting down before the place and patiently letting famine do its work. They must either act by assault, or else they must commit themselves to the orthodox procedure of sapping and mine-work.

The siege of Candia by the Turks in the seventeenth century lasted for a quarter of a century. The Venetians and their allies upon the whole enjoyed command of the sea and were supreme in local waters, and they were thus able to pour in supplies and reinforcements from time to time. The place was never in want of food although it contained within its walls a large civil population, the number of citizens having been swelled by refugees flocking from different parts of Crete as the Ottoman forces overran the island. The besiegers, on the other hand, suffered great difficulty in getting reinforcements. The Dardanelles were for a long time blockaded by the Venetian admirals, Mococenigo and Francesco Morosini; but the maritime power of the distant city on the Adriatic was already on the wane, and the Ægean and Levant were by no means permanently closed to the warships of the Sultan. The struggle was of a desperate character in its later stages, the garrison being succoured by adventurers from all over Europe, who bore themselves most gallantly in the fray but who generally wearied before long of the protracted operations. In the year 1667 alone, Candia sustained no less than 32 assaults. The garrison made 17 sorties, and it sprang 618 mines. It lost 3600 men, while the Moslem dead were reckoned to number 20,000. The place eventually capitulated on honourable terms, the defenders, together with all the civil population who wished to leave the island, being permitted to withdraw by sea with guns and all munitions of war.

The siege of Candia.

The fortress of Rosas, at the eastern end of the Pyrenees, although not a very formidable place of arms, played a

Rosas, 1794-95.

prominent part in certain phases of the Revolutionary and Napoleonic Wars. In the winter of 1794-95 it was besieged by the French general Perignon, at a time when there was a fleet of thirteen Spanish ships of the line in the harbour. It was kept victualled by the friendly fleet and was sustained by its encouraging presence; the wintry weather, moreover, militated against the prosecution of sap work of the besiegers. Nevertheless a practicable breach was at last made, and the fall of the fortress by assault had become a mere matter of hours, when the garrison embarked and evacuated the place altogether. This presents the advantage of having sea communications open in a new aspect. Although the fortress itself was lost to Spain for the campaign, its garrison was available for further service.

The siege of Tarragona in 1810. The defence of Tarragona in 1810 against Suchet is another good example. The works of the place were fairly efficient, the garrison was determined to hold out, and British war-vessels afforded some little occasional support with their fire. But it was the power of drawing supplies and reinforcements from over the sea which enabled the fortress to resist so gallantly and so long. There was never want of food at any time. The women and children were withdrawn by ship to a place of safety when the situation became critical. Reinforcements and ammunition arrived by water. Eventually, after a prolonged siege and much severe fighting, the French pushed their saps up close to the defences and forced their way in.

In these three cases, and also in that of the famous siege of Ostend early in the seventeenth century, the beleaguering army eventually overcame the defenders in spite of their sea-power. This is always likely to be the case if the siege is pressed with vigour by an adequate attacking force, and if the defending side cannot through the instrumentality of sea-power threaten the communications of the besiegers. But many instances can be quoted of maritime fortresses successfully withstanding all efforts of the assailants, thanks to command of the sea.

At the siege of Dunkirk by the Duke of York in 1793 the garrison received great assistance from French gunboats, the British fleet failing to put in an appearance when greatly needed although naval assistance had been promised the Duke: the defenders in consequence enjoyed all the advantages of command of local waters. It was very largely due to this that the place was able to make so spirited and protracted a defence, and that time was given the French to assemble considerable forces for its relief and so to compel the besiegers to withdraw. *The siege of Dunkirk in 1793.*

The case of Acre in 1799 comes naturally to mind. It was due to the presence of Sir S. Smith and his sailors that the ancient fortress held out at all. As already mentioned on p. 153, reinforcements for the garrison from the Dardanelles were in sight at the time when Napoleon, arrested in his works of approach and baffled in all attempts at assault, resolved to abandon the siege. But the reinforcements had been unable to disembark in time to participate in the active operations of defence owing to the ships being becalmed. *Acre, 1799.*

Sea command, unless it be backed up by military forces capable of operating against the rear of the besiegers, generally gives the besieged garrison encouragement rather than effective tactical assistance against regular attack. The supporting fleet can no doubt assist the defenders at points where the land fortifications approach the shore. But unless the fortress be so situated that, owing to the contour of the coast-line, the ships can bring fire to bear over extensive sections of the assailant's lines, they rarely can intervene very decisively. They have greater opportunities, it is true, than when operating against the besieged, because they have no coast batteries to fear and can run closer in. But as a general rule naval command is of im- *Assistance of fleet to garrison.*

portance rather from the point of view of keeping communications to the fortress open, than in consequence of the tactical support which it is likely to afford.

Siege of Rosas, 1808, and Tarifa, 1811. The siege of Rosas in 1808, however, affords an example of timely assistance to a hard-pressed garrison through the action of friendly war-vessels. "On the 9th," writes Lord Dundonald, "the citadel was attacked by General Reille and a breach effected; but Captain West, placing the *Meteor* in a position to flank the breach, and some boats to enfilade from the shore, prevented the assault." And a somewhat analogous case occurred at the siege of Tarifa in 1811 by General Leval. There the gun-fire of British war-vessels proved of great service to the garrison. Owing to the direction of the French attack the ships could effectively enfilade some of the breaching batteries which had with great labour been set up and armed, and they swept the approaches by which the besiegers were laboriously endeavouring to sap up to the ramparts. It is worthy of note that before the attacking force reached the outskirts of the place the defenders had already received timely reinforcements from Gibraltar by sea.

This depends largely on form of the fortress. Under modern conditions strongholds on promontories jutting out into the sea like Callao the port of Lima, like Sizeboli the rocky peninsula crowned with ancient battlements south of Bourgas on the Black Sea coast, which the Russians captured in the winter of 1829-30 previous to their passage of the Balkans, or like Calvi, memorable for Nelson's siege operations ashore, are out of date. Gibraltar, it is true, still remains one of the greatest fortresses in the world, but it is an exception to the general rule. The siege of such a place without control of the sea was ever a most difficult undertaking. And attack on a modern place of arms like Vladivostok, where the land defences consist of a chain of works across a strip of country analogous to an isthmus, must be a thankless task if the garrison is supported by a fleet: the guns of the ships take the assailant in flank and in reverse, and the besiegers are confronted, not merely by troops in prepared positions secure of supplies and ammunition, but also by hostile floating force which can injure them while itself immune from injury.

The siege of Gaeta by Massena in 1806 affords an interesting example of the siege of a fortified promontory, where the garrison received support from ships of war. A weak allied flotilla landed some of its ordnance to aid in the defence, and it gave some assistance with its guns by firing across the isthmus: owing to shoal water this fire could only be brought effectively to bear from one side. But, considering that Sir S. Smith had at the time a very respectable fleet at his disposal off the coast of Sicily and Calabria, and that this fleet was supreme in the waters of southern Italy, naval assistance to the beleaguered fortress appears to have been half-hearted and perfunctory; and the disparaging terms in which Sir J. Moore refers to the operations in his diary were perhaps better justified than some of his other criticisms of the sister service. For the Prince of Hesse, after making a most gallant resistance against a veteran army under a capable leader, was severely wounded and removed in a British ship; and his successor, lacking that strenuous support by naval power which in a fortress so situated was certain to exert great influence upon the result, and daunted by the resolute bearing and untiring exertions of Massena's forces, capitulated somewhat tamely in the end. *Gaeta, 1806.*

A belligerent holding a maritime fortress against the efforts of a besieging army may, in virtue of naval preponderance, be able to effect the relief of the place by landing troops to attack the enemy in rear, or may be able to threaten the hostile communications. The memorable success of the Danes at Fredericia in 1849, which has been already referred to on p. 307, is a case in point. As has been men- *Relief of a besieged fortress by landing troops in rear of besiegers. Examples.*

tioned earlier, the fortress of Malta was in 1565 relieved by the landing of an army from Sicily at the west end of the island. In 1628 Stralsund, when besieged by Wallenstein, was relieved by a Swedish army landed hard by. In 1811 General Graham and a portion of the garrison of Cadiz, which had long been invested by Victor, tried to raise the siege by embarking and proceeding to Tarifa: there they united with a considerable Spanish force and marched towards the invested stronghold, but in spite of the victory of Barossa the attempt failed. Operations of this kind, however, hardly come under the heading of attack and defence of fortified places, and they need not be further referred to here. Even supposing that the situation does not admit of action on these lines, even supposing that the enemy is too formidable for a force landed outside the immediate environs of the fortress to have any prospect of achieving the desired result, command of the sea still remains an invaluable asset to the garrison, as long as the besiegers cannot check the discharge of cargoes from on board ships within the harbour and cannot interrupt the flow of reinforcements arriving by water.

Sieges where maritime command has been in dispute. In the foregoing paragraphs this question of the siege of maritime fortresses has been discussed, first under the conditions where the besiegers have enjoyed maritime command, and afterwards under the conditions where that inestimable boon has been enjoyed by the besieged. But control of the sea is sometimes in dispute, and local naval preponderance sometimes changes from one side to the other during the course of operations. The importance of dominating local waters has been shown in earlier passages of this chapter, and it is obvious that the transfer of such dominion from one side to the other must transform the whole conditions under which the siege is being carried on. This can perhaps best be indicated by a few examples.

TYRE AND BARCELONA.

In ancient history the siege of Tyre by Alexander the Great illustrates the effect of the change of maritime command very forcibly. The Macedonian conqueror was not paramount at sea when he moved into Syria, and in attacking Tyre he entered upon a contest with a people noted above all others for their skill as mariners, and for their ingenuity, their daring, and their resolution in naval combats. And when the Tyrians retired with the aid of their ships to their island, and when Alexander began to create a mighty mole across the intervening channel to reach them in their fastness, it soon became manifest that without superiority in the local waters the besieging host was not likely to make rapid progress. Alexander was nothing if not thorough. Realising the nature of the strategical and tactical situation, he forthwith created a flotilla, he manned it with Greeks and other seafaring subject-peoples, and he speedily overthrew the Phœnician seamen on the element which they almost reckoned as their own. No sooner had maritime command passed over from besieged to besiegers, than the mole began to advance apace in spite of tempests and of sorties by the garrison, it spanned the intervening channel, and it finally reached the island, when superiority of force and the military skill and experience of Alexander soon gave the victory to the attacking side.

In 1706 a formidable army under Marshal Tessé aided by a powerful fleet was besieging Barcelona. The place was closely invested, siege-works were in progress, an abundant artillery was battering the defences, food was becoming scarce, and although the intrepid and adventurous Peterborough was harassing the land communications of the besiegers with guerillas, his forces were quite insufficient to take pressure off the fortress. A body of British troops under Stanhope, with a fleet under Leake, was coming from England, and Peterborough learnt that the armada was on its way to Catalonia. He thereupon collected his forces on the sea-coast, seized all available shipping, and then put off alone by boat to meet the fleet and to communicate with the military and naval leaders. The British fleet was known to be somewhat superior to that of the Comte de Toulouse blockading Barcelona, that admiral shirked encounter altogether and retired to Toulon, and thereupon Peterborough, Stanhope, and Leake sailed with their united forces into the harbour of the fortress. The breaches by this time were practicable, and the French troops were clamorous to storm them; but Tessé was a hesitating and cautious leader, and he delayed the assault till too late. With maritime control transferred to his opponents the marshal's position was extremely precarious in view of the propinquity to the sea of his land communications with France, which has already been noticed in chapter xvii. Fearing a serious disaster, he not only raised the siege, but he also retreated so precipitately that his siege train was abandoned, that his sick and wounded were left behind, and that even his tents were left standing in camp.

The great siege of Gibraltar. The great siege of Gibraltar lasted from June 1779 to February 1783. The fortress was continuously invested on its land side, and was for a great part of the time blockaded by the Spanish fleet. It was revictualled by Rodney in January 1780, the admiral on his way out having captured a convoy laden with food-stuffs. It was again revictualled in April 1781 by Admiral Darby. In 1782 the French mustered in great force to aid their allies by land and sea, and the memorable combined attack on it was made in September of that year, which ended so disastrously for the assailants. The following month Lord Howe arrived and revictualled the place a third time, and thus practically terminated the siege, although it was not actually raised till the next year. The command of Spanish waters had always been in the hands of the allies, except during brief intervals when the relieving fleets from England approached; but the temporary transfer of naval preponderance to the British for a short time on three occasions sufficed to enable Elliot and his devoted garrison to hold out.

The two sieges of Missolunghi by the Ottoman forces during the Greek War of Liberation also admirably illustrate the vicissitudes of a beleaguered stronghold on the coast, when maritime command is in dispute.

Missolunghi, 1822 and 1825-26.

During the first siege, in 1822, the patriot forces by land and sea had the upper hand, the place was only invested on the land side, and as supplies and reinforcements were poured in by sea the Turks soon abandoned the unpromising enterprise. It is indeed of interest only in its contrast to the later and greater siege, which began early in May 1825. The defences had been greatly developed and strengthened, largely owing to the energy and example of Lord Byron. The unhealthy low-lying village had become a formidable stronghold, and its capture promised to give the enemy considerable trouble. A Turkish army sat down before its walls, and a blockading fleet sailed into the Gulf of Patras to watch it from the side of the sea; but before much progress had been made the Greek admirals Miaulis and Sakhtouris hove in sight with a handy flotilla, attacked the Moslem shipping in the narrow waters throwing it into serious confusion, and poured supplies which were sorely needed into the beleaguered place of arms. So great was the effect of this victory that Missolunghi remained open on its seaward side for several months. But then a great Ottoman fleet arrived in the gulf, and during the month of November a rigid blockade was established by the Turkish navy, which was not again relaxed. Ibrahim Pasha with his Egyptians arrived to aid the Sultan's forces, and the siege was thenceforward prosecuted with relentless vigour by that capable and determined soldier. The garrison endured his attacks with unshaken fortitude till, in April 1826, food was all consumed. Then the stricken remnants made one desperate effort to cleave a way through the besiegers for themselves and for the sick, the women, and the children. The sortie failed. In the struggle which ensued the besiegers forced their way within the ramparts in overwhelming force, and the Egyptian and Turkish soldiery made short work of the survivors of the garrison, once the antagonists came to close quarters.

The siege of Cuddalore. Towards the close of the remarkable campaign in East Indian waters between Suffren and Hughes in 1783, a British army invested the weak French fortress of Cuddalore, on the Malabar coast south of Madras. Hearing of this, Suffren hastened thither. De Bussy, the French commander-in-chief, realising that the fate of the place depended upon the question of sea command, without hesitation embarked 1200 men from the garrison so as to fill up gaps in the *personnel* of the fleet, which was equipping itself for the impending battle with Hughes, who had followed Suffren. In the action which ensued neither side gained a clear tactical advantage, but Hughes sailed away north, and the French admiral thereupon promptly landed at Cuddalore the 1200 men whom he had borrowed, and landed 2400 men of his own in addition. De Bussy thus reinforced made a most vigorous sortie, which was only repulsed by the British after a severe struggle in which there were heavy casualties on both sides. A few days after the sortie, however, news arrived that peace was concluded; but had the operations continued, the British would almost certainly have been forced to raise the siege, in view of the presence of Suffren and his squadron.

Conclusion. To the sailor and the soldier there is something almost repellent in fixed defence. The one looks upon operations on the high seas as the true object of strategy, the other is drawn towards combinations on land of which mobility is the means and victory on the battlefield the end. But neither can wholly escape from the magnetism which the fortress is able to exert, in virtue of its natural functions in war. Those functions are to the weaker side protection, to the stronger side security of pivots upon which it founds its plan of offensive campaign. The more marked the inequality of force becomes, the more must the weaker side and the less need the stronger side lean on fixed defences, and as their importance to the one grows greater and their importance to the other grows less, they inevitably become more and more an objective for active operations to direct themselves against. The fleet worsted at sea flies to its maritime strongholds for shelter. The beaten army relies on its fenced cities to bar the way to the victorious foe, along the great routes of communication. And so the belligerent who has gained the upper hand finds the fortresses of the enemy acting as a loadstone which draws his mobile fleets and armies towards it, and which holds them as it were in thrall for a season, till the fortresses fall. Tactical conditions on land tend to substitute improvised lines of provisional works of the Plevna type, for those monuments of engineering ingenuity suggested by the names of Vauban and Cohorn.[3] But the coast battery is essentially a permanent work, nor does the evolution of arms of precision tend towards altering this. And as fortifications, whether provisional or permanent, cannot be expected to level themselves when an assailant approaches like the walls of Jericho, siege and blockade retain their place as one phase in the conduct of war which armies and navies find forced upon them.

The study of siege-works on land, and of their complement —blockade, torpedo-craft warfare, and countermining at sea —is in its more intricate details to a certain extent a question for the technicalist. But the general principles of carrying out an attack upon a modern stronghold are not difficult to understand, and it is only general principles with which this chapter has been concerned. We have recently seen the history of what occurred at Tyre and Carthage, on the shores of the Mediterranean at the dawn of civilisation, repeat itself on the other side of the world, by the shores of an ocean on the future control of which incalculable issues in peace and war may hang. Conflicts between mighty nations have hinged upon the siege and capture of maritime strongholds in all ages; and the course of the actual operations directed against those strongholds, as well as their result, has almost always indicated the inevitable interdependence between naval and military power.

CHAPTER XXII.

THE COMMAND OF INLAND WATERS AND WATERWAYS, AND ITS INFLUENCE UPON MILITARY OPERATIONS.

It is not easy to give a satisfactory and comprehensive definition of inland waters and waterways. Under the heading of inland waters come inland seas, lagoons, and lakes. Under the heading of waterways come estuaries, narrow straits, rivers, and canals. Operations depending upon the control of an inland sea obviously involve strategical conditions somewhat different from those which arise out of the question of command of some navigable river. It is only with waters of such depth and expanse as to be navigable by vessels capable of acting as fighting-ships, that we have to do. But even with this limitation the subject will be found to embrace so wide a field, that its examination in a single chapter cannot be of a very exhaustive character. *Explanation of what is meant by inland waters and waterways.*

It is one of the distinctive features of inland waterways, when the question of their control by mobile floating force comes to be considered, that they are generally to a great extent commanded from the shore. With few rivers is it the case that the banks are too far apart for modern artillery planted on one side or the other to sweep their channel from shore to shore. Canals are, from their nature, restricted in width. Those historic maritime defiles, the Bosporus and the Dardanelles, present the conditions of great navigable rivers, although it is the custom to look *Inland waterways are generally commanded from the shore, but inland waters often are not so commanded.*

upon them rather as straits, and although their waters are salt instead of being fresh. But inland seas and lakes are sometimes of great area. The Black Sea and even the Mediterranean are in a sense inland seas, although it is not with such great expanses of salt water as these that this chapter proposes to deal. Lake Superior is of approximately the same expanse as the Adriatic, and it is larger than the Sea of Azov, the command of which played so important a *rôle* in the early Russo-Turkish wars and in the Crimean war. On the surface of a lake of this size naval combinations on a most comprehensive scale can take place, and in its influence upon land operations around its shores it may in all respects resemble a stretch of the actual ocean.

Modern tactical conditions, governed as they are by armament, tend to increase the numbers of gulfs and bays and estuaries which may fairly be regarded as inland water. At the time of the great mutiny, the Nore was quite out of reach of the shore batteries at Sheerness; nowadays a fleet could not lie at the anchorage without exposing itself to very serious damage from the land. In the days when Admiral Byng wiped Spanish naval control of the coast of Sicily out of existence, war-vessels hugging the Calabrian coast were secure from gun-fire from the Messina side of the narrows: in the present day those straits present a very genuine maritime defile, a defile the power of using which in war depends upon the attitude of the Italian military forces. The great sea-fights of Salamis and of Actium took place in waters so narrow that powerful modern ordnance planted on the adjacent shores would have dominated the tactical situation from start to finish, even supposing the rival fleets to have consisted of up-to-date ships of war. The fighting fleets of old could navigate channels and creeks where only torpedo craft can manœuvre in the present day. The waterways about the mouth of the Rhine and in Holland, many of which are too shallow for the modern fighting-ship, were the scene of remarkable amphibious operations before and during the rise of the Dutch. But changed as are the conditions, there is something still to be learnt from the fighting of old on inland waters and waterways, just as there is something still to be learnt from the influence of sea-going fleets upon the course of the Punic wars and upon the siege of Ostend, and from the strategical shortcomings— such as they were—of La Galissonière with his fleet of sailing ships-of-the-line.

For purposes of convenience it will be best to deal first with inland seas and with lakes of great area. These present conditions very analogous to those which have been considered in some of the earlier chapters of this volume. To the military forces which enjoy that great advantage, command of them affords the power of transferring the sphere of action from point to point in security. It facilitates the movement of supplies, and it often affords to the army a secure and valuable line of communications. Bodies of troops based upon an inland sea dominated by a friendly flotilla have an assured place of refuge when in difficulties, if sufficient shipping to embark them be available. Such command, in fact, exerts an influence over a land campaign in progress in the neighbourhood, which is in many respects the counterpart of that which command of the sea exerts when the theatre of land operations is fixed in a maritime district. Inland seas and lakes of this kind are, however, comparatively speaking few. And many great sheets of water, like the Caspian Sea and like some of the lakes in the north-west of Canada, have never played any important part in war, and are never likely to do so in the future.[1]

But there is one point about naval warfare in such waters

Flotillas on them generally have to be improvised during war. which has a special interest. As deep-sea communication with them rarely exists, the flotillas which fight for mastery on their surface, or which by their existence at the outset of hostilities dominate their expanse throughout the operations, are generally local flotillas. They may be, and often have been, actually created during the course of the conflict. They naturally are composed of a different type of vessel altogether from that which secures the control of the ocean in struggles between maritime nations. In the numerous campaigns which have taken place in North America, the flotillas on the great lakes of the St Lawrence basin have often played a most important part, and in most of them the improvising of a local navy or navies while war was in progress has been a prominent and characteristic feature.

Great Lakes of North America. The history of Lakes Erie and Ontario and Champlain during the eighteenth century, and the early years of the nineteenth, is indeed remarkable for its wealth in dramatic incidents of war. In the struggles for the mastery between British and French, between the forces of Great Britain and those of the revolted colonies, and between the British Empire and the United States, the control of their waters has always been a governing factor at one stage of the campaign. The map at the end of this chapter illustrates the various points in connection with these great sheets of inland water, which are about to be discussed. All three of them are of such an area, that the artillery of a century ago when mounted in shore batteries could exert no appreciable influence over the question of their command in time **Question of ship-building in such cases.** of war. And it is interesting to note to how great an extent the securing of command of their waters was dependent upon energy and skill displayed in hastily improvised dockyards: supremacy on these lakes was often almost entirely a question of the comparative rapidity with which the belligerents were able to extemporise some sort of fighting flotilla.

QUESTION OF SHIPBUILDING. 395

In 1775 the celebrated General Arnold found himself **Examples.** driven to create a flotilla on Lake Champlain, when he was contemplating the invasion of Canada. He captured two vessels, and at the same time secured the material for equipping others. He was at the time fighting on the side of the Colonists, and he had operations against Quebec in view. Twenty years before this General Amherst had similarly been obliged to improvise a little fleet, so as to wrest command of the lake from some petty French vessels which at the moment dominated its broad expanse.

In the war of 1812-14 the building operations on Lake **Lake Ontario,** Ontario were a most important feature in the struggle for **1812-14.** the domination of its waters. The British had an excellent harbour, and they were furnished with building-slips and with other conveniences for the purpose at Kingston, which was then a rising centre of inland water traffic. The United States navy, on the other hand, had to depend upon Sackett's Harbour, which offered by no means the same advantages, but the Americans showed rare skill and resource in making the most of the place. On more than one occasion during the protracted struggle the fate of the rival flotillas trembled in the balance, and their power to hold their antagonists in check really hinged upon the work of the shipwrights, who carried on their labours almost entirely in these two ports. Mahan, speaking of Kingston and Sackett's Harbour, says, "Contrary to the usual conditions of naval warfare, the two ports, not the fleets depending upon them, were the decisive elements of the Ontario campaign." A decisive victory in action between the rival flotillas did not necessarily secure finality of result so long as the two busy dockyards remained untouched. Both sides realised this, but neither could capture the naval base of the other nor destroy its establishments.

The history of the war of 1812-14 in the extreme west **Lake Erie in** is rendered especially interesting by the extent to which **1812-14.**

the question of command of Lake Erie governed the course of the operations. It is no exaggeration to say that the question of victory or defeat in the theatre of conflict round this inland sea depended entirely upon the control of its waters. Nor were the vessels which played so important a part in the campaign formidable either from their nature or their numbers. A few brigs and armed schooners constituted the entire fighting fleets. At the outset the British were supreme on the lake, and their soldiery carried war successfully into territory now known as Ohio and Michigan, not wholly unaided by Red Indian levies. This went on for some months. Then Commander Perry managed to improvise an American flotilla at Presqu'isle and near the head of the Niagara River, round a nucleus which had been won from the British by an exploit of uncommon boldness. In due course Perry's flotilla attacked and overcame that which at the commencement of hostilities had roamed the lake unchallenged, and thereupon the situation on shore was transformed as if by magic. Up to that time the control of the waters had placed the British military commander in a position to land where he liked, and this control had, as Mahan expresses it, " hung over the frontier like a pall, until finally dissipated by Perry's victory." Not only were the British forces obliged to evacuate United States territory, but they were almost immediately driven entirely out of the angle between Lakes Erie and Huron, and were thrust back to the vicinity of Lake Ontario. The American naval victory on Lake Erie was decisive of the land campaign west of the Niagara Peninsula. The ground lost was not recovered by the British till the end of the war.

Command of Lake Erie, and Brock's overthrow of Hull.

The early days of this struggle on and round Lake Erie afford a very noteworthy example of command of an inland stretch of water enabling a military force to act on interior lines. The American general Hull was operating from about Detroit against the extreme western corner of Canada, as it was then known. Another force of United States levies was advancing against the Niagara frontier. The British general Brock, a brilliant soldier whose death in the fight of Queenston near Niagara Falls was a disaster to the British only second in importance to the naval defeat at the hands of Perry, was on the watch about the western end of Lake Ontario. He suddenly embarked at the eastern end of Lake Erie, and moved by water to Malden. From there he advanced into United States territory near Detroit, attacked Hull, and compelled the surrender of that commander and his force. This done Brock hastened back again by ship to the Niagara frontier, and was ready to oppose any hostile advance at that point, before the American troops heading for it were ready to deliver their blow. The British general had by dint of rare audacity and vigour abandoned one all-important line for a moment, had thrown himself upon the enemy advancing by another line, achieving a signal success, and had then hurried back to the point of main importance. It was a fine combination of war, which fully deserved the triumph with which it was crowned at Detroit, and its success as a whole. But it was only rendered possible by the fact that a British flotilla was dominating Lake Erie and was lending itself to the execution of amphibious operations.

It has been remarked upon above how greatly the question of the command of Lake Ontario in this war depended upon the rival bases of Kingston and Sackett's Harbour. The British made an abortive attempt upon the latter. On the American side a project for dealing with Kingston was at one time entertained, but it was abandoned without ever being put in execution. The Americans attacked Toronto, which served as a subsidiary British naval base; they burnt one vessel still on the stocks there and captured one schooner, but another escaped, and the effect on the lake

Importance of the bases on Lakes Erie and Ontario.

campaign was small. Considering the great importance of the two main naval bases on Lake Ontario, it is singular that neither belligerent made any attempt to destroy that of the other by a determined operation of war. The naval and military leaders hardly made the most of their opportunities. The circumstances of the case made war on the lake to a certain extent a war of posts; but the antagonists merely pawed at the posts, they did not strike.

A keener strategical insight was displayed by the naval leaders on and round Lake Erie. Previously to Perry's victory, and while that valiant sailor was straining every nerve to complete and equip his flotilla at Presqu'isle, the British military commander in the far west was most anxious to make an attack upon the shipyard there, and to destroy the potential hostile flotilla by a joint attack of ships and troops. The importance of dealing with the embryo hostile navy before it could do mischief, the influence which it would exert over the operations as a whole if it gained the upper hand, and the obligation of the army to co-operate in an attack upon it, seem to have been fully realised. But sufficient British troops to execute the project were not available on the spot. No reinforcements could be spared from the east. And so the design came to nothing, and Perry was left unmolested by military force, to put the finishing touches to his flotilla. Had an attack upon Presqu'isle been successful, Lake Erie would have remained in British hands, and the course of the land campaign in this, at that time remote, region must in consequence have been totally different.

In warfare of this nature a budding navy, or even a navy in full blossom, may generally be far more easily destroyed by military attack than is the case in land and sea operations on a greater scale. The forces are relatively small, and the class of fighting-vessel used on these inland waters is generally more susceptible to the damage which field artillery can inflict than the ships which go to form a seagoing fleet. Attacks directed against the naval bases assume, in fact, a position in a strategical sense of paramount importance, and the eventual command of a lake may be very largely dependent upon the judicious employment of military force at the outset.

During the various campaigns in the basin of the St Lawrence the fact that Lake Champlain is an expanse of water running north and south, and that it stretches along the direct route from New York to Montreal and its vicinity, was always a matter of great strategical importance. Owing to the topographical conditions of the region on either side of the lake—a region which was in those days virtually unexplored—the only line of operations for an army moving from the Hudson towards the lower St Lawrence ran along the shores of the lake. Control of its waters was therefore essential to an army advancing northwards from New York, or southwards from Montreal. A military force, no matter how superior it might be to that opposed to it, could not advance across the frontier in either direction by this great natural line of movement, as long as a hostile fleet was in a position to act on its flank or to cut its communications. The strategical position was, on a small scale, very similar to that already described in chapter xvii. in the case of Syria and the Riviera. And one of the closing scenes of that unfortunate conflict between this country and the United States early in the nineteenth century shows that, where a line of military operations runs along the edge of a great lake, the question of local command of the waters has just as great a strategical significance as maritime control has when the line of advance of an army skirts the sea-coast. The incident has been already referred to in chapter i., in illustration of another aspect of the interdependence between land operations and naval power. The British general Prevost, with a relatively speaking formidable army, advanced

Land communications running along a lake.

from about Montreal to invade the State of New York. The flotilla which was to aid his march along the shores of Lake Champlain was, however, badly beaten at Plattsburg. In consequence of its overthrow the control of the Lake Champlain passed definitely into the keeping of the war flotilla of the United States. General Prevost, brought to a standstill, paused for a while, and then fell back into Canada, judging—and Wellington approved his decision—that the contemplated operation had become impracticable now that a hostile navy was flanking his route.

Other phases of connection between naval and military operations illustrated by warfare on the Great Lakes. And it is interesting to note that the warfare on the Great Lakes illustrates other phases of the connection between naval and military operations. The difficulty of bottling up a fleet was exemplified by Perry's exploit at Presqu'isle in getting his ships out over an awkward bar, at a time when British control of Lake Erie was complete and when the British were perfectly well aware of its impending egress. While the British commanded Lake Ontario, the military line of communications between the west and the lower St Lawrence largely followed the water route from the upper end of the lake to Kingston. During the attack of the United States troops on Fort George—they had come by water and had landed some distance west of the fort—friendly gunboats co-operated with their guns, and contributed largely to the success which attended the enterprise. The naval operations were not on an imposing scale. The military forces put in the field by the belligerents were insignificant. Neither ashore nor afloat was the campaign at all times prosecuted with tenacity of purpose or with vigour of execution. But from the story of the not uneventful struggle one fact can safely be deduced. The strategical principles involved in amphibious war are the same, whether the fighting takes place on and around an inland sea, or whether the conflict has its scene in a region which is washed by the ocean.

But when we come to consider the question of command of estuaries, of straits, of rivers, and of canals, and when we begin to investigate the influence which such command exerts over military operations in their vicinity, a new factor has to be taken account of. Waterways of this character are necessarily to a great extent dominated by the land on either side, and naval control of them must be to a great extent contingent on military support. During the Crimean war the allied fleet for a time dominated the Gulf of Finland, although the shores on either side were held by Russia: they were operating on a wide expanse of water, where guns of the fortresses scattered along the enclosing shores could not reach them unless they challenged an encounter. But when, as for instance in the case of the Dardanelles, the sea narrows to a mere channel easily swept by shore batteries, its naval control does not depend so much upon brushing hostile fighting-ships aside or destroying them, as upon the relations in which the forces afloat stand to the forces on shore. To secure the control of a restricted waterway traversing territory in the hands of the enemy must necessarily be an operation of great difficulty, and modern engines of destruction undoubtedly tend to increase this difficulty. *Estuaries, straits, rivers, and canals.*

As a general rule, estuaries and rivers do not lend themselves to the passage of vessels of deep draught. The consequence is that in struggles to secure and to retain command of such waterways against hostile military force on shore, a navy is restricted to the use of small ships, and, unless these are especially constructed for the purpose, they may not be well adapted to withstand bombardment from the land. Navigation is, moreover, often intricate, and this may add greatly to the difficulties of effectively using a vessel's powers of offence. The channels can easily be blocked by sunken ships or by booms, and the development of submarine mining in the last half century has added greatly to the perils of naval operations conducted under such cir- *Generally a case of small vessels.*

cumstances. It is the same in the case of narrow straits like that of Messina, and like the arms of the sea which separate the Danish islands from each other and from Sweden, except that channels of this class can be passed by powerful battleships which have not much to fear from light artillery. The risk of submarine mines is much the same in either case. Canals, the naval command of which in war could seriously influence land operations in the territory which they traverse, are not numerous. Such artificial waterways are so narrow that their banks would have to be in occupation of friendly troops before warships could pass them; and if their use involves the passage of locks, there can be still less question of ships passing through them supposing the land on either hand to be in an enemy's occupation.

Only limited number of rivers navigable by fighting craft.

Only a limited number of rivers are navigable for fighting craft, and of these many, like the Amazon, the Volga, and the Yangtsekiang, have never played an important part in war owing to their geographical position. The Don and the Neva have both exerted a remarkable influence over naval and military history, in that they bore down the beginnings of Russian naval power to the sea, although the question of their control has not otherwise raised problems of strategical interest. The Danube, athwart the line of advance from Bessarabia to the Golden Horn, has acted rather as an obstacle to military movements than as a line of military or naval operations. As in the case of inland seas, it is to the New World that we have to look for the finest illustrations of the relations between the command of great navigable rivers and the course of campaigns in their basin, and the story of the Mississippi during the American Civil War stands alone as an example of a form of warfare possessing an interest which is all its own. The campaign on that great waterway will be so frequently referred to in the course of this chapter, that an outline sketch of its objects, and of the methods by which those objects were attained, will serve as a useful introduction.

The Federals, it will be remembered, commanded the sea from the outset. The upper waters of the Mississippi, and also of its great navigable tributary the Ohio, traversed States favouring the Union. But from Cairo down to the sea—the map facing p. 244 illustrates this remarkable amphibious campaign—the mighty river ran through Secessionist territory, and was navigated by a Secessionist flotilla.

The campaigns on the Mississippi in the American Civil War.

At an early stage of the great struggle the authorities at Washington began to realise the importance of this artery of communication to their opponents, and began to perceive that by getting it under their own control they would cut off the States of Texas, Louisiana, and Arkansas from those lying on the left bank of the river. From those undeveloped western States the Confederates drew supplies and reinforcements, while from their position they were not open to invasion from the north like Kentucky and Virginia, which abutted on prosperous and well-populated districts faithful to the Union. The seizure of the Mississippi by the North would cut Secessionist territory in two, it would open up a line of operations by which the eastern portion of that vast territory could be attacked from in rear, and it would, in consequence of Federal command of the sea, enable the military authorities on the Potomac to transfer troops by water from the Chesapeake to Arkansas, or from Illinois to the coast of the Carolinas.

Operations to gain control of the great waterway were set on foot from both ends. Kentucky was overrun, and the Ohio was secured in the north. In the south, the mouths of the Mississippi and New Orleans were captured from the side of the sea. And while a formidable river flotilla, organised on the Ohio, began to work down-stream from Cairo supported by an imposing military force, Farragut from the Gulf of Mexico operated northwards from the delta, displaying that resource and daring in his combinations, which has made his name famous among the seamen of the nineteenth century.

The Confederates for a time seem hardly to have paid sufficient attention to the strategical defence of the all-important waterway. A flotilla was organised. Batteries were equipped on its lowest reaches. Defences were erected commanding the channel some distance below Cairo, which gave the Federals considerable trouble. But it was not till the hostile naval and military forces converging towards each other from the north and south were practically in contact, that a supreme effort was put forth to contest the control of the river, and that Vicksburg, hastily fortified in the first instance and garrisoned with only an insignificant force, developed into a great place of arms held by an army, and became the scene of operations of war of surpassing interest which were to exert decisive influence over the course of the war as a whole.

Farragut, coming up from the south, ran past the batteries of Vicksburg at the end of June 1862, before they had blossomed into a formidable barrier. This was fifteen months after the outbreak of hostilities, when the strain of war was already beginning to tell upon the limited resources of the Confederation, and when a great blow struck in the west might have transformed the entire military situation from Texas to Maryland. But the river was falling. The admiral himself reported to Washington that an army of 15,000 to 20,000 men would be required to capture the growing centre of strategical force which was springing up. And shortly afterwards, the flotilla which had worked its way up the river by dint of so happy a combination of skill and resolution from the Gulf of Mexico, returned, with the exception of a few vessels, to New Orleans. Thereupon the formidable military forces of the Secessionists which were now gathered about Vicksburg, initiated active operations in a southerly direction. They recovered ground which had been lost. They created a new fortress at Port Hudson. And so the Union leaders, after they had for a brief space practically held command of the waterway from Cairo to the sea, found themselves confronted by two ugly-looking improvised strongholds which effectually separated their northern from their southern forces, and they were faced by a problem of extraordinary complexity owing to the nature of the country lying north of the mushroom fortress Vicksburg, a fortress which would have to be taken if the Mississippi was to cease to be a Confederate highway.

It took a year of chequered warfare in the swamps and "bayous" of the great river and of its meandering affluents, before Vicksburg and Port Hudson were in Federal hands. The two fortresses fell almost simultaneously in July 1863. From that time forward the fighting forces of the Union afloat and ashore dominated the great river. They used its channel as a line of communications and as an artery of supply. They cut off Arkansas and Louisiana from the rest of the Seceded States. And, using the river as a base, they began those active operations eastwards which carried Sherman to Atlanta in the heart of Georgia and from thence to the sea, and which led up to ultimate victory in the Atlantic watershed beyond the Alleghanies.

In the two years' struggle for possession of the Mississippi, the land forces of the North had co-operated loyally with the river flotillas, and often with rare effect. On the Confederate side also the troops and the ships had acted in close concert, both on the defensive and on the offensive. The details of these remarkable operations are worthy of the most careful study, for they present the finest illustration of a certain class of warfare to be found in history. Reference will be made farther on to certain incidents which occurred during the progress of the singular struggle. But looking at the question from the broad strategical point of view, the lesson of the Mississippi is that ships alone cannot secure the command of a river, even when they are handled with the utmost skill and fortitude. They must be supported by military force. In action the flotillas of the Union almost always overcame the Confederate vessels, which were not so powerful and which were less numerous. The land forces of the North were superior to those which confronted them. But the difficulties of the country through which the river ran from Memphis to Vicksburg hampered military movements to such an extent that the Federal army while moving southwards had no elbow-room, and that superiority of force could not be brought effectively into play in consequence.

Question of current.
In all naval operations on a river the current plays an important part, in that it increases or decreases the speed of vessels according as they are going up or down stream. The rate at which a ship is moving has a considerable effect upon its prospects of running past artillery placed on shore, and therefore when a flotilla is endeavouring to pass shore batteries, its chances of success are greater when it is descending than when it is ascending. Thus it has always been held to be far easier for a fleet to force the Bosporus and Dardanelles from the side of the Black Sea than from the side of the Ægean, the difference in speed amounting to several knots owing to the current.* At one time General Grant, operating against Vicksburg, wished some gunboats lying above the fortress to run past it for operations below. Admiral Porter professed himself ready to make the attempt, but he pointed out that once below the batteries his vessels would not be able to get up stream again past them. Some of the most brilliant exploits of the American Civil War arose out of the passage of formidable batteries by flotillas

* Duckworth[2] ran up the Dardanelles without difficulty in 1807, but his fleet was roughly handled coming down. The Turks were, however, taken by surprise the first time, while they were ready on the second occasion.

and individual ships; but the vessels were almost invariably running down stream and not up.

The question of current is important because, although the history of operations on the Danube, on the St Lawrence, and on the Mississippi and its great tributaries, seems to show that on these great waterways ships could generally run the gauntlet of batteries in the past, it remains to be seen whether this will prove to be the case in future. The very rapid fire and the great power of modern guns, added to their increased range and to their improved accuracy, make it certain that vessels running past batteries under the conditions of to-day will be hit many times, and will be hit hard, before they are out of danger. The application of armour will no doubt place the ship more on an equality with the shore gun. But adequate protection means an enormous weight, and it necessarily raises difficulties as to draught of water. It must, on the other hand, be remembered that river steamers of the present day possess great speed and ample manœuvring power, and that this tends in some measure to compensate for disadvantages which they suffer from increased efficacy of ordnance. For operations of this kind belligerents are generally at the outset unprepared. Flotillas adapted to the peculiar conditions have to be created, a process which must take a certain length of time. As far as the relative positions of a river navy and of batteries on shore are concerned, the probability is that in conflicts on inland waters of the future, the batteries will at first have the advantage, but that as operations proceed fighting-vessels adapted to this class of warfare will appear, and may be able to fully hold their own.
<small>Question whether in future armed river-vessels will be able to run past batteries.</small>

But guns mounted on the banks are not what a modern river navy has most to dread from an enemy on shore. It is in channels and narrow waters that submarine mines and torpedoes are especially formidable, and that the moral
<small>Submarine mines and torpedoes in river warfare.</small>

effect exerted by these engines of destruction is most far-reaching.[3] The course of amphibious campaigns on rivers, estuaries, and canals is certain to be greatly influenced henceforward by the ingenuity and resource displayed by the opposing sides in their use of floating and submerged explosives.

Submarine mining first attracted general attention in the War of Secession. Earlier attempts made so far back as the American War of Independence, the efforts of Fulton early in the nineteenth century, and crude machines such as those which the Russians tried in the Baltic in 1855, had led to very little result. And it is interesting to note that the Confederate engineers in the early days of the great struggle seem to have looked rather askance at this kind of warfare. As already mentioned on p. 116, their material was of a primitive description. But as the conflict progressed, as the fight became more embittered, and as the naval and military resources of the South were more and more driven back upon the defensive on shore and afloat, the submarine mine became a recognised weapon, and it was employed in defence of rivers with a considerable measure of success. A river flotilla operating in conjunction with a military force on one or both banks, has not perhaps much to fear from hostile mines. The troops as they advance can cut the wires. Countermining operations are generally highly effective, if deliberately carried out. It is when the ships are alone and are possibly exposed to hostile fire, that their progress is likely to be seriously impeded by mine-fields.

An incident in 1864 serves to bring into prominence the value of mines as a means of refusing passage of rivers, and at the same time offers an interesting example of the relations which exist between the naval command of waterways and military operations in their vicinity. The main line of communications of the Secessionist forces in Richmond

BOOMS AND OBSTRUCTIONS.   409

with the Carolinas and with the southern States generally, was a railway which crossed the river Roanoake about seventy miles from the city. The Roanoake runs into Pamlico Sound, and this the Federals held. With the idea of destroying the important railway bridges, a flotilla of seven gunboats was despatched on an expedition up this navigable river. The gunboats got safely almost to within striking resistance of their objective. Suddenly, however, they came upon a mine-field. All but two of the vessels were either sunk or disabled, and the expedition had to return to Pamlico Sound foiled in its project, and having effected nothing to damage the opposing side.

Rivers and canals can of course be blocked by booms and sunken obstructions. Their efficacy depends, however, almost entirely upon whether the obstacles are, or are not, defended by military force on the banks. Mere artificial barriers may cause delay, but they cannot permanently forbid passage to an energetically commanded flotilla. Farragut forced the elaborate obstructions below New Orleans, although these were protected by Confederate artillery and musketry fire: it proved, however, to be an operation of no little difficulty, and was in itself one of the finest of the many gallant exploits which enrich the annals of the fight for the Mississippi. But a skilfully designed combination of mine-fields, booms, and sunken obstructions might in the present day totally defeat all efforts of a mobile naval force, if this were unsupported by troops.

Booms and sunken obstructions.

In the Russo-Turkish war of 1877 the Russians at an early stage of the campaign succeeded in barring the channel of the Danube at two points near Galatz. By this method they shut off a portion of the river from the Ottoman seagoing fleet, which, it will be remembered, commanded the Black Sea and could run up the stream far above Galatz. Later on they fenced off a similar stretch between Nicopolis and Rustchuk and this enabled them to make their main

Russians on the Danube in 1877.

crossing of the formidable obstacle at Sistova within the protected reach. In these operations the object of the side controlling the channel was to prevent the military passage of the enemy across it, the enemy holding only one bank of the river. The strategical situation, in fact, differed very widely from that on the Mississippi. The purpose of the Russians was not so much to obtain control of the waterway themselves, or even to deprive their opponents of general control of it, as to get certain short stretches of it completely into their power, and to exclude hostile ships altogether from those stretches. The objective of the Ottoman flotilla was, or ought to have been, to keep the channel open by keeping constantly on the watch and on the move. Compared to that of the Mississippi, the story of the Danube in 1877 serves to bring out the strategical distinction between a waterway transverse to the general operations and thus forming in the main an obstacle, and a waterway coinciding with a general line of operations and thus forming a channel of movement and of communications. But the apathy of the Turks in the later campaign discounts its value as an illustration of this form of war, although the comparative ease with which the Russians barred off stretches of the river at will in defiance of the Ottoman fighting-ships, is a point deserving of special note.

During the course of some remarkable flotilla operations amid the "bayous" north of Vicksburg—"bayou" is a local term for the sluggish channels of tributaries of the Mississippi running through marshes covered with undergrowth—Admiral Porter's flotilla was nearly captured by the Confederate troops. These closed in in rear of his ships, and they constructed a barrier across the channel. He succeeded, however, in communicating with General Sherman who was not far off, and who brought a force up in boats and drove the enemy away.

Difficulties aris- In river operations, quite apart from the normal difficulties of navigation, a flotilla is exposed to the risk of the river falling, and of shallow stretches becoming impassable. After the fall of Vicksburg a Federal armada proceeded up the Red River, the troops being carried in steamers under protection by some fighting-ships. But after a time the waters began to fall, and the expedition found itself shut off from the Mississippi, not by a barrier created by the Secessionists, but by rapids which had sprung up with the decreasing volume of the stream and which forbade the descent of the vessels, even after they had been lightened. The troops were, however, promptly set to work to build up dams with timber and such other materials as came to hand, and by this means the depth of the river was so regulated that the flotilla was able to withdraw in safety to its starting-point. *ing from rivers rising and falling.*

It is only in alluvial valleys that obstructions could, under ordinary conditions, be circumvented and river defences turned by the expedient of digging canals for the shipping to pass through. Excavating channels for vessels, as a phase of military operations, is no new thing in war. Xerxes dug a canal through an isthmus in Macedonia on his way from the Dardanelles to Thessaly. In the days of Canute a canal was excavated round the southern end of London Bridge, then apparently a defensible structure, so as to enable the Danish flotilla to avoid the bridge and to gain the upper reaches of the tideway. A boat canal was dug by the British force below New Orleans before the unsuccessful attack on that city in 1814. In the campaign for the control of the Mississippi much labour was expended by the Federals in creating new channels by which hostile defences could be avoided; but these undertakings were rarely crowned with any success. Vicksburg is situated at the re-enterant of a great loop of the river, and a canal across this loop was cut by the troops of the Union; but, owing apparently to faulty design, the canal was a complete *Digging canals.*

failure and it was never used: it was seriously damaged by a sudden flood when nearly completed. Operations of this kind are hardly in keeping with an active plan of campaign, and that soldiers of so robust a type as Grant and Sherman should have wasted much time and expended much military labour on delving on a great scale in the swamps of an alluvial valley, shows the extraordinary character of the problem with which they had to contend.

Co-operation between flotilla and troops on banks, the essence of such operations.
From the above paragraphs it can be seen that a struggle for the command of a great inland waterway is always likely to lead to operations of an abnormal kind, and is certain to test the skill and resource of the opposing commanders to no small extent. The essence of such operations lies in the judicious application of amphibious force— in the co-operation of troops on the banks with vessels in the channel. Farragut's bold advance after the capture of New Orleans from the Gulf of Mexico to above Vicksburg was carried out almost entirely without the support of land detachments: it partook therefore of the character of a raid, and its influence over the course of the campaign was in consequence not of a decisive kind. The move down the river from Cairo, on the other hand, was carried out by a flotilla and an army acting in concert. The force on land and the force on the water moved hand in hand, extending their influence and their control southwards. What these won from the enemy, they kept.

Operating under these conditions, the military forces can afford great assistance to the ships; and, conversely, the flotilla can effectively second the efforts of the troops. If there are batteries sweeping the channel and jeopardising the ships, detachments working along the banks can take them in flank or in reverse: if there are barriers, booms, mine-fields, and so forth, in the stream, an army supporting the forces afloat can drive away the defenders of these obstructions, after which the display of a little ingenuity will soon overcome such impediment to navigation as they may offer. On the other hand, if the army operating along the general direction of the waterway be brought to a standstill by the enemy in position, warships following its course can take the adversary in flank and in reverse, and may thus be able to facilitate the solution of the tactical problem which confronts the troops. The movements of the military are greatly simplified if their impedimenta can be carried by water. And, as was often the case on the Mississippi, it will sometimes be practicable to convey the whole army in transports which follow the fighting flotilla, the troops only being landed when movements on shore are necessary to support the general advance by water, or when the circumstances of the case call for some set of operations of a purely military character based on the river. As an example of this kind of co-operation and of the peculiar situations which arise in this form of warfare, may be quoted General Pope's move down the Mississippi from Columbus, in association with the Federal flotilla.

A few miles below Columbus the river forms an inverted S, enclosing two horseshoes of land. Within the first bend of the stream there was in those days an island, which came to be know as Island No. 10. It was a narrow island about two miles long, and near the left bank. At the next loop, and situated on the right bank, was the town of New Madrid. The Confederates had fortified Island No. 10, as well as the left bank of the river above it, and they had also placed New Madrid in a state of defence. *Operations below Columbus on the Mississippi in 1862, as example.*

General Pope, advancing along the right bank of the Mississippi, had moved down to New Madrid before the flotilla was ready, and after a month's siege he captured the place. He then set up batteries on the right bank below the town to bar the river to the Confederate flotilla should it try to ascend the stream. The Confederates responded by erecting batteries along the left bank, at intervals below Island No. 10 down to Tiptonville. This was the situation when, a fortnight after the fall of New Madrid, the Federal ironclads and smaller vessels which had been fitting out higher up, steamed down from the north full of fight and approached Island No. 10.

But Commodore Foote, who was in command, found the defences too formidable to attack, and so a month passed in long-range bombardments which achieved no great results. All this time, however, Pope was not idle. His soldiers cut a canal through the swamps across the horseshoe north of the island, and by this means he enabled light vessels to pass from the upper Mississippi to New Madrid without running the gauntlet of the batteries. A number of transports were, moreover, got down through this artificial channel. Then one night, when all was ready, some of the Confederates' guns above Island No. 10 were spiked by an armed boat-expedition, and two or three nights later one of the Federal gunboats, taking advantage of a thunderstorm, dropped down past the island batteries, making the perilous passage in safety. Two nights later a second vessel descended. Next day the two ships together tackled the Confederate batteries above Tiptonville and silenced them after a short fight, whereupon General Pope's army at once began crossing the river near that point under protection of their guns.

The Secessionist army on the Kentucky side of the river now found itself caught in a regular trap. The swamps

ISLAND NO. 10.

which are shown on the sketch were impassable for troops, except along devious paths. The Federal gunboats swept the bank of the river. Part of General Pope's force barred the way southwards. There was no hope of escape, nor even any possibility of offering a creditable resistance in such a situation, and in consequence 7000 men laid down their arms, their capitulation being followed the same evening by the surrender of the garrison of Island No. 10.

From above the island to Tiptonville is only a distance of a few miles, even following the tortuous course of the river. The operations narrated above lasted over a period of nearly six weeks. But the brilliant success which, in the end, attended the well-considered co-operation between the naval and military forces of the North, fully justified the slow deliberation with which the operations were conducted. Not only was an important stretch of the great waterway definitely secured, but the enemy's advanced line of defence was broken through, and the hostile forces which had been especially detailed to guard the river against attack down stream, were wiped out of existence. The fighting round Island No. 10 is typical of the methods by which the troops and sailors of the Union gradually gained possession, not only of the great artery of the Mississippi, but also of other important waterways which swelled its volume. It serves to show how an army on shore, and sailors navigating inland waters, can mutually assist each other to gain the end in view. And it is of especial interest in that it took place at a time when the belligerents had little experience of this class of warfare, and when they were devising methods of war for which campaigns of the past afforded few precedents.

When one side has gained the control of some great inland waterway, and possesses the necessary transports capable of navigating its channels, troops can be very rapidly moved from point to point along its course. From the strategical point of view the command of a river like the Danube may

Inland water= ways as means of rapidly moving troops for strategical purposes.

confer upon a military commander even greater liberty of action than command of the sea does, because difficulties as to landing generally disappear. The best illustration of this in modern times is afforded by Lord Wolseley's campaign of 1882 in Egypt. By making use of the Suez Canal and landing at Ismailia, the British expeditionary force acted on interior lines against Arabi Pasha. The sudden move through the canal by the bulk of the army, while a brigade was left in Alexandria, came as a complete surprise to the Egyptians; and a firm hold was gained on a portion of the intended line of military operations before the defenders were in a position to offer effective resistance. It must be remembered that many of the estuaries of the Chesapeake, naval command of which played such an important part in the campaigns of Virginia related on pp. 289-296, might fairly be classed as inland waters. The conditions governing the command of a great river, or of a canal, differ widely from those upon which command of the sea depends. But once that command has been established, its strategical influence over land operations may be very similar to that which so often follows upon maritime supremacy.

Fortresses on rivers and estuaries. In olden times, and even down to within a century ago or less, the question of control of a river on which a fortress stood was of almost vital importance if that fortress came to be besieged. Many strongholds which have played a great part in history are situated upon navigable rivers. It is a natural situation for a centre of communications and an emporium of trade, and formerly fortifications sprang up round important cities almost as a matter of course, transforming them into fortresses. It was, moreover, also the practice to construct places of arms for the special purpose of dominating the channels of principal waterways from one or other bank. And when fixed defences placed on such a site came to be a military objective in war, command of the stream was necessarily a question of great importance, and the operations on its waters often lent a peculiar interest to struggles for the possession of the stronghold.

There are few more thrilling stories than that of the forcing of the boom at Derry and the relief of the devoted city.[4] A very few years later, at the opposite corner of Europe, Peter the Great, after failing in a first attempt upon the Turkish stronghold of Azov, made with military force alone, created a flotilla 300 miles up the Don: at his second attempt he by means of his ships cut the place off from the Ottoman navy which was cruising at the great river's mouth, and he forced it to capitulate. The many sieges of Antwerp, the siege of Dantzig, and the ever-memorable siege of Ismail, where Suvarof's gunboats played so important a part with their artillery, illustrate the same principle.[5] *Examples of attacks on fortresses so placed, under former conditions.*

In 1793 a Republican army was besieging Williamstadt in Holland. The assailants were pressing the garrison hard, and had established batteries on the glacis near the great navigable creek on which the stronghold lay. But three British gunboats pushed up the creek one night, and, coming abreast of the French batteries under cover of the morning fog, opened such a telling fire on them that they were abandoned. The same evening the siege was raised. This illustrates the importance of the command of the channel in such a case.

Under modern conditions a place of arms on a navigable waterway would, however, almost certainly be astride of its channel; and the control of the channel, at least within the area enclosed by the defence works, would almost necessarily be in the hands of the besieged. For such a fortress to be closely invested the command of the river must rest with the assailants, but from the conditions of the case these would hardly be in a position to use their war-vessels to much effect in the actual siege operations. *Changes introduced by modern conditions.*

Recent warfare has provided no examples of such a situation, and the course of operations arising out of it is matter of conjecture. But campaigns of the future may hinge upon the siege of a Coblenz as it exists to-day, a typical modern fortress astride a great navigable waterway. The efforts of a formidable army may yet be concentrated upon the capture of some Plevna, not like Vicksburg perched on a plateau overhanging the river, but covering a wide area on either side of a broad expanse of water, defended by booms and mine-fields and by all the other devices which ingenuity grafted on science can produce.[6]

The conquest of Canada as illustrating the subject treated of in chapter.
The campaign on the Great Lakes early in the nineteenth century, the fight for the Mississippi during the American Civil War, the operations on the Danube in 1877, the transfer of military force from Alexandria to the Bitter Lakes five years later, all serve to illustrate the interdependence which may exist between command of inland waters, and strategical combinations in the territory through which they run. There is, however, a war to which no reference has yet been made, every incident of which can be quoted as exemplifying the subject-matter of this chapter, and a sketch of which can hardly fail to be of some interest to a military or to a naval reader. It is a tale worth telling, a tale of daring and resolute endeavour, a tale the central episode of which every British schoolboy knows or ought to know even if its full significance is unappreciated, a tale of how the destinies of a whole continent were changed by the happy combination of military with naval force—a tale of the land and the sea.

The general plan of campaign.
To the elder Pitt the capture of Louisbourg, already referred to in former chapters, meant merely an advance by one stage on that road towards British domination of North America and towards the annexation of New France, which the Great Commoner had resolved that his country

should follow. One hundred and thirty years before, the English flag had waved for a brief period over the fortress of Quebec. But two subsequent attempts to wrest the key of the St Lawrence out of the hands of France had most signally failed, and all efforts made to reach the great river from the south by land had been repulsed by the holders of its banks and channel, and had come to nought. Pitt was resolved that what had been so well begun in Cape Breton Island should be carried through to its consummation, regardless of difficulties and dangers. Louisbourg was merely to be the opening scene in a mighty drama. He had set his heart on the total destruction of the enemy's power on the far side of the North Atlantic, and on adding to the dominions of the British crown the region of the great lakes and the lone land stretching from their shores towards the frozen north. And to carry his projects into execution he drew up a plan of campaign not ill calculated to achieve success, and he selected as his instruments commanders worthy of being entrusted with so difficult a task.

From the two sketch plans on page 429 the general scheme of the contemplated operations will be readily understood. There were to be three separate, converging lines of operations. A small force from Pennsylvania was to march to the Niagara and to gain a footing on Lake Ontario. A larger body of troops, under Amherst, was to move on Montreal by Lake Champlain. But it was upon the third expedition that Pitt mainly pinned his hopes. This was to be a conjunct naval and military enterprise. The force was to sail up the estuary of the St Lawrence and was to strike a decisive blow at the heart of French military power, the historic fortress of Quebec. That formidable stronghold once taken, a British force dominating Lake Ontario, and Montreal in Amherst's hands,—and the cause of France in North America was lost.

To command the army destined for Quebec, Pitt, scorning

The rival forces and commanders.

the claims of seniority and setting the cabals of court favourites at defiance, chose the young soldier whose leadership had contributed so greatly to the triumph of Louisbourg, Wolfe. And with Wolfe he associated a seaman not unworthy of participating in the most brilliant operation ever undertaken in unison by the British army and the British navy. It was not to be the fate of Admiral Saunders in years to come to command a fleet in battle on the open sea— no stately battleship nor greyhound cruiser bears his name; but by his strenuous and devoted support of his comrade in arms he made Wolfe's victory possible. And if his fame has been overshadowed by that of the general who fell at the moment of triumph in the Battle of the Plains, he ranks as an empire-builder among the very foremost of those naval and military chiefs who have made this country what it is.

Wolfe's force consisted of 9000 men. The transports and the fleet proceeded from Louisbourg up the estuary of the St Lawrence, and successfully braved the dangers of the intricate navigation of a channel which was then almost unknown. The passage of the armada up the tideway without pilots was of happy augury for future victory. The whole expeditionary force arrived in safety within striking distance of its formidable objective. And its arrival in the basin below Quebec caused no little consternation within the precincts of the famous fortress and capital of the French dominions in North America. But the commander of the defending army, the Marquis de Montcalm, alone was undismayed. A gallant and far-seeing soldier, whose prowess in fight British troops had learnt to appreciate by bitter experience the previous year, Montcalm combined with a natural genius for war, a fortitude in adversity, a strength of character, and a rectitude of purpose amid surroundings at once sordid and corrupt, which, even before the enemy was in the gate, had won for him the implicit confidence and warm regard of the sturdy settlers on whom the brunt of battle mainly was to fall. When on the 27th June the British armada disembarked its troops at the upper end of the Isle of Orleans, the French general, trusting to the efficient defences of the fortress and to the natural strength of the Heights of Abraham beyond it to make that side secure, moved the bulk of his army into position between the rivers Montmorency and St Charles, and there calmly awaited the next move of the invaders.

Arrival of Wolfe before Quebec.

Montcalm had the advantage of numbers; but a large part of his force consisted of half-trained militia, while Wolfe's army was an army of veterans. The French commander acted wisely when he adopted a defensive attitude, and when he left the initiative to his naval and military antagonists who now found themselves confronted with a problem of uncommon difficulty. An assault on the fortress was out of the question. Montcalm's forces in their lines of Beauport offered no attractions for a frontal attack. The river channel was dominated by the guns of Quebec. So Wolfe, after transferring part of his troops to Point Lévis where batteries were set up to bombard the city, moved the bulk of his army across the St Lawrence to a point below the outflow of the Montmorency so as to threaten the left flank of the French. Nor was the sister service inactive. A flotilla successfully ran the batteries of the fortress, proceeded up stream, and threatened the French line of supplies from Montreal and upper Canada. For a whole month, however, Montcalm remained quiescent, except for an abortive night raid against the batteries on Point Lévis. Then on the 31st of July Wolfe delivered a desperate attack upon the French left flank, part of the assaulting force crossing the Montmorency, and part of it being shipped across the main channel and landed in front of the enemy's position; but the assailants were beaten off with heavy loss, and during the month of August the rival forces remained face to face watching each other.

The Montmorency fight.

Difficulties of both sides.

The hopes of the defenders were rising high. Montcalm was, it is true, seriously inconvenienced by the British warships which had passed up the St Lawrence. His communications with Montreal were in jeopardy — he had indeed been constrained to detach part of his force to guard his right above the fortress. The gun-fire from Point Lévis was, moreover, laying the city of Quebec in ruins. Supplies were none too plentiful and were becoming a source of grave anxiety. But, on the other hand, the situation of the British was far from reassuring. The battlements of the fortress were untouched. The enemy's position at Beauport appeared to be unassailable. Summer was melting into autumn, and all ranks knew only too well that in a few weeks winter would lay its icy grip upon the land, would arrest the navigation of the St Lawrence, and would compel the expeditionary force to abandon the enterprise unless matters could be brought to a crisis beforehand. Worst of all, Wolfe, although undaunted by failure, was prostrated with a mortal sickness and incapacitated from active command. All ranks had learnt to revere this leader of men; he exerted over high and low who came in contact with him — even over those who merely saw him — a strange magnetic influence. And his absence at so critical and anxious a time added to the gloom which was beginning to spread through the invaders' bivouacs, and which augured ill for the ultimate success of an undertaking of which the full difficulties had scarcely been appreciated when the expeditionary force had first cast anchor off the Isle of Orleans.

Wolfe's great move up stream.

The one element of hope for the British lay in the command of that great waterway which at the moment divided their military forces into three detachments, one force on the left bank below the Montmorency, another on the Isle of Orleans, a third at Point Lévis. With the river absolutely under control of the attendant warships, Wolfe was

CONQUEST OF CANADA.

in a position to shift his troops about at will, and all the time he was lying grievously indisposed and racked with fever, a project was shaping itself in his fertile brain. Late in August a force of 1200 men was sent up the channel in transports to make feints at various points for a distance of thirty miles above Cap Rouge, so as to harass and perplex the French. Then Wolfe, still weak and ill, withdrew his men from the camp below the Montmorency to the Isle of Orleans, and on the 4th of September ships and transports carrying five months' provisions ran past the fortress batteries by night and joined Admiral Holmes' division, which had been operating up-stream. Next day seven battalions were quietly marched from Point Lévis to nearly opposite Cap Rouge. The troops left at the camp on the Isle of Orleans made demonstrations of attack, the batteries of Point Lévis bombarded Quebec with eager assiduity, below the city Admiral Saunders' fleet constantly threatened Montcalm's main position, and under cover of feints and alarms and cannonade the great transfer of military force from right to left was effectually concealed from the watchful eye of the French commander. Holmes' ships sailed up and down above the fortress, bewildering the detachments of defenders which were echeloned on that side by their mysterious movements. By every kind of stratagem and ruse which control of the waterway made practicable, the fact was disguised that the British general had massed the bulk of his resources some miles above the city which he had come to take, and that he was devising a singularly daring plan.

At last, on the night of the 12th, 1600 men in boats, under Wolfe himself, dropped down the channel from above Cap Rouge with the ebb tide, and pulled silently into the Anse de Foulon. Twenty-four volunteers scaled the rugged cliff and overpowered the picquet at the top by a sudden rush. The troops swarmed up the rocky pathway behind

The surprise of the Heights of Abraham and fall of Quebec.

them. And by early dawn, while Saunders with boats filled with troops and marines was making a pretence of landing on the Beauport flats, 4000 British soldiers were drawn up on the Heights of Abraham, ready to march upon Quebec.

Montcalm was detained for a brief space by Saunders. But no sooner did he learn that the British were in force close to Quebec than he hastened over from Beauport with all the troops he could collect, and formed them up for battle. But it was too late. In the combat which ensued Wolfe's army was victorious, both commanders falling in the fight. The French force, which consisted largely of militia, retreated in confusion. The vanquished army abandoned the city and fled in disorder round the British left by a devious route for thirty miles towards Montreal, leaving the invaders to devote all attention to the capture of the stronghold. The garrison made a show of resistance at first; but five days after the battle the commandant yielded, just at the moment when a considerable portion of the defeated army, which had been rallied by Lévis and had been joined by detachments from on guard above Cap Rouge, was rapidly approaching to make an effort to retrieve the situation. The relieving army retired. And a month later Saunders' fleet, accompanied by many transports conveying the sick and wounded, sailed down the St Lawrence, while a garrison of 7000 men under General Murray was left to hold the captured stronghold through the winter months against Lévis, a not unworthy successor of Montcalm, who, however, withdrew his troops to Montreal to prepare them for an early spring campaign.

An appreciation of Wolfe. Wolfe's death in the moment of victory has surrounded his final exploit with a halo of romance which has tended somewhat to obscure the more solid virtues of his leadership. "The horrors of the night, the precipice scaled by Wolfe, the empire he with a handful of men added to England,

and the glorious catastrophe of terminating life just when his fame began—ancient story may be ransacked and ostentatious philosophy thrown into the account, before an episode can be found to rank with Wolfe's." Pitt's speech in the House of Commons voiced the public estimate formed at the time of what the general had achieved, and it represents the opinion of his services which obtains to-day. His countrymen, dazzled by the triumph on the Heights of Abraham, have been inclined to forget what went before, to overlook the events which led up to that astonishing victory, to ignore the consummate skill with which control of the St Lawrence was turned to account, and to disregard the happy employment by himself and his naval associates of that liberty of strategic action which is an attribute of amphibious force. They have not appreciated at its full value Wolfe's masterly campaign, nor have they realised that this youthful, queer-looking, red headed, disease-stricken soldier from peaceful Westerham in Kent was a veritable Admirable Crichton among warriors,[7] an instrument in the hands of a maritime nation fashioned, as it were, for the express purpose of grafting a delicate and complex military enterprise upon dominion of the sea.

Nor did the capture of Quebec involve of necessity and at once an incorporation of the fair province of New France within the growing empire of the British people. Amherst's force, advancing northwards by the Champlain route, had made far from rapid progress. It had been brought to an abrupt standstill on the lake by a few insignificant, ill-armed, hostile vessels, which dominated its waters in default of anything to contest their supremacy. It had been necessary to call a halt, to establish building-slips, and to summon shipwrights from the coast so as to create a flotilla capable of wresting control of the lake from the French sailors. By the time that this had been accomplished the season was too far spent to continue the advance. This central detach-

Movements of the other columns.

ment of invaders went, therefore, into winter quarters, after having barely made its presence felt in the St Lawrence valley. The third expedition, on the other hand, had achieved a notable triumph in capturing Niagara, and in establishing itself firmly on Lake Ontario at the upper end of the coveted territory. So that when the campaign closed for the year, British troops were fixed fast at either end of the French possessions on the great North American waterway, and a force wintering on the shores of Lake Champlain was favourably situated for delivering a stroke at Montreal as soon as the melting of the winter snows should invite resumption of hostilities.

Preparations for 1760. Pitt was not the man to leave a task half finished. His plan for 1760 was that Amherst with a strong body of troops should advance down the St Lawrence from Lake Ontario, that a smaller force should push north from Lake Champlain, and that Murray with the garrison of Quebec should move on up the river, whenever the breaking of the winter ice which choked up the channel should permit fighting-ships and transports to reach the captured stronghold from the open sea.

Lévis' attack on Quebec. These fighting-ships and transports arrived at Quebec in the very nick of time. The troops left in the fortress were short of provisions, and they lacked the warm clothing necessary to withstand the rigours of a Canadian winter. They suffered severely, isolated as they were in the ruined city. A large proportion of the force was affected with scurvy, the whole of it was weak from want of food, and when the snows began to disappear Murray's little army was in no condition for undertaking active military operations. But no sooner did the ice begin to break than Lévis, bent on striking a blow before reinforcements could reach Quebec, came down from Montreal in transports which had fled up river before Holmes the previous year and which had found safety in its upper reaches. He landed above Cap Rouge and advanced upon the fortress. Murray, declining to lurk behind ramparts, moved boldly out to meet him, but was defeated with serious loss and was hustled back into the place. Then Lévis, seeing no prospect of success in an assault, set to work to recapture the lost stronghold by the regular process of a siege.

Both sides were in hopes that friendly ships might come from Europe and decide the issue in their favour. They were without definite news from home and knew not how events were shaping across the Atlantic, so that when, on the 9th of May, a frigate was descried some miles off beating slowly up the stream with no ensign flying, besiegers and besieged realised that the fate of New France depended upon the nationality of the approaching vessel. Owing to a mishap to the halyards, no flag floated over the citadel. But a sailor nimbly swarmed up the staff and showed the British colours from its peak. There was a moment's pause. Then the Union Jack ran up to the mast-head of the ship, and the worn-out garrison knew that they were safe. "Both officers and men mounted the parapets in the face of the enemy," the diarists of these stirring events tell us, "and huzzaed with their hats in the air for almost an hour. The garrison, the enemy's camp, the bay, and circumjacent country resounded with our shouts and the thunder of our artillery, for the gunners were so elated that they did nothing but fire and load for a considerable time." *The relief by sea-power.*

A week later two more ships of war arrived, and on the morrow the three together ran up the river past Quebec, fell upon the squadron which had brought down Lévis, some miles up stream, and after a sharp fight destroyed it. The French commander thereupon hastily abandoned the siege, leaving his guns in the trenches, and retreated by land to Montreal to there await the coming of the British columns: on the 8th September that city, menaced from three sides by converging armies, surrendered to the invaders; and thus Canada passed finally over to the British crown as prize of conquest.

The surrender of Montreal.   For Amherst, utilising the timber of the forests which then fringed the water's edge of Lake Ontario, had speedily created a flotilla of light craft suitable for river navigation. In this he had brought his army down the St Lawrence to the point where its rapids meet the tideway close to Montreal, not without suffering some loss in men and boats in passage of the cataracts, but practically unopposed by hostile troops. The force from Lake Champlain, no longer arrested by an enemy's flotilla on its waters, had made its way north to the vicinity of the city with little difficulty. And Murray, with his stores replenished and the efficiency of his garrison restored, had sailed up the St Lawrence in transports, convoyed by an imposing fleet. The three armies had met, their overwhelming strength had rendered further resistance useless, and Lévis was left no other alternative than capitulation. Victory had finally decided in favour of the side which in virtue of its maritime command controlled the lower reaches of the river at the outset, and which continued to extend its dominion over the waterway as part of a plan of offensive campaign.

Conclusion.   To deal with lakes and rivers in a work concerned with maritime preponderance may sound like paradox. But between control of such waters and command of the sea there is a close and intimate connection, and the strategical principles involved in relation to land operations are, as has been shown in this chapter, much the same in either case. The Mississippi was secured for the Federals, just as the lower St Lawrence fell into British hands in the time of Wolfe and Saunders, as a result of the resource and enterprise and seamanship of naval *personnel*. The operations on the Great Lakes in those years of desultory warfare between 1812 and 1814 can be likened to a maritime campaign in

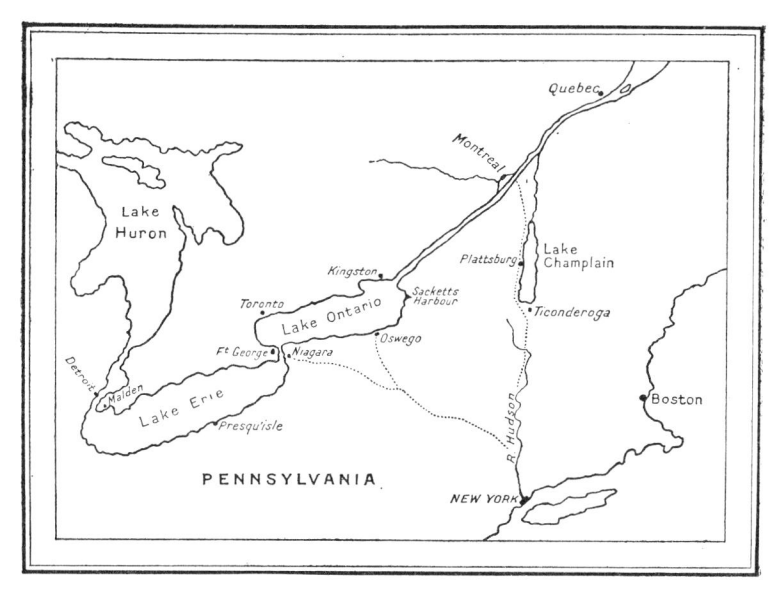

NORTH AMERICAN CAMPAIGNS, 1756-1814.

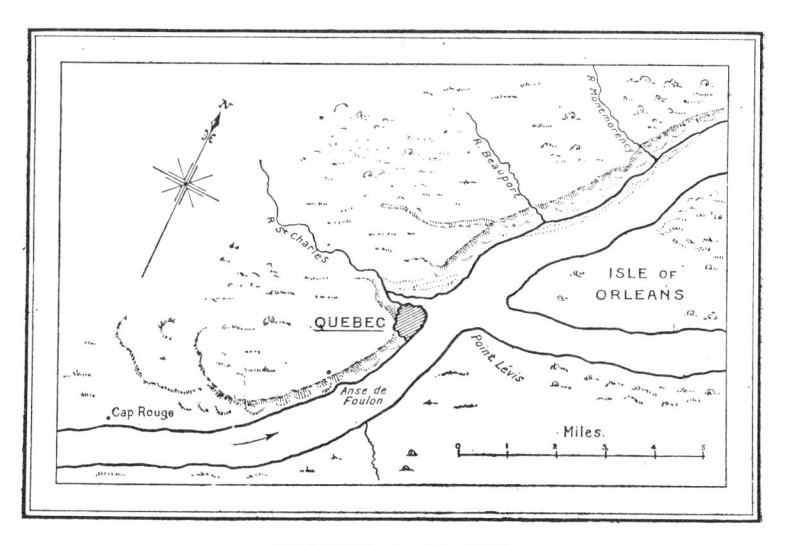

ENVIRONS OF QUEBEC.

miniature. In those conflicts in the New World the possession of the waterways served but as a means to an end; it merely established a firm foundation upon which plans of military action were to be built up. Such geographical conditions are, it is true, not found in every theatre of war. But if history teaches us nothing else, it teaches us that nations are apt to become involved in war in singular localities and under unwonted circumstances, and that the military and naval forces of a world-wide empire should be prepared for all eventualities.

CHAPTER XXIII.

SOME POINTS IN CONNECTION WITH EQUIPMENT, ORGANISATION, AND TRAINING OF NAVAL AND MILITARY FORCES FOR AMPHIBIOUS WAR.

IN the foregoing chapters an attempt has been made to explain the relations which exist between the establishing of control of the sea and the operations and disposition of military forces on land, between the action of armies carrying on a campaign in a maritime theatre of war and the power of transferring troops from place to place on the coast. It has been shown that an interdependence exists between fighting force afloat and fighting force ashore, each naturally supporting and succouring the other under certain strategical conditions. It has been proved by illustrations from the history of war that the land-service and the sea-service can co-operate in many situations which arise in struggles between maritime nations, and that they can mutually aid one another in bringing about the triumph of their side. But if the highest results are to be attained, there must not only be confidence and harmony between the naval forces and the military forces,—each must also be organised and equipped for the execution of amphibious operations under the circumstances created by the particular campaign, and each must be prepared to meet with experiences foreign to normal stereotyped forms of warfare.

Necessity for special organisation and equipment.

In discussing certain questions of organisation, training, and equipment suggested by what has gone before, the sea-service claims priority, and will therefore be considered first.

<small>Class of vessel required.</small>   The class of vessel by which dominion of the sea is attained in time of war is not necessarily that which is best suited for sustaining military operations ashore. In the present day maritime command is achieved by battle-ships, aided by cruisers, and assisted under certain conditions by torpedo craft. Gunboats and small armoured vessels drawing little water have no place in fleet-actions, and they are viewed with disfavour by authorities on the art of naval warfare who take that restricted view of the objects of sea-power in war which aims at nothing beyond destroying the enemy's forces afloat. But many situations are likely to arise in conflicts between seafaring nations where operations on shore are unavoidable, and where these cannot be prosecuted with the utmost vigour and effect, unless the troops have the support of fighting-ships in waters which may only be accessible to ships of limited dimensions.

"The greatest ships are the least serviceable," wrote Sir W. Raleigh some three centuries ago with his experiences on the American coast in mind, "are of marvellous charge and fearful cumber, less nimble, less maineable, and seldom employed, overpestered and clogged with great ordnance which only serves to overcharge the ships' sides in foule weather." That does not hold good in the present day on the high seas, nor is it the case even inshore if there be deep water; but the quaint language of the gallant author of the 'History of the World' is still applicable to much of the naval *matériel* likely to be at once available for amphibious operations in many possible theatres of war. The leviathan armour-clads, and even the more modest seagoing cruisers which are to be found in most modern navies, could not, at many points, otherwise favourable for landing an army, bring their guns effectively to bear in support of military forces about to disembark, without running ashore. Vessels of such heavy burthen could not even approach many stretches of coast-line where their ordnance might exert a great tactical influence on fights in progress. Torpedo-boats and destroyers are perhaps the highest forms of shallow-draught vessel capable of manœuvring close into the shore in most waters, which exists in the floating equipment of maritime nations; but formidable as are such craft for purposes of offence at sea, they are not designed to withstand the fire of even the lightest classes of artillery, and they would run great risks in river warfare from ordinary field troops.

It is not suggested that war-vessels should be especially constructed for this kind of work. That is neither necessary nor expedient. Gunboats and the smallest classes of cruiser can be easily adapted to the purpose. But adaptation takes time, unless preparations have been thought out, and unless fittings can be improvised speedily in the event of emergency. Half a century ago the two most powerful of naval nations despatched a great armament to the Baltic. There were line-of-battle ships and there were frigates and there were 10,000 men afloat in transports. There even were some fighting-ships propelled by steam-power, which was at the time still in its infancy as regards application to naval force. But the operations were a conspicuous failure, and in volume vi. of his fine history of the Royal Navy, Sir W. Clowes clearly explains the reason for the paltry results which were achieved by the allied fleets at the outset. "In the first year of the war neither Great Britain nor France was able to employ light-draught steam gunboats, and bomb- or mortar-vessels, because neither power possessed anything of the sort. Yet such vessels were absolutely requisite for effective operations in the bays and among the islands of the Baltic. . . . In the following year hundreds of craft of the kind were hurriedly and wastefully built or purchased." There is not the slightest reason to doubt that the French and British navies would in 1854 have satisfactorily performed the task for which they primarily existed, on the high seas against a hostile fleet. But the course of the war afforded them no opportunities for distinction out in open waters. The Russians shunned encounter with a superior foe, and naval operations on a great scale had no place in the struggle. In the northern theatre of war the actual injury caused by the imposing armada which the allies had got together, was confined to the blockade of a few ports which at the best laid claim to very little trade, and to the capture of some unimportant vessels. Its presence in the Baltic had, as shown in chapter xviii., the effect of detaining numbers of Russian troops in the neighbouring provinces; but the same, and probably even greater, effect would have been produced by ships better fitted for aggressive action. Command of the sea is undoubtedly the highest aim of a navy; but after accomplishing its primary duty there are other services which it may be called on to perform, if it is to play its part.

Question of projectile to be used by ships' guns.

And the effective co-operation of war-vessels with military force on shore, or which are in the act of disembarking, is not merely a question of the nature of the fighting craft which happen to be available. Except under circumstances where naval *personnel* is landed and becomes for the time being to all intents and purposes a body of troops, the sea-service can only participate in tactical operations ashore by artillery fire from on board ship. And, both as regards ammunition and as regards the art of gunnery, there is a marked difference between artillery fire against hostile troops and artillery fire against hostile vessels.

It is generally accepted by soldiers that shrapnel is the only projectile of much value against military forces in the open. Shell charged with high explosives are no doubt useful against buildings, and they are to a certain extent serviceable against earth-works and intrenchments; but in land warfare they take a second place. It is the custom to speak of a fleet covering a landing, and it is no doubt the case that at the expense of a great expenditure of ammunition from the powerful ordnance carried in modern fighting-ships, a bombardment with high explosive shells might lend material assistance to troops attempting a disembarkation in face of the enemy. But a far greater effect would unquestionably be obtained with accurately burst shrapnel. And the same thing applies to almost any conceivable case where a fleet is called upon to co-operate with an army during an engagement on the sea-coast. But unless the technical aspects of use of shrapnel be thoroughly understood its results are likely to be disappointing, and any inaccuracy in fuse-setting or in observation of fire may most seriously endanger friends whom the fire is intended to assist. The highest test of artillery training, from the soldier's point of view, is the maintenance of effective shrapnel-fire up to the last moment while friendly troops are closing with the enemy; and the standard of efficiency required to render this possible, whether it be in a battery on shore or whether it be in a gun's-crew on board ship, cannot be attained without elaborate training and without incessant practice.

Moreover, observation of fire, no matter what the nature of the projectile may be, differs very considerably according as the target fired at is on shore or is afloat. Nor can the art be acquired by watching gun-practice at some lonely crag which rears its crest above the waves. Proficiency can only be arrived at by experience on shore, and by watching the effect of artillery fire under varying conditions of weather and on different kinds of terrain in time of peace. War-vessels have grown to be such complicated machines, the engines of destruction which they

Observation of gun-fire ashore and afloat.

carry are so elaborate and so intricate, so much depends in naval warfare upon wireless telegraphy, signalling, and so forth, all of which demand aptitude, application, and knowledge if they are to be used to good purpose, that the *personnel* of a modern fleet has little leisure for studying methods of fighting only called for under special circumstances. In covering military disembarkations, or when participating in encounters between military forces ashore, the battleship or cruiser or gunboat acts only in an auxiliary capacity. It is not performing its primary and most obvious duty. To expect the naval gunner to attain the same standard of excellence as the artilleryman in employing shrapnel against troops on shore who are fighting in the dispersed formations of the present day, would be absurd. But some theoretical and practical experience in the technical work of artillery in the field, gained during courses of study at naval schools of gunnery by a small percentage of the complement of every fighting-ship, might prove of inestimable value on occasions where the land- and the sea-service are acting in concert.[1]

Japan the only nation with an army organised for amphibious warfare.

But if the ships composing modern fleets, and if the complements which they carry, do not always attain an ideal standard of perfection for the prosecution of amphibious operations of war, the same is also very generally the case with the military forces which must form their complement. With the solitary and significant exception of Japan, no important maritime country possesses an army organised and equipped with a view to land campaigns based upon control of the sea. And the nation which has the greatest experience of such warfare at its command, the nation which has been despatching military expeditions

---

[1] Why should not officers at the gunnery schools of our own navy spend a few days in artillery practice-camps at Okehampton or Salisbury Plain? They would acquire interesting experience and would receive a warm welcome.

across the seas for eight hundred years, the nation which looks with just pride to Quebec and Sebastopol, to Torres Vedras and Aboukir Bay, the nation which above all others requires an army designed, armed, and furnished for the express purpose of utilising to the full that liberty of action which naval preponderance confers upon military force, is still groping for an organisation to meet the class of warfare which, it may reasonably be assumed, will fall to its lot in the future.[1]

The cumbrous unwieldy units of all arms which serve so well where great modern armies are pitted against each other in a purely land campaign, are out of place in operations founded upon sea command and deriving their vitality from the power to transfer military force from one point to another by ship transport. Nations whose military strength lies in the combination of their fighting-resources ashore with predominance afloat, are well advised to organise their armies in a form suitable for over-sea expeditions. And in this the Japanese have shown the way. From the numerical point of view the military forces of Japan compare not unfavourably even with the Great Powers of Europe. They have succeeded in forming up in one line of battle a mass of troops only approached in modern times at Leipzig and at Gravelotte. And yet their military organisation is founded, not upon the army corps, but upon the division of all arms. They have realised during their long years of preparation—and war has proved the wisdom of their choice—that an island state, even supposing it can eventually muster forces in the field of such strength as to make an army corps organisation a tactical and administrative convenience, must embark on an oversea campaign with detachments of all arms framed on a smaller scale. They have learned, not by experience but by intuition, that the essence of amphibious strategy lies in compactness and mobility of the forces employed.

Question of organisation of field army.

438 EQUIPMENT, ORGANISATION, TRAINING.

Importance of portable artillery.

In the chapter on landings it was pointed out that a disembarkation in face of the enemy, always an undertaking of exceeding difficulty, has under modern tactical conditions become almost impracticable. But it is one of the privileges enjoyed by an expeditionary force about to land in hostile territory that, should the enemy be found drawn up in battle array at the point chosen beforehand for the disembarkation, a move can generally be made to some other spot on the coast where the foe is unprepared. But places suitable for the landing of an army are not numerous in all theatres of war, and it may prove impossible to find any point, compatible with the strategical conditions of the contemplated campaign, where a disembarkation on a large scale can be effected and where the enemy is not ready to dispute the landing. But because all ideal points of disembarkation are guarded, it does not follow that there may not be some small cove or stretch of beach unwatched by hostile forces, where light troops can be got on shore destined to operate from flank or rear against the enemy engaged in securing the more natural landing-places. By dint of subsidiary landings, the point of disembarkation which has been determined upon for the main body can be made good. Infantry and cavalry, unhampered by wheeled transport, can be got on shore and can be brought into action at places where there is no room for large bodies of troops to disembark, where the surroundings prohibit transports from discharging their cargoes of vehicles and stores, and where the ground abutting on the actual shore is of such a nature that wheeled guns moved by horse traction cannot be brought into action, however mobile they may be in other respects. Therefore a proportion of portable artillery—or mountain artillery as it is more generally called—is essential to a modern army about to make a descent on hostile territory. Without it, detachments of the other arms set on shore to gain a footing and to secure a base, are likely to find themselves opposed by guns to which they are not in a position to reply. The Japanese, whose army is organised for war and not for peace, made great use of portable artillery in the initial stages of their great campaign in 1904. Fully recognising the enormous importance of gun-fire in modern tactics, they took heed that some artillery should always be available at once as soon as a disembarkation had been effected. In this, as in most questions affecting the co-operation of naval and military forces and the conduct of operations based on the sea, there is much to be learnt from an army which has made its first essay in war on a grand scale with such brilliant promise.

Every detail had been thought out by the military authorities at Tokio in advance, in consultation with the Japanese Admiralty. Jetties, ready made, accompanied the troops, so that the disembarkation of stores could commence as soon as a footing had been gained on shore. The transfer of troops from ships to the land was carried out in localities where the natural facilities were limited, with the same precision as is customary when a debarkation takes place in some great military port. Every precaution had been taken to obviate the necessity of landing in face of the enemy, by detailing beforehand mobile troops capable of reaching the shore, ready for battle, at any point. *Advantage of all details being worked out beforehand.*

And inasmuch as the amount of ship transport available for conveying military force across the sea can never be unlimited, as, moreover, great bodies of troops cannot be trusted on the water till maritime preponderance is assured, any army organisation accepted by an insular Power, which does not take these strategical considerations into account, is likely to be inconveniently costly in time of peace and to be inappropriate to the circumstances of the case in time of war. An organisation which does not admit of the despatch of troops across the sea in anticipation of war, is a *Principles which must govern the military system of an insular Power.*

danger. An organisation which aims at mobilising troops ready for the field more rapidly than they can be despatched to the scene of action, is an anachronism.

It is pleasant to murmur "*Kriegmobil*" in the ear of an attendant aide-de-camp and to know that, within a week, army corps upon army corps will be converging along the lines of a cunningly contrived system of strategical railways, towards that borderland where a mighty conflict is impending. But what boots all this bustle if the frontier be the sea? These masses of men and vehicles and horses need many transports if their journey is to be continued beyond the coast-line of their own country. The aggregate of shipping which can in emergency be secured from even the largest of mercantile marines for conveyance of soldiers, is not after all unlimited. The ordinary cargo-tramp or passenger steamer cannot be transformed in an instant into a vessel suitable for carrying troops. And, quite apart from the question of provision of the requisite tonnage, the sea in the early days of some great war affords no sanctuary to the army crossing it against the machinations of the foe. There is nothing gained by the power to place troops in line of battle faster than they can be despatched to the theatre of operations. The rate at which troops can be mobilised in condition fit to take the field, depends upon their relative state of preparedness for war in time of peace; but it is the troops maintained in a high condition of efficiency in time of peace who cost most money, and who, when the element of time is taken into consideration, may give least value for that money. That element of time is a factor of paramount importance, and it governs the situation. If time be available, if from the conditions of the case it must be available, troops maintained in a state of comparative inefficiency in peace can be raised to the highest standard before they are wanted; and troops of this class are, if properly organised for the functions which they have to fulfil, far cheaper than those kept fit for action at a moment's notice. An insular Power which frames its military system with a view to the immediate readiness of a great army for service over-sea, is organising what it does not want, is organising what it cannot use, and is squandering its financial resources without adequate return owing to a misapprehension of strategical conditions.

But, on the other hand, the very fact that military forces are necessarily delayed by the circumstances of the case in reaching the scene of action, may be prejudicial to their prospects when they get there. The enemy may have benefited by their tardy appearance, and may have gained advantages strategical and moral. Therefore the army crossing the sea should be well supported, and machinery should exist to swell its numbers liberally from time to time in so far as maritime conditions permit of it. Behind the force first despatched to the theatre of war there should be abundant reserves, and there should be ample cadres in second line which, while waiting for their turn to proceed on service, are progressing from rudimentary acquaintance with the soldier's art towards that standard of efficiency which troops must possess if they are to make their mark in face of the enemy. An insular Power should, in fact, base its military system on the principle of having many categories in a progressive stage. The corps in the first category may be ten times as efficient, at the moment when war breaks out, as the corps in the fifth category, and it will probably cost ten times as much in peace time. But the organisation should be such that, by the time the fifth category is required, its component parts shall have attained the standard of excellence which is expected in the regular soldier, and that they shall be able to take their place in line of battle with credit to themselves and honour to their country.

442 EQUIPMENT, ORGANISATION, TRAINING.

Importance of adequate methods of communication and signalling between naval and military force acting in concert.

One more point deserves a passing notice. Macaulay draws a pathetic picture of the hard-pressed and almost-famished defenders of Derry gazing at the friendly fleet on Lough Foyle, but unable to communicate with it by signal. Signalling on any established system was in those days almost unknown at sea, and it was quite unknown on land. But even at a much later date, instances have occurred of military forces when acting in concert with ships of war being unable to communicate with them. When this is the case there is always a certain danger that misunderstandings may arise, and that the services may fail to co-operate effectively with each other at some critical juncture. It is not proposed to discuss the question in its technical aspects. The purpose here is merely to draw attention to a matter of considerable importance.

The perfection of the Japanese organisation for amphibious warfare has been already commented on in this chapter. This makes it the more interesting that in their war against China, in which the admirable nature of their arrangements and their genius for detail excited so much remark at the time, two noteworthy instances occurred of the army and navy firing on each other by mistake. On the morning after the Japanese had taken the forts defending Talienwan, the attendant fleet moved cautiously into the bay and opened fire on the works. No harm was done; but the bombardment seems to have been maintained for some little time before the officers on the war-vessels perceived that they were shelling their own men. The army returned the compliment some weeks later in another part of the theatre of war, and with interest. For on the night after the assaulting columns had captured the forts at Wei-hai-wei from the land side, they opened fire upon friendly torpedo-boats which had come to attack the boom. In this case the mistake had far more unfortunate results than that made at Talienwan; the Japanese flotilla was actually driven off, and the Chinese fleet thus got warning of the method of attack which the resolute foe intended to adopt. In consequence of the *contretemps* the onslaughts of the Japanese torpedo flotilla on subsequent nights were stubbornly resisted, and although they were successful in the end the triumph was only purchased after considerable loss.

Misunderstandings of this kind are certain to arise in war. Many instances occurred in the South African conflict of troops firing by misadventure on their own side. Some recent incidents in the North Sea and in Far Eastern waters appear to point to the conclusion, that neither the elaborate methods of naval signalling at night now in vogue, nor wireless telegraphy, have rendered it impossible that fighting-ships at sea should attack friendly vessels in the dark. There must alway be greater liability of error when two separate services are concerned, than when the operation is purely a military or purely a naval one. But this very fact makes it the more desirable that each should understand the signals and messages of the other, and that neither should, in conjunct undertakings, neglect to ascertain the movement and the progress of its partner. It is of course impossible to eliminate wholly the element of chance in such affairs; but that element can be much restricted by foresight, by training in peace time, and by that thorough understanding between the sailor and the soldier which means so much when they act together in concert in time of war.

And so we come back again to the point to which especial attention was drawn in the introductory chapter. It has been the purpose of this volume to show how naval preponderance and warfare on land are mutually dependent, if the one is to assert itself conclusively and if the other is to be carried out with vigour and effect. There is an intimate connection between command of the sea and control of the shore. But if the strategical principles involved in this connection are to be put in force to their full extent, if the whole of the machinery is to be set in motion, there must be co-ordination of authority and there must be harmony in the council chamber and in the theatre of operations. That is perhaps the most important lesson to be learnt from the many interesting and remarkable campaigns in which circumstances have brought into contact fighting forces afloat and fighting forces ashore. "United we stand, divided we fall," is a motto singularly applicable to the navy and army of a maritime nation and of a world-wide empire.

APPENDIX I.
TOWARD CONTINENTAL COMMITMENT, 1905:
THREE CALLWELL MEMORANDA

Strategic theory, military policy, and strategic planning repeatedly met in the pen of Charles E. Callwell in the course of 1905. Between the submission of the manuscript of *Military Operations* to its publisher in February and publication in July, the General Staff—including Callwell—conducted the first war game that considered seriously British military intervention in defense of Belgium in the event of a German invasion. Against the backcloth of the historic Anglo-French entente signed on 8 April 1904, of the simmering Franco-German crisis over Morocco, of a Russia much weakened by defeat at the hands of Britain's Japanese ally, and of the ever more menacing character of Admiral von Tirpitz's building program for the High Seas Fleet, for British military authorities 1905, if not a year of decision, assuredly was a year of emphatic strategic tilt toward European continental commitment.

As *Military Operations and Military Preponderance* appeared, British military and naval authorities were confronting a series of significant questions. First, if Britain were alone in a war with Germany (not to mention with France and/or Russia as well, for a truly worst-case assumption), what should the army and navy attempt? Second, if Britain were to fight Germany, but as an ally of France—over the excuse of German infringement of Belgian neutrality—again, what should the army and navy attempt? How best could Britain aid France in a struggle with Germany? Should Britain pose an essentially amphibious menace to North Germany (in which case, where, with what means, to what ends, on what time frame?); or, should Britain send her field army to Belgium or France ([a] to Antwerp, [b] to join on to the left wing of the French Army, or [c] to act independently in Northern France)? In the Summer and Fall of 1905 the War Office and the Admiralty exchanged memoranda on these matters. As head of the strategical section of the War Office's Directorate of Military Operations (ADMO, MO1), Callwell was a key figure in the exchanges.

By way of the briefest of summaries, after initially favoring the posing of an amphibious menace to North Germany (memorandum of 28 August 1905) in order to hold as many as "fully 400,000 German regular troops and Landwehr tight in the Baltic provinces" and thereby relieve the French of that measure of menace, the War Office swung rapidly to comprehensive rejection of any such scheme for peripheral diversion (memorandum of 3 October 1905). Indeed, by 15 November 1905 Col. William R. Robertson (ADMO, MO2) minuted the collective judgment of the General Staff to the effect that "no further action" was needed: the issue of the proper use of the British field army in a war with Germany was closed in favor of direct support for Belgium and France *in those countries*. The third memorandum reproduced here, dated 7 December 1906, appears to illustrate some unease on Callwell's part about the wisdom of the choice for, and proposed scale of, continental commitment. This rather puzzling document does not exactly read like a robust dissent from the 1906 General Staff orthodoxy that favored continental commitment, but it probably registers as serious a dissent as a characteristically team player like Callwell would allow himself.

The three Callwell memoranda are reproduced below, preceded by a summary chronology of the most relevant army-navy exchanges.

A "STRATEGIC MOMENT": CHRONOLOGY OF 1905

25 February	Callwell completes *Military Operations and Maritime Preponderance*.
20 March	*Report on Naval and Military Conference on Overseas Expeditions*, provides basic doctrine for amphibious warfare.
31 March	First Moroccan Crisis begins (Kaiser in Tangier).
April–May	General Staff war game (scenario: German invasion of Belgium, British intervention).
26 June	Admiral Fisher asks Capt. Charles Ottley, Director of Naval Intelligence (DNI), what Royal Navy could do to aid France in war with Germany.
27 June	DNI asks Admiral A. K. Wilson, Commander in Chief Channel Fleet, about British aid to France in war with Germany. Wilson suggests strategy of diversion.
Early July	Ottley drafts scheme for British amphibious diversion of German army.
20 July	Committee of Imperial Defence (CID) accepts Royal Navy proposal for creation of CID Sub-Committee on Combined Operations (never convened, because of War Office disinterest).
Early August	Naval Intelligence asks War Office informally for advice on feasi-

APPENDIX I: THREE CALLWELL MEMORANDA

	bility of strategy of diversion (raids, etc.).
17 August	Sir George Clarke, Secretary of CID, requests detailed report on British military aid to Belgium (ref. General Staff war game, April–May).
28 August	Callwell signs out initial War Office response to Naval Intelligence request of "early" August (probably written by Capt. Adrian Grant-Duff). (Memo: "British Military Action in Case of War with Germany").
28 August–very early October	Callwell on leave.
2 September	Capt. George A. Ballard, Assistant DNI, asks War Office to specify military objectives if Britain (a) has to act rapidly; (b) has time.
7 September	Grant-Duff asks Ballard how Army could help Navy.
9 September	Grant-Duff advises ADNI British amphibious diversions not useful to France ("British Military Action on the Baltic Coast in the event of a war between Germany and Great Britain and France in alliance").
26 September	Col. W. R. Robertson (WO, ADMO, MO2) writes minute deprecating uncleared War Office–Admiralty exchanges between junior officers.
29 September	General Staff memo in reply to CID request of 17 August. ("The Violation of Belgium During a

APPENDIX I: THREE CALLWELL MEMORANDA

	Franco-German War"). Assumes Germany invades Belgium following frustration on Franco-German border—thereby allowing British Army time to move to Belgium.
3 October	Callwell memo to ADNI, reversing his 28 August advice.
10 November	Major J. D. Fasson (German Sub-Section, DMO, MO2) submits memo on "The Feasibility of Landing a British Force of 100,000 Men on the Coasts of Germany; in the Event of Great Britain being in Active Alliance with France in a War against Germany, and the probable effect on the military situation." Argues that British Army of 100,000, so deployed, would be condemned to strategic irrelevance.
15 November	Robertson minute on the question of whether the Army should threaten to intervene in Belgium-France, or on the coasts of Germany, endorses 10 November study and concludes, "no further action."

APPENDIX I: THREE CALLWELL MEMORANDA

Memorandum, Colonel Charles E. Callwell
(ADMO, MO1), 28 August 1905
to Captain George A. Ballard [ADNI], British Military
Action in Case of War with Germany

Secret

BRITISH ALONE

(1) The British field army which might be dispatched to the continent in case of war may be put in round numbers at 120,000. The total number of Officers, N.C.O.'s and men which Germany possesses on a war footing amounts to 3,150,000; of these a large proportion would be in depôts etc., but it is reasonable to estimate that the actual field armies which the German Empire could dispose of within a few weeks of the commencement of war could not be less than 1,500,000 without considering line of communication troops etc. Thus the numerical odds against the British are overwhelming. It is a well known principle that command of the sea confers an extraordinary liberty of action upon an army contemplating descents on an enemy's coast and that it may compensate to a considerable extent for comparative numerical weakness; but in this case the superiority in strength of the defending side is altogether too great.

(2) The nature of the coastline appears to render a landing on the western side of Schleswig Holstein out of the question. On the eastern side, on the other hand, the conditions would appear to be favourable, especially within the "Little Belt." From the chart there would seem to be a choice of landing places, and it is quite possible that an army might be safely disembarked in this region and might gain a footing before the enemy came up on the scene in formidable force.

APPENDIX I: THREE CALLWELL MEMORANDA

(3) An army thus disembarked might be able to hold on with its back to the sea and its flanks secure for a considerable time, even against superior force; but it could do nothing alone, and, however favourable a tactical position it might take up, it would almost certainly eventually be driven to re-embark, probably losing part of its impedimenta during the process. Probably the best plan would be to capture the island of Alsen; it would be difficult for the Germans to expel a British military force from this island even if H. M. ships were unable to assist in the narrow channel near Sonderburg.

(4) But the fact remains that an operation of this character could not be undertaken without running considerable risks and that it would do no very serious injury to the enemy. It would give our antagonists an opportunity of bringing their great army into play. It might conceivably end in disaster. And it would most probably (except in the case of Alsen) merely result in the expeditionary force being driven away to sea again which would be interpreted as a moral victory by the enemy.

(5) It must be understood that there is no real objective for the expeditionary force. In case of war with that country Kiel is about the first place the Germans would think of, and they would mass troops there. An advance on Hamburg from about Lubeck Bay is obviously out of the question. There is nothing of any importance in Schleswig, nothing to destroy which would cause appreciable injury, nothing to capture.

BRITISH IN SUPPORT OF FRANCE

(6) Should the country be acting in alliance with France the situation would be totally different. Even if the 120,000 British troops merely occupied some limited tract of country in Schleswig or some other German maritime prov-

APPENDIX I: THREE CALLWELL MEMORANDA

ince they would afford immense assistance to our allies—greater assistance probably than they would on the Franco-German frontier. These 120,000 troops would probably hold fully 400,000 German regular troops and Landwehr tight in the Baltic provinces, and would relieve the French of all pressure by that very appreciable fraction of the formidable military forces of their antagonist.

(7) It is worth considering in some detail what should be the plan of campaign for the British army embarked for the Baltic in these circumstances. It might make simultaneous descents at several points and could certainly make feints of descent at several points. If kept concentrated it could probably occupy the whole of Schleswig. Although that province presents awkward natural obstacles to advance, it might conceivably be able to strike a really serious blow. But all this would have to be carefully considered in detail and these notes merely treat of the question in general terms.

NOTE. It is possible that in the event of war with Germany we should have serious trouble in South Africa absorbing a portion of our available military forces calculated upon above. It is not so much the German force in Damaraland itself as the fact of its being there which would give trouble. There would certainly be intrigues with the Boers and arms would be got through to the malcontents.

Letter and Memorandum, Colonel Charles E. Callwell
(ADMO, MO1)
to Captain George A. Ballard (ADNI)

War Office
London S.W.
3rd October 1905
My dear Ballard,

I enclose a further paper as to war with Germany. This must not be taken to be in any way authoritative but I think the C.G.S. and D.M.O. who are as you know away, would probably concur in it.

I am sorry if I to a certain extent mislead you in my first paper, but on these kind of matters second thoughts are often best, especially when first thoughts are the result of a hasty consideration of the subject.

(signed) C. E. Callwell

* * * * *

BRITISH MILITARY ACTION IN CASE OF WAR WITH GERMANY

(1) Further consideration of the subject makes it desirable to modify the expression of opinion in paragraphs (6) and (7) of a paper under above heading which was sent privately to the Naval Intelligence Department about 30th September.

(2) It seems doubtful if 120,000 troops if they made a successful descent on the Baltic coast would "contain" so many as 400,000 German regular troops and Landwehr, and relieve the French of that amount of pressure. The Germans have about 850,000 organised Landsturm for home defence, and although these troops would not be of the highest class or possess much manoeuvring power they should be able to offer a stolid resistance to the advance of an army of inferior numerical strength. The railways lend themselves to rapid concentration. And the German military authorities must be well aware that there is no satisfactory objective for an expeditionary force coming from oversea, apart from Kiel, the Kiel Canal, and Hamburg (these forming a group of objectives close to-

gether) and Wilhelmshafen, should part of their fleet be located there. The very fact of being at war with the French and British would compel the Germans to make these points secure in any case, and the idea of any attack upon them by an army of 120,000 may be dismissed as impracticable. Port Arthur has shown the difficulty of capturing a modern fortress, even when the attacking army has been able to devote its entire attention to the fortress itself.

(3) The mobilization of the British Army and the collection and preparation of transports would be known in Germany and it would probably be advantageous that it should be known. As long as this army remained in the United Kingdom it would constitute a certain menace to the German coasts. But it is probable that the most useful purpose to which it could be put would be to give support to the French Armies in the field.

(4) In a conflict of this kind Germany must inevitably feel the full power of sea pressure, in so far as closure of the coast line is concerned. But against this it is conceivable that the German Army might gain considerable successes on land against the French, such successes acting in some measure as a counterpoise to maritime collapse. An efficient army of 120,000 British Troops might just have the effect of preventing any important German successes on the Franco-German frontier, and of leading up to the situation that Germany, crushed at sea, also felt herself impotent on land. That would almost certainly bring about a speedy, and from the British and French point of view satisfactory, peace.

(5) C.I.D. Paper 20 A deals with the question of military policy to be adopted in the event of war with Germany and is worth perusal at the present time.

Memorandum from Colonel Charles E. Callwell to the DMO (Maj.-General John S. Ewart), 7 December 1906, Overseas Warfare. Military Forces Required for

SECRET

D.M.O.

(1) In connection with the question of army organization surely the first thing to decide is what is to be the strength of the force capable of being sent to a theatre of war overseas, and to decide this on broad grounds of policy and of strategy. For some reason we are to have a "striking force" of 150,000. Why? What is to be the military policy of the country? For years past that policy appears to have been that the army was not primarily intended for war on the continent. Is this changed?

(2) Putting the question of war on the continent on one side, the raison d'être for a "striking force" of 150,000 falls to the ground. In the various cases likely to arise we either do not want it or we could not use it if we had it. We do not want it to reinforce India in the event of war with Russia—the circumstances of the case call for gradual reinforcement. We do not want it for South Africa. We do not want it for small wars. We could not use it in defence of Canada in case of war with the United States, because it must take time to get command of the sea so as to be able to despatch troops across the Atlantic. Apart from war on the continent the organization of our army for oversea warfare should aim at the maintenance of a small "striking force" and of successive categories of troops of all arms to be despatched as it were in batches, the time available for mobilising the different categories and bringing them to a condition fit for taking the field varying from two months to six months. Accepting the new divisional organization we want:

APPENDIX I: THREE CALLWELL MEMORANDA

(a) 2 Divisions Regulars (with odds and ends and L. of C. troops) ready to go as soon as ships can be collected and one of them capable of being mobilised for a small war with the "special reserve." Transports, Ammunition Columns, etc., to be Regulars.

(b) 2 Divisions Regulars (with odds and ends) which would be ready to go in two months' time: L. of C. troops to be found from foreign garrisons relieved by troops on Militia basis: transport, Ammunit. columns etc., to be on Militia basis.

(c) 2 Divisions Regulars (with odds and ends) which would be ready to go in four months' time: L. of C. troops to be found from foreign garrisons relieved by troops on Militia basis: transport, Ammunition Columns etc., to be on Militia basis.

(d) 2 Divisions on Militia basis which would be ready to go in six months' time and which could start mobilising in the barracks vacated by the first two Divisions as soon as these sailed.

This would represent a field army of about 200,000. That should be our limit as regards enlisted troops whether on a Regular or on a Militia basis; but it is of course essential that the reserve to keep this army in the field shall exist or shall be capable of being formed by the time they are wanted.

(3) If war on the continent is to be the standard by all means let us have a "striking force" of 150,000—or more if possible. If it is not to be the standard then all we have to do in case of joining in military operations on the continent is to send what we have got i.e. 2 Divisions of the very best at once, 2 more Divisions in two months, and so on. We are not a great Military power and our alliance is sought for its naval not for its military advantage, but that is no reason why we should not throw such military forces as we have got into the scale.

(signed) 7/12/06 Cal

APPENDIX II.
CHARLES E. CALLWELL:
SUMMARY OF A MILITARY LIFE

2 April 1859	Born in London to Henry and Maud Callwell of Lismoyne, Co. Antrim.
January 1871–April 1876	Haileybury College.
1876–1877	Royal Military Academy, Woolwich.
January 1878	Commissioned into Royal Field Artillery (RFA) (awarded in July, for January).
March 1879	Joins F Battery, 3rd Brigade (F/3), (RFA), Dinapore, India.
January–May 1880	Afghanistan (2nd Afghan War). Takes heavy battery (Garrison Battery 10/11) to join Kabul Field Force.
Late 1880	In Peshawar, back with F/3.
25 January 1881	Arrives Durban for closing stage of First Boer War (sees no action).
Early December 1881	Back in London.
1882	With F/3 (redesignated X/1) at Woolwich; Brigade adjutant, Woolwich.
November 1883	Back in Dinapore, with A/1 (RFA).
June 1884	Sits Staff College exam at Simla—passes in first place.
Autumn 1884	Sails for England.
1885–1886	Staff College (twenty-five in Callwell's division).

APPENDIX II: SUMMARY OF A MILITARY LIFE

1886	Awarded Royal United Service Institution (RUSI) Gold Medal (Military) for essay on small wars.
March 1886	Promoted to captain.
1887	Posted to garrison artillery (RGA), Portsmouth.
Autumn 1887	Posted to RGA, Sheerness.
October 1887– September 1892	Appointed Staff Captain, Intelligence Division, War Office (WO), responsibility for Egypt, Sudan. "Visits" (i.e., spies in) Turkey, Greece (1888); Algiers, Oran (1889); Turkey (1890); Tangier, Morocco (1891); Norway, Germany, Austria, Rumania, Russia (1892).
September 1893– Autumn 1896	Brigade-Major of artillery, Western District (Devonport).
March 1896	Promoted to major; *Small Wars* published.
End of 1896– December 1899	Posted to 16 Battery, Southern Division, (RGA), Fort Ricasoli, Malta.
May 1897	Attached to Greek Army to observe Turko-Greek War.
1897–1899	"Amphibious rambles" around Mediterranean.
Early 1898	In Alexandria hoping, in vain, for attachment to Kitchener's expedition to Khartoum.
23 December 1899	Leaves Malta for South Africa.
24 January 1900	Arrives Durban with right half company of a heavy battery (two 5" breech-loading naval guns).

APPENDIX II: SUMMARY OF A MILITARY LIFE

February 1900	With Buller in Tugela combat and relief of Ladysmith.
January 1901– 26 July 1901	Commander RA, to Maj.-Gen. F. W. Kitchener. Desultory fighting from Lydenburg base in Transvaal.
31 July 1901	Appointed by H. H. Kitchener to a column command at Middleburg, Cape Colony, under Maj.-Gen. John French.
August 1901	Arrives Middleburg as brevet Lt.-Colonel, dated to November 1900.
Early August 1901	Column command (400 men) in constant action chasing Boer commandos in N. W. Cape Colony (Sutherland area).
Early November 1901	Fails to capture Van Deventer at Brand Kraal, possible blight on future career (displeasure of John French).
April 1902– 3 May 1903	Ships from Cape Town to Port Nolloth, Namaqualand to raise seige of Ookiep.
3 August 1903	Arrives in England. Garrison command, Spike Island, Cork Harbor, Ireland. Serves on RA committee to select gun (60 pdr) for mobile heavy batteries.
Spring 1903	Command of RGA depot, Dover.
Autumn 1903	Joins Dept. of Mobilization and Military Intelligence, Intelligence Div., WO (for second time), Strategical Sub-Div. (end of his regimental service). Responsibilities for

APPENDIX II: SUMMARY OF A MILITARY LIFE

	Overseas Empire and general questions of overseas defense.
4 October 1904	Head of Strategical Section of Directorate of Military Operations (ADMO, MO1).
October 1904	Promoted to brevet, then substantive, Colonel.
25 February 1905	Completes *Military Operations and Maritime Preponderance*.
28 August 1905	Signs out memo on "British Military Action in Case of War with Germany."
3 October 1905	Signs out much revised view on "British Military Action . . ."
19 December 1906	Drafts WO memo which "in effect 'turned' the [attack on the Dardanelles] project 'down.'"
October 1907	Made CB on ceasing to be ADMO, MO1.
October 1907– Early 1909	On half-pay. Odd jobs for WO (e.g., examines defenses of Cape Peninsula, South Africa). Journalism to supplement half-pay. Declines staff appointment "of relatively low standing." Retires.
1909–1913	Journalism. Attends British and foreign military maneuvers.
1911	Declines post of Commander in Chief, Chinese Army, offered by Lord Roberts (acting for Sun-Yat-sen).
April 1914	Visit to Ulster as sympathizer.
June 1914	"Private" visit to inspect German railways directed at Belgian-Luxemburg border.

460

APPENDIX II: SUMMARY OF A MILITARY LIFE

1 August 1914	Henry Wilson tells Callwell (to his surprise) he will replace him as DMO on mobilization.
August 1914– 29 December 1915	DMO (Operations and Intelligence), WO, as honorary Maj.-General.
3 September 1914	Invited to advise First Lord of Admiralty (Churchill) on Dardanelles operation; writes "decidedly discouraging memo."
August 1915	Helps E. Swinton (Acting Secretary, Committee of Imperial Defense) draft "get on or get out" Dardanelles memo.
September 1915	Gives up on Dardanelles adventure.
18 December 1915	Declines offer of D. Haig (C in C, BEF) to be his military secretary.
23 December 1915	Drafts Dardanelles evacuation memo for incoming CIGS (approved by Cabinet, 27 Dec.).
29 December 1915	Leaves WO position of DMO.
January 1916– February 1916	First mission to Russia for CIGS (W. Robertson) to examine real state of affairs.
March 1916– May 1916	Second trip to Russia for CIGS.
June 1916	Takes over WO branch in charge of munitions supply to Russia. Asked by Army Council to examine possible publication of Dardanelles documents (advises against).
October 1916	Declines offer by Lloyd George

461

APPENDIX II: SUMMARY OF A MILITARY LIFE

	(then Minister of State for War) to be his military secretary.
1917	Promoted to substantive Maj.-Gen. and created KCB. In charge of WO branch coordinating arms supplies to all Allies.
4 April 1917	WO representative on "Milner" Committee on Russian Supplies.
May 1917–June 1917	Acting Deputy CIGS.
Late December 1917	Sent as WO advisor to Dublin on military forces of a self-governing Ireland (abortive mission).
1917–1918	Advisor to Ministry of Munitions.
Early 1918	Callwell's branch of WO moved to the surveyor-general of supplies.
Early November 1918	Retires (again).
1 March 1921	Awarded Chesney Gold Medel of the RUSI "for his distinguished work in connection with military literature."
October 1927	Publishes the controversial book *Field-Marshal Sir Henry Wilson: His Life and Diaries*.
16 May 1928	Dies in London.

APPENDIX III.
SELECTED PUBLICATIONS OF CHARLES E. CALLWELL

"Notes on the Tactics of our Small Wars," *Proceedings of the Royal Artillery Institution* 12 (1881–1884): 531–52.

"Notes on the Strategy of our Small Wars," *Proceedings of the Royal Artillery Institution* 13 (1885): 403–20.

The Armed Strength of Roumania (London, 1886).

"Lessons to be Learnt from the Campaigns in which British Forces have been employed since the year 1865," *Journal of the Royal United Service Institution* 31 (1887): 357–412.

"Horse Artillery in Various Wars," *Journal of the Royal United Service Institution* 32 (1888): 801–4.

Wastage in War (London, 1890).

Hints on Reconnaissance in Little Known Countries (London, 1890).

Handbook of the Armies of the Minor Balkan States: Roumania, Servia, Bulgaria, Montenegro and Greece (London, 1891).

Military Report on North-Eastern Turkey in Asia (London, 1892).

Handbook on the Turkish Army (London, 1892).

"Naval Efficiency and Army Reform," *United Service Magazine* 7 (1893): 1244–50.

"Senoussi," *Blackwood's Magazine* (July 1894): 27–37.

Small Wars: Their Principles and Practice (London, 1896, 1899, 1906).

"With the Greeks: The Artillery of Domokos," *Proceedings of the Royal Artillery Institution* (1897): 505–10.

"A Glimpse of the Late War," *Blackwood's Magazine* (August 1897): 165–80.

The Effect of Maritime Command on Land Campaigns Since Waterloo (Edinburgh, 1897).
"The Army Problem: A Proposed Solution," *Blackwood's Magazine* (January 1898): 147–64.
"A Boer War: A Military Aspect," *Blackwood's Magazine* (August 1899): 259–65.
"The War Operations in South Africa," *Blackwood's Magazine* (May 1900): 734–48 (published pseudonymously as "By a Military Contributor").
"On the Move with Buller," *Blackwood's Magazine* (November 1900): 768–75.
The Tactics of Today (Edinburgh, 1902).
Military Operations and Maritime Preponderance: Their Relations and Interdependence (Edinburgh, 1905).
The Tactics of Home Defence (Edinburgh, 1908).
"The Defence of Fort Leternalkum," *Blackwood's Magazine* (April 1910): 457–71.
Tirah, 1897 (London, 1911).
"The Official Case Against Compulsory Service," *Blackwood's Magazine* (January 1911): 104–15.
"War Office Reminiscences," *Blackwood's Magazine* (August 1911): 154–70.
Service Yarns and Memories (Edinburgh, 1912).
"Some Peninsular Battlefields of a Century Ago," *Cornhill Magazine* 35 (1913): 349–62.
"After Two Years of It," *Blackwood's Magazine* (August 1916): 270–83.
"Introduction," to Lt.-Gen. Baron von Freytag-Loringhoven, *A Nation Trained in Arms or a Militia: Lessons in War from the Past and the Present* (London, 1918).
"The War Office in War Time," *Blackwood's Magazine* (December 1918): 775–87.
"The War Office in War Time—II," *Blackwood's Magazine* (January and March 1919): 23–33, 298–314.
The Life of Sir Stanley Maude (London, 1920).

APPENDIX III: SELECTED PUBLICATIONS

Experiences of a Dug-Out, 1914–1918 (London, 1921).
"Service Experts at War Councils," *The Nineteenth Century and After* (December 1921): 1062–71.
Stray Recollections, 2 vols. (London, 1923).
The Dardanelles (London, 1924).
"Introduction (and Notes)" to *The Autobiography of General Sir O'Moore Creagh* (London, 1926).
Field Marshal Sir Henry Wilson, His Life and Diaries, 2 vols. (London, 1927).
The History of the Royal Artillery from the Indian Mutiny to the Great War, Vol. I (1860–1899) (London, 1931), *Vol. II (1899–1914)* (London, 1937). With. Maj.-Gen. Sir John Headlam.

APPENDIX IV. TEXTUAL NOTES

CHAPTER 1

1. The view continues to be popular that in 1899 the Boer Republics missed their only strategic opportunity to beat the British by failing to deprive the enemy of his ability to proceed from the sea inland. "Both sides can now be seen to have made the most incredible strategic blunders; the Boers, who after all lost the war, made the more serious ones at the outset, both by besieging the three towns [Ladysmith in Natal, and Kimberley and Mafeking on the Bechuanaland Railway in Cape Colony] and thereby tying up their troops unnecessarily, and also by marching to Durban late in October 1899 before the British reinforcements had arrived in Natal. As Smuts [General Jan C. Smuts] and many of the younger men realized at the time, the rapid seizure of the few ports of South Africa [i.e., Cape Town, Port Elizabeth, East London, and Durban] would have placed the British in an almost hopeless position." Eversley Belfield, *The Boer War* (1975; London, 1993), ix–x. Belfield is correct in operational and strategic principle, but almost certainly wrong in practice, in that the Boers of October–November 1899 lacked the cohesion, not to mention the logistical necessities, to perform as Belfield specifies. The official history of the Boer War generally is not highly regarded for its independence of scholarship, but it does offer an excellent chapter (chapter six) on "The Navy in the Boer War" that includes valuable advice on joint planning and training. We are told, for example, that "joint action in manoeuvre will be valueless unless it is used to familiarise each service with the work of the other as it will be in the actual fighting of the time." Maurice Harold Grant, *History of the War in South Africa, 1899–1902* (London, 1910), 1:114. This good advice was ignored, of course.

2. Callwell is consistent throughout the book in this emphasis on the risks posed by enemy ships that survive battle at sea. This points to a persisting set of strategic, operational, and tactical questions, from Callwell's time of writing to the present, centered on the issue of how important is it to secure the actual destruction, rather than merely the containment, of inferior naval power? From Julian S. Corbett to the debate on the U.S. Navy's maritime strategy in the mid-1980s, the following proposition was debated: if we enjoy the benefit of maritime command, as it were by default, because the foe will not come out to be destroyed, should we hazard irreplaceable fleet units for the sake merely of capping an already effective strategy victory?

3. In 1810 no fewer that 619 British ships were taken in the *guerre de course,* the highest figure for any year of the Napoleonic War, for French privateer losses of 67. The figures for 1811 were 470 for 37, while for 1812 they were 475 for 34. The British losses look less awesome when it is appreciated that the average *annual* number of ships clearing the port of London in the period 1803–1813 was 15,211. J. Holland Rose, *Men and the Sea: Stages in Maritime and Human Progress* (Cambridge, 1935), 230. The annual loss numbers are taken from H. W. Wilson, "The Command of the Sea, 1803–15," in A. W. Ward, G. W. Prothero, and Stanley Leathers, eds., *The Cambridge Modern History, Vol. 9: Napoleon* (Cambridge, 1936), 242.

4. For example, Britain conducted the Boer War (1899–1902), and the United States the Vietnam War (1965–1973), with benefit of the absolute quality of sea control—really command—to which Callwell refers. Rarely in World War II, by way of contrast, did British or American sea control approximate a condition of command rather than preponderance.

5. As noted in the editor's introduction, Callwell frequently appears to pick his use of term—command, control, prepon-

derance, dominance, as well as sea, naval, maritime—for stylistic rather than substantive reasons.

6. The outstanding comparison of the worldviews of soldiers and sailors (and airmen) is J. C. Wylie, *Military Strategy: A General Theory of Power Control,* introduction by John B. Hattendorf (1967; Annapolis, Md., 1989), ch. 5.

7. "Conjunct expeditions" is the old-fashioned term for what has come to be called amphibious warfare. In Britain this has long been known as combined operations, and in the United States today it is known generically as joint operations or warfare. The words have changed, but not the meaning, save for the addition of air and space dimensions.

8. Given that both Britain and France were totally dependent upon sea lines of communication to their holdings in India, defeat at sea ultimately had to mean defeat on land. See Mahan, *Influence of Sea Power upon History*, ch. 12. See also G. S. Graham, *The Politics of Naval Supremacy: Studies in British Maritime Ascendancy* (Cambridge, 1965), ch. 2; and *Tides of Empire: Discursions on the Expansion of Britain Overseas* (Montreal, 1972), ch. 2.

9. Callwell's disdain for Napoleon's grasp of naval strategy was to be echoed by later writers. See Julian S. Corbett, *Some Principles of Maritime Strategy,* introduction by Eric J. Grove (1911; Annapolis, Md., 1988), 257–58; and G. J. Marcus, *The Age of Nelson: The Royal Navy, 1793–1815* (New York, 1971), 243.

10. In the 1580s and 1590s.

11. In addition to the problem of divided command to which Callwell refers, just about every possible misfortune of war attended the 1589 expedition, intended originally to eliminate the battered remainder of the Great Armada (of 1588) in the harbor at Santander, and then to move on and occupy Lisbon as an English base, raise Portugal against Spain, and even seize the Azores. The expedition suffered from lack of central command, lack of cohesion between land and sea el-

ements, uncertainty over objectives, and loss of surprise. Loss of surprise is almost always lethal to joint endeavors.

12. This episode was, alas, yet another black page in Britain's distinctly checkered history of amphibious enterprises. See J. H. Owen, *War at Sea under Queen Anne, 1702–1708* (Cambridge, 1938), ch. 3.

13. The prevention of the dynastic acquisition of Spain and its overseas empire either by the Bourbons of France or the Habsburgs of Austria.

14. Lord Mahon, *History of England*, 7 vols. (London, 1858).

15. This "sorry story" is visited in great detail in Richard Harding, *Amphibious Warfare in the Eighteenth Century: The British Expedition to the West Indies, 1740–1742* (Woodbridge, Suffolk, Eng., 1991), with an analysis which speaks usefully of joint warfare beyond the eighteenth century. Indeed, Harding's primary conclusion is identical to Callwell's: the need for close cooperation between the land and sea services.

16. 19 September 1757.

17. During the War of Austrian Succession (King George's War, in America), Louisbourg on Cape Breton Island surrendered on 16 June 1745. By the terms of the Treaty of Aix-la-Chapelle in 1748 Louisbourg was traded for Madras.

18. Belle Isle was captured in 1761; Martinique and Havana in 1762.

19. This is probably an exaggeration. See John Creswell, *Generals and Admirals: The Story of Amphibious Command* (Westport, Conn., 1952), chs. 3–6; and Harding, *Amphibious Warfare in the Eighteenth Century*.

20. The British evacuated Toulon on 19 December 1792. Corsica was captured on 10 August 1794 and was abandoned late in November 1796.

21. John Knox Laughton, *Studies in Naval History: Biographies* (1887; Annapolis, Md., 1970).

22. In World War II Britain resolved to prevent such a problem. On 3–4 July 1940 French naval forces at Oran were engaged and, by and large, sunk, while French units in Alexandria agreed to disarm themselves. Britain had two principal motives for the brutal action taken in 1940 against the navy of her erstwhile ally. First, to preclude even the possibility of Germany inheriting the French fleet. Second, Churchill believed that such bold and ruthless action would impress neutral (especially American) opinion on the issue of Britain's will to continue the fight.

23. Battles of La Hogue, 29 May–3 June 1692; the Battle of Malaga, 24 August 1704.

24. Walcheren in 1809, in common with Gallipoli in 1915, were both monumental failures in expeditionary warfare and both prompted deeply contentious public enquiries. See Gordon C. Bond, *The Grand Expedition: The British Invasion of Holland in 1809* (Athens, Ga., 1979).

25. There is no twentieth-century British equivalent to the belief of the U.S. Marine Corps on Guadalcanal in 1942 that they were viewed as expendable by a Navy concerned primarily with protecting its ships. To the contrary, the Royal Navy has accepted extraordinary risks in order to keep faith with dependent, and sometimes desperate, land forces. In 1941, as if the 1940 expeditionary rescue experience from Norway and France (Dunkirk primarily) were not enough, the sharpest of sharp ends of joint warfare afflicted the Royal Navy in the Mediterranean. With reference to the German sea-air threat to Crete, the Commander in Chief Mediterranean Fleet, Admiral Sir Andrew Cunningham "could only signal to all his ships: 'Stick it out. Navy must not let Army down. No enemy forces must reach Crete by Sea. . . .' The Navy did not let the Army down, and no German troops did reach Crete by sea. But to achieve this was taking what may without undue melodrama be termed the 'death ride' of the Mediterranean Fleet." Corelli Barnett, *Engage the Enemy More Closely: The Royal*

Navy in the Second World War (New York, 1991), 356.
26. Maj.-Gen. Sir William F. P. Napier, *History of the War in the Peninsula and in the South of France from the Year 1807 to the Year 1814*, 6 vols. (London, 1832–1840).
27. Writing in the Winter of 1904–1905, Callwell had the recent knowledge of only one official invasion enquiry. Before the outbreak of war in August 1914 there would be two more such enquiries, in 1907 and 1913. See H. R. Moon, "The Invasion of the United Kingdom: Public Controversy and Official Planning, 1888–1918," Ph.D. diss, London University, 1968; and John Gooch, "The Bolt from the Blue," in Gooch, *The Prospect of War: Studies in British Defence Policy, 1847–1942* (London, 1981), 1–34.

CHAPTER 2

1. The close dependence of galley fleets upon the shore is emphasized in John H. Pryor, *Geography, Technology, and War: Studies in the Maritime History of the Mediterranean, 649–1571* (Cambridge, 1988). "In the last days of galley warfare, sea power was just as much a matter of skilful use of coastal geography as it had ever been. Naval forces were in fact amphibious forces. Control of the sea lanes was achieved only through control of the coasts along which they passed" (177). The superior studies of galley warfare remain William Ledyard Rogers, *Naval Warfare Under Oars, 6th to 16th Centuries: A Study of Strategy, Tactics and Ship Design* (1940; Annapolis, Md., 1986); and John Francis Guilmartin, Jr., *Gunpowder and Galleys: Changing Technology and Mediterranean Warfare at Sea in the Sixteenth Century* (Cambridge, 1974).
2. "*Les Espagnols sur mer*": the Spaniards at sea. On 29 August 1350, in the Channel off Dungeness, Edward III's English fleet defeated a large Spanish force of forty armed merchantmen.

3. In company, later, with Corbett (*Some Principles of Maritime Strategy*, 261–79), though in contrast to Mahan, Callwell here implies some skepticism about the contemporary efficacy of convoy.

4. Presumably primarily because Germany, rather than France, is most likely to be Britain's principal enemy in a future great war.

5. See Callwell's 1897 study, *The Effect of Maritime Command on Land Campaigns Since Waterloo* (Edinburgh, 1897), ch. 2.

6. "The Battle of the Four Days" was waged from 11–14 June 1666 in the Second Anglo-Dutch War (1665–1667).

7. Furthermore, to amplify Callwell's argument, unlike Vice-Adm. Sir Horatio Nelson at Trafalgar on 21 October 1805, on 31 May 1916 Adm. Sir John Jellicoe commanded Britain's *only* battle fleet.

8. In 1822.

9. In 1759.

10. Which is to say from 480 B.C. to Callwell's time of writing, 1904–1905.

11. The first radio signal was transmitted by William Preece in 1892 (albeit only over a distance of 364 meters). Major advances were registered by Guglielmo Marconi from 1895 onward. Important, even radical, technical developments in radio were occurring as Callwell was writing this book. Given the command and communication needs of artillery, and the fact that Callwell was a very professional artilleryman, it is scarcely surprising that he was well attuned to the scientific and technical advances relevant to proficiency in war.

12. Probably the most dramatic and best known such case in the twentieth century is that of the German "pocket" battleship *Admiral Graf Spee* (12,100 tons, 6 x 11" guns, 26 knots), which in December 1939 was allowed only seventy-two hours by the government of Uruguay to make such repairs as she

could (to the damage sustained in a clash with three British cruisers) and clear territorial waters.

13. In 1675.

14. The wars of the twentieth-century have demonstrated that Callwell was too much the English gentleman, in this regard at least. Neutral states generally have been as even-handed, or otherwise, as it was prudent to be. Both Spain and Sweden elected in World War II to tilt in their neutral behavior in favor of the extant winning side. German U-boats were repaired in Spanish ports, while Germany treated the Swedish economy as an extension of her own and moved troops across Sweden as proved convenient.

15. In other words, there are still many parts of the world where neutral rights will not be allowed to override naval expediency. On 19 August 1759 Adm. Edward Boscawen ignored Portuguese neutrality and entered Lagos Bay to attack four French ships (under the command of Adm. Sabran de la Clue) which had (deliberately) run aground.

CHAPTER 3

1. In the memorable and slightly more subtle words of Basil H. Liddell Hart, "the object in war is to obtain a better peace." *Strategy: The Indirect Approach* (1941; London, 1967), 366.

2. Some of the problems with "this great truth" are outlined admirably in an article by Jan S. Breemer where the title tells all: "The Burden of Trafalgar: Decisive Battle and Naval Strategic Expectations on the Eve of World War I," *Journal of Strategic Studies* (March 1994): 33–62.

3. Callwell makes a point here that was to be validated by the naval history of both world wars. Even with the maturing of air power in the early years of World War II, Britain was unable reliably to reach major German warships sheltering in well defended home ports or Norwegian fiords.

4. Some conventional views of the continental-maritime nexus in British policy and strategy in the struggle with France from 1778 to 1783 are challenged usefully in N. A. M. Rodger, "The Continental Commitment in the Eighteenth Century," in Lawrence Freedman, Paul Hayes, and Robert O'Neill, eds., *War, Strategy, and International Politics: Essays in Honour of Sir Michael Howard* (Oxford, 1992), 39–55; and Daniel A. Baugh, "Why did Britain Lose Command of the Sea During the War for America?," in Jeremy Black and Philip Woodfine, eds., *The British Navy and the Use of Naval Power in the Eighteenth Century* (Leicester, Eng., 1988), 149–69.

5. On "the cardinal fault" of "ulterior objects" in naval policy, see Mahan, *Influence of Sea Power upon History*, 537.

6. This is an insightful analysis which demonstrates conclusively Callwell's strategic intellectual independence from Mahan. Callwell here describes almost precisely the German naval condition, or dilemma, of 1914–1918.

7. Audibert Ramatuelle, *Cours elementaire de tactique navales* (Paris, 1802). See Michael Depeyre, "Audibert Ramatuelle ou des Enseignments Perdus," in Hervé Coutau-Bégarie, ed., *L'Évolution de la penseé navale* (Paris, 1990), 1:79–88; and Brian Tunstall, *Naval Warfare in the Age of Sail: The Evolution of Fighting Tactics, 1650–1815*, ed. Nicholas Tracy (Annapolis, Md., 1990), 235–40.

8. Admiral Sébastian François de Bigot, Viscomte de Morogues, author of *Tactique navale ou traité des evolutions et des signaux* (Paris, 1763).

9. It would be difficult to express this very important point more clearly than does Callwell.

10. The German High Seas Fleet did not succumb to the temptation to fight for it's honor, as it were, early in the Great War. The rough handling the already critically weak German surface fleet received in Spring 1940 was a result not of naval bravado, but of the operational needs of the joint enterprise in Norway.

11. This was the orthodox view of Callwell's day; certainly it was reflected in the writings of Mahan and Corbett and in the beliefs of the Admiralty. Two great wars on from the writing of this book, however, it is plain that Callwell's first caveat—"when it takes the form of sustained effort"—is a less than stunningly perceptive truism, while his second caveat concerning "naval preponderance at its back" looks fragile in the light of the two Battles of the Atlantic. Of course, this is to be wise long after the event.

12. In common with everybody else in 1904–1905, Callwell, though impressed with the potential of the submarine, did not anticipate in the near term the development of a major, even possibly strategically decisive, submarine menace to maritime trade.

13. Sensible and conventional points to make in 1905, but to be proved wrong in 1917–1918 and 1939–1945.

14. Callwell makes an important distinction here, between the need for maritime preponderance for a "great land campaign based on the sea" and, by plain implication, the need for somewhat less achievement at sea if the joint expedition has more modest goals. The author may have been inspired by the useful distinction drawn by Rear-Adm. Philip H. Colomb between the objects of "(1) ravage and destruction [i.e., the raid]; (2) occupation and conquest [i.e., invasion from the sea]." *Naval Warfare: Its Ruling Principles and Practice Historically Treated* (London, 1891), ch. 10.

15. As Pryor makes very clear (*Geography, Technology, and War*), what Callwell here refers to as the "war of posts," the war for naval bases, always was a defining characteristic of galley warfare in the narrow seas of the Mediterranean.

CHAPTER 4

1. Eric Grove has provided the useful reminder that "such terms as 'sea communications' or 'sea lines of communication'

are dangerous in that they tend to mask the fundamental truth that maritime strategy is about *ships*, defined as the *means of movement* on or below the surface." *The Future of Sea Power* (Annapolis, Md., 1990), 22. (Emphasis in original.)

2. In 1904–1905, the time of Callwell's writing, the Royal Navy was a coal-burning fleet. Not until July 1913 did the First Lord of the Admiralty, Winston S. Churchill, announce in the House of Commons an historic wholesale shift in dependence of the Royal Navy from coal to oil. This was a bold move indeed, albeit a move necessary for enhancing the speed and readiness of warships. After all, Britain is an island partly made of coal, while in 1912–1913 the country had no known oil deposits securely at home.

3. The Treaty of Ryswick, 1697, concluded the War of the League of Augsburg, a.k.a. the Nine Years' War or King William's War (1688–1697).

4. Dunkirk was the principal home port for the French privateers who waged profitable private war on English shipping in the North Sea and the Channel. See J. S. Bromley, *Corsairs and Navies, 1660–1760* (London, 1987), ch. 5; and Patrick Crowhurst, *The French War on Trade: Privateering, 1793–1815* (Brookfield, Vt., 1989), 4–5.

5. *Plus ça change* . . . In anticipation of Italian belligerency, on 16 May 1940 the Royal Navy temporarily abandoned the Mediterranean sea-artery of empire in favor of the Cape route. Italy declared war on 10 June.

6. The Peace of Amiens, 1802–1803, heralded by the Treaty of Amiens, 27 March 1802.

7. The events of 1941–1942 work to show just how right Callwell was to emphasize the strategic importance of Malta.

8. A harbinger of the future was Adm. Sir Edward Hawke's blockade of Brest in 1759. See Geoffrey Marcus, *Quiberon Bay: The Campaign in Home Waters, 1759* (London, 1960), ch. 8, "Keeping the Sea"; and Ruddock F. Mackay, *Admiral Hawke* (Oxford, 1965), ch. 13.

9. Alas, Corbett did not add more volumes to *England in the Mediterranean: A Study of the Rise and Influence of British Power within the Straits, 1602–1713* (London, 1903). For the Mediterranean theater, or anywhere else for that matter, it would be difficult to overstate the importance of advanced bases in support of amphibious warfare, as well as for the prior achievement of maritime preponderance (Callwell's restricted point here). See Callwell, *Dardanelles*, 337–38, for just this argument. As the ANZACs were to be based in Egypt for their Gallipoli adventure, so U.S. Marines were to head from New Zealand for the southern Solomons twenty-seven years later.

10. Callwell's reference to "strategical positions" is distinctly Jominian. On the use of "strategy" and "strategic" see Colin S. Gray, *Explorations in Strategy* (Westport, Conn., 1996), ch. 1.

11. The Battle of Camperdown, 11 October 1797, one of the hardest fought naval battles in the history of the Royal Navy.

12. This uncompromisingly strong prediction would have looked particularly sound to U.S. naval planners in the early 1980s as they grappled with the challenge of defeating a Soviet Navy likely to adopt a broadly defensive "bastion" strategy.

13. During the interregnum in 1649–1650.

14. Not to mention the fleets of the Byzantines. See Colin S. Gray, *The Leverage of Sea Power: The Strategic Advantage of Navies in War* (New York, 1992), 118–29.

15. Adm. John van Galen blockaded Leghorn in 1652–1653 during the First Anglo-Dutch War. Adm. Edward Boscawen blockaded the French fleet in Toulon in 1759 during the Seven Years' War (1756–1763).

16. The Battle of Beachy Head, 10 July 1690, during the War of the League of Augsburg.

17. The enemy had been beaten at the Battle of the Saints,

12 April 1782, in the Anglo-French dimension to the War of American Independence.

18. This was to prove as true for the German U-boat campaigns of the two world wars, as it had been in past centuries for privateering campaigns. The U-boat pens still standing intact in French ports on the coast of the Bay of Biscay attest to the validity in Callwell's argument.

19. Technical-tactical developments soon would invalidate this statement.

20. The idea of close blockade of an inferior fleet was alive but not very well in the Royal Navy at the time of Callwell's writing. By 1912 the close blockade was officially defunct. See Arthur J. Marder, *From the Dreadnought to Scapa Flow: The Royal Navy in the Fisher Era, 1904–1919. Vol. I. The Road to War, 1904–1914* (London, 1961), 367–77.

21. The employment of submarines as commerce raiders naturally rendered entirely moot the question of how to handle "prizes."

22. The operational terms of engagement certainly were to improve as the century progressed, but Callwell was correct, the location of bases mattered deeply. By the early summer of 1940, the German Navy, weakened though it was by the exertions of the spring, now had geography very much on its side—at least as compared with its plight from 1914 to 1918. This argument is central to Wolfgang Wegener, *The Naval Strategy of the World War,* introduction by Holger H. Herwig (1929; Annapolis, Md., 1989).

CHAPTER 5

1. A thought more than a little reminiscent of Clausewitz's ideas on a "center of gravity." Carl von Clausewitz, *On War,* ed. Michael Howard and Peter Paret (Princeton, N.J., 1976), 595–97.

2. Although in a later period supremacy at sea could be sought via an initial air assault on a naval "post" (e.g., Pearl Harbor, Taranto), or by threatening a "post" in defense of which the enemy believes he must offer battle.

3. The extensive experience of anti-submarine warfare in the twentieth century proves beyond a shadow of a doubt that "the operations of cruisers in the open sea" are not cost-effective—at least they were not in the 1910s or the 1940s.

CHAPTER 6

1. But, as Callwell recognized, this is a rule of prudence and not a Law of War. This question took on great significance for policy in the winter of 1914–1915. Churchill allowed himself to believe what he wanted to believe about the effectiveness of naval gunfire, particularly when it took the form of 15" rifles from the *Queen Elizabeth* super-Dreadnought. See Winston S. Churchill, *The World Crisis, 1911–1918* (London, 1938), pt. 2, ch. 7.

2. Alfred Thayer Mahan, *Lessons of the War with Spain and Other Articles* (Boston, 1899).

3. On 13 April 1904, the Russian fleet commander, Vice Adm. Stepan Osipov Makarov, went down with his ship, the *Petropavlovsk,* when she struck a mine (the mine exploded the ship's magazine and *its* stock of mines as well), during the Russo-Japanese War (1904–1905). See Vice Adm. S. O. Makarov, *Imperial Russian Navy: Discussion of Questions in Naval Tactics,* introduction by Capt. Robert B. Bathurst (1898; Annapolis, Md., 1990), xxxiii–xxxv.

4. Callwell was correct, as usual. The attempt to force the Dardanelles strictly with naval force was abandoned on 18 March 1915 after the bombarding squadron lost three pre-Dreadnought battleships (the *Bouvet, Irresistible,* and *Ocean*)

and suffered damage to a battlecruiser (*Inflexible*) when they ran across a line of undetected mines.

CHAPTER 7

1. Even though he proceeds to qualify the advice, and even though he is right to keep in view the prospect of hard fighting, still it has to be admitted that this is an unfortunately simple-mindedly sentiment, as expressed.
2. Had World War I concluded as a draw, the naval balance could have had particular significance in the shaping of the post-war settlement. In 1940, Winston Churchill was none too subtle in his hints to Franklin Roosevelt to the effect that the United States ought to worry about the disposition of the surviving assets of the Royal Navy in the event of British defeat at home.
3. Callwell is wrong here; at least he is wrong with reference to the blockaded High Seas Fleet of Germany in 1914–1918. Living conditions of wartime service in an inactive fleet, added to the sense of being confined to the bench in the struggle for national survival, created a crisis of low morale. See Holger H. Herwig, *"Luxury" Fleet: The Imperial German Navy, 1888–1918* (London, 1980), chs. 11–12.
4. In the Battle of Minorca, 20 May 1756, Adm. John Byng secured only a tactically indecisive result—as was typical of pre-Nelsonian naval battle in the eighteenth century—following which he returned to Gibraltar, which left the French at liberty to take Port Mahon. Byng was recalled, court-martialled, found guilty, and shot. Embarrassed politicians are prone to hunt for scapegoats. The Byng execution was a robust variant of what was meted out to those designated as guilty after the Walcheren failure of 1809, the Dardanelles failure of 1915, and the persistent failures by the British Army in North Africa in 1941–1942.

5. Lt.-Gen. Sir Ralph Abercromby was the very fine leader of the military element of the joint expedition that conducted a successful opposed landing at Aboukir Bay in Egypt on 8 March 1801. He was killed in battle two weeks later, thereby assuring that his military reputation would lose none of its well deserved luster.

6. A rare historical error by Callwell. The proper date was 2 April 1801.

7. By 1814 "the French Navy totalled 103 of the line and 157 frigates." Marcus, *Age of Nelson*, 426.

CHAPTER 8

1. This 1905 judgment by Callwell has found persuasive echoes down the years. The same judgment permeates Marder, *From the Dreadnought to Scapa Flow,* vol. 5 (London, 1970), ch. 12; John Creswell, *British Admirals of the Eighteenth Century: Tactics in Battle* (Hamden, Conn., 1972); and John Horsfield, *The Art of Leadership in War: The Royal Navy From the Age of Nelson to the End of World War II* (Westport, Conn., 1980). Wayne Hughes is exactly right when he advises that "Men Matter Most." Wayne P. Hughes, Jr., *Fleet Tactics: Theory and Practice* (Annapolis, Md., 1986), 26–28. In his celebrated study *Generals and Generalship* (New York, 1943), Gen. Sir Archibald Wavell argued that "military history is a flesh-and-blood affair, not a matter of diagrams and formulas or of rules; not a conflict of machines but of men" (24). The would-be "information warrior" of today should take heed.

2. In 1799 Captain, later Rear Adm., Sir Thomas Troubridge, was engaged in assisting local Italian resistance to French invaders.

CHAPTER 9

1. Every geographically specialized form of armed force has its equivalents to "fixed defences on shore." Air power has defended airfields and space power could have protected launch sites. Armies, of course, can seek sanctuary and support either behind fortifications or dispersed so as to evade enemy targeteers.
2. See Colin S. Gray and Roger W. Barnett, "Reflections," in Gray and Barnett, eds., *Seapower and Strategy* (Annapolis, Md., 1989), 371–86.

CHAPTER 10

1. War being a two-sided affair, at the very least, it is important to remember that the measure of *our* interest in the sea has to be the measure of *our enemy's* interest. Callwell is entirely correct in pointing out the all but unique vulnerability of Britain to pressure at sea, but one should not deduce that the naval strength of a truly continental power like Germany is of a "luxury" kind. The course of two world wars demonstrated that Germany was obliged to seek effective answers of both a military and naval kind to the strategic leverage of British sea power.
2. It is useful to register the following hierarchy of descending authority: (1) *vision* of the kind of national security condition desired; (2) *policy* choice; (3) *grand strategy* on the choice among policy instruments; (4) *military strategy* (and naval and air strategy, and so forth); (5) *operations* at the theater level of war; and (6) *tactics*. Callwell recognizes a much more simple universe wherein there is (1) military policy, (2) strategy, and presumably (3) tactics.
3. Whether or not specific contemporary conditions allow this purportedly immense competence to amphibious power,

Callwell is to be praised for emphasizing here the limitations of "purely naval force" and, generally, the strategic merit in joint endeavor. He is always reminding his readers, as one should expect of a strategically sophisticated army officer, that the leverage of naval force is achieved in application *forward from the sea,* to pick a form of words not entirely at random.

4. This is a permanent truth about the course of economic warfare, as well as about a maritime supply blockade in particular.

5. This is one of the best paragraphs in the book. Indeed, as noted earlier, it is possible, even probable, that Julian Corbett found some inspiration here for his observation on the apparently disappointing consequences of Trafalgar.

6. This remains quite a popular belief, but, on balance, it is probably not true, at least it is incorrect as stated with reference to the Civil War as a whole. The truth of the matter is that "to have a chance to win, the Confederacy had to industrialize, and it did." Richard E. Beringer, Herman Hattaway, Archer Jones, and William N. Still, Jr., *Why the South Lost the Civil War* (Athens, Ga., 1986), 59.

7. This thought bears more than a trivial resemblance to at least a part of the argument in Halford J. Mackinder's 25 January 1904 lecture "The Geographical Pivot of History." Reprinted in Mackinder, *Democratic Ideals and Reality* (New York, 1962), 240–64. Mackinder predicted that the completion of great transcontinental railways was transforming the economic, political, and strategic relations between sea power and land power in favor of the latter. While Callwell was head of the strategical section of the Directorate of Military Operations in the War Office from 1904 until 1907, Mackinder was barely a mile away working as director of the London School of Economics from 1903 to 1908. Needless to add, perhaps, Mackinder's seminal lecture before the Royal Geographical Society in January 1904 was delivered less than

a year prior to Callwell undertaking the writing of *Military Operations*. Given the measure of Callwell's and Mackinder's apparent agreement on the implications of railways for the strengthening of continental states in conflict with insular ones, it is to Callwell's credit as an independent thinker that his text emerged with an amphibious emphasis.

8. In World War I this problem presented itself to Britain vis-à-vis possible contraband heading for Germany via Holland, Denmark, Norway, and Sweden. See A. C. Bell, *A History of the Blockade of Germany and of the Countries Associated with Her in the Great War, Austria-Hungry, Bulgaria, and Turkey, 1914–1918* (London, 1937); and Gerd Hardach, *The First World War, 1914–1918* (Berkeley, Calif., 1977), ch. 2.

9. What Callwell knew to be correct about the inefficiency of economic blockade in 1904–1905, and nothing in subsequent decades suggested plausibly to be false, many people who should have known better declined to believe in 1990–1991 in the case of Iraq.

10. In 1914–1916, Britain was prepared to go to strategically self-damaging lengths in non-rigorous conduct of the economic blockade because of sensitivity to America's interests. As a neutral power, the United States posed a major challenge to whatever strategic efficacy economic blockade otherwise might have had as a weapon in the world war. In World War II, Japan closed her eyes to the trans-Pacific supply of war-related material that was shipped from North America to Vladivostok. Rather than face war with the USSR, Japan preferred to ignore the flow of Soviet-flagged American ships that were delivering material critically important to the war effort of their German ally's most lethal foe.

11. This eloquent paragraph is mainly superficially Mahanian. Callwell's talk of "steady pressure" appears to bear the intellectual signature of the author of these familiar words: "It is not the taking of individual ships or convoys, be

they few or many, that strikes down the money power of a nation; it is the possession of that overbearing power on the sea which drives the enemy's flag from it, or allows it to appear only as a fugitive." *Influence of Sea Power upon History,* 138. Callwell's concluding sentence provides a massive counterpoint of complementary strategic common sense.

12. Corbett, *England in the Mediterranean,* 2:242.

CHAPTER 11

1. As Callwell himself demonstrates persuasively in *Maritime Command,* chs. 3, 8.

2. French preponderance at sea might have counted for much more than it did had the war become truly protracted. Michael Howard, *The Franco-Prussian War: The German Invasion of France, 1870–1871* (London, 1961), 389, is useful.

CHAPTER 12

1. The great siege of Malta by the Turks, 1565. Richard I, Coeur de Lion's "armament destined for Palestine," 1191.

2. Sir William Laird Clowes, *The Royal Navy: A History from the Earliest Times to the Present,* 7 vols. (London, 1897–1903). See the discussion of "fleet in being" in Corbett, *Some Principles of Maritime Strategy,* 209–27.

3. Mahan, *Lessons of the War with Spain.* Reprinted in Allan Westcott, ed., *Mahan on Naval Warfare: Selections from the Writings of Rear Admiral Alfred T. Mahan* (Boston, 1918), 242–43.

4. In December 1796.

5. The year should be 1854. The Allied expedition left Varna on 7 September and began landing in the Crimea on 13 September.

6. Compare these words by Callwell with the following thoughts expressed in 1911 by Julian Corbett: "If we have gained complete command, no invasion can take place, nor will it . . . be attempted. If we have lost it completely no invasion will be necessary, since, quite apart from the threat of invasion, we must make peace on the best terms we can get." *Some Principles of Maritime Strategy*, 239.

CHAPTER 13

1. An example for all time of Callwell's topic here is Gen. Douglas MacArthur's amphibious triumph at Inchon, 15 September 1950. See Col. Robert D. Heinl, Jr., "Inchon, 1950," in Merrill L. Bartlett, ed., *Assault from the Sea: Essays on the History of Amphibious Warfare* (Annapolis, Md., 1983), 337–53.

2. With specifically insular reference, in his *History of United States Naval Operations in World War II,* Samuel Eliot Morison was to repeat the sense in this argument by Callwell. "As the transports that had brought the Marines to this unpleasant island [Guadalcanal] disappeared over the horizon on the afternoon of 9 August [the Japanese had won the naval Battle of Savo Island in the early hours of that day], escorted by all combat ships still afloat, General Vandergrift knew that he was in for a rough, tough time. No ground force, not even United States Marines, can long hold a remote island against an enemy who commands the surrounding seas and the routes to its own bases." *Vol. V: The Struggle for Guadalcanal, August 1942–February 1943* (Boston, 1968), 65.

3. This is a nice distinction, made even more eloquent by its "joint" presentation with both maritime and continental illustration. "It was worried, but it was not endangered," is both stylistically pleasing and analytically sophisticated. This

complex case discussed by Callwell merits further treatment by defense professionals who perennially must cope with menaces of modest seeming dimensions.

CHAPTER 14

1. For Callwell's firsthand experiences in the Turko-Greek War of 1897, see his *Stray Recollections,* vol. 2, ch. 15.
2. See Callwell, *Maritime Command,* ch. 5.
3. See David Walder, *The Short Victorious War: The Russo-Japanese Conflict, 1904–05* (London, 1973); Newton A. McCully, *The McCully Report: The Russo-Japanese War, 1904–05* (1906; Annapolis, Md., 1977); Richard Connaughton, *The War of the Rising Sun and Tumbling Bear: A Military History of the Russo-Japanese War, 1904–5* (London, 1988); and Julian S. Corbett, *Maritime Operations in the Russo-Japanese War, 1904–05* (1912–1914; Annapolis, Md., 1994).
4. See Callwell, *Maritime Command,* ch. 3.

CHAPTER 15

1. As, for example, in Antoine Henri de Jomini, *The Art of War* (1838, 1862; London, 1992), 188–96.
2. Respectively, Jomini, *The Art of War*; and Edward Bruce Hamley, *The Operations of War Explained and Illustrated* (1866; Edinburgh, 1909).
3. This need not be the case in modern conditions. In May 1940 the British army discovered that an enemy able to command, or at least seriously to dispute, the overhead aerial flank can render life intolerable in a coastal enclave. The enemy overhead—not to mention his artillery—poses threats both to the army ashore and to the viability of the sea lines of communication of the coastal enclave. There are no perma-

nent tactical or operational laws pertinent here either from one period to another or in different cases in the same period. Whether or not a military force can be tolerably secure in a coastal enclave depends entirely upon the unique circumstances in question.

4. See Corbett, *Some Principles of Maritime Strategy*, pt. 1, chs. 5–6; and B. H. Liddell Hart, "Marines and Strategy," *Marine Corps Gazette* (July 1960): 22–31.

5. Surprise is a necessary, though it may not always be a sufficient, condition for success in the conduct of opposed landings. There will be occasions when the very fact of immediate tactical opposition to a landing will follow from poor operational security. Callwell's careful phrasing covers, for example, the case of the surprise, all but unopposed landings at Ari Burnu (ANZAC Cove) on 25 April, and at Suvla Bay, 6 August 1915. The lack of powerful immediate resistance to these landings did not suffice for the expeditionary troops to achieve operational success by exploiting their initial lodgements ashore. Overall, however, Gallipoli in 1915, in common with the Dieppe raid of 19 August 1942, illustrates the sense in Callwell's argument. Loss of operational security in amphibious warfare is typically fatal to the prospects for success.

6. As noted in the editor's introductory essay, even by the relaxed standards of his day Callwell's comments about Jews often crossed the line into the offensive column.

7. Thomas Babington [Lord] Macaulay, *The History of England*, ed. Hugh Trevor-Roper (London, 1986). Originally published in five volumes (London, 1848–1861).

CHAPTER 16

1. See the stimulating analysis in Correlli Barnett, *Britain and Her Army, 1509–1970: A Military, Political and Social Survey* (1970; London, 1974), especially pp. 248–49.

2. Callwell almost certainly is in error here. Although the maritime enterprise against, though not the original concept of the raid on, Sebastopol, was an operational success, the war could not be won by action around the Black Sea littoral alone. The fighting in the Crimea was expensive for the Tsar, but it was the sea-based threat to the center of gravity of the Russian Empire in, or from, the Baltic, that generated the strategic leverage necessary for a satisfactory peace. See Andrew D. Lambert, *The Crimean War: British Grand Strategy Against Russia, 1853–56* (Manchester, Eng., 1990).

3. See the map on p. 306, and see Callwell, *Maritime Command*, 202–15.

4. See the memoranda by Callwell reproduced in Appendix I.

CHAPTER 18

1. Thomas Carlyle, *The History of Friedrich II of Prussia, called Frederick the Great*, 6 vols. (London, 1858–1865).

2. This view is very much in line with Callwell's 1897 opinion that "the influence of the Baltic campaign upon the struggle in the Crimea was enormous." *Maritime Command*, 180. Basil Greenhill and Ann Giffard, *The British Assault on Finland, 1854–1855: A Forgotten Naval War* (London, 1988), 340–41, support Callwell's argument. However, not everyone in the War Office in 1905 shared Callwell's appreciation of the strategic history of the Crimean War. In December 1905 Julian Corbett was informed by Capt. Edward Slade, director of the war course at the Naval College (Greenwich), that the War Office had rejected the idea of the Navy's Baltic scheme. Corbett's biographer writes that "a few days later [than 16 December 1905, actually, as just noted, on 26 December] he [Slade] stated that the basis for the War Office objection was that the Baltic Sea operations of 1854 had no influence on

the Crimean War." Donald M. Schurman, *Julian S. Corbett, 1854–1922: Historian of British Maritime Policy from Drake to Jellicoe* (London, 1981), 42–43.

3. It is also common sense, as well as being the purest Jomini. See *Art of War,* 70.

CHAPTER 19

1. "Naval artillery against forts" is a subject of enduring "joint" interest. This sensible paragraph by Callwell—who, it should not be forgotten, himself had commanded coastal artillery batteries and garrisons, as well as heavy field guns on campaign—presages the debate over the effectiveness, actual and potential, of naval gunfire at the Dardanelles in 1914 and 1915. For a glimpse at some of the terms of long subsequent debate, see Arthur J. Marder, "The Dardanelles Revisited: Further Thoughts on the Naval Prelude," in Marder, *From the Dardanelles to Oran: Studies of the Royal Navy in War and Peace, 1915–1940* (London, 1976), 1–32.

CHAPTER 20

1. This seemingly innocuous interpolation expresses recognition en passant of an absence of experience that was to have the most dire of consequences in 1914 in East Africa and in 1915 at Gallipoli. In the blunt words of Correlli Barnett: "Amphibious strokes especially demand meticulous preparation; they demand the highest possible standard of efficiency and organization in fighting troops, supporting services and formation headquarters. The Dardanelles expedition lacked all these essentials. *As too often before with British maritime adventures all was hasty improvisation."* *Britain and Her Army,* 384. (Emphasis added.) Somewhat after

the fashion of the U.S. Army Air Forces, and then the USAF itself, repeatedly having to relearn the lessons of yesteryear about the need for competence in close air support of ground forces, so the British army and the Royal Navy in war after war had to rediscover the practical skills necessary to effect amphibious ways in combat. The condition to which Callwell pointed accurately, the absence of opposed landings "on a great scale of recent years," in effect characteristically is lethal to the maintenance, let alone acquisition, of competence in the techniques needed for amphibious forced entry.

2. These sage words by Callwell in 1905 could as well have been written to condemn Gallipoli in 1915, or Dieppe in 1942: charge by charge he hits the mark.

3. Callwell returns to this key topic in his book *Dardanelles*, 74–75.

4. It is ironic that the British often have shown more professional skill in the organization and conduct of amphibious retreat than amphibious assault. Writing about the retreat from Gallipoli, Barnett judges that "the evacuation itself was a masterpiece of staffwork and deception, showing what might have been achieved in the original landings, had it not been for haste, unreadiness and improvisation." *Britain and Her Army,* 385.

5. Callwell ought to be correct here, especially if one adds in the hindering effect of hostile air power. The historical experience of amphibious withdrawal under fire, actual or potential, in the twentieth century, however, does not provide a ringing endorsement for Callwell's prudent judgment. Practice confounds theory, yet again.

CHAPTER 21

1. The exemplar of this argument is provided by the better part of a millennium of Byzantine experience with the security of their capital city on the Bosphorous, Constantinople. Besieger after besieger through the centuries learnt that the

city might be taken only if it was isolated from assistance by land and by sea. This point is developed in Gray, *Leverage of Sea Power*, 118–29. Also see Hans Delbrück, *History of the Art of War Within the Framework of Political History. Vol. III: The Middle Ages* (1923; Westport Conn., 1982), 195; and, for the dénouement, Steven Runciman, *The Fall of Constantinople, 1453* (Cambridge, 1965).

2. Linear terminology, too tightly transferred from its home environment, is inclined to mislead when it appears in relation to operations at sea or in the air. As with lines of communication, so patrol lines conjure up visions of linear control that the size of the maritime environment—not to mention the weather—easily can mock. The arrival of the means of overhead reconnaissance, of sonar, and of radar, certainly renders sea passage more readily monitored than before, but still it is well to remember that barriers of various kinds at sea tend to be more notional than physical.

3. Sébestian Le Prestre de Vauban (1633–1707), military engineer of genius, appointed France's commissary general of fortifications in 1678. In addition to constructing thirty-three new fortresses, and modernizing three hundred others, on France's frontiers, he wrote authoritative textbooks on the attack (1701) and the defense (1706) of fortified places. Baron Menno van Coehoorn (1641–1704), Dutch military engineer who invented a "new system" of fortification and of methods of active defense. He was appointed engineer-general of fortifications in the Dutch Republic in 1695.

CHAPTER 22

1. Callwell surely is correct about the strategic irrelevance of the lakes in N. W. Canada, but his like judgment about the Caspian was to be falsified little more than ten years after his time of writing. The Caspian Sea was the focus of intense,

if modest-scale, military, and some naval, activity from 1915 to 1919. The Caspian may be a "closed sea," but in the period just cited it was a hub connecting combatant Russian "Whites," combatant Russian Bolsheviks, the Baku oilfields, Turkish interests in the East, British interests in the East, and so forth. It was a dynamic mixture. See the once "secret" (in India), British "lost" official history, Brig.-Gen. F. J. Moberly, *History of the Great War: Operations in Persia, 1914–1916*, introduction by G. M. Bayliss (1929; London, 1987), especially chs. 9–11.

2. Rear Adm. Sir John Duckworth.

3. It might be said that mines came of age in the Russo-Japanese War, which still was underway as Callwell was writing these words. His judgment on the operational effect of mines was to prove sounder than was that of the Royal Navy. Marder observes that although "[Admiral Sir John] Fisher was impressed with the use of mines in the Japanese war . . . he seems to have believed that submarines allowed the mine to be dispensed with. Down to 1914 mines were not regarded in the Navy as formidable weapons whether for offence or defence. They were looked upon as rather expensive luxuries in an unimportant branch of naval warfare." *Dreadnought to Scapa Flow*, 1:328. The Royal Navy was not to be the only first-class navy in this century to look down with disdain upon the humble mine.

4. Macaulay, *History of England*, 316–17.

5. In December 1790, during the Russo-Turkish War of 1787–1792, Count Alexander Vasilievich Suvorov (1729–1800) stormed the Turkish fortress of Ismail and massacred most of its garrison.

6. During the Russo-Turkish War of 1877–1878 the Russians were delayed by the conduct of a five-month siege of the Turkish fortress town of Plevna in Bulgaria (19 July–10 December 1877).

7. The Butler in J. M. Barrie's play of the same name. The Admirable Crichton assumes the leadership role—in this case

of an amphibious enterprise, notwithstanding the British practice of coordinated, rather than unified, command—by virtue of his superior personal qualities.

CHAPTER 23

1. Callwell's concept here is all but indistinguishable from the thinking in the U.S. Marine Corps in the very early 1920s that eventually (1933) led to creation of the two-brigade strong Fleet Marine Force. Those two brigades were, of course, to grow to six divisions (plus specialist units) by September 1944.

INDEX.

ABERCROMBY, SIR J., capture of Mauritius by, 134 note.
Abercromby, Sir R., references to, 35, 134 note; at the Helder, 138; landing of, in Aboukir Bay, 157, 224, 355-358.
Aberdeen, references to, 248, 325.
Abo, burning of Swedish galleys at, 131.
Aboukir Bay, references to, 35, 38, 40, 182, 215, 236, 359, 437; Abercromby's landing in, 157, 224, 351, 355-358.
Abraham, Heights of, appearance of Wolfe on, 424; reference to, 425.
Acquia Creek, Federal base at, 292.
Acre, Napoleon's siege-train captured on way to, 36; attack on, in 1840, 115; Napoleon and Sir S. Smith at, 153, 154; Ibrahim Pasha at, 320; references to, 321, 322; Sir S. Smith at the siege of, 381.
Actium, battle of, 392.
Adige, River, reference to, 315.
Admiralty, the, and Wellington, 3, 19, 20; reference to, 119; remarkable letter from, to Wellington, 137, 138; rebuke of Nelson by, 157; St Vincent's Memorandum to, 159.
Adrianople, Peace of, 255; Diebich advances to, 258.
Adriatic, references to, 73, 122, 185, 188, 272, 392; the defile north of the, 314-316; command of, in 1848-49, 315, 316.
Ægean, Greeks get command of, after Salamis, 130; references to, 185, 186, 187, 188, 379, 406; control of, by Greeks, in Turko-Greek war, 249, 250; move of Suliman Pasha from the Adriatic to the, 272; campaign in, in 1822, 317-319.
Agosto, action off, 34.
Aix, Isle of, reference to, 326.
Aix-la-Chapelle, Peace of, 96, 192.
Akhalkali, capture of, 254.
Akhalsik, capture of, 254.
Albemarle, at Havana, 135; landing of, at Havana, 346.
Aleppo, capture of, by Ibrahim Pasha, 321.
Alexander the Great, siege of Tyre by, 408.
Alexandria, Napoleon and Nelson at, 39, 40; typical of commercial port, 76; references to, 158, 209, 215, 216, 224, 236, 282, 322, 349, 356, 385, 416, 418.
Algeria, troops brought from, to France, 189; landing in, 224.
Algiers, Exmouth's attack on, 111, 125; Charles V.'s expedition against, 225-228, 230.
Alleghanies, references to, 274, 405.
Alma, battle of, 269, 270, 303; as illustrating warships helping troops, 339, 340.
Alps, references to, 286, 287, 313.
Alsen, references to, 305, 307.
Amazon, River, reference to, 402.
American Civil War, commerce destroying in, 101; as demonstrating limitations of sea-power, 171, 172; Federals capture base in, 108, 109; references to, 273, 274, 277, 289-295, 408, 409, 410, 411, 413-415; the Mississippi in, 403-406.
American Independence, War of,

497

faulty naval strategy of, 60 ; references to, 63, 408 ; the campaign of Newport in, 144-146 ; the campaign of Yorktown in, 237-240.

Amherst, General, and Boscawen, 14 ; attack of, on Louisbourg, 98, 135 ; references to, 193, 353, 419 ; delayed by bad weather in landing at Louisbourg, 344 ; creates flotilla on Lake Champlain, 395 ; operations of, in 1759, 425, 426 ; operations of, in 1760, 428.

Amiens, Peace of, references to, 55, 73, 100, 181.

Anapa, capture of, 253 ; reference to, 274.

Anatolia, references to, 187, 253, 321.

Andalusia, references to, 280, 325.

Andes, references to, 209, 284.

Andrea Doria, in charge of Charles V.'s fleet, 226 ; reference to, 227.

Anse de Foulon, landing of Wolfe at, 423.

Anson, Lord, reference to, 28 ; and La Jonquière, 213.

Anticosti, Walker's disaster off, 35.

Antietam, battle of, 292 ; reference to, 294.

Antony, reference to, 23.

Antwerp, Walcheren expedition and, 142 ; acquired by Napoleon to remedy deficiency of Channel ports, 76, 141 ; General Graham at, 132 ; importance of, to Napoleon, 167 ; as example of fortress on river, 370, 417.

Appleton, at Leghorn, 45, 46.

Appotamox, Lee's surrender at, 295.

Arabi Pasha, reference to, 416.

Arabia, reference to, 322.

Arbuthnot, Admiral, and Newport, 144, 145 ; reference to, 160.

Argentina, reference to, 209.

Arkansas, references to, 403, 405.

Armenia, references to, 185, 187, 188, 253, 255, 256.

Arnold, in Virginia, 237 ; on Lake Champlain, 395.

Artillery, effect of introduction of, on bases, 68 ; action of, on land against ships, 112, 132, 135 ; landing, from fleet, 166, 167 ; effect of, on conveyance of troops by sea, 195 ; effect of improvements in, on tactical intervention of warships in land fights, 338-340 ; at Miraflores, 341 ; effect of modern, on landings, 359, 360 ; fire of, damaged own side at St Cas, 367 ; effect of, from ships on sieges, *ib.*, 377 ; landing of, from ships for sieges, 377, 378 ; effect of, on inland waters generally, 407, 408 ; question of naval, for firing against shore, 434-436 ; portable, required for amphibious operations, 438, 439.

Asia Minor, references to, 47, 129, 130, 186, 318, 344.

Astorga, reference to, 301.

Atlanta, Sherman's march from, to the sea, 273 ; reference to, 405.

Attica, references to, 130, 318.

Austerlitz, references to, 8, 301.

Austria, Austrian, Austrians, references to, 115, 141, 170, 171, 314, 315, 322 ; at Messina, 132, 133 ; in campaign of 1859, 286, 287 ; in Italy in 1809, 328 ; at Loano, 336 ; in the Riviera, 340, 374.

Azov, Peter the Great at, 417.

Azov, Sea of, importance of, in Crimean War, 250, 251, 304 ; part played by, in early Russo-Turkish wars, 302 ; reference to, 392.

BACON, quotation from, 296.

Badiley, off Leghorn, 45, 46 ; reference to, 68.

Balaclava, as base, 225, 232, 303 ; references to, 247, 269 ; battle of, 270.

Balearic Islands, reference to, 279.

Balkans, references to, 258, 274, 382.

Balmaceda, reference to, 224.

Baltic, expeditions to, 3 ; references to, 47, 171, 329 ; rise of Russian sea-power in the, 302 ; British action in the, in 1807, 328 ; unsuitable ships used in the, 433, 434.

Baltimore, reference to, 295.

Bantry Bay, Hoche's expedition in, 30 ; references to, 198, 206.

Barbadoes, reference to, 213.

Barbarossa, campaign of Charles V. against, 134, 135 ; reference to, 344.

Barbary Corsairs, galleys of the, 26 ; Admiral Spragge and the, 33 ;

INDEX. 499

British operations against, 68; reference to, 149; Charles V. and the, 226-228.
Barbary States, reference to, 73.
Barcelona, Peterborough at, 12; English fleet and, 70; reference to, 268; Noailles and Russell at, 311; siege and relief of, in 1708, 385, 386.
Barossa, battle of, 384.
Barrington, Admiral, capture of St Lucia by, 107; and D'Estaing, 214, 215, 217.
Base, Bases, naval, question of, 65, 66; always indispensable to sea-power, 67; influence of acquisition of, in Mediterranean, 68-74; as harbours of refuge, 74, 75; importance of, early recognised, 75; fortresses as, 77-82; secure, necessary for commerce-destroying, 79, 80; need of secure, 81, 82; importance of, being properly defended, 85-87; fortified, essential to weaker side, 88, 89; for torpedo craft, 89, 90; of enemy as objectives, 94, 95; examples of capture of hostile, 95-98; attack of, sometimes necessary to destroy fleet within, 99; attack of, for commerce-destroying, 99-102; captured, may form *point d'appui* for further naval operations, 102, 103; chance of capturing valuable material in, 103, 104; conclusions as to attacks on, 105, 106; securing, during operations, 106; examples of securing, 107-109; occupation of islands as, 109; the British chain of, 178, 179; on Lake Ontario, 395; Mahan on, on lakes, *ib.*; importance of, on Lakes Erie and Ontario, 397, 398.
Base (land), Wellington's shift of, to Santander, 259, 260.
Basque Roads, Cochrane in, 33; reference to, 356.
Bastia, siege of, 17; reference to, 108.
Batoum, reference to, 187.
Battery, Batteries, ships *versus*, 112-115; ships against, on rivers, 406-408.
Battle of the Four Days, reference to the, 32.

Battleships cannot be improvised at short notice, 2.
Beachy Head, battle of, 79; references to, 203, 204.
Beauport, Montcalm's position at, 421.
Belisarius, capture of Palermo by, 377.
Bellasis at Cadiz, 11.
Belleisle, capture of, 14, 180, 327; exchange of, for Minorca, 181; bad weather delays landings at, 344; the landing at Lomarie in, 355.
Berlin Decree, reference to, 173.
Bermuda, acquisition of, 178.
Berry, Sir E., reference to, 212.
Bertie, Admiral, at Mauritius, 134.
Bertrand, quotation from, 358.
Bessarabia, references to, 259, 269, 270, 402.
Beyrout, reference to, 321.
Bilbao, campaign of, as illustrating liberty of action, 288.
Biscay, Bay of, merchant vessels not secure in, even before 1812, 3; references to, 181, 198, 276, 344.
Biscay (Province), reference to, 288.
Biserta, reference to, 113.
Bitter Lakes, reference to, 418.
Black Sea, references to, 185, 247, 252, 253, 254, 255, 257, 296, 329, 382, 392, 406; in Russo-Turkish wars, 187, 188; affording opportunity for acting on interior lines, 274.
Blake, references to, 18, 74, 78, 129, 147, 149, 344; off the Tagus, 45; bases of, in the Mediterranean, 68; attack of, on Santa Cruz, 80, 113, 114, 125; attack of, on Porto Farina, 113; death of, 114.
Blenheim, reference to, 9.
Bligh, General, expedition of, to French coast, 365-368.
Blockade, Blockading, reference to, 31; question of, fortresses, 119; Nelson on, *ib.*; difficulties of, 120, 121; Mahan on, 121; effect of, of coasts, 172, 173; question of, of islands, 175, 176; question of, of besieged maritime fortress, 372-375, 378.
Blocking, entrances to harbour from within, 121; entrances from with-

500 INDEX.

out, *ib.*, 122; examples of, 122, 123.
Boadicea, reference to, 134 note.
Boats, beaching of, 35; much the same for landing purposes as formerly, 229, 230, 344; run same risk from fire as formerly, 358-360.
Bœotia, reference to, 318.
Boer, Boers, reference to, 266.
Bolivia, references to, 284, 285.
Bomarsund, capture of, 329.
Bombardment, Japanese, of Port Arthur, 113; heavy expenditure of ammunition in, 115; question of, 118; of fleets from the land, 132-134.
Bompart, Commodore, disaster to, off Lough Swilly, 209.
Bonifaccio, Straits of, reference to, 370.
Boom, Booms, references to, 33, 118; use of, in river warfare, 409; Farragut's passage of, *ib.*
Boscawen, Wolfe's appreciation of, 14; references to, 15, 98, 135, 353; and De la Clue, 47, 49; off Toulon, 58.
Bosporus, references to, 187, 247, 258, 321, 406.
Bosquet, reference to, 157.
Boston, references to, 98, 295; British advance from, against Bunker's Hill, 334.
Bougie, Spragge at, 33.
Bourbon Isle, references to, 82, 101.
Bourgas, capture of, 258, 382; as base, 259.
Bradley, Mr, quotation from, 353, 354.
Brest, Conflans at, 58; as shelter for French fleets, 78; references to, 86, 141, 150, 151; blockades of, 104, 120, 128; attack of Tollemache on, 282, 283, 351, 352.
Bridport, Lord, references to, 30, 165; Hoche's expedition evades, 206, 207.
Bristol, reference to, 177.
Bristol Channel, references to, 266, 267.
Brittany, Hoche's start from, 30; references to, 180, 197, 204.
Brock, General, campaign of, on Lake Erie, 397.

Brown, Lieutenant, at Louisbourg, 354.
Brueys, Admiral, references to, 213, 215, 243.
Bruix, Admiral, escape of, from Brest, 86; in the Mediterranean, *ib.*, 87.
Buckingham, Duke of, attack of, on the Isle of Rhé, 373.
Buenavista, reference to, 280.
Bulgaria, references to, 188, 207, 253, 258, 259, 272.
Bull Run, battle of, 290, 291.
Bunker's Hill, battle of, as example of warships helping troops, 334.
Buonaparte. *See* Napoleon.
Buonaparte, Joseph, reference to, 260.
Burgos, reference to, 171.
Burgoyne, reference to, 144.
Burgundy, Duke of, attacks Calais, 123.
Burnside, General, operations of, 292.
Byazid, capture of, 254.
Byng, Admiral, at Cape Passaro and Messina, 132, 133; landing of guns by, for siege, 377; reference to, 392.
Byng, Admiral, and La Galissonière, 56-58; references to, 71, 205.
Byron, Admiral, and D'Estaing at Grenada, 213, 214, 216.
Byron, Lord, at Missolunghi, 387.

CABANAS, feint at, 346.
Cadiz, expedition of 1702 to, 11, 352; references to, 12, 39, 86, 107, 150, 151, 160, 202; St Vincent off, 38; Vivonne's designs against, 46; roomy harbour of, 75; and Trafalgar, 79; blockades of, 104, 128; destruction of Rosily's fleet in, 140, 141, 147; Stanhope's contemplated attack on, 326; landing near, in 1702, 352; attempted relief of, 384.
Cairo (America), 403, 404, 405.
Cairo (Egypt), reference to, 236.
Cairo, blowing up of the, 116.
Calabria, descent of Sir J. Stuart on, 267; reference to, 383, 392.
Calais, Spanish Armada off, 33; Duke of Burgundy's attack on, 123; references to, 198, 242; re-capture of, by French, 333.

INDEX. 501

Callao, *Huascar* at, 118; references to, 210, 382.
Calvi, siege of, 17; references to, 18, 108; Nelson as to ships attacking batteries at, 112, as old fortress on promontory, 382.
Camaret Bay, reference to, 283.
Camperdown, battle of, references to, 76, 139; the, 138.
Canada, first step towards conquest of, 98; references to, 177, 192, 264, 395, 400; conquest of, result of sea-power, 192, 193; the story of the conquest of, 418-428.
Canal, dug at Carthage, 122; question of digging, 411; examples of digging, *ib.*, 412; campaign of 1882 as example of strategical use of a, 416.
Canaries, the, reference to, 80.
Canaris at Ipsara, 154, 155.
Candia, the siege of, 302, 379.
Canning, quotation from, 328.
Cannon. *See* Artillery.
Canute, canal dug by, round London Bridge, 411.
Cap Rouge, references to, 423, 424, 426.
Cape Breton, references to, 97, 192, 419.
Cape Colony, reference to campaign in, 273.
Cape de Verdes, Porto Praya in, 48.
Cape Horn, reference to, 210.
Cape of Good Hope, reference to, 48; troops brought from Mauritius to, in a cruiser, 201.
Cape Peninsula, capture of, 103, 336.
Cape Town, reference to, 273.
Capua, Troubridge's expedition against, 156, 157.
Carlist War, incident in the, 287, 288.
Carlyle, quotation from, 326.
Carnatic, reference to, 82.
Carolina, North, reference to, 261.
Carolina, South, reference to, 261.
Carolinas, Cornwallis in the, 238; Sherman's campaign in the, 260, 261, 295; reference to, 403.
Carracks at L'Espagnols sur Mer, 26.
Carribean Sea, reference to, 54.
Cartagena (South America), Vernon and Wentworth at, 12, 13; references to, 17, 150; as naval base, 75.

Cartagena (Spain), reference to, 86.
Carthage, references to, 25, 389; Nepheris at siege of, 96; Roman dam at, 111, 122, 372, 373.
Carthaginians, reference to, 37; defeat of, at Ecnomus, 210, 211.
Caspian, reference to, 393.
Castlereagh, letter of Moore to, 300.
Catalonia, Catalonian, references to, 12, 268, 279, 310, 311, 326, 385; effort of English fleet on, coast in reign of William III., 311.
Cattaro, reference to, 272.
Caucasus, references to, 253, 256.
Cervera, Admiral, at Santiago, 128, 136.
Ceuta, reference to, 280.
Ceylon, reference to, 134 note; question of attack on, 175, 176.
Champlain, Lake, references to, 19, 394, 419; creation of flotillas on, 395, 425, 426; land communications running along, 399, 400; Prevost's campaign on, *ib.*; Amherst's campaign on, 425, 426; final advance from, 428.
Chancellorsville, the battle of, 293, 295.
Charente, reference to, 326.
Charles II., reference to, 9; and the Mediterranean, 65, 74.
Charles V., references to, 191, 229; attack of, on Goletta, 134, 135; attack of, on Algiers, 225-228.
Charles XII., landing of, in Zealand, 346.
Charles Edward, expedition of, 198.
Charleston, references to, 21, 108, 109, 157, 239, 260, 261; landing of guns to attack, 160, 161.
Chatham, Lord. *See* Pitt.
Chatham, Lord (General), and Admiral Strachan, 18, 142.
Cheraw, reference to, 262.
Cherbourg, references to, 76, 326, 366.
Chesapeake, the, references to, 54, 206, 224, 265, 289, 291, 416; De Grasse in, 59; in the campaign of Yorktown, 238, 239, 243; in the Virginian campaigns, 291-295.
Chesmé Bay, fire-ships in, 33.
Chickahominy, River, reference to, 291.
Chili, the liberation of, 191; creation

2 F

of fleet by, 191, 210; war between, and Peru as illustrating liberty of action, 283-287, 296.
Chilian, Chilians, bombardment of Callao, 118; disembarkations of, army in Peru, 224; reference to, army, 287; at battles before Lima, 340, 341.
Chilian War of Independence, references to, 32, 209, 210.
China, harmony between army and navy in, 20; Hong Kong ceded by, 178.
Chinese, destruction of, fleet at Weihai-wei, 118, 135, 147, 442; defeat of, navy in Korea Bay, 205; deceived by Japanese feint, 281.
Chiogia, the campaign of, 122, 123.
Chios, Turkish attack on, 318.
Choiseul uses Minorca as a bait, 58.
Chorillos, reference to, 341.
Cinque Ports, reference to, 243.
Cintra, Convention of, inquiry as to, 230.
Circassia, references to, 253, 256, 274.
Clacton-on-Sea, reference to, 232.
Clinton, General, references to, 21, 238; action of, as to Newport, 144-146; quotation from, 145, 146; attack of, on Charleston, 160; sends force to relieve Cornwallis, 206; in the campaign of Yorktown, 239, 240.
Clive, reference to, 7.
Clowes, Sir W. L., on fleet in being, 203; quotation from, as to fleets in Baltic, 433, 434.
Clyde, River, reference to, 268.
Coal, question of, 67, 84; consumption of torpedo craft and submarines, 89, 90.
Coaling-stations, importance of, 84, 85; necessity of security for, 85; importance of capturing enemy's, 94.
Coast batteries. See Batteries.
Coast-lines, form of, as affecting strategy, 264-267.
Coblentz, a typical modern fortress on a river, 418.
Cochrane, in Basque Roads, 33; references to, 145, 192, 356; at Rosas, 153, 382; on the coast of Catalonia, 311; quotation from, 382.

Cochrane, Captain, in charge of boats at Abercromby's landing, 356.
Cohorn, reference to, 389.
Colbert, reference to, 17.
Colliers, inconvenience to fleet of guarding its, 67.
Collingwood, references to, 22, 137; blockade of Cadiz by, 141; action of, in aid of Spanish patriots, 310, 311.
Colombo, acquisition of, 179.
Colonies, sea-power and distant, 175, 176; question of attacks on, 189 193.
Columbia, reference to, 261.
Columbus, reference to, 413.
Command of the sea. See Maritime preponderance.
Commerce, sea-power and, 52, 55; damage to British, in Indian Ocean, 100, 101; effect of destruction of maritime, 176-178.
Commerce-destroyers, action of, 61; war of, 62; Mahan on, ib.; question of bases for, 84, 85; coaling stations essential for, 85, 88; attack on bases for, 99-101; influence of steam on, 101, 102; of the Confederates, 101; effect of successful, 177.
Commerce-destroying. See Commerce-destroyers.
Commonwealth, the, references to, 45, 78.
Communications, Communication, line of, question of, at sea, 66, 67; importance of, to an army, 246; drain which, make on an army, ib., 247; French, compared to Wellington's in Peninsula, 247; advantage of maritime, ib., 248; superiority of maritime, to land, 248; influence of steam on question of maritime, 249; examples to show value of maritime, 249-261; sea cannot be used as, without maritime preponderance, 250; Sea of Azov as, in Crimean War, 251; example of maritime, ib., 252; Russo-Turkish war as illustrating value of maritime, 252-259; question of, following the coast-line, 309-322; examples of, parallel to sea, 310-316; passing through an isthmus, 316, 317; examples

INDEX. 503

of, passing through an isthmus, 317-319; Syrian campaigns as examples of, 320-322; running along lake, 399, 400.

Confederate, Confederates, Confederation, references to, 108, 136, 274; States of, poor in natural resources, 171, 172; Sherman's devastation of, territory, 260, 261; in Virginia, 289-295; position of, as regards the Mississippi, 403; campaign of, on Mississippi, 403-406; and submarine mines, 408, 409; in the "bayous," 410; on the Red River, 411; about New Madrid, 413-415.

Conflans, in Brest, 58.

Containing power of amphibious force, explanation of, 323, 324; Kinglake on, 324; examples of, 324-326; Canning on, 327; Crimean War as illustrating, 328-330; war in Far East as illustrating, 330, 331.

Contraband, question of, 173, 174.

Convoy, sailing under, 3; failure of, in Indian Ocean, 101.

Conway, River, reference to, 248.

Copenhagen, capture of fleet in, 104; Nelson and batteries of, 112; references to, 114, 129; capture of Danish fleet at, 139, 161.

Corbett, Mr, references to, 74 note, 183; quotation from, 179.

Cordilleras, reference to, 284.

Cordova and D'Orvilliers, 204.

Corinth, Gulf of, references to, 317.

Corinth, Isthmus of, references to, 317-319, 324; the Turks in the, 317.

Cornice, the, reference to, 314.

Cornwallis, Lord, investment of, in Yorktown, 59; references to, 206, 243; during the campaign of Yorktown, 238-240; case of, as showing communications completely cut, 250.

Cornwallis, (Admiral) (Commodore), reference to, 165; and De Ternay, 206.

Corsica, the army and navy in, 17; references to, 32, 202; as a naval base, 72; operations to secure, 72; occupation of, to secure base, 108.

Coruña, Ormonde's expedition from, 197; references to, 202, 275, 276, 367; Sir J. Moore at, 300, 301; question of evacuating, 300; the embarkation at, 363.

Cotton, Admiral, off Cadiz, 141.

Cove of Cork, reference to, 75.

Craig, General, at the Cape, 103, 336, 337.

Crete, Napoleon and Nelson pass, 39, 40; reference to, 379.

Crillon, Duc de, captures Minorca, 72; the siege of Fort St Philip by, 373, 374.

Crimea, invasion of, to destroy Sebastopol, 105; references to, 131, 225; French and Turkish troops carried to, in warships, 200, 208, 216; danger of such a move as that to, in the present day, 219.

Crimean War, harmony between the services in, 20; references to, 63, 150, 166, 201, 296, 401; general effect of sea-power in, 187, 188; importance of Sea of Azov in, 250, 251; as example of "interior lines," 269, 270; as example of hold given on land by sea-power, 302-304, 308.

Cromwell, arrangements of, as to Penn and Venables, 11; references to, 68, 149; and Montague, 149; advance of, on Wexford, 248, 249; on the Firth of Forth, 335.

Cruiser, Cruisers, cannot be equipped at short notice, 2; evil of tying, to bases, 85.

Crusaders, reference to, 350.

Crusades, reference to, 149.

Cuba, references to, 75, 143, 219, 339.

Cuddalore, reference to, 83; the siege of, 388.

Culloden, reference to, 248.

Cumberland, Duke of, communications of, with Aberdeen, 248.

Current, question of, 406, 407; in the Dardanelles, 406; in the Mississippi, *ib.*, 407.

Cyprus, Louis IX. in, 281, 349.

D'ACHÉ, Lally and, 7; and Mauritius, 82.

Daiquiri, Shafter's landing at, 346.

Dalmatia, reference to, 185.
Dalny, reference to, 316.
Dalrymple, General, proposes to send a force against Rosily's fleet, 141.
Damietta, Napoleon's siege train shipped from, 36, 153; Louis IX. conceals intentions as to, 282; landing of Louis IX. at, 349, 350.
Dane, Danes, struggle of, against Germany, 305-308, 319; and Swedes at Charles XII.'s landing in Zealand, 346; at Fredericia, 383.
Danish navy, carried off to England, 104; destruction of, by Nelson, 112.
Dantzig, siege of, 417.
Danube, references to, 141, 142, 185, 187, 254, 269, 274, 315, 402, 407; the, in 1828, 257, 258; crossing of the, in 1877, 258; the campaign of 1877 on, 408, 410, 418.
Darby, Admiral, re-victuals Gibraltar, 386.
Dardanelles, as refuge for Ottoman fleets, 78; Xerxes crosses, 129; references to, 154, 247, 318, 319, 320, 321, 381, 411; as a waterway, 401; current in, 406; Duckworth's passage of, 406 note.
Darius, reference to, 130, 296.
De Burgh, General, reference to, 158.
De Bussy at Cuddalore, 388.
De Chafferault, Wolfe's reference to, 135.
D'Estaing, and Howe, 28, 238; operations of, in North America, 144; and Byron, 213, 214; and Barrington 214, 215; at Savannah, 228.
De Grasse, in the Chesapeake, 59; references to, 79, 109, 242; arrival of, in North America, 146; in the campaign of Yorktown, 206, 239, 240.
De la Clue, and Boscawen, 47, 49; in Toulon, 58.
D'Orvilliers and Cordova in the Channel, 204.
De Ruyter, references to, 28, 32, 34, 109, 200.
De Ternay, arrival of, at Newport, 144; operations of, 145, 146; references to, 206.
Deal, reference to, 348.
Deane, reference to, 18.

Declaration of Paris as to privateering, 102.
Decrès, difficulties of, with Napoleon, 8.
Dee, River, reference to, 248.
Demaratus, advice of, to Xerxes, 324.
Denmark, references to, 139, 264; campaigns in, in 1843, 1849, 305-308.
Derry, the relief of, 417; difficulty as to signals at, 441.
Detroit, Brock and Hull at, 397.
Dettingen, reference to, 138.
Devins, General, on the Riviera, 314; at the battle of Loano, 336.
Devon, Devonshire, references to, 114, 266, 267.
Dewey, Admiral, victory of, at Manilla, 116.
Diebich, campaign of, in Turkey, 258, 259.
Disembarkation. *See* Landing.
Dnieper, River, reference to, 133.
Dniester, River, reference to, 270.
Docks. *See* Dockyards.
Dockyards, need of, 68; first class, generally in home ports, 75; necessity for, in present day, 81, 82; necessity for secure, 85; importance of capture of, 94.
Domokos, reference to battle of, 249.
Don, River, reference to, 251, 256, 402, 417.
Doris in command of Persians at Marathon, 364.
Dorset, reference to, 266.
Douro, River, reference to, 231.
Dover, Straits of, 31, 204; reference to, 199; Hubert de Burgh and, 241-243.
Drake, at Lisbon, 11; action of, at Lagos, 107; references to, 125, 151.
Dromop, reference to the, 26.
Drury, General, at St Cas, 366, 367.
Dublin, reference to, 248.
Duckworth, expedition of, to Minorca, 14, 159; reference to, 86; passage of Dardanelles by, 406 note.
Dunbar, battle of, 335.
Duncan, Admiral, at Camperdown, 138.

Dundas, at Toulon, 16; in Corsica, 17.
Dunkirk, references to, 71, 228; the siege of, in 1793, 381.
Dupleix, and La Bourdonais, 6, 7; reference to, 83.
Düppel, reference to, 305; Danes retire to, 306; attacks on, *ib.*, 307.
Durban, reference to, 272.
Dutch, in the Mediterranean, 68; nature of, harbours, 76; references to, 101, 133, 348, 349, 355; Colombo conquered from, 179; and Spanish troops in Channel, 199; capture of, ships in Saldanha Bay, 200; at Muizenberg, 336, 337.
Dutch fleet, navy, references to, 45, 160; value of, 53; capture of, by Pichegru, 131; defeat of, at Camperdown, 138; capture of, 139.
Dutch Wars, references to, 45, 150.

EAST LONDON, reference to, 272.
Ecnomus, battle of, 210.
Edinburgh, references to, 30, 335.
Edward I., communications of, in Wales, 248.
Edward III., reference to, 26.
Egmont, Count, at Gravelines, 333.
Egypt, reference to operations in, 20; naval brigades in, *ib.*; Napoleon's advance from, into Syria, 36; Napoleon's expedition to, 38-43, 207, 209; references to, 39, 40, 41, 125, 185, 202, 243, 280, 281; reference to campaign in, 98; object of British expedition to, 181, 182; troops brought from, to European theatre of war, 186, 188; French army maintains itself in, for three years, 236; defile leading along the Levant coast from, 320-322; crusade of Louis IX. to, 349, 350; Abercromby's landing in, 355-358.
Elba, Badiley and Van Galen off, 45; used as base, 72; General de Burgh at, 158.
Electrical communications, effect of, 24, 37, 38.
Elizabethan era, reference to, 10, 75.
Elliott, General, at Gibraltar, 387.

Elphinstone. *See* Keith.
Embarkation, Embarkations, in face of opposition generally a case of retreat, 362, 363; a rearguard operation as a rule, 362; examples of opposed, 364, 365; difficulty of opposed, increased under modern conditions, 365; artillery covering, *ib.*; the, at St Cas, 365-368.
'England in the Mediterranean,' reference to, 74 note; quotation from, 179.
Enos, references to, 188, 272.
Erie, Lake, references to, 394, 398, 400; in 1812-14, 395, 396; command of, and Brock's overthrow of Hull, 396, 397; importance of bases on, 398.
Erzerum, references to, 187, 256; capture of, 255; Russians advance to, 257.
Espartero, attempt of, to relieve Bilbao, 287, 288.
Esquimalt, acquisition of, 178.
Essex, reference to, 266.
Esthonia, reference to, 329.
Eugene, Prince, reference to, 249; advance of, on Toulon, 314; communications of, north of Adriatic, *ib.*
Euphrates, River, reference to, 321.
Eustace the Monk and Hubert de Burgh, 241, 242,
Exmouth, Lord, references to, 28, 137; attack of, on Algiers, 111, 124.

FALSE BAY, reference to, 336.
Farragut, Admiral, at Mobile, 115, 116, 129; campaign of, on the Mississippi, 404, 412.
Federal, Federals, secure Port Royal, 108; sinking of, gunboat *Cairo*, 116; references to, 136; superiority of, fighting forces on land decided issue of war, 172; in Georgia, 274; in Virginia, 289-295; importance of Mississippi to, 403; campaign of, on Mississippi, 403-406; attempt of, on the Roanoke, 408, 409; on the Red River, 411; canals dug by, *ib.*, 412; in campaign of Island No. 10, 413-415.

INDEX.

Feints, opportunities for, at landings, 281, 282; largely made use of at landings, 345; examples of, 346, 347.

Ferdinand, Prince, reference to, 327.

Ferrol, expedition to, in 1800, 140; reference to, 202.

'Fight with France for North America,' quotation from, 353, 354.

Finland, Gulf of, references to, 302, 329, 401.

Finland, reference to, 131.

Fire-ships, functions of, 33; records of, *ib.*, 34.

Fixed defences, objections to, 88; discussion of the crusade against, 91; weaker side at sea and, 164, 165.

Flanders, expedition to, 3; references to, 71, 349; the campaign in, 160; contest between Dutch and Spanish in, 199.

Fleet, Fleets, rapidity with which, could formerly be created, 32, 33; injury inflicted on enemy by destroying, 51, 52; destruction of enemy's, the primary object in naval war, 52-55; need of bases for, 65-77; fortresses as refuges for, 77, 78; need of depots and dockyards for, 81, 82; objection to tying, to bases, 85-87; importance of capturing enemy's, 94; question of attack of, on fortresses, 111-118; land operations directed against, 126-143; in fortress " contains" floating force outside, 127; destruction of, at Mycale, 129, 130; capture of, by Pichegru, 131; capture of, at Sveaborg, *ib.*; destruction of, at Abo, *ib.*; destruction of, at Messina, 132, 133; destruction of, at Ochakof, 133; bombardment of, at Antwerp, *ib.*, 134; destruction of, at Wei-hai-wei, 134; destruction of, at Goletta, *ib.*, 135; destruction of, at Louisbourg, 135; destruction of, at Procida, *ib.*; destruction of, at Santiago, 136; capture of, in Zuyder Zee, 139; destruction of Rosily's, 140, 141; Walcheren expedition undertaken to destroy, 142.

"Fleet in being," references to, 88, 104, 121, 138; doctrine of the, 203; definition of, by Clowes, *ib.*; Mahan on, *ib.*; Torrington on, 204; discussion of, 204-211; examination of principle of, in sailing days, 211, 212; examples of failure of, 213-215; effect of, under modern conditions, 216-221; Japanese action as regards, 220, 221; effect of, after an army has landed in hostile territory, 236, 237; Hubert de Burgh's, 242.

Flemings, Flemish, reference to, 33; landing of, in Walcheren, 348, 349.

Florida, reference to, 143.

Flushing, Napoleon's preparations at, 142; capture of, 143.

Fog, Fogs, effect of, 34, 35, 198.

Foote, Commodore, in campaign of Island No. 10, 414.

Fornelles, landing in Bay of, 346.

Fort George, capture of, 400.

Fort Monroe, reference to, 291.

Fort Royal, as naval base, 75; reference to, 158.

Forth, Firth of, references to, 30, 264, 268, 335.

Fortress, Fortresses, weaker fleet repairs to shelter of, 60; object of naval, 77; as refuges for floating force, 78, 113; difficulty of dealing with, from the sea, 78; importance of, to beaten fleet, 79; need of, for commerce-destroyers, *ib.*; need of, for merchant shipping, 80; example of attacks on, from the sea, *ib.*, 81; essential to the weaker side, 88, 89; floating force generally unsuitable for attacking, 111-113; ships *versus*, 112, 113; examples of attacks of ships on, 113-116; influence of submarine mining on, 116, 117; influence of torpedo craft on, 117, 118; improbability of fleets attacking, in future, 118; blockade of, 119-121; blocking entrance to, from without, 121, 122; blocking entrance to, from within, 121; sealing up, by mines from without, 123, 124; land operations generally necessary to attack naval, 124, 125; difficulty of attacking,

INDEX. 507

when sheltering fleets, 127; employment of naval *personnel* in defence of, 150-152.
Foyle, Lough, reference to, 441.
Franco-German War, effect of sea-power in, 189; reference to, 246.
Fredericia, references to, 305, 307; battle of, 307; siege of, 383; relief of, *ib.*
Frederick Charles, Prince, reference to, 307.
Frederick the Great, references to, 171, 326, 327.
Fredericksburg, operations round, 293.
Friant, General, at Aboukir Bay, 356, 357.
Frontiers, form of, as compared to coast-lines, 264-266.
Fulton, reference to, 408.
Funen, references to, 305, 307.

GAETA, as example of fortress on promontory, 370; the siege of, 383.
Galatz, reference to, 409.
Galicia, references to, 140, 202, 276, 300.
Galissonière, La, operations of, off Minorca, 56-59; references to, 205, 393.
Galleys, of Barbary Corsairs, 26; supersession of, 27; could not ride out storms, *ib.*; destruction of, at Abo and Sveaborg, 131; Massena organises flotilla of, at Genoa, 376.
Genghis Khan, reference to, 197.
Genoa, Keith at, 21; galleys at siege of, 26, 376; references to, 286, 287, 313, 340; siege of, 374; war between, and Venice, 122, 123; question of blockade at siege of, 374.
George II., orders of, for Bligh's expedition, 365.
George III., reference to, 181.
Georgia (America), references to, 238, 295, 405; Sherman's march from, 260, 262; the march of Sherman through, 273, 274, 289.
Georgia (Asia), references to, 253, 256.
German, Germans, Germany, armies at gates of Paris, 129; invasion of France, 189; references to, 199, 265, 327; wars of, with the Danes, 305-308.

Gettysburg, battle of, 293, 294.
Gibraltar, reinforcements at, could not be sent to Santander, 3; need for naval base above gut of, 9; reinforcements expected from, at Toulon, 16; straits of, 31; references to, 47, 53, 54, 74, 115, 141, 161, 179, 300, 326, 382; Byng returns to, 56; Boscawen returns to, 58; capture of, by Rooke, 70, 125; Rooke's fleet beats batteries of, 111; failure of allied bombardment of, 115; Montague and, 149; captured practically by naval force alone, 179; imaginary case of landing in Bay of, 268; Lord St Vincent at, 278-281; great siege of, 297, 386, 387; Godinot bombarded by cruisers in, bay, 333.
Godinot, General, march of, to Tarifa, 333.
Golden Horn, the, references to, 187, 259, 317, 402.
Goldsboro, reference to, 261.
Goletta, reference to, 113; destruction of Barbarossa's flotilla in, 134, 135.
Graham, General, on the Scheldt, 133; attempt of, to relieve Cadiz, 384.
Grant, Ensign, at Louisbourg, 354.
Grant, General, references to, 260, 290; campaign of, in Virginia, 294, 295; at Vicksburg, 406.
Gravelines, battle of, as example of warships helping troops, 333, 334.
Gravelotte, reference to battle of, 437.
Gravenstein, reference to, 306.
Graves, Admiral, and De Grasse, 59, 239; arrival of, in North America, 144.
Great Central Railway, reference to, 248.
Great Northern Railway, reference to, 248.
Greece, references to, 25, 317, 324, 344; struggle of, for freedom, 32; Xerxes' invasion of, 129; Ibrahim Pasha in, 237; war between, and Turkey, 249, 250; a peninsula, 265.
Greek War of Liberation, fire-ships in the, 33; attack on Ipsara during, 154, 155; sea-power aids Turks to assemble forces for, 186, 187;

"fleet in being" in, 207; Isthmus of Corinth in the, 317-319; sieges of Missolunghi during, 387, 388.
Grenada, capture of, by D'Estaing, 213; reference to, 214.
Grey, General, in the West Indies, 14.
Guadaloupe, as base for privateers, 100, 101; reference to, 105.
Guantanamo, landing at, 224.
"Guerre de course." See Commerce-destroyers.
Guildhall, the, Chatham's monument in, 177.
Gunpowder drives out galleys, 26.
Guy of Flanders, Count, the landing of, in Walcheren, 348, 349.

HALIFAX, reference to, 103; acquisition of, 178.
Hamburg, typical of commercial port, 76.
Hamilcar Barca, reference to, 25.
Hamilton, Sir W., reference to, 212.
Hamley, reference to, 263.
Hampton Roads, reference to, 136.
Hannibal, reference to, 23.
Harbours, artificial, creation of, in modern times, 76.
Harbours, natural, importance of, 76.
Harbours of refuge, need of, for fleets, 78, 79.
Hardy, Admiral (Sir C.), opposed to D'Orvilliers and Cordova, 204.
Hardy, Admiral (Sir T.), reference to, 137.
Harper's Ferry, references to, 292, 293.
Haultain, Admiral, action of, towards Spanish troops, 199.
Havana, capture of, 14; as naval base, 75; captures at, 80, 81; references to, 100, 177; attack on Morro Castle at, 114; capture of ships in, 135; feint on occasion of descent on, 346.
Hawke, at Rochefort, 13; references to, 34, 59; and L'Etendeur, 213.
Helder, the, expedition to, 138, 139; references to, 144, 160, 166, 299; landing at, delayed by bad weather, 344.
Hellas, Hellenes. See Greece, Greeks.

Hellespont. See Dardanelles.
Henry VI., reference to, 123.
Henry VII. See Richmond.
Henry VIII., reference to, 335.
Herbert, Admiral. See Torrington, Lord.
Hesse, Duke of, at Gibraltar, 70, 179.
Hesse, Prince of, defence of Gaeta by, 383.
Hoche, expedition of, to Ireland, 30; references to, 198, 216; troops carried on fighting-ships in expedition of, 200; expedition of, evades Bridport, 206, 207; and the Royalists at Quiberon, 337.
Holbourne, Admiral, dispersion of fleet of, 28.
Holland, references to, 62, 72, 75, 76, 138, 139, 301, 393, 417; form of frontier of, 264.
Holmes, Admiral, operations of, on the St Lawrence, 423, 426.
Holstein, references to, 305, 308.
Homs, battle of, 321.
Hong Kong, acquisition of, 178.
Hood (General), references to, 274.
Hood, Lord, at Toulon, 15-17, 302; off Corsica, 17; references to, 34, 109, 137; effect of not having Minorca on operations of, 72, 96; effect of failure of, to burn establishments at Toulon, 98.
Hooker, General, operations of, 293; reference to, 294.
Hopkins, Lieutenant, at Louisbourg, 354.
Hotham, Admiral, reference to, 17; on the Riviera, 21; in the Ligurian Sea, 36; and Devins, 336.
Howe, Lord (Commodore), and D'Estaing, 28, 238; reference to, 34; at the St Cas embarkation, 365-368; services of, 366, 367; relief of Gibraltar by, 386.
Huascar at Callao, 118.
Hubert de Burgh and the French invasion in 1216, 242, 243.
Hudson, the, references to, 238, 239, 399.
Hughes, action of, as regards base, 83; and Trincomalee, 86, 103; at Cuddalore, 388.
Hull, General, defeat of, by Brock, 396, 397.

INDEX. 509

Hull, reference to, 232.
Humber, the, reference to, 248.
Hunter, General, move of, from Natal to Orange Free State, 272, 273.
Huron, Lake, references to, 396.

IBRAHIM PASHA, invasion of Greece by, 207 ; position of, after Navarino, 236, 237, 243 ; the campaign of, in Syria, 320-322 ; at Missolunghi, 387.
Illinois, reference to, 403.
Imperieuse, the, references to, 328, 356.
India, sea-power decided fate of, 7 ; form of frontier of, 264.
Indian Ocean, question of sea-power in, 67, 82, 83 ; commerce destroying in, 101, 102.
'Influence of Sea-Power upon History,' quotations from, 53, 56, 57, 83, 86, 100.
'Influence of Sea-Power upon the French Revolution and Empire,' quotations from, 8, 9, 47, 100, 101 ; references to, 62, 170, 171.
Inkerman, battle of, 270.
Inshore flotillas, remarks as to, 35, 36.
Interior lines, sea-power confers opportunities for acting on, 266-269 ; Crimean War as example of, 269, 270 ; principle of, 270, 271 ; examples of, in campaign round Black Sea, 271, 272 ; move of Suliman Pasha as example of, 272 ; examples of, from South African War, *ib.*, 273.
Invasion of England, dispersion of attempts at, by storms, 197, 198 ; influence of torpedo craft on, 217, 218 note.
Inverness, reference to, 248.
Ipsara, the Turkish attack on, 154, 155.
Ischia, reference to, 135.
Island No. 10, campaign of, 413-415.
Islay, reference to, 181.
Isle of France. *See* Mauritius.
Isle of Orleans, references to, 421, 422, 423.
Ismail, gunboats at siege of, 417.
Ismailia, reference to, 416.
Isthmus, communications through an, 316, 317 ; examples of influence of sea-power in, 317-319.

Italy, references to, 312, 313, 315, 383 ; length of coast-line of, 265 ; toe of, 267.

JACKSON, STONEWALL, campaigns of, in Virginia, 290, 291 ; death of, 293 ; reference to, 295.
Jamaica, capture of, 178.
James I., reference to, 199.
James River, the *Merrimac* in the, 136 ; reference to, in the campaigns of Virginia, 291, 292, 294, 296.
Japan, Japanese, commerce destroying in, waters, 102 ; references to, fleet, 112, 117, 259 ; at Wei-hai-wei, 128, 134, 147 ; size of, army at Port Arthur, 156 ; situation of, as insular power, 168 ; reference to, 196 ; Kublai's expedition against, 197 ; impeded by fogs, 198 ; attitude of, as regards "fleet in being," 220, 221 ; landings near Port Arthur, 224, 225 ; secure Talienwan, 225 ; use made by, during advance through Korea, 252 ; an insular power, 265 ; liberty of action of, 278 ; advantages enjoyed by, in Far East compared to Russians, 304, 305 ; Russian uncertainty as to, intentions, 330 ; at Nanshan, 337, 338 ; landings in Korea, 359 ; descent on Liaotung, 361 ; blockade by, of Port Arthur, 375 ; only country organised for amphibious war, 436-439 ; mistakes of, at Talienwan and Wei-hai-wei, 442, 443.
Java, capture of, 101.
Jean de Vienne, wooden fortress of, 27 ; draws Richard II. into Scotland, 325.
Jena, reference to, 301.
Jervis. *See* St Vincent.
John, Archduke, reference to, 328.
John, King, references to, 241, 242.
Johnstone, Commodore, at Porto Praya, 48.
Jomini, reference to, 263 ; quotation from, as to Coruña, 300.
Julius Cæsar, landing of, at Walmer, 347, 348.
Justinian, reference to, 377.
Jutland, references to, 266, 308 ; invasions of, 305, 306, 307.

KAMISH, as base, 225, 232, 303; references to, 247, 269.
Kars, capture of, 187; capture of, 254, 257; references to, 256, 257, 274.
Keith, Lord, as a soldier, 21, 156; reference to, 73; and Minorca, 86, 87; quotation from, 87; at capture of Cape Peninsula, 103; landing of sailors by, after Aboukir, 157, 158; at Saldanha Bay, 200; at the battle of Muizenberg, 336, 337; gunboats of, at Genoa, 340, 374, 376.
Kennington Cove, reference to, 353.
Kent, Kentish, references to, 27, 241, 347.
Kentucky, references to, 403, 414.
Kerry, reference to, 216.
Khertch, coal captured at, 103; reference to straits of, 251; secrecy as to expedition to, 281.
Kinchau Bay, reference to, 338.
Kinglake, quotation from, 324; reference to, as to the Alma, 339, 340.
Kingston, British base at, on Lake Ontario, 395, 397, 400.
Kinsale, shelters Rupert, 78; escape of Rupert from, 120.
Kiriakof, General, reference to, 340.
Kleber, reference to, 237.
Knights of St John (Malta), reference to, 6; restoration of Malta to, 73.
Kolding, reference to, 305.
Komorn, reference to, 370.
Konia, battle of, 321, 322.
Korea, defeat of Chinese fleet in Bay of, 128, 205; references to, 198, 220, 221, 249, 259, 278; Japanese communications in, 252; a peninsula, 264; Japanese landings in, 359.
Kornilof, Admiral, lands sailors at Sebastopol, 153; "fleet in being" of, in Sebastopol, 208, 216; fortification of Sebastopol by, 303.
Kowshing, case of the, 196.
Kronstadt, Swedish landing at, 352, 353, 355; as example of fortress on an island, 370.
Kublai sends expedition against Japan, 197.
Kurdistan, reference to, 187.

Kuropatkin, General, reference to, 330.
Kustenji, references to, 257, 259.
Kwang Tung, reference to, 137.

LA BOURDONAIS, and Dupleix, 6, 7; action of, at Mauritius, 82.
La Fayette in Virginia, 239.
La Hogue, reference to, 18; Russell victor of, 70, 311.
La Jonquière, defeat of, by Anson, 213.
Lacedemonians, reference to, 287.
Laconia, reference to, 324.
Ladysmith, relief of, 272.
Lagos, Boscawen and De la Clue at, 47, 49; Drake at, 105, 107.
Lakes, general question of, 393, 394; flotillas on, generally improvised during war, 394; examples of improvising flotillas on, 395; importance of bases in, warfare, 397, 398; land communications along, 399, 400.
Land operations, reason why, are generally necessary to secure bases, 125; directed against fleet and shipping, 127-146; employment of sailors on, 148-158.
Landing, Landings, effect of bad weather on, 223; example of, in exposed situations, 224; nature of risks run in, in exposed situations, 225-229; of Charles V. at Algiers as example, 225-228; British, at Ostend, 228, 229; character of coast-line affects question of, 230, 231; attack by hostile ships during, 234, 235; question of, at night, 235, 361, 362; often delayed by bad weather, 344; generally takes place on open beach, *ib.*; false impression that opposed, are generally successful, 345; subsidiary, 345; examples of feints to secure, 346, 347; examples of opposed, under ancient conditions, 347-350; examples of opposed, under more modern conditions, 351-358; difference between conditions of, formerly and to-day, 359-361; at awkward places generally best carried out by sailors, 361.
Landing-places, usual nature of, 223-225.

INDEX. 511

Languedoc, references to, 286, 311.
Latakia, reference to, 321.
Latouche Tréville, Nelson and, 165.
Laughton, Professor, quotation from, 15.
L'Espagnols sur Mer, battle of, 26.
L'Etendeur and Hawke, 213.
Leake, failure of, to understand Mediterranean problem, 10; attack on Minorca by, 74, 125; lands guns at St Philip, 377; at Barcelona, 385, 386.
Lee, references to, 261; campaigns of, in Virginia, 274; the campaigns of, in Virginia, 290-295.
Leghorn, affair of the *Phœnix* at, 45, 46; serves as base to British, 68, 72; references to, 78, 313.
Leipzig, reference to battle of, 437.
Leith, reference to, 30.
Leon, reference to, 276.
Lepanto, rapid creation of fleet after, 32.
Leslie and Cromwell, 335.
'Lessons of War with Spain,' quotation from, 112.
Leval, General, siege of Tarifa by, 382.
Levant, the, references to, 26, 36, 45, 47, 73, 181, 185, 320, 322, 349, 379; command of, in Syrian wars, 320-322.
Lévis, reference to, 193; rallies French forces retreating from Quebec, 424; operations of, 426, 427; surrender of, 428.
Liaotung, references to peninsula, 221, 225; coast-line of, 231; Japanese descent on, 361.
Liaoyang, reference to, 330.
Libya, reference to, 210.
Lido, the, at Venice, 122, 123.
Ligurian Sea, reference to, 36.
Lima, references to, 209, 224, 382; capture of, 285, 286, 341.
Lincoln, Prince Louis defeated at, 242.
Line of communications. *See* Communications.
Lion, Gulf of the, references to, 39, 42.
Lisbon, reinforcements at, could not be sent to Santander, 3; Drake and Raleigh at, 11; Drake at, 107; references to, 158, 203, 259,
275, 276, 300, 325; Wellesley aimed at, 225; as base for British, 298.
Lissa, attack on defences of, 115.
Lithuania, reference to, 329.
Liverpool, typical of commercial port, 76.
Llewellyn, reference to, 248.
Loano, battle of, 314; battle of, as illustrating warships aiding troops, 336.
Lomarie, the landing at, 355.
Lombardy, references to, 287, 314, 315.
London Bridge, canal dug round, 411.
London, references to, 177, 248, 282.
'Lost Possessions of England,' quotation from, 58.
Loudon, expedition of, to Louisbourg, 206.
Louis IX., ruse of, 281, 282; landing of, at Damietta, 349, 350.
Louis XIV., galleys of, 26; and William III., 69; in War of Spanish Succession, 70; inaction of, after Beachy Head, 204; preparations of, at Brest, 282; and Catalonia, 311.
Louis XV., action of, as to Louisbourg, 97, 98, 192.
Louis Napoleon. *See* Napoleon III.
Louis, Prince, invasion of England by, 241-243.
Louisbourg, Boscawen at, 14; references to, 28, 192, 351, 361, 418; as naval base, 75; importance of, 97; effect of capture of, 97, 98; exchanged for Madras, 98; dismantling of, 103; French ships captured in, 135; sailors assisted in defence of, 153; Loudon's expedition to, 206; the landing at, 344, 353, 354; capture of, merely a step towards securing St Lawrence, 418.
Louisiana, references to, 403, 405.
Lynchburg, reference to, 261.
Lynedoch, Lord. *See* Graham, General.

MACAULAY, quotation from, as to Marlborough, 282, 283; on Pitt's policy of raids, 327; reference to, 441.
Macdonald, reference to, 8.

M'Clellan, references to, 205, 294, 296; shift of base by, 277, 291; campaigns of, in Virginia, 291, 292.
Macedonia, reference to, 185; Turkish advance into Greece from, 317-319.
Maddalena, Nelson based on, 73; as example of fortress covering group of islands, 370.
Madras, references to, 7, 85, 86, 98, 383; exchanged for Louisbourg, 98.
Madrid, Napoleon takes, 275; reference to, 276.
Magenta, battle of, 287.
Mahan, quotations from, 8, 9, 47, 53, 56, 57, 83, 86, 100, 112, 116, 120, 159, 396; on principles of naval strategy, 52, 56, 57; references to, 59, 140, 205; on commerce destroying, 62; on naval bases, 83, 86; on bases for commerce destroying, 82, 83; on ships *versus* batteries, 112; on mines in civil war, 116; account of, of effect of sea-power on Napoleonic wars, 170, 171; on "fleet in being," 203, 219; likens sea to a great common, 277; on Napoleon in the Riviera, 314; on bases in lake warfare, 395.
Mahon, Lord, quotations from, 12, 13, 327, 352.
Mahon, Port, references to, 47, 56, 57, 71, 87, 181, 205, 279, 281, 373.
Maida, the battle of, 267, 299.
Maine, reference to, 143.
Malabar Coast, reference to, 388.
Malacca, Straits of, reference to, 83.
Malaga, reference to, 115.
Malden, Brock lands at, 397.
Malplaquet, reference to, 138.
Malta, Turkish admiral and general quarrel during expedition to, 6; Napoleon at, 39, 150; reduction of, 39; references to, 65, 125, 179; value of, 73, 74; Nelson's anxiety as to, 159; question of attack on, 175; first attempt to relieve, 197; Mustapha's embarkation at, 364; relief of, 384.
Maltese at siege of Valetta, 372.
Malvern, reference to, 291.
Mamelukes, reference to, 43.

Manassas, references to, 290, 292, 294, 295.
Manchuria, reference to, 78; effect of fogs on campaign in, 198; nature of coast-line of, 231; campaign in, as illustrating liberty of action conferred by sea-power, 278; strategical aspect of campaign in, 304, 305, 308; advantages enjoyed by Japanese in, 330.
Manila, Admiral Dewey at, 116.
Marathon, reference to, 23; embarkation after, 364, 365.
Marco Polo, reference to, 197.
Marengo, reference to, 301.
Maritime command. *See* Maritime preponderance.
Maritime preponderance, reasons for using this term, 1-4; extent of, in Peninsular War, 3; importance of bases to, 65-77; great aim of naval warfare to secure, 163, 164; the limitations of, in securing the objects for which war is undertaken, 170-183; importance of, to scattered empires for the purpose of concentrating military force for war, 184-194; examined from the point of view of "fleet in being," 203-221; effect of loss of, after an army has landed, 233-244; liberty of action conferred by, on military force, 266-296; the hold which, gives an army upon coast districts, 297-308; influence of, when a line of operations or communications follows the coast, 309-322; tendency of, to contain military force, 323-331; influence of, upon sieges of maritime fortresses, 369-390.
Market Bosworth, reference to, 197.
Marlborough, views of, as to Mediterranean, 9, 10; reference to, 12; on Cadiz, 70; importance of scheme of, against Toulon, 71, 98; and the attack on Brest, 282, 283.
Marmont, reference to, 247.
Marseilles, references to, 58, 286.
Martinique, attack on, 14, 299; Fort Royal in, 75; Mahan on, 100; restored to France, *ib.*; reference to, 58.
Maryland, invasion of, 292; references to, 293, 404.

INDEX. 513

Massachusetts, reference to, 28.
Massena, references to, 9, 247, 298 ; defence of Genoa by, 374 ; siege of Gaeta by, 383.
Matapan, Cape, reference to, 207.
Mauritius, La Bourdonais at, 6, 82 ; references to, 83, 105, 179 ; Mahan on, 101 ; attack on, 101, 134 ; troops brought from, in cruisers to South Africa, 201.
Meadows, General, captures St Lucia, 214.
Medina Sidonia, reference to, 199.
Mediterranean, Marlborough's views as to, 9 ; references to, 26, 30, 32, 34, 38, 39, 41, 46, 47, 56, 58, 86, 87, 96, 98, 125, 149, 175, 185, 187, 188, 189, 213, 236, 247, 286, 310, 311, 312, 313, 373, 374 ; effect of British acquisition of bases in, 68-74.
Medway, reference to, 109.
Mehemet Ali, reference to, 25 ; aids Sultan against Greeks, 186 ; war of, against the Sultan, 320-322.
Melas, Keith and, 21 ; at the siege of Genoa, 374.
Melville, Lord, despatch of, to Wellington, 3 ; despatches of, to Wellington, 20 ; quotations from, 137, 138, 141 ; letter from, as to blockade of San Sebastion, 372.
Memphis, reference to, 406.
Menou, references to, 181, 236 ; position of, in Egypt, 237 ; action of, at time of Abercromby's arrival, 356, 358.
Mentschikof, Prince, action of, as to Russian fleet, 131 ; position of, as regards supplies in Crimea, 251 ; army of, 269 ; evacuation of Sebastopol by, 303.
Merrimac, the destruction of the, 136 ; references to, 205, 291.
Messina, references to, 104, 154, 267, 369 ; destruction of fleet in, 132, 133 ; guns landed from fleet at, 377 ; strategical aspect of Straits of, 392, 402.
Meteor, the, at Rosas, 382.
Mexico, Gulf of, reference to, 101, 265, 412.
Miaulis, Admiral, at Missolunghi, 387.
Michigan, reference to, 396.

Midland Railway, reference to, 248.
Milan, reference to, 287.
Milan Decree, reference to, 173.
Miltiades at Marathon, 365.
Mincio, River, reference to, 315.
Minden, reference to, 138.
Mine-fields, influence of, on fortresses, 116, 117 ; in the American Civil War, 116 ; effect of, at Santiago and Port Arthur, 117 ; in inland waters, 408, 409 ; examples of, on rivers, *ib.*
Minho, reference to the, 231.
Minorca, question of seizing, 10 ; Duckworth and, 14, 159 ; the story of Byng and La Galissonière at, 56-59 ; references to, 63, 95, 150, 205, 224, 299, 377 ; capture of, in 1707, 71 ; effect of loss of, *ib. ;* restoration of, 72 ; recapture of, by Duc de Crillon, *ib. ;* want of, in 1793, *ib. ;* capture of, in 1798, 73 ; Keith and, 86, 87, 157 ; capture of, as showing value of bases, 106 ; captured by large land force, 125 ; excitement over the loss of, 180 ; Belleisle exchanged for, 181 ; the expedition to, in 1798, 278-281 ; landing at, in 1798, 346.
Miraflores, battle of, effect of guns of warships at, 341.
Mississippi, references to, 116, 172, 260, 409, 410, 411, 413, 414, 415, 418, 428 ; importance of campaigns on, 402-407 ; operations below Columbus on the, 413-415.
Missolunghi, the sieges of, 387, 388.
Missouri, reference to, 265.
Mitchell, Admiral, Dutch fleet surrenders to, 139.
Mobile, Farragut's attack on, 115, 129.
Mococenigo, reference to, 379.
Monckton, Rodney and, 14 ; reference to, 15.
Mondego, River, Wellesley's landing in estuary of, 224, 225 ; damage to boats at, 230 ; reference to, 231.
Monitor, the, and the *Merrimac*, 136, 205.
Monk, reference to, 18.
Mont Cenis, reference to, 286.
Montague, Admiral, reference to, 149 ; quotation from, *ib.*
Montcalm, reference to, 193 ; char-

acter of, 420, 421; operations of, in 1759, 421-424; death of, 424.
Monte Cristo, battle of, 45.
Monte Video, expenditure of ammunition at, 115.
Montenegro, references to, 188, 272.
Montenotte, reference to, 314.
Montmorency, River, references to, 421, 422.
Montreal, references to, 399, 419, 422; Lévis advances from, 426; fall of, 428.
Moore, Sir J. (Colonel), references to, 16, 140, 277; in Corsica, 17; quotations from, 139; advance of, towards Burgos, 171; views of, as to troops on voyages, 202; campaign of, as illustrating liberty of action, 275, 276, 296; strategy of, 299-301; letter of, to Castlereagh, 300; defeat of Soult by, 363, 367; on Sir S. Smith, 383.
Moors, the, reference to, 69.
Mordaunt at Rochefort, 13.
Morea, the, references to, 187, 324; Ibrahim Pasha in, 207, 242; Turkish advances into, 317-319.
Morlaix, reference to, 366.
Morocco, reference to, 185.
Morogues, views on naval warfare of, 57.
Morosini, reference to, 379.
Morro Castle, at Havana, 115.
Moscow, reference to, 55.
Motley, quotation from, 333.
Muizenberg, battle of, as illustrating warships aiding troops, 336, 337, 339.
Mukden, reference to, 330.
Mukhtar Pasha, campaign of, in Armenia, 188, 256, 257.
Murad, reference to, 187.
Murray, General, reference to, 193; defence of St Philip by, 374; left in command at Quebec, 426; defeated near Quebec, 427; advance of, on Montreal, 428.
Musselburgh, reference to, 335.
Mustapha, at Malta, 6; the embarkation of, 364,
Mutiny (Indian), naval brigade in, 20, 158.
Mutiny (Nore), reference to, 392.
Mycale, Persian fleet destroyed by land attack at, 130.

NAMAQUALAND, Boer invasion of, 273.
Nanshan, the battle of, 337, 338; reference to, 342.
Napier, on Admiralty and Wellington, 20; quotation from, 260; reference to, 275.
Naples, used as base by British fleet, 47, 72; references to, 134, 267; Sir J. Stuart at, 328.
Napoleon, failure of, to understand naval questions, 8, 9; references to, 30, 72, 75, 76, 98, 109, 125, 141, 150, 173, 209, 213, 224, 226, 236, 237, 247, 267, 289, 374; on the Riviera, 36, 314; advance of, into Syria, 36; expedition of, to Egypt, 38-43, 207, 278; quotation from, 57; on the Walcheren expedition, 143; and Sir S. Smith at Acre, 153, 154; and Antwerp, 167; opposed to all Europe, 171; object of British expedition to Egypt to deprive, of a valuable asset, 181, 182; on "fleet in being," 218, 219; campaign of, in 1814, 271; and Sir J. Moore, 275, 276, 300, 301; scheme of operations of, in Peninsula, 300, 301; advance of, into Syria, 320; position of, in 1807, 326, 327.
Napoleon III., arbitration of, 49; reference to, 189; joins in war of 1859, 286.
Narborough, Sir J., reference to, 69.
Natal, form of frontier of, 265, 266; reference to, 273.
Nauplia, reference to, 318.
Naval Brigade, Brigades, references to, 20, 158.
Naval command. *See* Maritime preponderance.
Naval Discipline Act, reference to, 169.
Naval warfare, objects of, 51-64; distinction between, and warfare generally, 170-183.
Navarino, battle of, destruction of Turkish naval power at, 187; references to, 207, 243; effect of, 236, 237, 252.
Nelson, in Corsica, 17; references to, 18, 22, 30, 33, 36, 76, 79, 86, 87, 129, 137, 139, 182, 209, 237, 278; on the Riviera, 21; quota-

INDEX. 515

tions from, 31, 208; pursuit of Napoleon by, 38-43, 207; strategy of, 55; sent back into Mediterranean, 72; based on Maddalena, 73; attempt of, on Santa Cruz, 158, 361, 362; at Calvi and Copenhagen, 112; on blockade, 119; rebuke of, by the Admiralty, 157; recognition of need of military force by, 158; anxiety of, as to Malta, 159; and Latouche Tréville, 165; on destruction of transports, 212, 213; plan of, in case he met Napoleon's expedition to Egypt, 213; shows how to attack fleet in a bay, 215; criticism by, of Hotham, 336; at Calvi, 382.

Nepheris, with reference to Carthage, 96, 122, 372.

Neutrality, violation of, examples of, 45-49; position of, question in present day, 49; Dutch violation of English, 199.

Neutrals, attitude of, formerly and now, 43-50.

Neva, River, references to, 302, 402.

New England, Louisbourg captured by, colonists, 192.

New France. *See* Canada.

New Madrid, references to, 413, 414.

New Orleans, references to, 294, 403, 404, 411, 412.

New York, as naval base, 75; expedition to Louisbourg from, references to, 98, 144, 238, 239, 294, 399.

New York (state), reference to, 400.

Newbern, reference to, 262.

Newcastle, reference to, 266.

Newport, the story of, as illustrating interdependence of land- and sea-power, 144-146; reference to, 249.

Nezib, battle of, 321.

Niagara Fort, capture of, 426.

Niagara (river), (frontier), references to, 396, 397.

Nice, reference to, 314.

Nicopolis, reference to, 409.

Nile, battle of, some units of beaten squadron left after, 2; Napoleon's position after the, 182, 236, 237; references to, 86, 138, 165.

Nile Delta. *See* Egypt.

Noailles, Duc de, attack of, on Barcelona, 311.

Nore, reference to mutiny at, 392.

Norfolk, fall of, 136.

Normandy, references to, 197, 204, 366.

Norreys at Lisbon, 11.

North Foreland, reference to, 242.

Nova Scotia, references to, 28, 97.

Novara, the battle of, 316.

OARS, ancient ships driven by, 25.

Ochakof, destruction of Turkish fleet at, 133.

Octavian, reference to, 23.

Odessa, references to, 254, 269.

O'Hara, General, at Gibraltar, 279, 280.

Ohio, reference to, 396.

Ohio, River, reference to, 403.

Okehampton, reference to, 436 note.

Oku, General, quotation from, as to Nanshan, 338.

Old Fort, landing of allies at, 269.

Old Pretender, the, reference to, 197.

Omar Pasha, move of, to Redoute Kale, 271.

Ontario, Lake, references to, 394, 419, 426, 428; in 1812-14, 397; question of bases on, *ib.*, 398.

Ookiep, reference to, 273.

Oporto, reference to, 202.

Orange Free State, references to, 266, 272.

Orders in Council, reference to, 173.

Ormonde, Duke of, at Cadiz, 12, 13, 352; attack of, on Vigo, 80, 136; expedition of, from Coruña driven back by storm, 197.

Osman Pasha, references to, 188, 259.

Ostend, British landing at, 228, 229; siege of, 380, 381.

Othman, reference to, 258.

Ottoman Empire. *See* Turkey.

Oudenarde, reference to, 138.

Over-sea possessions, question of operations against, 175, 176.

PALERMO, Vivonne at, 34, 35; taking of, by Belisarius, 377.

Palestine, references to, 185, 187, 197, 320.

Pamlico Sound, references to, 261, 409.

Pamunky, River, references to, 291, 294.

Panama, Isthmus of, strategical aspect of, on land, 319.
Paoli, reference to, 108.
Papal States, troops brought from, to France, 189.
Paris, reference to, 129; defence of, 189.
Paris, Treaty of, privateering abolished by, 102.
Parma, Duke of, reference to, 199.
Paskievich, the campaigns of, 187, 253-256.
Passaro, Cape, Byng's victory at, 132.
Patras, Gulf of, reference to, 387.
Paul Jones in the Firth of Forth, 30.
Pausanias left by Xerxes in Greece, 130.
Peel, Captain, reference to, 158.
Pellew. *See* Exmouth, Lord.
Peloponnesus. *See* Morea.
Pelusium, ancient landing at, 344.
Peniche, reference to, 231.
Peninsula, expeditions to, 3; Admiralty correspondence with Wellington as to, 19, 20; references to, 201, 296; communications in, 202; Wellesley's landing in, 224; Sir J. Moore's campaign in, 275, 276.
Peninsular War, Admiralty and Wellington during, 20; question of complete maritime control during, 20, 233, 234; Wellington's strategy in the, 298-302; Moore's strategy in the, 299-301.
Penn and Venables in West Indies, 11; references to, 21, 149.
Pennsylvania, reference to, 419.
Perekop, Isthmus of, sea in vicinity of, shallow, 319, 337.
Perignon, General, at siege of Rosas, 380.
Perpignan, reference to, 310.
Perry, Commodore, exploits of, on Lake Erie, 396, 397, 398, 400.
Persano, Admiral, at Lissa, 115.
Persia, Persian, references to, 25, 130, 324, 364, 365.
Peru, liberation of, 191; reference to, 210; Chilian landings in, 224; war between, and Chili as illustrating liberty of action, 283-287, 296.

Peruvians in battles before Lima, 341.
Peter the Great at Azov, 417.
Peterborough, references to, 12, 299; relief of Barcelona by, 385, 386.
Petersburg, reference to, 261; campaign round, 294, 295.
Petropavlovsk, the, blowing up of the, 117.
Pevensey Bay, landing of William the Conqueror at, 27.
Phalerum, Doris arrives at, 367.
Philippines, reference to, 143.
Phœnicians, references to, 109, 385; leave Persians at Samos, 130.
Phœnix, story of the, 45, 46.
Piali at Malta, 6.
Pichegru, capture of Dutch fleet by, 131, 139.
Piedmont, references to, 73, 286, 316.
Pinkie Cleugh, battle of, 335.
Pisani at Chiogia, 122, 123.
Pitt (elder), reconciliation of navy with army by, 10, 13, 14; war policy of, 98, 299; monument to, in Guildhall, 177; policy of raids of, discussed, 326, 327; references to, 418, 419; plan of campaign of, in North America, 419; quotation from, as to Wolfe, 424, 425; plan of, for 1760, 426.
Pitt (younger), war policy of, 101.
Plattsburg, reference to, 19, 21, 400.
Plevna, reference to, 259, 418.
Plymouth Sound, reference to, 114.
Po, River, references to, 141, 286, 315, 374; basin of, 312, 314; Archduke John in valley of, 328.
Pocock, Admiral, ships of, suffer at Havanna, 114.
Point Lévis, references to, 421, 422, 423.
Pondicherry, La Bourdonais at, 7.
Pope, General, campaign of, in Virginia, 292; campaign of, below Columbus, 413-415.
Pope, the, and Charles V., 226.
Porcupine, the, Jervis and, 159.
Port, Ports. *See* Harbours.
Port Arthur, references to, 37, 104, 105, 117, 133, 152, 154, 156, 166, 221, 316; as shelter for Russian fleet, 99; material captured in, 104; blocking entrance

INDEX. 517

to, 111; question of bombardment of, by ships, 112, 113; blowing up of *Petropavlovsk* at, 117; attempts to block entrance of, 121, 123; the lesson of, 128, 129, 147; compared to Mycale, 130; attack on Russian fleet at, by torpedo craft, 217; failure of Russian torpedo craft in, *ib.*; Japanese landings near, 361; question of blockading, 374, 375; long-range fire of fleet at, 376.
Port Elizabeth, reference to, 223, 272.
Port Hudson, references to, 293; fortified, 405.
Port Louis, capture of, 134.
Port Mahon. *See* Mahon.
Port Royal, capture of, by Federals, 108, 109.
Port Said, reference to, 344.
Porter, Admiral, references to, 406, 410.
Portland, reference to, 76.
Porto Farina, Blake's attack on, 113; reference to, 149.
Porto Praya, Suffren at, 48.
Portsmouth, references to, 47, 152.
Portugal, Portuguese, ships not safe on coast of, even before 1812, 3; references to, 45, 47, 247, 300; position of, in time of war, 48; communications in, 202; coast-line of, 230, 231; Wellington's shift of base from, to Santander, 259, 260; position of Wellington in, 298; danger of, during War of Spanish Succession, 325, 326.
Potemkin at Ochakof, 133.
Poti, capture of, 253; reference to, 254, 255.
Potomac, River, references to, 290, 292, 293, 294, 295, 403.
Presqu'isle, Perry's base on Lake Erie, 396, 400; proposal to capture, 398.
Prevost, General, at Plattsburg, 19, 399, 400; reference to, 21.
Privateer, Privateers, reference to, 100; effect of, *ib.*, 101; abolition of, 102; Wexford a nest of, 248, 249; anxiety caused to Wellington by, 250.
Procida, capture of gunboats at, 135, 136.

Provence, reference to, 286.
Prussia, reference to, 171.
Psariots, reference to, 154.
Pulteney, expedition of, to Ferrol, 140.
Punic War, Wars, reference to first, 25.
Pursuit, inadequate, before time of St Vincent and Nelson, 78, 79.
Pyrenees, references to, 233, 247, 259, 298, 312; the defile east of the, 310, 311.

QUEBEC, fire-ships below, 33; Walker's expedition to, 35; references to, 98, 135, 177, 224, 374, 437; example of fortress on river, 370; the campaign of, in 1760, 419-428; siege of, 424, 426; relief of, 427.
Queenston, Brock killed at, 397.
Quiberon, reference to, 177; the descent of *emigrés* on, 337.
Quinqueremes, of Greeks and Romans, 26.
Quinteros, landing in Bay of, 224.

RADETZKY, Marshal, campaigns of, in North Italy, 315, 316.
Raglan, Lord, reference to, 302.
Raleigh, in West Indies, 10; on size of warships, 432.
Ramatuelle, Mahan on, 56, 57; reference to, 59.
Rameses III., quotation from, 345.
Ramillies, references to, 9, 12, 71.
Rapahannock, River, references to, 292, 293.
Rapidan, River, reference to, 292.
Red River, campaign on the, 411.
Redoute Kale, move of Omar Pasha to, 271.
Re-enterant frontiers, references to, 266, 267.
Regulus, reference to, 25.
Reille, General, at Rosas, 382.
Revel, as shelter to Russian fleets, 78; Swedish attack on, 114; reference to, 329.
Reynier, General, at Maida, 267.
Rhé, attack on island of, 373.
Rhine, River, reference to, 393.
Rhode Island, reference to, 145.
Rhone, River, reference to, 312.
Richard Cœur de Lion, armada of, dispersed by storm, 197.

2 G

Richard II. drawn to Scotland by Jean de Vienne, 324.
Richelieu, Duc de, attack of, on Minorca, 56; references to, 63, 71, 95, 205, 208, 278.
Richmond, Duke of, expeditions of, to England, 197.
Richmond, references to, 260, 289, 408; fall of, 261; importance of, 289; in Virginian campaigns, 291, 294.
Rio de Janiero, reference to, 76.
River warfare, generally a case of small vessels, 401; campaign of Mississippi as example of, 403-407; question of current in, 406; question whether in future armed vessels can pass batteries in, 407; submarine mines in, *ib.*, 408; campaign of 1877 on Danube as example of, 409, 410; Porter in the "bayous" as example of, 410; difficulties in, due to rise and fall, 411; digging canals in, 412, 413; co-operation between flotilla and troops in, *ib.;* campaign of Island No. 10 as example of, 413-415.
Riviera, operations on the, 21; inadequate blockade of the, 36; defile of the, 312-314; references to, 332, 340, 399; tactical intervention of ships in, 335, 336.
Roanoke, River, effect of mine-fields on, 409.
Roberts, Lord, reference to, 272.
Rochambeau, at Newport, 144-146; references to, 206, 249.
Rochefort, expedition to, 13; secret as to, allowed to leak out, 282; Carlyle on expedition to, 326; Howe at, 367.
Rochelle, La, reference to, 373.
Rodney, and Monckton, 14; ineffective pursuit by, 79; references to, 100, 109; arrival of, in North America, 145; and Newport, 145, 146; recognition of need of military force by, 158; revictualling of Gibraltar by, 386.
Roman, Romans, reference to, 37; at Carthage, 111; make dam at Carthage, 122; at Ecnomus, 210, 211; at landing at Walmer, 347, 348.

Rome, garrison of, withdrawn, 189.
Rooke, failure of, to understand Mediterranean problem, 10; at Cadiz, 11, 352; capture of Gibraltar by, 70, 125, 150; reference to, 74; attack of, on Vigo, 80, 136; beats down fire of Gibraltar batteries, 111; at battle of Malaga, 115; lands guns at Gibraltar, 161; sends fleet to Adriatic, 314.
Rosas, Cochrane at, 153, 328; siege of, in 1794-95, 379, 380; siege of, in 1808, 382.
Rosily, Admiral, destruction of fleet of, in Cadiz, 140, 141.
Roumania, references to, 253, 258, 269.
Roumelia, reference to, 253.
Rupert, Prince, references to, 18, 45; in the Tagus, 45; in Kinsale, 78; escape of, from Kinsale, 120; at battle of Texel, 200.
Russell, quotation from, 71, 72; on the coast of Catalonia, 311.
Russia, Russian, reference to war of, with Sweden, 26; benevolent neutrality of England towards, in 1770, 47; value of, Far Eastern fleet in 1904, 52; Japanese fleets only risked against, squadron at sea, 113; sunken, fleet at Port Arthur, 128; sinking of, fleet at Sebastopol, 131; sinking of, fleet at Port Arthur, 147; justified in landing sailors at Port Arthur, 154; references to, 171, 208; a widely extended empire, 184; fleet in Sebastopol during allied move to the Crimea, 200, 208; failure of, torpedo craft in Port Arthur, 217; commerce destroying in 1904, 220; sudden attack on, fleet, *ib.;* army supplied across Sea of Azov, 251; position of, in 1828, 253; difficulties of, in Crimean War, 304; position of, compared to that of Japan in Far Eastern War, *ib.*, 305; fleet in Mediterranean in 1770, 317; comes to aid of Sultan against Mehemet Ali, 320; at Nanshan, 338; at the Alma, 339, 340; on the Danube in 1877, 409, 410; in the Baltic during the Crimean War, 434.

INDEX. 519

Russo-Turkish War, 1828-29, Russia commanded sea in, 187 ; as illustration of question of communications, 252-256, 257, 258 ; as illustrating "interior lines," 274.

Russo-Turkish War, 1877-78, Turks commanded sea in, 188 ; as illustration of question of communications, 256, 257, 258, 259 ; as illustrating "interior lines," 272 ; passage of Danube in, 409, 410.

Rustchuk, references to, 258, 409.

SACKETT'S HARBOUR, American base at, 395 ; attack on, 397.

Sailing days, risks of storms during, 28 ; uncertainty as to time in, 29 ; comparison of, with steam, *ib.;* effect of wind in, 30, 31 ; difficulties of blockade in, 31 ; difficulties of attacking anchored transports in, 214, 215 ; "fleet in being" in, 215, 216.

Sailing-ships, advantage of, over rowing vessels, 27.

Sailing-ships of war, introduction of, 27 ; assisting troops, 340.

Sailors, question of employing, ashore, 144-158 ; advantage of employing, ashore under certain circumstances, 148 ; question of employing, on fixed defences, 150-152 ; landing on emergency duty, 152, 153 ; examples of employing, ashore, 152-154 ; disadvantage of employing, ashore, 154, 155 ; employing, ashore generally only permissible on small scale, 156, 157 ; no objection to landing, if they can be spared, 157, 158 ; landings at awkward places best carried out by, 361, 362.

St Arnaud, Marshal, reference to, 302.

St Bernard, references to, 8, 374.

St Cas, the affair of, 365-368.

St Charles, River, reference to, 421.

St Domingo, reference to, 11 ; Penn and Venables at, 179.

St Helena, reference to, 143.

St Lawrence, Wolfe on the, 14, 299 ; importance of Louisbourg with reference to the, 97 ; references to, 98, 193, 224, 394, 399, 400, 407 ; the campaign on the, in 1759, 419-426 ; the campaign on the, in 1760, 426-428.

St Lucia, capture of, as base by Barrington, 107 ; references to, 109, 179, 217 ; Barrington and D'Estaing at, 214, 215.

St Malo, expeditions to, 326, 327, 366.

St Martin's, siege of, 373.

St Paul's Bay, embarkation of Turks at, 364.

St Petersburg, reference to, 329.

St Philip, Fort, references to, 56, 279 ; the siege of, by de Crillon, 373, 374 ; siege of, in 1708, 377.

St Roque, Godinot marches from, 333.

St Vincent, battle of, references to, 72, 138, 165.

St Vincent, Cape, references to, 47, 72.

St Vincent, Lord, and Grey, 14 ; instructions of, to Duckworth, *ib.;* references to, 15, 17, 73, 79, 137, 165 ; sends Nelson to Toulon, 38 ; strategy of, 55 ; gains victory off Cape St Vincent, 72; sends Nelson back into Mediterranean, *ib.;* on bases, 85 ; quotation from, *ib.;* succeeded by Keith, 86 ; on military forces, 159, 160 ; quotation from, 159 ; and the United Service Club, 160 note ; story of, and the attack on Minorca in 1798, 278-281.

Sakhtouris at Missolunghi, 387.

Salamanca, reference to, 300.

Salamis, references to, 23, 25, 37, 392 ; battle of, 129.

Saldanha Bay, troops captured on fighting-ships in, 200.

Salient frontiers, remarks on, 265-267,

Salisbury Plain, reference to, 436 note.

Samos, Persian fleet at, 131.

Sampson, Admiral, at Santiago, 120, 121 ; quotation from, 143.

San Fiorenzo, reference to, 108.

San Sebastian, as example of fortress on promontory, 370; siege of, 372, 373.

San Stefano, Peace of, 257.

Santa Cruz, Blake's attack on, 80, 113, 114, 124, 129 ; Nelson's design for attacking, 158; Nelson's attack on, 361, 392.

Santander, reinforcements from Gibraltar and Lisbon could not be despatched to, 3; Wellington's shift of base to, 259, 260; Espartero at, 288.

Santiago de Cuba, relations between United States admiral and general at, 7, 8; mines in, harbour, 117; attempt to block entrance to, 121; the lesson of, 128, 129, 143; references to, 136, 219, 224, 346; long-range fire of fleet at, 376.

Saracens, references to, 282, 349.

Saratoga, references to, 144, 237.

Sardinia (Island), British based on, 68, 72; Spain offers Temple a base in, 69; reference to, 73.

Sardinia (Kingdom), reference to, 314; war between, and Austria, 315, 316.

Sardinian army at Messina, 132.

Saumarez, Admiral, in the Baltic, 131.

Saunders, Admiral, Wolfe and, 14; references to, 33, 428; selected by Pitt to co-operate with Wolfe, 420; operations of, 420-424.

Savannah, references to, 108, 238; Sherman at, 260; Sherman's march to, 274.

Savona, reference to, 36.

Savoy, Duke of, attack of, on Toulon, 314, 335.

Scandinavia, reference to, 265.

Scheldt, the, references to, 133, 156; Walcheren expedition directed against, 142; Ostend expedition directed against canals of, 228.

Schleswig, reference to, 266; invasion of, 305; in the Danish wars, 305-308; as an isthmus, 319.

Schofield, operations of, in concert with Sherman, 262.

Scilly Islands, Sir C. Shovel lost on the, 34.

Scipio, action of, against Nepheris, 96; attempt of, to block entrance to Carthage, 122, 372.

Scotland, reference to, 248; strategical conditions of, in wars with England, 264, 268.

Scott, Sir W., quotation from, 30.

Sea, command of. *See* Maritime preponderance.

Sea, control of. *See* Maritime preponderance.

Seamen. *See* Sailors.

Sea-power. *See* Maritime preponderance.

Sebastopol, as refuge for Russian fleet, 99; references to, 104, 115, 150, 188, 200, 219, 247, 251, 254, 269, 270, 304; attacked partly because of Russian fleet, 105; naval attack on, 115; sinking of fleet in, 131; action of Kornilof at, 153; the flank march to, 225; landing of guns from fleet for siege of, 377, 378.

Sedan, reference to, 189.

Servia, reference to, 272.

Seven Years' War, references to, 10, 98, 192, 205, 299; the question of growth of British over-sea trade in the, 177, 178; England's assistance to Prussia in, 326, 327; Pitt's policy of raids in, *ib.*

Shafter, General, at Santiago, 117, 128, 376; objective of, 136; orders to, 143; delayed by false report of "fleet in being," 219; landing of, at Daiquiri, 346.

Sha-ho, River, reference to, 330.

Shantung, reference to, 281.

Sheerness, reference to, 392.

Shenandoah Valley, references to, 291, 294.

Sheridan and the "sugar islands," 177, 178.

Sherman, General, capture of Port Royal by, 108, 109; campaign of, in the Carolinas, 260, 261; march of, to the sea as illustrating liberty of action, 273, 274; references to, 289, 296, 405, 412; relief of Porter's flotilla by, 410.

Shipbuilding, nations can generally carry out, during war, 2; progress of, 24, 26, 27, 35; rapidity of, formerly, 32.

Shipka Pass, Suliman Pasha at, 188, 272; reference to, 258.

Shovel, Sir C., failure of, to understand Mediterranean problem, 10; loss of, 34; at Toulon, 114, 160, 314; at the battle on the Var, 335, 336.

INDEX. 521

Shrapnel, question as to warships using, against shore, 434, 435.
Shumla, reference to, 258.
Siberia, reference to, 330.
Sicily, references to operations in, 33, 34; in Napoleon's expedition to Egypt, 40, 41; Vivonne's attack on, 46; British based on ports of, 72; references to, 73, 133, 135, 197, 202, 267, 383, 384; Sir J. Stuart and, 328.
Sidi Feruch, landing at, 224.
Siege, sieges, command of sea vital in, of maritime fortress, 369; where attacking side has sea command, 371-378; assistance of warships in, 376, 377; where defending side has sea command, 378-384; where maritime command is in dispute, 384-388.
Siege-train, capture of Napoleon's, by Sir S. Smith, 36; taken from Dublin to Wexford by sea, 249.
Signalling, importance of, between land and sea forces, 441-443.
Silistria, siege of, 269.
Simon's Bay, Simonstown, acquisition of, 179; references to, 336, 337.
Sistova, reference to, 258.
Sizeboli, reference to, 382.
Smith, Sir S., on coast of Syria, 36; landing of sailors by, at Acre, 153, 154, 381; on coast of Calabria, 267, 383; at the landing in Aboukir Bay, 356, 357; and Gaeta, 383.
Snowdon, reference to, 248.
Soliman the Magnificent, references to, 6, 258.
Solway, reference to, 264.
Somerset, reference to, 267.
Soult, reference to, 247; and Sir J. Moore, 276, 301, 363, 367.
South Africa, maritime command undisputed in war in, 1; naval brigades in, 20, 158; war in, as illustrating effect of sea-power, 190; troops brought from Mauritius in cruiser in early part of war in, 201; examples of "interior lines" in, 272, 273; reference to, 443.
South Wales, reference to, 267.
Southampton, reference to, 232.

Spanish Armada, references to, 28, 204, 224; fire-ships and the, 33; escape of the, 79; cause of disaster to, 204.
Spanish Succession, War of, references to, 26, 70, 75, 80; effect capture of Toulon would have had on, 71, 98; Peterborough's exploits in, 299; campaign in Catalonia during, 310; shift of Stanhope during, 325, 326.
Sparre at Cadiz, 11.
Spartans, Demaratus on the, 324.
Speedy, reference to the, 356.
Spezia, reference to, 152.
Spithead, reference to, 47.
Splügen, reference to, 8.
Spragge, Admiral, at Bougie, 33.
Stanhope, Colonel (General), quotations from, 12, 71, 326; references to, 74, 249; capture of Minorca by, 125; contemplated attack by, on Cadiz, 326; at siege of St Philip, 377; arrival of, at Barcelona, 385, 386.
Steam, introduction of, 29; comparison of, with sailing days, *ib.*; did away with uncertainty, *ib.*; influence of, on commerce destroying, 84, 85.
Stopford, Admiral, attack of, on Acre, 115.
Storm, storms, effect of, in ancient times, 25; of 1705, 28; examples of dispersion of expeditions by, 197; effect of, on invasions of England, *ib.*, 198; question of, during landings, 225; during Charles V.'s operations at Algiers, 227; at Balaclava, 232.
Strachan, Admiral, and Lord Chatham, 18.
Stralsund, relief of, 384.
Stronghold. *See* Fortress.
Stuart, General (Swedish), landing of, in Zealand, 346.
Stuart, Sir C., in Corsica, 17, 86.
Stuart, Sir J., reference to, 16; at Maida, 267; expedition of, to Naples, 328.
Submarine mines. *See* Mine-fields.
Submarines, reference to, 33; bases required for, 89; radius of action of, *ib.*, 90; effect of, on transports at anchor, 235.

Suchet at siege of Tarragona, 380.
Suez Canal in campaign of 1882, 416.
Suez, Isthmus of, 316, 319, 322.
Suffren, at Porto Praya, 48; references to, 59, 109; in want of base, 83; in the Indian Ocean, *ib.;* and Trincomalee, 86, 103, 125; at the siege of Cuddalore, 388.
Suliman Pasha, move of, from Adriatic to Ægean, 188, 272; at the Shipka Pass, 188.
Sunium, Cape, reference to, 364.
Superior, Lake, size of, 392.
Sussex, reference to, 27.
Suvarof, reference to, 249; at siege of Ismail, 417.
Sveaborg, attack on, 111, 329; destruction of Swedish fleet at, 131.
Swede, Sweden, Swedish, references to, 26, 28, 202, 346; attack of, fleet on Revel, 114; destruction of, fleet at Sveaborg and Abo, 131; Russians challenge supremacy of, in Baltic, 302; attack on Kronstadt, 352, 353; at Stralsund, 384.
Swilly, Loch, defeat of Bompart off, 209.
Swiss frontier, length of, 265.
Sydney, reference to, 76.
Syracuse, Nelson at, 40; reference to, 197.
Syria, references to, 25, 36; campaign in, 320-322.

TACTICAL intervention of warships, general considerations of, 332, 333; examples of, 333-337; in case of an isthmus, 337, 338; battle of Nanshan as example of, 338; how influenced by progress in artillery, 338-340; how influenced by steam, 340.
Tagus, Rupert in the, 45, 78; references to, 107, 173, 202, 231, 276.
Talienwan, reference to, 316; Japanese warships fire on own side at, 442.
Tampa, General Shafter at, 219.
Tangier, Vivonne at, 46, 49; acquisition of, 69; reference to, *ib.;* abandonment of, 75, 311; Herbert at, 152.
Tarapaca, Chilians take, 285.

Tarifa, march of Godinot to, 333; siege of, 382; Graham starts from, to relieve Cadiz, 384.
Tarragona, the siege of, 380.
Tauric Chersonese. *See* Crimea.
Taurus Mountains, Ibrahim Pasha crosses, 321.
Tecumseh, blown up by mine, 116.
Tegethoff, reference to, 59; at Lissa, 115.
Telegraph, effect of, 37, 38; influence of, on commerce-destroyers, 102.
Temple, Sir W., reference to, 69.
Tenedos, fire-ships at, 33.
Teneriffe, reference to, 113.
Tennessee, reference to, 273.
Territorial waters, question of, 44.
Tessé, Marshal, siege of Barcelona by, 385, 386.
Texas, references to, 265, 403, 404.
Texel, the, Pichegru at, 131; troops carried in fighting-ships at battle of, 200.
Thames, reference to, 216, 248.
Thebes, inscription on temple at, 345.
Thermopylæ, references to, 25, 287, 324.
Thessaly, Xerxes passes through, 129; references to, 186, 249, 411.
Thiebault, General, quotation from, 374.
Thiers, admission of, as to Napoleon, 8.
Ticino, reference to, 286.
Tiptonville, references to, 414, 415.
Todleben, at Sebastopol, 303.
Togo, Admiral, blocking of entrance to Port Arthur by, 111, 121.
Tokio, reference to, 330.
Tollemache, the attack of, on Brest, 282, 283; the landing of, at Brest, 351, 352.
Toronto, American attack on, 397.
Torpedo-boat stations, question of, 89, 90; reference to, 218 note.
Torpedo-boats, craft, reference to, 85; need of bases for, 89, 90; radius of action of, *ib.;* action of, against fortresses, 117, 118; at Wei-hai-wei, 118; effect of, as regards transports, 216, 217; with references to invasion of England, 217, 218 note; attack of, during

INDEX. 523

landings, 235; unsuitable for amphibious operations, 433.
Torquay, reference to, 232.
Torres Vedras, the lines of, 298, 299; reference to, 437.
Torrington, Lord, action of, at Tangier, 152; father of the "fleet in being," 202, 203; references to, 204, 205, 216.
Toulon, Marlborough's plans against, 9; Hood at, 15-17; Keith at, 21; references to, 31, 78, 141, 150, 160, 216, 278; rapid creation of fleet in, 32; Napoleon at, 38; Napoleon's departure from, *ib.;* Nelson off, 39, 41; Boscawen and De la Clue at, 58; Nelson sent to, 72; roomy harbour of, 75, 151; importance of Marlborough's scheme against, 98; probable result if Hood had destroyed everything in, *ib.;* material left in, 104; attack on, by Duke of Savoy and Shovel, 335; Nelson on blockading, 119; scale of attack on, in 1717, 156; Nelson off, 165; Napoleon and the British at, 301; Tourville retires to, 311; as typical fortress, 369.
Toulouse, fight of, with Rooke at Malaga, 115; blockade of Barcelona by, 386, 387.
Tourville, at Palermo, 33; action of, after Beachy Head, 79; reference to, 204; abandons blockade of Barcelona, 311.
Trafalgar, battle of, some units of defeated squadron left after, 2; nature of preponderance after, 3; references to, 8, 73, 140, 167, 171; question of pursuit after, 79; the last echo of, 140, 141, 147; French naval position after, 141.
Transcaucasia, references to, 256, 257.
Transvaal, reference to, 266.
Trebizond, references to, 187, 254, 256.
Trincomalee, in campaign between Hughes and Suffren, 86; capture of, by Suffren, *ib.*, 103; references to, 109, 125.
Tripoli (Africa), reference to, 185.
Tripoli (Syria), reference to, 322.
Triremes of Greeks and Romans, 26.

Troubridge, junction of, with Nelson, 39, 41; at Capua, 156, 157.
Tunis, reference to Bay of, 97; Dey of, 113; references to, 134, 135, 211, 226.
Turk, Turkish, expedition to Malta, 6; destruction of, fleets by fireships, 33; defeat of, fleet by Russians, 47; reinforcements at Acre, 153; attack of, fleet in Ipsara, 154, 155; failure of, attack on Malta, 197; invasion of Greece, 317; invasion of Greece in 1822, 317-319; fleet at Perekop, 337; at Missolunghi, 387, 388; capture of, stronghold of Azov, 417.
Turkey, rapidly created new fleet after Lepanto, 32; Russian war with, in 1770, 47; references to, 115, 181; extent of, in 1788, 133; as example of importance of sea command to scattered empire, 185-189; war between, and Greece, 249, 250; position of, on Black Sea in 1828, 253; fight of Venice against, 301; Mehemet Ali's campaign against, 320-322.
Turkish Empire. *See* Turkey.
Turko-Greek War, maritime communications in, 249, 250.
Tuscany, Grand Duke of, reference to, 46.
Tuscany, references to, 45, 73, 208, 313.
Tweed, references to, 264, 335.
Two Sicilies, kingdom of, references to, 157, 299.
Tyre, siege of, 385, 389.

"ULTERIOR objects," doctrine of, 55-59.
United Kingdom, attempted invasions of, dispersed by storm, 197, 198; peculiar position of, as regards dependence on naval force, 168, 169, 170; question of invasion of, 217, 218 note.
United Service Club, the, reference to, 160 note.
United States, British fleet did not enjoy unquestioned control of sea even before war with, in 1812, 3; claim of, against Portugal, 48, 49.
Upnor Castle, reference to, 109.

VALENCIA, Valencian, reference to, 12; reference to ports, 69.
Valetta, Napoleon reduces, 39; value of, 74; references to, 159, 364; siege of, 372.
Valladolid, Napoleon at, 301.
Valparaiso, Chilians create fleet at, 210; reference to, 224.
Van Galen, off Leghorn, 45; reference to, 78.
Var, River, references to, 313; battle on the, 335, 336.
Varna, references to, 200, 219, 258, 259; capture of, 257, 258; assembly of allies at, 269; siege of, 274.
Vauban, at Brest, 282; reference to, 389.
Vaubois, General, defends Valetta, 372.
Venables and Penn in the West Indies, 11; reference to, 21, 149; capture of Jamaica by, 178, 179; landing of, at Guantanamo, 224.
Venetia, Venetians, rebellion in, 315; the, at siege of Candia, 379.
Venetian colonies. *See* Venice.
Venice, Genoese attack on, 122, 123; grip of, on her over-sea possessions, 301.
Vernon and Wentworth at Cartagena, 12, 13.
Vicksburg, references to, 293, 406, 410, 411, 412; development of, by the Confederates, 404; capture of, 405; references to, 406, 410, 411, 412, 418.
Victor at Cadiz, 384.
Vienna, Peace of, reference to, 55.
Vigo, references to, 12, 202; attack on ships in, 80; troops in attack on, 136.
Villaret Joyeuse, the defeat of, by Howe, 367.
Villeneuve, references to, 31, 141.
Virginia, Federal troops and navy worked hand in hand in, 172; references to campaign of, 205, 416; Federal landings in, 224; the campaign of Cornwallis in, 238-240; references to, 243, 260, 261, 403; Lee in, 274; the campaign of, as illustrating liberty of action, 289-296, 403, 416.

Vistula, references to, 171, 328.
Vittoria, battle of, 3, 260.
Vivonne, Duc de, at Palermo, 33, 34; at Tangier, 46, 49.
Vladivostok, effect of commerce-destroyers from, 102; Russian forces contained at, 330; as example of fortress on promontory, 370.
Volga, River, reference to, 402.
Volo, Gulf of, disaster to Xerxes' fleet off, 25.
Voltri, ships fail to help troops at, 340.
Vosges, failure of French to destroy, tunnels, 104.

WALCHEREN, expedition to, 18; object of the, expedition, 141, 142, 167; references to, 147, 161; landing of Count Guy of Flanders in, 348, 349.
Walker, Sir H., disaster to, 35.
Wallenstein at Stralsund, 384.
Walmer, landing of Julius Cæsar at, 347, 348.
War of American Independence. *See* American Independence.
War of Greek Liberation. *See* Greek Liberation.
War of Secession. *See* American Civil War.
War of Spanish Succession. *See* Spanish Succession.
Warren, Admiral, assists in capture of Louisbourg, 97.
Warren, Admiral (Commodore), expedition of, against Ferrol, 140; defeats Bompart, 209.
Washington (General), dissatisfaction of, with his allies, 54; plans of, 144; in Newport campaign, 145, 146; in the campaign of Yorktown, 206, 238-240, 243; reference to, 249.
Washington, references to, 289-295, 403.
Water, question of, for fleets formerly, 65, 66.
Waterloo, reference to, 109.
Waterways, inland, definition of, 391; generally commanded from shore, *ib.*, 392; command of, a case of small vessels, 392, 393; question of current in, 406.

Wei-hai-wei, torpedo craft at, 118; the lesson of, 128, 129; compared to Mycale, 130; object of Japanese attack on, 134; Japanese feints before landing to attack, 281; Japanese fire on own torpedo-boats at, 442.

Wellesley, Sir A. *See* Wellington.

Wellington, despatch from Melville to, 3; references to, 16, 240, 247, 250, 304; and the Admiralty, 19, 20, 233; landing of, at the Mondego, 224, 225, 231; shift of base by, to Santander, 259, 260; strategy of, at Torres Vedras, 298-302; letter from Melville to, as to San Sebastian, 372; approves Prevost's decision to retire after Plattsburg, 400.

Wentworth, and Vernon at Cartagena, 12, 13.

West, Captain, at Rosas, 382.

West Indies, West Indian Islands, Drake and Raleigh in, 10; Cromwell and, 11; fight for, 54; fall of France in, 71; effect of capture of, in Seven Years' War, 100, 178; references to, 101, 107, 145, 149, 158, 159, 202, 213.

Westerham, reference to, 425.

Wexford, siege of, 248, 249.

White House, M'Clellan's base at, 291.

White Sea, operations in, 329.

William III., policy of, in Mediterranean, 9, 311; opposition of, to Louis XIV., 69; and Cadiz, 70; first expedition of, to England dispersed by storm, 197; references to, 203, 283.

William of Orange. *See* William III.

William the Conqueror, landing of, at Pevensey, 27; driven back by strong winds, 197.

Williamstadt, siege of, 417.

Wilmington, reference to, 238; force despatched to, 261.

Wireless telegraphy, effect of, 38; influence of, on commerce-destroyers, 102.

Wittgenstein, campaign of, in Bulgaria, 257, 258.

Wolfe, on St Lawrence, 12; references to, 13, 159, 193, 224, 299, 361, 428; quotation from, 14; at the landing at Louisbourg, 353, 354; selection of, to command army for Quebec, 420; operations of, before Quebec, 420-424; death of, 424; services of, 425, 426.

Wolfe Tone, capture of, 209.

Wolseley, Lord, use made of Suez Canal by, 416.

Wörth, reference to, 189.

XERXES, fleet of, damaged off Volo, 25, invasion of Greece by, 129, 130; and Demaratus, 324.

YANGTSEKIANG, River, reference to, 402.

Yellow Sea, fogs in, 198.

Yen Toa, the landing at, 361.

York, Duke of, at the Helder, 138; at the siege of Dunkirk, 381.

York, River, reference to, 291.

Yorkshire, reference to, 248.

Yorktown, references to, 20, 54, 146, 206, 250, 291; Cornwallis at, 59, 243; account of the campaign of, 238-240.

Yorktown peninsula, M'Clellan in, 205.

ZEALAND (Island), landing of Charles XII. in, 346.

Zeeland, reference to, 349.

Zuyder Zee, Pichegru's dash across, 131; capture of Dutch fleet in, by Mitchell, 139.

THE END.

ABOUT THE EDITOR

Colin S. Gray has been professor of international politics and director of the Centre for Security Studies at the University of Hull (U.K.) since 1993. He studied at the universities of Manchester and Oxford. He was on the directing staff of the International Institute for Strategic Studies, London, and the Hudson Institute, Croton-On-Hudson, New York, before becoming founding president of the National Institute for Public Policy in Fairfax, Virginia, in 1981. He held a presidential appointment from 1982–1987, serving on the President's General Advisory Committee on Arms Control and Disarmament, and in 1987 he was honored by the U.S. Navy with its Superior Public Service Award.

He has written *The Leverage of Sea Power* (New York, 1992), *The Navy in the Post-Cold War World* (University Park, Pa., 1994), and edited (with Roger W. Barnett) *Seapower and Strategy* (Annapolis, Md., 1989). His other books include *Strategic Studies and Public Policy* (Lexington, Ky., 1982), and *War, Peace and Victory* (New York, 1990).

He is a strategic theorist and defense analyst who finds as much time for military history as daily demands permit. He is completing a book on "Strategy in the Twentieth Century." He teaches and writes about modern strategy as very much a joint endeavor—a conviction and approach that helps explain his longstanding interest in Charles E. Callwell.

The Naval Institute Press is the book-publishing arm of the U.S. Naval Institute, a private, nonprofit society for sea service professionals and others who share an interest in naval and maritime affairs. Established in 1873 at the U.S. Naval Academy in Annapolis, Maryland, where its offices remain today, the Naval Institute has more than 85,000 members worldwide.

Members of the Naval Institute receive the influential monthly magazine *Proceedings* and discounts on fine nautical prints and on ship and aircraft photos. They also have access to the transcripts of the Institute's Oral History Program and get discounted admission to any of the Institute-sponsored seminars offered around the country.

The Naval Institute also publishes *Naval History* magazine. This colorful bimonthly is filled with entertaining and thought-provoking articles, first-person reminiscences, and dramatic art and photography. Members receive a discount on Naval History subscriptions.

The Naval Institute's book-publishing program, begun in 1898 with basic guides to naval practices, has broadened its scope in recent years to include books of more general interest. Now the Naval Institute Press publishes about 100 titles each year, ranging from how-to books on boating and navigation to battle histories, biographies, ship and aircraft guides, and novels. Institute members receive discounts of 20 to 50 percent on the Press's nearly 600 books in print.

For a free catalog describing Naval Institute Press books currently available, and for further information about subscribing to Naval History magazine or about joining the U.S. Naval Institute, please write to:

Membership & Communications Department
U.S. Naval Institute
118 Maryland Avenue
Annapolis, Maryland 21402-5035
Telephone: (800) 233-8764
Fax: (410) 269-7940